EARLY JUDAISM

EARLY JUDAISM

A Comprehensive Overview

Edited by

John J. Collins *and* Daniel C. Harlow

WILLIAM B. EERDMANS PUBLISHING COMPANY
GRAND RAPIDS, MICHIGAN / CAMBRIDGE, U.K.

Published 2012 by

Wm. B. Eerdmans Publishing Co.

2140 Oak Industrial Drive N.E., Grand Rapids, Michigan 49505 /
P.O. Box 163, Cambridge CB3 9PU U.K.

Printed in the United States of America

18 17 16 15 14 13 12   7 6 5 4 3 2 1

Library of Congress Cataloging-in-Publication Data

Early Judaism: a comprehensive overview / edited by
    John J. Collins and Daniel C. Harlow.
       p.   cm.
    Includes bibliographical references and index.
    ISBN 978-0-8028-6922-7 (pbk.: alk. paper)
    1. Judaism — History — Post-exilic period, 586 B.C.-210 A.D.
    2. Jews — History — 586 B.C.-210 A.D.
    I. Collins, John Joseph, 1946-   II. Harlow, Daniel C.

    BM176.E342   2012
    296.09′01 — dc23

2012032136

www.eerdmans.com

Contents

v

Preface

The last fifty years or so have witnessed a burgeoning interest in the field of Second Temple Jewish Studies. This interest has been prompted in large part by the publication of the Dead Sea Scrolls, but there has also been renewed interest in the Apocrypha and Pseudepigrapha and in the Greco-Jewish writings from the Diaspora. The *Eerdmans Dictionary of Early Judaism*, published in 2010, was a first attempt to provide a comprehensive reference work for this expanding field.

Naming and delimiting the field have posed, and continue to pose, a problem. The old German label *Spätjudentum* (Late Judaism) had derogatory connotations, and in any case was largely based on the rabbinic literature, from a later period. The Second Temple period, strictly defined, includes most of the Hebrew Bible, while several major nonbiblical, nonrabbinic works (Josephus, some apocalypses), were composed after the destruction of the Temple in 70 c.e. "Early Judaism" has been the accepted name for the Judaism of the Hellenistic and early Roman period in the Society of Biblical Literature, and this is the name we have adopted here. The boundaries of the period are admittedly fuzzy. The primary focus falls on the period between Alexander the Great in the late fourth century b.c.e. and the emperor Hadrian and the Bar Kokhba Revolt in the early second century c.e. It is impossible to study this period, however, without taking some account of the Persian period and the postexilic biblical books, on the one hand, and of the subsequent development of rabbinic Judaism on the other.

The present volume reprints the thirteen major essays that constituted the first part of the *Dictionary*. We have made corrections and other emendations, and added some recent works to the bibliographies, but the essays stand as they were published in the *Dictionary*. We have also pulled from the *Dictionary* the alphabetical entries on Philo and Josephus. Together, we believe, these essays provide a comprehensive and authoritative overview of Judaism in the Hellenistic and early Roman periods.

Since some of the essays have been coauthored, we would like to indicate the division of labor. In the essay "Jewish History from Alexander to Hadrian," Chris Seeman wrote the section "From Alexander to Pompey" and Adam Marshak the section "From Pompey to Hadrian." In the essay on Philo, Greg Sterling write the "Overview" and "Achievement" sections; David Runia, the section on *Questions and Answers on Genesis and Exodus;* Maren Niehoff, the sections on the *Allegorical Commentary* and *Exposition of the Law;* and Annewies van den Hoek, the section on "Apologetic Treatises." In the essay on Josephus, Steve Mason wrote the following sections: the introduction, *Vita, Jewish Antiquities,* and "New Approaches"; James McLaren write the section on the *Jewish War,* and John Barclay, the one on *Against Apion.* It is our hope that it will serve the interests of both students and scholars.

JOHN J. COLLINS
DANIEL C. HARLOW

Contributors

JOHN M. G. BARCLAY J. B. Lightfoot Professor of Divinity, University of Durham, England

MIRIAM PUCCI BEN ZEEV Professor of Jewish History, Ben Gurion University, Beersheva, Israel

KATELL BERTHELOT Chargée de recherche au Centre National pour la Recherche Scientifique, Aix-en-Provence, France; Centre de Recherche Français de Jérusalem, Israel

JOHN J. COLLINS Holmes Professor of Old Testament Criticism and Interpretation, Yale Divinity School, New Haven, Connecticut

ERICH S. GRUEN Gladys Rehard Wood Professor of History and Classics, Emeritus, University of California, Berkeley

DANIEL C. HARLOW Professor of New Testament and Early Judaism, Calvin College, Grand Rapids, Michigan

JAMES L. KUGEL Professor of Bible and Director, Institute for the History of the Jewish Bible, Bar-Ilan University, Ramat-Gan, Israel

ADAM KOLMAN MARSHAK Lecturer in Classical Studies, Gann Academy, Waltham, Massachusetts

STEVE MASON Kirby Laing Professor of New Testament Exegesis, School of Divinity, History and Philosophy, University of Aberdeen, Scotland

JAMES S. McLAREN Senior Lecturer in Theology, Australian Catholic University, Fitzroy, Victoria

MAREN R. NIEHOFF Associate Professor in Jewish Thought, Hebrew University of Jerusalem, Israel

DAVID T. RUNIA Master of Queen's College and Professorial Fellow, University of Melbourne, Australia

LAWRENCE H. SCHIFFMAN Vice Provost for Undergraduate Education, Yeshiva University, New York, New York

CHRIS SEEMAN Assistant Professor of Theology, Walsh University, North Canton, Ohio

GREGORY E. STERLING The Reverend Henry L. Slack Dean of the Divinity School, Yale University, New Haven, Connecticut

LOREN T. STUCKENBRUCK Chair in New Testament and Early Judaism, Ludwig-Maximilian-Universität, Munich, Germany

EIBERT TIGCHELAAR Research Professor, Faculty of Theology, Katholieke Universiteit, Leuven, Belgium

EUGENE ULRICH John A. O'Brien Professor of Hebrew Scriptures, University of Notre Dame, Indiana

ANNEWIES VAN DEN HOEK Lecturer in Hellenistic Greek, Harvard Divinity School, Cambridge, Massachusetts

JAMES C. VANDERKAM John A. O'Brien Professor of Hebrew Bible, University of Notre Dame, Indiana

JÜRGEN K. ZANGENBERG Professor of New Testament Exegesis and Early Christian Literature, Leiden University, The Netherlands

Abbreviations

Abr.	*De Abrahamo*
Aet.	*De aeternitate mundi*
Ag. Ap.	*Against Apion*
Agr.	*De agricultura*
Alleg. Interp.	*Allegorical Interpretation*
Anim.	*De animalibus*
Ant.	*Jewish Antiquities*
b.	Babylonian Talmud tractate
2 Bar.	*2 Baruch (Syriac Apocalypse)*
B.C.E.	Before the Common Era
Bib. Ant.	*Biblical Antiquities*
C.E.	Common Era
CAP	*Aramaic Papyri of the Fifth Century* B.C., ed. A. C. Cowley. Oxford, 1923.
CD	Cairo Genizah copy of the *Damascus Document*
chap(s).	chapter(s)
Chron.	Chronicles
CIJ	*Corpus Inscriptionum Judaicarum*, ed. J.-B. Frey. Vatican City, 1936-1952.
CIL	*Corpus Inscriptionum Latinarum*, 18 vols. Berlin, 1862-1989.
CJZC	*Corpus jüdischer Zeugnisse aus der Cyrenaika*, ed. G. Lüderitz. Wiesbaden, 1983.
Col.	Colossians
Congr.	*De congressu eruditionis gratia*
Contempl.	*De vita contemplativa*

Cor.	Corinthians
CPJ	*Corpus Papyrorum Judaicarum,* ed. V. Tcherikover and A. Fuks, 3 vols. Cambridge, Mass., 1957-1964.
Dan.	Daniel
Dem.	*Demai*
Det.	*Quod deterius potiori insidiari soleat*
Deut.	Deuteronomy
DJD	Discoveries in the Judaean Desert
DSD	*Dead Sea Discoveries*
Ebr.	*De ebrietate*
Eph.	Ephesians
Exod.	Exodus
Ezek.	Ezekiel
Flacc.	*In Flaccum*
frag(s).	fragment(s)
Gal.	Galatians
Gen.	Genesis
Gen. Rab.	*Genesis Rabbah*
Gr.	Greek
Hev	Naḥal Ḥever
Hist. Eccl.	*Ecclesiastical History*
HTR	*Harvard Theological Review*
IJO	*Inscriptiones Judaicae Orientis,* ed. D. Noy et al., 3 vols. Tübingen, 2004.
ILS	*Inscriptiones Latinae Selectae,* ed. H. Dessau, 3 vols. In 5 parts. Berlin, 1892-1916.
Isa.	Isaiah
J.W.	*Jewish War*
Jas.	James
Jer.	Jeremiah
JIGRE	*Jewish Inscriptions of Graeco-Roman Egypt,* ed. W. Horbury and D. Noy. Cambridge, Mass., 1992.
JJS	*Journal of Jewish Studies*
Josh.	Joshua
JQR	*Jewish Quarterly Review*
JRRW	*Jewish Rights in the Roman World: the Greek and Roman Documents Quoted by Josephus Flavius,* ed. M. Pucci ben Zeev. Tübingen, 1998.
JSHRZ	Judische Schriften aus Hellenistische-Römischer Zeit

JSJ	*Journal for the Study of Judaism*
JSJSup	Journal for the Study of Judaism Supplement
JSS	*Journal of Semitic Studies*
Jub.	*Jubilees*
KhQ	Khirbet Qumran
L.A.B.	*Liber Antiquitatum Biblicarum*
LCL	Loeb Classical Library
Leg.	*Legum allegoriae*
Legat.	*Legatio ad Gaium*
Lev.	Leviticus
LXX	Septuagint
m.	Mishnah tractate
Macc.	Maccabees
Magn.	*To the Magnesians*
Mart. Pol.	*Martyrdom of Polycarp*
Matt.	Matthew
Meg.	*Megilla*
Migr.	*De migratione Abrahami*
Mos.	*De vita Mosis*
MT	Masoretic Text
Mur	Murabbaʿat
Mut.	*De mutatione nominum*
Neh.	Nehemiah
no(s).	number(s)
Num.	Numbers
O.	Ostracon
OG	Old Greek
Opif.	*De opificio mundi*
P.	papyrus
P.Ḥev	*Aramaic, Hebrew and Greek Documentary Texts from Naḥal Ḥever and Other Sites, with an Appendix Containing Alleged Qumran Texts (The Seiyâl Collection II),* ed. H. M. Cotton and A. Yardeni. Oxford, 1997.
P.Polit.Jud.	*Urkunden des Politeuma der Juden von Herakleopolis (144/3\-133/2 v. Chr.),* ed. K. Maresch and J. M. S. Cowey. Wiesbaden, 2001.
P.Yadin	*The Documents from the Bar Kokhba Period in the Cave of Letters,* vol. 1, *Greek Papyri,* ed. N. Lewis. Jerusalem, 1989.

PAM	Palestine Archaeological Museum
par(s).	parallel(s)
Phil.	Philippians
Phld.	*To the Philadelphians*
Praem.	*De praemiis et poenis*
Praep. Evang.	*Praeparatio Evangelica*
Prob.	*Quod omnis probus liber sit*
Prov.	Proverbs
Prov.	*De providentia*
Ps(s).	Psalm(s)
Ps. Philo	Pseudo-Philo
Q	Qumran
1Q, 2Q, etc.	Numbered Caves of Qumran
1QH	*Hodayot* or *Thanksgiving Hymns* from Qumran Cave 1
1QIsa^{a,b}	First or second copy of Isaiah from Qumran
1QM	*Milḥamah* or *War Scroll* from Qumran
1QpHab	*Habakkuk Pesher* from Qumran
1QS	*Serek Hayaḥad* or *Rule of the Community* from Qumran Cave 1
1QS^a	*Rule of the Congregation* from Qumran Cave 1
1QS^b	*Rule of Blessings* from Qumran Cave 1
4QDan^a	First copy of Daniel from Qumran Cave 4
4QGen^b	Second copy of Genesis Scroll from Qumran Cave 4
4QJer^{a,c,d}	First, second, and fourth copies of Jeremiah from Qumran Cave 4
4QJosh^a	First copy of Joshua from Qumran Cave 4
4QJudg^b	Second Copy of Judges from Qumran Cave 4
4QMMT	*Miqṣat Maʿasê ha-Torâ* or *Some of the Works of the Law* from Qumran Cave 4
4QNum^b	Second copy of Numbers from Qumran Cave 4
4QpaleoExod^m	Paleo-Hebrew Exodus scroll from Qumran Cave 4
4QSam^{a,b}	First or second copy of Samuel from Qumran Cave 4
4QtgJob	Job Targum from Qumran Cave 4
4QtgLev	Leviticus Targum from Qumran Cave 4
11QPs^{a,b}	First or second copy of Psalms from Qumran Cave 11
11QT	*Temple Scroll* from Qumran Cave 11
11QtgJob	Job Targum from Qumran Cave 11
QE	*Questions on Exodus*
QG	*Questions on Genesis*

Rev.	Revelation
RevQ	*Revue de Qumran*
Rom.	Romans
Šabb.	*Šabbat*
Se	(Naḥal) Seʾelim
Se nab.	(Naḥal) Seʾelim Nabataean
SEG	*Supplementum Epigraphicum Graecum,* ed. A. Chaniotis et al.
Šeqal.	*Šeqalim*
Sib. Or.	*Sibylline Oracle(s)*
Sir.	Sirach
Somn.	*De somniis*
SP	Samaritan Pentateuch
Spec.	*De specialibus legibus*
t.	Tosefta tractate
T. Jos.	*Testament of Joseph*
T. Sim.	*Testament of Simeon*
TAD	*Textbook of Aramaic Documents from Ancient Egypt,* ed. B. Porten and A. Yardeni. Jerusalem, 1986-1999.
tg	Targum
Thess.	Thessalonians
Virt.	*De virtutibus*
vol.	volume
Wis.	Wisdom of Solomon
y.	Yerushalmi (Palestinian or Jerusalem Talmud tractate)

Chronology

60-66	Roman procurators Festus, Albinus, and Florus deal with brigands and popular uprisings in Judea
62	Roman governor Flaccus seizes Jewish Temple tax from Apamea, Adramyttium, Laodicea, and Pergamum in Asia Minor
64	Fire in Rome; death of James (brother of Jesus), Paul, and Peter
66	Anti-Jewish riots in Alexandria; Tiberius Julius Alexander enforces reprisals
66-70	First Jewish Revolt against Rome
68-69	Year of the four emperors (Galba, Otho, Vitellius, and Vespasian)
69-79	Vespasian, emperor
70	Jerusalem Temple destroyed by Romans; *fiscus Iudaicus* imposed on Jews in lieu of Temple tax
73/74	Masada, the last refuge of Jewish rebels under Eleazar ben Ya'ir, falls to Romans; Oniad temple at Leontopolis in Egypt destroyed by Romans
79-81	Titus, emperor
80-90	Beginnings of rabbinic academy at Yavneh (Jamnia); House of Hillel gains ascendancy over the House of Shammai; Yoḥanan ben Zakkai is the leading rabbinic sage in Palestine
81-96	Domitian, emperor
90-115	Gamaliel II is the leading rabbinic sage
96-98	Nerva, emperor
98-117	Trajan, emperor
100-135	Ishmael ben Elisha and Akiba ben Joseph are the leading rabbinic sages
116-117	Diaspora Jewish uprisings in Egypt, Cyprus, and Cyrene
117-138	Hadrian, emperor
132-135	Bar Kokhba Revolt
200	Rabbi Judah the Patriarch edits the Mishnah

Maps

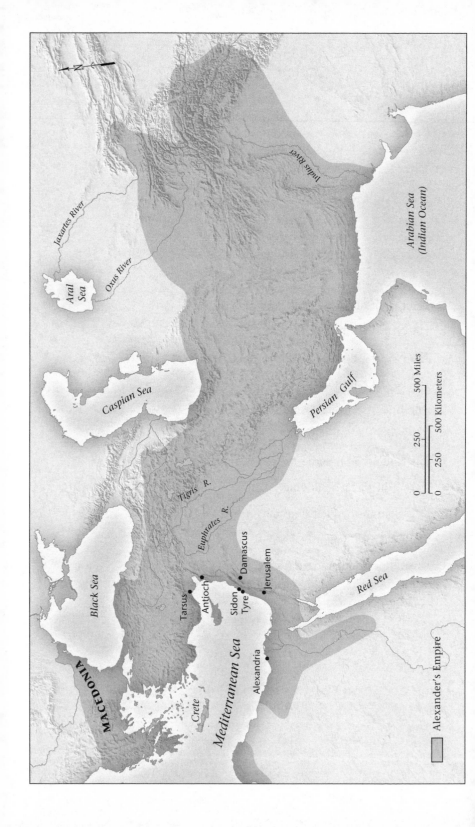

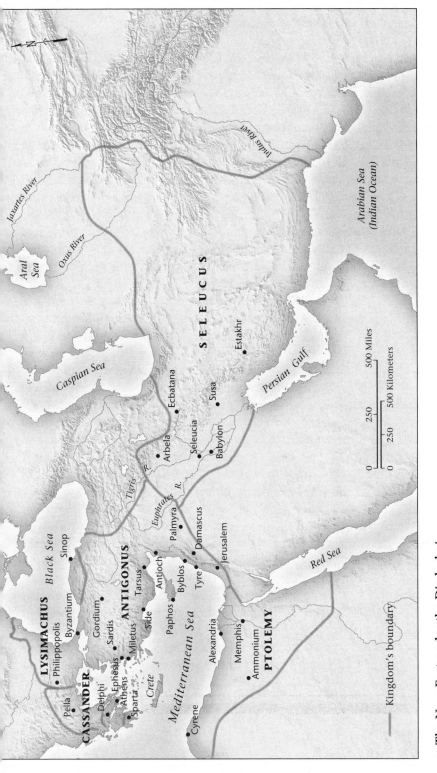

2. The Near East under the Diadochoi

3. The Near East under the Ptolemies

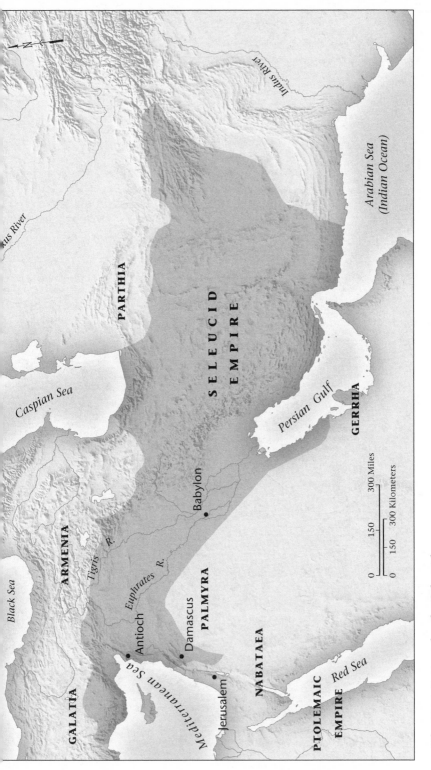

4. The Near East under the Seleucids

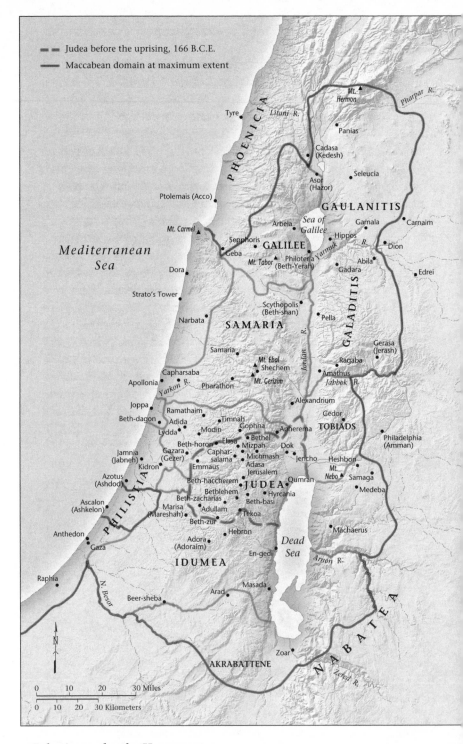

Legend:
- Judea before the uprising, 166 B.C.E.
- Maccabean domain at maximum extent

Tyre
PHOENICIA
Litani R.
Mt. Hermon
Pharpar R.
Panias
Cadasa (Kedesh)
Asor (Hazor)
Seleucia
GAULANITIS
Ptolemais (Acco)
Arbela
Sea of Galilee
Gamala
Carnaim
Mt. Carmel
Sepphoris
GALILEE
Hippos
Dion
Geba
Mt. Tabor
Philoteria (Beth-Yerah)
Yarmuk R.
Abila
Mediterranean Sea
Dora
Gadara
Edrei
Strato's Tower
Scythopolis (Beth-shan)
Pella
GALADITIS
Narbata
SAMARIA
Samaria
Mt. Ebal
Shechem
Mt. Gerizim
Ragaba
Gerasa (Jerash)
Capharsaba
Pharathon
Amathus
Jabbok R.
Apollonia
Yarkon R.
Joppa
Ramathaim
Alexandrium
Beth-dagon
Adida
Timnah
Gedor
Lydda
Modin
Gophna
Apherema
TOBIADS
Gazara (Gezer)
Beth-horon
Elasa
Bethel
Dok
Philadelphia (Amman)
Jamnia (Jabneh)
Caphar-salama
Mizpah
Michmash
Jericho
Heshbon
Kidron
Emmaus
Adasa
Jerusalem
Mt. Nebo
Samaga
Azotus (Ashdod)
Beth-haccherem
Qumran
Medeba
Bethlehem
Hyrcania
Ascalon (Ashkelon)
PHILISTIA
Beth-zacharias
Beth-basi
Marisa (Mareshah)
Adullam
Tekoa
Anthedon
Beth-zur
Machaerus
Gaza
Adora (Adoraïm)
Hebron
Dead Sea
En-gedi
Arnon R.
Raphia
IDUMEA
Masada
NABATEA
N. Besor
Beer-sheba
Arad
AKRABATTENE
Zoar
Zered R.

0   10   20   30 Miles
0   10   20   30 Kilometers

5. Palestine under the Hasmoneans

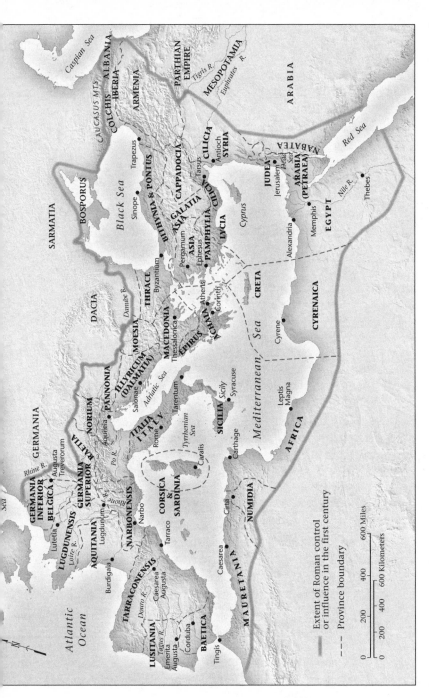

6. The Roman Empire in the First Century C.E.

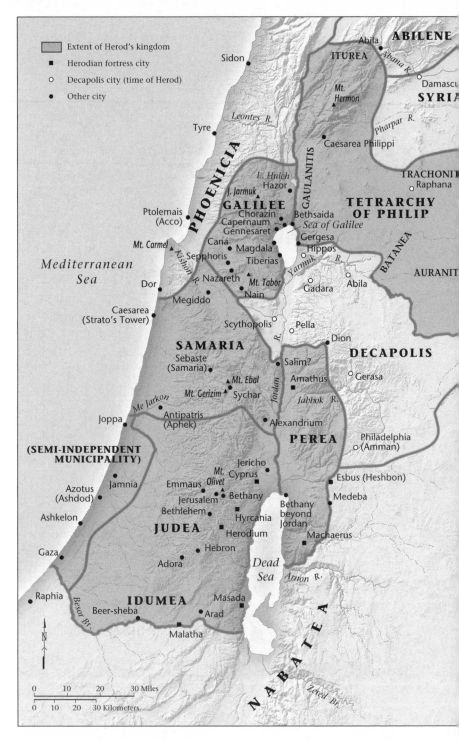

7. The Kingdom of Herod the Great

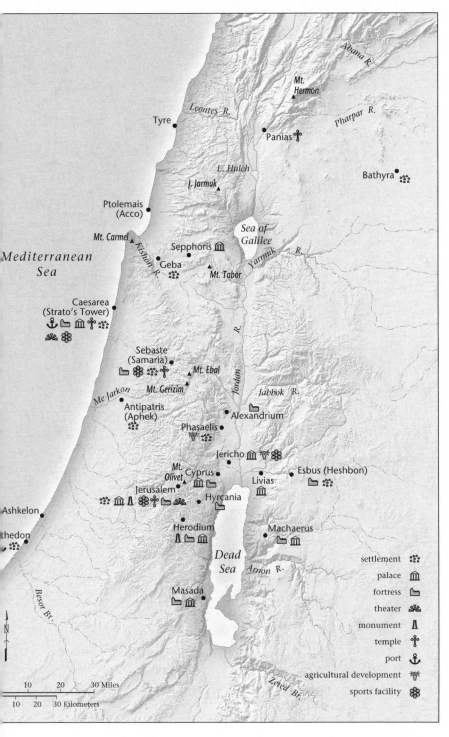

Herod the Great's Building Projects

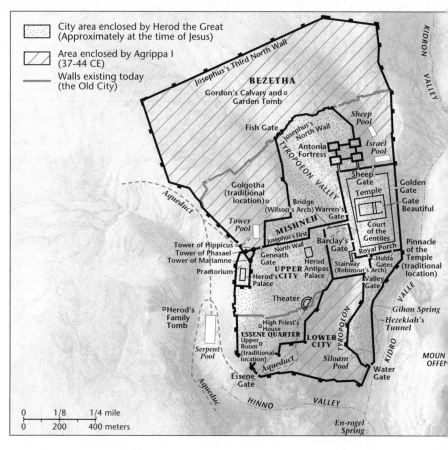

Josephus's Third North Wall

KIDRON VALLEY

BEZETHA

Gordon's Calvary and Garden Tomb

Fish Gate

Josephus's North Wall

Sheep Pool

Israel Pool

Antonia Fortress

Sheep Gate

Golgotha (traditional location)

Temple

Golden Gate

Gate Beautiful

Bridge (Wilson's Arch)

Warren's Gate

Aqueduct

Tower Pool

MISHNEH

Josephus's First North Wall

Court of the Gentiles

Tower of Hippicus
Tower of Phasael
Tower of Mariamne

Gennath Gate

Barclay's Gate

Royal Porch

Pinnacle of the Temple (traditional location)

Praetorium

Herod's Palace

UPPER CITY

Herod Antipas Palace

Stairway (Robinson's Arch)

Hulda Gates

Valley Gate

Theater

VALLE

Herod's Family Tomb

High Priest's House

ESSENE QUARTER

Upper Room (traditional location)

LOWER CITY

Gihon Spring

Hezekiah's Tunnel

TYROPOEON

KIDRO

Serpent Pool

Siloam Pool

Water Gate

MOUN OFFEN

Aqueduct

Essene Gate

Aqueduc

HINNO

VALLEY

En-rogel Spring

0   1/8   1/4 mile
0   200   400 meters

9. Jerusalem in the First Century C.E.

The Dead Sea Region

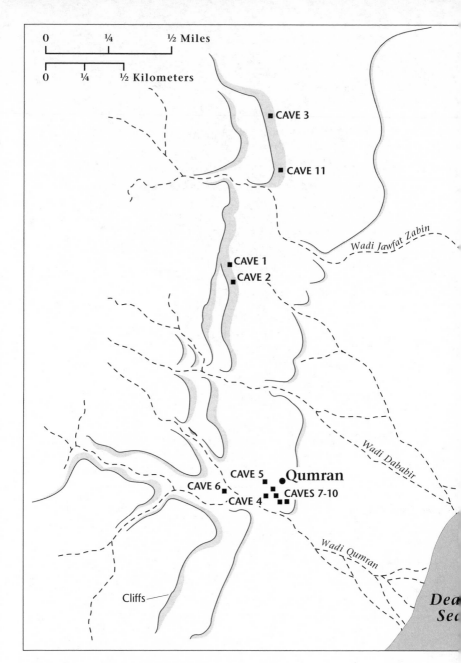

11. Location of the Qumran Caves

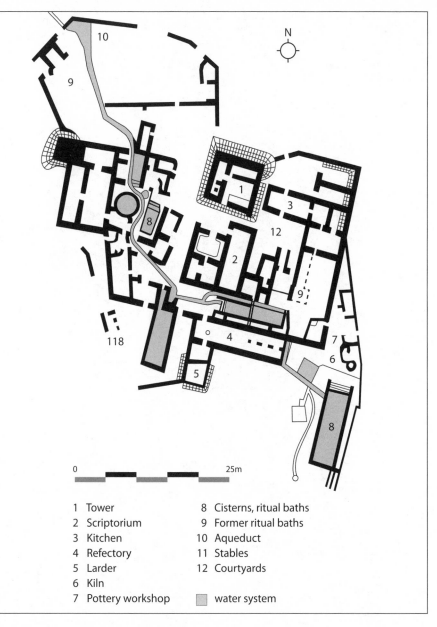

1 Tower	8 Cisterns, ritual baths
2 Scriptorium	9 Former ritual baths
3 Kitchen	10 Aqueduct
4 Refectory	11 Stables
5 Larder	12 Courtyards
6 Kiln	
7 Pottery workshop	▨ water system

Site Plan of the Qumran Settlement

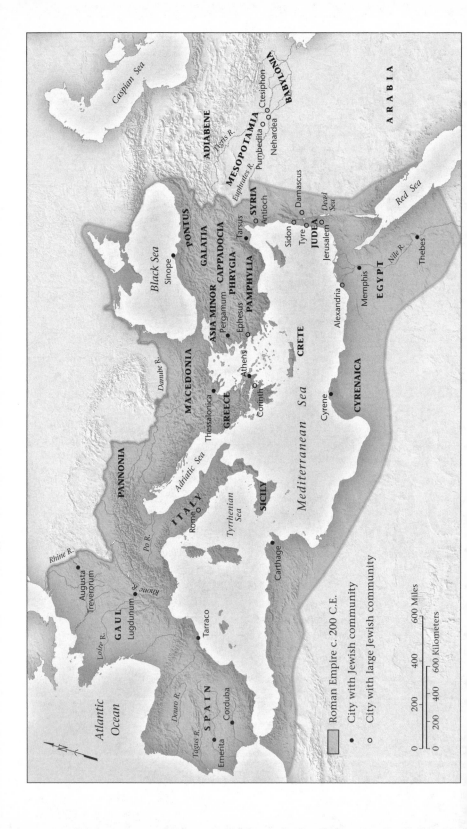

Roman Empire c. 200 C.E.
• City with Jewish community
○ City with large Jewish community

0   200   400   600 Miles
0   200   400   600 Kilometers

Atlantic Ocean

Rhine R.
Augusta Treverorum
GAUL
Lugdunum
Loire R.
Rhone R.

SPAIN
Douro R.
Tagus R.
Emerita
Corduba

Tarraco

Po R.
ITALY
Rome
Tyrrhenian Sea
SICILY
Carthage

PANNONIA
Mt. Alps
Adriatic Sea

Danube R.

MACEDONIA
Thessalonica
GREECE
Athens
Corinth

Mediterranean Sea

CRETE

CYRENAICA
Cyrene

Black Sea
Sinope
PONTUS
GALATIA
ASIA MINOR
CAPPADOCIA
Pergamum
PHRYGIA
Ephesus
PAMPHYLIA

Caspian Sea

ADIABENE
MESOPOTAMIA
Tigris R.
Euphrates R.
Pumbedita
Nehardea
Ctesiphon
BABYLONIA

Tarsus
SYRIA
Antioch
Damascus
Sidon
Tyre
JUDEA
Jerusalem
Dead Sea

ARABIA

Red Sea

EGYPT
Nile R.
Alexandria
Memphis
Thebes

Early Judaism in Modern Scholarship

John J. Collins

Judaism in the period between the conquests of Alexander the Great in the fourth century B.C.E. and the last Jewish revolt against Rome in the early second century C.E. has been characterized in various ways. For German scholars of the late nineteenth and early and mid-twentieth century, such as Emil Schürer and Wilhelm Bousset, this was *Spätjudentum,* "Late Judaism." The "lateness" was relative to the teaching of the prophets, and bespoke decline as well as chronological sequence. The decline reached its nadir in rabbinic Judaism, understood as a religion of the Law.

After the Holocaust, this way of characterizing ancient Judaism was widely (but not universally) recognized as not only offensive but dangerous. It was also inaccurate. On any reckoning, the history of Judaism since the Roman period is longer than the preceding history. Moreover, it is now increasingly apparent that the religion of ancient Israel and Judah before the Babylonian conquest was significantly different from the "Judaism" that emerged after the Exile. It has often been assumed that the reforms of Ezra in the fifth century marked the beginning of Judaism, but in fact we have little historical knowledge about these reforms, or indeed about Ezra himself. Shaye Cohen has argued persuasively that the Greek word *Ioudaios* originally meant "Judean," a usage that never disappears, but that "in the latter part of the second century B.C.E. is supplemented by a 'religious' or 'cultural' meaning: 'Jew'" (Cohen 1999: 3; Mason 2007 disputes the supplementary meaning). The word "Judaism" derives from the Greek *Ioudaismos,* which first occurs in 2 Maccabees (2:21; 8:1; 14:38), as does its counterpart *Hellenismos* (4:13). The Jewish, or Judean, way of life was certainly recognized as distinctive before this. It was noted by Hecataeus of Abdera at the beginning of the Hellenistic period (ca. 300 B.C.E.). The right of Judeans, even communities living outside of Judah, to live according to their ancestral laws was widely recognized by Hellenistic rulers, who were probably continuing Persian policy. But there are good grounds for regarding "Judaism" as a phenomenon of the Second Temple period. Accordingly, the period under review in this volume belongs to the early history of Judaism, even if the beginnings should be sought somewhat earlier.

While some biblical books (Daniel and probably Qoheleth) date from the Hellenistic age, the primary evidence for Judaism in this period lies in literature and other evidence dated "between the Bible and the Mishnah" (Nickelsburg 2005). Accordingly, this has sometimes been called the "intertestamental" period. While this term does not have the derogatory character of *Spätjudentum,* it does reflect a Christian perspective. Moreover, it obscures the fact that the New Testament itself provides evidence for Judaism in this period, and that some of the important Jewish writings (e.g., Josephus, *4 Ezra, 2 Baruch*) are contemporary with or later than some of the Christian Scriptures. In recent years, it has become customary to use the label "Second Temple Judaism" for this period (Stone 1984). Again, several relevant Jewish authors (most notably Josephus) worked after the destruction of the Second Temple, but the inaccuracy can be excused on the grounds that many of the later writings are still greatly preoccupied with the Temple and its destruction, and that the restructuring and reconceptualizing of the religion that we find in rabbinic literature did not occur immediately when Jerusalem fell. The Second Temple period, however, must begin with the Persians, and includes the editing, if not the composition, of much of the Hebrew Bible.

In this volume, we are mainly concerned with the evidence for Judaism between the Bible and the Mishnah. There is still overlap with the later biblical books, and the rabbinic corpus, compiled centuries later, also contains material relevant to the earlier period. No characterization, and no exact delimitation, is without problems, but "Early Judaism" seems the least problematic label available. (The designation "Middle Judaism," suggested by Gabriele Boccaccini [1991], might be applied more appropriately to the Middle Ages. It is hardly appropriate for prerabbinic Judaism.) The conquests of Alexander are taken as the *terminus a quo,* on the grounds that they marked a major cultural transition. Several extant postbiblical Jewish writings date from the third or early second century B.C.E., prior to the Maccabean Revolt, which has often served as a marker for a new era (e.g., in Schürer's *History*). The reign of Hadrian (117-138 C.E.) and the Bar Kokhba Revolt (132-135 C.E.) are taken to mark the end of an era, but not the end of Judaism by any means. The rabbinic literature, which later tradition would take as normative, took shape in the following centuries, but it did so in conditions that were very different from those that had prevailed before the great revolts.

The Recovery of the Pseudepigrapha

For much of Western history, there were relatively few sources for Judaism between the Bible and the Mishnah. The Apocrypha, or deuterocanonical books, were traditionally (and still are) part of the Bible of the Catholic Church. This is a very small selection of Jewish literature from the period 200 B.C.E. to 100 C.E. It includes the books of Maccabees, major wisdom books (Ben Sira and Wisdom of Solomon) and pious tales (Tobit, Judith), but apocalyptic writings are conspicuous by their absence. (2 Esdras, which includes the apocalypse of *4 Ezra,* is included in the Apocrypha but not in the deuterocanonical books that are part of the Catholic Bible.) The history of the period was well known because of the books of Maccabees and the writings of Josephus. In recent years these sources have been supplemented by archaeology (Meyers and Chancey 2012), but few additional literary sources that shed light on the history have surfaced. Also, the great corpus of Philo of Alexandria's works was transmitted by Christians, because of its similarity to the writings of the church fathers. The Hellenistic Jewish literature was of marginal interest for orthodox Jewish scholarship in the nineteenth century, but it was the subject of some important studies, notably in the work of Jacob Freudenthal (1874-1875; see Niehoff in Oppenheimer, ed. 1999: 9-28).

There exists, however, an extensive class of writings attributed to Old Testament figures that is not included in the Apocrypha. These writings are called "pseudepigrapha" (falsely attributed writings). There is also a small number of pseudepigraphic writings attributed to figures of pagan antiquity, most prominently the Sibyl. Most of the Greek and Latin writings relating to the Old Testament, such as the *Testaments of the Twelve Patriarchs,* were collected by J. A. Fabricius in his *Codex Pseudepigraphus Veteris Testamenti* in 1713. But many important works were preserved only in less widely known languages, such as Ethiopic, Syriac, and Old Church Slavonic. The translations from Ethiopic of the *Ascension of Isaiah* (1819) and *1 Enoch* (1821) by Richard Laurence inaugurated a new era in the study of ancient Judaism. During the latter half of the nineteenth century, several more important pseudepigrapha came to light — *Jubilees*, 2 and 3 *Baruch*, 2 *Enoch*, the *Apocalypse of Abraham*, and the *Testament of Abraham*. These discoveries greatly enlarged the corpus of apocalyptic works from around the turn of the era and potentially provided resources for a new view of ancient Judaism. At the beginning of the twentieth century, there were landmark editions of the collected Pseudepigrapha in German (Kautzsch 1900; Riessler 1928) and English (Charles 1913), but editions of the individual books had been available from the late nineteenth century.

The Relevance of Rabbinic Writings

This newly available material was not immediately integrated into the study of ancient Judaism. Emil Schürer's *Geschichte des jüdischen Volkes im Zeitalter Jesu Christi* (1886-1890) included surveys of Jewish literature (divided between "Palestinian Jewish" and "Hellenistic Jewish" literature), but his depiction of Jewish religion is drawn heavily from rabbinic writings. This is especially true of his treatment of "Life under the Law," in which he drew primarily from the Mishnah, but even his account of messianic belief integrated data from the Pseudepigrapha with rabbinic beliefs. In the judgment of George Foote Moore, the chapter on the Law "was conceived, not as a chapter of the history of Judaism but as a topic of Christian apologetic; it was written to prove by the highest Jewish authority that the strictures on Judaism in the Gospels and the Pauline Epistles are fully justified" (Moore 1921: 240). Schürer's work was a mine of information and historical detail. Its enduring value can be seen in the degree to which its structure, and much of its detail, are retained in the English edition revised by Geza Vermes and his collaborators. The revisers "endeavoured to clear the notorious chapter 28, *Das Leben unter dem Gesetz* — here re-styled as 'Life and the Law' — and the section on the Pharisees . . . of the dogmatic prejudices of nineteenth-century theology" (Vermes et al. 1973-1987: 2:v; cf. 464 n. 1). Nonetheless, Schürer's introductory claim is repeated: "The chief characteristic of this period was the growing importance of Pharisaism . . . the generalities of biblical law were resolved into an immense number of detailed precepts . . . this concern with the punctilious observance of the minutiae of religion became the hallmark of mainstream Judaism" (Vermes et al. 1973-1987: 1:1). Likewise, the section on messianism retained the systematic presentation, which synthesizes data from rabbinic sources and the Pseudepigrapha.

The first scholar to offer a reconstruction of Jewish religion based primarily on the Pseudepigrapha was Wilhelm Bousset, whose *Religion des Judentums im neutestamentlichen Zeitalter* first appeared in 1903. It was greeted by a storm of criticism from Jewish scholars (Wiese 2005: 159-215). Bousset's view of Judaism was more differentiated than that of Schürer. In addition to the legalistic aspect of Pharisaism, he also detected a universalistic strand on which the teaching of Jesus could build. Some of his Jewish critics objected to "this dogmatic reduction of Judaism to a 'praeparatio evangelica'" (Wiese 2005: 180). But there was also a fundamental disagreement on the question of appropriate sources. Felix Perles praised Bousset's treatment of the piety of apocalyptic and Hellenistic Judaism but objected to the prominence accorded to this material and the lack of a systematic description of "normative Judaism," as represented by rabbinic literature. Bousset, he claimed, had missed the "center of the Jewish religion" (Perles 1903: 22-23; Wiese 2005: 181). Bousset responded that one must differentiate between "the scholarship of the scribes," which became normative after 70 C.E., and the more diverse "popular piety" of the earlier period, and he charged that Perles was "incapable of understanding the richer and more diverse life of Jewish popular religion before the destruction of the Jewish nation, because he is focused on the Mishnah and the Talmud and the entire later history of the scribes" (Bousset 1903b; Wiese 2005: 186). Few scholars would now accept Bousset's characterization of the Pseudepigrapha as "popular religion" without qualification, but the issue of the relevance of rabbinic literature for the Second Temple period persists as a live issue down to the present.

R. H. Charles, the scholar who did most to advance the study of the Pseudepigrapha, did not attempt a comprehensive study of ancient Judaism. While his own work focused largely on the apocalypses, he held that "Apocalyptic Judaism and legalistic Judaism were not in pre-Christian times essentially antagonistic. Fundamentally their origin was the same. Both started with the unreserved recognition of the supremacy of the Law" (Charles 1913: vii). Charles viewed the apocalyptic material positively, as a bridge between the prophets and early Christianity. His view of Judaism in this period as comprising two main strands is one of the major paradigms that has been adapted with various nuances in later scholarship (see VanderKam in Boccaccini and Collins 2007).

Perles's criticisms of Bousset were echoed almost two decades later by the American Christian scholar, George Foote Moore:

The censure which Jewish scholars have unanimously passed on *Die Religion des Judentums* is that the author uses as his primary sources almost exclusively the writings commonly called Apocrypha and Pseudepigrapha, with an especial penchant for the apocalypses; and only secondarily, and almost casually the writings which represent the acknowledged and authoritative teachings of the school and the more popular instruction of the synagogue. This is much as if one should describe early Christianity using indiscriminately for his principal sources the Apocryphal Gospels and Acts, the Apocalypses of John and Peter, and the Clementine literature. (Moore 1921: 243)

While acknowledging the problem of the date of the rabbinic material, Moore insisted: "it is clear that the author ought not to have called his book *Die Religion des Judentums,* for the sources from which his representation is drawn are those to which, so far as we know, Judaism never conceded any authority, while he discredits and largely ignores those which it has always regarded as normative" (244).

But as F. C. Porter pointed out in his review of Moore's own masterwork (Moore 1927-1930), "When Moore speaks of the sources which Judaism has always regarded as authentic, he means 'always' from the third century A.D. onward. . . . Was there then no other type of Judaism in the time of Christ that may claim such names as 'normative,' 'normal,' 'orthodox'?" (Porter 1928; cf. Neusner 1981: 9). More fundamentally, one might question whether notions of normativity are appropriate to a discussion of the history of a religion at all. As Jacob Neusner, with all due appreciation for Moore's goodwill, pointed out: "Moore's is to begin with not really a work in the history of religions at all. . . . His research is into theology. It is organized in theological categories, not differentiated by historical periods at all" (Neusner 1981: 7). Neusner was no less critical of Jewish scholarship at the beginning of the twentieth century. The attempt to draw a direct line from the Hebrew Bible to a "normative" Judaism defined by the rabbis was an anachronism, motivated by apologetics (Neusner 1984: 101; Wiese 2005: 213).

The mantle of Moore was taken up half a century later by E. P. Sanders, with some qualifications. Sanders recognizes that the tannaitic literature (i.e., literature traditionally ascribed to the period between 70 and 200 C.E.) cannot be assumed to provide "an accurate picture of Judaism or even of Pharisaism in the time of Jesus and Paul, although it would be surprising if there were no connection" (Sanders 1977: 60). He also recognizes that Jewish literature from this period, including the tannaitic literature, is very varied. Yet he argues that "a common pattern can be discerned which underlies otherwise disparate parts of tannaitic literature" (Sanders 1977: 70), which he describes as "covenantal nomism." The Law must be seen in the context of election and covenant. It provides for a means of atonement, so that the covenantal relationship can be reestablished or maintained. All who are maintained in the covenant will be saved. Salvation, then, does not depend on purely individual observance of the Law. Sanders finds this pattern not only in tannaitic literature but also in the Dead Sea Scrolls, Apocrypha, and Pseudepigrapha, with the single exception of *4 Ezra* (Sanders 1977: 422-23). He concludes that his study "lends no support to those who have urged that apocalypticism and legalism constitute substantially different religious types or streams in the Judaism of the period" (Sanders 1977: 423) and denies that apocalypticism constituted a distinct type of religion (Sanders 1992: 8). The case for the compatibility of concern for the Law with apocalyptic beliefs finds strong support in the Dead Sea Scrolls.

In Sanders's view, "covenantal nomism does not cover the entirety of Jewish theology, much less the entirety of Judaism" (Sanders 1992: 262). It is nonetheless an aspect of "common" or "normal" Judaism. Mindful of the criticism directed at Moore, Sanders is careful to qualify the word "normative": "whatever we find to have been normal was based on internal assent and was 'normative' only to the degree that it was backed up by common opinion — which has a good deal of coercive power, but which allows individuals who strongly dissent to break away" (Sanders 1992: 47). The pillars of common Judaism were the belief in one God, the Scriptures, especially the Torah, and the Temple. Within a common framework, considerable variation was possible. Sanders's approach is focused on practice rather than belief. Even when he draws his data from Josephus or other Second Temple sources, the kinds of issues on which he focuses are generally similar to those that predominate in the Mishnah. Apocalyptic speculations about the heavens or the end of history tell us little about the authors' daily observances.

Sanders's portrait of common Judaism is less vulnerable to critique than Moore's normative Judaism, and it enjoys wide acceptance (see, e.g., Goodman 2002: 38). It does not deny that diversity existed but places the emphasis on what all (or at least most) Jews had in common. One could also place more emphasis on diversity with equal validity. The other end of the spectrum from Sanders is occupied by Jacob Neusner, who insists on

7

speaking of "Judaisms" rather than "Judaism" (e.g., Neusner, Green, and Frerichs 1987: ix). The plural has been adopted by some scholars (e.g., Boccaccini) but is infelicitous: to speak of "a Judaism" requires the over-arching concept of "Judaism" in the singular. While Neusner's insistence that each corpus of Jewish literature (say, the Dead Sea Scrolls) be analyzed in its own right and not read through the lens of another corpus (say, the Mishnah) is salutary, it does not follow that each corpus represents a distinct religious system. Insistence on radical diversity distorts the data just as much as an essentialist approach that would exclude ostensibly Jewish material that does not conform to a norm (see the remarks of Green 1994: 298 on Sanders's *Paul and Palestinian Judaism:* "Paul's writings are analyzed in juxtaposition to Judaism rather than as part of it").

In his recent attempt at a sweeping characterization of early Judaism, Seth Schwartz is sharply critical of Neusner: "I reject the characterization of Judaism as multiple, as well as the atomistic reading of the sources that justifies it" (Schwartz 2001: 9). He continues: "The notion that each piece of evidence reflects a discrete social organization is obviously wrong." It is not apparent, however, that Neusner associates his different "Judaisms" with "discrete social organizations." Schwartz goes on to distinguish broadly between "apocalyptic mythology" and "covenantal ideology" (Schwartz 2001: 78-82). He regards these as "incongruous systems": "The covenant imagines an orderly world governed justly by the one God. The apocalyptic myth imagines a world in disarray, filled with evil; a world in which people do not get what they deserve. God is not in control in any obvious way; indeed the cosmology of the myth is dualist or polythe-ist. . . ." The accuracy of this sketch of "the apocalyptic myth" might be questioned, especially with regard to whether God is in control, but there is no doubt that there are real differences here. Schwartz notes "the re-peated juxtaposition of the covenant and the myth in ancient Jewish writing" and infers that "though the systems are logically incongruous, they did not for the most part generate social division." Thus he agrees with Sanders that "apocalyptic Judaism" was not a separate entity. He is also du-bious about "covenantal Judaism." Rather, he supposes that "the apocalyptic myth" was "a more or less fully naturalized part of the ideology of Juda-ism." Insofar as he recognizes "incongruous systems," Schwartz may not be as far removed from Neusner as he thinks, although the latter would surely insist on a greater variety of systems. At the same time, Schwartz can avoid the impression of fragmentation that is conveyed by Neusner's insistence on multiple Judaisms.

The Place of the Pseudepigrapha

In his critique of Bousset, Moore acknowledged that critical use of the rabbinic writings is difficult, but he argued that the critical problems presented by the Pseudepigrapha are no less difficult: "How wide, for example, was the currency of these writings? Do they represent a certain common type of 'Volksfrömmigkeit,' or did they circulate in circles with peculiar notions and tendencies of their own? How far do they come from sects regarded by the mass of their countrymen as heretical?" (Moore 1921: 244). Perhaps the most fundamental question to be asked about the use of the Pseudepigrapha in the reconstruction of ancient Judaism is whether they are in fact Jewish at all. Most of these texts were preserved by Christians, not by Jews. Robert Kraft has argued repeatedly that these texts should first be understood in their Christian context (Kraft 1994; 2001). At the same time, it is incontrovertible that some pseudepigraphic writings which were preserved only by Christians were composed by Jews in the centuries around the turn of the era. Fragments of most sections of *1 Enoch,* and of *Jubilees* were found in Aramaic and Hebrew, respectively, among the Dead Sea Scrolls. It does not necessarily follow that all pseudepigrapha attributed to Old Testament figures are of Jewish origin. Since most Christian literature refers explicitly to Christ, and Christians often added references to Christ to Jewish writings, the tendency has been to assume that any Old Testament pseudepigraphon that has nothing explicitly Christian in it is in fact Jewish.

This tendency has recently been challenged by James Davila (2005). We have a considerable corpus of writings from antiquity that are indisputably Jewish, because of their language or the context of their discovery (most notably, the Dead Sea Scrolls). On the basis of these texts Davila attempts to identify "signature features" that can reliably indicate the Jewish origin of a work:

- substantial Jewish content, and evidence of a pre-Christian date;
- compelling evidence that a work was translated from Hebrew;
- sympathetic concern with the Jewish ritual cult;
- sympathetic concern with Jewish Law/Torah and halakah;
- concern with Jewish ethnic and national interests. (Davila 2005: 65)

These "signature features" are not necessarily foolproof, but they can help establish a balance of probability. They enable Davila to authenticate as

Jewish a work like 2 *Baruch*, which was clearly written by a Torah-observant Jew, against the objections of Rivkah Nir (2003), who argues that several of its apocalyptic motifs are typical of Christianity rather than Judaism (Davila 2005: 131). He rightly argues that Nir's concept of ancient Judaism is "narrow to the point of being procrustean," as she does not even include works like *1 Enoch* and *Jubilees* in her control corpus of Jewish material. He also defends the Jewish origin of the *Similitudes of Enoch* (*1 Enoch* 37–71), which shows no interest in Torah observance, and which was regarded as a late Christian work by J. T. Milik (1976: 89-98). In this case the conclusive consideration is the apparent identification of Enoch, not Jesus, with the Son of Man in *1 Enoch* 71:14 (Davila 2005: 134). The identification, though, is not as unambiguous as Davila claims (Collins 1998: 187-91), but it is inconceivable that a Christian author would have allowed any ambiguity as to the identification of the Son of Man. Other cases are more difficult to decide. The Jewish origin of *Joseph and Aseneth* has been questioned forcefully by Ross Kraemer (1998) and Rivka Nir (2012). Davila fails to detect either Jewish or Christian signature features that would decide the issue (Davila 2005: 193). Neither does the *Testament of Job* offer any decisive evidence, although it fits quite comfortably in the context provided by the oldest attestation, in Christian circles in Egypt in the early fifth century C.E. He also finds the *Testament of Abraham* congenial to a late antique Christian setting. Less plausibly, he finds nothing in the Wisdom of Solomon "that prohibits or even renders unlikely its having been written by a gentile Christian in the second half of the first century CE" (Davila 2005: 225). But there is no parallel for Christian composition of a pseudepigraphic writing in the name of an Old Testament figure at such an early date, and the retelling of the exodus story in Wisdom of Solomon 11–19 surely meets the criterion of concern for Jewish ethnic and national interests. Davila's reasoning is not persuasive in every instance, but he has advanced the discussion by showing that the evidence for Jewish origin is much clearer in some instances than in others.

There is plenty of evidence that Christians sometimes composed works in the names of Old Testament figures (e.g., Isaiah, Ezra, Elijah, Daniel). It is also plausible that they inserted explicit Christian passages into Jewish works to render them more suitable for Christian devotion (see, e.g., Harlow 1996 on 3 *Baruch;* Collins in Charlesworth 1983: 330-53 on *Sibylline Oracles* 1 and 2). The more extensive the Christian redaction, the more hazardous the reconstruction of the underlying Jewish work becomes. The most celebrated problem case in this regard is the *Testaments of the Twelve Patriarchs.* This collection is clearly Christian in its present form. One of its distinctive features is the expectation of a messiah from Levi and Judah, who is evidently identified as Christ. He will be priest and king, God and man (*T. Sim.* 7:2). He is referred to as "the lamb of God" (*T. Jos.* 19:6). *Testament of Judah* 24 speaks of a man from the tribe of Judah, for whom the heavens will be opened and in whom no sin will be found. Scholars have argued that each of these references can be justified in a Jewish context, or that they are Christian insertions in a text that is basically Jewish (Charles 1913: 291). The cumulative evidence, however, is far more easily explained on the assumption of Christian authorship (de Jonge 1953).

Nonetheless, there are good reasons to think that the *Testaments* draw heavily on Jewish traditions. The association of the messiah with both Levi and Judah inevitably recalls the two messiahs of the Dead Sea Scrolls. Partial parallels to the *Testament of Levi,* in Aramaic, and to the *Testament of Naphtali,* in Hebrew, have been found among the Dead Sea Scrolls. It is possible, however, that these were source documents used by the Christian authors of the *Testaments* (de Jonge 2000). We do not have conclusive evidence for a Jewish *Testaments of the Twelve Patriarchs* (as distinct from apocryphal writings associated with individuals such as Levi). The ethical teachings of the *Testaments* can be explained satisfactorily in the context of either Hellenistic Judaism or early Christianity.

In cases where the Christian elements are not extensive, and somewhat incongruous, a stronger case can be made for Jewish authorship. The fifth *Sibylline Oracle* contains only one overtly Christian verse (arguably two) in a composition of 531 verses. Verse 257 qualifies the "exceptional man from the sky" with the line "who stretched out his hands on the fruitful wood." The following verse says that he will one day cause the sun to stand. Most commentators excise either one or both verses as an interpolation (Collins in Charlesworth 1983: 399). The reference to causing the sun to stand could be regarded as part of the interpolation because of a play on Jesus/Joshua). Davila allows that this is possible, but finds it unnecessary: "Sibylline Oracles 5 as a whole reads comfortably as a work by a Jewish-Christian who was outraged by the Roman destruction of Jerusalem and who put after-the-fact prophecies in the mouth of the Sibyl both to condemn the Romans and the other polytheistic nations and to predict the coming of Jesus as the eschatological redeemer" (Davila 2005:189). But while the outrage over the destruction is loud and clear in this work, the identification of Jesus as the eschatological redeemer is perceptible only in this one passage, and is not very explicit even there. Davila notes that *Sibylline Oracles* 5 shows no interest in circumcision, dietary laws, or the Sabbath, and virtually reduces the Law to idolatry and sexual sins. But this is quite typical of Jewish writings from the Hellenistic Diaspora (Collins 2000: 155-85). As this example shows, the identification of a given text as Jewish depends on the profile of Judaism one is willing to accept. In some cases, arguments against Jewish provenance reflect a narrow, normative view of Judaism (Efron 1987: 219-86 on the *Psalms of Solomon;* Nir on *2 Baruch*). This is not true of Davila, however, and the questions may be justified in some cases. The boundaries of Judaism cannot be restricted to concern for the Torah or covenantal nomism. Conversely, arguments for Jewish diversity based on pseudepigraphic texts of uncertain origin cannot bear the full weight of evidence unless they are supported by parallels in texts that are clearly Jewish.

The Place of Apocalypticism

The controversy over the use of the Pseudepigrapha in the reconstruction of early Judaism is due in large part to the prominence of apocalyptic literature. Even pseudepigraphic books that are not formally apocalypses, such as the *Sibylline Oracles,* the *Psalms of Solomon,* or the *Testaments of the Twelve Patriarchs* have much in common with them, especially in their view of history and eschatology. Only one apocalyptic writing, the book of Daniel, was included in the Hebrew Bible, and the apocalyptic tradition was rejected by rabbinic Judaism. The noncanonical apocalypses were transmitted by Christians, and were not preserved in Hebrew or Aramaic, although Aramaic fragments of *1 Enoch* and Hebrew fragments of *Jubilees* have been found in the Dead Sea Scrolls. It has been said that apocalypticism is the mother of Christian theology. R. H. Charles saw it as the link between biblical prophecy and early Christianity, and the view that it was "the child of prophecy" has always been popular in English-language scholarship (Rowley 1944). Bousset, in contrast, attributed its rise to Zoroastrian influence. Other sources, both biblical (wisdom literature, von Rad 1965: 2:315-30) and foreign (Babylonian traditions, e.g., Kvanvig 1988) have occasionally been proposed. Only in the last quarter of the twentieth century has apocalypticism been recognized as a phenomenon in its own right rather than as a mutation (or degeneration) of something else (Collins 1998: 26-42).

After the great burst of creative energy expended on the Pseudepigrapha in the late nineteenth and early twentieth centuries, this literature received little scholarly attention for more than half a century. (This neglect must be seen in the context of a general shift in focus from history of religion to biblical theology in this period.) Many of the more influential scholars who addressed it, such as Rowley and von Rad, were biblical scholars who naturally enough tried to assimilate the strange noncanonical material to biblical categories. Much of the scholarship that purported to deal with "apocalyptic" actually dealt with postexilic prophecy or with the letters of Paul. The discovery of the Dead Sea Scrolls, however, led to renewed interest in Judaism between the Bible and the Mishnah. From the 1970s onward there was extensive work on the Pseudepigrapha both in the United States and in Europe, which bore fruit in the two-volume translation of Old Testament Pseudepigrapha edited by Charlesworth (1983-1985), which included much more material than the older edition of Charles, and the German series of fascicles *Jüdische Schriften aus hellenistisch-römischer Zeit*. Now the apocalypses came to be studied in the context of the contemporary pseudepigraphic literature and the Dead Sea Scrolls. This in turn led to a change in focus from "apocalyptic" as a kind of theology, usually studied with an eye to its relevance for the New Testament, to the literary genre apocalypse (Koch 1972; Collins ed. 1979).

Three results of the study of the genre are noteworthy. First, apocalypses are not only concerned with historical eschatology (the end of the present age) in the way familiar from Daniel and the book of Revelation. They are also, even primarily, revelations of heavenly mysteries (Rowland 1983). A whole subtype of the genre is concerned with otherworldly journeys, and this material is important for the early history of Jewish mysticism (Himmelfarb 1993). Second, since only one book in the Hebrew Bible, Daniel, could be said to exemplify the genre, discussion of "apocalyptic" or "protoapocalyptic" in the prophetic literature became increasingly dubious. Third, the genre is not peculiar to Judaism and Christianity, but has important parallels in Persian tradition and throughout the Greco-Roman world, especially in the case of the heavenly journeys (Hellholm 1983).

Another byproduct of the focus on the genre apocalypse and on the context of the Pseudepigrapha was increased interest in the collection of writings known as *1 Enoch*. Charles had already realized that some parts of *1 Enoch* were older than Daniel. Interest was greatly increased by the publication of the Aramaic fragments found among the Dead Sea Scrolls (Milik 1976). The Italian scholar Paolo Sacchi argued that the root of apocalypticism should be found in the *Book of the Watchers* (*1 Enoch* 1–36), one of the earliest segments of the tradition (Sacchi 1997). The generative question was the origin of evil, and the answer was that it was brought to earth by fallen angels. Sacchi tended to identify apocalypticism with the Enochic tradition, in contrast even to the book of Daniel. His student, Gabriele Boccaccini, has proceeded to argue, in Neusnerian fashion, that *1 Enoch* testifies to "Enochic Judaism," which he further identifies with the Essenes, whom he regards as the parent movement of the Qumran sect (Boccaccini 1998).

Even if one were to grant that the *Book of the Watchers* is the earliest Jewish apocalypse, the whole phenomenon cannot be defined only on the basis of its earliest exemplar. The differences between Daniel and Enoch show only that there was some diversity within apocalypticism, and that it should not be restricted to a single social movement. Again, while the books of Enoch were preserved at Qumran (except for the *Similitudes*), they were not the only, or even the primary source of sectarian ideology, and there is no evidence whatever that would warrant identifying them with the Essenes. Nonetheless, the early Enoch books attest to a kind of Judaism that is significantly different from the covenantal nomism of "common Judaism." As George Nickelsburg has argued, "the general category of covenant was not important for these authors" (Nickelsburg 1998: 125). Enoch rather than Moses is the mediator of revelation. Unlike the book of *Jubilees,* which is closely related to Enoch in some respects, there is no attempt to read back Mosaic legislation into the primeval period. Even the *Animal Apocalypse,* which touches on the exodus and the ascent of Mt. Sinai in the course of a "prophecy" of the history of Israel, conspicuously fails to mention either the making of a covenant or the giving of the Law. In all of this there is no polemic against the Mosaic Torah, but the Torah is not the explicit frame of reference. Moreover, the Enoch literature attests to a soli-lunar calendar different from the lunar calendar that was observed in the Jerusalem Temple (at least in later times), but similar to the one found in *Jubilees* and the Dead Sea Scrolls.

The idea of a movement within Judaism that is not centered on the Mosaic Torah may seem anomalous in the context of the Hellenistic age, but it was not without precedent. The biblical wisdom literature is distinguished precisely by its lack of explicit reference to either the Mosaic Torah or the history of Israel, and it retains this character as late as the book of Qoheleth, which may be roughly contemporary with the early Enoch literature. Charles, then, was not correct when he claimed that "apocalyptic Judaism" "started with the unreserved recognition of the supremacy of the Law." At least in the case of the early Enoch literature, this was not the case.

What is true of the Enoch literature, however, is not necessarily true of all the Pseudepigrapha, or even of all apocalyptic literature. The book of *Jubilees* adapts the myth of the fallen angels from *1 Enoch* (Segal 2007: 103-43), and shares with it the solar (364-day) calendar. It can be viewed as an example of "rewritten Bible," or biblical paraphrase, but it is also an apocalypse, in the sense that it is a revelation mediated by an angel. But the recipient of the revelation is none other than Moses, and the content is a paraphrase of the book of Genesis. Moreover, this paraphrase is informed throughout by a keen interest in halakic issues. The sectarian writings of the Dead Sea Scrolls are at once apocalyptic and focused on the exact interpretation of the Law of Moses. The Torah also plays a central role in the apocalypses of *4 Ezra* and *2 Baruch*, which were composed after the destruction of the Temple, at the end of the first century c.e. The relationship between apocalyptic literature and the Torah is illustrated most vividly by *4 Ezra*. At the end of the book, Ezra is commissioned to replace the books of the Law that had been burnt. He is given a fiery liquid to drink, and inspired to dictate the books. In all, ninety-four books are written. Of these, twenty-four are made public so that the worthy and unworthy may read them. But the seventy others are kept secret, in order that they may be given to the wise among the people. The extra or hidden books contain "the spring of understanding, the fountain of wisdom and the river of knowledge." *4 Ezra* is neither critical of the Torah nor opposed to it, but it claims to have further revelation, which provides the context within which the Torah must be understood. This claim of higher revelation is one of the defining characteristics of apocalyptic literature. In the words of Seth Schwartz, "it was a way of compensating for the deficiencies of the covenantal system" (Schwartz 2001: 83). The covenant promised life and prosperity to those who observed it and threatened disaster to those who did not, but life evidently did not work this way. One of the major topics of apocalyptic revelation was judgment after death and the contrasting fates of the righteous and wicked in the hereafter. Belief in life after death was not confined to apocalyptic literature; the immortality of the soul was widely accepted in Greek-speaking Judaism, and the Pharisees, who may have subscribed to apocalyptic ideas to various degrees, believed in resurrection. But belief in the judgment of the dead and a differentiated afterlife is first attested in Judaism in the books of *Enoch* and Daniel, and it is the primary factor that distinguishes apocalyptic eschatology from that of the prophets (Collins 1997b: 75-97).

The Dead Sea Scrolls

The most important development for the study of early Judaism in the past century was undoubtedly the discovery and eventual publication of the Dead Sea Scrolls. The scrolls were found in proximity to a ruined settlement at Khirbet Qumran, south of Jericho, by the Dead Sea. Cave 4, where the main trove of texts was found, is literally a stone's throw from the site. Most scholars have assumed that the texts constituted the library of a sectarian settlement at Qumran (VanderKam 1994: 12-27). The Roman writer Pliny says that there was an Essene settlement in this region (*Natural History* 5.73), and there are extensive parallels between the rule books found at Qumran, especially the *Serek Ha-Yaḥad,* or *Community Rule,* and the accounts of the Essenes by Philo and Josephus (Beall 1988). Both the association with the site and the identification with the Essenes have been contested, often vociferously, in recent years (Galor, Humbert, and Zangenberg 2006). Norman Golb has insisted that such an extensive corpus of scrolls could have come only from the Jerusalem Temple, and that the multiplicity of hands belies composition in a single community (Golb 1995). With regard to the identification with the Essenes, the main point in dispute has been the issue of celibacy, which is noted by all ancient writers on the Essenes but is never explicitly required in the scrolls. Also, the accounts of the Essenes do not hint at messianic expectation or at the kind of apocalyptic expectations found in the *War Scroll* and other texts at Qumran.

The discussion has been obscured by a tendency among scholars to think of Qumran as a single, monastery-like institution. In fact, the rule books make clear that there was a network of communities, which could have as few as ten people, at various locations. The accounts of the Essenes (other than Pliny) also emphasize that they had many settlements. Josephus notes that there were two orders of Essenes, one of which accepted marriage. One of the rule books found at Qumran, the so-called *Damascus Document,* also appears to distinguish between "those who live in camps and marry and have children" and others who presumably do not. It is unlikely that all the scrolls were copied at Qumran. An alternative scenario is that Essenes from other settlements fled to Qumran in face of the advancing Romans in 68 C.E. and brought their scrolls with them. This would account for the high number of sectarian texts and also for the presence of different editions of the rule books in the caves.

In any case, it is clear that the corpus of texts found at Qumran includes many that were not sectarian in origin, although they may been used in a sectarian context. These include the biblical books, but also compositions like the books of *Enoch* and *Jubilees,* which apparently were composed before the formation of the sect in the middle or late second century B.C.E. and circulated more widely. But also many texts that were not known before the discovery of the scrolls may have been in broader use in the Judaism of the time. Yet the scrolls cannot be taken as a random sampling of Second Temple literature. On the one hand, the proportion of clearly sectarian texts, including sectarian rule books, is too great. On the other hand, several important writings from this period are conspicuously absent from Qumran. These include 1 Maccabees, the propagandistic history of the Hasmonean family, and the *Psalms of Solomon,* which has often been suspected of Pharisaic ideology. Nothing in the Dead Sea Scrolls can be identified as Pharisaic, and only one text (4Q448, the *Prayer for King Jonathan*) can be read as supportive of the Hasmoneans. The corpus is not narrowly sectarian, in the sense of containing only sectarian literature, but it is nonetheless selective and excludes some literature for ideological reasons.

The first scrolls were discovered on the eve of the Arab-Israeli war that led to the division of Palestine. When partition occurred, Qumran was on the Jordanian side of the border. The seven scrolls originally found in Cave 1 (*Community Rule, War Scroll, Hodayot, Habakkuk Pesher, Genesis Apocryphon,* and two copies of the book of Isaiah) were acquired by Eliezer Sukenik and his son Yigael Yadin, but Jewish scholars would have no access to the rest of the corpus until after the Six-Day War in 1967. The international team appointed to edit the fragments included no Jewish scholars. The first phase of scholarship on the scrolls, then, was dominated by Christian scholars, and Christian interests took priority. There were many comparisons of the community behind the scrolls to early Christianity, and such matters as eschatology and messianism received great attention (see, e.g., Cross 1995). In 1967, however, both Qumran and the Rockefeller Museum, where the scrolls were stored, came under Israeli control. This did not at first lead to any change in the editorial team, but it had a profound impact on scholarship in another way. Yadin, who was a general in the Israeli army, appropriated a long text, known as the *Temple Scroll,* from the antiquities dealer Kando, and he published it a decade later (Yadin 1977, 1983). This scroll contains a rewriting of biblical laws, and its interests are primarily halakic. Its publication aroused new interest in the aspects of the scrolls that were continuous with rabbinic rather than with Christian interests. Even more revolutionary was the disclosure in 1984 of a halakic work known as 4QMMT (Qimron and Strugnell 1994). This document is apparently addressed to a leader of Israel, and it outlines the reasons for the separation of a sectarian group from the majority of the people. The reasons had to do with issues of calendar and purity, and the scroll shows that halakic issues (issues of religious law) were vital to the raison d'être of the sect. The positions taken on these issues typically disagreed with those associated with the Pharisees in rabbinic literature and agreed with those of the Sadducees on some points. The scroll showed beyond any doubt that the kinds of issues debated in the Mishnah and Talmud were of great concern already in the late Second Temple period (Schiffman in Oppenheimer 1999: 205-19), and that in this respect any account of Judaism based only on the Apocrypha and Pseudepigrapha would be incomplete.

A third phase in the study of the scrolls began when the entire corpus became generally available in the early 1990s, and the editorial team was greatly expanded under the leadership of Emanuel Tov. It is now possible to get a more balanced view of the entire corpus.

Whatever their relation to "Enochic Judaism," the scrolls testify to the pervasive authority and influence of the Mosaic Torah. They provide important evidence about the development of the biblical text. The majority of the textual witnesses are close to the Masoretic Text, but there were also other textual forms in circulation. In some cases it is difficult to decide whether a given text is a variant form of the biblical text or a deliberate adaptation of it, in the manner of "rewritten bible," such as we find in *Jubilees*. The *Temple Scroll* reinterprets the legal traditions of Leviticus and Deuteronomy by presenting them in rewritten form as a revelation to Moses. In this way the writer's interpretation of the biblical laws is invested with the authority of the revelation at Sinai. Some scholars have argued that the *Temple Scroll* was intended to replace the Torah as the definitive law for the end of days (Wacholder 1983; Wise 1990: 184). Others argue that it presupposes the authority of the biblical text and is intended as a companion piece and guide to its interpretation (Najman 1999). It is, however, presented as a direct revelation from God, and it does not acknowledge the more familiar Torah. While it probably presupposes the validity of that Torah on some matters, it would seem to supersede it on the issues that it actually discusses. The scrolls also contain many examples of explicit commentary, most notably in the pesharim, which date from the first century B.C.E. and are the oldest extant formal biblical commentaries. The commentaries are primarily on prophetic texts, including Psalms, and relate them to the history of the sect and the "end of days." Especially interesting is the so-called *Pesher on Genesis* (4Q252), which combines a paraphrase of the flood story with a pesher-style interpretation of the Blessing of Jacob in Genesis 49.

The scrolls also provide ample evidence for an extensive literature associated with biblical figures, in the manner of the Pseudepigrapha (Dimant 1994; Flint in Flint and VanderKam 1998-1999: 2:24-66). Since most of this literature is fragmentary, it is difficult to be sure of the literary genre of many compositions. Related to the Enoch literature is a fragmentary *Book of Giants*. Possible apocalypses found at Qumran include the *Visions of Amram*, which describes dualistic angelic-demonic powers, the so-called *Aramaic Apocalypse* or *Son of God* text (4Q246), the *New Jerusalem* text (a vision in the tradition of Ezekiel 40–48), and a "four kingdoms" prophecy in which the four kingdoms are symbolized by four trees (4Q552-553). There are also prophecies after the fact attributed to Daniel (4Q243-244, 245) and a similar text, 4Q390, variously identified as *Pseudo-Moses* or *Jeremiah Apocryphon*. There are Aramaic texts relating to Levi and Qahath, and an Aramaic *Genesis Apocryphon*. The Aramaic literature found at Qumran is not perceptibly sectarian.

Since so many of the scrolls are dependent on biblical texts, there is a tendency to assume derivation from biblical prototypes. In some cases, this is justified. There are Targums of Leviticus and Job, and the *Genesis Apocryphon* and *Aramaic Levi Document* are obviously related to the biblical text. But this literature is not all derivative. The *Prayer of Nabonidus* may have been a source for the book of Daniel, but it does not depend on it, and at least some of the pseudo-Daniel literature also appears to be independent. The text sometimes known as *Proto-Esther* (4Q550) is related to Esther only insofar as both are tales set in the Persian court. The book of Tobit, which is included in the Apocrypha and is found at Qumran in both Hebrew and Aramaic, is another example of a narrative work that is not derived from a biblical story, although it draws on various biblical motifs. The scrolls also expand significantly our corpus of nonbiblical wisdom literature, including an extensive and important text, 4QInstruction (Goff 2007). Fragments of Ben Sira were also found. The corpus of liturgical texts is also enlarged (Nitzan 1994; Falk 1998). The sapiential and liturgical texts are in Hebrew, but in many cases they are not necessarily sectarian. The scrolls, then, support the view that Jewish literature in the late Second Temple period was quite diverse. Some of it certainly shared the halakic interests of the later rabbis, but much of it also exhibited concerns similar to those attested in the Apocrypha and Pseudepigrapha.

The most distinctive literature found in the scrolls consists of sectarian rule books (Metso 1998). The *Community Rule* and *Damascus Document* describe a complex sectarian movement that had more than one form of community life. They exhibit important parallels with Greek voluntary associations (Weinfeld 1986; Gillihan 2011), but they are conceived in terms of membership in a new covenant. These rules show extensive similarity to the descriptions of the Essenes in Philo and Josephus, with regard to admission procedures, common property, and community life. The Essenes were not the only sectarian movement to emerge in Judaism in the last centuries before the turn of the era. Rather, sectarianism was a feature of the age, and the scrolls are an important witness to the phenomenon (Baumgarten 1997).

The movement described in the scrolls has often been called an "apocalyptic community," with good reason (Collins 1997c). The *War Scroll* and the Treatise on the Two Spirits in the *Community Rule* are prime examples of what Seth Schwartz has called "the apocalyptic myth" (Schwartz 2001: 74-82). Yet the community does not seem to have used the literary form of apocalypse to any significant degree. In this case, the Torah of Moses was unequivocally regarded as the primary source of revelation. Moreover, the figure called the Teacher of Righteousness was revered as the authoritative interpreter, and rendered pseudonymous mediators such as Enoch or Daniel superfluous. In this respect, the sect was quite unique. It shows, however, that there was no necessary conflict between the veneration of the Torah and interest in apocalyptic revelations.

Judaism and Hellenism

Throughout the period under consideration in this volume, Jews lived in a world permeated by Hellenistic culture. The pervasiveness of Hellenistic influence can be seen even in the Dead Sea Scrolls (where there is little evidence of conscious interaction with the Greek world), for example, in the analogies between the sectarian communities and voluntary associations.

Modern scholarship has often assumed an antagonistic relationship between Hellenism and Judaism. This is due in large part to the received account of the Maccabean Revolt, especially in 2 Maccabees. The revolt was preceded by an attempt to make Jerusalem into a Hellenistic *polis*. Elias Bickerman (1937) even argued that the persecution was instigated by the Hellenizing high priest Alcimus, and in this he was followed by Martin Hengel (1974). Yet the revolt did not actually break out until the Syrian king, Antiochus IV Epiphanes, had disrupted the Jerusalem cult and given the Temple over to a Syrian garrison. The revolt was not directed against Hellenistic culture but against the policies of the king, especially with regard to the cult. Judas allegedly sent an embassy to Rome and availed himself of the services of one Eupolemus, who was sufficiently proficient in Greek to write an account of Jewish history. The successors of the Maccabees, the Hasmoneans, freely adopted Greek customs and even Greek names. Arnaldo Momigliano wrote that "the penetration of Greek words, customs, and intellectual modes in Judaea during the rule of the Hasmoneans and the following Kingdom of Herod has no limits" (Momigliano 1994: 22; see also Hengel 1989; Levine 1998). Herod established athletic contests in honor of Caesar and built a large amphitheater, and even established Roman-style gladiatorial contests. He also built temples for pagan cults, but not in Jewish territory, and he had to yield to protests by removing trophies, which involved images surrounded by weapons, from the Temple. In all cases where we find resistance to Hellenism in Judea, the issue involves cult or worship (Collins 2005: 21-43). Many aspects of Greek culture, including most obviously the language, were inoffensive. The revolt against Rome was sparked not by cultural conflict but by Roman mismanagement and social tensions.

Because of the extensive Hellenization of Judea, the old distinction between "Palestinian" Judaism and "Hellenistic" (= Diaspora) Judaism has been eroded to a great degree in modern scholarship. Nonetheless, the situation of Jews in the Diaspora was different in degree, as they were a minority in a pagan, Greek-speaking environment, and the Greek language and cultural forms provided their natural means of expression (Gruen 1998, 2002). The Jewish community in Alexandria, the Diaspora community of which we are most fully informed, regarded themselves as akin to the Greeks, in contrast to the Egyptians and other *Barbaroi.* The Torah was translated into Greek already in the third century B.C.E. Thereafter, Jewish authors experimented with Greek genres — epic, tragedy, Sibylline oracles, philosophical treatises (Goodman in Vermes et al. 1973-1987: 3:1.470-704; Collins 2000). This considerable literary production reached its apex in the voluminous work of the philosopher Philo in the early first century C.E. This Greco-Jewish literature has often been categorized as apologetic, on the assumption that it was addressed to Gentiles. Since the work of Victor Tcherikover (1956), it is generally recognized that it is rather directed to the Jewish community. Nonetheless, it has a certain apologetic dimension (Collins 2005: 1-20). It is greatly concerned to claim Gentile approval for

Judaism. In the *Letter of Aristeas,* the Ptolemy and his counselors are greatly impressed by the wisdom of the Jewish sages. *Aristeas* affirms that these people worship the same God that the Greeks know as Zeus, and the roughly contemporary Jewish philosopher Aristobulus affirms that the Greek poets refer to the true God by the same name. The Sibyl praises the Jews alone among the peoples of the earth. Philo, and later Josephus, is at pains to show that Jews exhibit the Greek virtue of *philanthrōpia.*

To some degree, Hellenistic Jewish authors wrote to counteract perceptions of Jews that circulated in the Hellenistic world (Berthelot 2003). Already at the beginning of the Hellenistic era, Hecataeus of Abdera wrote that Moses had introduced "a somewhat unsocial and inhospitable mode of life." He told a garbled story of Jewish origins which conflated the Jews with the Hyksos, the Syrian invaders of the second millennium B.C.E. whose memory in Egypt was accursed. The story was elaborated by the Egyptian historian Manetho. It is unlikely that either Manetho or Hecataeus knew the exodus story in its biblical form, or that either had more than an incidental interest in the Jews. The association of the Jews with this tradition was highly negative. Many of the negative stereotypes and calumnies of the Jews were collected by the Alexandrian grammarian Apion in the first century C.E. We owe their preservation, ironically, to the refutation by Josephus, in his tract *Against Apion.*

There has been a tendency in modern scholarship to find in this material the roots of anti-Semitism (Gager 1983; Schäfer 1997). But the portrayal of Jews was not uniformly negative (Feldman 1993: 177-287). Moses was often praised as a lawgiver, even already by Hecataeus. Moreover, we should bear in mind that the Jews were by no means the only ethnic group in the Hellenistic world who were subjected to ridicule (Isaac 2004). In the first century C.E., however, antagonism moved beyond ridicule to violence, in the form of a virtual pogrom in 38 C.E. Violent conflict would eventually consume the Jewish Egyptian community in the revolt under Trajan (Pucci ben Zeev 2005). The alleged anti-Semitism in Alexandria must be seen in the concrete historical and social circumstances of this conflict

Jews had prospered in Egypt in the Ptolemaic period, despite occasional tensions. Some had served as generals in Ptolemaic armies. Philo's family became wealthy bankers. In the Roman era, however, their fortunes declined, and there were pogroms in Alexandria in the time of Caligula and again in 66 C.E. The classic explanation of this conflict was offered by Tcherikover, who made good use of papyrological evidence (1959: 296-332; Tcherikover and Fuks 1957-1964; cf. Modrzejewski 1995). For purposes of taxation, the Romans drew a sharper line between citizen and noncitizen than was the case the Ptolemaic era. Jews responded by trying to infiltrate the gymnasium, as a way of attaining citizenship. The Alexandrians resisted, and conflict ensued. The evidence for this construction of events is admittedly fragile, as Erich Gruen especially has pointed out (Gruen 2002: 54-83). It is doubtful whether the Jews actually sought citizenship, which would presumably have entailed some acknowledgment of the Greek gods (Kasher 1985). Rather, they wanted a status equal to that of citizens. What is apparent is that the Roman conquest of Egypt intensified ethnic rivalry in Alexandria. The Alexandrian citizens were jealous of their diminished status. Jews resented being classified with Egyptians. The role of the Roman governor in manipulating the conflict for his own ends is less than clear. The details of the case are a subject of ongoing debate (Collins 2005: 181-201; Gambetti 2009).

Diaspora Judaism, no less than its counterpart in the land of Israel, had its frame of reference in the Torah, which in its Greek translation is the great wellspring of Greco-Jewish literature. Many of the fragmentary writings can be described as parabiblical, even if they are cast in Greek forms. The retelling of the exodus in the form of a Greek tragedy by one Ezekiel is a case in point. There has been growing appreciation in recent years of the role of exegesis of the Torah as a unifying element across the full spectrum of ancient Judaism (Kugel 1998).

Egyptian Judaism, however, was distinctive in important ways. Philo, the greatest exegete of Alexandrian Judaism, viewed the Torah through a prism of Greek philosophy, which led to a very different understanding from anything we find in Hebrew or Aramaic sources. Few Alexandrian Jews would have shared Philo's philosophical sophistication, but virtually all the writings we have from this community use Greek literary forms and categories to appropriate the biblical tradition. In contrast to the Dead Sea Scrolls, the Diaspora literature makes minimal reference to halakic issues or purity laws. It does, however, insist on Jewish monotheism, and frequently ridicules pagan idolatry. It also insists on the superiority of Jewish sexual ethics and the fact that Jews refrain from infanticide. These were matters which enlightened Greeks could, in principle, appreciate, and they are indicative of the self-image cultivated by Diaspora Jewry. Complete assimilation to the Gentile way of life certainly occurred. (The most famous example is Philo's nephew, Tiberius Julius Alexander, who became prefect of Egypt and assisted in putting down the Jewish revolt against Rome.) But the Jewish community as a whole preserved a distinct identity, even while embracing most aspects of Hellenistic culture other than idolatry. (On the degrees of assimilation and acculturation, see Barclay 1996.)

Conclusion

The story of modern scholarship on early Judaism is largely a story of retrieval. None of the literature of this period was preserved by the rabbis. The Greek literature of the Diaspora may not have been available to them. Much of the apocalyptic literature and of the material in the Dead Sea Scrolls was rejected for ideological reasons. The recovery of this literature in modern times presents us with a very different view of early Judaism than was current in the nineteenth century, and even than more recent accounts that impose a rabbinic paradigm on the period in the interests of normativity.

No doubt, our current picture of early Judaism is also incomplete. Despite the important documentary papyri from the Judean Desert dating to the Bar Kokhba period (Cotton in Oppenheimer, ed. 1999: 221-36), descriptions of the *realia* of Jewish life still rely heavily on rabbinic sources that are possibly anachronistic. The overdue study of women in this period is a case in point (Ilan 1995). One of the salutary lessons of the Dead Sea Scrolls is that they revealed aspects of Judaism that no one would have predicted before the discovery. And yet this was only the corpus of writings collected by one sect. To do justice to early Judaism we would need similar finds of Pharisaic, Sadducean, and other groups, and further documentary finds similar to those that have shed at least limited light on Egyptian Judaism and on Judah in the Bar Kokhba period.

BIBLIOGRAPHY

Barclay, John M. G. 1996. *Jews in the Mediterranean Diaspora*. Edinburgh: Clark.
Baumgarten, Albert I. 1997. *The Flourishing of Jewish Sects in the Maccabean Era: An Interpretation*. Leiden: Brill.
Beall, Todd S. 1988. *Josephus' Description of the Essenes Illustrated by the Dead Sea Scrolls*. Cambridge: Cambridge University.
Berthelot, Katell. 2003. *Philanthropia Judaica: Le débat autour de la 'misanthropie' des lois juives dans l'antiquité*. Leiden: Brill.
———, and Daniel Stökl Ben Ezra. 2010. *Aramaica Qumranica: Proceedings of the Conference on the Aramaic Texts from Qumran in aix-en-Provence, 30 June–2 July 2008*. Leiden: Brill.

Bickerman, Elias J. 1937. *Der Gott der Makkabäer.* Berlin: Schocken.

Boccaccini, Gabriele. 1991. *Middle Judaism: Jewish Thought, 300 B.C.E.–200 C.E.* Minneapolis: Fortress.

———. 1998. *Beyond the Essene Hypothesis: The Parting of the Ways between Qumran and Enochic Judaism.* Grand Rapids: Eerdmans.

———, ed. 2005. *Enoch and Qumran Origins: New Light on a Forgotten Connection.* Grand Rapids: Eerdmans.

Boccaccini, Gabriele, and John J. Collins, eds. 2007. *The Early Enoch Literature.* Leiden: Brill.

Bousset, Wilhelm. 1903a. *Die Religion des Judentums in neutestamentlichen Zeitalter.* Berlin: Reuther und Reichard.

———. 1903b. *Volksfrömmigkeit und Schriftgelehrtentum: Antwort auf Herrn Perles' Kritik meiner 'Religion des Judentums im N.T. Zeitalter.'* Berlin: Reuther und Reichard.

Charles, R. H., ed. 1913. *The Apocrypha and Pseudepigrapha of the Old Testament.* 2 vols. Oxford: Clarendon.

Charlesworth, James H., ed. 1983-1985. *The Old Testament Pseudepigrapha.* 2 vols. New York: Doubleday.

Cohen, Shaye J. D. 1999. *The Beginnings of Jewishness: Boundaries, Varieties, Uncertainties.* Berkeley: University of California Press.

Collins, John J., ed. 1979. *Apocalypse: The Morphology of a Genre.* Semeia 14. Missoula, Mont.: Scholars Press.

———. 1997a. *Jewish Wisdom in the Hellenistic Age.* Louisville: Westminster John Knox.

———. 1997b. *Seers, Sibyls and Sages in Hellenistic-Roman Judaism.* Leiden: Brill.

———. 1997c. *Apocalypticism in the Dead Sea Scrolls.* London: Routledge.

———. 1998. *The Apocalyptic Imagination: An Introduction to Jewish Apocalyptic Literature.* 2nd ed. Grand Rapids: Eerdmans.

———. 2000. *Between Athens and Jerusalem: Jewish Identity in the Hellenistic Diaspora.* 2nd ed. Grand Rapids: Eerdmans.

———. 2005. *Jewish Cult and Hellenistic Culture: Essays on the Jewish Encounter with Hellenism and Roman Rule.* Leiden: Brill.

Cross, Frank Moore. 1995. *The Ancient Library of Qumran.* 3d ed. Sheffield: Sheffield Academic Press.

Davila, James R. 2005. *The Provenance of the Pseudepigrapha: Jewish, Christian, or Other?* Leiden: Brill.

Dimant, Devorah. 1994. "Apocalyptic Texts at Qumran." In *The Community of the Renewed Covenant: The Notre Dame Symposium on the Dead Sea Scrolls.* Ed. Eugene Ulrich and James VanderKam. Notre Dame: University of Notre Dame Press, 175-91.

Efron, Joshua. 1987. *Studies on the Hasmonean Period.* Leiden: Brill.

Fabricius, J. A. 1713. *Codex Pseudepigraphus Veteris Testamenti.* Leipzig: Liebezeit.

Falk, Daniel K. 1998. *Daily, Sabbath, and Festival Prayers in the Dead Sea Scrolls.* Leiden: Brill.

Feldman, Louis H. 1993. *Jew and Gentile in the Ancient World: Attitudes and Interactions from Alexander to Justinian.* Princeton: Princeton University Press.

Flint, Peter W., and James C. VanderKam, eds. 1998-1999. *The Dead Sea Scrolls after Fifty Years: A Comprehensive Assessment.* 2 vols. Leiden: Brill.

Gager, John G. 1985. *The Origins of Anti-Semitism: Attitudes toward Judaism in Pagan and Christian Antiquity.* Oxford: Oxford University Press.

Galor, Katharina, Jean-Baptiste Humbert, and Jürgen Zangenberg, eds. 2006. *Qumran: The Site of the Dead Sea Scrolls: Archaeological Interpretations and Debates.* Leiden: Brill.

Gambetti, Sandra. 2009. *The Alexandrian Riots of 38 c.e. and the Persecution of the Jews: A Historical Reconstruction.* Leiden: Brill.

Gillihan, Yonder Moynihan. 2011. *Civic Ideology, Organization, and Law in the Rule Scrolls: A Comparative Study of the Covenanters' Sect and Contemporary Voluntary Associations in Political Context.* Leiden: Brill.

Goff, Matthew J. 2007. *Discerning Wisdom: The Sapiential Literature of the Dead Sea Scrolls.* Leiden: Brill.

Golb, Norman. 1995. *Who Wrote the Dead Sea Scrolls? The Search for the Secret of Qumran.* New York: Scribner.

Goodman, Martin. 2002. "Jews and Judaism in the Second Temple Period." In *The Oxford Handbook of Jewish Studies.* Ed. M. Goodman. Oxford: Oxford University Press, 36-52.

Green, William S. 1994. "Ancient Judaism: Contours and Complexity." In *Language, Theology and the Bible: Essays in Honour of James Barr.* Ed. S. E. Balentine and J. Barton. Oxford: Oxford University Press, 293-310.

Gruen, Erich S. 1998. *Heritage and Hellenism: The Reinvention of Jewish Tradition.* Berkeley: University of California Press.

———. 2002. *Diaspora: Jews amidst Greeks and Romans.* Cambridge: Harvard University Press.

Harlow, Daniel C. 1996. *The Greek Apocalypse of Baruch (3 Baruch) in Hellenistic Judaism and Early Christianity.* Leiden: Brill.

Hellholm, David. 1983. *Apocalypticism in the Mediterranean World and the Near East.* Tübingen: Mohr Siebeck.

Hengel, Martin. 1974. *Judaism and Hellenism: Studies in Their Encounter in Palestine in the Early Hellenistic Period.* 2 vols. Philadelphia: Fortress.

———. 1989. *The Hellenization of Judaea in the First Century after Christ.* Philadelphia: Trinity Press International.

———. 1990. "Der alte und der neue Schürer." *JSS* 35: 19-64.

Himmelfarb, Martha. 1993. *Ascent to Heaven in Jewish and Christian Apocalypses.* New York: Oxford.

Ilan, Tal. 1995. *Jewish Women in Greco-Roman Palestine: An Inquiry into Image and Status*. Tübingen: Mohr Siebeck.

Isaac, Benjamin. 2004. *The Invention of Racism in Classical Antiquity*. Princeton: Princeton University Press.

Jonge, Marinus de. 1953. *The Testaments of the Twelve Patriarchs: A Study of Their Text, Composition and Origin*. Assen: van Gorcum.

————. 2000. "The Testaments of the Twelve Patriarchs and Related Qumran Fragments." In *For a Later Generation: The Transformation of Tradition in Israel, Early Judaism and Early Christianity*. Ed. Randall A. Argall, Beverly A. Bow, and Rodney A. Werline. Harrisburg, Penn.: Trinity Press International, 63-77.

Kasher, Aryeh. 1985. *The Jews in Hellenistic and Roman Egypt*. Tübingen: Mohr Siebeck.

Kautzsch, Emil. 1900. *Die Apokryphen und Pseudepigraphen des Alten Testaments*. Tübingen: Mohr.

Koch, Klaus. 1972. *The Rediscovery of Apocalyptic*. Naperville, Ill.: Allenson.

Kraemer, Ross S. 1998. *When Aseneth Met Joseph: A Late Antique Tale of the Biblical Patriarch and His Egyptian Wife, Reconsidered*. Oxford: Oxford University Press.

Kraft, Robert A. 1994. "The Pseudepigrapha in Christianity." In *Tracing the Threads: Studies in the Vitality of Jewish Pseudepigrapha*. Ed. John C. Reeves. Atlanta: Scholars Press, 55-86.

————. 2001. "The Pseudepigrapha and Christianity Revisited: Setting the Stage and Framing Some Central Questions." *JSJ* 32: 371-95.

Kugel, James L. 1998. *Traditions of the Bible: A Guide to the Bible As It Was at the Start of the Common Era*. Cambridge: Harvard University Press.

Kvanvig, Helge S. 1988. *Roots of Apocalyptic: The Mesopotamian Background of the Enoch Figure and of the Son of Man*. Neukirchen-Vluyn: Neukirchener Verlag.

Laurence, Richard. 1821. *The Book of Enoch the Prophet*. Oxford: Oxford University Press.

Levine, Lee. I. 1998. *Judaism and Hellenism in Antiquity: Conflict or Confluence?* Seattle: University of Washington Press.

Lim, Timothy, and John J. Collins, eds. 2010. *The Oxford Handbook of the Dead Sea Scrolls*. Oxford: Oxford University Press.

Mason, Steve. 2007. "Jews, Judaeans, Judaizing, Judaism: Problems of Categorization in Ancient History." *JSJ* 38: 457-512.

Metso, Sarianna. 1997. *The Textual Development of the Qumran Community Rule*. Leiden/New York: Brill.

Meyers, Eric M., and Mark A. Chancey. 2012. *Archaeology of the Land of the Bible: From Cyrus to Constantine*. New Haven: Yale University Press.

Milik, J. T. 1976. *The Books of Enoch*. Oxford: Clarendon.

Modrzejewski, Joseph Mélèze. 1995. *The Jews of Egypt: From Rameses II to Emperor Hadrian.* Princeton: Princeton University Press.

Momigliano, Arnaldo. 1994. *Essays on Ancient and Modern Judaism.* Chicago: University of Chicago Press.

Moore, George Foote. 1921. "Christian Writers on Judaism." *HTR* 14: 197-254.

————. 1927-1930. *Judaism in the First Centuries of the Christian Era: The Age of the Tannaim.* 3 vols. Cambridge: Harvard University Press.

Najman, Hindy. 1999. *Seconding Sinai: The Development of Mosaic Discourse in Second Temple Judaism.* Leiden: Brill.

Neusner, Jacob. 1981. *Judaism: The Evidence of the Mishnah.* Chicago: University of Chicago Press.

————. 1984. *Das pharisäische und talmudische Judentum.* Ed. Hermann Lichtenberger. Tübingen: Mohr Siebeck.

Neusner, Jacob, William S. Green, and Ernst Frerichs, eds. 1987. *Judaisms and Their Messiahs at the Turn of the Christian Era.* Cambridge: Cambridge University Press.

Nickelsburg, George W. E. 1998. "Enochic Wisdom: An Alternative to the Mosaic Torah?" In *Hesed ve-emet: Studies in Honor of Ernest S. Frerichs.* Ed. Jodi Magness and Seymour Gitin. Atlanta: Scholars Press, 123-32.

————. 2005. *Jewish Literature between the Bible and the Mishnah.* 2d ed. Minneapolis: Fortress.

Nir, Rivka. 2003. *The Destruction of Jerusalem and the Idea of Redemption in the Syriac Apocalypse of Baruch.* Atlanta: Society of Biblical Literature.

————. 2012. *Joseph and Aseneth: A Christian Book.* Sheffield: Sheffield Phoenix.

Nitzan, Bilhah. 1994. *Qumran Prayer and Religious Poetry.* Leiden: Brill.

Oppenheimer, Aharon, ed. 1999. *Jüdische Geschichte in hellenistisch-römischer Zeit: Wege der Forschung, Vom alten zum neuen Schürer.* Munich: Oldenbourg.

Perles, Felix. 1903. *Bousset's Religion des Judentums im neutestamentlichen Zeitalter kritisch untersucht.* Berlin: Peiser.

Porter, F. C. 1928. Review of *Judaism in the First Centuries of the Christian Era: The Age of the Tannaim* by G. F. Moore in *Journal of Religion* 8: 30-62.

Pucci ben Zeev, Miriam. 2005. *Diaspora Judaism in Turmoil, 116/117 CE: Ancient Sources and Modern Insights.* Leuven: Peeters.

Qimron, Elisha, and John Strugnell. 1994. *Qumran Cave 4, V. Miqṣat Ma'aśê Ha-Torah.* DJD 10. Oxford: Clarendon.

Rad, Gerhard von. 1965. *Theologie des Alten Testament.* 4th ed. Munich: Kaiser.

Riessler, Paul. 1928. *Altjüdisches Schrifttum ausserhalb der Bibel.* Augsburg: Filer.

Rowland, Christopher. 1983. *The Open Heaven: A Study of Apocalyptic in Judaism and Early Christianity.* New York: Crossroad.

Rowley, H. H. 1944. *The Relevance of Apocalyptic.* London: Athlone.

Sacchi, Paolo. 1997. *Jewish Apocalyptic and Its History.* Sheffield: Sheffield Academic Press.

Sanders, E. P. 1977. *Paul and Palestinian Judaism*. Philadelphia: Fortress.

————. 1985. *Jesus and Judaism*. Philadelphia: Fortress.

————. 1990. *Jewish Law from Jesus to the Mishnah*. London: SCM.

————. 1992. *Judaism: Practice and Belief, 63 BCE–66 CE*. Philadelphia: Trinity Press International.

Schäfer, Peter. 1997. *Judeophobia: Attitudes toward the Jews in the Ancient World*. Cambridge: Harvard University Press.

Schiffman, L. H. 1999. "Halakha and History: The Contribution of the Dead Sea Scrolls to Recent Scholarship." In *Jüdische Geschichte*. Ed. A. Oppenheimer. Munich: Oldenbourg, 205-19.

Schürer, Emil. 1886-1911. *Geschichte des jüdischen Volkes im Zeitalter Jesu Christi*. 2 vols. Leipzig: Hinrichs (1886-1890; 3d ed., 3 vols., 1898-1901; 4th ed., 1901-1909, with index volume, 1911; English translation of 3d ed.: *A History of the Jewish People in the Time of Jesus Christ*, 3 vols., Edinburgh: Clark, 1890-1893).

Schwartz, Seth. 2001. *Imperialism and Jewish Society, 200 B.C.E. to 640 C.E.* Princeton: Princeton University Press.

Segal, Michael. 2007. *The Book of Jubilees: Rewritten Bible, Redaction, Ideology and Theology*. Leiden: Brill.

Stone, Michael E., ed. 1984. *Jewish Literature of the Second Temple Period*. Assen: Van Gorcum; Philadelphia: Fortress.

Tcherikover, Victor. 1956. "Jewish Apologetic Literature Reconsidered." *Eos* 48: 169-93.

————. 1959. *Hellenistic Civilization and the Jews*. Philadelphia: Jewish Publication Society.

Tcherikover, Victor, and Alexander Fuks. 1957-64. *Corpus Papyrorum Judaicarum*. 3 vols. Cambridge: Harvard University Press.

VanderKam, James C. 2010. *The Dead Sea Scrolls Today*. Rev. ed. Grand Rapids: Eerdmans.

Vermes, Geza et al., eds. 1973-1987. *The History of the Jewish People in the Age of Jesus Christ (175 B.C.–A.D. 135) by Emil Schürer: A New English Edition Revised and Edited*. 3 vols., vol. 3 in 2 parts. Edinburgh: Clark.

Wacholder, Ben Zion. 1983. *The Dawn of Qumran: The Sectarian Torah and the Teacher of Righteousness*. Cincinnati: Hebrew Union College.

Weinfeld, Moshe. 1986. *The Organizational Pattern and the Penal Code of the Qumran Sect*. Göttingen: Vandenhoeck & Ruprecht.

Wiese, Christian. 2005. *Challenging Colonial Discourse: Jewish Studies and Protestant Theology in Wilhelmine Germany*. Trans. B. Harshav and C. Wiese. Leiden: Brill.

Wise, Michael O. 1990. *A Critical Study of the Temple Scroll from Qumran Cave 11*. Chicago: Oriental Institute.

Yadin, Yigael. 1977. *Megillat ha-Miqdash*. 3 vols. Jerusalem: Israel Exploration Society.

————. 1983. *The Temple Scroll*. 3 vols. Jerusalem: Israel Exploration Society.

Jewish History from Alexander to Hadrian

Chris Seeman and Adam Kolman Marshak

From Alexander to Pompey

The conquests of Alexander the Great had far-reaching consequences for the Jews. In the course of a single decade (334-324 B.C.E.), Jewish communities everywhere found themselves subjects of a new world empire ruled by Macedonians and connected with Greek culture (see map 1). Macedonian monarchs would continue to dominate the Near East for the next three centuries, while Hellenism itself would cast a still longer shadow over the region and its peoples.

These new realities carried with them both peril and prospect for the Jews of Asia Minor, the Levant, Egypt, Mesopotamia, and Iran. The inability of Alexander's successors to hold together his far-flung dominions condemned those lands to chronic interstate warfare and incessant dynastic instability. Physical displacement, economic hardship, political factionalism, enslavement, and other woes are prominent themes of this era. But Jews could also benefit from the opportunities created by so volatile an environment. Some found ready employment in the military and bureaucratic sectors of the Hellenistic states. Others engaged in interregional trade networks and participated in the cosmopolitan life of Greek cities. By the second half of the first century B.C.E., the Hasmoneans were able to forge a sovereign, Jewish state in Palestine — the first in almost 500 years. The Hellenistic age brought Jews into contact with a wider world; it also brought them to the notice of that world. When the Roman general Pompey set foot in Palestine in 63 B.C.E., the Jews had become a people to be reckoned with.

Before Alexander

Before the conquests of Alexander, all Jews (so far as we are aware) resided within the confines of the Persian Empire. Stretching from Anatolia in the west to Afghanistan in the east and from the Caspian steppe in the north to Upper Egypt in the south, the multiethnic domain of the Achaemenid dynasty sustained numerous Jewish communities. Most of these are known to us only through indirect or retrospective testimony. Thus, our present understanding of Jewish life on the eve of Alexander's conquests is imperfect, especially outside of Palestine.

An obscure biblical allusion and a stray Aramaic inscription *may* attest to a Jewish presence in Asia Minor before Alexander, but their interpretation and dating are contested. In the absence of stronger evidence, it is more defensible to treat the Jewish settlement of western Anatolia as a Hellenistic development.

The Babylonian Diaspora is a major focus of the prophetic corpus of the Hebrew Bible. The later flowering of talmudic culture in that region spawned a wealth of traditions concerning the Jews of Mesopotamia. But the historicity of the latter is often suspect, and the former deals mostly with the Neo-Babylonian period. This gap in reliable testimony is partly remedied by economic documents that locate individual Jews (as well as at least one predominantly Jewish town) in the Babylon-Borsippa and Nippur regions. As yet, there is no cuneiform evidence for a Jewish presence in the city of Babylon itself during Achaemenid times.

Less certain still is the extent of pre-Hellenistic Jewish penetration of lands of the Zagros arc — Armenia, Adiabene, Media, Elam — or the vast Iranian plateau beyond. Late antique sources attest to an Achaemenid deportation of Jews to distant Hyrcania around 340 B.C.E., and the subsequent appearance of "Hyrcanus" as a Jewish name has been cited as corroboration for this tradition. It is possible, however, that the alleged deportation has been chronologically misplaced and that it actually happened six centuries later.

The geopolitical situation of Palestine has traditionally linked it with Egypt. The Bible is rife with references to pro-Egyptian factions collaborating with allies on the Nile. Such interstate cooperation appears to have supplied the occasion for the emergence of a Jewish military colony at Elephantine (Yeb) in Upper Egypt. Although there were certainly other Jewish settlements in Egypt, the Elephantine garrison is the only one whose persistence into Achaemenid times has been verified by papyri. Unfortunately, this documentation peters out by the end of the fifth century B.C.E. One Hellenistic text, the largely fictional *Letter of Aristeas,* claims additional colonists settled in Egypt with the advent of Persian rule, but no precise chronology is offered. Still, it is a reasonable inference that there were Jews living in Egypt at the time of Alexander's capture of that country in 332 B.C.E. The pattern of military settlement certainly continued under Macedonian rule.

We are better informed about Palestinian Jewry than any other, though the picture remains woefully incomplete. Survey archaeology has revealed a gradual demographic expansion during late Achaemenid times, as well as significant commercial involvement with the Greek world via the Phoenician coast. Recent excavations on Mt. Gerizim have firmly dated the construction of a Samaritan temple there to the mid-fifth century, though it remains unclear whether or to what extent this event reflects the developed Jewish-Samaritan rivalry of the Hellenistic period.

The wars of Alexander and his successors undoubtedly disrupted Jewish life in the late fourth century, but the core areas of Jewish settlement persisted and, in time, expanded. By the time of Pompey, Jews could be found not only within the lands of the former Persian Empire, but also in the Aegean, the Greek mainland, North Africa, even the city of Rome. The consolidation of the Hasmonean state in the late second and early first centuries extended Jewish settlement (or at least control) over much of Palestine, transforming Judea from a minute, land-locked, temple community into a major regional power. In Achaemenid times, many Jews — perhaps a majority — inhabited the hinterlands of the great urban centers of the Near East. This was to change during the age of Alexander. In the course of the Hellenistic period, many Jews would be drawn to the Greek *polis* and would absorb and appropriate its culture (selectively) as their own. This development, more than any other, propelled the creative genius of early Judaism.

Alexander and the Diadochoi

The principal Greek and Roman historians who chronicled the campaigns of Alexander make no mention of the Jews, who appear to have played little or no active role in the titanic clashes of that decisive decade. The first-century-C.E. Jewish historian, Flavius Josephus, conjures up a very different picture. In his account, Alexander visited Jerusalem after his capture of Gaza in 332, attributed his victories to the favor of the Jewish god, guaranteed all Jews the right to live by their ancestral laws, and invited any who wished to join the Macedonians in their war against Persia (*Ant.* 11.325-39). Hecataeus of Abdera (or, more likely, a Jewish pseudepigrapher writing in his name) preserves episodes involving Jewish soldiers in Alexander's forces (*apud* Josephus, *Ag. Ap.* 1.192, 200-204). Although judged to be fictional by most scholars, these and other imaginative reconstructions reflect the fact that Jews did serve in the armies of the Hellenistic monarchies.

Alexander died in 323 without a viable heir and apparently without any clear instructions for choosing one. The result was a series of ultimately unsuccessful attempts by his former companions to prevent the fragmentation of Alexander's realm. The rival maneuverings of these generals, collectively dubbed the Diadochoi ("Successors") by later historians, turned the lands of the Near East into an incessant battleground (see map 2). The loss of Alexander's natural kin to attrition removed the Macedonian royal house as a putative object of common allegiance, impelling each of the Diadochoi in turn to proclaim himself king. The failure of the strongest of these to achieve ascendancy over his rivals at the Battle of Ipsus in 301 B.C.E. precipitated a division of territory that would eventually harden into three relatively stable monarchies: Antigonid Greece, Seleucid Asia, and Ptolemaic Egypt.

References to Jewish fortunes during the early wars of the Diadochoi are sparse. The Alexandrian historian Agatharchides of Cnidus relates that Ptolemy I captured Jerusalem, probably in 312 B.C.E. (*apud* Josephus, *Ag. Ap.* 1.209-11; cf. *Ant.* 12.6). The *Letter of Aristeas* states that Ptolemy enslaved some of its inhabitants and relocated others to Egypt, absorbing roughly a third of the latter into his defense forces. *Aristeas*'s numbers (100,000 deportees) are clearly exaggerated; but even if the story oversimplifies a more complicated series of population transfers, it surely reflects at least one source of Egypt's Jewish population during the early Hellenistic period. Josephus also claims Jews served in the armies of Seleucus I (ruled 305-281) and were rewarded with citizenship in the cities he founded (*Ant.* 12.119). As with the Ptolemaic tales, this tradition smacks of retrospection by later Jewish inhabitants of these cities — especially those of the Seleucid capital at Antioch (*Ant.* 12.120-24). A precise chronology of early Jewish settlement within the Ptolemaic and Seleucid realms is not recoverable.

The Third Century

The Ptolemaic Empire dominates the historical record of Jewish life in the third century B.C.E. (see map 3). From the Battle of Ipsus until the Seleucid seizure of Palestine in 198, roughly half the world's Jews were subjects of the House of Ptolemy. (Of the other half, we possess virtually no evidence for this period.) From an Egyptian core, centered on the maritime metropolis of Alexandria, the Ptolemies projected their power across the eastern Mediterranean. Cyrenaica, Cyprus, Crete, the islands of the Aegean, the coasts of Anatolia and the Levant, along with much of the Syrian and Palestinian hinterlands, all felt the hand of Ptolemaic rule.

Egypt itself provides the greatest wealth of documentation for Jews in the Ptolemaic realm. Third-century papyri reveal Jewish military settlements in the Fayyum, while funerary inscriptions from the vicinity of Alexandria indicate an early concentration of Jews there. This picture is reinforced by inscriptions from Schedia and Arsinoe-Crocodilopolis dedicating prayer houses to Ptolemy III (ruled 246-221 B.C.E.). The presence of one such building at Schedia on the Nile may also lend some credence to Josephus's claim that Jews had been involved in official oversight of river traffic (*Ag. Ap.* 2.64).

The vexed and ultimately insoluble problem of dating the *Letter of Aristeas* need not detain us. Most scholars conjecture a late second- or early first-century-B.C.E. setting; but whatever the date of its creation, *Aristeas* must have postdated (probably by several generations) the actual event of the Pentateuch's translation into Greek. Since there is no convincing reason to question Alexandria as the site of the translation, we may infer that, by the end of the third century, the Ptolemaic capital supported a Greek-speaking Jewish population numerous enough to warrant such an extensive undertaking. It is unnecessary to account for the existence of this community by any single event or cause. A century of Ptolemaic rule, along with the city's economic importance, is sufficient grounds for Alexandria's reputation as the largest urban Jewish settlement of the Hellenistic age.

The Libyan pentapolis of Cyrenaica was incorporated into the Ptolemaic realm already by the late fourth century. Predictably, Josephus attributes the origins of Jewish presence there to an act of Ptolemy I, bent on consolidating his hold over this tenuous frontier (*Ag. Ap.* 2.44). More substantial testimony for Jewish habitation of North Africa emerges only in the first century B.C.E., and so can tell us little about its possible beginnings two hundred years earlier (*Ant.* 14.115).

As for Jewish settlement elsewhere in the Ptolemaic Empire (apart from Palestine), we have no direct third-century evidence. The book of 1 Maccabees, probably composed in the late second century B.C.E., contains a list of cities and countries, including Cyrene and many other communities that fell within the zone of Ptolemaic hegemony (1 Macc. 15:22-23). This list, which refers to a Roman request that the addressees extradite any Jews who may be seeking asylum among them, has sometimes been construed as evidence for Jewish habitation in those places. This, however, is neither stated nor implied in the passage, which is itself historically suspect. It is possible that Jews penetrated the islands and coasts of the Ptolemaic-controlled Mediterranean by this time or earlier, but firmer statements to this effect must await new discoveries.

Our two primary sources for the history of Ptolemaic Palestine itself are Josephus and the so-called Zenon Papyri. Numismatic and archaeological data contribute to the assessment of this written testimony but also complicate its interpretation. Josephus's narrative focuses upon the fortunes of the Tobiads, a clan of Jewish notables who achieved prominence as collaborators and mediators of Ptolemaic rule. These colorful tales depict Judea as a distinct ethnic unit within Palestine whose tributary relations with Alexandria are mediated by the high priest in Jerusalem — until, that is, this role is transferred to the Tobiads. Tensions with his countrymen (possibly coincident with the conquest of Palestine by the Seleucids) eventually prompt Hyrcanus, one scion of the family, to withdraw to Transjordan, where he establishes himself as an independent strongman (*Ant.* 12.154-222).

Josephus's account suffers from historical inaccuracies, and many features of the Tobiad cycle are patently folkloric. The Zenon Papyri, a dossier detailing the economic activities of an agent of the chief finance minister for Ptolemy II, reveals a much more centrally controlled fiscal regime than that envisioned by Josephus (see fig. 16). Being occasional by its very nature, Zenon's correspondence can offer only vignettes of Ptolemaic Palestine, not a comprehensive panorama. No reference is made in them, for example, to the high priest (or the Tobiads) as the nexus of Ptolemaic administration. Strikingly, though, one papyrus does verify a Tobiad military presence in Transjordan a half century prior to Hyrcanus's settling in that region. Excavations have positively identified 'Araq el-Amir and its environs with the fortified estate Josephus attributes to Hyrcanus (and possibly with the military colony of Hyrcanus's ancestor, Tobias, associated by Zenon with "Birta in Ammanitis"). But scholarly consensus on the chronology of the surviving structures has yet to be achieved. What does emerge with certainty is that the institution of military settlement continued to be an important anchor for Macedonian control in the region, and that Jews could and did acquire power and prominence in other areas of life through that initial channel.

Another avenue of inquiry into the history of third-century Palestine is afforded by coinage. A series of small silver denomination, dubbed by numismatists "Yehud coins," crosscuts the boundary between the Persian and Hellenistic eras, and is coextensive with the period of Ptolemaic rule. Two features of these coins have attracted historical notice. The first is the fact that the name of the local governor (who apparently had acted as the minting authority under the Persians) disappears from the third-century issues. This absence, combined with the centrality of high priests in the literary sources, has led many to the conclusion that the Jewish high priest assumed an enlarged secular role under the Ptolemies. In addition to the *Letter of Aristeas* and the Tobiad romance, other texts referential to this period (1 Macc. 12:20-23; Sirach 50; 3 Maccabees 2; Hecataeus *apud* Diodorus 40.3.5-6) are unanimous in presenting the high priest as representative and leader of the Jewish people. These portraits may well be idealized, but the presumption that they reflect some degree of reality remains a defensible hypothesis. The modification of the coin legend *Yehud* to *Yehudah* on the later groups may indicate an administrative reorganization (perhaps during the reign of Ptolemy II). Advocates of the high priest-as-political-leader thesis often see the coins as indirect corroboration that the office was melding into a combination of cultic, diplomatic, and municipal roles. Enticing as these theories are, the numismatic evidence remains mute and therefore amenable to other interpretations. Whatever else they may point to, the coins do reveal that the coming of Ptolemaic rule did not involve a total break with existing institutions.

But Ptolemaic rule was not to last. Seleucus I's claim upon the lands of the Levant was never forgotten by his heirs, who, over the course of the third century, launched no fewer than five successive campaigns to recover the region. The last of these, fought between 202 and 198, definitively wrested Palestine from the Ptolemies, ushering in a century of Seleucid dominance (see map 4).

Antiochus III

With the reign of Antiochus III (223-187 B.C.E.), Jewish history became inextricably bound up with the fortunes of the Seleucid dynasty. When he came to power, Antiochus presided over a failing empire. Challenged internally by secessionist forces and confined from without by Ptolemy IV, the young monarch spent the better part of two decades reconsolidating Seleucid hegemony over Syria, Asia Minor, Mesopotamia, Iran, and central Asia. Jews appear to have played some role in this process. Josephus reproduces the text of a letter announcing Antiochus's decision to transplant 2,000 Jewish families from Mesopotamia and Babylonia to western Asia Minor, in hopes of establishing a loyalist presence in the rebellious satrapies of Phrygia and Lydia (*Ant.* 12.148-53).

The letter is not dated but cannot have been penned earlier than 213, the year Antiochus completed his reduction of Anatolia and began turning his attention to eastern affairs. If authentic, it supplies the earliest unambiguous testimony for Jewish settlement here. It also implies that Antiochus had reason to trust the Jewish communities of Babylonia and Mesopotamia. The justifications offered in the letter, however, are less than convincing (devotion to their God and loyalty toward the king's forefathers), prompting some to regard the document as a pious fiction — but one undoubtedly concocted by Jewish inhabitants of the regions mentioned. (Other documents in Josephus relating to Asia Minor in the late second and mid-first century B.C.E. provide ample evidence for Jews living there.)

The death of Ptolemy IV in 204 B.C.E. offered Antiochus a window of opportunity to recapture the southern Levant (which he had been forced to evacuate after an abortive conquest a decade and a half earlier). The details of the Fifth Syrian War that followed are imperfectly known. For the Jews of Palestine, the decisive turning point was the Battle of Panion (200 B.C.E.), which put Ptolemaic forces on the run. Subsequent coastal victories over Sidon (199) and Tyre (198) sealed Seleucid control over the region. According to Polybius (*apud* Josephus, *Ant.* 12.136), Jerusalem was captured soon after Panion, the Jews having assisted Antiochus in dislodging the city's Egyptian garrison (*Ant.* 12.138).

Josephus adduces two documents of Antiochus regarding Jerusalem and its people in the aftermath of Panion. The first promises royal financial underwriting for the Temple service and its physical repair from damages suffered in the conflict, mandates restoration to their homes of war captives and other displaced persons, guarantees the Jews shall live according to their traditional laws, exempts Temple personnel and other notables from certain taxes, and offers partial remission of tribute until the city and its hinterland recover from the ravages of war (*Ant.* 12.138-44). The second document asserts the sanctity of the Temple and its city, upholding purity regulations defined by "the ancestral law" and prescribing a fine to be paid in the event of their violation (*Ant.* 12.145-46).

The first of these documents is presented as a letter from Antiochus to a "Ptolemy" (probably to be identified with the Seleucid governor of Coele-Syria and Phoenicia attested in other contemporary sources). Its historicity is today generally accepted on the grounds that it conforms in most respects to known patterns of Seleucid beneficence. The second document is more problematic because it lacks a preamble identifying the king as its author. Some of the prohibitions it mandates find echoes in the *Temple Scroll* from Qumran (thought to have been composed half a century later). If Antiochus did promulgate such a decree, its stipulations were clearly governed by Jewish conceptualities, rather than conventional Hellenistic notions of temple inviolability.

Having secured his southern frontier against Egypt, Antiochus trained his gaze westward to the remaining Ptolemaic dependencies along the coasts of Anatolia. But his ambitions went beyond neutralizing the Ptolemaic Empire. In that same year (197), the Romans defeated Philip V of Macedon, erstwhile hegemon of Antigonid Greece. Stepping into this political vacuum, Antiochus crossed the Hellespont in 196 and began projecting Seleucid power into Europe. Four years later, the king's involvement in Greece precipitated war with Rome. Repulsed by Roman arms, Antiochus withdrew to Asia, where he was defeated at the Battle of Magnesia late in 190. Two years later, the humbled monarch ratified the Peace of Apamea, whose terms included a sizable war-indemnity, the transfer to Rome of royal hostages as surety for the king's good behavior, and a total ban on military involvement in Anatolia or Europe.

Antiochus himself died the following year on campaign in the east. But the terms of Apamea remained in force, and would have a significant impact on Seleucid relations with Judea for the next twenty-five years. The imperative to raise money to pay off annual installments of the indemnity frequently strained Seleucid resources. It may be that the attempt by Seleucus IV (Antiochus's son and successor) to plunder the Jerusalem Temple treasury a decade after Apamea reflects these pressures (2 Maccabees 3). The shadow of Apamea undoubtedly also increased the willingness of Antiochus' descendants to accept monetary bribes from rival Jewish aspirants to the high priestly office, setting a precedent that would persist even after the indemnity was paid off. Another long-term effect of Apamea on Jewish-Seleucid relations was the political instability it engendered. The treaty's stipulation that a scion of the House of Seleucus be held hostage in Rome created, in effect, a potential usurper "waiting in the wings." Dynastic rivalry resulting from this heightened the claimants' need to solicit support from their subjects. The factionalism fueled by this dynamic would prove to be one of the central engines of Jewish history during the second half of the second century B.C.E.

Antiochus IV

Upon the death of Seleucus IV, his younger brother Antiochus IV seized power. Our principal source for Jewish history during the early years of the new Antiochus's reign is 2 Maccabees, which focuses on events in Palestine. Central to this narrative is the Seleucid-backed acquisition of the high priesthood by two successive candidates, and the civil strife ensuing from their rivalry. The first of these, Jason, secured not only the high priesthood but also the king's permission "to establish, through his authority, a gymnasium and an *ephebeion,* and to enroll the Antiochenes in Jerusalem" (2 Macc. 4:9). Having been granted these requests in exchange for a hefty donation to the royal coffers, Jason proceeded to promote a Greek way of life in Jerusalem among "the noblest of the young men" and among his fellow priests (2 Macc. 4:11-15).

No scholarly consensus exists as to the meaning of the petition concerning "the Antiochenes in Jerusalem." This group is mentioned on only one other occasion, in the context of a delegation sent by Jason to an athletic competition held in the Phoenician city of Tyre (2 Macc. 4:19). The dominant view is that Jason was requesting a Greek city to be founded within Jerusalem ("Antioch in Jerusalem"), and that the ephebic institutions he established were intended for the training of a citizen body for the new *polis.* This interpretation trades on Antiochus's attested reputation elsewhere in the empire as a *ktistēs* (city-founder). However, given its unusual wording, other readings of this line are possible. Whatever the nature of Jason's actions as high priest, the key historical issue is whether these actions contributed to the political strife that erupted a decade later.

It is not at all obvious that they did. When Jason's high-priestly tenure was terminated three years later by the bribe of one Menelaus, the author of 2 Maccabees attributes this to the latter's corruption, not to any dissatisfaction with Jason's policies (4:23-25). Having lost royal support, Jason took refuge in Transjordan, leaving Menelaus in possession of the high priesthood. For his part, Menelaus, finding himself unable to pay off his royal patron by legitimate means, consolidated his position (so the hostile narrative claims) by doling out Temple vessels as gifts to Seleucid officials and neighboring cities, and by engineering the murder of Onias when the ex–high priest threatened to expose his sacrilege (2 Macc. 4:32-34). Nefariousness, not Hellenism, appears to have motivated Menelaus's behavior.

During the winter of 170/169, Antiochus invaded Egypt, preemptively halting Ptolemaic designs to recapture his Levantine possessions. By the following summer, the king controlled most of Lower Egypt and had installed a pliant youth on the throne. But this détente swiftly deteriorated, prompting a second Seleucid invasion in 168. Though victorious in battle, Antiochus was compelled to call off the campaign under threat of Roman intervention.

In the course of his contest with Egypt, Antiochus paid two visits to Jerusalem that seriously tried the allegiance of his Jewish subjects. The first involved a fleecing of the Temple's adornments, probably with a view to replenishing the king's war chest in the wake of his Egyptian expedition. The second visitation came in response to a violent upheaval among the Jews themselves. While the king was occupied with Egypt, the ex–high priest, Jason, marched against Jerusalem at the head of an army, intent on deposing Menelaus and his supporters (an objective he failed to achieve). Antiochus, unable or unwilling to discriminate aggressors from defenders, brought down bloody slaughter upon Jerusalem. Not long after this debacle, the king dispatched a sizeable force to garrison Jerusalem indefinitely, an event (according to our hostile sources) accompanied by gratuitous violence and brutality. Menelaus remained in power, guarded by the Seleucid garrison (the "Akra"), which also came to serve as a place of refuge for Jewish loyalists of Antiochus's regime.

Some scholars are skeptical of the Maccabean narrative, contending that the king's repressive measures are unintelligible, unless the Jerusalemites as a whole had in fact attempted to cast off Seleucid rule. The absence of direct testimony for such a revolt necessarily renders any speculation moot. Yet even if the revolt hypothesis were substantiated, it would not account for Antiochus's actions following his installation of the Akra: the suppression of Judaism itself. A litany of horrors describing this unparalleled persecution are paraded in both Maccabean accounts: the Temple and its worship were profaned in every conceivable way, its altar rededicated to Olympian Zeus; other altars were erected throughout Judea and cultic celebrations prescribed in honor of Dionysus and the king's birthday; Torah scrolls were burned, and anyone found in possession of one or abiding by its laws was put to death (1 Macc. 1:41-61; 2 Macc. 6:1-11). According to 2 Maccabees, similar resolutions were adopted by the neighboring coastal town of Ptolemais (2 Macc. 6:8-9).

The Maccabean tradition offers no credible explanation for this unprecedented revolution in Seleucid policy. Second Maccabees simply casts Antiochus into the biblical mold of the arrogant tyrant who unwittingly executes God's judgment upon rebellious Israel. First Maccabees alleges a royal decree, addressed to all Seleucid subjects, demanding "that all become one people, and that each abandon his [own] customs" (1 Macc. 1:41-42). If Antiochus ever issued such a decree, its implementation is nowhere in evidence (except, of course, in Judea itself). In fact, nowhere in either account is there any insinuation that the king's suppression of Judaism extended to Jews living elsewhere in the Seleucid realm. Whatever the motivation for the Antiochene persecution, Palestine was its sole focus.

The persecution itself lasted approximately three years. Jewish responses ranged from outright collaboration with (or acquiescence in) the king's policies, to passive noncooperation, to willing martyrdom or militant resistance. The last of these take center stage in the Maccabean accounts, making it difficult to analyze the others. In particular, the tradition downplays the role of Menelaus and his supporters in bringing the persecution to an end through negotiation, a development attested in a dossier of letters preserved in 2 Maccabees. The Maccabean narrative focuses instead upon the purification and rededication of the Temple half a year later and continued Jewish (i.e., Maccabean) dissatisfaction with the Seleucid-backed high priesthood.

Antiochus himself did not personally preside over the Judean theater for long. Financial pressures and the imperative to reassert Seleucid sovereignty over the eastern satrapies drew him away in 165; he named his under-aged son, Antiochus V, coruler under the supervision of a guardian, Lysias. Cuneiform sources confirm that Antiochus IV died on campaign in the east near the end of the following year. News of the king's death precipitated the first of many succession struggles that would influence Judean affairs for the next half century.

The Maccabean Revolt

Armed resistance to Antiochus IV's decrees quickly gravitated around the priestly family of Hashmonay (hence, "Hasmoneans"). Following the death of the family's patriarch Mattathias in 166, his son Judas Maccabaeus assumed leadership of the insurgency. Over the next two years, Judas distinguished himself in battle against local Seleucid commanders. But it was not until 164 that Lysias himself undertook a full-scale expedition to stamp out the revolt. The Seleucid vizier combined his military efforts against Judas with diplomatic overtures toward other Jewish groups. In spite of the success of these negotiations, Judas fought on.

On the military front, Lysias's expedition failed to achieve its goal. He besieged Judas in the strategic town of Beth Zur, but withdrew to Antioch before taking it. This withdrawal enabled Judas to enter Jerusalem and take control of the Temple Mount, which he appointed priests to cleanse and re-dedicate. The joint decision by "Judas and his brothers and all the assembly of Israel" (1 Macc. 4:59) to commemorate the event as an annual festival, and his garrisoning of Jerusalem and Beth Zur, indicate that by the end of 164 Judas had acquired recognition by a significant segment of his countrymen.

The death of Antiochus IV constrained Lysias to devote the better part of the following year to consolidating his power as guardian of the royal heir. This respite gave Judas and his brothers an opportunity to launch expeditions into the surrounding territories where Jews were a vulnerable minority in need of protection. One result of these raids was the relocation of Jewish refugees to Judea, thus increasing Judas's reservoir of potential recruits for his growing forces. Early in 162, Judas felt his position strong enough to launch a direct attack against the Akra.

This bold move provoked Lysias to lead a substantial force into Judea in May of that year with the boy-king Antiochus V in tow. Judas's forces were overwhelmed and forced to retreat, while Lysias and the king pressed on to Jerusalem and besieged the Temple Mount. Within two months, however, news of an insurrection at Antioch by a rival general brought the siege to a standstill. A truce with the Temple's defenders was affected, but Judas's fortifications were demolished. The absence of Judas from 1 Maccabees' narrative of events following his defeat by Lysias is conspicuous. Second Maccabees claims he was received by the king in conjunction with the truce; but this account also denies that Judas was defeated, thus casting suspicion on its reliability. Either way, the events of 162 were a setback for the Maccabean movement.

The deterioration of Judas's position continued. Later that same year, a new aspirant to the Seleucid throne, Demetrius I, seized power in Syria and executed Lysias along with Antiochus V. This abrupt regime change prompted an embassy from the Jews led by one Alcimus, who obtained from Demetrius the high priesthood (Menelaus having been done away with by Antiochus V). Alcimus received military assistance in subjugating Judas and his agitators. This precipitated a series of military engagements between Syrian forces and Alcimus's Jewish opponents, culminating in Judas's death in the spring of 161.

It was in the midst of these campaigns, immediately following a dramatic victory over Demetrius's general, Nicanor, that Judas is said to have sent an embassy to Rome seeking friendship and alliance. According to 1 Maccabees, the Senate acceded to Judas's request, conferring a treaty of mutual assistance and delivering a heated letter of condemnation to Demetrius (1 Macc. 8:23-31). The authenticity of the treaty and its attendant letter has had its share of detractors, but there are no persuasive reasons for rejecting either document out of hand. The more pertinent question is why Judas would have appealed to Rome in the first place. Second Maccabees reports the involvement of Roman envoys in negotiations conducted between Lysias and the Jews three years earlier, but their role appears to have been marginal (2 Macc. 11:34-38); it supplied no obvious precedent for Judas's action in 161. Nor is it likely that Judas seriously expected Roman arms to defend the Maccabean cause. A more plausible interpretation would see the overture as a propaganda ploy on Judas's part to shore up his claim to act as representative and defender of the Jewish people. Conversely, a senatorial rebuke of Demetrius, casting him in the role of aggressor, would serve to discredit Alcimus's regime. Whatever its intent, Judas's Roman mission had no tangible impact on the ground. It did, however, set in motion a tradition of diplomacy that Judas's successors would intermittently draw upon as part of their arsenal of legitimation.

Alcimus died (seemingly of natural causes) not long after Judas's own demise. Demetrius made no move to appoint a new high priest, and apparently no candidates stepped forward. This anomalous state of affairs would persist for seven years, indicating that the contending Jewish factions had reached some kind of stalemate. During this period, Judas's surviving supporters gathered around his brother Jonathan, who continued to agitate the status quo. The stalemate broke down around 158, when Jonathan's enemies summoned a Seleucid force to eliminate his guerilla band. The plan backfired when the commander of this force made peace with Jonathan and returned to Antioch. But the position of the Maccabean group did not change dramatically until 153.

In that year, the rule of Demetrius was challenged by a pretender, Alexander Balas, who established himself at Ptolemais. This development strategically positioned Judea as a potential asset to both contenders. Jonathan exploited the situation, eventually siding with Balas, who appointed him high priest and friend of the king. Alexander's final victory over Demetrius in 152 or 151 further strengthened Jonathan's authority as a Seleucid appointee, securing him immunity from domestic rivals. Subsequent struggles for the Seleucid throne over the next decade replayed this scenario. For Jonathan, the downfall of one monarch merely meant the prospect of new honors from the next. Local "renegades" occasionally attempted to stir up trouble for him, but they could be dealt with by bribery. In short, Jonathan maintained his legitimacy through exactly the same methods employed by his high-priestly predecessors — Jason, Menelaus, and Alcimus. Jonathan is often thought to be the "Wicked Priest" referred to in the biblical commentaries *(pesharim)* from Qumran. The "wickedness" in question, however, has to do with his opposition to the sectarian leader known as the Teacher of Righteousness, not with his political machinations.

In 143, Jonathan fell victim to the game of kings in which he had embroiled himself. His brother Simon took up his mantle by rejoining the fray, obtaining the high priesthood from Demetrius II, son of the monarch whom Judas had fought against. Like other Seleucids before him, Demetrius sweetened the deal with numerous concessions, releasing Judea from tribute, acknowledging Simon's possession of all Maccabean strongholds, and inviting Jewish troops to enroll in the royal forces. For these achievements, Simon was credited with the "removal of the yoke of the Gentiles" (1 Macc. 13:41). Notably though, Demetrius's concessions did not cede control over the Akra. But by June of 141, Simon had starved its inhabitants into submission, thus bringing all of Jerusalem under his power. The last memorial of Antiochus IV's infamy had been swept away.

The following year, a great assembly of the Jewish people commemorated Simon, who had "fought off the enemies of Israel and established its freedom" (1 Macc. 14:26). In recognition of these achievements, a resolution was passed that Simon

> ... should be their leader and high priest indefinitely (until a trustworthy prophet should arise), and that he should be their general, and that he should be given custodianship of the sanctuary and that he should appoint men over its functions and over the countryside and over the weapons and over the fortresses, and that he should be obeyed by all, and that all contracts in the country should be written in his name, and that he should wear purple and gold. And it shall be forbidden for any-

one of the people or of the priests to abrogate any of these things or to oppose things said by him or to convene an assembly in the country without him or to wear purple or to put on a golden buckle, and whoever acts contrary to these things or abrogates any of them shall be liable for punishment. (1 Macc. 14:41-45)

The pro-Maccabean narrative in which this decree is embedded presents it as a spontaneous, voluntary, unanimous expression of the popular will. The dictatorial character of the privileges bestowed upon Simon belie that image, indicating the presence (or prospect) of significant internal challenges to his leadership. Simon's death at the hands of a would-be usurper half a decade later lends weight to this interpretation, as does the extradition clause in a Roman diplomatic missive penned on his behalf (1 Macc. 15:16-21). The Simon decree signals a shift in the orientation of the Maccabean movement toward *de facto* monarchy.

Beyond the cleansing of the Temple, the repeal of Antiochus IV's decrees, and the removal of the Akra garrison, it is notoriously difficult to discern what the ultimate aims of the Maccabean revolt actually were. Resistance to Seleucid authority cannot be disentangled from the Maccabees' struggles against native rivals who enjoyed Seleucid support. Once the possibility of negotiation with the Macedonian overlord had become a viable option, Judas and his brothers embraced it wholeheartedly as a tool of entrenchment against their Jewish adversaries. In time, the descendants of Simon would achieve enduring political independence from Seleucid suzerainty; but this achievement was ultimately a function of Seleucid weakness, not of Hasmonean strength.

The Oniads in Egypt

Another Jewish family narrative surfaces during the latter half of the second century. Excluded from office by the upheavals of the Seleucid-backed high priesthood, Onias IV, son of the murdered high priest of the same name, fled to Egypt. There he obtained a land grant and permission from the reigning monarchs (Ptolemy VI and Cleopatra II) to erect a temple modeled on that of Jerusalem in the eastern Nile Delta. Conflicting sources obscure the precise timing and intent of this undertaking, but it is evident that (as so often with Jewish settlement in the Hellenistic age) the Oniad district and its temple functioned as a military colony, providing internal security for Lower Egypt, as well as supplying manpower for the Ptolemaic army when called upon.

Although Jewish inhabitants of the region embroiled themselves in Egyptian conflicts as late as Julius Caesar's Alexandrine War (48 B.C.E.), testimony for the career of the Oniad family itself is confined to the period of the dynastic intrigues of Cleopatra II and Cleopatra III (145-102 B.C.E.). In his refutation of Apion's diatribe against the Jews of Alexandria, Josephus tells of two Jewish generals, Onias and Dositheos, who supported Cleopatra II's claim to the throne against her brother, Physcon, and his Alexandrian partisans, following the death of her husband in 145 (*Ag. Ap.* 2.49-56). Although Josephus does not explicitly connect this Onias with the expatriate Jerusalemite, the probability of their identification seems quite strong. (The identity of Dositheos and his relationship to Onias cannot be determined with certainty.) Two sons of Onias IV — Chelkias and Ananias — likewise emerge as generals during the reign of Cleopatra III (whose titulature and propaganda reveal a consistent effort to win over and maintain the allegiance of her mother's traditional support base). In 103, Chelkias and Ananias led an Egyptian army into Palestine against the queen's would-be usurper, her elder son Ptolemy Lathyrus. Chelkias fell in battle, but Ananias (if Josephus is to be believed) influenced Cleopatra's decision to forge an alliance with the Judean king, Alexander Jannaeus (*Ant.* 13.324-55).

After this episode, information on the Oniads dries up. But epigraphic evidence testifies to the continued vitality of the community Onias founded. More than seventy Jewish funerary inscriptions have been recovered from Tell el-Yahudiyya (ancient Leontopolis) dating as late as the early second century C.E. One epitaph explicitly names the "Land of Onias" as the patrimony of the deceased (*JIGRE* 38). Like the Maccabean narrative, the Oniad saga illustrates the capacity of Jews to operate within the framework of the Hellenistic monarchies. But whereas the Oniads were absorbed into the Ptolemaic hierarchy, the relationship of the Hasmoneans to the Seleucid state was to develop along quite a different path.

The Hasmonean Dynasty

Seleucid interference in Judean affairs was not ended. But unlike earlier ventures, which had as their goal the elimination of the Maccabean insurgents, containment or curtailment of Hasmonean power now became their prime objective. Ongoing dynastic quarrels were complicated by an increasingly belligerent Parthian menace. The Parthian annexation of Babylonia in 140 posed a major threat to the coherence of Macedonian rule in the east, and the invaders' readiness to play off one Seleucid against another compounded the crisis. The diversion of energies to meet these pressing new problems loosened the Seleucids' grip on their ambitious Jewish clients. In response, Simon's successors applied themselves to the pursuit of Hellenistic statecraft.

Territorial acquisition commenced in earnest under Simon's son, John Hyrcanus I (ruled 135/134-104), who extended Hasmonean hegemony into Idumea, Samaria, and Galilee (see map 5). Aggrandizement accelerated during the tenure of Hyrcanus's own sons, who pushed their conquests as far north as Iturea, while absorbing much of the Transjordanian and coastal zones. The transition to Hasmonean rule was not a smooth one. The Samarian campaign resulted in the demolition of the temple on Mt. Gerizim, intensifying Jewish-Samaritan animosity. Circumcision and adherence to Jewish laws became mandatory for continued residence within the newly subjugated Idumean and Iturean domains. Pompey's later liberation of Greek cities controlled by the Hasmoneans signals both the extent of their military success and the unwelcome, imposed character of their rule.

Militarism demanded manpower, which in turn required money. Hyrcanus is said to have plundered the tomb of David in order to buy off Antiochus VII and to supplement his own force with mercenaries. His son, Alexander Jannaeus (ruled 103-76), is known to have continued this practice, his territorial gains doubtlessly enhancing his purchasing power. With the development of standing armies beholden to their Hasmonean paymaster rather than to their fellow countrymen came overt monarchic assertion. Hyrcanus's son, Aristobulus I (ruled 104-103), was the first to claim royal honors, and Jannaeus followed suit. And with kingship came dynastic struggles whose divisive potential and destructive impact was only amplified by the resources at each side's disposal. Between 67 and 63 B.C.E., the sons of Jannaeus — Aristobulus II and Hyrcanus II — became embroiled in a contest for the kingship that ultimately terminated the career of the Hasmonean state.

Already under Hyrcanus I, Hasmonean pretensions met with Jewish resistance. Internal opposition reached its apogee during Jannaeus's reign. So intense was their detestation of the king that his enemies actually appealed to the reigning Seleucid monarch for assistance in ousting him. The ouster failed. But the brutality of Jannaeus's repressive regime thwarted any possibility of peace between himself and his alienated subjects. (Qumran texts remember him as the "Lion of Wrath.") A more conciliatory situation appears to have developed under Jannaeus's wife, Shelamzion (Salome) Alexandra, who succeeded him (ruled 76-67).

According to Josephus, a key ingredient in Alexandra's success was her cultivation of the Pharisees, a group whose existence is first mentioned in the context of the time of Jonathan. Josephus himself ascribes anti-Hasmonean activity to Pharisaic instigation, a thesis that gains some plausibility from his claim that Jannaeus crucified 800 members of the sect. Alexandra, at any rate, placated the populace by involving the Pharisees in her administration. It is clear, however, that for some Jews, the excesses of Jannaeus and the sectarian flip-flopping of Hyrcanus were symptoms of a more fundamental wrong: monarchic rule itself. When the contentious sons of Alexandra appealed to Pompey for arbitration of their competing claims in 63 B.C.E., they were challenged by a third party, comprising more than 200 of the most prominent men of Judea. Virulently opposed to both Hasmoneans, these Jewish notables demonstrated to the Roman general that their own forebears

> had negotiated with the Senate, and had received the leadership of the Jews as a free and autonomous people — the title of king not having been taken, but with a high priest set over the nation. But that now these men [Aristobulus II and Hyrcanus II] were holding power by virtue of the fact that they had annulled the ancestral laws and had unjustly reduced the citizenry to slavery; for by a mass of mercenaries and by outrages and by many impious murders they had acquired royal power for themselves. (Diodorus 40.2)

The significance of this indictment, delivered at so pivotal a moment in Jewish history (the eve of Rome's first direct intervention into Judean affairs), lies not in the historical veracity of its claims (which are debatable). Its importance lies rather in the contrast it draws between two visions of early Judaism: the ideal temple-community, governed by the Torah and presided over by a high priest; and the historical contingencies of a sovereign state, struggling to maintain its independence amidst the successor-kingdoms of Alexander the Great. In 63 B.C.E., both the Hasmonean princes and their aristocratic opponents viewed Rome as the key to preserving their vision.

From Pompey to Hadrian

The period from the conquest of Jerusalem by Pompey the Great in 63 B.C.E. to the violent repression of the revolt under the emperor Hadrian in 135 C.E. was one of both tremendous accomplishments and incredible setbacks for the Jews as a people and Judea as a kingdom (see map 6). This period began with the violation of the Jerusalem Temple and ended with the expulsion of the Jews from Jerusalem, during which the city morphed from the Jewish city of Jerusalem to the Roman *polis* Aelia Capitolina. At the same time, Hadrian changed the name of the province from Judea to Syria Palestina.

This is not to say that life for Jews in Judea during this period was a perpetual nightmare. Indeed, for the majority of the 200 years from Pompey's conquest to Bar Kokhba's revolt, Jews in Judea lived in peaceful coexistence within the Roman Empire. Moreover, during this period, Jews were spreading all over the Diaspora and settling in or expanding within the major cities of the empire. Significant populations of Jews could be found in Egypt, Asia Minor, Syria, the Greek islands, and even Rome itself. Thus, although many of the major events in this period were ruinous for the Jews, there were prolonged periods of peace and prosperity.

The End of Hasmonean Rule and the Rise of the Antipatrids

The twenty-year period from Pompey's siege of Jerusalem to the accession of Herod the Great was one of almost constant civil war between two factions of the Hasmonean family led by John Hyrcanus II and Judah Aristobulus II, the sons of Alexander Jannaeus and Salome Alexandra. Both sides appealed to Rome for support. Pompey sided with Hyrcanus, and in response Aristobulus and his supporters barricaded themselves within fortresses and the Temple itself. Pompey and his army besieged Jerusalem and the Temple, and in the ensuing siege, the city was badly damaged. Aristobulus's faction was massacred inside the Temple precinct itself, and Pompey himself violated the sanctity of the Temple by entering the Holy of Holies. After establishing order in the city, Pompey restored Hyrcanus to the high priesthood but stripped him of his royal title and political authority.

During the next nine years, an Idumean family, the Antipatrids, rose to preeminence in the Hasmonean court. They first achieved prominence during the reign of Alexander Jannaeus when he appointed an Idumean noble named Antipas as *stratēgos* of Idumea. It is likely that Antipas's son, Antipater, succeeded him. Antipater quickly became the real power behind the Hasmonean throne. He was a consummate politician who excelled at cultivating and exploiting friendships with local rulers as well as with leading Romans. Antipater first secured the friendship of Pompey and then of Julius Caesar when he eclipsed Pompey. In 48 B.C.E., Julius Caesar found himself besieged in Alexandria by native Egyptians. Antipater came to his aid by enlisting the support of local rulers as well as personally leading an army into Egypt. In recognition of his support, Caesar bestowed Roman citizenship on Antipater and his family (*J.W.* 1.187-94; *Ant.* 14.127-39).

Although Antipater was now clearly the main man at court, he still had powerful enemies, who assassinated him in 43 B.C.E. (*J.W.* 1.225-26; *Ant.* 14.280-84). Herod and his brother Phasael, who had been appointed *stratēgoi* of Galilee and Judea respectively (47 B.C.E.), assumed the leadership of their family as well their father's position as the dominant courtiers of the Hasmoneans. Their power and influence increased further in 42, when Marc Antony appointed them tetrarchs (*J.W.* 1.244; *Ant.* 14.326). However, in 40 the Parthians and their ally, the Hasmonean Mattathias Antigonus, the son of Aristobulus II, invaded Judea and besieged Jerusalem. While on a diplomatic mission to the Parthians, Phasael and Hyrcanus were arrested and imprisoned. Phasael chose to commit suicide by dashing his head against a rock. Herod, on the other hand, fled to Rome to secure its support against the Parthians and Antigonus. With the support and lobbying of the triumvirs Antony and Octavian, the Roman senate proclaimed Herod King of Judea and promised him military aid in his war against Antigonus (*J.W.* 1.282-85; *Ant.* 14.381-89). It took Herod three years to defeat Antigonus and capture Jerusalem, but in the spring of 37 B.C.E. he entered Jerusalem as both *de jure* and *de facto* King of Judea (*J.W.* 1.349-57; *Ant.* 14.476-91).

Herod, King of Judea and Client of Rome

Herod the Great was arguably the most powerful and influential Jewish monarch in history. During his long reign (40-4 B.C.E.), he amassed extraordinary wealth, implemented an elaborate and comprehensive building program, and transformed Judea from a small petty kingdom into an economic center of the eastern Mediterranean (see maps 7-8). Jerusalem, too, changed from a crowded and dilapidated provincial city into a major pilgrimage site and tourist attraction of the Greco-Roman world (see map 9). Despite his significant achievements, Herod's reign was not a smooth one. In his early years, one of his major concerns was establishing and maintaining his own legitimacy. As a usurper who had risen to power through Roman support, his claims to legitimacy were somewhat suspect. In addition to legitimacy issues, he also had to contend with the ambitions of Cleopatra, who wanted to reclaim the Ptolemaic Empire and annex Judea to her kingdom. Through astute political maneuvering, he was able to keep Cleopatra at bay and rule in relative security until 30 B.C.E. In that year, Herod's patron Antony, along with Cleopatra, was defeated by Octavian Caesar at the Battle of Actium. Like his father before him, Herod wisely saw the benefit of switching loyalties, so he quickly sailed to Rhodes to persuade the victorious Octavian that he could fit well into his new regime as a loyal and friendly client king. Octavian confirmed Herod's position and enlarged his kingdom (*J. W.* 1.386-97; *Ant.* 15.187-201). For the next twenty-six years, Herod provided a stable and friendly ally on the eastern border and promoted economic development and Romanization in Judea. As a reward for his services, Octavian, who after 27 B.C.E. was known as Augustus, bestowed upon Herod additional territories such as Trachonitis, Batanea, and Auranitis in 24/23 B.C.E. and Ulatha and Paneas in 20. He also ceded Herod control of the copper mines on Cyprus and half of their revenue. Thus, by the end of his reign, Herod ruled over a kingdom that rivaled all previous Jewish monarchies in size, wealth, and importance within the Mediterranean world.

Despite his numerous political and economic successes, Herod's reign was also marked by considerable domestic difficulties. His relationship with his Jewish subjects was periodically strained partially due to his somewhat ambiguous attitude toward Judaism. Internal dissension among his own family also caused Herod numerous problems and resulted in the execution of three sons and one wife as well as several other relatives and friends. Finally, a series of riots and disturbances broke out after his death in 4 B.C.E. Such social disorder suggests considerable dissatisfaction with the regime among many of his subjects. Despite these failings, Herod achieved enough legitimacy and security during his reign to rule without any significant threat to the stability of his kingdom. Furthermore, he was able to bequeath his kingdom to his three chosen successors, his sons Herod Archelaus, Herod Antipas, and Herod Philip.

Herod's Sons and Successors

After Herod's death, there was a struggle among his sons over who was going to succeed him, and the rival delegations traveled to Rome to solicit the princeps' opinion. In the end, Augustus chose to honor Herod's last will and divide the kingdom among the three named sons. Archelaus received Judea, Samaria, and Idumea, but only the title of ethnarch instead of king. Herod Philip, who became a tetrarch, received Batanea, Trachonitis, Auranitis, and other nearby territories. Finally, Galilee and Perea went to Herod Antipas, who received the title of tetrarch (*J.W.* 1.14-15, 20-38, 80-100; *Ant.* 17.219-49, 299-320). These three brothers ruled Herod's territory with varied success for the next thirty years.

Archelaus's short reign was a disaster from the beginning. His cruelty and oppressive measures enraged his subjects, and in 6 c.e. Augustus banished him to Vienne in Gaul. Judea then became a province governed by a procurator (*J.W.* 1.39-79, 111-17; *Ant.* 17.250-98, 339-55). His half-brother Herod Philip, on the other hand, ruled in relative peace for approximately thirty-eight years, and although little is known of his reign, it seems to have been successful and benign. Jews were a minority in his kingdom, and most of the inhabitants were of Syrian or Arab descent. During his reign, he rebuilt the city of Paneas and renamed it Caesarea Philippi in honor of himself and Augustus. He also expanded and embellished Bethsaida, renaming it Julias, in honor of Augustus's daughter Julia (*J.W.* 1.168; *Ant.* 18.28). When Philip died childless in 34 c.e., the emperor Tiberius attached his realm to the province of Syria (*Ant.* 18.106-8).

Of the three successors to Herod the Great, Herod Antipas is the one about whom we know the most. He reigned for more than forty years, longer than either of his brothers, and throughout his reign he was a valuable ally and client king to Rome. He rebuilt Sepphoris in Galilee and Betharamphtha in Perea, renaming them Autocratoris and Livias, respectively (*J.W.* 1.168; *Ant.* 18.27). His most expansive urban project, however, was the construction of a new capital city, Tiberias, in honor of the emperor Tiberius. According to coin evidence, this city was dedicated in the twenty-fourth year of Antipas's reign (19/20 c.e.). Although pious Jews initially refused to live in the city because of its construction atop a graveyard, eventually it became a center of Jewish learning and study (*J.W.* 1.168; *Ant.* 18.36-38).

As with his father, Antipas's personal life was less stable than his political rule. After several years of marriage, he abandoned his first wife Phasaelis, the eldest daughter of King Aretas IV, and married his niece,

Herodias, who had also been married to two of Antipas's half-brothers, Herod Philip and Herod son of Mariamne, the daughter of Simon Boethus. As a result, he incurred the wrath of both his former father-in-law and the charismatic preacher John the Baptist (Mark 6:14-29; Matt. 14:1-12; Luke 3:19-20; *Ant.* 18.116-19). Antipas's defeat in battle against Aretas and his army was seen by his subjects as just punishment from God for the execution of John (*Ant.* 18.113-16).

Despite his defeat by the Nabatean army, Antipas's positive relationship with Tiberius enabled him to survive on his throne. However, upon the death of Tiberius in 37 C.E. and the accession of Gaius Caligula, Antipas's status severely declined. One of Gaius's early acts was to appoint Antipas's nephew Herod Agrippa, who was also Herodias's brother, king in the territory of Herod Philip. Herodias, who was supposedly jealous of her brother's rise in power, believed that her husband also should receive the royal title. She therefore urged him to go to Rome and petition the new emperor. However, because of the machinations of Herod Agrippa, who disliked and distrusted his uncle, Gaius decided that Antipas was a traitor and exiled him to Lugdunum in Gaul (present-day Lyon). Because of her status as Agrippa's sister, Gaius was willing to permit Herodias to retain her property and not go into exile with her husband. Nevertheless, she voluntarily chose to share Antipas's fate (*J.W.* 1.181-83; *Ant.* 18.237-54).

Judea under Roman Rule (6-41 C.E.)

Meanwhile, since Archelaus's deposition in 6 C.E., a Roman prefect or procurator had governed Judea and Samaria, beginning with Coponius. Josephus's narratives provide most of the information about this period in Judean history, although the Gospels also provide some information, specifically about Pontius Pilate. Coin evidence and some archaeological material supplement Josephus's testimony, but for the most part scholars rely upon Josephus's account. In general, his depiction of the Roman administrators is decidedly negative, and he asserts that their mismanagement played a fundamental role in the downward spiral of the relationship between Rome and its Judean subjects. In this first stage of Roman occupation, however, Josephus's narrative is rather neutral, and the majority of these early governors receive minimal mention, which suggests somewhat peaceful interactions (*Ant.* 18.2, 29, 31-35). The sole exception to this is the tenure of Pontius Pilate (26-36 C.E.).

Outside of literary sources such as Philo, Josephus, and the Gospels, the name Pontius Pilate appears in only one inscription, which records his dedication of a *Tiberieum* and was discovered in the theater at Caesarea. In the literary sources, two main images appear. In the Gospels, Pilate is depicted as the blameless instrument of Roman justice. In both Philo and Josephus, however, he appears as a ruthless administrator who openly offended Jewish sensibilities and reveled in brutal methods of suppressing dissent. Philo calls him "a man of inflexible, stubborn and cruel dispositions" whose tenure was characterized by "venality, violence, robbery, assault, abusive behavior, frequent executions without trial, and endless savage ferocity" (*Legat.* 301–2). On more than one occasion, Pilate blatantly disrespected Jewish religious sensibilities, and his response to their complaints was often to resort to violence (*J.W.* 2.169-77; *Ant.* 18.55-62, 85-87). Finally, in ca. 36/37 c.e., he was recalled by the governor of Syria, Lucius Vitellius, and ordered to return to Rome to explain his conduct to the emperor.

Things were relatively quiet in Judea until the winter of 39/40 c.e., when the non-Jewish minority of Jamnia erected an altar to the imperial cult, which the Jewish inhabitants of the town promptly destroyed. The imperial procurator in Jamnia, Gaius Herrenius Capito, reported the incident to the new emperor, Gaius Caligula, who was enraged at the supposed insult to his majesty. He ordered the new governor of Syria, Publius Petronius, to march into Judea with two of the four legions stationed in Syria and to erect a golden statue of Gaius in the Temple. If the Jews resisted, Petronius was ordered to suppress them by force (*J.W.* 2.184-85; *Ant.* 18.261-62; Philo, *Legat.* 198–207). Realizing that Jewish resistance was inevitable, Petronius attempted to delay constructing the statue.

Herod Agrippa I

In the midst of Petronius's delaying tactics, Herod Agrippa, the grandson of Herod the Great and ultimately his successor as King of Judea, also took up the Judean cause. He had been educated in Rome alongside the imperial family, in particular the future emperor Claudius (*Ant.* 18.143, 165). With the rise of Gaius to the throne, Agrippa finally achieved prominence. He had become close friends with Gaius, and his friendship was rewarded with the tetrarchy of his recently deceased uncle Herod Philip (*J.W.* 2.181; *Ant.* 18.237). After the banishment of Antipas in 39 c.e. Caligula enlarged Agrippa's kingdom by annexing Galilee and Perea (*Ant.* 18.252).

Agrippa arrived in Italy in the midst of the statue crisis. Through either a letter (*Legat.* 261–334) or a banquet (*Ant.* 18.289-301), Agrippa successfully persuaded Gaius to forgo his plans for the statue, at least temporarily. However, both Philo and Josephus describe Gaius reneging on his promise not to place the statue in the Temple, and only the emperor's assassination saved the Jews from open conflict with Rome (*Legat.* 337–38; *J.W.* 2.202-3; *Ant.* 18.302-9). This incident only increased tensions between Rome and Judea.

Shortly before the assassination of Gaius, Agrippa returned to Rome, and after the emperor's murder, Agrippa was a crucial advisor to his successor, Claudius, and helped to secure his accession as emperor (*J.W.* 2.204-13; *Ant.* 18.236-67). As a reward for his services, Claudius appointed Agrippa king over the territory once ruled by his grandfather. Claudius also appointed Agrippa's brother Herod as ruler of Chalcis in Lebanon (*J.W.* 2.215-17; *Ant.* 18.274-77).

Herod Agrippa returned to Judea and governed it for the next three years (41-44 C.E.). He sought to further enhance the prestige of Judea. To this end, he initiated a building program around the Levant that, while not equaling his grandfather's, still enabled him to enhance his status and that of his kingdom. Among other projects, he built a theater in Berytus and a new city wall in Jerusalem across the northern edge of the city that enclosed the suburb of Bezetha. This wall, however, was not completed during Agrippa's reign because the governor of Syria, Vibius Marsus, was suspicious of Agrippa's intentions and persuaded Claudius to prohibit its completion. Jewish rebels hastily completed this wall after the outbreak of revolt in 66 C.E.

As part of this campaign to aggrandize his position within the eastern Mediterranean, Herod Agrippa called together a meeting of the region's rulers at Tiberias, including the kings of Commagene, Emesa, Armenia Minor, and Pontus, as well as his brother, the ruler of Chalcis. Although Marsus feared that Agrippa was planning a revolution at this meeting, this is extremely unlikely. More likely, Agrippa was seeking to establish himself as the preeminent client king of the Roman East. His efforts, therefore, were directed more toward his neighbors than toward Claudius.

During Passover in 44 C.E., Agrippa traveled to Caesarea to attend the games being held there in honor of Claudius. According to Josephus, in the midst of the festival, Agrippa fell ill with violent pains and died five days later (*Ant.* 19.343-52; Acts 12). At the time of his death, Agrippa's heir and namesake, Herod Agrippa II, was approximately seventeen. Because of the age and inexperience of the younger Agrippa, Claudius returned Judea to the rule of a Roman procurator (*J.W.* 2.220; *Ant.* 18.362-63).

The Road to Revolution (44-66 C.E.)

Despite its size and importance to both the Roman economy and political system, when Judea again became a Roman province following the death of Agrippa I, it was not upgraded to proconsular status. Instead, as before, an equestrian procurator governed from Caesarea under the supervision of the governor of Syria. For the next twenty years, these procurators would govern a province that became increasingly unstable and hostile to Roman rule. Ultimately, their mismanagement of the province would be one of the major causes of the outbreak of the Great Jewish Revolt in 66 C.E. Josephus attributes the outbreak of revolution in 66 C.E. to the following other factors: Roman oppression, socioeconomic tensions, religious incitement, and quarrels with local Gentiles. Some scholars have added another factor ignored by Josephus: the failure of the Judean elite to control the province and its restive population (Goodman 1987). As with any complex event, it is more likely that the culmination of these factors, as opposed to one or another, caused the revolt.

The First Jewish Revolt

Revolution broke out in Judea in the early summer of 66 C.E. Some Jewish young men had parodied the greed and stinginess of the procurator Florus. In response, he marched to Jerusalem and demanded that the elders of the city hand over the youths for punishment. The local authorities refused to comply, and Florus let loose his soldiers upon the city. According to Josephus, he even crucified some Jewish *equites* (*J.W.* 2.294-308). Some members of the Jerusalem ruling elite attempted to defuse the situation, but this proved impossible. Florus made the situation more volatile by demanding a public display of submission and ordering the Jewish populace to greet the two cohorts he had sent to Jerusalem as reinforcement of the city garrison. However, the soldiers of these cohorts behaved so arrogantly toward the populace that more riots broke out, forcing Florus to withdraw to Caesarea. Meanwhile, Herod Agrippa II and his sister Berenice, who had heard about the disturbances in the city, tried to appeal for calm. Nonetheless, their efforts ultimately failed, and they were expelled from the city (*J.W.* 2.309-14, 334-35, 343-406). In May/June of 66 C.E., some of the young priests, incited and led by the captain of the Temple, Eleazer ben Ananias, terminated the sacrifices offered daily at the Temple on behalf of the emperor. In essence, this served as an open proclamation of revolution and war.

Fighting broke out between various factions over both control of the city and the resumption of the daily sacrifices. This internecine fighting became even more violent when *sicarii* led by a certain Menahem ben Judah entered the city and joined with Eleazer. Eleazer's father and uncle, who were the leaders of the faction trying to avoid war with Rome, were murdered by Menahem and his men, and the soldiers sent into the city by Agrippa II to restore order either joined the rebels or were driven out of the city. A small contingent of Roman auxiliaries, who found themselves trapped inside the city, tried to escape, but were killed by Eleazer's men. The rebellion thus quickly became unavoidable and irrevocable.

Given this situation, Jews from all over Judea took the opportunity to rise up against their non-Jewish neighbors and vice versa. Seeing that the situation had gotten out of control, the governor of Syria, Cestius Gallus, collected a large army including the Twelfth Legion and some auxiliaries supplied by Agrippa and began marching south to Judea. Gallus reached Ptolemais in September and secured Galilee with little opposition. However, in October, his forces met Jewish rebels, who plundered his baggage train before he had even reached Jerusalem. Nevertheless, Gallus marched his army to Jerusalem and seized the northern suburbs, especially the district of Bezetha, with little difficulty. Despite this success, Gallus quickly determined that he could not take the city that year, so he ordered a retreat to the coast, but this withdrawal was completely disorderly, and the Jewish army took the opportunity to inflict heavy casualties on the retreating Roman forces.

At this point, the Jewish rebels now began to organize themselves as a revolutionary government. Joseph ben Gurion and Ananus ben Ananus became joint leaders of the provisional government, and they appointed generals to conduct the war. Josephus himself was selected to be the general of the forces in Galilee. In Rome, Nero dispatched Titus Flavius Vespasianus, who had distinguished himself in the invasion of Britain during the reign of Claudius. By June of 67 C.E., Vespasian reached Galilee with his army, which had secured the region through brutal tactics. Josephus, who lacked proper troops and armaments, was reduced to protecting little more than small hilltop fortresses and was finally captured at the siege of Jotapata. He managed to ingratiate himself with Vespasian by hailing him as the next emperor of Rome. The other Jewish resistance fighter in the region, John of Gischala, attempted to continue the war against Vespasian, but he was forced to flee to Jerusalem in the late summer of 67.

Back in Jerusalem, the situation was becoming increasingly unstable. The population was dissatisfied with the provisional government because of its inability to hold Galilee. Dissatisfaction only increased in the spring of 68 when Vespasian began to march toward and encircle Jerusalem. Opposition to Ananus was bolstered partially by rural peasants, who had fled into the city because their homes and farms had been captured or threatened by the Roman army. In this hotbed of factionalism rose a new group of elite priests, who described themselves as Zealots because of their zeal for the Temple and its cult. These Zealots accused the provisional government of not prosecuting the war with enough enthusiasm. Such a charge may have been unfair, but it was strengthened by the reality that many original members of Ananus's faction, including Josephus, had by this time defected to the Roman side. Regardless, the Zealots ultimately barricaded themselves within the Temple, where they were soon joined by John of Gischala and his men as well as a large force of Idumeans who had come to Jerusalem to defend the city. This new faction was able to overthrow the provisional government and execute Ananus and his closest supporters, including Josephus's friend and patron Joshua ben Gamala. Now firmly in power, John and the Zealots began a bloody purge of their enemies within the city.

Meanwhile, back in Rome Nero committed suicide, and with his death ended Vespasian's mandate as imperial legate. Because of this development, Vespasian suspended his campaign and waited to see what would happen. His campaign resumed in May/June of 69, and by the time that he was proclaimed emperor in July, his army had recovered the land previously conquered and had just finished encircling Jerusalem again. For a second time, the Roman campaign against Jerusalem was suspended as Vespasian turned to securing control of the empire.

While the Romans were engaged in a civil war known as the "Year of the Four Emperors," the Jews in Jerusalem were involved in their own civil war. In the year 68 some of the factional leaders, whom John and the Zealots had ousted from power, left the city and joined the army of Simon bar Gioras, a commander in the battle against Cestius Gallus who had been sidelined by Ananus's government. With Ananus now dead, Simon entered the fray, again capturing Hebron in the spring of 69 and then camping outside of Jerusalem. With the help of the Idumeans, who had become disenchanted with the Zealots and John, Simon was able to seize control of all of Jerusalem except the Temple itself. John eventually split from the Zealots and occupied the outer precincts of the Temple, while the Zealots holed up in the inner Temple. This tripartite division of the city lasted until Vespasian's son Titus and his army arrived before the walls of Jerusalem in March of 70 and began to besiege the city. With the arrival of the Roman army, the three factions set aside their differences and began coordinating their defenses.

Titus could have tried to starve the city into submission, but the new Flavian regime needed a magnificent victory, and so he determined to take the city by force. By May of 70, the Romans had captured the third wall. The Antonia fortress fell in June, and by August the Romans had captured and burned the Temple itself. As autumn began, the Roman army focused its attention on crushing any pockets of resistance that remained in the Upper City. It then turned its attention to the handful of Herodian fortresses occupied by the Jewish resistance. The most famous of these, Masada, was not taken until 73/74, after its defenders committed mass suicide.

Judea was placed under the control of a praetorian legate, and a legion was permanently stationed in Jerusalem. Vespasian also established a veteran colony at Emmaus to keep the peace (*J.W.* 7.217). The Temple was not rebuilt, and its plundered riches were transported to Rome, where they played a central role in the Flavian triumph. Simon Bar Gioras, who had been captured in the siege, was also taken to Rome, forced to march in the triumph, and then ritually executed (*J.W.* 7.153-55). The Jewish political state ceased to exist. With the loss of the Temple, the people of Judea were forced to survive in radically different circumstances.

The Jewish Diaspora from Pompey to 70 C.E.

The late Hellenistic and early Roman periods saw a tremendous expansion of the Jewish Diaspora. By the first century C.E., large and prosperous Jewish communities existed all over the Mediterranean from Syrian Antioch to Asia Minor and from Greece to Alexandria in Egypt (see map 13). There was some settlement in Italy and in Rome, but there is no evidence for Jews in the western Mediterranean until the late Roman period. Although there were some Jews living in the countryside, in general during the Roman period, the Diaspora was an urban phenomenon. In cities such as Alexandria, Jews lived in self-regulating communities, which were isolated either by law or by custom.

The heart of any Diaspora community was the synagogue, and each Jewish community had at least one, although larger communities had several. These synagogues evolved into more than just meeting places. Especially after the destruction of the Temple in 70, they became the main location for religious expression and communal interaction. The Septuagint, a Greek translation of the Hebrew Bible composed in Alexandria, was the most standard version of Scripture in the Diaspora. Indeed, for Jews such as Philo, the Septuagint had divine authority.

In terms of religious practice, there was a certain amount of regional variation among Diaspora communities. Nevertheless, according to the often-negative comments by non-Jewish authors, the religious practices of Diaspora Jews were quite similar to those in Judea. Diaspora Jews practiced circumcision, kept kosher, and observed the Sabbath. During the reign of Herod the Great, an embassy of Ionian Jews appealed to the king to intercede with Marcus Agrippa on their behalf. One of their complaints was that their Gentile neighbors were dragging them into court on Shabbat and their other holy days (*Ant.* 16.27). Such an incident attests to the importance of Sabbath observance for Diaspora Jews. The Diaspora also supported the Temple in Jerusalem by paying the half-shekel tax incumbent upon all Jewish men. In the Ionian Jews' petition to Herod, another of their complaints was that the money they had raised to be sent to Jerusalem was being unlawfully seized by the non-Jewish government (*Ant.* 16.28). Further evidence of this practice appears in a speech by Cicero in 59 B.C.E. in which he defended the proconsul of Asia, Lucius Valerius Flaccus (*Pro Flacco* 28.66-69).

In general, Diaspora Jews seem to have coexisted peacefully with their non-Jewish neighbors. The massacres and violence perpetrated by both sides in the wake of the First Revolt probably reflect local conflicts and disputes that had originated years before and about whose causes and origins we can only speculate. Roman officials usually protected Jewish rights and interests, and a number of edicts and letters that appear in Josephus's narratives show Roman leaders such as Caesar, Antony, Augustus, and Agrippa upholding Jewish rights and condoning their religious, political, and social distinctiveness (*Ant.* 14.186-267, 306-23; 16.166-73). Violations did occur, but in most cases the Roman government quickly remedied the situation. When Marcus Agrippa heard about the offenses against the rights of the Jews of Ionia, he immediately ruled in their favor (*Ant.* 16.58-61). When the Jews of Asia and Cyrenaica again experienced discrimination and the confiscation of the money they had raised for the Temple tax, they complained directly to Augustus, who ruled in their favor (*Ant.* 16.160-65). Although these incidents testify to periodic tension between Jews and non-Jews, in general Diaspora Jews were tolerated by their pagan neighbors.

The Diaspora community about which we know the most is Alexandria. The Jewish community of this city had thrived under the later Ptolemies because of direct royal patronage. During this period, the Jews enjoyed a civil status almost equal to that of their Greek neighbors. However, the situation changed with the end of the Ptolemaic dynasty. When Augustus took control of the country, he demoted them to a status equivalent to that of the native Egyptians because it was consistent with his policy of entrusting the government and political power to the Greeks of the eastern Mediterranean. Such relegation was extremely irksome to many Alexandrian Jews, who felt themselves to be fully immersed within the wider Greco-Roman culture, despite maintaining their distinct Jewish identity. The history of Alexandrian Jewry during the Roman period is marked by a consistent drive to remove the ignominious burden of the *laographia* (poll tax) and achieve *isopoliteia* (political autonomy).

The troubles of the Alexandrian Jews reached a dangerous level in 38 c.e., when the newly appointed King Herod Agrippa I visited Alexandria on his way to Judea. His presence in the city stirred up an unruly mob of non-Jews, who publicly insulted him by parading a local madman into the arena and using him to parody Agrippa. Then the mob started calling for graven images to be placed within the synagogues of the city. As a result, the mob attacked and desecrated the synagogues and eventually started attacking the Jews themselves, shutting them off into one section of the city and causing hundreds of casualties. Homes were ransacked and businesses were destroyed (Philo, *Flacc.* 25–85, 95–96). In his *Embassy to Gaius*, Philo again describes the anti-Jewish riots of 38, but in this text he blames the violence on Emperor Gaius and the anti-Jewish Alexandrians rather than on the Alexandrians and Flaccus.

Once peace had been restored to the city, both sides sent embassies to Gaius in order to exonerate themselves of blame for the riots and to seek an imperial edict codifying the position of the Jews within the city. According to Philo, the emperor was stirred against the Jews by a small group of Alexandrian advisors, especially a certain Helicon. Ultimately, neither embassy achieved its goal of receiving an official answer from Gaius. At the time of his murder, the issue was still open. Claudius finally settled the matter when he ordered both sides to behave but told the Jews that they lived in a city not their own and warned them not to aim for more than what they had (*CPJ* 153; the edict of Claudius, as reported by Josephus in *Ant.* 19.280-91 is much more positive toward the Jews than the papyrus, and is of doubtful authenticity).

Roman Jews also experienced mixed relations with their non-Jewish neighbors. The Jewish community in the city of Rome was composed mostly of the descendants of slaves brought to the capital after Pompey's conquest in 63 B.C.E. and that of Gaius Sosius in 37. This community had expanded during the early Principate, and under Augustus many of these slaves received their freedom. Despite their new liberty, these Jews largely remained within the lower classes of the city, living across the Tiber in Trastevere. Yet even in the face of the usual toleration granted by the government, the Jews of Rome periodically experienced official persecution, such as their expulsion under Tiberius (Tacitus, *Annales* 11.85; Suetonius, *Tiberius* 36; Josephus, *Ant.* 18.65-84) and later under Claudius (Acts 18:2; Suetonius, *Claudius* 25; Dio 60.6). During both expulsions, it is unlikely that many Jews actually went farther than Rome's suburbs. Even if they did, the Jewish community quickly returned. By the end of the Roman period, as evidenced by the catacombs in Rome, a large Jewish population inhabited the city.

Judea between the Revolts

The tragic outcome of the Great Revolt substantially changed life in Judea, but it also had a strong ripple effect on the Diaspora as well. Jerusalem and the Temple were destroyed and the priesthood disbanded. The Sanhedrin ceased to function, and the old ruling class vanished. Although Herod Agrippa II was rewarded for his loyalty in 75 C.E. with additional territory in Lebanon and the *ornamenta praetoria,* he received no new territory in Judea. And yet, Jewish life managed to continue. The prestige of the priesthood persisted, and individual priests were still receiving tithes, but as their religious utility declined, so too did their influence and power. It is highly likely that the Jews of this period continued to hope for a restoration of the Temple. Both Josephus and the author of *1 Clement* write under the assumption that the Temple would be rebuilt and the priesthood restored. In practice, however, Judaism became localized and centered on the village synagogue. The local scribes, whose skill at interpreting Torah had made them influential, filled the power vacuum, and some of these scribes ultimately became the rabbis.

Rabbinic tradition tells of the fortuitous escape and surrender of Yoḥanan ben Zakkai during the siege of Jerusalem. According to the story, while other rabbis such as Simon ben Gamaliel participated fully in the revolt and defense of Jerusalem, ben Zakkai decided that resistance was futile. He therefore smuggled himself out of the city as a corpse and then surrendered to the Romans. He impressed Vespasian by predicting his accession as emperor. Vespasian therefore granted ben Zakkai's request to found a new center of Jewish law at Yavneh (Jamnia). In the generations following ben Zakkai, the rabbis continued to study Torah and attempted to rebuild Jewish religious and cultural life. It is not entirely clear how much political or religious power the rabbis actually possessed during this early period, and it is likely that acceptance of their leadership by Jews was gradual and perhaps only in its infancy when rebellion again broke out in Judea in 132 C.E.

The Diaspora between the Revolts

Few Jews in the Diaspora had been inspired to join in the revolt of 66. There was a brief uprising in Alexandria, but it was short-lived. Roman retaliation against the Jews also included the forced closure of the Oniad temple at Leontopolis in 72 and its precincts in 73, even though it had never been a center of unrest or disloyalty since its foundation in the mid-second century B.C.E. Titus's destruction of the Jerusalem Temple in 70, however, severely strained Diaspora Jews' loyalty. Further complicating matters was the imposition after 70 of the *fiscus Iudaicus,* an annual payment made to Jupiter Capitolinus by all Jews, regardless of gender, in lieu of payment of the Temple tax. This tax weighed heavily on the Jews, especially the poorer ones with large households, and its rigorous application by the emperor Domitian only made conditions worse (Suetonius, *Domitian* 12).

In Alexandria, local conditions and grievances made the status of the Jewish community quite unstable. A single papyrus, the *Acta Hermaisci,* recounts rival embassies from Alexandria to Emperor Trajan only a decade before the outbreak of another uprising. Although the account has been heavily fictionalized, it speaks to the tensions between Alexandrian Jews and non-Jews. Some scholars have argued that there were additional factors leading up to the rebellions (Pucci Ben Zeev 2005). In particular, rebels who had fled Judea after the suppression of the First Revolt continued to cause problems, which only heightened tensions between Jews and non-Jews. There was a general rise in messianic aspirations and expectations of Rome's collapse, especially after an earthquake that occurred in Antioch during a visit of Emperor Trajan in 115.

In 115/116, these tensions exploded into full-scale revolt in Egypt, Cyrene, Cyprus, and Mesopotamia. This revolt, also called the War of Quietus after the general Lusius Quietus who suppressed the revolt in Mesopotamia, raged until 117. In Egypt, the Jewish rebels managed to take over much of the countryside including the Athribite district, the Fayum, Oxyrhynchus, and the nome of Herakleopolis. To the south, fighting broke out in the districts of Apollinopolis Magna, Hermopolis, Kynopolis, and Lycopolis. In Alexandria itself the rebellion seems to have involved destruction of pagan shrines, such as the shrine of Nemesis near Alexandria and the tomb of Pompey (Appian, *Bella Civilia* 2.90). In Cyrene, the rebels, who were led by a certain Andreas (Dio 68.32.1) or Lukuas (Eusebius, *Hist. Eccl.* 4.2.3), killed several thousand non-Jews and destroyed several statues of the gods as well as several temples and sanctuaries, including the temples of Zeus and Hecate and parts of the sanctuaries of Apollo and Asclepius. Finally, perhaps in fear of a Roman military arrival by sea, the rebels smashed up the road connecting Cyrene to its port (*CJZC* 24-25). In Cyprus, a man named Artemion led an attack on the Gentile population and razed the city of Salamis. Not much information is known about the uprising in Mesopotamia except that Trajan sent Lusius Quietus to suppress the rebellion. It is possible that the Jews were simply one part of a general anti-Roman revolt within the region, and that the inhabitants there preferred Parthian control to Roman.

The Roman response to the uprisings in Cyrene, Cyprus, and Egypt was swift and brutal. Trajan sent two forces to put down the rebellion: the VII Claudia legion to Cyprus and Quintus Marcius Turbo, with a large fleet and a number of legions, to Egypt and Cyrene. Egyptian papyri also indicate that local non-Jewish militias fought alongside the legions. Turbo sailed into Alexandria and defeated the rebels over the course of several battles in which his army killed several thousand Jews.

The results of the war were cataclysmic for the Jewish populations of Egypt, North Africa, and Cyprus. Jews were banished from Cyprus and were prohibited from setting foot on it on pain of death. After the revolt, there is no more evidence for Jewish settlement in the countryside of Egypt or Cyrene. Tragically, the great Jewish community of Alexandria disappeared and seems to have been destroyed, although there are a few traces of Jews left in the city afterward. Outside of the region under revolt, however, there does not seem to have been any anti-Jewish backlash. In the following years, large swaths of North African territory needed to be resettled and repopulated. Trajan and his successor Hadrian used confiscated Jewish property to fund the reconstruction efforts, especially the rebuilding of pagan temples.

The Bar Kokhba Revolt

After suppressing the Jews of Mesopotamia, Lusius Quietus was elected consul, and Trajan then appointed him governor of Judea. There are no specific details concerning any war in Judea related to the Diaspora uprisings of 115-117, and none of the Greek or Latin sources refers to fighting in Judea during this period. Rabbinic sources (*Seder ʿOlam Rabbah* 30; *m. Soṭah* 9:14) do mention a "War of Kitos" that occurred fifty-two years after Vespasian's war and sixteen years before the Bar Kokhba Revolt. Like these two wars, the "War of Kitos" saw the passage of sumptuary laws by the rabbis and a prohibition of teaching Greek. Nevertheless, the rabbinic sources are ambiguous at best. Rabbinic tradition preserves an account of two martyrs, Julianus and Pappus, who supposedly died under Trajan, but these deaths could have taken place anywhere (*m. Soṭah* 9:14; *Megillat Taʿanit* 29).

However, war and rebellion soon came to Judea, led by a charismatic leader, Shimon ben Kosiba. Later rabbinic sources claim that Ben Kosiba received the support of Rabbi Akiba, who renamed the revolutionary leader Bar Kokhba (Aramaic for "Son of the Star") in reference to the prophecy in Num. 24:17 ("A star will come out of Jacob; a scepter will rise out of Israel"). Bar Kokhba does not make any messianic claim in his letters, but on his coins he is called "prince *(naśiʾ)* of Israel," a title that had a long history of messianic associations.

The immediate causes of the war are unclear because we lack a detailed narrative of its course. It is likely that economic distress, hatred of the Romans, and anger over the destruction of the Temple played major roles in inciting Jews to rebel. Further, land confiscations probably exacerbated economic hardship, and religious factors also seem to have been influential. According to the *Historia Augusta,* the revolt began because Hadrian issued an edict prohibiting circumcision (14.2). The ban was part of a wider, empire-wide prohibition on mutilation, including castration, but Hadrian must have known how the Jews would respond. Dio suggests that the emperor also had decided to turn Jerusalem into a new pagan city, Aelia Capitolina (Dio 69.12.1-2), and perhaps this prohibition was connected to that larger plan.

The rebellion's territorial extent is also unclear, but most evidence suggests a concentration in the part of Judea closest to Jerusalem and the Dead Sea. The Jews seem to have had some success in the beginning, but it is not clear if the Jewish rebels ever managed to seize Jerusalem. The rebel letters found in the desert refer to Herodium and not Jerusalem as the insurgent headquarters, and their last stronghold was Bethar, not Jerusalem.

The Romans responded seriously to this new threat, and Hadrian sent Gaius Julius Severus from Britain to take over command of Judea in 134 C.E. Dedicatory inscriptions indicate that legions from all over the empire were sent to Judea, but otherwise there is no indication of troop size or makeup. The paucity of evidence from Greco-Roman authors suggests hesitancy on the part of the imperial government to mention a brutal suppression of rebellion, which did not fit well with Hadrian's image of benevolent patronage of the provinces.

According to Dio, the Romans killed more than 500,000 Jews and destroyed 50 towns and 785 villages in the suppression of the revolt. He also claims that they enslaved many of the survivors (Dio 69.14.3). Although these numbers likely are inflated, the bones discovered in the Judean Desert caves testify to Roman thoroughness and ruthlessness. Rabbinic sources state that many sages were martyred, including Rabbi Aqiba, and a period of strict persecution followed in which Jews could not practice many facets of their religion, including studying Torah, observing the Sabbath, and circumcising their sons. Indeed, Jews did not receive permission to circumcise their sons until after Hadrian's death. Perhaps the most long-lasting and devastating result of the war, however, was the expulsion of the Jews from Jerusalem (now called Aelia Capitolina) and its territory (Justin, *Apology* 7.6). Hadrianic coins celebrated the new city with a Greek figure representing it, and a temple dedicated to Hadrian was constructed atop the Temple Mount itself. Thus, what began as an attempt to liberate the Jews of Judea ultimately led to their death and to their enslavement and expulsion from the Holy City. With the failure of the Bar Kokhba Revolt, a major period of Jewish history comes to an end.

BIBLIOGRAPHY

Bagnall, Roger S. 1976. *The Administration of the Ptolemaic Possessions outside Egypt.* Leiden: Brill.

Bar-Kochva, Bezalel. 1989. *Judas Maccabaeus: The Jewish Struggle against the Seleucids.* Cambridge: Cambridge University Press.

Barclay, John M. G. 1996. *Jews in the Mediterranean Diaspora.* Edinburgh: Clark.

Berlin, Adele M., and J. Andrew Overman, eds. 2002. *The First Jewish Revolt: Archaeology, History, and Ideology.* London: Routledge.

Bickerman, Elias J. 1980. "La Charte séleucide de Jérusalem." In *Studies in Jewish and Christian History (Part Two).* Leiden: Brill, 44-85.

———. 1979. *The God of the Maccabees: Studies on the Meaning and Origin of the Maccabean Revolt.* Leiden: Brill.

Bouché-Leclercq, Auguste. 1903-1907. *Histoire des Lagides.* 4 vols. Paris: Leroux.

———. 1913-1914. *Histoire des Séleucides (323-64 J.-C.).* 2 vols. Paris: Leroux.

Brutti, Maria. 2006. *The Development of the High Priesthood during the Pre-Hasmonean Period: History, Ideology, Theology.* Leiden: Brill.

Cohen, Getzel M. 2006. *The Hellenistic Settlements in Syria, the Red Sea Basin, and North Africa.* Berkeley: University of California Press.

Doran, Robert. 2011. "The Persecution of Judeans by Antiochus IV: The Significance of Ancestral Laws." In *The "Other" in Second Temple Judaism: Essays in Honor of John J. Collins.* Ed. Daniel C. Harlow et al. Grand Rapids: Eerdmans, 423-56.

———. 2012. The Second Book of Maccabees. Hermeneia. Minneapolis: Fortress.

Eshel, Hanan. 2008. *The Dead Sea Scrolls and the Hasmonean State.* Grand Rapids: Eerdmans.

Fischer, Thomas. 1980. *Seleukiden und Makkabäer: Beiträge zur Seleukidengeschichte und zu den politischen Ereignissen in Judäa während der 1. Hälfte des 2. Jahrhunderts v. Chr.* Bochum: Studienverlag Dr. Norbert Brockmyer.

Gafni, Isaiah. 1984. "The Historical Background." In *Jewish Writings of the Second Temple Period.* Ed. Michael E. Stone. Assen: Van Gorcum; Philadelphia: Fortress, 1-31.

Gambetti, Sandra. 2009. *The Alexandrian Riots of 38 C.E. and the Persecution of the Jews: A Historical Reconstruction.* Leiden: Brill.

Gera, Dov. 1998. *Judaea and Mediterranean Politics, 219 to 161 B.C.E.* Leiden: Brill.

Goodblatt, David. 2006. *Elements of Jewish Nationalism.* Cambridge: Cambridge University Press.

Goodman, Martin. 1987. *The Ruling Class of Judea: The Origins of the Jewish Revolt AD 66-70.* Cambridge: Cambridge University Press.

Grabbe, Lester L. 1992. *Judaism from Cyrus to Hadrian.* 2 vols. Minneapolis: Fortress.

Grainger, John D. 1997. *A Seleukid Prosopography and Gazetteer.* Leiden: Brill.

Green, Peter. 1990. *Alexander to Actium: The Historical Evolution of the Hellenistic Age.* Berkeley: University of California Press.

Gruen, Erich S. 1993. "Hellenism and Persecution: Antiochus IV and the Jews." In *Hellenistic History and Culture.* Ed. P. Green. Berkeley: University of California Press, 238-55; 256-74.

————. 2002. *Diaspora: Jews amidst the Greeks and Romans.* Cambridge: Harvard University Press.

Hengel, Martin. 1989. *The Zealots: Investigations into the Jewish Freedom Movement in the Period from Herod I until 70 A.D.* Trans. David Smith. Edinburgh: Clark.

Hoehner, Harold. 1972. *Herod Antipas.* Cambridge: Cambridge University Press.

Hölbl, Günther. 2001. *A History of the Ptolemaic Empire.* London: Routledge.

Johnson, Sara R. 2004. *Historical Fictions and Hellenistic Jewish Identity.* Berkeley: University of California Press.

Jones, A. H. M. 1938. *The Herods of Judea.* Oxford: Clarendon.

Kasher, Aryeh. 1985. *The Jews in Hellenistic and Roman Egypt.* Tübingen: Mohr Siebeck.

————. 1990. *Jews and the Hellenistic Cities in Eretz-Israel: Relations of the Jews in Eretz-Israel with the Hellenistic Cities during the Hellenistic and Roman Era (332 BCE–70 CE).* Tübingen: Mohr Siebeck.

Kokkinos, Nikos. 1998. *The Herodian Dynasty: Origins, Roles in Society and Eclipse.* Sheffield: Sheffield Academic Press.

Lipschits, Oded et al., eds. 2007. *Judah and the Judeans in the Fourth Century B.C.E.* Winona Lake: Eisenbrauns.

Lüderitz, Gert, ed. 1983. *Corpus Jüdischer Zeugnisse aus der Cyrenaika.* Wiesbaden: Reichert.

Mendels, Doron. 1992. *The Rise of Jewish Nationalism: Jewish and Christian Ethnicity in Ancient Palestine.* New York: Doubleday.

Meshorer, Ya'akov. 2001. *A Treasury of Jewish Coins: From the Persian Period to Bar Kokhba.* Nyack, N.Y.: Amphora.

Mittag, Peter Franz. 2006. *Antiochos IV. Epiphanes: Eine politische Biographie.* Berlin: Akademie.

Modrzejewski, Joseph Méléze. 1995. *The Jews of Egypt: From Rameses II to Emperor Hadrian.* Princeton: Princeton University Press.

Mørkholm, Otto. 1966. *Antiochus IV of Syria.* Copenhagen: Nordisk Forlag.

Netzer, Ehud. 2006. *The Architecture of Herod, the Great Builder.* Tübingen: Mohr Siebeck.

Neusner, Jacob. 1969. *A History of the Jews in Babylonia,* vol. 1, *The Parthian Period.* Leiden: Brill.

Price, Jonathan. 1992. *Jerusalem under Siege: The Collapse of the Jewish State 66-70 C.E.* Leiden: Brill.

Pucci Ben Zeev, Miriam. 2005. *Diaspora Judaism in Turmoil, 116/117 CE: Ancient Sources and Modern Insights.* Leuven: Peeters.

Rajak, Tessa. 2002. *Josephus: The Historian and His Society.* 2d ed. London: Duckworth.

Richardson, Peter. 1996. *Herod: King of the Jews and Friend of the Romans.* Columbia: University of South Carolina Press.

Rooke, Deborah W. 2000. *Zadok's Heirs: The Role and Development of the High Priesthood in Ancient Israel.* Oxford: Oxford University Press.

Schäfer, Peter. 1995. *The History of the Jews in Antiquity: The Jews of Palestine from Alexander the Great to the Arab Conquest.* Luxembourg: Harwood.

———, ed. 2003. *The Bar Kokhba War Reconsidered.* Tübingen: Mohr Siebeck.

Schalit, Abraham. 1969. *König Herodes: Der Mann und sein Werk.* Berlin: de Gruyter.

Schürer, Emil. 1973-1987. *The History of the Jewish People in the Age of Jesus Christ.* Rev. and ed. G. Vermes, F. Millar, and M. Goodman. 3 vols. Edinburgh: Clark.

Schwartz, Daniel R. 1990. *Agrippa I: The Last King of Judea.* Tübingen: Mohr Siebeck.

———. 2008. *2 Maccabees.* Berlin: de Gruyter.

Schwartz, Seth. 2001. *Imperialism and Jewish Society, 200 B.C.E. to 640 C.E.* Princeton: Princeton University Press.

Shatzman, Israel. 1991. *The Armies of the Hasmonaeans and Herod.* Tübingen: Mohr-Siebeck.

Sievers, Joseph. 1990. *The Hasmoneans and Their Supporters.* Atlanta: Scholars Press.

Smallwood, E. Mary. 1976. *The Jews under Roman Rule from Pompey to Diocletian.* Leiden: Brill.

Tcherikover, Victor. 1959. *Hellenistic Civilization and the Jews.* New York: Jewish Publication Society. (Reprint: Peabody, Mass.: Hendrickson, 1999, with a preface by John J. Collins.)

Trebilco, Paul R. 1991. *Jewish Communities in Asia Minor.* Cambridge: Cambridge University Press.

VanderKam, James C. 2004. *From Joshua to Caiaphas: High Priests after the Exile.* Minneapolis: Fortress.

Wilker, Julia. 2007. *Für Rom und Jerusalem. Die herodianische Dynastie im 1. Jahrhundert n. Chr.* Frankfurt am Main: Verlag Antike.

Yadin, Yigael. 1963-2002. *The Finds from the Bar Kokhba Period in the Cave of Letters.* 3 vols. Jerusalem: Israel Exploration Society.

———. 1966. *Masada: Herod's Fortress and the Zealot's Last Stand.* New York: Random House.

Judaism in the Land of Israel

James C. VanderKam

Judaism as a designation for the entire phenomenon of the Jewish ways of living and believing is a Greek term *(Ioudaismos)* first attested in 2 Macc. 2:21; 14:38. It is related to the name for the land where many Jews lived — the land of Judah or Judea — and seems to have been coined as a way of contrasting traditional Jewishness with Hellenism *(Hellenismos;* see 2 Macc. 4:13). This essay will focus on Judaism as it came to expression in the land of Israel.

The Land of Israel

The Scriptures repeatedly mention God's promise that the descendants of Abraham and Sarah would possess the land (Gen. 12:7; 13:14-17; 15:7, 17-21; etc.), and the book of Joshua shows how that promise came to fruition (e.g., Josh. 21:43-45). The people of Israel lived in the promised land for centuries, but finally their sins, according to the Deuteronomistic History (2 Kings 21:10-15; etc.), so sorely tried the divine patience that YHWH invoked the curses of the covenant upon them, and gave them into the power of their enemies, who torched Jerusalem and the Temple and exiled many from the land. Decades later a return to the land began and a new temple was constructed on the site of the old one. Though a large number of Jewish people by this time lived in the various diasporas, the land of Israel remained a powerful symbol for them, yet this spiritual and national force did not necessarily impel them to live there. The Temple was a center for pilgrimages and gifts in addition to being the place where sacrifices were continually offered. The prophets had looked forward to a day when the dispersed people of God would be gathered to their home (e.g., Isa. 11:10-16; Ezek. 37:15-28), and that longing comes to expression in some of the literature written when the Second Temple stood, although the vast majority of Diaspora Jews remained where they were.

The Temple

One phenomenon related to and underscoring the centrality of the land of Israel, one that exercised a strong attraction for Jews everywhere, was the Temple in Jerusalem. Other Jewish temples existed — one at Elephantine in Egypt and later one in Leontopolis, also in Egypt — but the sanctuary in Jerusalem held a special place. Ezra 6:13-18 dates the completion and dedication of the Second Temple to the sixth year of King Darius (515 B.C.E.); that building complex (with repairs) apparently lasted until 20 B.C.E. when King Herod began completely rebuilding it on a grander scale (see fig. 65). Herod's temple was to be destroyed with the city of Jerusalem in 70 C.E.

If the Second Temple followed the structural plan of Solomon's temple (see 1 Kings 6:2-6), the building itself would have had three rooms — the nave or vestibule, the Holy Place, and the Holy of Holies — along with several altars. These would have been set within at least two large courts and would have been surrounded by other structures required for the personnel and materials of sacrificial worship and other sanctuary-related activities. The Herodian temple area (see Josephus, *Ant.* 15.391-420; *Ag. Ap.* 2.102-4) included four courts with ever greater degrees of holiness: one accessible to all, including non-Jews, one for all Jews including women, one for Jewish men, and one for priests only (see figs. 66-67). At various places there were marble columns and porticoes with steps and walls between enclosures. Only the high priest, on the Day of Atonement, could enter the Holy of Holies, the innermost room of the Temple itself.

Because of the central place occupied by the Temple in Jerusalem, the priests who served there exercised important functions in society, and some of them became its leading officials. According to the scriptural genealogies and laws, all qualified males of the tribe of Levi were clergy, but only the members of this tribe stemming from Aaron's line were priests (Num. 8:5-26; see also Exod. 28:1-3; 29:1-37). The Levites performed other duties at the sanctuary and served the priests, the sons of Aaron (Num. 18:1-7; 4:46-49). At the head of the body of priests stood the high priest, who, in the early centuries of the Second Temple period, came from the family of Joshua/Jeshua (the first high priest of the Second Temple), who held the post in hereditary succession (Neh. 12:10-11). The high priest seems at times to have exercised political power as well, serving as the chief national official in the absence of a governor. Those Hasmoneans who held the high-priestly office from 152 until the Roman conquest in 63 B.C.E. were not only heads of the cultic establishment but also chiefs of state and commanders of the army. During the years of Roman rule and before the defeat and destruction of Jerusalem in 70 C.E., the high priests continued to be influential leaders in dealing both with Jewish and Roman officials.

There were too many priests to allow all of them to serve at the Temple complex at the same time. 1 Chronicles 24:7-18 contains a list dividing the priests into twenty-four groups, one of which served at the Temple for a week, after which it was replaced by the next group on the list (Josephus, *Ant.* 7.365-66; *Ag. Ap.* 2.108). In this system, therefore, most of these divisions of priests were on duty at the Temple for only two weeks each year (twenty-four groups each serving two weeks would fill forty-eight weeks so that four would have to serve a third week) and at the great festivals when more of them were needed because of the large numbers of people bringing offerings. The Levites may have been organized in a similar way; from among their ranks came the singers and gatekeepers at the Temple (1 Chronicles 25–26; *Ant.* 7.367).

Worship at the Temple followed and built upon the prescriptions in the Mosaic Law. Animal and grain offerings with their libations were regularly made there. Each day, as the Law prescribed, there were two sacrifices of a lamb with accompanying grain and liquid offerings — the morning and evening sacrifices described in Exod. 29:38-42; Num. 28:3-8 (see 1 Chron. 15:40; 2 Chron. 8:11; 31:3). There were other mandated sacrifices for the Sabbaths, the first of each month, and for the festivals (Numbers 28–29), and passages such as Leviticus 1–7 describe the many kinds of sacrifice — their contents, who offers them, and the occasions for them. The priests were the ones who performed the procedures carried out at the altar (Num. 18:1-7; 1 Chron. 6:49-53), and for their support priests received prescribed parts of offerings other than the whole burnt offering (e.g., Lev. 2:3, 10; 5:13; 6:16-18, 26, 29; 7:6-10, 14, 31-36; Num. 18:8-20) as well as other gifts.

The festivals constituted an important if less frequent part of worship at the Temple in Jerusalem. The Law of Moses commanded that an Israelite male was to present himself before the Lord three times each year: at the

Festival of Unleavened Bread, the Festival of Weeks, and the Festival of Tabernacles (Exod. 23:14-17; 34:18-24; Deut. 16:1-17). It came to be understood that the Jerusalem Temple was the place where one appeared before YHWH; as a result, thousands of Jews would travel to Jerusalem to celebrate those holidays, whether from the land or the Diaspora. Deuteronomy also stipulated that Passover be held at the sanctuary; consequently, large crowds converged on Jerusalem on the prescribed date (1/14); they could remain there for the Festival of Unleavened Bread, which followed immediately (from 1/15 to 1/21). The Day of Atonement (7/10) involved elaborate rites at the Temple, including several trips in and out of the Holy of Holies by the high priest (Leviticus 16). During Hasmonean times another Temple-related festival — Hanukkah — was added to the list in the Hebrew Bible; it celebrated and remembered the reconsecration of the Temple in 164 B.C.E. after it had been defiled.

Worship at the Temple also involved music. There are references in the literature to the singing of the Levites, with the books of Chronicles being especially rich in passages relating to this levitical function. They present the Levites as singers at the time of David and his royal successors, but these books may reflect more of the situation in Second Temple times when they were compiled. In 1 Chron. 6:31-48 David appoints Levites to provide music at the house of the Lord; among them are Asaph and Kohath, whose names are found in the titles of some psalms (sons of Korah: Psalms 42, 44–49, 84–85, 87–88; Asaph: Psalms 50, 73–83; in 1 Chron. 16:7-36 Asaph and his kin sing from Psalms 105, 95, and 106; see also 2 Chron. 29:25-30; 35:15). The king ordered the singers and instrumentalists to perform at the times of sacrifice, Sabbaths, and festivals (1 Chron. 23:30-31). When Jews presented their Passover offerings, the Levites sang the Hallel psalms (Psalms 113–18; *m. Pesaḥ.* 5:7).

The large costs incurred in connection with the forms of worship at the Temple and the maintenance of the structures were met through different means. As noted, support for the priests, who had no land to supply them with their needs, came from the parts of sacrifices allotted to them by the Law, and they also received one of the tithes mentioned in the Scriptures. The Law provided that the Levites, who also lacked land, should receive tithes from the Israelites (cf. Deut. 14:28-29), and they in turn were to give a tithe from their tithe to the priests (Num. 18:21-32). Tobit 1:6-7 gives a summary of the firstfruits contributions and the clerically related payments as the protagonist describes his religious practice before he was exiled from his land: "I would hurry off to Jerusalem with the firstfruits of the crops and the firstlings of the flock, the tithes of the cattle, and the first shearings of the sheep. I would give these to the priests, the sons of Aaron, at the altar; likewise the tenth of the grain, wine, olive oil, pomegranates, figs, and the rest of the fruits to the sons of Levi who ministered at Jerusalem."

In addition to these means of support for the clergy, the sources disclose other revenues. First, several foreign monarchs who ruled Judea made contributions to the Temple. This is attested for three Persian kings (Ezra 6:1-5 [Cyrus], 8-10 [Darius I]; 7:15-23 [Artaxerxes I]) and for the Seleucid rulers Antiochus III (Josephus, *Ant.* 12.138-44) and Seleucus IV (2 Macc. 3:2-3; cf. 1 Macc. 10:40). The passage from 2 Maccabees claims: "it came about that the kings themselves honored the place and glorified the temple with the finest presents, even to the extent that King Seleucus of Asia defrayed from his own revenues all the expenses connected with the service of the sacrifices." Ezekiel had envisaged that the prince in Jerusalem would pay for the sacrifices on holidays and Sabbaths (45:17; see also 45:22–46:15), but in reality it was foreign rulers who did so. Second, the Jewish populace worldwide supported the Temple through a tax. Exodus 30:11-16 records an imposition of one-half shekel that each Israelite male twenty years of age and above was to pay as an atonement; YHWH ordered Moses: "You shall take the atonement money from the Israelites and shall designate it for the service of the tent of meeting" (30:16; 38:25-28, where it is apparently for construction of the tabernacle; see also 2 Chron. 24:4-14; Josephus, *Ant.* 3.194-96). Exodus attaches the payment to a census Moses was to take and does not say how often the Israelites were supposed to pay it. In the time of Nehemiah the people not only pledged to bring wood for the offerings at the Temple, the firsts of the crops and herds, and the tithes (10:34-39), but also obligated themselves to pay an annual tax of one-third of a shekel "for the service of the house of our God: for the rows of bread, the regular grain offering, the regular burnt offering, the Sabbaths, the new moons, the appointed festivals, the sacred donations, and the sin offerings to make atonement for Israel, and for all the work of the house of our God" (Neh. 10:32-33). The reader does not learn why the amount of this levy differed from the one in Exodus 30, but later one finds references in the sources to an annual half-shekel payment (see Matt. 17:24-27; *m. Šeqal.* 4:1-5) — one that Josephus mentions several times and indicates that it applied to Jews in the Diaspora as well as those in the land (*Ag. Ap.* 2.77; *Ant.* 16.163; 18.312-13 [Babylon]; see Philo, *Spec.* 1.76-78). After Jerusalem was destroyed in 70 C.E., the Romans redirected the tax monies to the temple of Jupiter Capitolinus in Rome (*J.W.* 7.218). It is interesting that a text from

Qumran decrees that the tax be paid only once in a person's lifetime (4Q159 1 ii 6-7) — perhaps a polemical view based on Exod. 30:11-16.

Festivals

Besides the daily and other sacrifices and ceremonies performed regularly at the Temple in Jerusalem, the cycle of festivals was centered there. As noted above, the Passover (1/14) and the three pilgrimage festivals took place at the sanctuary as the Mosaic Law directed. For the Passover, the representative of each household presented the paschal lamb at the Temple, where it was sacrificed. The Festival of Unleavened Bread, lasting from 1/15 to 1/21, coincided with the barley harvest; the Festival of Weeks, occurring at some unspecified point in the third month, marked the wheat harvest; and the Festival of Booths, celebrated on 7/15-21, came at the end of the entire harvest season. Each of the three pilgrimage holidays was also a firstfruits festival that required presentation of a part of the relevant crop at the sanctuary. The two additional firstfruits festivals mandated in the *Temple Scroll* (of wine and oil) would have taken place at the Temple, if they were ever implemented (11QT^a 19:11–23:2). The Second Passover (2/14; for individuals who, for certain legitimate causes, were not able to celebrate the Passover in the first month [see Num. 9:6-14]) also was a Temple festival, while the ceremonies for the Day of Atonement (7/10) necessarily took place at the Temple (Leviticus 16). The book of Esther provides the dramatic story that gave rise to the holiday called Purim (lots), but there was no requirement that it be observed at the sanctuary. And Hanukkah, an eight-day festival commemorating and celebrating the rededication of the Temple in 164 B.C.E. (1 Macc. 4:36-59; 2 Macc. 10:1-8), was by definition associated with the Temple, but there was no requirement that one had to travel there to mark it properly.

Each of the festivals summarized in Leviticus 23 and Numbers 28–29 required sacrifices at the Temple beyond the daily ones offered, and the firstfruits holidays, as noted, involved the appropriate offering from the harvest of that season. This meant that the Temple became a very busy and crowded place on these occasions. As a result, the priests who happened to be on duty at the Temple at the time of a major festival were not able to handle the large increase in sacrifices and related activities; they were augmented by priests from the other rotations.

It is not possible to infer from the way in which the Pentateuch dates festivals the nature of the calendar by which they were calculated. In the priestly portions of the Torah, the months are designated with ordinal numbers and the days are, of course, numbered as well. But no text indicates whether a solar calendar, a lunar calendar, or a combination of the two was used as the system in Second Temple times for the very practical issue of determining when public festivals occurred. Exodus 12:1 identifies the month of the Passover as the first month of the year; hence, for dating festivals, a Spring inception of the year was assumed. Psalm 104:19 could be taken as an indication that lunar considerations were involved in dating festivals (as they were later): "You have made the moon to mark the seasons [or: the festivals]; the sun knows its time for setting." But nothing specific should be inferred from the verse. Sirach 43:6-8, after a section extolling the wonders of the sun, has been adduced as evidence that by the early second century B.C.E. the moon determined festal dates. Note in particular 43:6-7: "It is the moon that marks the changing seasons, governing the times, their everlasting sign. From the moon comes the sign for festal days, a light that wanes when it completes its course." One prominent trait of 1 Enoch 72–82, Jubilees, and the sectarian literature from Qumran is the prominence of a solar year lasting 364 days; the festival dates are determined according to it.

It is appropriate to append a short reference to synagogues to this survey of information about the Temple and worship in the land of Israel. It would seem that having only one temple could prove inconvenient for those who lived some distance from it, even though the area of Jewish settlement was not very large and a person was not often required to be at the Temple. Also, the traditional form of sacrificial worship at the Jerusalem Temple (the only place where it could be effected) may not have met all the religious needs of Jewish people. Whatever the reasons may have been, at some point or very gradually in the Second Temple period, synagogues, local places for worship and study, began to appear, perhaps at first in the Diaspora (there are third-century-B.C.E. references from Egypt), but also in the land of Israel (the earliest evidence is from the first century B.C.E.). The Gospel of Luke documents the presence of a synagogue at Nazareth and the importance of Scripture reading and exposition in the Sabbath service there (Luke 4:16-30; notice that 4:15 refers to synagogues in Galilee). Others are known from Herodium, Masada, and Gamla (see fig. 51), and there are references to synagogues in Jerusalem (e.g., Acts 6:8-9). The synagogue was a place for communal activities (see the Theodotus Inscription [fig. 24]) including reading, studying, and expositing the Scriptures and prayer. Synagogues appear not to have been seen as rivals in some sense to the Temple but rather as complements to it.

Institutions

The Temple was a dominant institution in the Judaism as practiced in the land, and later in the period synagogues served key functions, but there were other institutions that played central roles in society. Some information has survived regarding the political organization of the Jewish people in their land. A fundamental fact of life throughout the centuries of early Judaism was that Judah/Judea was under foreign control (Persia, the Hellenistic kingdoms of the Ptolemies and Seleucids, Rome), with the exception of a few decades when the Hasmoneans controlled the state and were somewhat independent of the Seleucid administration.

There was a governor in Jerusalem at a number of times, although the evidence is insufficient to show that there was always an officer of this sort. Sheshbazzar (Ezra 5:14) and Zerubbabel (Hag. 1:1), perhaps both descendants of David, are called governors in the late sixth century, and Nehemiah, who refers to his predecessors in the office (Neh. 5:15), served in the same capacity in the second half of the fifth century. An official named Bagohi/Bagoas/Bigvai was the governor at the end of the century according to one of the Elephantine papyri (*TAD* A4.7 = *CAP* 30), and a certain Hezekiah is called governor on some coins from the end of the Persian and perhaps the beginning of the Hellenistic periods. After this, there is a lengthy gap in attestations of a governor, and it may be that the high priest became the chief of state. This appears to be the case in the Tobiad Romance and also in Jerusalem as pictured at the beginning of the historical account in 2 Maccabees (3:1–4:6). In all of the narratives in 1-2 Maccabees, there is no mention of a governor other than a member of the Hasmonean family (the governor Philip in 1 Macc. 5:22 is a foreigner imposed from without for a short time).

When the Hasmoneans became high priests (starting in 152 B.C.E.), they continued serving as political leaders and army commanders. Beginning either in the short reign of Aristobulus I (104-103 B.C.E.) or in that of Alexander Jannaeus (103-76), these rulers called themselves kings. They retained that office (with one queen, Salome Alexandra) until the Roman conquest of the area in 63 B.C.E. Yet, even after this date a high priest such as Hyrcanus II enjoyed very high positions in society and is still called *king* a few times, and Antigonus briefly claimed the royal office (40-37 B.C.E.). Josephus indicates that in the first century the aristocratically constituted state of the Jews was led by the high priests (*Ant.* 20.251), although this was done under Roman supervision.

Herod's appointment as king by the Roman senate profoundly changed the political landscape. From the time of his reign (37-4 B.C.E.) until the destruction of Jerusalem (and beyond), he and his descendants were dominant rulers among the Jews in the land. Herod held the office of king, and two of his sons (Antipas [4 B.C.E.–39 C.E.] and Philip [4 B.C.E.– 33/34 C.E.]) were tetrarchs in parts of their father's realm, while Archelaus (4 B.C.E.–6 C.E.), who inherited the rule of Judea, served as ethnarch until he was deposed for his incompetent and violent rule. In Judea the Romans then assumed more direct control by appointing prefects (from 6 to 41), among whom the best known is Pontius Pilate (26-36/37). King Agrippa I briefly reunited the kingdom of his grandfather Herod the Great (between 37 and 44) before dying at a young age. Following his death in 44 C.E., the Romans again assumed closer control by appointing procurators, an arrangement that lasted until the end of the revolt. During this latter period, Agrippa's son Agrippa II came to have a significant influence in Jewish political and religious affairs.

A second institution that seems to have occupied an important place in Jewish society was the council of elders (*gērousia* in Greek) or Sanhedrin, if, as seems likely, the two terms refer to the same type of body. There are references in Ezra to "the elders" as an influential group, but whether they constituted a ruling body is not said (Ezra 5:5, 9; 6:7, 14; in these passages they are involved in rebuilding the Temple and negotiations about it). Apart from the book of Judith (e.g., 4:8), which has a weak claim to historicity, the earliest mention of a council of elders is in Josephus's citation of the letter issued by Antiochus III (223-187 B.C.E.) regarding the Jewish people: he says they with their senate *(gērousia)* greeted him when he visited the city (*Ant.* 12.138); later the king mentions the Jewish form of government and lists the senate among the groups exempt from three taxes (12.142). In 2 Macc. 4:4 the senate is the body that sends representatives to King Antiochus IV to press a case against the actions of the high priest Menelaus (vv. 43-50). In subsequent times the term continues to be used in official letters in which the leaders of the Jews are listed (e.g., 2 Macc. 1:10) or addressed (2 Macc. 11:27; 1 Macc. 12:6; 13:36 [where they are called "the elders"; see also 11:23; 12:35]; 14:20, 28 [in the section regarding the decree honoring Simon]). Josephus reports that Gabinius, a Roman official, set up five sanhedrins in Jewish territory in the 50s B.C.E. (*Ant.* 14.91), but not long afterward the historian relates the story of young Herod's trial before the Sanhedrin (14.165-79). From this episode the judicial nature of the group's work is clear, although it was definitely intimidated by the military power of Herod. The Sanhedrin as a judicial body is also evidenced in the trial of Jesus (Mark 14:53-65, where the members are identified as the high priest, the chief priests, elders, and scribes; Matt. 26:59-68; Luke 22:66-71) and that of his brother James (*Ant.* 20.199-203). The book of Acts, among several references to the council, includes Paul's appearance before it; there the members are the high priest along with representatives of the Pharisees and the Sadducees (22:30–23:12). Rabbinic sources know of a Sanhedrin that was a gathering of scholars who, among other activities, discussed matters of religious law. How that picture relates to the earlier references in Josephus and other Greek sources is not entirely clear.

Groups

As in any society, there were various groups among the Jewish people in the land of Israel. The sources for the earlier centuries of the period are sparse, but they indicate differing perspectives on some issues. So, for example, Ezra stands as a representative of a separatist point of view, one absolutely opposed to intermarriage with people of other races and nationalities; the book that bears his name includes information about many who had felt free to engage in exogamy and who were forced to dismiss their families. A number of scholars have argued that a fundamental tension existed in Judean society in the early Second Temple period between those who found fulfillment of promises in the restored community and Temple and those of a more visionary bent who looked for more spectacular realizations of God's plans for his people. Those expectations found expression in some late prophetic literature and perhaps in some texts with traits that would later characterize the apocalypses.

During the early Hellenistic period there is evidence for some Jewish people who had greater ties with the Ptolemaic government (the Tobiad family, for one), while others seem to have favored the Seleucid administration (note the friendly reception of Antiochus III at Jerusalem). But the most famous division in Jewish society, one that became unmistakable in the early second century B.C.E., is the one between those Jews who were more open to aspects of Greek culture and those who opposed the adoption of Greek ways. The contrast should not be pictured as absolute, since Hellenistic influence, such as the spread of the Greek language, was multifaceted and in part religiously neutral. But 2 Maccabees describes a situation in which a group of Jews, led by the usurping high priest Jason and with the approval of the Seleucid monarch Antiochus IV (175-164 B.C.E.), introduced into Jerusalem the central institutions of Greek education and citizenship — a gymnasium and an ephebate. 1 Maccabees 1:11 presents the perspective embraced by such people in these words: "In those days certain renegades *(paranomoi)* came out from Israel and misled many, saying, 'Let us go and make a covenant with the Gentiles around us, for since we separated from them many disasters have come upon us.'" The author adds that not only was the gymnasium built in Jerusalem but these people "removed the marks of circumcision, and abandoned the holy covenant. They joined with the Gentiles and sold themselves to do evil" (v. 15). Later, when the worship of a different god was set up in the Jerusalem Temple, not all Jews were opposed to the innovation although some, under Hasmonean leadership, violently fought it.

In the context of the early Hasmonean period, specifically in his account of the reign of Jonathan as high priest and leader, Josephus (*Ant.* 13.171-73) reports that there were three sects or schools of thought *(haireseis)* among the Jews and lists them as the Pharisees, the Sadducees, and the Essenes. Josephus mentions members of these groups in various places in his narratives and devotes a couple of sections to describing them, especially in *J.W.* 2.119-66 (see also *Ant.* 18.11-22). The information from Josephus regarding these groups can be supplemented from the Dead Sea Scrolls and from the New Testament. Rabbinic literature, too, refers to Pharisees and Sadducees.

About the Pharisees Josephus reports that they were known for their skill and accuracy in interpreting the Law of Moses (*J.W.* 2.162), and to this he adds that "the Pharisees had passed on to the people certain regulations handed down by former generations and not recorded in the Laws of Moses" (*Ant.* 13.297 [trans. R. Marcus]). This appears to be the oral Torah known from other sources, a tradition of commentary and interpretation that allowed the Pharisees to apply the ancient law to changed circumstances. Josephus, who mentions this Pharisaic trait while describing disagreements between Pharisees and Sadducees at the time of John Hyrcanus (134-104 B.C.E.), says that these regulations of the Pharisees were not accepted by the Sadducees, who insisted "that only those regulations should be considered valid which were written down (in Scripture), and that those which had been handed down by former generations need not be observed" (13.297). The meaning of this distinction in views between the two groups has received much scholarly discussion, but it is clear enough that at issue between the two was the proper way for interpreting and applying the Mosaic Law, which both of course accepted as authoritative for practice. A number of the controversies between Jesus and the Pharisees reported in the Gospels present a similar picture of the Pharisees. When the "Pharisees and scribes" asked Jesus why his disciples "break the tradition of the elders" since they did not follow the practice of washing their hands before they ate, he answered: "And why do you break the commandment of God for the sake of your tradition?" (Matt. 15:3; see also v. 6; he cites their view about identifying goods as an offering and thus not using them to support parents as a violation of the fourth commandment).

Josephus identifies the Pharisees as an influential group within Jewish society. He claims that there were some 6,000 of them (*Ant.* 17.42) but says they were able to bring the masses to their side and even compel rulers to act in accord with their teachings (*Ant.* 13.288, 298; 18.15). Whether that was always true may be debated, but Josephus does tell about two periods when the Pharisees were especially influential with Hasmonean rulers and thus in the state. The background to his story about John Hyrcanus's break with the Pharisaic party is that they were in his favor before this. In fact, Josephus calls John Hyrcanus a disciple of theirs; how long this relationship had existed and whether it obtained in the time of his predecessors is not said. When Hyrcanus, convinced they had maligned him by telling him he should give up the high priesthood, changed to the side of the Sadducees, the Pharisees lost power and Jews were forbidden to practice their regulations. The dominance of the Sadducees with the Hasmonean rulers continued through the violent reign of Alexander Jannaeus, who apparently killed many Pharisees, but with his successor, his wife Salome Alexandra (76-67 B.C.E.), the situation was reversed and the Pharisees regained a position of dominance. After this time the evidence becomes sketchy, and it is not apparent whether Pharisees continued to enjoy political as well as religious prominence.

Regarding their beliefs, Josephus mentions their moderate position on the issue of what he calls fate: they believed that both divine and individual human aspects were involved in human actions so that people had a measure of responsibility for what they did. According to him, they also anticipated a resurrection for the righteous and eternal punishment for the wicked. There is support for some of this description in Acts 23, where the

Pharisees are identified as the members of the Sanhedrin who accept the belief that a resurrection would occur. It adds that they also believed there were angels and spirits.

The next group in Josephus's list, the Sadducees, he describes generally in contrast to the Pharisees. Their view of fate, for example, was not the moderate or balanced approach of the Pharisees: the Sadducees are supposed to have denied there was any thing such as fate that influenced human behavior, explaining rather that people are responsible for what they do. As noted above, the Sadducees rejected the validity of the tradition adopted by the Pharisees and insisted that the scriptural law alone was valid. It is difficult to imagine that the Sadducees had no tradition of how to interpret or apply scriptural law; whatever their way of interpreting may have been, it must have been different from the Pharisaic one. Acts 23:8 summarizes some of their theological disagreements with Pharisees in this way: "The Sadducees say that there is no resurrection, or angel, or spirit; but the Pharisees acknowledge all three." In his appearance before the Sanhedrin, Paul, who identifies himself as a Pharisee, exploits the difference by appealing to the resurrection.

Josephus adds that, while the Pharisees were influential among the masses of the people, the Sadducees, whose number he does not estimate (although he says there were few of them), appealed to the wealthy. In the episode in which John Hyrcanus broke with the Pharisees, he is said to have gone over to the Sadducean side. As a result, the Sadducees were not dominant in the period before this time in his reign, but they retained their position of influence throughout the rest of Hyrcanus's reign and apparently through that of Aristobulus I (104-103 B.C.E.) and of Alexander Jannaeus (103-76), before the Pharisees returned to their previous status. Josephus presents, for later times, a strange situation: the few Sadducees were people of the highest rank, but when they assumed an office, they were compelled to follow the dictates of the Pharisees because the people otherwise would refuse to tolerate them (*Ant.* 18.17). The point is related to the question whether the high priests — people who enjoyed the very highest rank — were Sadducees. The name Sadducee may be related to Zadok, the leading priest in the time of David and Solomon, and an ancestor of the Second Temple high priests. John Hyrcanus, a high priest, became a devotee of the Sadducees, and his sons Aristobulus I and Alexander Jannaeus may have been as well. But here the evidence grows very thin. In fact, the only other high priest who is identified as a Sadducee is Ananus ben Ananus who briefly held the office in 62 C.E. Josephus says that

Ananus followed the Sadducean school and that Sadducees were noted for being harsher than others in judgment (*Ant.* 20.199). A high priest is mentioned in connection with Sadducees in Acts 5:17, but he is not identified as a Sadducee.

The Essenes, Josephus's third group, are the one he describes at the greatest length (*J.W.* 2.119-61), perhaps because his source material was more complete or their unusual character made them more interesting. He estimated there were some 4,000 of them throughout the land (*Ant.* 18.21) and describes them as living a very disciplined form of life and gathered into communities of self-help and support. In their communities the members gave up their private property to the group so that the needs of all could be met. They avoided marriage, although there was a type of Essenes who did take wives and have children. They worked hard and were frugal in their ways; they were also known as the strictest in their keeping of the Sabbath. One of the topics regarding the Essenes that Josephus describes at some length is the process, several years in length, of admission into the group. He also notes their meetings and the rules that prevailed at them. Their view of fate, he reports, was that it determined everything — exactly the opposite of the view he attributes to the Sadducees; they also studied the writings of the ancients and were accurate predictors of events.

Scholarly interest in the Essenes increased with the discovery and study of the Dead Sea Scrolls. Most experts have identified the group responsible for the scrolls at Qumran as a small band of Essenes, so the scrolls can now fill in the information from Josephus and elsewhere regarding the Essenes. It may be that Josephus's comment about the Essenes' view regarding fate is exemplified in 1QS 3:13–4:26, where the divine governance of the universe and human actions through two opposing spirits is the subject. The scrolls community also practiced a community of goods, and their entry procedures very much resemble the ones noted by Josephus.

The scrolls probably allow us to see some of the controversies that separated the Essenes and the Pharisees. Several writers refer to their opponents as "the ones who look for smooth things," probably a punning allusion to the Pharisees. These writers accuse them of taking a more relaxed approach to the Law of Moses and thus of violating the covenant. Some scrolls, especially the copies of 4QMMT, express some legal positions that are attributed to the Sadducees in rabbinic sources. This does not mean that the authors of the Scrolls were Sadducees, since they disagree with the Sadducees on basic theological points (e.g., fate); it probably means that both the Essenes and the Sadducees adopted conservative, stricter understandings of the Law.

The community of the Dead Sea Scrolls illustrates the fact that the social makeup of early Judaism was more complex than our other sources suggested. Before they were discovered between 1947 and 1956, there was only a hint or two in the literature that such a group existed; there was no indication that it had a large library indicative of extensive study and much more. The scrolls reveal a community that had in protest separated itself physically from other Jews and that apparently did not participate in worship at the Temple in Jerusalem. In the wilderness of Judea they pursued the way of life they thought was revealed in the Scriptures and looked to the day when, in a final war between the sons of light and the sons of darkness, the former would win a great victory and a new age would dawn.

These were not the only groups in the land of Israel in the later Second Temple period. Josephus also speaks of a fourth "philosophy" whose members refused to accept human rule, although in other respects they agreed with the Pharisees (*Ant.* 18.23). Josephus considered them and their violent ways instrumental in causing the revolt against Rome in 66 c.e. (*Ant.* 18.6-10).

Literature

There is no doubting that Jews in the land of Israel wrote a sizable literature in the centuries when the Second Temple stood, and a considerable amount of it has survived to the present in one form or another, that is, in whole or in part, in the original language or in translation. Rarely is there information about exactly when a book was written or who wrote it, but texts of a variety of literary genres were composed in the period. A number of those works are now incorporated into the Hebrew Bible, although it is not always certain which books date from the Second Temple era. There would be a large amount of agreement among experts about the following as coming from the postexilic age:

Final form of the Pentateuch
1-2 Chronicles
Ezra
Nehemiah

Esther
Many of the psalms
Ecclesiastes
Daniel
Third Isaiah (Isaiah 56–66)
Joel
Haggai
Zechariah
Malachi

Perhaps there are other books or parts of books in the Hebrew Bible stemming from the years after the initial return from exile.

It is generally agreed that there was no canon of Scripture until perhaps the very end of the Second Temple period, but it is evident that there were ancient writings that exercised considerable influence and were acknowledged to contain God's words. Those books would have included Genesis through Deuteronomy and the prophetic works and Psalms and probably more, but it is not possible, given the evidence at hand, to decide exactly which books were considered authoritative and by whom.

In the later centuries of the period, Jews continued to write, and many of their compositions have survived to the present. One difficulty is that it is not always clear which books were written in Israel and which in the Diaspora. A possible indicator of location is language (if we happen to know the original language of the work): a book written in Hebrew or Aramaic is more likely to have been written in Judea (or Babylon) than in Egypt, while a work in Greek has a better chance of coming from Egypt or some other part of the Hellenistic world. But one should not exclude the possibility that a Greek work comes from Israel. One other note should precede the survey of Jewish literature from Israel: in a sense Josephus, a prolific author whose works are invaluable for understanding early Judaism, is a writer from Israel. He spent the first thirty years or so of his life in Judea, where he was a prominent priest and occupied important positions. But the Judean Jew Josephus actually wrote his histories *War* and *Antiquities* and his *Life* and *Against Apion* while he was living in Rome after the end of the Jewish revolt in 70 c.e. In that sense he is a Diaspora writer. He seems to have composed *War* in a Semitic language, but only the Greek version exists today.

It is convenient to divide the books and other works that were probably written in Israel into different, rather general literary categories.

85

History

An important component of the Hebrew Scriptures is the set of histories that trace the great events of Israel's sacred and not so sacred past (Genesis, Exodus, Numbers, Joshua, Judges, 1-2 Samuel, 1-2 Kings, 1-2 Chronicles, Ezra, Nehemiah). Writing in this vein continued in early Judaism. The most prominent example is 1 Maccabees. It is likely that the work was written in Hebrew. It presents a historical review of the period from Alexander the Great to the death of the Hasmonean Simon (from the late fourth century to 134 B.C.E.), but it covers the first centuries of this period in a few sentences and concentrates its attention on the approximately forty years from about 175 to 134. The author is an advocate of the Hasmonean family, beginning with Mattathias, who sounded the call to revolt against the policies of Antiochus IV Epiphanes, and continuing with his sons Judas, Jonathan, and Simon, who led the nation in its struggle for the right to practice their traditional religion and to freedom from foreign rule. At first they led forces that were opposed to the suppression of ancestral religious practices and to the desecration of the Temple. After regaining the Temple Mount from Seleucid and renegade Jewish control, they purified the Temple and inaugurated the festival of Hanukkah to commemorate the event (it lasts eight days, beginning on 9/25). After Judas died in battle, leadership of the Hasmonean forces fell to Jonathan, who, in 152 B.C.E., was appointed the high priest. He held the office until his capture and death in 142, when his brother Simon assumed the leadership and the high priesthood. Simon was killed in 134, and the book ends with a notice about the reign of his son John Hyrcanus I. Despite its strong pro-Hasmonean bias, the book is a profoundly important history for the period covered. The author quotes official documents and offers a careful chronology of events. The book was written no later than 104 B.C.E. (the death of John Hyrcanus); it was translated into Greek and became a part of the Greek Bible (it is in Roman Catholic and Orthodox Bibles today but is considered apocryphal by Protestants and Jews).

The other major histories of the period that are extant are Josephus's *War* and *Antiquities,* although, as indicated above, they were not written in Judea. *War* is primarily an account of the First Jewish Revolt against Rome (66-70 C.E.) with a long prologue beginning just before Hasmonean times. *Antiquities* begins with the scriptural stories (from the beginning of Genesis) and follows them to the end (Esther, Ezra-Nehemiah material) before continuing with events until Josephus's own time. His coverage of large parts of the post-Hebrew Bible period is sketchy because of inadequate source material, but he offers extensive accounts from the Hasmonean period to the mid-first century C.E. and is often the only source of information about these times.

Stories

A number of narrative works that do not appear to be historical in intent express, often in highly entertaining ways, the theological and ethical views of the authors.

The book of Tobit may have been written in Israel, although it is not impossible that it comes from somewhere in the eastern Diaspora. It was composed in Aramaic. Copies of it have been found in Qumran Cave 4 (4Q196-199 in Aramaic [see fig. 40], 4Q200 in Hebrew). The work tells the parallel stories of two pious Jews whose lives had become tragedies, although they maintained their religious fidelity in dire circumstances, and who were delivered through the agency of the angel Raphael. The book commends pious deeds by Diaspora Jews such as almsgiving, care for fellow Jews, praise of God, prayer, and endogamy.

The book of Judith was written in Hebrew, although it is available only in a Greek translation. The author paints a confusing situation blending Babylonian, Persian, and perhaps other times, but its aim is to describe the deliverance God gave to his beleaguered people through the hand of a woman named Judith, whose extraordinary piety and remarkable bravery and cleverness brought about victory for the Jews in the land when the great general Holophernes and his massive army wished to destroy them. The book also presents an interesting example of a proselyte in the form of Achior the Ammonite.

Legal Texts

From early in the Second Temple period there is little evidence of legal literature in the sense of laws such as those in the Pentateuch. Those books may have reached their final form early in the period, but from the centuries that followed no such texts are attested until the literature found at Qumran. Among the scrolls are different sorts of works that deal with and expound the law of Moses; these are in addition to the numerous copies of the pentateuchal books found there. Examples are 4QMMT (see fig. 48), which lists more than twenty legal points on which the group differs from those whom they address; and the *Temple Scroll* (see fig. 46), which describes a grand future temple and all that will accompany it, such as the festivals, and represents and paraphrases a large part of the material in Exodus 25 through Deuteronomy. Additional texts, only fragmentarily preserved, deal with various aspects of the Law (e.g., ones that treat issues of purity and impurity [4Q274-279]; calendar texts [4Q317-330]). Other sorts of legal texts, ones that supply laws specifically for the group, are the *Rule of the Community* (see fig. 41) and the *Damascus Document,* the latter of which includes a lengthy halakic section. The legal texts from Qumran show that the kind of reflection that was later codified in the Mishnah and the Talmuds was at home in a much earlier time and was practiced by a group representing a very different point of view from the one found in the rabbinic works.

Wisdom Literature

A major sapiential work, the Wisdom of Ben Sira, was written in Hebrew (more than half of which has been recovered) at some time in the early second century B.C.E. The lengthy book (51 chapters) stands in the tradition of Proverbs, offering wise teachings on a range of practical issues. It marks an additional step in the sapiential tradition by teaching that the place where wisdom is to be found is in the Law of Moses (see also Bar. 3:9–4:4) and that the essence of wise behavior is to fear God. Ben Sira also differs from earlier wisdom literature by surveying Israel's history and the divine guidance in it. The Hebrew work was rendered into Greek by the author's grandson, whose preface explains the situation, purpose, and time of the translation.

A second example of a wisdom text is 4QInstruction, a work represented in several copies among the Dead Sea Scrolls (4Q415-418, 423; 1Q26). It offers prudent instructions to a younger person on familiar topics, but it also has characteristics which distinguish it from its predecessors in the wisdom tradition. One expression that appears a number of times is "the secret of what is/will be" — apparently meaning the secret teaching about the true character of the creation and of history. The work also incorporates eschatological teachings into a wisdom work.

Scriptural Interpretation

Throughout early Judaism, interpretation of older scriptures was an important exercise. This is evident in the Hebrew Bible (e.g., Daniel 9) and outside it. Among the most interesting examples are a series of commentaries found at Qumran. These pesharim or interpretations offer comments on scriptural prophetic texts; they cite a passage and then explain it before proceeding to the next passage in the book (occasionally more than one book is involved). The best-preserved examples are the commentaries on Nahum (4Q169) and Habakkuk (1QpHab; see fig. 43); altogether seventeen copies of pesharim have been identified (1QpHab; 1Q14-16; 4Q161-71, 173), treating Isaiah, Hosea, Micah, Nahum, Habakkuk, Zephaniah, and several Psalms. These lemmatized commentaries allow the reader to see how the Qumran community understood the ancient prophecies to be coming true in their own day; they also disclose some information about that time and important characters in their world. Other types of commentaries are not tied to particular texts but are more thematic and thus treat texts from various places in the scriptures. Among them are the *Florilegium* (4Q174) and the *Melchizedek* text (11Q13).

Scriptural interpretation may be the rubric under which to survey a set of works called by scholars Rewritten Bible or, better, Rewritten Scriptures. These texts take the contents of an older scriptural work, in whole or in part, and re-present them. At times the representation is so close to the original that the difference is practically negligible (*Reworked Pentateuch* from Qumran is an example), while in others there is a wide difference (such as in the *Book of the Watchers* [*1 Enoch* 1–36]). The representation can accomplish several goals, such as clarifying obscure passages, adding to or subtracting from the older text in various ways to communicate the old message in a new form. Familiar examples that fall into this broad and diverse category are parts of *1 Enoch*, the *Aramaic Levi Document*, the *Genesis Apocryphon*, the *Book of Jubilees*, and the *Temple Scroll*. *1 Enoch* 1–36 (the *Book of the Watchers*) in part treats passages about Enoch and the immediate pre-flood period in Genesis 5–6 but expands considerably through an elaborate story of angels who descend, marry women, and have gigantic children whose misdeeds, with the illicit teachings of the angels, cause the flood. Enoch is presented as a mediator between God and the sinful angels and also as a traveling companion of angels on a tour of the world. The *Aramaic Levi Document* takes the rather problematic scriptural character Levi and greatly exalts him as a divinely appointed priest, the ancestor of a priesthood, and the recipient of revelations. The Aramaic *Genesis Apocryphon* (see fig. 42) offers stories from the early chapters of Genesis until chap. 15 (where the manuscript breaks off). The book of *Jubilees* more closely adheres to its scriptural base as it retells the stories from Genesis 1 to Exodus 24, all of which was revealed to Moses on Mt. Sinai. It packages them in its theologically eloquent chronology of fifty jubilee units and emphasizes the one, frequently renewed covenant between God and the chosen line, the importance of separating from the nations, the need to keep the Sabbath properly, and the significance of following the correct calendar of 364 days in a year. The *Temple Scroll* is a rewriting of the remaining parts of the Pentateuch (beginning with Exodus 24), while the *Reworked Pentateuch* is at times classified as scriptural and at times as Reworked Scripture.

Also within the area of scriptural interpretation are targums, Aramaic translations and interpretations of the Hebrew Scriptures. Although the major targums *(Onqelos* and *Jonathan)* date from much later times, the presence of Aramaic renderings of Job (4Q157; 11Q10) and apparently Leviticus (4Q156) at Qumran illustrates that this type of exercise has ancient roots.

Apocalypses

Several works give an account of revelatory experiences granted to exemplary leaders; the revelations to them disclose information about the future and the heavenly world. Among the apocalypses, perhaps the oldest is the Enochic *Apocalypse of Weeks* (*1 Enoch* 93:1-10; 91:11-17), which divides all of history and the future judgments into ten "weeks" (long units of time). Other early instances are the various revelations in Daniel 7–12, which "predict" the attacks on Jews and Judaism by Antiochus IV as the climax of evil and distress before the deliverance of the people of God. The *Animal Apocalypse* (*1 Enoch* 83–90) may come from nearly the same time. It surveys scriptural history, symbolizing almost all characters as various kinds of animals, and pictures a new age after the final woes caused by the nations that rule Israel and the judgment on the sinners. A number of other works fit in this category: the *Similitudes of Enoch* (*1 Enoch* 37–71), the *Testament of Moses, 4 Ezra,* and *2 Baruch.* The first two of these may have been written around the turn of the eras, while the latter two offer apocalyptic reflection upon the destruction of Jerusalem and the Temple.

In some of the apocalypses a messianic leader plays a role in the final drama (e.g., *Animal Apocalypse, Similitudes of Enoch, 4 Ezra, 2 Baruch*).

Poetic and Liturgical Works

The Psalms incorporated into the Hebrew Psalter served various functions in Temple worship and presumably in other settings as well, but these 150 poems hardly comprise the totality of poetic writing in the period. Again, the Qumran texts have offered abundant examples of such compositions. The *Hodayot* or *Thanksgiving Hymns* are sectarian poetic compositions which celebrate the greatness of God and his goodness to those whom he has chosen and other teachings of the group (such as divine predestination of events). Another set of poems has been labeled *Noncanonical Psalms* (4Q380-381). Among the scrolls are also texts that contain prayers for certain occasions (daily [4Q503] and festival [4Q507-509] prayers) and blessings for each day (4Q504-506; see also the *Berakhot* or *Blessings* texts, 4Q286-290). Considerable interest attaches to the *Songs of the Sabbath Sacrifice* (4Q400-407; 11Q17), which describes the heavenly worship on the first thirteen Sabbaths of a year and assumes a unity between the angelic worship offered in the celestial sanctuary and the worship offered by humans on earth. Poetry of a different nature is found in the *Psalms of Solomon*, a first-century-B.C.E. work that, among other topics, speaks bitterly about the Hasmonean rulers and about Pompey, the Roman general who took Jerusalem in 63 B.C.E. *Psalms of Solomon* 17 and 18 also offer some important statements about a Davidic messiah.

Other texts were written, but the above survey should suffice to give an idea of the range of Judean literature composed in the period of early Judaism.

Commonalities

The surviving evidence exhibits a richness and diversity in Judaism of the Second Temple era, a diversity so great that some have resorted to the neologism "Judaisms" to express it. Yet, despite the undoubted diversity present in the texts, there are fundamental beliefs and practices that would have been accepted by virtually all Jews during those centuries and that justify retaining the singular noun Judaism.

Monotheism

There were some Jews who rejected this doctrine, but the data, both Jewish and foreign, indicate that belief in one God was a defining characteristic of Judaism. Jews confessed that God was one and that he was the creator and sustainer of all, and non-Jews recognized monotheism as a trait that made Jews different from most others. In obedience to the second commandment, Jews made no representation of the God they worshiped, and in this regard, too, they were distinctive. The Temple in Jerusalem was unusual in that it contained no visible representation of the deity; in the time of the first Temple, he was thought to be enthroned upon the Ark of the Covenant between the cherubim, but there was no object representing him.

Covenant

The one God had entered into a covenant with Abraham, the ancestor of the Jews and, later, with his descendants, the people of Israel. The covenant remained valid and binding; it not only defined a relationship between YHWH and his people but also took the concrete form of stipulating the way of life that the descendants of Abraham were to follow in order to remain in covenantal fellowship with him. The most specific form of that definition was the Law of Moses, which therefore had to be obeyed and interpreted as new situations arose. Among the laws that regulated the covenantal behavior of Jewish people, several stood out as particularly important and known to non-Jews: an aniconic worship of the one God and rejection of all other deities and idols associated with them, Sabbath observance, circumcision, food laws, festivals, and separation from others because of the theological danger of intermarriage and impurity.

The history of the covenantal relationship that obtained between God and Israel took on special importance as evidence of divine election and guidance and as a source of lessons to be learned about the consequences of obedience or disobedience. Covenant violation was regarded as the root cause for catastrophes such as the destruction of Jerusalem and the Temple; the wise could learn from such instances and act accordingly. Amid disaster, Jews entertained hopes for a restoration of grander times; one such hope was for a messianic leader from David's line.

With the loss of the center — Jerusalem and the Temple — in 70 c.e. and carnage and loss throughout the land, an era in Jewish history ended and a new one began. Of necessity, the leadership of the nation changed, with no Jewish political leader and no class of priests in influential positions, but so rich was the heritage of Judaism that other aspects of it came to the fore as it moved into the age of the Tannaim and their work. Even the brutal Roman quashing of the Bar Kokhba Revolt (132-135 C.E.), another disaster for the land and its populace, did not prevent the Jewish people from surviving, from continuing to believe in the one God, and from adhering to the covenant and the way of life entailed in it.

BIBLIOGRAPHY

Ådna, Achim. 1999. *Jerusalemer Tempel und Tempelmarkt im 1. Jahrhundert n. Chr.* Wiesbaden: Harrassowitz.

Charlesworth, James H., ed. 1983-1985. *The Old Testament Pseudepigrapha.* 2 vols. Garden City, N.Y.: Doubleday.

Collins, John J. 1998. *The Apocalyptic Imagination: An Introduction to Jewish Apocalyptic Literature.* 2d ed. Grand Rapids: Eerdmans.

Falk, Daniel K. 1998. *Daily, Sabbath, and Festival Prayers in the Dead Sea Scrolls.* Leiden: Brill.

Grabbe, Lester L. 1992. *Judaism from Cyrus to Hadrian.* 2 vols. Minneapolis: Fortress.

———. 2000. *Judaic Religion in the Second Temple Period: Belief and Practice from the Exile to Yavneh.* London: Routledge.

Hengel, Martin. 1974. *Judaism and Hellenism.* 2 vols. London: SCM; Philadelphia: Fortress.

Henze, Matthias, ed. 2012. *A Companion to Biblical Interpretation in Early Judaism.* Grand Rapids: Eerdmans.

Kampen, John. 2011. *Wisdom Literature.* Grand Rapids: Eerdmans.

Kugel, James L. 1998. *Traditions of the Bible: A Guide to the Bible As It Was at the Start of the Common Era.* Cambridge: Harvard University Press.

Levine, Lee I. 2002. *Jerusalem: Portrait of the City in the Second Temple Period (538 B.C.E.–70 C.E.).* Philadelphia: Jewish Publication Society.

Mantel, Hugo. 1961. *Studies in the History of the Sanhedrin.* Cambridge: Harvard University Press.

Mendels, Doron. 1987. *The Land of Israel as a Political Concept in Hasmonean Literature.* Tübingen: Mohr Siebeck.

Murphy, Frederick J. 2002. *Early Judaism: The Exile to the Time of Jesus.* Peabody, Mass.: Hendrickson.

Nickelsburg, George W. E. 2005. *Jewish Literature between the Bible and the Mishnah.* 2d ed. Minneapolis: Fortress.

Rajak, Tessa. 2002. *Josephus: The Historian and His Society.* 2d ed. London: Duckworth.

Richardson, Peter. 1996. *Herod: King of the Jews and Friend of the Romans.* Columbia: University of South Carolina Press.

Rubenstein, Jeffrey L. 1995. *The History of Sukkot in the Second Temple and Rabbinic Periods.* Atlanta: Scholars Press.

Safrai, Shmuel. 1965. *Pilgrimage at the Time of the Second Temple.* Tel-Aviv: Am Hassefer (in Hebrew).

Sanders, E. P. 1992. *Judaism: Practice and Belief 66 BCE–66 CE.* London: SCM; Philadelphia: Trinity Press International.

Schiffman, Lawrence H. 1991. *From Text to Tradition: A History of Judaism in Second Temple and Rabbinic Times.* New York: KTAV.

———. 1998. *Texts and Traditions: A Source Reader for the Study of Second Temple and Rabbinic Judaism.* New York: KTAV.

Schürer, Emil. 1973-1987. *The History of the Jewish People in the Age of Jesus Christ.* Rev. and ed. G. Vermes, F. Millar, and M. Goodman. 3 vols. Edinburgh: Clark.

Segal, Judah Benzion. 1963. *The Hebrew Passover from the Earliest Times to A.D. 70.* Oxford: Oxford University Press.

Sievers, Joseph. 1990. *The Hasmoneans and Their Supporters: From Mattathias to the Death of John Hyrcanus I.* Atlanta: Scholars Press.

Stone, Michal, ed. 1984. *Jewish Writings of the Second Temple Period: Apocrypha, Pseudepigrapha, Qumran Sectarian Writings, Philo, Josephus.* Assen: Van Gorcum; Philadelphia: Fortress.

Ulfgard, Håkan. 1998. *The Story of Sukkot: The Setting, Shaping, and Sequel of the Biblical Feast of Tabernacles.* Tübingen: Mohr Siebeck.

VanderKam, James C. 2001. *An Introduction to Early Judaism.* Grand Rapids: Eerdmans.

———. 2004. *From Joshua to Caiaphas: High Priests after the Exile.* Minneapolis: Fortress.

———. 2012. *The Dead Sea Scrolls and the Bible.* Grand Rapids: Eerdmans.

———, and Peter W. Flint. 2002. *The Meaning of the Dead Sea Scrolls: Their Significance for Understanding the Bible, Judaism, Jesus, and Christianity.* San Francisco: HarperSanFrancisco.

Zahn, Molly M. 2011. *Rethinking Rewritten Scripture: Composition and Exegesis in the 4QReworked Pentateuch Manuscripts.* Leiden: Brill.

Judaism in the Diaspora

Erich S. Gruen

A Roman army destroyed the Temple in Jerusalem in 70 C.E. For the Jews of antiquity the loss of the Temple not only constituted a devastating blow but signaled an enduring trauma. The reverberations of that event still resonate. The day of the Temple's destruction, which, by a quirk of fate or (more probably) fabrication, coincides with that on which Jerusalem fell to the Babylonians six and a half centuries earlier, continues to receive annual commemoration in Israel. For many it shaped the consciousness of the Jewish Diaspora through the centuries to follow. The eradication of the center that had given meaning and definition to the nation's identity obliged Jews to alter their sights, accommodate to a displaced existence, and rethink their own heritage in the context of alien surroundings.

The Extent of the Jewish Diaspora

The focus on the consequences of the Temple's destruction, however, overlooks a fact of immense significance: the Jewish Diaspora had a long history prior to Rome's crushing of Jerusalem. Indeed, the notion of removal from the homeland is lodged deeply in the mythology of the nation. The curse of Cain, condemned to perpetual wandering over the earth, symbolizes it. So do the years of enslavement and oppression in Egypt prior to the exodus, followed by years of meandering in the wilderness. And that was just the beginning. The record of Jewish experience included the "Babylonian captivity" in the sixth century B.C.E., ostensibly a serious dislocation from the homeland. The story may contain exaggeration and embellishment but does not deliver pure fiction. And, whatever the historicity of the

95

"Return" from that displacement, the Diaspora was already a fact, not to be reversed. Jews dwelled in Egypt in the sixth century, as papyri from a Jewish military colony at Elephantine reveal. And an archive of documents from Babylon attests to Jews in a variety of trades and professions even after their supposed restoration to Judah.

The pace quickened, however, and the scattering multiplied from the late fourth century B.C.E. The conquests of Alexander the Great sent Greeks into the Near East in substantial numbers. The collapse of the Persian Empire prompted a wave of migration and relocation. New communities sprang up, old ones were repopulated or expanded. Mobility increased, and a host of settlements beckoned to the restless and the adventurous. As Greeks found the prospects abroad enticing, so also did the Jews. A burgeoning Jewish Diaspora, it appears, followed in the wake of the Greek Diaspora.

Precise numbers elude us. But they were clearly substantial. By the late second century B.C.E., the author of 1 Maccabees could claim that Jews had found their way not only to Egypt, Syria, Mesopotamia, and the Iranian plateau, but to the cities and principalities of Asia Minor, to the islands of the Aegean, to Greece itself, to Crete, Cyprus, and Cyrene. We know further of Jewish communities in Italy, including large settlements in Rome and Ostia. The Greek geographer Strabo, writing at the end of the first century B.C.E. (and he had no axe to grind on the subject), remarked that there was hardly a place in the world that did not possess members of this tribe and feel their weight. And all of this occurred well before the demolition of the Temple. Even without explicit figures we may be confident that Jews abroad far outnumbered those dwelling in Palestine — and had done so for many generations (see map 13).

The fact needs to be underscored. Diaspora life in the Second Temple period was no aberration, not a marginal, exceptional, temporary, or fleeting part of Jewish experience. In important ways it constituted the most characteristic ingredient of that experience. The Temple stood in Jerusalem. Yet the vast majority of Jews dwelled elsewhere. The physical and emotional world of the Jews cannot be grasped without placing the Diaspora under scrutiny.

What motivated the mass migration? Some of it, to be sure, was involuntary and unwelcome. Many of those who found themselves abroad had come as captives, prisoners of war, and slaves. Conflicts between the Egyptian and Syrian kingdoms in the third century B.C.E. caused periodic dislocation. Internal upheavals in Palestine in the following century created some political refugees and forced settlements. Roman intervention in the Near East temporarily accelerated the process. Pompey's victories in Judea in 63 B.C.E., followed by battles on Palestinian soil over the next three decades, brought an unspecified number of Jews to Italy as human booty, the victims of conquest.

Compulsory displacement, however, cannot have accounted for more than a fraction of the Diaspora. A host of reasons could motivate Jews to migrate voluntarily. Overpopulation in Palestine may have been a factor for some, indebtedness for others. But more than hardship was involved here. The new and expanded communities that sprang up in consequence of Alexander's acquisitions served as magnets for migration. In a mobile society, a range of options presented themselves. Large numbers of Jews found employment as mercenaries, military colonists, or enlisted men in the regular forces of Hellenic cities or kingdoms. Others seized opportunities in business, commerce, or agriculture. All lands were open to them.

The Jewish Conception of Diaspora

How did Jews conceptualize the Diaspora? What sort of self-perception shaped the thinking of those who dwelled in Antioch, Alexandria, Rome, Cyrene, Ephesus, or anywhere outside Judea? The biblical reverberations of the scattering of Israel possessed a decidedly somber character, a dark cloud cast upon Jews whose memories of the homeland grew ever dimmer. The book of Leviticus had declared that divine retaliation for their sins would disperse Israelites among the nations. The anger of YHWH, so one reads in Deuteronomy, would pursue them in foreign lands where they would worship false gods and idols. Jeremiah's pronouncements reinforced the message: the Israelites who turn their backs on YHWH will live as slaves of alien lords in alien parts, scattered among strange peoples where they will endure God's punishment until their destruction. And Daniel warns that failure to heed divine commandments will provoke God to order the dispersal of Israel. Diaspora thus appears to emblematize enforced expulsion from the homeland, a condemnation for wickedness, with sinners languishing abroad in distant parts under the oppressive sway of hostile strangers.

Yet dire biblical forecasts may bear little relevance to Diaspora life in the Hellenistic and Roman periods. Historical reality stands in the way. Can one plausibly conceive of Jews living abroad in countless numbers over many generations mired in misery and longing for the land of their forefathers? The scenario is preposterous. A sense of displacement did not dominate Jewish consciousness in communities strewn around the Mediterranean. It is noteworthy that Jews seem to have felt no need to fashion a theory of Diaspora. Those who inhabited a world of Greek culture and Roman power did not wrestle with or agonize over the fact of dispersal. It was an integral part of their existence and a central element of their identity.

The very term "Diaspora" is a Greek one. It rarely appears as a noun in Hellenistic Jewish authors. And it nowhere serves as a translation of *galut* or *golah* with the connotation of "exile." In fact, the authors of the Septuagint normally rendered such terms as "colony" or a version of "colony." In normal Greek usage the word carried no negative overtones and, in fact, Hellenic colonies generally developed fully independent existences. The founding of Jerusalem is ascribed to Moses by a Greek author who labels it a "colony" and gives it a positive meaning. Jews evidently picked up this phraseology from the Gentiles. Philo alludes to the Hebrews led out of Egypt by Moses as a "colony." And movement in the other direction receives the same designation: the Jews of Palestine sent out colonies to places all over the Mediterranean and the Near East. The migration generated a sense of pride, not an embarrassment or a lament. Jewish intellectuals did not fill their writings with complaints about being cut off from the center and confined to a truncated, isolated, and subservient existence. One hears no agonizing rationalizations, justifications, or apologias for Diaspora. That itself is telling.

Just how the Jews did feel about their circumstances abroad escapes direct notice. Indirect evidence has to suffice. And generalizations that encompass the Mediterranean world would be hazardous, if not downright misleading. The experience of Jewish communities in Asia Minor may have little bearing on that of the Jews in Babylon or Cyrene or Rome. The very notion of "Diaspora Judaism" suggests a uniformity that is unlikely to have existed. Circumstances differed and reactions varied. It would be an error to imagine that Jews everywhere faced a choice of either maintaining tenacious adherence to a segregated existence or assimilating fully to an alien culture. There was much room in between, and Jews doubtless ranged themselves on all parts of the spectrum. Each individual area struck its balance differently and constructed its own peculiar mixture. It was rarely a conscious or calculated process.

Synagogues in the Diaspora

But common ground did exist. Substantial evidence attests to the near ubiquity of synagogues. The term itself, *synagōgē,* may not always have been applied. Other designations like *proseuchē* (prayer house) or *hieron* (holy place) also appear. And the reference may be to a gathering or an assemblage rather than to a building. No model or pattern held throughout. A diversity of functions, physical characteristics, and institutional structures preclude any notion of uniformity. But impressive and widespread testimony demonstrates that the synagogue (in whatever form) could serve as a means to promote communal activity among Jews and advance a sense of collective identity. The evidence comes from literary texts, inscriptions, papyri, and archaeological finds that disclose outlines of the structures themselves. The bulk of it dates to the period after destruction of the Temple. But ample attestation in the Second Temple era shows the broad geographical range of the synagogue.

A sanctuary at Elephantine in Upper Egypt served a Jewish military colony as early as the sixth century B.C.E. That may have been exceptional, but it signals the natural inclination of Jews, wherever they were, to find a medium for expressing common interests. By the mid-third century, inscriptions reveal synagogues (termed *proseuchai*) in Middle Egypt, dedicated by Jews in honor of the Ptolemies, the ruling family of the land. Royal favor extended to the Jewish *proseuchai,* even to the extent of granting the formal status of places of asylum, commonly accorded to pagan temples, a notable mark of official approval. A plethora of synagogues stood in Alexandria, noted by literary sources and epigraphic texts. The latter provide the standard formulas whereby the dedicators establish their *proseuchē* on behalf of Ptolemy and his household. Egyptian Jews were fully comfortable in hailing the Gentile rulers while simultaneously dedicating their synagogues to the "Most High God." No tension or inconsistency troubled the two concepts. Jewish synagogues were a familiar part of the Egyptian landscape.

Jews also settled in Cyrenaica in significant numbers. Synagogues clearly sprang up. One inscription honors donors whose gifts helped to repair the synagogue in a Cyrenaic town. That a graphic declaration of gratitude to benefactors should be put on public display, in addition to the structure itself, which they hoped to refurbish, demonstrates that Jews took open pride in the maintenance of their own institutions and in announcing that maintenance to any interested party in the larger community.

Jews were to be found all over Asia Minor. The travels of Paul and his colleagues brought them regularly to Jewish synagogues of that region. And Roman pronouncements, collected through the documentary researches of Josephus, guaranteed the rights of Jews to construct and assemble in synagogues.

The institution surfaces quite strikingly in Greek cities on the north and east coasts of the Black Sea. A remarkable group of documents from the first century C.E. records the emancipation of slaves by Jews in the synagogues of those cities and provides for the continued association of the freedmen with the Jewish community, which took responsibility for their guardianship — a clear sign of collective solidarity.

Numerous other examples can illustrate the geographic spread of the synagogue. Paul's journeys, for example, took him to synagogues in various cities of Macedon and Greece. An actual structure, almost certainly a synagogue, emerged from excavations at the island of Delos in the Aegean. That a Jewish community settled in that holy site, the legendary birthplace of Apollo, dramatically attests to the comfort of Jews and their own institutions even in a key center of pagan religion. Jews indeed went as far from the homeland as Italy to establish thriving communities. The presence of Jews in Rome is well attested not only by literary texts but by funerary epitaphs from the Jewish catacombs that convey the names of at least eleven synagogues in the city. And archaeologists have unearthed the remains of a synagogue in Ostia, the principal harbor of Rome, situated near the bank of the Tiber. Here, as often elsewhere, the finds disclose characteristic Jewish features like an apsidal structure for Torah scrolls and images like the menorah, lulav, shofar, and ethrog, thus making the identification clear. Jewish synagogues of the Second Temple period stretched from the Black Sea to North Africa, and from Syria to Italy.

The synagogue supplied a vehicle for a wide range of activities that promoted the shared interests of Jews. These included study and instruction; discussion of the Scriptures, traditions, law, and moral teachings; prayers, rituals, and worship; communal dining, celebration of festivals, and commemoration of key events in Jewish history; adjudication of disputes, passage of decrees, meetings of members; maintenance of sacred monies, votive offerings, dedicatory inscriptions, and archives of the community. To be sure, not all synagogues performed all these functions. Local circumstances doubtless dictated numerous divergences. But the spectrum of services was broad. And they did not occur in hidden enclaves. Synagogues stood in public view; congregations had their own officialdom, leaders, and representatives; Gentiles frequently remarked about Sabbath services; inscriptions announced decisions of the membership; and the letters and decrees of Roman spokesmen gave public sanction to Jewish practices, most of which took place in the synagogue. The impressive testimony demonstrates the existence of thriving and vigorous Jewish communities, self-assured in the exhibition of their traditions and their special character.

The Jews' Participation in Social and Political Life

Explicit testimony on how Jews led their lives in the scattered cities of the Diaspora is hard to come by. But most of the fragmentary indications, clues, and indirect signs suggest circumstances in which they could both partake of the social and cultural environment and maintain a separate identity. These were not mutually exclusive alternatives.

One might note, for example, the gymnasium, that most Hellenic of institutions. The gymnasium was a conspicuous feature of Greek education, at least for the elite, in communities throughout the Mediterranean. It catered to the corps of ephebes, the select youth of upper-echelon families, the training ground for generations of Hellenic leadership in the urban centers of Greek migration. That institution would appear to be the last place available to Jews. Yet unmistakable traces of their participation in gymnasia do exist. Ephebic lists include Jews in places as different as Alexandria in Egypt, Cyrene in North Africa, Sardis in western Asia Minor, Iasos in southwestern Asia Minor, and Korone in southern Greece. So even the preeminent bastion of Hellenism, the gymnasium, was, at least in several sites, open to Jews.

The fullest information on Jewish life abroad (and it is very skimpy) comes from Egypt, where the papyri allow us to peer selectively into some corners of social and economic experience. The evidence, reinforced by some literary and epigraphic testimonia, shows that Jews served in the Ptolemaic armies and police forces, reached officer rank, and received land grants. Inscriptions in Aramaic and Greek from Alexandrian cemeteries disclose Jews, evidently mercenary soldiers, buried alongside Greeks from all parts of the Hellenic world. Jews had access to various levels of the administration as tax-farmers and tax-collectors, as bankers and granary officials. They took part in commerce, shipping, finance, farming, and every form of occupation. And they could even reach posts of prestige and importance. Juridically, the Jews, like other Greek-speaking immigrants to

Egypt, were reckoned among the "Hellenes" — not singled out for prejudicial discrimination.

The nature of Jewish civic status remains obscure and controversial. The Jews did have an established place in Alexandria by the end of the first century B.C.E. Strabo, who had no Jewish agenda, reports that the Jews had a large portion of the city allotted to them, and had their own official, an ethnarch, to govern them, decide disputes, and oversee contracts and decrees. He plainly implies that Jews governed their own internal affairs but also took part in a larger Alexandrian entity to which they owed allegiance. Other evidence shows that they lived in all parts of the city, not restricted to a ghettoized existence. They could label themselves "Alexandrians," a term that carried more than geographic designation. The Roman emperor Augustus, in fact, referred to them on a bronze stele as "citizens of the Alexandrians." Whatever that means, it signals an acknowledged role in the political process of the city, a feature independently attested by Philo, who notes that Alexandrian Jews "shared in political rights." Although we lack precise data, Jews clearly had some claim on civic prerogatives, just as they had on the social and economic life of the city.

Elsewhere, the political status of Jews receives only occasional mention. At Herakleopolis in Egypt, recent papyrological finds reveal the existence of a Jewish *politeuma*, a self-governing body that could, among other things, adjudicate cases involving both Jews and non-Jews. A comparable *politeuma* existed in Cyrenaica, and we possess evidence indicating that Jews could serve in the governing body of the larger Cyrenaic community as well. Citizen privileges of some sort also belonged to the Jews of Antioch, as they did for those in Sardis and the Ionian cities of Asia Minor. Moreover, Jews were eligible for Roman citizenship, well outside the city of Rome. Paul, a Jew from Tarsus and a Roman citizen, is only the most celebrated example. Just what prerogatives this involved and how far they were exercised remain controversial. But no barriers, it appears, excluded Jews from becoming full-fledged beneficiaries of Roman power.

The Jews' Participation in Cultural and Intellectual Life

One can go further. Jews had access even to cultural life in the upper echelons of Hellenistic society. Jewish authors were well versed in most, perhaps all, forms of Hellenic writings. Those conversant with the conventions included epic poets like Theodotus and Philo, tragic dramatists like Ezekiel, writers of history like Demetrius and Eupolemus, philosophers like Aristobulus, composers of novellas and historical fiction like the authors of the *Letter of Aristeas*, 3 Maccabees, and *Joseph and Aseneth,* and those who engaged in cosmology and mythography like Pseudo-Eupolemus, and the authors of the *Sibylline Oracles.* The capacity to produce such works demonstrates that the writers could partake of higher education and engage deeply with Hellenic cultural traditions. They were themselves an integral part of the intelligentsia. Most of the names known to us come from Alexandria. But, as we have seen, gymnasium education was available to Jews elsewhere and doubtless spawned writers whose reputations do not survive.

Jewish writers clearly showed a wide familiarity with the genres, forms, and styles of Greek literature. They wrote in Greek and they adapted Greek literary modes. But they employed those conventions to their own ends. Jewish intellectuals may have embraced Hellenic canons of literature, but they had no interest in recounting the tale of Troy, the labors of Herakles, the house of Atreus, or the Greco-Persian wars, let alone the myths of the Olympian gods. Their heroes were Abraham, Joseph, and Moses. They appropriated Hellenism to the goals of rewriting biblical narratives, recasting the traditions of their forefathers, reinvigorating their ancient legends, and shaping the distinctive identity of Jews within the larger world of Hellenic culture. The challenge for the Jews was not how to surmount barriers, cross boundaries, or assimilate to an alien society. In a world where Hellenic culture held an ascendant position, they strove to present Judaic traditions and express their own self-definition through the media of the Greeks — and even to make those media their own.

A particularly striking example can illuminate the point. Tragic drama is perhaps the quintessential Greek medium. This did not render it off limits to the Jews. The Alexandrian writer Ezekiel, working within the tradition of classical tragedy, produced a play, the *Exagōgē,* based on the story of Moses leading the Israelites out of Egypt. Ezekiel hewed closely to the narrative line contained in the book of Exodus, while employing the conventions of the Greek theater. But he inserted some creativity of his own. This included a remarkable scene in which Moses recounts a dream vision of God sitting on a throne, summoning Moses to him, handing over his diadem and scepter, and departing. The dramatist here not only exalts the grandeur of Moses but reconceives Moses's relationship with God. The celestial realm appears as analogous to royal governance on earth. Moses's ascension to the throne and acquisition of kingly emblems signal his appointment as YHWH's surrogate in governing the affairs of men. This had clear resonance to the contemporaries of Ezekiel. Moses's role as executor of God's will on earth, with absolute authority, reflected royal rule in the Hellenistic realms. The author thus reinvents the position of Moses on the model of Hellenistic kingship while making him the precursor of Hellenistic kingship itself. Moses as supreme judge would expound the Law for all nations. The Israelite hero becomes a beacon for humankind, a representative of the divinity, described in phraseology that struck responsive chords among Ezekiel's Hellenic or Hellenized compatriots. The tragic poet had effectively commandeered a preeminent Greek genre and deployed it as a source of esteem for his Jewish readership.

Another celebrated composition illustrates both the intersection of Jew and Gentile in the Diaspora and the emphasis on the special qualities of the Jews. The *Letter of Aristeas* was drafted by a Hellenized Jew from Alexandria, probably in the second century B.C.E. It purports to recount the events that led to the translation of the Hebrew Bible into Greek. That undertaking came about in Alexandria around the middle of the third century, an episode of the highest importance for Diaspora Jewry. The need for a Greek Bible itself holds critical significance. It indicates that many Jews dwelling in the scattered communities of the Mediterranean had lost their mastery of Hebrew but nonetheless clung to the centerpiece of their tradition. If they were to read the Bible, it would have to be in Greek. The initial rendering or renderings eventually congealed into what became known as the Septuagint. For the vast majority of Jews living in the Greco-Roman period, it *was* the Bible.

The *Letter of Aristeas* ascribes the translation's origin to the initiative of the court of Ptolemy II, ruler of Egypt in the mid-third century. As the narrative has it, the impetus came from the chief librarian in Alexandria, who persuaded King Ptolemy to authorize the addition of "the laws of the Jews," evidently the Pentateuch, to the shelves of the great library. This required translation, for the available Hebrew texts were carelessly and improperly drawn up. Ptolemy composed a letter to the high priest in Jerusalem, requesting translators. The high priest graciously complied and selected seventy-two Jewish scholars, six from each tribe, experts in both languages, to do the job. The Jewish sages reached Alexandria, where they were warmly welcomed, Ptolemy himself paying homage to the sacred scrolls that they had conveyed from Jerusalem. Indeed, he went beyond that to organize a seven-day banquet (serving kosher food!), during which the king put a different question to each of his seventy-two guests, largely concerning the appropriate means of governing wisely, and found reason to praise every one of them for his sagacity. The translators then repaired to the island of Pharos, where they went to work, periodically comparing drafts, agreed upon a common version, and completed their task in precisely seventy-two days. The priests and leaders of the Jewish community in Alexandria pronounced it a definitive version, not a line of it to be altered. Ptolemy joined them in admiration, paid reverence to the new Bible, and lavished gifts upon the Jewish scholars.

Such is the gist of the tale. None can doubt that it issued from the pen of a Jewish author cloaked in the garb of a learned official at the court of Ptolemy II. The particulars, of course, are largely, if not entirely, fictitious. But the author's creation holds high significance. The *Letter of Aristeas* offers a showcase for the familiarity of Jewish intellectuals with diverse features and forms of Greek learning from ethnographic excursuses to textual exegesis and allegorical interpretation. The author is plainly steeped in Hellenic literature. On the face of it, this treatise would seem to be the most telling attestation of a cultural convergence between Judaism and Hellenism — at least as viewed from the Jewish side. The Hellenistic monarch promotes the project, and the Jewish scholars carry it out. The translators act at the behest of the king to enhance the pagan library, while the king pays deep homage to the sacred books of Israel. The pseudonymous narrator, Aristeas, even declares to Ptolemy that the Jews revere God, overseer and creator of all, who is worshipped by everyone, including the Greeks, except that they give him a different name, Zeus.

Yet cross-cultural harmony and blending do not tell the whole story. Another dimension carries equal importance. The *Letter of Aristeas,* while fully conversant with Hellenic literary genres, adapted that knowledge to advertise the advantages of Jewish tradition. The distinctiveness of the Jews is never in question. The god to whom all bear witness, even though the Greeks may call him Zeus, is the Jewish god. The high priest happily sends Jewish scholars to Alexandria to render the Bible into Greek, but he reminds the Greeks of the superiority of the Jewish faith, ridiculing those who worship idols of wood and stone fashioned by themselves. He insists that Mosaic Law insulated the Hebrews from outside influences, erecting firm barriers to prevent the infiltration of tainted institutions. And the high priest observes that the Jews offer sacrifice to God to insure the peace and renown of the Ptolemaic kingdom — a neat reversal of the patron-client relationship.

One can go further. The seven-day symposium may have been a fundamentally Hellenic practice, but the Jewish sages answered every query by the king with swift and pithy answers, adding a reference to God in each response, and earning the admiration not only of Ptolemy and his courtiers but of all the Greek philosophers in attendance, who acknowledged their inferiority to the sagacity of the guests. Ptolemy applauds and commends every answer by a Jew, no matter how commonplace and banal. The king hardly emerges as discerning or discriminating. The *Letter of Aristeas,* to be sure, portrays Ptolemy as a wise, gentle, and generous ruler, a man of deep cultivation and learning. But the author carries his portrait somewhat beyond the sober and the plausible. He makes Ptolemy deferential to a fault. The king bows no fewer than seven times to the Hebrew scrolls upon their arrival in Alexandria, even bursts into tears at the sight of them, and then proclaims that the date of their arrival would henceforth be celebrated as an annual festival. The author extends this form of caricature to the Greek philosophers as well, turning them into awestruck witnesses of the superiority of Jewish learning. In short, the *Letter of Aristeas,* that quintessential text of harmony and collaboration between Jew and Gentile in a Diaspora setting, simultaneously underscores the distinctive character — and the precedence — of Jewish values.

The very idea of rendering the Hebrew Bible into Greek has profound significance for the Diaspora. The historicity of the tale in the *Letter of Aristeas* is a secondary issue. Ptolemy II may or may not have had a hand in its creation. His reputation for learning made him a logical figure to whom a later writer could ascribe such an initiative. The need of Jews abroad to comprehend the holy books and laws of their tradition in the language that was now their own played a greater role. And, more fundamentally, the work of translation represents a signal instance of Jewish pride and self-esteem. It signified that the Jews had a legitimate claim on a place in the prevailing culture of the Mediterranean. Their Scriptures did not belong to an isolated and marginal group. They contained the record and principles of a people whose roots went back to distant antiquity but who maintained their prestige and authority in a contemporary society — and in a contemporary language. That may be the clearest sign that the Jews perceived themselves as an integral part of the Hellenistic cultural world.

Maintaining Jewish Identity

Jewish comfort and familiarity with the Hellenistic world in no way entailed abandonment or compromise of their distinctive identity. Terms like "assimilation" and "accommodation" deliver misleading impressions that are best avoided, suggesting that the Jews needed to transform themselves in order to fit into an alien environment. On the contrary, they unabashedly called attention to their own characteristic features.

The issue of endogamy, for instance, recurs in Second Temple literature. The book of Tobit, among other things, exhorts those dwelling in the Diaspora to adhere to the teachings of their fathers, to hold their coreligionists to the highest ideals, and to reinforce the solidarity of the clan. The work enjoins Jews in the lands of the Gentiles to maintain their special identity through strict endogamy, a theme that runs throughout the tale, thus assuring survival of the tribe. The author of Tobit may indeed take the point too far, deliberately so, with a touch of irony. He has almost every character in the narrative, even husbands and wives, greet one another as brother and sister, with numbing repetition. This is endogamy with a vengeance, perhaps a parody of the practice — but also testimony to the practice. The author himself is evidently not partial to clannishness. He has Tobit's deathbed speech offer a broader vision in which Jerusalem will eventually encompass Jew and Gentile alike, attracting all the nations of the world to its light.

The matter of endogamy surfaces prominently also in the Jewish novella, *Joseph and Aseneth,* a grandiose elaboration on the brief scriptural notice of Joseph's marriage to the daughter of an Egyptian priest. The romantic story underscores in no uncertain terms Joseph's unbending resistance to marriage outside the clan, relenting only when Aseneth abandons all her heresies, smashes her idols, and seeks forgiveness through abject prayers to the god of Joseph. The author here too, by exaggerating Joseph's priggishness and Aseneth's debasement, may suggest the disadvantages of taking endogamy to extremes. But the importance of the practice as highlighting Jewish particularity is plain.

Jews seem quite uninhibited in displaying in the Diaspora traits peculiar to their ancestral traditions. One need only think of those practices remarked upon most often by Greek and Roman authors: observance of the Sabbath, dietary laws, and circumcision. The institution of the Sabbath frequently drew comment, generally amused comment. Pagan writers found it quite incomprehensible that Jews refused to fight on the Sabbath — thus causing Jerusalem to fall on three different occasions. And even if the prohibition did not cause disaster, it seemed a colossal waste of time: why did Jews waste one-seventh of their lives in idleness? Comparable mirth directed itself against the abstention from eating pork. Even Emperor Augustus, in reference to the notorious intrigues and murders that took place in the household of Herod, famously observed that "it's better to be Herod's pig than his son." That quip implies that the Jewish dietary restriction was well known among the Romans. Satirists indeed had a field day with it. Petronius, author of the *Satyricon,* concluded that, if Jews don't touch pork, they must worship a pig-god. And Juvenal characterized Judea as a place where a long-standing indulgence permits pigs to reach a ripe old age. As for circumcision, it provided much grist for the jokesters' mill. Philo reports that circumcision called forth considerable ridicule from non-Jews. Among the instances of this was Juvenal's claim that Jews are so exclusive that they would not even give directions in the street to anyone who was not circumcised. None of this amounts, as has often been thought, to "anti-Semitism." It represents mockery rather than animosity. But it demonstrates that Diaspora Jews had no qualms (and no fears) about practicing their conventional customs, thereby denoting their differences from Gentiles.

In fact, what struck pagan writers most was not Jewish assimilation but Jewish separateness. That emerges in Juvenal's quip noted above. It recurs also in a comment by his contemporary, the historian Tacitus, who claimed that Jews took up circumcision precisely in order to express their distinctiveness from all other people. The impression of Jewish separatism appears, in fact, as early as the first extant Greek writer to take note of the Jews, Hecataeus of Abdera, a historian of the late fourth century B.C.E. Hecataeus, in an account generally favorable to Jews, indicates that they tended to keep to themselves and shun the company of others.

The uncommon character of their customs both provided bonds among Diaspora Jews everywhere and announced their differences from other peoples. The surviving evidence underscores this again and again. The collection of an annual tax to be sent to the Temple from Jewish communities throughout the Mediterranean exemplifies it. So does the regular celebration of festivals that mark major milestones in the history of the nation. The Jews of Egypt kept the Passover at least as early as the fifth century, as the Aramaic papyri from Elephantine attest. Scattered testimony reveals observance of Shavuot, Sukkot, and Yom Kippur in Jewish communities outside Palestine, conspicuous links to ancient tradition. Later feasts have strong Diaspora connections. The Purim festival began in the Persian period, according to the book of Esther, and was celebrated annually by the Jews of Persia. A comparable anniversary occurred in Alexandria to celebrate a Jewish triumph, according to the narrative of 3 Maccabees. And the

Jews of Jerusalem invited their compatriots in Egypt to commemorate the purification of the Temple in their own Diaspora location.

As noted earlier, the structures in which Jews of the Diaspora met often carried the designation of *proseuchai* or prayer houses. That term applies regularly to Jewish meeting places in Egypt but also in the Bosporan region, in Delos, in Halicarnassus, and doubtless in other communities where the evidence fails us. The implication seems clear enough: such gatherings included prayers, acts of worship of some sort that gave voice to the particular Jewish relationship with the divinity. Such places of assemblage, whether called *proseuchē* or *synagōgē*, served also as a site for collective Torah study and for other instructional activity that reinforced the continued commitment to Jewish tradition.

Philo, the learned Alexandrian Jew, places particular emphasis upon this aspect of synagogue activity, noting that the laws were read out to weekly meetings on the Sabbath. Priests or elders, according to Philo, took responsibility for reading and commenting on the sacred laws, even keeping the congregation at it for hours, and providing them with great impetus toward piety. In Philo's portrayal, perhaps somewhat shaped by his own philosophic proclivities, congregants sit in their synagogues, read their sacred books, and discuss at length the particulars of their ancestral philosophy. He reckons the synagogue as a Jewish replica of a philosophical academy. The presentation may be slightly skewed but surely not far off the mark.

The book of Acts portrays Paul repeatedly entering Jewish synagogues in various cities of the Diaspora, in Thessalonica, Athens, Corinth, and Ephesus, and arguing with Jews about the meaning of the Scriptures. Close attention to holy writ obviously remained central to Jewish activity outside Palestine — and to Jewish self-perception. The vitality of the Torah was undiminished. The stimulus for translation into Greek suffices to establish that. And, as Philo reports, the completion of the project receives annual celebration on the island of Pharos, where the translators allegedly worked, a strong signal of Jewish pride in the heritage that marked them out from others.

The tenacious adherence to signature principles occurred perhaps most obviously in the Jewish insistence upon rejecting idolatry. The affirmation did not consist, strictly speaking, in pitting monotheism against polytheism. Jewish intellectuals recognized that Greek philosophic thinking often expressed itself in terms of a supreme deity or a single divine principle. What Jews resisted unequivocally was the worship of deities in the form of images. Such practice they reckoned as profaning the spiritual essence of God. The stance, of course, derives from the biblical command-ment against graven images, and the struggle against idolaters fills the pages of the Torah and the Deuteronomistic history. The principle re-tained its power in the Second Temple. As we have seen, even the *Letter of Aristeas,* a prime document for accord between the Jewish and Hellenic worlds, draws the line firmly at idolatry, denouncing in harshest terms those who fashion their own gods in wood or stone and thus fundamen-tally misconceive the nature of divinity. Aseneth's acceptance of Joseph's god could come only when she pulverized every idol in the household. And the assault on idolatry gains voice also in the *Sibylline Oracles,* com-posed by Jews who emphasized the failings and offenses of Gentiles. The incorporeal character of God represented an unshakable principle. Jewish aniconism was conspicuous and widely acknowledged by non-Jews. Some found it peculiar and puzzling, even akin to atheism. Others admired it. The Roman historian Tacitus held up the Jewish practice as a worthy con-trast with animal worship indulged in by Egyptians and with emperor worship, which Tacitus deplored. Indeed the most learned of Romans, the great scholar Varro, in the late first century B.C.E., praised the imageless conception of the deity, likening it to ancient Roman custom as genuine piety before the Romans began to set up images and adulterate their creed. But whether questioning or admiring, pagan references to Jewish an-iconism make clear that perseverance in this principle that set Jews apart from their neighbors received widespread notice. They erected no façade of assimilation.

Gentile Attraction to Judaism

The insistence on distinctiveness, however, did not entail a closed society. Indeed the accessibility of Judaism to the outsider, a striking feature often overlooked, merits attention. A considerable number of non-Jews found Judaism enticing. We can no longer recover the reasons, and they doubt-less varied from place to place, and person to person. Some may have been attracted by its great longevity, by the ethical precepts, by the rigorous ad-herence to the Law, by the discipline demanded in its practices, by the so-cial bonding of the synagogues, by the celebration of its festivals, or by the reputation not only for Eastern wisdom but for skills in both the practical and the occult sciences. We can only speculate on the motives. But the fact of Gentiles entering into Jewish society in some fashion is incontrovertible. This did not require conversion — nor necessarily an abandonment of previous identity and associations. It might take the form of imitating the Jewish way of life up to a point, like observing the Sabbath, or adopting certain codes of behavior, or taking part in synagogue activities, or providing material support for the Jewish community. The Jews did not turn such people away.

We hear of several non-Jews who held Judaism in high esteem and showed genuine interest in it. The Gospel of Luke mentions a Roman centurion at Capernaum as one who loved Jews and had built them a synagogue. According to Philo, the Roman prefect of Syria had gained familiarity with Jewish philosophy and piety. Josephus indicates in several contexts the attraction of eminent women to Judaism, including even the wife of the emperor Nero. Gentile reverence for Jewish laws and mores appears with some frequency in Josephus's works.

Indeed, if Josephus is to be believed, pagans everywhere included observers of the Sabbath, people who adopted Jewish dietary practices, or those who attempted to imitate the Jews in their internal concord, their philanthropy, their skill in the crafts, and their adherence to the Law even under duress. Philo makes a similar claim, asserting that almost all people, especially those who place a premium upon virtue, pay homage to Jewish laws. The Jewish authors, to be sure, are hardly unbiased witnesses. But their statements, however exaggerated and embroidered, do not arise out of the void.

Non-Jewish sources supply corroboration. The Roman satirist Juvenal, writing in the early second century c.e., refers in sardonic fashion to the appeal that Jewish practices have in Rome. He alludes to fathers who revere the Sabbath and follow Jewish dietary restrictions. Their sons then go further: they worship a deity of the sky, draw no distinction between consuming swine's flesh and cannibalism, and even engage in circumcision. A very different text, the Christian book of Revelation, composed about the same time, denounces those who falsely claim to be Jews but are not so. This may refer to Gentiles who have adopted Jewish behavior and institutions — without becoming Jews.

Such persons seem even to have a name. "God-fearers" serves as the conventional designation (even if not technical terminology) for Gentiles seriously drawn to an association with Judaism or the Jewish community. The Acts of the Apostles contain several references to "those who fear God" or "those who revere God," denoting Gentiles who were closely and sympathetically involved with the Jewish community and who lived in accord with at least some of its precepts. The terminology has a parallel in Josephus, who attributes the wealth of the Temple to contributions both from Jews and from "those who worship God" all over the world. Closely comparable phrases appear in inscriptions of somewhat later periods from a wide variety of regions ranging from Italy to the Black Sea. Gentiles in substantial numbers participated in some fashion (doubtless in diverse fashions) in Jewish synagogues and communities — and they were clearly welcomed.

Relations with the Homeland

An important question remains. How did Diaspora Jews relate to the homeland? Did the land of Israel beckon to those dwelling in distant places, a prime objective of the displaced, the principal means of realizing the destiny of the people for whom the "Return" represented the fulfillment of Yahweh's promise? Or had the Jews instead assimilated to life abroad, finding gratification in the concept that their identity resided in the "Book," not in any territorial legitimation. For such Jews, restoration to the homeland was irrelevant and superfluous; the land of their residence rather than the home of the fathers constituted the cardinal attachment.

The dichotomy misleads and deceives. The whole idea of valuing homeland over Diaspora or Diaspora over homeland is off the mark. Second Temple Jews need not have faced so stark a choice.

The Bible, of course, has YHWH promise eventually to return the children of Israel from the most remote regions to the land of their fathers. And similar comments recur in Jewish Hellenistic writers who deplore the dispersal and forecast the ingathering of the exiles, as in the book of Tobit, the *Psalms of Solomon,* and *Jubilees.* But in each instance the termination of exile and the return to the homeland are connected to the reconstruction of the Temple. As a symbol of the faith, its demolition at the hands of Babylon had caused heartbreak and longing. But a comparable condition did not hold in the Hellenistic Diaspora. The Temple stood again in Jerusalem. And few Jews abroad were held there by constraint.

The generally satisfactory circumstances of the Diaspora defused any widespread passion for the "Return." Jews, as we have seen, generally formed stable communities at places quite distant from Judea, entered into the social, economic, and political life of the nations they joined, and aspired to and obtained civic privileges in the cities of the Hellenistic world. Josephus maintains that Jews have every right to call themselves Alexandrians, Antiochenes, or Ephesians. And Philo refers to his home as "our Alexandria." An inscription from the Phrygian city of Acmonia, set up by a Jew or group of Jews, alludes to the fulfillment of a vow made to the "whole *patris*." This records a conspicuous and public pronouncement of local loyalty. Philo confirms the sentiment in striking fashion: Jews consider the holy city as their "metropolis," but the states in which they were born and raised and which they acquired from their fathers, grandfathers, and distant forefathers they adjudge to be their *patrides*. That fervent expression denies any idea of the "doctrine of return." Diaspora Jews, in Philo's formulation at least, held a fierce attachment to the adopted lands of their ancestors.

None of this, however, diminished the sanctity and centrality of Jerusalem in the Jewish consciousness. The city's aura retained a powerful hold on Jews, wherever they happened to reside. Even the pagan geographer Strabo observed the Jews' devotion to their sacred "acropolis." Numerous other texts characterize Palestine as the "Holy Land." That designation appears in works as different as 2 Maccabees, the Wisdom of Solomon, the *Testament of Job*, the *Sibylline Oracles*, and Philo. Most, if not all, of those texts stem from the Diaspora. They underscore the reverence with which Jews around the Mediterranean continued to regard Jerusalem and the land of their fathers. But the authors who speak with reverence do not demand the "Return." Commitment to one's local or regional community was entirely compatible with devotion to Jerusalem. The two concepts in no way represented mutually exclusive alternatives.

What meaning, then, did the notion of a homeland have for Jews dwelling in scattered Mediterranean communities? They never yielded the principle. Jewish attitudes here, as in many other regards, corresponded with those of their pagan neighbors. Loyalty to one's native land represented a frequent sentiment in the rhetoric of the Hellenistic world. Philo more than once endorses the idea that adherence to one's native land held singular power. He puts failure to worship God on a level with neglecting to honor parents, benefactors, and native land. It does not follow, however, that Diaspora Jews set their hearts upon a return to the fatherland. Broad pronouncements about love of one's country accord with general Hellenistic expressions. They do not require that those native environs be reinhabited for life to be complete.

Jerusalem as concept and reality remained a powerful emblem of Jewish identity — not supplanted by the Book or disavowed by those who dwelled afar. It appears again and again in the texts of Second Temple authors as a symbol of the highest appeal. Yet this tenacious devotion did not entail a widespread desire to pull up stakes and return to the fatherland.

Jews reminded themselves and others every year of their commitment to Jerusalem. The reminder came in the form of a tithe paid to the Temple annually by Jews all over the Mediterranean. The ritualistic offering carried deep significance as a bonding device. That fact is vividly illustrated by an episode in the mid 60s B.C.E. A Roman governor of the province of Asia (essentially northwestern Asia Minor) banned the sending of gold by the Jews of the region to Jerusalem. This was part of a broader Roman policy and did not apply to Jews alone. But the solidarity of Jewish reaction was impressive. Word got back in great haste to the Jewish community in Rome. Demonstrations mobilized and strong pressure mounted on the Roman government by Jews in the city expressing concern in unequivocal terms for their compatriots abroad. The event underscores the importance of Jewish commitment to provide funds annually to the Temple from Italy and from all the provinces of the Roman Empire. Clearly the plight of Asian Jews who were prevented from making their contributions had powerful resonance among fellow Jews far off in Rome. The latter expressed their sentiments in no uncertain terms. Jerusalem and the Temple remained emblematic of their common purpose across the Mediterranean.

References to the gravity of the tithe abound. Josephus proudly observes that the donations came from Jews all over Asia and Europe, indeed from everywhere in the world, for countless years. When local authorities interfered with that activity, Jews would send up a howl to Rome — and usually get satisfaction. Areas beyond the reach of Roman power also tithed consistently. Jewish communities in Babylon and other satrapies under Parthian dominion sent representatives every year over difficult terrain and dangerous highways to deposit their contributions in the Temple. The value of paying homage to Jerusalem was undiminished. That annual act of obeisance constituted a repeated display of affection and allegiance, visible evidence of the unbroken attachment of the Diaspora to the center.

The remittance, however, did not imply that Jews viewed the Diaspora as no more than a temporary exile to be terminated by an ingathering in Jerusalem. Indeed, it implied the reverse. The yearly contribution proclaimed that the Diaspora could endure indefinitely — and quite satisfactorily. The communities abroad had successfully entrenched themselves; they were now mainstays of the center. Their fierce commitment to the tithe did not signify a desire for the "Return." It rendered the Return unnecessary.

A comparable institution reinforces that inference: the pilgrimage of Diaspora Jews to Jerusalem. Major festivals could attract them with some frequency and in substantial numbers. According to Philo, myriads came from countless cities for every feast, over land and sea, from all points of the compass, to enjoy the Temple as a serene refuge from the hurly-burly of everyday life abroad. Josephus informs us that the women's court at the Temple was large enough to accommodate those who resided in the land and those who arrived from abroad — a clear sign that numerous female pilgrims came with some regularity.

The Holy City was a compelling magnet. But the demonstration of devotion did not entail a desire for migration. Pilgrimage, in fact, by its very nature, signified a temporary payment of respect. Jerusalem possessed an irresistible claim on the emotions of Diaspora Jews, forming a critical part of their identity. But home was elsewhere.

The self-perception of Second Temple Jews projected a tight solidarity between center and Diaspora. Images of exile and separation did not haunt them. What affected the dwellers in Jerusalem affected Jews everywhere. The theme of intertwined experience and identity recurs with impressive frequency and variety in Second Temple literature. The two letters affixed to the beginning of 2 Maccabees illustrate the point. The Jews of Jerusalem take for granted the intimate relationship that exists with their brethren in Egypt. The preamble of the first letter greets them as "brothers" to "brothers" and alludes to their common heritage: God's covenant with Abraham, Isaac, and Jacob. And the concluding lines of the second letter make reference to the desired reunion of all Jews in the holy site. The latter delivers a summons to Egyptian Jews to attend the newly instituted festival, thus to celebrate the purification of the Temple, a reaffirmation of the solidarity among Jews everywhere. It reflects the practice of pilgrimage, not a program to dissolve the Diaspora.

The *Letter of Aristeas* makes an equally forceful statement about the connection between Jerusalemites and other Jews. King Ptolemy's missive to the high priest in Judea asserts that his motive in having the Hebrew Bible rendered into Greek is to benefit not only the Jews of Egypt but all Jews throughout the world, including those yet unborn. One may legitimately question whether the king ever made such a statement. But the Jewish author of the *Letter* conceived or conveyed it. And that is the point. At the conclusion of the work, when the scholars from Jerusalem complete their translation and have it read out to the Jews of Egypt, the large assembly bursts into applause, a dramatic expression of the unity of purpose.

Historical events reinforce the evidence of literary creations. As we have seen, the demonstrations of Roman Jews on behalf of their compatriots in Asia whose contributions to the Temple were in jeopardy reveal a strong sense of Jewish fellowship across the Mediterranean. Another, very different, episode adds conformation. At the height of the Roman civil war, Julius Caesar found himself besieged in Alexandria in 48/47 B.C.E. A troop of three thousand Jewish soldiers marched to his rescue. But Egyptian Jews who dwelled at Leontopolis, site of a long-standing Jewish enclave, blocked their path. The stalemate, however, was swiftly broken. The Jewish commander overcame the resistance of the Leontopolitans by appealing to their common nationality and their common loyalty to the high priest in Jerusalem. No further persuasion proved necessary. The Jews of both Leontopolis and Memphis declared themselves for Caesar and helped to turn the tide of war. The connection between Judea and Diaspora held firm.

A similar conclusion derives from quite a different occasion. The death of Herod the Great in 4 B.C.E. prompted a major discussion in Rome on the future of the regime. Fifty envoys came to Rome from Judea urging Emperor Augustus to put an end to the rule of the Herodian family. And 8,000 Jews resident in Rome, so we are told, joined their fellow Jews in this lobbying effort. A network of connections across the Mediterranean made it possible. And the interests coincided. When a pretender to the throne of Herod emerged, claiming to be a reincarnation of one of Herod's sons, he found widespread support from Jews in Crete, in Melos, and in Rome itself. The network was extensive. Such events provide a revealing window upon the lively interest and occasionally energetic engagement of Diaspora Jews in the affairs of Palestine.

The affiliations emerge most dramatically in the grave crises that marked the reign of the emperor Caligula (37-41 C.E.). Bitter conflict erupted in Alexandria, bringing harsh sufferings upon the Jews of that city. And a still worse menace loomed over Jerusalem when the eccentric and unpredictable Roman emperor proposed to have a statue for pagan worship installed in the Temple. When Alexandrian Jews were attacked, says Philo (a contemporary of the events), the word spread like wildfire. Reports swept not only through all the districts of Egypt but from there to the nations of the East and from the borders of Libya to the lands of the West. Philo's claims of such speedy communications may stretch a point, but the concept of tight interrelationships among Jews of the Diaspora is plain and potent.

With regard to news of Caligula's decision to erect a statue in the Temple, Philo's description is telling: the most grievous calamity fell unexpectedly and brought peril not to one part of the Jewish people but to the entire nation at once. The disaster was averted, thanks in part to a letter of the Jewish prince Agrippa I, a friend of the emperor and recent recipient of a kingdom among the Jews. Agrippa urgently alerted Caligula to the gravity of the situation. He made it clear that an affront to Jerusalem would have vast repercussions: the Holy City was not merely the metropolis of Judea but of most nations in the world since Jewish colonies thrived all over the Near East, Asia Minor, Greece, Macedon, Africa, and the lands beyond the Euphrates. The image of Jerusalem binding together Jews everywhere in the world remained central in the self-perception of the Diaspora.

A moving passage elsewhere in Philo encapsulates this theme. Although he thrived in the Diaspora, enjoyed its advantages, and broadcast its virtues, Philo nevertheless found even deeper meaning in the land of Israel. He interprets the Shavuot festival as a celebration of the Jews' possession of their own land, a heritage now of long standing, and a means whereby they could cease their wandering. Philo saw no inconsistency or contradiction. Diaspora Jews might find fulfillment and reward in their communities abroad. But they honored Judea as a refuge for those who were once displaced and unsettled — and the prime legacy of all.

Josephus makes the point in a quite different context but with equal force. In his rewriting of Numbers he places a sweeping prognostication in the mouth of the Mesopotamian priest Balaam. The priest projects a glorious future for the Israelites: they will not only occupy and hold forever the land of Canaan, a chief signal of God's favor, but their multitudes will fill all the world, islands, and continents, outnumbering even the stars in the heavens. That is a notable declaration. Palestine, as ever, merits a special place. But the Diaspora, far from being a source of shame to be overcome, represents a resplendent achievement.

The respect and awe one paid to the Holy Land stood in full harmony with a commitment to the local community and allegiance to Gentile governance. Diaspora Jews did not bewail their fate and pine away for the homeland. Nor, by contrast, did they shrug off the homeland and reckon the Book as surrogate for the Temple. Palestine mattered, and it mattered in a territorial sense — but not as a required residence. Gifts to the Temple and pilgrimages to Jerusalem announced simultaneously one's devotion to the symbolic heart of Judaism and a singular pride in the accomplishments of the Diaspora.

None of this, of course, suggests that the experience of Jews in the Diaspora was everywhere and always untroubled, serene, and harmonious. Outbursts of violence and turbulence occasionally shattered their existence. Most notoriously, tensions among Greeks, Egyptians, and Jews in Alexandria, exacerbated by insensitive Roman overlordship, resulted in a bloody assault on Jews in 38 C.E. A quarter century later, the outbreak of Jewish rebellion against Roman rule in Palestine also had reverberations in the Diaspora. The Jews of Alexandria were victimized by a riot in 66 C.E. and, when they retaliated, encountered fierce Roman reprisals administered by Tiberius Julius Alexander, himself a Jew now in Roman service. The temple at Leontopolis in Egypt, which had stood for more than two centuries, also suffered destruction in that upheaval. A still wider Diaspora rebellion occurred in 116 C.E., involving Jews in Cyrene, Egypt, Cyprus, and possibly Mesopotamia. What caused these uprisings remains unknown. But the Roman crackdown, ordered by the emperor Trajan, was harsh, terminating the existence of many Jewish communities in these regions.

Episodes of this sort cause little surprise in the circumstances of rivalries and tensions in multiethnic societies. What is noteworthy, however, is their remarkable rarity. Given that our sources dwell on violence and upheaval when they can, the relative absence of such turmoil in our evidence is particularly significant. Even in Egypt, over a period of four centuries, the outbreak of hostilities is very much the exception rather than the norm. Elsewhere in the Diaspora, in Italy, mainland Greece, Asia Minor, and Babylon, no serious disquiet stands on record — and Jewish communities continued to thrive.

BIBLIOGRAPHY

Applebaum, Shim'on. 1979. *Jews and Greeks in Ancient Cyrene.* Leiden: Brill.
Barclay, John M. G. 1996. *Jews in the Mediterranean Diaspora.* Edinburgh: Clark.
————, ed. 2004. *Negotiating Diaspora: Jewish Strategies in the Roman Empire.* London: Clark.
Bartlett, John R., ed. 2002. *Jews in the Hellenistic and Roman Cities.* London: Routledge.
Cappelletti, Silvia. 2006. *The Jewish Community of Rome from the Second Century B.C. to the Third Century C.E.* Leiden: Brill.
Cohen, Shaye J. D., and Ernest S. Frerichs, eds. 1993. *Diasporas in Antiquity.* Atlanta: Scholars Press.

Collins, John J. 2000. *Between Athens and Jerusalem: Jewish Identity in the Hellenistic Diaspora.* 2d ed. Grand Rapids: Eerdmans.

―――. *Jewish Cult and Hellenistic Culture.* JSJSup 100. Leiden: Brill, 2005.

Cowey, James M. S., and Klaus Maresch, eds. 2001. *Urkunden des Politeuma der Juden von Herakleopolis (144/3–133/2 v. Chr.) (P. Polit. Iud.): Papyri aus Sammlungen von Heidelberg, Köln, München und Wien.* Wiesbaden: Westdeutscher Verlag.

Feldman, Louis H. 1993. *Jew and Gentile in the Ancient World.* Princeton: Princeton University Press.

Gafni, Isaiah M. 1997. *Land, Center, and Diaspora.* Sheffield: Sheffield Academic Press.

Goodman, Martin, ed. 1998. *Jews in a Graeco-Roman World.* Oxford: Clarendon.

Grabbe, Lester L. 2000. *Judaic Religion in the Second Temple Period: Belief and Practice from the Exile to Yavneh.* London: Routledge.

Gruen, Erich S. 2002. *Diaspora: Jews amidst Greeks and Romans.* Cambridge: Harvard University Press.

―――. 1998. *Heritage and Hellenism: The Reinvention of Jewish Tradition.* Berkeley: University of California Press.

Hachlili, Rachel. 1998. *Ancient Jewish Art and Archaeology in the Diaspora.* Leiden: Brill.

Honigman, Sylvie. 2003. *The Septuagint and Homeric Scholarship in Alexandria.* London: Routledge.

Horbury, William, and David Noy. 1992. *Jewish Inscriptions of Graeco-Roman Egypt.* Cambridge: Cambridge University Press.

Kasher, Aryeh. 1985. *The Jews in Hellenistic and Roman Egypt: The Struggle for Equal Rights.* Tübingen: Mohr Siebeck.

Levine, Lee I. 2000. *The Ancient Synagogue.* New Haven: Yale University Press.

Linder, Amon, ed. 1987. *The Jews in Roman Imperial Legislation.* Detroit: Wayne State University Press.

Modrzejewski, Joseph M. 1995. *The Jews of Egypt from Ramses II to the Emperor Hadrian.* Philadelphia: Jewish Publication Society.

Overman, J. Andrew, A. Thomas Kraabel, and Robert S. MacLennan, eds. 1992. *Diaspora Jews and Judaism.* Atlanta: Scholars Press.

Pucci Ben Zeev, Miriam. 1998. *Jewish Rights in the Roman World: The Greek and Roman Documents Quoted by Josephus Flavius.* Tübingen: Mohr Siebeck.

―――. 2005. *Diaspora Judaism in Turmoil, 116/117 CE.* Leuven: Peeters.

Rajak, Tessa. 2001. *The Jewish Dialogue with Greece and Rome: Studies in Cultural and Social Interaction.* Leiden: Brill.

―――. 2009. *Translation and Survival: The Greek Bible of the Ancient Jewish Diaspora.* Oxford: Oxford University Press.

Rutgers, Leonard V. 1995. *The Jews in Late Ancient Rome.* Leiden: Brill.

Smallwood, E. Mary. 1976. *The Jews under Roman Rule.* Leiden: Brill.

Tcherikover, Victor. 1961. *Hellenistic Civilization and the Jews.* Trans. S. Applebaum. Philadelphia: Jewish Publication Society of America. Rpt. Grand
Rapids: Baker Academic, 1999.

Trebilco, Paul R. 1991. *Jewish Communities in Asia Minor.* Cambridge: Cambridge
University Press.

Williams, Margaret H. 1998. *The Jews among the Greeks and Romans: A Diaspora
Sourcebook.* London: Duckworth.

The Jewish Scriptures: Texts, Versions, Canons

Eugene Ulrich

The texts that eventually came to constitute the canonical books of the Hebrew Bible or Old Testament display a pattern of developmental growth in their composition. Like a cross-section of a tree with multiple rings, they show repeated stages of new growth from their beginnings, which are usually lost in the darkness of history, continually until the end of the Second Temple period. This developmental growth did not cease until some time after the destruction of the Temple in 70 C.E., when it halted rather abruptly.

The Composition of the Scriptural Texts

The popular imagination, formed as early as rabbinic times, envisioned a few holy men (e.g., Moses, Samuel, Isaiah, Daniel) as the authors of the books that bear their names, similar to classical or modern authors who individually compose and publish books under their own name. Prior to the Enlightenment, however, several attentive readers began to raise suspicions about those views of authorship, and buoyed by the Enlightenment, questions concerning authorship gained momentum, resulting in sustained, critical analysis of the literary character of the biblical books. The overwhelming conclusion of this international and interconfessional scholarship was that the books of the biblical anthology were composed in stages. Small units of what usually began as oral material — stories, laws, songs, proverbs — were gathered into larger, growing literary complexes. Earlier source materials were brought together into a unified work by an anonymous person who is usually labeled an editor or redactor. Tradents and scribes passed on the traditions, faithfully retaining the earlier message, and at times creatively adapting them to address newer concerns that affected the successive communities. Textual critics detected further minor developments within the major stages of the compositions, noting additions to, losses from, and errors in the text of each book after it had been composed and as it continued to be recited or copied from generation to generation. Thus the Scriptures were seen to be composed over the course of approximately a millennium, from source materials in the premonarchic and monarchic periods to within a generation or so of the fall of the Second Temple in 70 C.E.

No manuscript evidence survives from the early centuries to provide clear details for a reconstruction of the history of Israel's religious and cultural literature. The scholarship described above was theoretical, based not on manuscripts but on literary and historical clues embedded within the works themselves. But the general results of that vast modern library of theoretical scholarship have now been solidly confirmed by abundant documentary evidence provided by the scriptural manuscripts from Qumran.

Thus there are two distinct periods in the history of the biblical text: a formative period of developmental growth and pluriformity until the time of the Jewish revolts against Rome, eclipsed by the period of a uniform text tradition since the second century C.E. The dynamics of these two periods account for the character of the textual witnesses preserved and the transmission history of these books.

The Texts in the Early Second Temple Period

As the liberated Judean exiles returned from Babylon to Jerusalem and environs, they gradually rebuilt the Temple, the walls, and the city. Religious leaders also assumed the responsibility of reconstituting the literary heritage from the monarchic culture as well as producing new religious works that attempted to help the people refocus their understanding of their relationship with God after the disaster.

The literary heritage from the monarchic era — which would have been primarily transmitted orally, even if priests or scribes possessed written copies — was rich and diverse. Early Israel in all likelihood had some kind of oral accounts of its formation as a people; it seems inconceivable that they lacked any traditional accounts of their origins. Martin Noth posited five themes of oral traditions that were eventually woven together to form what became the Tetrateuch or Hexateuch: the promise to the patriarchs, the guidance out of Egypt, the wandering through the wilderness, the revelation at Sinai, and the occupation of the land. Historically it is unlikely that any single group experienced the events behind all five of these traditions. Rather, different groups experienced different events which eventually were memorialized in these themes, and some individuals wove the themes together, probably adding new insights and commentary, to form what could be called a national epic. As the unity among the disparate groups developed, all groups increasingly accepted all components of the tradition as "our" story, giving it a pan-Israelite significance.

In addition to the origins narratives, various preexilic traditions would have survived in the memory of the people, including the Deuteronomistic History, or at least many of the tribal, royal, military, and religious traditions which served as the sources of that History. Included also in that early heritage were collections of sayings of and stories about prophets, such as Elijah, Elisha, Amos, Hosea, and Isaiah of Jerusalem, as well as collections of priestly rituals, liturgical hymns, and wisdom instructions.

For the most part Second Temple tradents or scribes assiduously recited or recopied those traditions as accurately as they could, but occasionally there were creative minds that sought to revise and expand the texts with insights addressing new situations and making the works meaningful to the current generation. A priestly edition of the Torah was produced and interwoven into the earlier origins traditions to help the people understand that the ancient covenant was not ephemeral and did not necessarily rest on land, autonomous kingship, and the historical process, but rather was eternal and rested on theocracy, Temple liturgy, and adherence to Torah. The Deuteronomistic History was also updated, putting heavier emphasis on the curse which would result in war, defeat, and exile from the land that had flowed with milk and honey. In contrast, certain prophetic collections with oracles of judgment were supplemented with much-needed oracles of salvation or consolation (e.g., Amos 9:11-15, and Isaiah 40–55 joined to Isaiah 1–33).

New compositions were also produced in reaction to the shocking loss of independence, land, king, and temple. In addition to the expanded and retheologized editions of the Torah and the Deuteronomistic History, Second Isaiah joyously trumpeted the exiles' imminent and glorious return to Jerusalem, typologically promising a new creation, new exodus, new covenant, and new Jerusalem. Job may be seen as an attempt to understand and deal with life and the God-human relationship after the Exile. New psalms emphasized themes of lament and the ideal of Torah as wisdom. New works, such as Chronicles and Ezra, Haggai and Zechariah, also depicted the efforts at restoring the Temple, the religion, and the people.

Recognition of the Literature as Scripture

Many if not all of these works originated as, and were generally viewed as, humanly produced literature; indeed, Sir. 44:1-15 could be seen as an ancient witness to this view. There is a spectrum of theological views concerning the divine origin of the Scriptures, but here the focus must be on how the human community came to recognize these books as divinely authored. They served a variety of purposes: the early narrative strands of the Pentateuch and the Deuteronomistic History served as a national epic and national history; Leviticus, Psalms, and Esther were used for the liturgy; *Jubilees,* the Deuteronomistic History, Proverbs, Job, Qohelet, and Ben Sira contributed to religious, moral, and practical education; the Song of Songs, Tobit, and Ruth were models for human love and loyalty; and Daniel provided a model for courage in perilous times. The literature grew as community literature, and countless tradents and copyists contributed to its dynamic development from its earliest origins as sayings, reports, songs, and other materials into books sufficiently well known and treasured to assure that they would be transmitted as important for successive generations. Just as the community formed the literature, so too the literature formed the community as it moved through history.

Of the many works produced, some came to be regarded as sacred Scripture; that is, they were regarded as in some sense having God as author. There is little evidence for reconstructing this important transition, but certain contributing factors can be proposed.

First, God was increasingly understood to be speaking through the texts to the people. For the Greeks the *Iliad* and the *Odyssey* held essential religious importance, but they were principally seen as national epics. Similarly, the early hexateuchal narratives originally would likely have been perceived more as a national epic than as "Scripture." Just as the gods spoke in the Homeric poems, so too did God speak in Israel's texts. But once the priestly portions were incorporated, especially the legal materials listed as divinely spoken on Sinai, and insofar as the divine source was reinforced by the preaching of the Torah as articulating God's will, it is quite easy to understand how God came to be viewed as the author. Already by the early second century B.C.E., *Jubilees* clearly attests this: "The LORD revealed to him . . ." (*Jub.* 1:4), and "The angel of the presence spoke to Moses according to the word of the LORD, saying: 'Write the complete history of the creation . . .'" (*Jub.* 2:1).

The divine authorship envisioned on Sinai was extended to material that had presumably been simply the priests' ritual handbook for Temple sacrifices. It is quite plausible that editorial framing in the Second Temple period transformed the priests' handbook of directions for performing the various offerings. The directions in Leviticus 1–7 may at an earlier point have begun with "When any of you bring an offering of livestock to the LORD, you shall . . ." (1:2b), proceeded with the detailed sacrificial directions, and then ended with "This is the ritual of the burnt offering, the grain offering, the sin offering, the guilt offering, the ordination offering, and the sacrifice of well-being" (7:37). The editorial framing of those priestly directions would then have introduced the section with "The LORD called Moses and spoke to him from the tent of meeting, saying, 'Speak to the people of Israel and say to them'" (1:1-2a), and concluded it with "which the LORD commanded Moses on Mount Sinai, when he commanded the people of Israel to bring their offerings to the LORD, in the wilderness of Sinai" (7:38; cf. also 4:1-2a; 5:20; 27:1-2a, 34). According to this view, the priestly ritual handbook was transformed into a divinely authored book.

Just as Moses relayed God's word in the Torah, certain prophets were seen to deliver God's message to the king and people. But eventually the entire prophetic book, including stories about the prophets and the full editorial framework, was considered divine revelation. With the passage of time a book containing God's word became a divinely revealed book.

Similarly, the Psalms, which originated as humanly composed hymns to God, were elevated to the status of divinely authored Scripture. The largest Psalms scroll from Qumran states explicitly the divine source of David's Psalter: "All these he spoke through prophecy that was given to him from the Most High" (11QPs^a 27:11). The divinely inspired prophetic nature of the Psalms is echoed in the Acts of the Apostles: "Since he was a prophet. . . . Foreseeing this, David spoke of the resurrection of the Messiah . . ." (Acts 2:30-31).

Second, additions that enhanced the theological, pious, or festival-oriented nature of a text seem to have been influential in considering a book as Scripture. For example, the theological material in Proverbs 1–9 may well have been the factor that achieved scriptural status for that book.

The older section starting in chapter 10 had probably been much more regarded as a collection of commonsense folk wisdom and pithy sayings. But the additions — such as "the LORD created [Wisdom] at the beginning" (8:22) and she was beside him "When he established the heavens . . . , when he made firm the skies above" (8:27-30) — helped transform the collection so that one could seek and "find the knowledge of God" (2:5). The not-excessively pious Qohelet may have gained scriptural status once the more traditional appendix, urging the reader to "fear God and keep his commandments" (Eccl. 12:9-14) was added. The same status may have been gained for the book of Esther with the addition of the institution of the feast of Purim (Esth. 9:18-32).

Third, hermeneutical innovation also contributed to sacralization. The Song of Songs, which like the Psalms originated as human literature, was sublimated through a hermeneutical lens into a meditation on God's love for Israel.

The book of Daniel also provides an interesting example. There was a growing cycle of Danielic materials, which perhaps drew on the righteous figure of Dan(i)el, laconically mentioned in Ezek. 14:14, 20, and which attached his name to traditions such as the anonymous Jewish healer in the Prayer of Nabonidus (4Q242). The cycle (1) achieved the form of a small literary collection of wisdom tales during the Persian period (Daniel 2–6); (2) developed into a larger collection due to the persecution of Antiochus IV (Daniel 1–12) and yet a larger collection with the Additions (1–14); and (3) continued to emerge in the form of other Pseudo-Daniel traditions (4Q243-245). Out of that developing cycle, the collections of chapters 1–12 and of 1–14 were accepted by different communities as Scripture, though not the earlier or later materials.

Other factors that may also have contributed to the recognition of Israel's literature as divinely authored Scripture were the increasing antiquity of a work, the educational or liturgical settings in which this literature was proclaimed to be speaking in the name of God or articulating the will of God, and the "resignification" or adaptability of the texts to the current community's ongoing life, whereby they could readily identify their situation with one in which God had favored Israel in the past.

Religious leaders and pious people sincerely trying to understand and articulate the divine will produced the religious classics of Israel. As generation after generation pondered their religious traditions in light of their current historical, political, and social reality, in one sense, the word *about* God became the word *of* God. The communities continued to hear it repeated as such, and eventually they recognized and described it explicitly as such.

Early Translations: Aramaic and Greek

Another possible indication that the Torah was considered authoritative Scripture before the middle of the Second Temple period is the translation of those texts into the vernacular languages. The *Iliad* and the *Odyssey*, despite their central cultural importance when the Romans took over the Greek culture, were apparently never translated into Latin in antiquity. A summary of the *Iliad* is attributed to Baebius Italicus in Nero's time, but it is a brief (only 1,070 hexameters) pedestrian version of the majestic original. By contrast with the Homeric poems, which were not translated, the Torah was translated in subsequent centuries into languages that the people could understand. The texts were important not only for the educated and cultured, and spoke not only of the past; they were central to the ongoing life of the whole community and had to be applicable to the future situations that the people might encounter. So the Scriptures were translated into Aramaic and Greek, the respective languages of the Persian Empire and the Jewish community in Babylon, and of the Hellenistic Empire and the Jewish community in Alexandria.

The Babylonian destruction and exile caused many fractures in Israel's life, including that of language. Aramaic was the imperial language of the Persian Empire, and Greek the language that the successors of Alexander attempted to impose upon their conquered territories. Though there was resistance to Greek culture, an increasing number of Jews became Aramaic or Greek speakers, creating a need for translations. Because the texts were important for community identity and had to be applicable to the future situations and foreign surroundings in which the Jewish people would find themselves in the Diaspora, the Scriptures were translated into languages that the people could understand.

There is no early evidence, but it seems likely that by the third century B.C.E. the Jewish community in Babylon had begun to translate the Torah and possibly also prophetic books into Aramaic. We do not know whether these were complete, written translations or oral, functional explanations of the Hebrew. The latter scene is mirrored in Neh. 8:8, narrated probably in the fourth century: accompanying a public reading from the Hebrew scroll, the Levites translated it and gave the sense, so that the people could understand. The earliest extant manuscripts are a Targum of Leviticus (4QtgLev) from the late second or early first century B.C.E. and two of Job (4QtgJob, 11QtgJob) from the middle of the first century C.E. Apart from these Qumran texts, the witness of the Targums for text-critical purposes is reduced, however, irrespective of the date when complete Targums of the Torah and other books were finally written down, since all preserved Targum texts have subsequently been revised to agree with an early precursor of the Masoretic Text (MT). It is difficult to have confidence that any specific readings provide premishnaic evidence.

Unlike the nebulous situation regarding early Aramaic translations, the probability is strong that the Jewish community in Alexandria had translated the Torah into Greek during the third century B.C.E. The legendary *Letter of Aristeas* elaborately narrates such an early translation, though it is generally believed to have been written in support of a version making claims for hegemony about a century later. Nevertheless, plausible examples of quotations in the late third and the second century B.C.E. as well as manuscript evidence make a third-century date for the translation close to certain. Demetrius the Chronographer already in the late third century quotes the Greek Genesis, and Eupolemus in the mid-second century uses the Greek Chronicles, which probably means that the more important Prophets had already been translated as well. Moreover, in the last third of the second century Ben Sira's grandson translated his grandfather's work and only casually mentions the translation of the Torah and the Prophets and other books, which suggests that those translations were not recent but had become widely known. Finally, the discovery of second-century manuscripts of Greek Pentateuchal books both in Egypt and in Palestine (already showing noticeable development) makes a third-century translation probable. Again, this unprecedented fact of translation may be a strong indicator that the Torah had become regarded as authoritative Scripture.

The Value of the Early Versions

The Targums generally do not help penetrate to ancient forms of the text other than those inherited in the MT collection. The Old Greek (OG) translation, on the other hand, provides for many books an invaluable witness to Second Temple textual forms that have otherwise perished. Whereas prior to the middle of the twentieth century the value of the LXX for text-critical purposes was often denigrated, the discovery of Hebrew manuscripts from Qumran vindicated the veracity of the LXX. Scrolls such as 4QDeut[q], 4QSam[a,b], and 4QJer[b,d] display in Hebrew the type of texts from which the OG had been faithfully translated.

Those manuscripts have illuminated the first of four levels that must be taken into account when dealing with the individual Hebrew parent text from which the original translation was made. Previously, it had mainly been presumed that the parent text was virtually identical with the form in the MT, but the abundant variant editions unearthed at Qumran have freed critics from that myopic vision. One must seriously consider that the Greek is a witness to a Hebrew text that may simply be no longer available.

The second level is that of the act and product of the translation itself. Due to the many sources of possible variation from the parent Hebrew, the Greek often presented a text at odds even with the parent Hebrew it did use. Those sources included, for example, errors or damaged spots in the Hebrew manuscript, the uncertainty involved in understanding an often ambiguous consonantal Hebrew, misreading or misunderstanding of the Hebrew on the part of the translator, and different division of sentences due to lack of punctuation. Thus, though the translator was usually attempting to translate the Hebrew source text faithfully, unintended variants were inevitable. It is often declared that every translation is an interpretation. In a restricted sense that is correct; of course, the translator must interpret what the meaning of the original is. But the degree of interpretation is at times exaggerated to include theological *Tendenz,* or even "actualizing exegesis," whereby the translator deliberately changed the ancient text to highlight some current event or view. Despite the attractiveness and relatively heightened significance of such theological interpretation — if it were correct — the creative exegesis is usually to be assigned to the scholar proposing it. In light of the pluriform Hebrew and Greek manuscripts from Qumran, a Herculean burden of proof falls on one who would claim that the translator saw and understood one message in the Hebrew and deliberately produced a different message in the translation. A distinction must also be made between the meaning that the translator produced and the diverse possible meanings that later interpreters might derive from that wording.

Messages different from the Hebrew could and did result from a third level. Roughly six centuries of copyists' transmission elapsed between the original translation and the earliest full copies of the LXX dating from the fourth century c.e. It must be presumed that textual variants, both inadvertent errors and intentional corrections or supplements, began to affect the Greek texts from the earliest copies that scribes attempted to produce, just as happened with the Hebrew. Some variants entered the text through cross-fertilization from variant Hebrew formulations. Theological changes also occasionally occurred during the transmission process, clearly exemplified in passages such as LXX Ps. 13:3, with a long insertion quoted from Rom. 3:3-10, and other patently Christian additions in the transmitted texts, for example, at Pss. 50:9 and 95:10. Variants at the transmission level multiplied voluminously over the centuries and are seen now flooding the critical apparatus of the Göttingen Septuagint editions.

A fourth level visible in LXX manuscripts took the texts in a different direction. While variants multiplied and spread in the LXX transmission, certain Jewish scholars labored to unify the developing LXX text, revising it toward conformity with what they presumed was the "original" Hebrew text, which for them happened to be the collection of texts now in the MT, the only collection then known. This recensional process — seen primarily in the work of Aquila, Symmachus, and (proto-)Theodotion, and culminating in Origen's Hexapla — instead of unifying the ongoing Greek manuscript tradition, rather infiltrated and complicated it. To use the LXX critically, it is important to work with the first and second levels, sifting out influence from the third and fourth levels.

In addition to serving as a valuable window into ancient Hebrew text forms, the LXX also provides luminous witness to the understanding of the Scriptures in late antiquity. The Greek texts also developed a life of their own, soon no longer moored to the precise meaning of the Hebrew originals, becoming the Scriptures of both Christian and Greek-speaking Jewish communities. The Old Latin and the "daughter versions" (e.g., the Armenian, the Bohairic, etc.) were translated from the LXX and serve indirectly as witnesses to possible alternate Hebrew texts, but all the remaining versions witness uniformly to the MT collection.

Surprising Texts from the Late Second Temple Period

Starting in the latter half of the third century B.C.E., light begins to shine on the textual landscape, thanks to the discovery of more than two hundred scriptural manuscripts in caves near Qumran and at other sites along the western side of the Dead Sea. The scriptural scrolls provide a wide-ranging parade of textual surprises that deserve close review.

Exodus

An extensively preserved manuscript of Exodus written in the Paleo-Hebrew script and dated to approximately the middle of the first century B.C.E. surprised scholars shortly after the discovery of Cave 4. 4Qpaleo-Exod^m routinely displayed the expanded text edition that was well known from the Samaritan Pentateuch (SP). In every instance where it is preserved, it displays the major expansions beyond the MT and the LXX that are exhibited by the SP. Where it is not extant there is also no reason to suspect that it did not agree with other SP expansions, except for one instance. It apparently did not have space to contain the lengthy extra commandment added in the SP at Exod. 20:17b after the traditional commandments. That specifically Samaritan commandment (though taken from Deuteronomy 11 and 27, common to MT, SP, and LXX) to build an altar at Mt. Gerizim evidently was not in 4QpaleoExod^m, just as it is lacking in the MT and the LXX. It seems clear, then, that there were at least two variant editions of the text of Exodus in circulation within Jewish circles during the first century B.C.E. Evidently both were used and enjoyed equal status. 4QpaleoExod^m was damaged at one point, and someone carefully sewed a patch over the large hole and reinscribed the lost words. This repair would not have happened if the manuscript were not needed for use. The Samaritans made use of that secondary, expanded edition and apparently made only one theological change in two forms: they added the commandment that Israel's central altar was to be built on Mt. Gerizim, and in the recurring formula they stressed that God had chosen Mt. Gerizim, not Jerusalem, as that central shrine where his name should dwell. Thus, the "Samaritan" Exodus was mainly a general Jewish text of Exodus. And that secondary, expanded edition that lacked the two specifically Samaritan changes continued to be used by Jews and was still being copied around the middle of the first century B.C.E. There does not appear to be any evidence that the Jews and Samaritans were aware of or concerned about the specific text-type.

Numbers

Scholars were generally slow in digesting and accepting that new evidence from 4QpaleoExod^m, but the most extensively preserved scroll of the book of Numbers provided confirmatory evidence with a profile similar to that of the Exodus scroll. 4QNum^b, written in the Jewish script and dating from the latter half of the first century B.C.E., also exhibits agreement with the additions in the SP beyond the traditional text as in the MT and LXX. But like 4QpaleoExod^m, it does not have the specifically Samaritan readings. It thus confirms the pattern seen in Exodus, that Palestinian Judaism knew at least two editions of the book of Numbers, and that the Samaritans used the secondary, already expanded Jewish tradition exemplified in 4QNum^b. Again, both editions of Numbers were apparently in use by Jews in the late Second Temple period.

Joshua

The oldest manuscript of Joshua also provided a surprise, but in a different direction. 4QJosh^a, from the latter half of the second or the first half of the first century B.C.E., presented a sequence of important episodes that was strikingly at variance with the order of events in the traditional MT. In the scroll, Joshua evidently builds the first altar in the newly entered land at Gilgal, immediately after he has traversed the River Jordan and led all the people safely across. That is, the episode occurs at the end of chapter 4, thus prior to the circumcision and Passover and then the ensuing conquest. The scroll's sequence seems natural and logical, and one might expect that the sanctification of the land by the building of the first altar, the recitation of the Torah, the rite of circumcision, and the celebration of Passover would be the inaugural episodes of the occupation of the Promised Land. In contrast, the MT locates the building of the first altar at the end of chapter 8, placing it on Mt. Ebal, which causes numerous problems. Commentators have had to struggle with that odd location, for it requires a march (including the women and children, 8:35) of twenty miles from Ai up to Ebal, the construction of the altar, then a return march south, back to Gilgal. Meanwhile, Joshua would have left that important altar abandoned in enemy territory, and, whereas Gilgal remained an important shrine (1 Sam. 11:14-15; 2 Kings 2:1), Mt. Ebal is otherwise insignificant. The problem is worsened since Josh. 9:1 logically and syntactically follows 8:29, not 8:35, suggesting that the insertion of vv. 30-35 at the end of chapter 8 is in a secondary position. Moreover, the LXX presents yet a slightly different order, though it is in basic agreement with the MT regarding the location of the altar. But perhaps the strongest confirmation of the sequence in 4QJosh^a is provided by Josephus (*Ant.* 5.20) and Pseudo-Philo (*L.A.B.* 21:7), who also place the altar at Gilgal and who must have used as their source a biblical text that agreed with the Qumran scroll. Josephus even adds further support (*Ant.* 5.45-57) insofar as he does not narrate a building of the altar where the MT places it, between the conquest of Ai (Josh. 8:1-29) and the Gibeonites' ruse (Joshua 9). An additional piece of the puzzle is provided by the SP, which reads "Mount Gerizim," in agreement with an Old Greek papyrus and the Old Latin, which reads "Garzin," at Deut. 27:4, the command that is the basis for this episode in Joshua. Thus 4QJosh[a] evidently provides a more original form of the narrative. The placement of that first altar in the land has serious consequences, of course, and the most plausible reading of the textual evidence is that 4QJosh[a] has the earliest sequence and that a northern faction (Samarians or Samaritans) secondarily rearranged the location of the altar at their sacred shrine on Mt. Gerizim. At a third stage, in counterreaction, southerners (Judeans or rabbis), due to religious polemics, simply changed the name of the mountain from Gerizim to Ebal, despite the anomaly created.

Judges

The oldest manuscript of the book of Judges (4QJudg[a]), dating from about 50-25 B.C.E., survives in but a single small fragment. It contains Judg. 6:2-6 followed directly by vv. 11-13. It lacks 6:7-10, a separate unit whose style differs from the preceding and following verses and appears to be a later theological insertion. Thus, again, the Qumran text of Judges exhibits an early, short form of Judges 6, and the MT has a secondary, theologically expanded version.

Samuel

4QSam[a], dating from near the mid-first century B.C.E., contains a form of text that included a complete paragraph that is not present in the MT, the LXX, or any other extant version. It narrates the oppression by Nahash the Ammonite that introduces the material now found in 1 Sam. 11:1 in the MT and other texts. The fragment itself contains a case of a scribal skip of the eye (parablepsis), which lends support to the probability that the passage was lost in the MT tradition through the same kind of error. Parallel to Josephus's agreement with 4QJosh[a], he also shows that he used a text of

Samuel like 4QSam[a], since he also narrates the content, details, and wording of that otherwise lost paragraph (*Ant.* 6.68-69).

Isaiah

The Great Isaiah Scroll (1QIsa[a]; see fig. 44) was the first and most dramatic biblical manuscript to gain widespread fame. Especially because the text displays multifaceted disagreement with the traditional MT, the assumption was made that it was a Qumran text of Isaiah, that is, that its unusual features were specifically due to the "sect" that lived at Qumran and copied it there. A second Isaiah scroll (1QIsa[b]) was also found in Cave 1 and by contrast was quite close to the MT. It did indeed show that the medieval MT of Isaiah had been copied with great accuracy over the intervening thousand years. But whereas the two scrolls were first categorized as one authentic text and one "vulgar" Qumran text, in fact they demonstrated — though scholars could not yet realize it — the two principal lessons for the biblical text from the new discoveries. The MT is, for the most part, an accurate copy of some ancient text for each book; but importantly, there were also valuable variant editions of many books in antiquity that had been lost or discarded. Though the linguistic and orthographic profile of 1QIsa[a] is generally secondary to that of the MT, its textual profile is earlier in numerous cases. 1QIsa[a] demonstrates that the MT displays a recurring pattern of a sentence or more added to the text; in seven instances the MT inserts secondary expansions of up to four verses where 1QIsa[a] preserves the earlier short text.

Jeremiah

While several scrolls show that the edition they represent is at variance with the MT, the scrolls of Jeremiah provide an example of two variant, successive editions of the book visible among the scrolls themselves. Small fragments of two manuscripts, 4QJer[b] and 4QJer[d], both from the second century B.C.E., display in Hebrew the earlier, shorter edition with one arrangement of the book that formed the basis of the OG translation. In contrast, both 4QJer[a], from ca. 225-175 B.C.E., and 4QJer[c], from the latter part of the first century B.C.E., have the later, more expanded edition with a variant arrangement in agreement with the MT. Just as 4QJer[b] and the

OG show that verses 6-8 and 10 are a secondary insertion into chap. 10 in the MT, 4QJer[a], though it agrees with the MT in its overall edition, nonetheless exposes a large secondary addition of eight verses in the MT at Jer. 7:30-34; 8:1-3. The original scroll, copied ca. 225-175 B.C.E., lacked this lengthy pair of passages; but a later scribe, palaeographically dated a century or more later, about 100-50 B.C.E., inserted them into the old text. He squeezed three lines of tiny script into a horizontal space in the text, continued with four lines written down the left margin, and, since there was yet more text, wrote a final line upside down in the bottom margin (DJD 15: 155 and plate 24). That this two-part passage was not part of the original Jeremiah text is suggested by the fact that it is not closely related to the context, that the prose insertion interrupts the flow of the poetic verse 7:29 into another logically following poetic verse 8:4, and that the original scribe's omission of it would have required an unparalleled parablepsis involving about twelve lines of text.

Psalms

The evidence from Qumran and Masada also demonstrates that there were at least two editions of the Psalter in antiquity. One manuscript from Masada has Psalm 150 followed by a blank sheet at the end, showing that it represented the same 150-psalm edition handed down in the MT. Cave 11, however, held a beautiful and generously preserved scroll with Psalms that was so different from the MT that many scholars, especially in the early decades, considered it as nonbiblical. 11QPs[a] (see fig. 45) contains thirty-nine Psalms known from the MT plus ten additional compositions. Shortly after it was published, there was a vigorous debate concerning its nature, whether biblical or not. Its editor, James A. Sanders, considered it a biblical scroll and thus listed "Ps" in the title, but other major scholars challenged this classification. Their challenges included the following reasons: (1) the psalms that are familiar as biblical psalms are presented in a sequence that differs repeatedly from that of the MT; (2) the scroll includes additional "nonbiblical" psalms not found in the MT; (3) it was characterized as "liturgical," because even within the biblical Psalm 145 an antiphon is repeatedly added in contrast with the MT; (4) it includes in the midst of the Psalms a prose piece, "David's Compositions"; and (5) the tetragrammaton is written in the Paleo-Hebrew script, not in the normal Jewish script used for the remainder of the scroll.

But in light of the accumulating evidence from the biblical manuscripts, each of those objections collapsed, and the scroll is being increasingly acknowledged as an alternate edition of the biblical Psalter in ancient Judaism. (1) The MT Psalter does not have a rigorously or clearly intentionally arranged sequence to its psalms; some deliberate groupings can be postulated, but there is no discernible comprehensive plan. (2) Four of the so-called noncanonical compositions are in fact psalms found in Greek and Syriac manuscripts, and two others are found at other places in the MT or LXX, namely, 2 Sam. 23:1-7 and Sir. 51:13-30. The remaining psalms were hitherto unknown but had been composed in the ancient style of the biblical psalms, not in that of the later Qumran *Hodayot*. They were clearly originally Hebrew psalms, even if not eventually accepted into the MT edition of the Psalter. (3) 11QPs^a is indeed a liturgical scroll, but so is the MT Psalter by its very nature. The antiphon interspersed in Psalm 145, "Blessed be the LORD, and blessed be his name forever and ever," is totally derived from verse 1 of Psalm 145, and it is systematically repeated in the identical manner in which the antiphon "For his faithfulness endures forever" is repeated in Psalm 136 in the MT. (4) "David's Compositions" stakes an explicit claim for prophetic inspiration and thus scriptural status of the Psalter. It may have originally been positioned not *within* the collection but at the *end* of an earlier edition of the collection (before Psalms 140, 134, and 151 were appended), thus functioning as a quasi-colophon with the claim for scriptural status. (5) The use of the Paleo-Hebrew script for the divine name in a text written in the Jewish script had earlier been considered an indication that the text was not biblical, but several other biblical scrolls in the Jewish script have also been identified that write the tetragrammaton in the Paleo-Hebrew script. Finally, two additional manuscripts (11QPs^b and 4QPs^e) apparently witness to the 11QPs^a edition, whereas none of the ancient manuscripts found at Qumran unambiguously supports the MT sequence of Psalms against the 11QPs^a sequence.

The (Reworked?) Pentateuch

Four sets of fragments, three of them containing text from four or all five books of the Pentateuch, still pose challenges that deserve exploration. First, it remains undecided whether 4Q364-367, to which yet a fifth manuscript (4Q185) has been linked, represent copies of the same composition or only similar variant forms of pentateuchal development. Second, the classification is still debated. In large part the fragments present a running text of the Pentateuch but have frequent additions, possibly a few omissions, and variant sequences. Accordingly, they were first published as "4QReworked Pentateuch"; that is, the variants were deemed to outweigh the agreements, and thus they were not the Pentateuch but beyond the Pentateuch. A number of scholars, however, having digested the lessons from the many variant, developing editions of the biblical books — that additions, omissions, and altered sequences are characteristic of the biblical text in the Second Temple period — have increasingly recognized these texts as a yet later form (or forms) of the Pentateuch, and thus refer to it as 4QPentateuch. It seems to be moderately developed beyond the expanded Jewish version seen in 4QpaleoExod^m and 4QNum^b and used by the Samaritans; in fact, many of its variants agree with the SP, though none are sectarian. Other scholars remain somewhere in a middle position between "Pentateuch" and "reworked Pentateuch," searching for a proper category and term.

Similar Examples from the MT, SP, and OG

Once taught by the variant editions posed by the biblical scrolls, scholars could recognize similar examples long available in familiar sources. The MT was recognized as containing revised and expanded editions when compared with the OG, in the Tabernacle account (Exodus 35–40), the account of David's induction into Saul's service (1 Samuel 17–18), and the book of Jeremiah. The SP was recognized as witnessing the already expanded Jewish editions of the pentateuchal books with only slight theological changes. The OG of Daniel was seen as an expanded form of the edition in the MT — the reverse process compared with the situation in Jeremiah.

The Greek papyrus 967 may well also display an edition of Ezekiel that is earlier than the edition now attested by the MT and the LXX. It has the order of chapters as 36, 38, 39, 37, and 40, and lacks 36:23c-38. Analysis suggests that this was the early form translated from a Hebrew text with that order. A later Hebrew editor transposed chap. 37 into its present (MT) position and added the last section of chap. 36 (vv. 23c-38) at the same time as a suitable eschatological introduction into chap. 37. Other ancient sources join the biblical texts in adding their witness. Josephus, for example, as seen above, used biblical texts similar to 4QJosh^a and 4QSam^a, rather than the forms in the MT, for his *Jewish Antiquities*.

Lessons from the Biblical Scrolls

In light of this review of the parade of biblical manuscripts from Qumran and the major variants in the MT, SP, and OG that can be seen and appreciated in clearer focus due to the Qumran scrolls, what lessons do they offer? The first headline that immediately flashes is "textual pluriformity." The pluriformity, however, is not chaos but shows patterns that can be clearly seen and intelligibly classified. There are four principal categories of variation detectable through comparison of the Qumran manuscripts, MT, SP, and OG: (1) orthography, (2) individual textual variants, (3) isolated insertions, and (4) revised and expanded editions. Studies show that these four types of variation operate on different levels unrelated to each other.

Orthography

The six centuries of the Second Temple period saw noticeable development in the Hebrew language, and especially its spelling practices. Scribes, through the insertion of *matres lectionis,* made early contributions to the interpretational process that concluded with the Masoretes' vocalization of the texts. Since the text was sometimes ambiguous, the tendency toward fuller spelling was helpful for correct reading and preservation of correct understanding. The *matres* were inserted at times unintentionally, at times intentionally, insofar as the source text may have had one spelling, but the scribe nonetheless inadvertently or consciously wrote the word as he customarily spelled it, regardless of the source text. Usually the fuller form simply indicated the correct form more clearly and involved no change in meaning. For example, in Isa. 8:19 the ambiguous *ha-'bwt,* which could mean "ancestors," was correctly vocalized in 1QIsa[a] as *ha-'ôbôt,* "ghosts," and similarly in the MT as *ha-'ōbôt.* But in Isa. 40:6 the ambiguous *w'mr* was interpreted in the MT as third person, whereas it was clarified as first person in 1QIsa[a].

Individual Textual Variants

The human difficulty in accurately copying large amounts of complicated text resulted in readings that differed from the parent text for virtually every ancient manuscript. Many variants were unintentional (e.g., numerous types of errors, inadvertent substitution of *lectiones faciliores,* loss of letters, loss of one or more words through inattention or parablepsis); others were intentional (clarifying insertions, scribal correction [whether correct or not], additional information, linguistic smoothing, euphemistic substitutions, literary flourishes, theological ideas). This general phenomenon is well known, and the traditional handbooks on textual criticism primarily deal with this level, describing general rules of thumb that remain well founded for judging variants.

Isolated Insertions

Learned scribes occasionally inserted into the text they were copying what they considered an appropriate piece of additional material. Comparisons between the Scrolls, the MT, the SP, and the LXX highlight insertions of up to eight verses now in one text, now in another. Depending upon the genre of book being copied, the insertions provided information (2 Sam. 5:4-5 in MT vs. 4QSam^a), offered instruction (Isa. 2:22 in 1QIsa^a MT vs. LXX), solved nomistic inconsistencies (Lev. 17:4 in 4QLev^d SP vs. 11QpaleoLev^a MT), stemmed from piety (Isa 2:9b in 4QIsa^a 4QIsa^b MT LXX vs. 1QIsa^a), added prophetic apparitions (Judg. 6:7-10 in MT vs. 4QJudg^a), introduced apocalyptic tendencies (Isa. 2:10 in 4QIsa^a 4QIsa^b MT LXX vs. 1QIsa^a, plus many "on that day" passages in Isaiah), or simply added similar material (Isa. 34:17b–35:2 in MT LXX vs. 1QIsa^a; Jer. 7:30–8:3 in MT 4QJer^a ^{2m} vs. 4QJer^{a*}) or contrasting material (Jer. 10:6-8, 10 in MT vs. 4QJer^b LXX). The prophetic books especially are replete with such expansions, and results of this activity have penetrated all texts; indeed, it seems to have been a widespread factor in the development of all the biblical books. If such interpretive insertions are isolated and not linked as part of a series, they are classified in this category. If there are a number of coordinated patterned sets showing substantial harmonizations, revisions, or insertions, these would form a new edition of a book.

New and Expanded Editions of Biblical Books

The most influential method by which the texts developed in major ways was through successive revised and expanded editions of each book. From their earliest, shadowy beginnings the texts solidified and developed by faithful repetition but also by occasional creative, updated editions to form the books as we begin to see them when manuscript evidence becomes available. Source-critical examples, such as the retheologizing of the older monarchic traditions in light of the destruction and exile (traditional P), and more specifically the insertion of the P flood story into the older J story in Genesis 6–9, help illustrate the phenomenon. Those new editions were achieved not through displacement of the old but through combination of the new with the old. A more sustained and documented example is the four or five successive editions of the book of Exodus. Exodus 35–40 is preserved in two successive editions; the OG is presumably the earlier edition (edition $n + 1$) and the MT the later (edition $n + 2$), developed from the Hebrew parent text used by the OG. Then 4QpaleoExod^m displayed an expanded edition (edition $n + 3$) based on but expanding the edition as in the MT, while the SP exhibited the same general edition as 4QpaleoExod^m but with such significant theological changes (albeit not significant quantitative changes) that it could be regarded as a fourth edition (edition $n + 4$). There is now even a fifth, if 4QRP is considered 4QPentateuch (edition $n + 5$). A similar pair of successive editions for Numbers was seen in 4QNum^b, while for Genesis the MT, SP, and LXX all clearly show intentionally revised editions of the two extended passages in chaps. 5 and 11.

The Nature of the Biblical Text

Before the discovery of the scrolls in 1947, scholars generally viewed the MT, the SP, and the LXX as three main, but not equal, text types. The MT, in a purified form, was seen as the "original" Bible; Gesenius had shown that the SP was derivative from the MT and thus farther from the "original," and the LXX was usually denigrated as an inaccurate translation where it disagreed with the MT. The SP and the LXX were occasionally helpful, to be sure, but the prevailing mentality was that the MT represented the closest extant form of the *Urtext*. The *Urtext* theory was championed by Paul de Lagarde in the late nineteenth century. It envisioned a single original Hebrew text that was no longer extant in its pure form but that could largely be recovered through the MT with comparative analysis of the SP, the LXX, and the versions. Paul Kahle in the middle of the twentieth century unsuccessfully challenged it with his *Vulgärtexte* theory, seeing a plethora of variant texts overshadowed by the MT, the SP, and the

LXX; but the genetic relationship between all texts argued strongly against it. The *Urtext* theory probably emerged from three factors: (1) the absence of evidence, because only a single Hebrew text form had been transmitted to posterity after the Second Jewish Revolt in 132-135 C.E.; (2) the traditional religious view, that the biblical text was the word that God spoke to Moses and the Prophets and the Sages, and thus was unique; and (3) early scholarly views, that the books were "documents" or major written compositions by single authors or compilers. Thus, the purified MT was ultimately God's word, and the diverse manuscripts that survive attest to the errors that human scribes have allowed to penetrate it.

But just as the invention of the telescope and accurate observation of astronomical data allowed the Copernican heliocentric cosmology to eclipse the unquestioned Ptolemaic-medieval geocentric cosmology, so too the discovery of the biblical scrolls and accurate observation of the data they provide have eclipsed the view of the MT as the textual center of the Hebrew Bible. Though the biblical scrolls from the Judean Desert were early assumed to be sectarian, the more they are studied, the more it is obvious that there is nothing sectarian about them; they constitute the most ancient and authentic witness to what the texts of the Jewish Scriptures were like at the time of the origins of Christianity and rabbinic Judaism.

The Qumran biblical manuscripts — and in their light, the LXX, the expanded Jewish text used as the basis for the SP, the biblical texts used by Josephus, and citations in the New Testament and rabbinic writings — make it clear that the MT was not the textual center. They all attest to a measured pluriformity in the scriptural texts. A number of lessons thus emerged. First, the scrolls did confirm that the medieval codices of the MT had for over a millennium been very accurately hand-copied from texts like 4QGen^b, 1QIsa^b, and 4QJer^{a,c}. But they also confirmed that the SP (in light of 4QpaleoExod^m and 4QNum^b) and the LXX (in light of 4QDeut^q, 4QSam^{a,b}, and 4QJer^{b,d}) preserved equally important witnesses to alternate ancient forms of the Hebrew biblical text otherwise lost.

Second, scholars realized not only that the MT is not "the original text" or the *Urtext* of the Hebrew Bible, but that it is not "a text" at all. Like the LXX, it is a varied collection of texts — a different type of text for each of the books — each being simply a copy of one of the editions of that book that was circulating in late Second Temple Jewish circles. Again, the MT is not "the original text"; it is rather the only collection of texts in the *original language* that had been preserved (beyond the Samaritan community) since the second century C.E.

Third, there was a revival of theories making major advances in charting the history of the biblical text. The discoveries at first supported the position of the three main text types, since various scrolls agreed with the MT, the LXX, and the SP. Large fragments of 4QSam[a,b] (agreeing with the LXX) and 4QpaleoExod[m] (agreeing with the SP) were published early, and thus W. F. Albright and, more substantially, Frank Moore Cross posited three localities as producing the three local text types, seeing a textual development of "one-into-three" — the presumed original into the MT, the LXX, and the SP. But numerous differences in the scrolls from these three types led to further theories. Shemaryahu Talmon, noting the pluriformity, saw rather a "many-into-three" situation, noting that out of the many textual traditions only three survived. Socio-religiously only three communities survived the Roman destruction: the rabbis, the Samaritans, and the Christians, each preserving their own set of texts. But the numerous disagreements in the scrolls also dethroned the LXX and the SP from their positions as the other two "main text types." Seeing the numerous disagreements as well as the agreements, Emanuel Tov expanded the view, classifying a number of scrolls as "nonaligned" with either the MT, the SP, or the LXX.

Prior to the Jewish revolts against Rome, however, there was no "standard text" — whether MT, SP, or LXX — with which texts should be "aligned" or should be judged "non-aligned," and thus those four categories appeared anachronistic for classifying the scrolls. Thus, the present author proposed a series of successive revised and expanded editions of each of the biblical books, noting that the pluriformity and great variation in the texts were not chaotic, but patterned in the four principal categories of variation discussed above. Each book had its own history and developed along its own trajectory. The main lines of development resulted from the creative revised and expanded editions of each book. Each copy of whichever edition displayed its own particular individual textual variants, and further copies would either reproduce the orthographic profile of the source text or show modernizing tendencies in spelling practices. Occasionally, scribes would put into the text isolated interpretive insertions that had become either customary oral supplements or marginal glosses, and these would become an accepted part of the transmitted text. Each of the four kinds of variation took place independently of the other three. The MT, the LXX, and the SP should not be regarded as "the three main text types" but are merely manuscript copies for each book in their collection, each copied more or less accurately from one or other of the available editions of that book. Thus, the Masoretic texts must be judged on a par with and according to the same criteria by which the LXX, the SP, the scrolls, the versions, and all other texts are judged, word by word.

From Collection of Scriptures to the Canon of Scripture

The discussion thus far has centered on individual texts, since the books developed separately and were written on separate scrolls during the Second Temple period. By the third or fourth century c.e., however, the collection of texts coalesced into a single text. Books considered to have divine authority formed a special group distinct from other works. The group of five books seen as the revelation to Moses became "the book of Moses" (4QMMT C10), though the authoritative status of *Jubilees* in certain circles raises the question whether the category of Torah was strictly confined to the five books. The book of Moses together with an undefined collection of prophetic books (including, for most Jewish groups, Psalms and Daniel) formed a special collection of authoritative Scripture — "the Law and the Prophets" — during the late Second Temple period and New Testament times. Many other works, some of which would, and others of which would not, become part of the Writings, or Poetic and Wisdom books, were still finding their place in the first century c.e. By approximately the third century, though the scroll format apparently continued in Jewish circles, at least for Christians the codex gradually supplanted the scroll as the preferred form, and the texts that had been placed only in a mental category were now transformed into a physical unity, a single text: the Old Testament. Thus, the idea of a collection of sacred texts originated in Judaism, but explicit discussion of a canon of sacred Scriptures and physical reproduction of it apparently arose in Christian circles.

"Canon" is a theological *terminus technicus* denoting the definitive, official list of inspired, authoritative books that constitute the recognized and accepted body of sacred Scripture which forms the rule of faith for a major religious group, that definitive list being the result of inclusive and exclusive decisions after serious deliberation. Jews, Catholics, Protestants, Orthodox, and others have differing lists of books as their canon, but the definition of "the canon of Scripture" remains the same for all, and the process leading up to the establishment of the canon was an analogous process for each.

There is no solid evidence from the Second Temple period regarding the specific books in the canon and at best inconclusive evidence for anything beyond "the Law and the Prophets." The Prologue to Ben Sira is clearest with "the Law and the Prophets and the other books of our ancestors" (8–10; cf. 1–2, 24–25). But this could mean either a tripartite or a bipartite collection: either (1) the Law, (2) the Prophets, and (3) the Writings; or (1) the Scriptures (i.e., the Law and the Prophets) and (2) other important religious literature helpful toward instruction and wisdom (like Ben Sira itself). Whereas both the bipartite and the tripartite (albeit quite vague for the third category) positions are defensible, in contrast, the oft-cited reference to a tripartite canon in 4QMMT C10 ("in the book of Moses [and] in the book[s of the P]rophets and in Dav[id . . .]") requires serious scrutiny. The DJD editors' interpretation as an attestation of a tripartite canon is highly dubious on at least five levels: questionable placement of a fragment (4QMMT^d frg. 17), paleographic transcription of several letters, reconstruction of the composite text in light of disagreements between the manuscripts, awkward syntax, and the content denoted by the last phrase (*wbd??*[ ]). That is, two of the three sections, "the book[s of]" the Prophets, and "David," may well disappear from the alleged tripartite reference. Appeals to other biblical references — such as in Ben Sira's own work and 1 and 2 Maccabees — are likewise unpersuasive, unless one takes a maximalist approach in which mere knowledge of or allusive mention of a book means that it, or even its entire category of books, was already considered canonical. Only toward the end of the first century C.E. does Josephus write of an exclusive twenty-two-book collection, and *4 Ezra* mentions a set of twenty-four books for the public alongside seventy to be distributed among the wise. Thus, the absence of any clear mention of a tripartite collection of Scriptures prior to the late first century C.E. weighs in favor of a bipartite collection envisioned in the Prologue to Ben Sira.

Terminological Distinctions

For clarity and to avoid maximalist overinterpretation, it is essential to distinguish between terms or realities that are closely associated with the concept of canon but are not identical with it. An *authoritative* work is one which a group, whether secular or religious, recognizes and accepts as determinative for its conduct, and as of a higher order than can be overridden by the power or will of the group or any member. An example would be a constitution or law code. A book of *Scripture* is a sacred authoritative work believed to have God as its ultimate author, which the community recognizes and accepts as determinative for its belief and practice; it is not necessarily a fixed text but may be still developing and circulating in several textual forms. *A collection of authoritative Scriptures,* as opposed to a canon, is an open collection to which more books can be added. Certainly such a collection was recognized as fundamental to the Jewish religion from sometime in the first half of the Second Temple period; at that time it was probably confined to the Law of Moses, as attested by the OG translation of the Pentateuch and the Samaritan canon. According to the distinction between "a collection of authoritative books" and "an authoritative collection of books," throughout the Second Temple period the collection was growing and thus there was not yet a canon.

A *canon,* as defined above, is a religious body's official, definitively debated and permanently decided, exclusive list of inspired, authoritative books that constitute its recognized corpus of sacred Scripture. The *Bible,* in the singular, denotes a textual form of the collection of canonical books. In contrast to the canon, which is the normative list of the books, the Bible is the text of that collection of books, conceived of as a single anthology, and usually presented physically as such. Thus, the term is probably anachronistic prior to the codex format of the collection. "The Scriptures" can be an open collection, but the "Bible" connotes an already closed collection.

The *canonical process* is the journey of the many disparate works of literature within the ongoing community from their early stages when they began to be considered as somehow authoritative, through the sifting and endorsement process, to the final judgment concerning their inspired character as the unified and defined collection of Scripture — that is, until the reflective judgment of recognition that officially constituted the canon. *Canon* as such is a static concept, the result of a retrospective conclusion that something has come to be. Until that final decision is reached, *process toward canon* or *canonical process* is preferable. Some speak of an "open canon" or of "adaptability" as the primary characteristic of the canon; but the canon is by definition closed, and so an "open collection" is preferable; and adaptability is a function, not the essence, of the canon — how it is used, not what it is.

The Evidence from Qumran for the Process toward Canon

In the absence of clear early written discussion, surveying the Qumran evidence can be somewhat illuminating, especially since it generally agrees with the New Testament evidence. Criteria of varying strengths for canon or scriptural status would be: (a) a title of the canon or its parts, or a list of its books; (b) formulas that introduce explicit quotations of Scripture; (c) books explicitly quoted as Scripture; (d) multiple copies of a book; (e) books on which commentaries were written; and (f) books that were translated into the vernacular languages.

Unfortunately, the Dead Sea Scrolls provide no conclusive evidence for determining the exact contents of the collection that the covenanters considered the authoritative books of Scripture or whether they even discussed the question. But that they regarded the Law and the Prophets as divinely revealed Scripture is clear from statements such as "[God] commanded through Moses and all his servants the prophets" (1QS 1:1-3), "As you said through Moses" (1QM 10:6), and "As God said through Isaiah the prophet" (CD 4:13). Thus, there is (a) no clear evidence for a canon of Scripture, but (b) certitude regarding the Law and the Prophets as Scripture. (c) Isaiah and the Minor Prophets are quoted nine times each, the Pentateuchal books (except for Genesis) and Ezekiel one to five times each; the only others are Psalms and Daniel at two times each, and one each for Jeremiah, Proverbs, and *Jubilees.* The Former Prophets and the remainder of the Writings are never quoted (except for the prophetic oracle in 2 Samuel 7). (d) There are (including 4QPentateuch) thirty-six copies of Deuteronomy and Psalms, twenty-four of Genesis, twenty-two of Exodus, twenty-one of Isaiah, eighteen of Leviticus, fourteen of *Jubilees,* twelve (or twenty?) of *1 Enoch,* eleven of Numbers, eight of the Minor Prophets and Daniel, six of Jeremiah, Ezekiel, and Job, and five of Tobit. The Former Prophets and the Writings all have four or fewer copies — fewer than the *Community Rule,* the *Damascus Document,* the *Hodayot,* and the *War Scroll.* (e) Exegetical commentaries treat only the Law and the Prophets (Isaiah, the Minor Prophets, and Psalms). Finally, (f) the Qumran texts show only the Torah (and possibly *1 Enoch*) translated into Greek, while Aramaic targums were rare: one for Leviticus and two for Job. The Greek Minor Prophets scroll from Naḥal Ḥever, however, adds valuable evidence. Since this scroll from the turn of the era is already in revised Greek form, it indicates that the original Greek translation of the main prophetic books had also been accomplished at least by the first century B.C.E.

Admittedly, the evidence for each criterion is only suggestive; but the combination is quite persuasive. It is clear that the books of the Torah and the Prophets (including Psalms and Daniel) were considered Scripture. *Jubilees* and *1 Enoch* have a strong claim. Job and possibly Proverbs qualify.

But regarding the Former Prophets and the remainder of the Writings, it can only be claimed that the literature was known to the Qumran covenanters; it may or may not have been considered Scripture, though the presence of four copies of Canticles presumably indicates that it was read at least as spiritual allegory.

Shifts in the Process toward Canon

While the terminology regarding the canonical process may be clarified, and the evidence from Qumran may witness to certain Scriptures but no canon yet, the waters remain largely uncharted for the more important and intriguing issue of the socio-political struggles and theological debates that formed the path to the eventual canon. A few turns in the path, however, can be seen.

First, there was a shift from national literature to sacred Scripture, described above. Some works of Israel's literature became recognized as having divine origin and thus were regarded as sacred Scripture.

Second, there was a shift in the understanding of revelation. Whereas revelation had been seen as dynamic and a continuing possibility, gradually it was viewed as verbal and recorded in the distant past. This gets expressed in the ancient (and a lingering modern) conviction regarding the cessation of prophecy.

Third, there was a shift from a religion centered primarily on the Temple and its rituals to a religion centered on its texts. This was a result of the destruction of the Temple and the ability of shared texts to function as a unifying force even for a people spread throughout Diaspora communities.

Fourth, vague consciousness had to give way to clear decisions regarding the scriptural status of books toward the periphery. The new focus on sacred texts as Judaism's centripetal force required new questions, scrutiny, debate, and decisions about the relative status of various texts. While all Jews recognized the sanctity of the Torah and most recognized divine revelation in a collection of prophetic books, now decisions had to be made concerning which books belonged in the "Prophets" collection and whether extra books might also deserve to be accorded supreme authority.

Fifth, a dramatic shift replaced textual pluriformity with uniformity. Throughout the Second Temple period, the texts were characterized by fluidity, pluriformity, and creativeness in composition. But the shocks of the two revolts and the increased importance of the texts precluded further development. This shift, which froze each book in a single textual form, happened quite abruptly in the late first or early second century c.e.; it is often referred to as "stabilization," but "freezing" or "termination of development" is more accurate, since it was not a textual process but simply a cessation.

Sixth, the format of the books of the Scriptures shifted from individual scrolls to codex. Whereas a scroll usually contained one or at most two books, a codex could contain a large number of books. Thus, decisions whether a book was recognized as sacred Scripture were more pressing when considering its inclusion in, or exclusion from, a single collection between front and back covers.

At the end of the lengthy process of composition and development of the Scriptures from their beginnings and through the late shifts just described, came the Romans. After two failed revolts by the Jews, the Qumran covenanters were no more; the Samaritans remained apart; the Jewish followers of Jesus inherited a large, not yet delimited collection of Scriptures emphasizing the prophetic writings. The rabbis eventually restricted the collection to twenty-four books, rejecting *1 Enoch,* Ben Sira, and others; de-emphasizing certain apocalyptic and messianic aspects; and focusing on the sapiential rather than prophetic character of the Psalms and Daniel.

BIBLIOGRAPHY

Abegg, Martin, Peter Flint, and Eugene Ulrich. 1999. *The Dead Sea Scrolls Bible: The Oldest Known Bible Translated for the First Time into English.* San Francisco: HarperSanFrancisco.

Auwers, J.-M., and H. J. De Jonge, eds. 2002. *The Biblical Canons.* Leuven: Leuven University Press and Peeters.

Cross, Frank Moore, and Shemaryahu Talmon, eds. 1975. *Qumran and the History of the Biblical Text.* Cambridge: Harvard University Press.

Dávid, Nóra, Armin Lange, Kristin De Troyer, and Shani Tzoref, eds. 2012. *The Hebrew Bible in Light of the Dead Sea Scrolls.* Göttingen: Vandenhoeck & Ruprecht.

Fernández Marcos, N. 2000. *The Septuagint in Context: Introduction to the Greek Versions of the Bible.* Trans. W. G. E. Watson. Leiden: Brill.

Flint, Peter W., and James C. VanderKam, eds. 1998. *The Dead Sea Scrolls after Fifty Years: A Comprehensive Assessment.* 2 vols. Leiden: Brill.

Harl, Marguerite, Gilles Dorrival, and Olivier Munnich. 1988. *La Bible grecque des*

Septante: Du judaïsme hellénistique au christianisme ancien. Paris: Cerf and C.N.R.S.

Hendel, Ronald S. 2010. "Assessing the Text-Critical Theories of the Hebrew Bible after Qumran." In *The Oxford Handbook of the Dead Sea Scrolls.* Ed. Timothy H. Lim and John J. Collins. Oxford: Oxford University Press, 281-302.

Herbert, Edward D., and Emanuel Tov. 2002. *The Bible as Book: The Hebrew Bible and the Judaean Desert Discoveries.* London: British Library and Oak Knoll Press.

Lim, Timothy H. 2010. "Authoritative Scriptures and the Dead Sea Scrolls." In *The Oxford Handbook of the Dead Sea Scrolls.* Ed. Timothy H. Lim and John J. Collins. Oxford: Oxford University Press, 303-22.

McDonald, Lee M., and James A. Sanders, eds. 2002. *The Canon Debate.* Peabody, Mass.: Hendrickson.

Mulder, Martin Jan, ed. 1988. *Mikra: Text, Translation, Reading and Interpretation of the Hebrew Bible in Ancient Judaism and Early Christianity.* Assen: Van Gorcum; Philadelphia: Fortress.

Purvis, James D. 1968. *The Samaritan Pentateuch and the Origin of the Samaritan Sect.* Cambridge: Harvard University Press.

Sanderson, Judith E. 1986. *An Exodus Scroll from Qumran: 4QpaleoExod^m and the Samaritan Tradition,* Atlanta: Scholars Press.

Schiffman, Lawrence H., and James C. VanderKam, eds. 2000. *The Encyclopedia of the Dead Sea Scrolls.* 2 vols. New York: Oxford University Press.

Shepherd, David. 2004. *Targum and Translation: A Reconsideration of the Qumran Aramaic Version of Job.* Assen: Van Gorcum.

Sokoloff, Michael. 1974. *The Targum to Job from Qumran Cave XI.* Ramat-Gan: Bar-Ilan University.

Talmon, Shemaryahu. 2010. *Text and Canon of the Hebrew Bible.* Winona Lake, Ind.: Eisenbrauns.

Tov, Emanuel. 1999. *The Greek and Hebrew Bible: Collected Essays on the Septuagint.* Leiden: Brill.

―――. 2008. *Hebrew Bible, Greek Bible, and Qumran: Collected Essays.* Tübingen: Mohr Siebeck.

―――. 2012. *Textual Criticism of the Hebrew Bible.* 3d ed. Minneapolis: Fortress; Assen: Royal Van Gorcum.

Trebolle Barrera, Julio. 1998. *The Jewish Bible and the Christian Bible: An Introduction to the History of the Bible.* Leiden: Brill; Grand Rapids: Eerdmans.

Ulrich, Eugene. 1999. *The Dead Sea Scrolls and the Origins of the Bible.* Grand Rapids: Eerdmans; Leiden: Brill.

―――. 2010. *The Biblical Qumran Scrolls: Transcriptions and Textual Variants.* Leiden: Brill.

―――, and Peter W. Flint. 2010. *Qumran Cave 1.II: The Isaiah Scrolls. Part 1: Plates and Transcriptions; Part 2: Introductions, Commentary, and Textual Variants.* DJD 32. Oxford: Clarendon.

VanderKam, James C. 2012. *The Dead Sea Scrolls and the Bible.* Grand Rapids: Eerdmans.

————, and Peter W. Flint. 2002. *The Meaning of the Dead Sea Scrolls: Their Significance for Understanding the Bible, Judaism, Jesus, and Christianity.* San Francisco: HarperSanFrancisco.

Van der Ploeg, J. P. M., and A. S. van der Woude. 1971. *Le Targum de Job de la Grotte XI de Qumrân.* Leiden: Brill.

Early Jewish Biblical Interpretation

James L. Kugel

Scripture was, by all accounts, a major interest, if not to say an obsession, among a broad spectrum of Jews in the Second Temple period. People argued, sometimes violently, about the meaning of this or that verse in the Torah (Pentateuch), or about the proper way to carry out one or another of its laws. People also *wrote* a great deal about Scripture: numerous compositions that have survived from the Second Temple period seek to explain various scriptural prophecies and songs and stories, and even those books that are not explicitly exegetical are usually replete with allusions to Scripture and scriptural interpretation. Moreover, a whole new institution emerged in this period, the synagogue, a place where people might gather specifically for the purpose of studying Scripture; indeed, the synagogue went on to become a (one might even say *the*) major Jewish institution, both within the land of Israel and in the Diaspora.

But perhaps the most striking evidence of Scripture's importance comes from the Dead Sea Scrolls, a collection of writings found at Qumran, south of Jericho. This library, apparently the possession of a particular Jewish community that flourished at the end of the Second Temple period, is itself a most impressive thing, consisting of roughly 800 individual manuscripts. (It was no doubt still larger at one point: some of its original contents have certainly been lost to the depredations of nature or human hands.) The library contained not one or two copies of what was to become our Hebrew Bible, but, for example, thirty-six different manuscripts of the Psalms, twenty-nine copies of Deuteronomy, and so forth. In all, these scriptural manuscripts made up a little more than a quarter of the library's total contents. But the remaining three-quarters were scarcely less tied to Scripture: nearly all of these other compositions seek, in one way or another, to explain, allude to, or expand upon things found in biblical books. Indeed, the rules governing the daily life of the community that lived at Qumran specify that the study of Scripture is to be a steady, ongoing activity: "Anywhere where there are ten people, let there not be lacking a man expounding the Torah day and night, continuously, concerning the right conduct of a man with his fellow. And let the [Assembly of the] Many see to it that in the community a third of every night of the year [is spent] in reading the Book and expounding the Law and offering blessings together" (1QS 6:6-8).

In short, Scripture was on nearly everyone's mind. The words of Ps. 119:97 — "How I love your Torah; I speak of it all day long" — might have served as the motto of *all* the different Jewish communities and sects in Second Temple times. Now when one stops to consider this state of affairs in its larger context, it should appear more than a little strange. After all, religious piety elsewhere in the ancient Near East consisted principally of the offering of animal sacrifices at one or another sanctuary, participation in mass religious revels with singing and dancing, or solemn rites to ward off evil and demonic forces. None of these elements was absent from Second Temple Judaism, but along with them, and ultimately displacing them, was the oddest sort of act: reading words written centuries earlier and acting as if they had the highest significance for people in the present age. How did this come about?

The Rise of the Bible

The idea of a specific set of writings called the Bible did not exist before the end of the Second Temple period. Before that, there existed a somewhat inchoate group of books considered sacred by one or more of the various religious communities that flourished during this period. The heart of Scripture, all communities agreed, was the Torah or Pentateuch, that is, the biblical books of Genesis, Exodus, Leviticus, Numbers, and Deuteronomy. These books were attributed to the authorship of Moses, and from an early time their laws in particular were looked to for guidance in matters of daily life. Along with them were other works — historical writings covering the period from the death of Moses to later times; prophetic books and visions associated with various figures from the past; psalms, hymns, and similar works, many attributed to King David; wise sayings and other wisdom writings, some attributed to King Solomon; and so forth. Some of these texts were actually composed within the Second Temple period, but many went back far earlier, to the time before the Babylonian Exile in the sixth century B.C.E. For example, most modern scholars agree that large parts of our biblical books of Isaiah, Hosea, Amos, and Micah go back to the eighth century B.C.E.; to a still earlier period belong a number of other texts — for example, some of the songs and psalms found in the Bible, along with a portion of the historical and legendary material later included in different books.

If these texts had thus been preserved for hundreds of years before the start of the Second Temple period, they must have played some active role in the lives of those who preserved them. After all, the parchment or papyrus on which texts were generally written begins to disintegrate after a century or so; recopying books was a tedious, and expensive, process. If these writings were nonetheless saved and recopied, it seems likely that, far back into the biblical period, people were using them for some purpose. Ancient laws were no doubt written down to preserve their exact wording, so that they might be explicated and applied to real-life cases; if psalms and hymns were similarly recorded, it was probably because they were an actual part of the liturgy in use at one or another ancient sanctuary; tales of past heroes and their doings were written down to be read in court or at festive occasions; and so forth.

Nevertheless, it is only some time after the return from the Babylonian Exile at the end of the sixth century B.C.E. that we begin to find frequent reference to the Scripture (principally the Pentateuch) and its interpretation. This is truly the time when these ancient texts begin to move to center stage in Judaism. Several factors combined to make Scripture so important.

One of these is a rather universal phenomenon. Scripture may have come to play a particularly important role in Judaism, but in many religions and civilizations (some of them quite unrelated to Judaism), writings from the ancient past also play a special role — the Vedas in Hinduism, the Zoroastrian Avesta, the writings of Confucius, and so forth. What is behind this phenomenon? With regard to premodern societies, our own view of knowledge as a dynamic, ever-expanding thing is rather inappropriate. In such societies people generally conceived of knowledge as an altogether static, unchanging thing, and they therefore tended to attach great significance to the wisdom found in writings from the ancient past. Indeed, as the chronological distance between such writings and themselves increased, so too did the esteem in which these ancient pronouncements were held. After all, what the ancients knew, or what had been revealed to them, was timeless truth, part of that great, static corpus of knowledge; it could never be displaced by later insights (nor would anyone want it to be).

Israel's ancient writings had no doubt long enjoyed a similar cachet. But added to this were several more specific things that heightened the role of Scripture in the early postexilic period. The first was the fact of the Babylonian Exile itself. Though it lasted scarcely more than half a century, it profoundly disrupted things for the exiled Jews. Institutions like the royal court, the Jerusalem Temple, and other formerly crucial centers were no more; soon, the traditions and ways of thought associated with them began to fade. Instead, the exiles' heads were now filled with foreign institutions, a foreign language, and a way of thinking that hardly bothered to take account of the tiny nation from which they had come. Under such circumstances, Israel's ancient writings offered an island of refuge. Here, the royal court and the Jerusalem Temple still lived in their full glory; here the God of Israel still reigned supreme, and His people and their history occupied center stage; and here was the exiles' old language, the Judean idiom, written down in the classical cadences of its greatest prophets and sages. It seems altogether likely that, during those years in Babylon, such writings as had accompanied the Judeans into exile only grew in importance — if not for all, then at least for some significant segment of the population. And once the exile was over, these same ancient texts continued in this role: they were the history of the nation and its pride, a national literature and more than that, a statement about the ongoing importance of the remnants of that kingdom, for its God, and for the world.

The Mode of Restoration

When the Babylonian Empire collapsed and its conqueror, the Persian king Cyrus, issued his famous decree (538 B.C.E.) allowing the exiled Judeans to return to their homeland, the ancient writings took on an additional, and still more central, role. After all, not all the exiles took up Cyrus's offer. Some had settled into life in Babylon, whatever its hardships, and were loath to make the long trek back to an uncertain future in their ancestral home. The returnees were thus a self-selected group. All of them had, in one way or another, resolved to go back to the place of an earlier existence. No doubt their motives varied, but this *mode of restoration,* of going back to what had been before, was common to all.

But how exactly could one know what had been before? The landscape itself was mute; one could not pick up a rock or interrogate a tree to find out. The past lived only in those same ancient writings, and to the extent that the returnees sought consciously to restore their land and themselves to a former way of being, their first point of reference was necessarily what those texts said or implied about how things had been before the Exile. Israel's ancient writings thus acquired a potentially *prescriptive* quality. What they said about the past could easily be translated into a potential program for the future.

Of course, the returnees were not all of one mind. Some wished only to settle down to life as residents of an obedient province in the Persian Empire, while others clung to the hope that their nation would soon find the opportunity to shake off foreign rule and return to political independence, indeed, to regain the political and military preeminence that had existed in the days of David and Solomon. Descendants of the former power elites — members of prominent families and clans, not to speak of the royal dynasty and the hereditary priesthood — must have hoped that the old social order would be re-created. Others — visionaries, prophets, reformers of various allegiances — saw in the return from exile just the opposite prospect, an opportunity to reshuffle the social deck. But precisely because all were in this *mode of restoration,* they all sought to use accounts of the past to justify their own plans for the future.

One of the most striking illustrations of this mentality is the biblical book of Chronicles, composed, according to most scholars, relatively early in the postexilic period. Although much of this book simply repeats material narrated in the biblical books of Samuel and Kings, modern scholarship has revealed subtle changes introduced here and there by the author of Chronicles, changes that embodied his own definite program for the future. He believed, for example, that the Davidic monarchy should be restored, and he looked forward to a day when the inhabitants of Judah would join forces with their northern neighbors in Samaria to form a great, United Kingdom as in days of old. He also had his own ideas about the Temple, the priesthood, and the very nature of God. Yet he did not put these ideas forth in the form of a political manifesto or religious tract. Instead, he presented them as part of a history of preexilic times, in fact, a crafty rewriting of that history that would stress all that he believed in while suppressing everything else. Why did he do so? The apparent reason is that he, and the rest of his countrymen, looked to the past for guidance about what to do in their own time.

The Laws of the Pentateuch

Of all the writings that made up Israel's Scripture, it was probably the laws of the Pentateuch that played the most important role in restored Judea These laws covered all manner of different things: civil and criminal law Temple procedure, ethical behavior, ritual purity and impurity, proper diet, and so forth. Nowadays, a country's laws do not play a very active part in most people's lives — certainly not in their religious lives. Someone who breaks the law may have to pay a fine or even go to prison, but this in itself has no particular spiritual dimension. Likewise, someone who upholds the law may be proud to be a good citizen, but nothing more. In restored Judea, by contrast, the laws of the Pentateuch were held to come from God and this automatically gave them a wholly new significance. To break a law ordained by God was not merely to commit a crime; it was to commit a sin. Likewise, observing the laws and doing what they said was not merely good citizenship but a form of divine service, a way of actively seeking to do God's will. This view of things may have existed in preexilic times, but it became particularly prominent after the return from exile.

Perhaps it was the very course of recent events that made Second Temple Jews so concerned with biblical law. Many of them must have asked themselves why their homeland had been conquered by the Babylonians, and why the Babylonian Empire had in turn collapsed shortly thereafter. Some, no doubt, gave to these questions a purely practical answer: the Babylonian army was simply stronger than that of little Judah, so it won; similarly, once the Medes and the Persians had combined forces, they easily overcame the Babylonians and took over their whole empire. But the Bible contains a different, more theological explanation: God *allowed* His people to be conquered as a punishment for their failure to keep His laws, the great covenant He had concluded with their ancestors. "Surely this came upon Judah at the command of the LORD" (2 Kings 24:3). By the same token, lest anyone think it was by any merit of the Babylonians that Judah had been overcome, He subsequently dispatched the Persian army to reduce them to ruin. So now, returned to their ancient homeland, the Judeans (or at least some of them) set out to draw the obvious theological conclusion and avoid repeating their ancestors' mistake. This time they would scrupulously obey all of God's commandments; this time, everyone would be an expert in the application of divine law, so that there would be no mistakes (Jer. 31:31-34).

There was probably another, more practical side to the importance attributed to these ancient laws. The Bible reports that the Persian administration actually adopted them as part of the Israelite legal system to be instituted in their new colony. The Persian king Artaxerxes I is thus reported to have written a letter to Ezra, a Jewish priest and sage who took over as a leader of the reestablished community:

> "And you, Ezra, according to the God-given wisdom you possess, appoint magistrates and judges who may judge all the people in the province [of Judah] who know the *laws of your God;* and you shall teach those who do not know them. All who will not obey the law of your God and the law of the king, let judgment be strictly executed on them." (Ezra 7:25-26)

It may always be, of course, that one or another element in the Bible is the result of exaggeration or wishful thinking on the part of the biblical historian, but skepticism in this case is probably unwarranted. Other, extrabiblical sources have shown the Persians to have generally been enlightened rulers who sought to accommodate their subject peoples by, among other things, maintaining the local legal system; it would simply have been good sense to adopt such an approach with the Judeans as well.

The Rise of Biblical Interpreters

For all such reasons, Scripture came to be a major focus of attention in the Second Temple period. But Scripture needed to be interpreted in order to be understood. So it was that a new figure emerged in Judean society, the biblical interpreter, and he would soon become a central force in postexilic society.

One of our first glimpses of this new figure at work is found in the biblical account of Ezra's public reading of the Torah to the assembled returnees in Jerusalem:

> When the seventh month came — the people of Israel being settled in their towns — all the people gathered together into the square before the Water Gate. They told the scribe Ezra to bring the book of the Law of Moses, which the LORD had given to Israel. Accordingly, the priest Ezra brought the Law before the assembly, both men and women and all who could hear with understanding. This was on the first day of the sev-

enth month. He read from it facing the square before the Water Gate from early morning until midday, in the presence of the men and the women and those who could understand; and the ears of all the people were attentive to the book of the Law. The scribe Ezra stood on a wooden platform that had been made for the purpose. . . . And Ezra opened the book in the sight of all the people, for he was standing above all the people; and when he opened it, all the people stood up. Then Ezra blessed the LORD, the great God, and all the people answered, "Amen, Amen," lifting up their hands. Then they bowed their heads and worshiped the LORD with their faces to the ground. Also Jeshua, Bani, Sherebiah, Jamin, Akkub, Shabbethai, Hodiah, Maaseiah, Kelita, Azariah, Jozabad, Hanan, Pelaiah, the Levites, *helped the people to understand the law,* while the people remained in their places. So they read from the book, from the Law of God, *with interpretation.* They gave the sense, so that the people understood the reading. (Neh. 7:73b–8:8)

A few things stand out in this account. It is not at Ezra's initiative, but that of the people, that this great public reading is said to have taken place. Apparently, "all the people" knew that this great book of law (presumably our Pentateuch) existed, but they were still somewhat fuzzy about its contents. So they willingly stood for hours, "from early morning until midday," in order to hear its words firsthand. It is remarkable that this assembly included "both men and women and all who could hear with understanding," that is, children above a certain age: the Torah's words were, according to this passage, not reserved for some elite, or even for the adult males of the population, but were intended for the whole people to learn and apply. But — most significantly for our subject — this public reading is accompanied by a public *explanation* of the text. The Levites "helped the people to understand the Law, while the people remained in their places"; thus, "they read from the book, from the Law of God, *with interpretation*."

Why should Scripture have needed interpreters? No doubt the need began with very down-to-earth matters. After all, every language changes over time, and by the Second Temple period some of the words and expressions used in preexilic texts were no longer understood. Even such basic concepts as *get, take, need, want, time,* and *much* were expressed with new terms by the end of the biblical period; the old words had either shifted their meaning or dropped out of the language entirely. Under such circumstances, some sort of interpreter would be necessary to make the meaning of the ancient text comprehensible. The same was true with regard to other things — names of places that no longer existed or histori-cal figures or events long forgotten or social institutions that had ceased to be.

In addition to such relatively mundane matters, however, interpreters ultimately came to address far broader and more consequential questions. As already discussed, the returning exiles had looked to texts from the an-cient past in order to fashion their own present, and this way of approach-ing Scripture as *prescriptive for the present* went on long after the return from exile was an established fact; interpreters continued to look to these ancient writings for a message relevant to their own day. But at first glance, at least, much of Scripture must have seemed quite irrelevant. It talked about figures from the distant past: what importance could their stories have to a later day other than preserving some nostalgic memory of people and events long gone? Why should anyone care about laws forbidding things that no one did any more anyway, indeed, things that no one even understood anymore? Part of the interpreter's task was thus to make the past relevant to the present — to find some practical *lesson* in ancient his-tory, or to reinterpret an ancient law in such a way as to have it apply to present-day situations, sometimes at the price of completely distorting the text's original meaning. It appears that interpreters only gradually as-sumed these functions, but as time went on, they became more daring in the way they went about things while, at the same time, settling into a more important and solid niche in Judean society.

In the case of Ezra's reading, we have no way of knowing what sort of interpretation was involved. Was it a matter of explaining an odd word or phrase here or there? Or were the interpreters (as one ancient Jewish tradi-tion has it) actually translating the whole text word-for-word, presumably into Aramaic, then the *lingua franca* of the Near East? Or did they go be-yond even this, explaining how this or that biblical law was to be applied — what was involved in "doing no work" on the Sabbath, for example?

Interpretation inside the Bible

If the Bible provides no solid leads in the case of Ezra's reading, it does of-fer a number of other examples of ancient biblical interpretation; in fact, the most ancient examples of biblical interpretation that we have are found within the Bible itself, where later books explain or expand on things that appear in earlier books. Often, the things that ancient interpreters felt called to comment upon were apparent inconsistencies or contradictions within the biblical text. Take, for example, the law in Exodus about the Passover meal:

> Tell the whole congregation of Israel that on the tenth of this month they are to take a lamb for each family, a lamb for each household. If a household is too small for a whole lamb, it shall join its closest neighbor in obtaining one; the lamb shall be divided in proportion to the number of people who eat of it. Your lamb shall be without blemish, a year-old male; you may take it from the sheep or from the goats. . . . They shall eat the lamb that same night; they shall eat it roasted over the fire with unleavened bread and bitter herbs. Do not eat any of it raw or boiled in water, but roasted over the fire, with its head, legs, and inner organs. (Exod. 12:3-9)

This passage could hardly be less ambiguous: the Passover meal was to feature the meat of a lamb (though, apparently, goat meat was also acceptable, "from the sheep or from the goats"), and it was not to be boiled, but roasted. But if so, then how is one to explain this passage from Deuteronomy?

> You shall offer the Passover sacrifice to the LORD your God, from the *flock and the herd,* at the place that the LORD will choose as a dwelling for his name. You shall *boil it* and eat it at the place that the LORD your God will choose; the next morning you may go back to your tents. (Deut. 16:2, 7)

The phrase "from the flock and the herd" presumably means that a calf or a bull would be just as acceptable as a lamb or goat, and whichever animal was chosen, its meat was apparently to be boiled — precisely what the earlier passage had forbidden. What was a person to do?

The author of the book of Chronicles, an early postexilic work, seems to have been aware of the contradiction between these two texts, since he addressed at least part of it in his own history:

> They [the Israelites] slaughtered the Passover offering, and the priests dashed the blood that they received from them, while the Levites did the skinning. . . . Then they *boiled the Passover offering in fire* according to the ordinance. . . . (2 Chron. 35:13)

"Boiled" — the same word used earlier by Deuteronomy — need not necessarily mean "boiled in water," this passage suggests; instead, it might just be a circumlocution for roasting, that is, "boiling in fire." If so, then there really was no contradiction between the Exodus and Deuteronomy passages — both of them really meant "roast"; it was just that Deuteronomy had, for some reason, not used that word explicitly.

Another little problem found within an early book of the Bible was addressed by a later one; this time, the issue concerned the inheritance rights of the firstborn son. According to biblical law, the firstborn son was to receive a larger portion of his father's estate — just because he was the firstborn. But what happened if the father had two wives and wished to give precedence to the son of his other wife, even though that son was not his first? This was probably not an uncommon situation, since the law in Deuteronomy is quite emphatic:

> If a man has two wives, and one of them is favored over the other, and
> if both the favored one and the other have borne him sons, the first-
> born being the son of the disfavored one; then on the day when he
> wills his possessions to his sons, he is not permitted to grant the son of
> the favored wife preference over the son of the other, who is the first-
> born. Instead, he must acknowledge as firstborn the son of the one
> who is not favored, giving him a double portion of all that he has;
> since he is the first issue of his virility, the right of the firstborn is his.
> (Deut. 21:15-17)

The firstborn son is to get the double portion no matter how the father feels about the boy's mother. But if so, then how does one explain what happened in the biblical story of Jacob and his sons? Jacob marries Leah and Rachel, but it is clear from the start that Rachel is his favorite (Gen. 29:17-18). Nevertheless, Reuben, Leah's son, is Jacob's oldest boy, so by rights the double portion is to be his. As things turn out, however, Reuben gets pushed aside: it is Joseph, Rachel's son, who effectively ends up with the extra inheritance (Gen. 48:5-6). To later readers of Scripture, this surely seemed to be a blatant violation of biblical law. To make matters worse, Reuben kept being referred to as Jacob's "firstborn" (Exod. 6:14; Num. 1:20; 26:5; etc.). Was he — and if so, why did he lose his inheritance?

Once again, the author of Chronicles went out of his way to explain an apparent contradiction in the text:

The sons of Reuben, the firstborn of Israel [that is, Jacob]. (He *was* the firstborn, but because he defiled his father's bed, his birthright was given to the sons of Joseph son of Israel, so that he is not enrolled in the genealogy according to the birthright.) (1 Chron. 5:1)

In Reuben's case, the Chronicler explains, an exception was made to the general rule because of Reuben's egregious sin with his father's concubine (Gen. 35:22). He was still, in genealogical terms, the firstborn, but the firstborn's special inheritance (the "birthright") was given instead to Joseph, Rachel's son.

Interpretations outside the Bible

Biblical scholars have been diligent in uncovering little spots of interpretation such as these within the Hebrew Bible itself: later versions of earlier laws sometimes modify their wording or reconfigure their application; original biblical prophecies are sometimes supplemented or rearranged to stress the new interpretation now given to them; later editors sometimes inserted phrases that glossed earlier texts whose wording was no longer understood. But considered as a whole, these inner-biblical interpretations pale before the great body of ancient interpretation that has been preserved outside of the Jewish Bible, in works composed from about the third century B.C.E. to the second century C.E. and beyond. This was the golden age of biblical interpretation, the period in which various groups of (largely anonymous) interpreters put their stamp on the Hebrew Bible and determined the basic way in which the Bible would be interpreted for the next 2,000 years.

The writings in which their interpretations are attested are quite varied. Some of them are originally Jewish compositions included in Christian Bibles — identified there as "Deuterocanonical Books" or "Old Testament Apocrypha" — works such as the Wisdom of Jesus Ben Sira (second century B.C.E.) and the Wisdom of Solomon (first century B.C.E. or C.E.). Others are categorized as "pseudepigrapha," compositions falsely ascribed to ancient figures from the Bible but actually written in a later period — works such as the book of *Jubilees* (early second century B.C.E.) or the *Testament of Abraham* (first century B.C.E. or C.E.). Much ancient biblical interpretation is also preserved in the Dead Sea Scrolls; some of these texts go back to the third century B.C.E. or earlier. Ancient translations, such as the Old Greek (Septuagint) translation of the Pentateuch (third century B.C.E.) or various targums, translations of the Bible into Aramaic (probably originating in the first century C.E. or earlier, though later material was often added in the process of transmission), also contain reflections of ancient biblical interpretation. Hellenistic Jewish writers such as Philo of Alexandria (ca. 20 B.C.E.–ca. 50 C.E.) and Josephus (ca. 37–100 C.E.) also present a great deal of biblical interpretation — part of it entirely of their own fashioning, but much else gathered from or influenced by the work of earlier interpreters. Christian writings of the first two centuries C.E., including the New Testament and other early compositions, also contain a good deal of biblical interpretation — much of it rooted in pre-Christian exegesis. Finally, later Jewish writings such as the Mishnah (put in its final form around 200 C.E.), along with the Tosefta and the tannaitic midrashim (both from roughly the same period), contain a great deal of exegetical material, much of it continuing the line of earlier biblical interpretation. Considered together, this is a vast body of writings, many times greater than the Hebrew Bible itself. In studying it, scholars are able to piece together a developmental history of how the Bible was understood starting early in the second B.C.E. or so and continuing through the next three or four hundred years — a crucial period in the Bible's history.

A note about the form of biblical interpretation: relatively few of the above-mentioned texts are written in the form of actual *commentaries,* that is, writings that cite a biblical verse and then explain what the interpreter thinks the verse means. Such commentaries did exist — they were the preferred genre of Philo of Alexandria, and commentary-like texts have been found as well among the Dead Sea Scrolls. But the favorite form for transmitting biblical interpretation in writing was *retelling.* Most writers simply assumed that their readers would be familiar with the biblical text, indeed, familiar with the exegetical problems associated with this or that verse. So he or she would retell the text with little interpretive insertions: a word no longer understood would be glossed or replaced with a word whose meaning everyone knew; an apparent contradiction would be resolved through the insertion of an explicative detail; the retelling would take the trouble to explain *why* A or B had done what they did, or *how* they did it, thereby answering a question left open in the laconic biblical version of the same story. Such retellings are a common phenomenon in ancient interpretation: the *Book of Jubilees,* the *Genesis Apocryphon* from Qumran, and Pseudo-Philo's *Book of Biblical Antiquities* are good examples of compositions that are, from start to finish, interpretive retellings. So, in a sense, are Aramaic targums such as that of *Pseudo-Jonathan* or *Neofiti;* they "translate" the Pentateuch into Aramaic, but with so many interpolations that they are actually more like retellings than real translations.

The Four Assumptions

Why was this a crucial period? Because, as already mentioned, these interpreters established the general way in which the Bible was to be approached for the next two millennia — indeed, to a certain extent, their approach is still with us to this day. Their way of reading and explaining texts was anything but straightforward — it was a highly ideological (and idealistic) form of exegesis, one that relied on a somewhat idiosyncratic combination of very close reading and great exegetical freedom. The interpretations these ancient sages came up with soon acquired the mantle of authority; they were memorized and passed on from generation to generation, sometimes modified in one or more details, but basically maintained as *what the Bible really means* for hundreds and hundreds of years.

As best we can tell, the ancient interpreters were a highly varied lot. Some lived in the land of Judea and were steeped in the Hebrew language and traditional Jewish learning. A few others, however, seem to have lived elsewhere and had a thoroughly Hellenistic education and orientation — for example, the author of the Wisdom of Solomon or Philo of Alexandria, both of whom wrote in Greek, alluded to Greek philosophical ideas, and generally cited Scripture in its Septuagint translation. (Some contemporary scholars doubt that Philo was even competent to read the Hebrew Bible in the original.) And even among those interpreters who inhabited Judea there was great variety: the author of *Jubilees* was a would-be religious innovator and a bit of a rebel; his contemporary, Ben Sira, was quite the opposite, a creature of the establishment who would probably have refused to sit at the same table with *Jubilees'* author. Pharisees battled with Sadducees over matters of interpretation, and the proprietors of the Dead Sea Scrolls (most likely to be identified with a third group, the Essenes) disagreed with both these other groups; some of them, having withdrawn to the desert, vowed to keep their own interpretations of Scripture hidden from all but the members of their own community, meanwhile waiting for the "day of vengeance" when God would strike down the other groups for their false teachings and errant practices.

And yet, for all their diversity, all these ancient interpreters went about the business of interpreting in strikingly similar fashion. It seems as if they all had, as it were, the same general set of marching orders; or, to put it differently, they all shared the same basic assumptions about *how* Scripture is to be interpreted and what its message ought to be. This is most surprising. It would appear likely that if they all shared the same basic approach — one which, as we will see, was very much influenced by the ancient Near Eastern concept of "wisdom" — this was because they were all descended, directly or otherwise, from a "wisdom"-influenced way of thinking about Scripture that existed even before these various groups of interpreters developed.

However these groups of ancient interpreters came to exist, modern scholars can, in examining their writings, deduce the basic assumptions underlying their way of explaining biblical texts. These assumptions may be broken down into four fundamental postulates:

1. All ancient interpreters assumed that scriptural texts were basically *cryptic;* that is, while the text may say A, often what it really means is B.
2. They also assumed that, although most of Scripture had been written hundreds of years earlier and seemed to be addressed to people back then, its words nevertheless were altogether *relevant* to people in the interpreters' own day — its stories contained timeless messages about proper conduct; its prophecies really referred to events happening now, or in the near future; its ancient laws were to be scrupulously observed today, even if they seemed to refer to situations or practices that no longer existed; and so forth. In a word, the basic purpose of Scripture was to *guide* people nowadays; although it talked about the past, it was really aimed at the present.
3. On the face of it, Scripture included texts written by different prophets and sages, people who lived hundreds of years apart from one another and who came from different strata of society. Nevertheless, these diverse writings were assumed to contain *a single, unitary message.* That is to say, Scripture's different parts could never contradict one another or disagree on any matter of fact or doctrine; indeed, what Scripture taught would always be perfectly consistent with the interpreters' own beliefs and practices, whatever they might be (Greek philosophical doctrines; common historical or geographical lore; the halakic teachings of later postbiblical teachers). In short, Scripture was altogether *harmonious* in all its details and altogether true; carried to its extreme, this approach postulated that there was not a single redundancy, unnecessary detail, or scribal error in the text: everything was perfect.

4. Some parts of Scripture directly cite words spoken by God, "And the LORD said to Moses . . ." and so forth. Other parts, however, are not identified as divine speech — the whole court history of King David and King Solomon, for example, or the book of Psalms, whose words are addressed *to* God. Nevertheless, ancient interpreters came to assume that all of Scripture was *of divine origin,* that God had *caused* ancient sages or historians or psalmists to write what they wrote, or that their writings had somehow been divinely guided or inspired. In short, all of Scripture came from God and all of it was sacred.

How Interpretation Worked

To see how these assumptions combined to shape the way in which interpreters interpreted, it might be appropriate to consider an actual text from the Bible, the biblical account of Abraham's near-sacrifice of his beloved son Isaac:

> And it came to pass, after these things, that God tested Abraham. He said to him, "Abraham!" and he answered, "Here I am." He said, "Take your son, your only son Isaac, whom you love, and go to the land of Moriah. Then sacrifice him there as a burnt offering on one of the mountains that I will show you." So Abraham got up early in the morning and saddled his donkey. He took two of his servants with him, along with his son Isaac; he cut the wood for the burnt offering and then set out for the place that God had told him about. On the third day, Abraham looked up and saw the place from afar. Abraham told his servants, "You stay here with the donkey while the boy and I go up there, so that we can worship and then come back to you."
>
> Abraham took the wood for the burnt offering and put it on his son Isaac; then he took the fire and the knife, and the two of them walked together. But Isaac said to his father Abraham, "Father?" and he said, "Here I am, my son." And he said, "Here is the fire and the wood, but where is the lamb for the burnt offering?" Abraham said, "God Himself will provide the lamb for the burnt offering, my son." And the two of them walked together.
>
> When they came to the place that God had told him about, Abraham built an altar and arranged the wood on it. He then tied up his son Isaac and put him on the altar on top of the wood. Abraham picked up

the knife to kill his son. But an angel of the LORD called to him from heaven, and said, "Abraham, Abraham!" And he said, "Here I am." He said, "Do not harm the boy or do anything to him. For now I know that you fear God, since you have not withheld your son, your only son, from me." And Abraham looked up and saw a ram caught in a thicket by its horns. Abraham went and took the ram and sacrificed it as a burnt offering instead of his son. (Gen. 22:1-13)

Ancient interpreters were no doubt troubled by a number of elements in this story. Did not the very fact of divine omniscience seem to make this divine "test" of Abraham unnecessary? Surely God knew how it would turn out before it took place — He knew, as the angel says at the end of the story, that Abraham was one who "fears God." So why put Abraham through this awful test? Equally disturbing was Abraham's apparent conduct vis-à-vis his son. He never tells Isaac what God has told him to do; in fact, when Isaac asks his father the obvious question — "I see fire and the wood for the sacrifice, but where is the sacrificial animal?" — Abraham gives him an evasive answer: "God Himself will provide the lamb for the burnt offering, my son." This actually turns out to be true; God does provide a ram at the last minute — but Abraham had no way of knowing this at the time. Along with this is Abraham's problematic coldness. God orders him to sacrifice his son, who, God reminds him, is "your son, your only son Isaac, whom you love," and Abraham does not utter a word of protest; in fact, the text says explicitly that Abraham "got up early in the morning," as if eager to carry out the deed.

Such problems were clearly on the minds of ancient interpreters when they commented on this story, and they did their best to find a solution to them. It is important to stress that ancient interpreters generally were not out to arrive at a modern-style critical or objective reading of Scripture's words. In keeping with Assumption 2, they began with the belief that Scripture had some important lesson to teach *them,* and in the case of this story, it had to be a positive lesson about all concerned — not only Abraham and Isaac, but about God as well. If that lesson was not immediately apparent, then it had to be searched for through a careful weighing of every word, since, in keeping with Assumption 1, the meaning of any biblical text could be hidden: it might say A when it really meant B.

With regard to the first question mentioned above — why should God need to test anyone if He is omniscient? — interpreters set their eye on an apparently insignificant detail, the opening clause of the passage: "And it came to pass, after these things. . . ." Such phrases are often used in the Bible to mark a transition; they generally signal a break: "The previous story is over, and now we are going on to something new." But the word "things" in Hebrew *(děbārîm)* also means "words." So the transitional phrase here could equally well be understood as asserting that some words had been spoken, and that "it came to pass, after these *words,* that God tested Abraham." What words? The Bible did not say, but if some words had indeed been spoken, then interpreters felt free to try to figure out what the words in question might have been.

At some point, an ancient interpreter — no one knows exactly who or when — thought of another part of the Bible quite unrelated to Abraham, the book of Job. That book begins by reporting that Satan once challenged God to test His servant Job (1:6-12; 2:1-6). Since the story of Abraham and Isaac is also described as a divine test, this interpreter theorized that the "words" mentioned in the opening sentence of the passage ("And it came to pass, after these *words,* that God tested Abraham . . .") might have been, as in the book of Job, words connected to the hypothetical challenge spoken by Satan to God: "Put Abraham to the test and see whether He is indeed obedient enough even to sacrifice his own son." If one reads the opening sentence with this in mind, then the problem of why God should have tested Abraham disappears. Of course God knew that Abraham would pass the test — but if He nevertheless went on to test Abraham, it was because some words had been spoken leading God to take up a challenge and prove *to Satan* Abraham's worthiness. One ancient interpreter who adopted this solution was the anonymous author of the *Book of Jubilees.* Here is how his retelling of the story begins:

> There were *words* in heaven regarding Abraham, that he was faithful in everything that He told him, [and that] the Lord loved him, and in every difficulty he was faithful. Then the angel Mastema [i.e., Satan] came and said before the Lord, "Behold, Abraham loves his son Isaac and he delights in him above all else. Tell him to offer him as a sacrifice on the altar. Then you will see if he carries out this command, and You will know if he is faithful in everything through which you test him." Now the Lord knew that Abraham was faithful in every difficulty which he had told him. . . . *(Jub.* 17:15-16)

Here, the "words" referred to in Gen. 22:1 are words of praise uttered by the other angels. "And it came to pass, after these *words*" were uttered, that Satan felt moved to challenge God concerning his faithful servant. God takes up the challenge, but the author of *Jubilees* goes to the trouble to assure his readers that there was really no need for God to test Abraham, since "the LORD knew that Abraham was faithful in every difficulty which he had told him" and would certainly pass this test as well.

As noted, this revised version of the biblical story contains a lesson for today (Assumption 2): Abraham was faithful to God, even when put to a very difficult test; you should be too, and you will be rewarded as Abraham was. It also illustrates Assumption 3, the idea that the Bible is not only internally consistent, but that it agrees with the interpreter's own beliefs and practices — in this case, the belief that an all-knowing God would have no need to put Abraham to the test. (As a matter of fact, however, the idea of divine omniscience is never stated outright in the Hebrew Bible — apparently, this notion did not come into existence until later on.) Finally, it is thanks to Assumption 1, that the Bible speaks cryptically, that this interpretation was possible: When the Bible said "after these things," although this looked at first glance like a common transitional phrase, what it really meant was "after these words," and it thereby intended readers to think of the book of Job and the divine test with which that book begins.

All this was well and good, but interpreters still had not completely resolved the matter of what God knew beforehand. They were still troubled by the way the test ended:

> The angel of the LORD called to him from heaven and said, "Abraham! Abraham!" and he said, "Here I am." He said, "Do not put your hand on the boy or do anything to him; for *now I know* that you fear God, since you have not withheld your son, your only son, from Me." (Gen. 22:12)

"*Now* I know" certainly seems to imply "I did not know before." Why should God say such a thing if He was really omniscient? To this problem, too, the book of *Jubilees* had an answer:

> Then I [the angel who narrates the book of *Jubilees*] stood in front of him [Abraham] and in front of Mastema [Satan]. The Lord said: "Tell him not to let his hand go down on the child and not to do anything to him, because I know that he is one who fears the Lord." So I called to him from heaven and said to him: "Abraham, Abraham!" He was startled and said, "Yes?" I said to him, "Do not lay your hands on the child and do not do anything to him, because now I know that you are

one who fears the Lord. You have not refused me your firstborn son."
(*Jub.* 18:9-11)

This passage is basically a rewording of the biblical verse cited above, Gen.
22:12, but the author of *Jubilees* has done something that the biblical text
did not: he has supplied the actual instructions that God gave His angel
before the angel cried out to Abraham. God instructs the angel, "Tell him
not to let his hand go down on the child and not to do anything to him, because I know that he is one who fears the Lord."

The author of *Jubilees* loved little subtleties. God's instructions to the
angel are identical to what the angel says in Genesis — except for one
word. God does not say "*now* I know"; He simply says, "I know." For the
author of *Jubilees,* such a scenario explained everything. The angel may not
have known how the test would turn out, but God certainly did. "I *know*
that he is one who fears the Lord," He tells the angel in *Jubilees* — in fact,
I've known it along! Thus, the words that appear in Genesis, according to
Jubilees, do not exactly represent God's command, but the angel's rewording of it. It is the angel who only now found out what God had known all
along.

As for Abraham's hiding his intentions from Isaac — once again it all
depends on how you read the text. Ancient interpreters noticed that the
passage contains a slight repetition:

> Abraham took the wood for the burnt offering and put it on his son
> Isaac; then he took the fire and the knife, *and the two of them walked to-*
> *gether.* But Isaac said to his father Abraham, "Father?" And he said,
> "Here I am, my son." And he said, "Here is the fire and the wood, but
> where is the lamb for the burnt offering?" Abraham said, "God Himself
> will provide the lamb for the burnt offering, my son." *And the two of*
> *them walked together.* (Gen. 22:6-8)

Repetition is not necessarily a bad thing, but ancient interpreters generally
felt (in keeping with Assumption 3) that the Bible would not repeat itself
without purpose. Between the two occurrences of the clause "and the two
of them walked together" is the brief exchange in which Abraham apparently hides his true intentions from Isaac. Here Abraham's words were, at
least potentially, ambiguous. Since biblical Hebrew was originally written
without punctuation marks or even capital letters marking the beginnings
of sentences, Abraham's answer to Isaac could actually be read as two sen-

tences: "God Himself will provide. The lamb for the burnt offering [is] my son." (Note that Hebrew has no verb "to be" in the present tense; thus, this last sentence would be the same whether or not the word "is" is supplied in translation.) Read in this way, Abraham's answer to Isaac was not an evasion but the brutal truth: "You're the sacrifice, Isaac." If, following that, the text adds, "And the two of them walked together," this would not be a needless repetition at all: Abraham told his son that he was to be the sacrifice, and Isaac agreed; then the two of them "walked together" in the sense that they were now of one mind to carry out God's fearsome command. Thus, in keeping with Assumptions 1 and 3, the apparent repetition was no repetition at all, and Abraham's apparent evasion was actually an announcement to Isaac of the plain truth. The conduct of both Abraham and Isaac was now above reproach: Abraham did not seek to deceive his son, and Isaac, far from a mere victim, actively sought to do God's will no less than his father did. Indeed, their conduct might thus serve as an example to be imitated by later readers (Assumption 2): even when God's decrees seem to be difficult, the righteous must follow them — and sometimes they turn out merely to be a test.

But did interpreters actually believe their interpretations? Didn't they know they were distorting the text's real meaning? This is always a difficult question. It seems likely that, at least at first, ancient interpreters were sometimes quite well aware that they were departing from the straightforward meaning of the text. But with time, that awareness began to dim. Biblical interpretation soon became an institution in ancient Israel; one generation's interpretations were passed on to the next, and eventually they acquired the authority that time and tradition always grant. *Midrash,* as this body of interpretation came to be called, simply became what the text had always been intended to communicate. Along with the interpretations themselves, the interpreters' very *modus operandi* acquired its own authority: this was how the Bible was to be interpreted, period. Moreover, since the midrashic method of searching the text carefully for hidden implications seemed to solve so many problems in the Bible that otherwise had no solution, this indicated that the interpreters were going about things correctly. As time went on, new interpretations were created on the model of older ones, until soon every chapter of the Bible came accompanied by a host of clever explanations that accounted for any perceived difficulty in its words.

Words and Verses

One final point about the "how" of ancient biblical interpretation: it always worked via a scrupulous examination of the precise wording of the biblical text. Even when the issues addressed by interpreters were broader — divine omniscience, Abraham's character, Isaac's apparent passivity — these were always approached through the interpretation of a specific verse, indeed, sometimes through a single word in the verse. "Do you want to know what 'after these things' means in the story of Abraham and Isaac? It means *after these words*." "Do you know why *the two of them walked together* is repeated? The second time is a hint that Abraham had just told Isaac he was to be sacrificed, and he agreed." It was always from such precise points of wording that larger issues were approached.

Ancient biblical interpretation was thus, no matter how broad its intentions, formally an interpretation of single verses. And this is what enabled specific interpretations to travel so widely. Teachers in school as well as preachers in synagogue or church would, in the course of explaining a biblical text, inevitably pass on an insight into this or that verse: "Here is what it is really talking about!" Thereafter, all the listeners would know that such was the meaning of that particular verse, and they would think of it every time the verse was read in public; indeed, they would pass on the explanation to others. Since the biblical text was known far and wide and often cited — the Torah, in particular, was learned by heart at an early age — a clever answer to a long-standing conundrum would circulate quickly throughout the population.

Nowadays, such verse-centered interpretations are known as *exegetical motifs* — "motifs" because, like musical motifs, they were capable of being inserted into different compositions, reworked or adapted, and combined with other motifs to make a smooth-running narrative. After a while, retellers sometimes did not even bother to allude to the particular biblical verse in question, but simply incorporated the underlying idea into their retelling. Thus, for example, the idea that Abraham had explained to Isaac that "the lamb for the burnt offering [is you,] my son," and that Isaac, far from fleeing, had willingly embraced his martyrdom, shows up in a variety of retellings, some of them terse, but others lovingly expanding on the basic idea:

> Going at the same pace — no less with regard to their thinking than with their bodies . . . they came to the designated place. (Philo, *Abr.* 172)

This is indeed intended as a precise explanation of the two occurrences of "and the two of them walked together" in the Genesis tale; the first refers to their physical walking (what Philo designates as the motion of "their bodies"), whereas the second refers to their agreement that Isaac should be sacrificed (Philo's "with regard to their thinking").

> Remember . . . the father [= Abraham], by whose hand Isaac would have submitted to being slain for the sake of religion. (4 Macc. 13:12)

> When the altar had been prepared (and) he had laid the cleft wood upon it and all was ready, [Abraham] said to his son: "My child, myriad were the prayers in which I beseeched God for your birth, and when you came into the world, I spared nothing for your upbringing. . . . But since it was by God's will that I became your father and it now pleases Him that I give you over to Him, bear this consecration valiantly. . . ." The son of such a father could not but be brave-hearted, and Isaac received these words with joy. He exclaimed that he deserved never to have been born at all if he were to reject the decision of God and of his father. . . . (Josephus, *Ant.* 1.228-32)

> And as he was setting out, he said to his son, "Behold now, my son, I am offering you as a burnt offering and I am returning you into the hands of Him who gave you to me. But the son said to the father, "Hear me, father. If [ordinarily] a lamb of the flocks is accepted with sweet savor as a sacrifice to the Lord, and if such flocks have been set aside for slaughter [in order to atone] for human iniquity, while man, on the contrary, has been designated to inherit this world — why should you be saying to me now, 'Come and inherit eternal life and time without measure?' Why if not that I was indeed born in this world *in order to* be offered as a sacrifice to Him who made me? Indeed, this [sacrifice] will be the [mark of] my blessedness over other men. . . ." (Ps.-Philo, *L.A.B.* 32:2-3)

The Wisdom Connection

It was suggested above that the common ancestor of all the diverse biblical interpreters of ancient Judaism and Christianity was the ancient Near Eastern sage, who pursued what the Bible calls "wisdom." Wisdom was an international pursuit, and a very old one; some of the earliest texts that we possess from ancient Sumer and Babylon and Egypt are collections of proverbs, the favorite medium for transmitting wisdom. What wisdom was is not given to easy summary, but its basic premise was that there exists an underlying set of rules (including, but not limited to, what we would call "laws of nature") that governs all of reality. The sage, by studying the written words of earlier sages as well as through his own, careful contemplation of the world, hoped to come to a fuller understanding of these rules and, hence, come to know how the world works. His wise counsel was therefore sought by kings and princes, and he was often a teacher who trained the next generation of sages.

At a certain point in Second Temple times, the job description of the Jewish sage was changed. Now, instead of contemplating the proverbs of previous generations, it was the Torah that occupied the sage's attention: he became a biblical interpreter. In a sense, this transformation takes place before our eyes, in books like the Wisdom of Ben Sira (or: Sirach). The second-century-B.C.E. author is, in many ways, a traditional sage: his book is full of clever, pithy proverbs, many of them his own rewording of the insights from earlier generations and centuries. But along with this traditional sort of wisdom writing, Ben Sira also explains laws and stories from the Bible; indeed, his book concludes with a six-chapter review of biblical heroes and the lessons their stories are designed to impart. This is because, for him, it is the Torah that is the great repository of wisdom. Indeed, he says as much in an extended paean to wisdom in the middle of his book, in which Wisdom (here personified as a woman) tells of her own existence.

"I came forth from the mouth of the Most High, and covered the earth like a mist. I dwelt in the highest heavens, and my throne was in a pillar of cloud. Alone I compassed the vault of heaven and traversed the depths of the abyss." (Sir. 24:3-5)

But God then orders Wisdom to transfer her headquarters out of heaven and take up residence on earth:

He said, "Make your dwelling in Jacob, and in Israel receive your inheritance. . . ." [So] I took root in an honored people, in the portion of the Lord, His heritage. (Sir. 24:8, 12)

In recounting this, Ben Sira is not merely being a proud Jew who asserts that wisdom is the peculiar possession of his own people. Rather, he has something more specific in mind:

All this is the book of the covenant of the Most High God, the Torah that Moses commanded us as an inheritance for the congregations of Jacob. (Sir. 24:23)

In other words, Wisdom *is* the Pentateuch, "the book of the covenant of the Most High God." Thus, if you wish really to know how the world works, to know about the underlying set of rules that God established for it, then the Pentateuch is your basic resource.

The wisdom connection apparent in Ben Sira explains much about the character of ancient biblical interpretation — not only for him, but for his contemporaries and predecessors as well. For when these sages-turned-exegetes approached the Pentateuch, they brought to their reading of it many of the same expectations and interpretive techniques that they had used in reading collections of proverbs and other wisdom compositions. Thus, the full meaning of a proverb was not immediately apparent; its words had to be studied and sifted carefully before they would yield their full significance. So too did all of Scripture have to be scrutinized, since the meaning of a particular word or phrase or prophecy or story might similarly be hidden from view. And just as proverbs were full of lessons for today, so biblical texts, even though they seemed to talk about the past, were likewise understood to have a message for the present; indeed, those two favorite opposites of ancient wisdom, the "righteous" and the "wicked," might turn out to be embodied in a biblical narrative about the (altogether righteous) Abraham or Jacob, and such (altogether wicked) figures as Lot or Esau. The insights of wise proverbs were part of a single weave of divine wisdom, the great pattern underlying all of reality; even when one proverb seemed to contradict another (see Prov. 26:4-5), there really was no contradiction. Similarly, the Bible, the great compendium of divine wisdom, could contain no real contradiction; careful contemplation of its words would always show that they agree. Finally wisdom, although it was transmitted by different sages in different periods, truly had no human author; these tradents were merely reporting bits and pieces of the great pattern that had been created by God. Similarly, the books of Scripture may be attributed to different authors, but all of them, since they are full of divine wisdom, truly have only one source, God, who guided the human beings responsible for Scripture's various parts. The various characteristics mentioned here are, it will be noticed, none other than the Four Assumptions shared by all ancient interpreters. It seems likely, therefore, that these common elements all derive from the wisdom heritage of the earliest interpreters, going back at least to the time of Ezra, "a *sage* skilled in the law of Moses" (Ezra 7:6). Although Scripture's interpreters included people from many different orientations and walks of life, wild-eyed visionaries, priests and temple officials, experts in law and jurisprudence, and so forth — *all* appear to have been touched by this crucial consilience of scriptural interpretation and ancient Near Eastern wisdom.

*   *   *

Such was biblical interpretation in early Judaism. To modern eyes, some of it may not appear to be interpretation at all; certainly some of the claims made about the meaning of this or that verse or passage seem to us highly fanciful, if not patently apologetic or forced, though in fairness one ought to note that modern biblical commentaries are themselves not entirely free of such traits, even if they are usually more subtle about their intentions. But whatever one's judgment of the work of these interpreters, their importance can scarcely be gainsaid. It is not just that, as mentioned earlier, they determined the basic way that the Bible would be approached for the next two millennia. Their Four Assumptions continued to be assumed by all interpreters until well after the Renaissance and the Protestant Reformation of the sixteenth century; indeed, they are, to a great extent, still with us today. But still more important was the effect that these ancient interpreters had on their own contemporaries. Had they not succeeded in persuading their listeners that biblical texts did indeed have a message vital to people in their own day; and that the biblical corpus was perfectly consistent and harmonious, free of any error or defect; indeed, that these texts had been given by God for the purpose of guiding humans on their path, if only they were clever enough to understand the hidden meaning of many of its verses — had they not succeeded in getting these basic ideas and this basic approach across through myriad examples of actual interpretations, it seems quite unlikely that the writings of ancient Israel would ever have become what they did, the centerpiece of two great biblical religions, Judaism and Christianity.

BIBLIOGRAPHY

Anderson, Gary. 2001. *The Genesis of Perfection: Adam and Eve in Jewish and Christian Imagination*. Louisville: Westminster John Knox.

Borgen, Peder. 1997. *Philo of Alexandria: An Exegete for His Time.* Leiden: Brill.

Campbell, Jonathan G. 2004. *The Exegetical Texts.* Companion to the Qumran Scrolls. London: Clark.

Charlesworth, James H., and Craig A. Evans, eds. 1994. *The Pseudepigrapha and Early Biblical Interpretation.* Sheffield: Sheffield Academic Press.

Endres, John C. 1987. *Biblical Interpretation in the Book of Jubilees.* Washington, D.C.: Catholic Biblical Association of America.

Evans, Craig A., ed. 2004. *From Prophecy to Testament: The Function of the Old Testament in the New.* Peabody, Mass.: Hendrickson.

Feldman, Louis H. 1998. *Josephus's Interpretation of the Bible.* Berkeley: University of California Press.

Fishbane, Michael. 1985. *Biblical Interpretation in Ancient Israel.* Oxford: Clarendon.

Henze, Matthias, ed. 2005. *Biblical Interpretation at Qumran.* Grand Rapids: Eerdmans.

———, ed. 2012. *A Companion to Biblical Interpretation in Early Judaism.* Grand Rapids: Eerdmans.

Hirschman, Marc G. 1996. *A Rivalry of Genius: Jewish and Christian Biblical Interpretation in Late Antiquity.* Albany: SUNY Press.

Kugel, James L. 1990. *In Potiphar's House: The Interpretive Life of Biblical Texts.* San Francisco: HarperSanFrancisco.

———. 1998. *Traditions of the Bible: A Guide to the Bible As It Was at the Start of the Common Era.* Cambridge: Harvard University Press.

———. 2001. *Studies in Ancient Midrash.* Cambridge: Harvard University Press.

———. 2006. *The Ladder of Jacob: Ancient Interpretations of the Biblical Story of Jacob and His Children.* Princeton: Princeton University Press.

———. 2007. *How to Read the Bible: A Guide to Scripture, Then and Now.* New York: Free Press.

———. 2012. *A Walk through Jubilees: Studies in the Book of Jubilees and the World of Its Creation.* Leiden: Brill.

———, and R. A. Greer. 1986. *Early Biblical Interpretation.* Philadelphia: Westminster.

Moriya, Akio, and Gohei Hata, ed. 2012. *Pentateuchal Traditions in the Late Second Temple Period: Proceedings of the International Workshop in Tokyo, August 28-31, 2007.* Leiden: Brill.

Mulder, M. J., and H. Sysling, eds. 1988. *Mikra: Text, Translation, Reading and Interpretation of the Hebrew Bible in Ancient Judaism and Early Christianity.* Assen: Van Gorcum; Philadelphia: Fortress.

Najman, Hindy. 2003. *Seconding Sinai: The Development of Mosaic Discourse in Second Temple Judaism.* Leiden: Brill.

Najman, Hindy, and Judith Newman, eds. 2004. *The Idea of Biblical Interpretation.* Leiden: Brill.

Nitzan, Bilhah. 2010. "The Continuity of Biblical Interpretation in the Qumran Scrolls and Rabbinic Literature." In *The Oxford Handbook of the Dead Sea Scrolls*. Ed. Timothy H. Lim and John J. Collins. Oxford: Oxford University Press, 337-50.

White Crawford, Sidnie. 2008. *Rewriting Scripture in Second Temple Times*. Grand Rapids: Eerdmans.

Zahn, Molly M. 2010. "Rewritten Scripture." In *The Oxford Handbook of the Dead Sea Scrolls*. Ed. Timothy H. Lim and John J. Collins. Oxford: Oxford University Press, 323-36.

Zakovitch, Y. 1992. *An Introduction to Inner-Biblical Interpretation*. Even-Yehudah: Reches (in Hebrew).

Apocrypha and Pseudepigrapha

Loren T. Stuckenbruck

The terms "apocrypha" and "pseudepigrapha" mean, respectively, "hidden things (books)" and "books falsely ascribed/inscribed." However, under the problematic headings of "Old Testament Apocrypha" and "Old Testament Pseudepigrapha" they have come to designate collections or groups of ancient Jewish writings which were either composed during the Second Temple period or which preserve traditions that arguably go back to that time. Thus these designations, as conventionally used today, are not descriptive and do not always reflect the way they (and the concepts underlying them) were sometimes used in antiquity. It is the ancient background, especially as now informed by the writings preserved among the Dead Sea Scrolls, which may suggest that what "apocrypha" and "pseudepigrapha" appropriately signify may need to be rethought. Since the contemporary use of these terms is largely determined by developments after the Second Temple period, the present discussion will review their use in Christian and Jewish tradition from late antiquity through the post-Reformation and then consider how they were being applied by some of the Jewish writers who composed them.

Apocrypha

Apocrypha during and since the Reformation and Counter-Reformation

Most commonly, the term "Apocrypha" refers to a collection of writings that fall outside the canons of the Hebrew Bible (Old Testament) and New

Testament, but that are nonetheless included in some modern Christian translations of the Bible, usually between the Old and New Testaments. In modern translations this group of writings consists of the following: 1 Esdras (= *3 Ezra*), 2 Esdras (= *4, 5,* and *6 Ezra*), Tobit, Judith, Additions to the Book of Esther, Wisdom of Solomon, Sirach (or Ecclesiasticus), Baruch and Letter of Jeremiah, the Prayer of Azariah and the Song of the Three Young Men, Susanna, Bel and the Dragon, Prayer of Manasseh, 1 Maccabees, and 2 Maccabees. However, traditional Protestant and Catholic definitions and judgments of the value of these writings have diverged.

Among the Protestant Reformers, the value attributed to the "Apocrypha" was not entirely uniform. Martin Luther, whose translation of the Bible (completed in 1534) did not include 1 and 2 Esdras among the Apocrypha, defined Apocrypha as "books which are not considered equal to the Holy Scriptures" while being "profitable and good to read." Other reformers, such as Oecolampadius, adopted a similar view, while translations such as the Dutch Bible (1526) and the Swiss-German Bible (1527-1529) preface the "Apocrypha" with statements, respectively, that these books, which are not found in the Hebrew Bible of the Jews, are "not in the canon" and "are not reckoned as biblical." A more discriminating statement about their value was offered in 1520 by Andreas Bodenstein of Karlstadt *(De Canonicis Scripturis Libellus):* some works (Wisdom of Solomon, Sirach, Tobit, Judith, 1 and 2 Maccabees) outside the Hebrew canon are "holy writings" and their content "is not to be despised" (sections 114, 118), while others (1 and 2 Esdras, Baruch, Prayer of Manasseh, Prayer of Azariah, Song of the Three Young Men, Susanna, Bel and the Dragon) are so problematic that they are "worthy of a censor's ban." Thus, despite the inclusion of "Apocrypha" in a number of Protestant translations, sentiments comparable to those of Karlstadt were widely held (e.g., the Belgic Confession 1561, the Synod of Dort 1618-19, Westminster Confession 1647) and have led to the removal of these writings in many translations of the Bible until today.

The widespread criticism of the Apocrypha among Protestant Reformers led the Roman Catholic Church to a response during the first Council of Trent. In Session VI of the deliberations in 1546, the delegates pronounced a curse against any who were not prepared to recognize all those books contained in the Latin Vulgate Bible. (Although many Latin manuscripts had also included 1 and 2 Esdras and the Prayer of Manasseh, the Council denied them the canonicity accorded to the other books. These were reinstated as appendices to the New Testament in the

Clementine Bible published in 1592.) Since Sixtus of Sienna (1566), many Roman Catholic scholars have referred to Old Testament writings not included in the Jewish Hebrew Bible as "Deuterocanonical," a term that is meant not so much to imply their secondary or inferior status as rather to acknowledge that their canonicity had not been formalized by ecclesiastical authorities until a more recent time.

Apocrypha in Orthodox Traditions

It is important to remember that the term "Apocrypha," while playing an important role in Protestantism, has been of only little significance in other traditions. In this respect, we may draw attention to eastern Orthodox confessions, such as the Greek, Russian, Syriac, and Ethiopic churches, which have defined their biblical canons in a way that includes some of the "Apocrypha" and, indeed, even further writings (which vary in each tradition). Each of these ecclesiastical traditions includes a core of these writings within their Bible, while the determination of what constitutes Scripture as a whole varies, depending on factors such as the form and shape of traditions received into their respective languages, use in liturgy, other issues in emerging self-definition, and the understanding of "canon."

Among the Orthodox traditions, some thirteen writings regarded by the Council of Trent as "Deuterocanonical" have acquired some form of biblical status. While five of these appear as material attached to the end of other books (Psalm 151, Letter of Jeremiah [to Baruch], Additions to Esther, and Additions to Daniel in Prayer of Azariah, Song of the Three Young Men, Susanna, and Bel and the Dragon), the remaining seven have been transmitted as free-standing works (Tobit, Judith, Wisdom of Solomon, 1 and 2 Maccabees, Sirach, and Baruch).

In the Greek Orthodox Church, after some debate, these writings were labeled as "Deuterocanonical" during the Synod of Jerusalem of 1672; however, they are more often referred to as "things which are read" (Gr. *anagignōskomena*). Not found in the Hebrew Bible, but transmitted as part of the Greek Old Testament, this group of books also includes Prayer of Manasseh, 1 Esdras, and 3 Maccabees (while 4 Maccabees, transmitted in a more limited number of biblical manuscripts, is now placed in an appendix). The affirmation of the validity of the "Deuterocanonical" writings by the Synod was more a commendation than a dogmatic pronouncement, so that opinion regarding their canonical status in the Church has varied.

Beyond the core list, the Russian Orthodox Church, drawing on a tradition that received the Greek Bible, included in its first published Bible in Old Church Slavonic (in Ostrog 1581) a list of writings that differs slightly from that of Greek Orthodoxy: Prayer of Manasseh, 2 Esdras (= 1 Esdras), 3 Esdras (= 2 Esdras), and 3 Maccabees. Here one may notice not only the difference in nomenclature for the Esdras books but also the complete absence of 4 Maccabees. The status of these books, however, has not been rigorously maintained in subsequent centuries, so that they now have an ambivalent place and function within the biblical canon.

The Ethiopian Orthodox Church has an understanding of canon that has not operated with the same degree of fixedness as found in other traditions. Moreover, unlike most of the Orthodox churches, the Ethiopic tradition did not inherit the Greek Bible. Many biblical manuscripts copied in Classical Ethiopic (Ge'ez) tradition contain Prayer of Manasseh (where it follows immediately upon 2 Chron. 33:12), 1 Esdras, 2 Esdras 3–14 (= *4 Ezra*, without the Christian additions in chaps. 1–2 and 15–16), *1 Enoch*, and *Jubilees*. The degree of recognition accorded the latter two works and, indeed, a number of books in the Old Testament may have varied during the early stages of their reception and consolidation into the Ethiopic tradition. For example, while there is little or no evidence that the scriptural status of *Jubilees* was ever questioned, other works could be regarded as "disputed" (Chronicles, Esther, Job, Proverbs, Ecclesiastes, Song of Songs), while some of these and even others could be labeled as "noncanonical" (Ezra-Nehemiah, 1 Esdras, 2 Esdras, Tobit, Judith, Wisdom of Solomon, Ecclesiastes, Baruch, *1 Enoch, Ascension of Isaiah, 4 Baruch*).

It is not clear whether the West-Syrian Orthodox traditions (e.g., Syriac Orthodox and Monophysite Orthodox churches), such as the Ethiopian, initially received an Old Testament based on the Hebrew Bible or derived it from the Greek. Although the Peshitta, the standardizing Syriac translation of the Bible, transmitted the Jewish Bible as its Old Testament, the Old Testament writings not in the Hebrew Bible were soon added to this tradition. Not only did the fourth-century fathers Aphrahat and Ephrem treat them as part of their Bible, but these writings are copied in the earliest complete Syriac Bibles whose manuscripts may date back as early as the sixth century. Significantly, one of these early manuscripts, designated *7a1*, even contained 2 *Baruch*, 4 *Ezra*, and 4 Maccabees. Moreover, the oldest Syriac version of the Psalter from the twelfth century (now in Baghdad, the Library of the Chaldaean Patriarchate) includes five additional psalms (Psalms 151–155), of which Psalm 151 corresponds to the same document by that name in the Greek Psalter and, together with Psalms 154 and 155, is preserved in Hebrew among the Dead Sea manuscripts (11Q5). In addition, a fourth-century document called *Canons of the Apostles,* the Syriac text of which goes back to at least the seventh century, includes Judith, Tobith, and Ben Sira in its list of "accepted books."

Apocrypha in Greek Codices of the Bible

The "Apocrypha" are sometimes casually defined as those books or parts of books found in the Septuagint but not in the Jewish Hebrew Bible. If we consult the three prominent Greek codices that contain the Old Testament writings — Codices Sinaiticus (fourth century), Vaticanus (fourth century), and Alexandrinus (fifth century) — the following books come into view:

Sinaiticus	Vaticanus	Alexandrinus
Greek Esther	Greek Esther	Greek Esther
Judith	Judith	Tobit
Tobit	Tobit	Judith
1 Maccabees		1 Maccabees
		2 Maccabees
		3 Maccabees
4 Maccabees		4 Maccabees
Wisdom of Solomon	Wisdom of Solomon	Wisdom of Solomon
Sirach	Sirach	Sirach
		Psalms of Solomon
1 Baruch	1 Baruch	1 Baruch
Epistle of Jeremiah	Epistle of Jeremiah	Epistle of Jeremiah
	Susannah	Susannah
	Bel and the Dragon	Bel and the Dragon
		Psalms and Odes (including Prayer of Manasseh)

In addition, two somewhat later biblical codices preserve copies of several of these writings: Marchalianus (sixth/seventh century) includes 1 Baruch, Epistle of Jeremiah, Susannah, and Bel and the Dragon, while Venetus (eighth century) has Greek Esther, Judith, Tobit, 1-4 Maccabees,

Wisdom of Solomon, Sirach, 1 Baruch, Epistle of Jeremiah, Susannah, and Bel and the Dragon. Furthermore, the partially preserved Cologne–Chester Beatty Papyrus 967 (second-third century) contains fragmentary versions of Susannah and Bel and the Dragon alongside several biblical books (Esther, Ezekiel, Daniel). Finally, like Codex Alexandrinus, the seventh-century Codex T transmits the Prayer of Manasseh among the Odes appended to the Psalms.

The manuscript tradition thus reflects a fluid understanding of where the boundaries for the literature not preserved in Hebrew lie. The manuscripts attest the following works, which are omitted from modern collections of the "Apocrypha" or "Deuterocanonicals": *Psalms of Solomon*, 3 and 4 Maccabees. This fluidity is echoed by the Syriac manuscript *7a1* (see above) and, of course, the Ethiopic Orthodox tradition.

At the same time, two works not found in the Greek but preserved in many Latin manuscripts have found their way into this collection: 2 Esdras (chaps. 3–14 of which = *4 Ezra*) and the Prayer of Manasseh (first attested in Syriac manuscripts in the ninth century and in Latin manuscripts from the thirteenth century, but also found in the Cairo Geniza).

"Apocrypha" in Antiquity

Luther's view of "apocrypha" as profitable to read without being Scripture goes back to Jerome. The prefaces to his Latin translations of Jewish and Old Testament writings (ca. 405 C.E.) make it clear that for Jerome "apocrypha" such as Wisdom of Solomon, Sirach, Tobit, Judith, and 1 and 2 Maccabees could be read for edification in the church; however, the church does not receive them "among the canonical books," and they should not be used to establish doctrine (so Jerome's prologues to the book of Kings [= *Prologus Galeatus*], Judith, Tobit, and the books of Solomon).

Jerome's use of the term "apocrypha" was, however, not consistent. He not only could admit in the translation prefaces a certain overlap between what he called "apocrypha" and "pseudepigrapha" (e.g., in the case of Wisdom of Solomon), he could even appear to equate the two terms altogether. In a letter (107.12) written in the year 403, he instructs a certain Laeta to have her daughter "avoid all apocryphal writings" because they cannot be read for "the truth of the doctrines they contain," they "are not actually written by those to whom they are ascribed," and they have "many faults" that "have been introduced into them." This negative assessment of "apocrypha" did not mean Jerome denied them all religious value; but it takes "great prudence *(grandis . . . prudentiae)* to find gold in the mire *(in luto)*."

This last-mentioned understanding of "apocrypha" was a widely held view among Jerome's contemporaries and is reflected in the later Roman Catholic tradition. For example, Cyril of Jerusalem (mid-third century) had applied the term to "disputed" works that are not acknowledged by all; the church should neither study nor read them, so that they are best avoided altogether. For Cyril of Jerusalem Scripture consists of "twenty-two books of the Old Testament that were translated by the seventy-two translators" of the Septuagint, though both this numeration and his description of the individual books themselves makes it clear that, except for 1 Baruch (regarded as an appendix to Jeremiah), this did not include any of the works that Jerome would have called apocrypha in any sense (*Catechetical Lectures* 4.33). Rufinus, an older contemporary of Cyril, was more explicit in distinguishing between three groups of writings (*Expositio Symboli* 34): (a) "canonical" works, that is, the "twenty-two" books of the Old Testament; (b) "ecclesiastical" books — Wisdom of Solomon, Sirach, Tobit, Judith, 1-2 Maccabees — that may be read but not in order to confirm faith; and (c) "Apocrypha," that is, falsely ascribed writings (pseudepigrapha) and heretical books that should not be received in the church at all, as indicated in the preface to a list of "apocrypha" in the Gelasian Decree (fifth century). This last use of the term is aptly illustrated as early as the late second century c.e. by Irenaeus who, in his *Against Heresies* (1.20.1), referred to the existence of "an unspeakable number of apocryphal and spurious writings" that confuse the foolish and ignorant. Similarly, Origen in the third century c.e. declared that certain writings are called *apocryphae* because "many things in them are corrupt and contrary to true faith" (*Commentary on Song of Songs;* cf. also *Commentary on Matthew* 10.18.13.57). The equation of "secret" books with deception, though applied by Irenaeus (and Origen) to inauthentic traditions about Jesus, would in time be applied to "pseudepigraphal" Jewish compositions as well.

In summary, Jerome's twofold use of "apocrypha" would be picked up, respectively, in the Reformation (Luther) and Counter-Reformation (Council of Trent). The Protestant "Apocrypha" had their counterpart in the Roman Church's "Deuterocanonicals," while the latter has regarded "Apocrypha" as the remaining (mostly pseudepigraphal) religious writings from Jewish antiquity.

The reason for the use of "apocrypha" to designate noncanonical works during the fourth century may be found in the widespread notion of "hidden" or "sealed" books in Greco-Roman and especially Jewish antiquity (Dan. 8:26; 12:4, 9-10; *Sib. Or.* 11.163-71; *4 Ezra* 12:37; 14:5-6; 14:44-47; *2 Bar.* 20:3-4; 87:1; implied in *Jub.* 1:5; *1 Enoch* 82:1-3; 107:3; *2 Enoch* 35:1-3). In a number of Jewish apocalyptic writings, authors sometimes presented themselves (or, rather, those ancient figures whose names they were using) as having been instructed by God or an angel to "seal" or "hide" their works. This fictional instruction functioned as a way of explaining how such works attributed to such ancient authors had not been in circulation until the present. The existence of these books was a "secret" until the time when they actually appeared. A closely related idea is the instruction that a writer "seal" the book so that its contents will not be accessible until the appropriate time.

In this regard, three texts in particular seem to have exercised some influence: Daniel, *4 Ezra*, and *2 Baruch*. (a) The book of Daniel presents itself as an apocryphal work. The writer is told to "seal up the vision" given to him, "for it refers to many days from now" (8:26). This instruction is then echoed in 12:4 ("keep the words secret and the book sealed until the time of the end"), while according to 12:9-10 the seer, who has completed writing down his revelations, is to consign his work "to remain secret and sealed until the time of the end." This self-presentation of Daniel is closely bound up with the view that the special revelation in this book will be comprehended only by the wise (12:10). (b) *4 Ezra* picks up similar ideas in several passages. In 12:37-38 the command that the seer record his visions is accompanied by the directive that he deposit them "in a hidden place"; similar to Daniel, the hidden status of the writing establishes its contents as teaching for "the wise . . . whose hearts . . . are able to comprehend and keep these secrets." In a later passage (14:5-6) the figure of Moses himself is presented as having been the recipient of a double revelation (cf. Deut. 29:29), one being open and available to all, the other being secret and restricted in access. While the generally available teaching refers to the Mosaic Torah, the esoteric teaching involves "the secrets of the times" and "the end of the times." Near the end of the book (14:44-47), the seer, who patterns himself after Moses, claims to have been given, along with five men with him, ninety-four books to record during forty days of revelation. Of these books, the twenty-four to be made public are to be read by "the worthy and unworthy," while the remaining seventy are to be given to "the wise" in whom there are "the springs of understanding," "the fountains of wisdom," and "the river of knowledge." The association of esoteric revelation with more discerning readers is reminiscent of Daniel. It is tempting to see here a distinction between "canonical" and "noncanonical" writings. However, the force of the passage emphasizes that both groups of writings, though distinct, are equally revelatory. Indeed, if from *4 Ezra* 12:37-38 one has the impression that the activity behind *4 Ezra* itself is "hidden," in 14:37-48 the writer presents himself as the primary mediator among those who produced all ninety-four books (without even mentioning Moses). It was only later, for example, in the fourth century c.e., that Epiphanius of Salamis (*De Mensuris et Ponderibus* 10, Armenian), perhaps influenced by *4 Ezra* 14, turned the partition of the same number of writings into a classification of first- and second-rank books in the Septuagint: twenty-two works of the Old Testament and seventy-two "apocryphal" works. This ranking, however, says less about *4 Ezra* itself than about ideas of canonicity that had developed by Epiphanius's time. (c) In *2 Baruch* the seer, having been instructed to seal divine commands given to him (20:3-4), concludes his work by saying, "I folded it, sealed it cautiously, and bound it to the neck of the eagle. And I let it go and sent it away" (87:1).

The passages just cited from Daniel and *4 Ezra* make clear that their intended reception among a more exclusive class of "wise" readers underscores their special value rather than having anything to do with any measure of inferiority later associated with the term "apocrypha" as, for example, would later be the case with Rufinus and Jerome. Instead, revelation for a privileged group would have underscored its particular value. An analogy for this may be detected in Jesus' exclusive teaching of parables to his disciples preserved in the Synoptic Gospels (see Mark 4:10-11; Matt. 13:10-11; Luke 8:9-10).

The self-presentation of Daniel, *4 Ezra*, and *2 Baruch* as "hidden" works shows the degree to which the term "apocrypha" does not describe the character of those books that would later be collected under this designation. Indeed, while Daniel came to be understood as "biblical," *4 Ezra* was treated as "deuterocanonical" or "apocryphal," and *2 Baruch* was assigned to the "pseudepigrapha."

Recent Use of "Apocrypha" as a Title for Ancient Documents

Whereas the notion of "hiddenness" is part of the literary technique employed by the authors of Daniel, *4 Ezra*, and *2 Baruch,* the term "apocryphon" has more recently been applied more loosely to those writings that represent or contain traditions whose existence was unknown before they were discovered in modern times. This is the case with a number of documents from the Dead Sea Scrolls, of which the more prominent examples would be *Genesis Apocryphon* (1Q20), *Apocryphon of Moses* (1Q22, 1Q29, 2Q21, 4Q375, 4Q376, 4Q408), *Apocryphal Prophecy* (1Q25, 2Q23, 6Q12), 2QApocryphon of David (2Q22), 4QApocryphal Lamentations (4Q179, 4Q501), 4QApocryphal Daniel (4Q246), 4QApocryphal Pentateuch A (4Q368), 4QApocryphon of Joshua (4Q378), 4QApocryphon of Jeremiah (4Q383, 4Q385a, 4Q387, 4Q387a, 4Q388a, 4Q389-390), 4QApocryphon of Elisha (4Q481a), 4QApocryphon of Malachi (5Q10), and 11QApocryphal Psalms (11Q11). While the titles assigned to some of these works have varied, here "apocryphon" has functioned as a designation for a previously unknown tradition related to a biblical book or figure. As such, the term could be a source of confusion, since it has been made to refer to neither "apocrypha" in the senses it has acquired in Catholic and Protestant circles nor to works which formally use "hiddenness" as a way of presenting themselves.

Coherence of the "Old Testament Apocrypha"

If neither the technical nor ecclesiastical usage is properly descriptive, how are the books called "apocrypha" in Protestant tradition to be characterized? First, we may recognize that the great codices from the fourth and fifth centuries as well as the Protestant "Apocrypha" or Roman Catholic "Deuterocanonicals" include very different kinds of literature: (a) Several works were composed as supplementary materials to already existing biblical books: Esther (expansions with further chapters in Greek); additions to Daniel (Prayer of Azariah, Song of the Three Young Men, Susannah, and Bel and the Dragon); and 1 Baruch and the Epistle of Jeremiah. (b) Two of the works are historiographical: 1 and 2 Maccabees. (c) Two may be classified as literary tales: Tobit and Judith. (d) Liturgical prayer is also included: Prayer of Manasseh (see also *Psalms of Solomon,* Psalms and Odes, and Psalm 151). (e) The sapiential or wisdom literature is represented by Ben Sira and Wisdom of Solomon. Finally, (f) *4 Ezra* is an apocalyptic vision. The only sense in which these diverse compositions are all "apocrypha" is if one eschews any etymological meaning and simply regards them as a modern (and somewhat fluid) collection of books.

Second, these writings were originally composed in different languages. For several of the documents an original composition in Hebrew or Aramaic is confirmed through the evidence from the Dead Sea Scrolls. Most chapters of Tobit are found in fragments from one Hebrew manuscript (4Q200) and in four Aramaic manuscripts (4Q196-199); Hebrew texts of Ben Sira exist in two manuscripts from the Qumran caves (2Q18 [from 6:14-15 or 1:19-20 and 6:20-31]; 11Q5 21:1–22:1 [from Sirach 51]) and the Ben Sira scroll from Masada (fragmentary text of 39:27–44:17); Psalm 151 is found in 11Q5 col. 28, though, unlike in the Greek Orthodox Psalter, it is divided into two psalms separated by a *vacat* and carrying their own superscriptions (151A in 11Q5 28:3-12; 151B in 28:13); and, finally, Hebrew texts for Psalms 154 and 155 from the Syriac Psalter are preserved, respectively, in 11Q5 18:1-16 and 24:3-17.

In addition, linguistic studies have made it likely that several documents preserved only in Greek or Latin versions derive from now-lost Semitic versions: Judith, 1 Esdras, Epistle of Jeremiah (preserved in a Greek fragment from Qumran, 7Q2), Prayer of Azariah, the Song of the Three Young Men, Bel and the Dragon, and 1 Maccabees. Interestingly, Jerome claims to have known Semitic versions of Tobit (Aramaic), Ben Sira (Hebrew), 1 Maccabees (Hebrew), and Judith (Hebrew). Less certain is whether and to what extent a Semitic version lies behind the Greek texts of 1 Baruch, Prayer of Manasseh, and Susanna. On the other hand, several of the works were originally composed in Greek. These are Greek Esther, Wisdom of Solomon, 2 Maccabees, and 3-4 Maccabees.

Third, though it is impossible to be precise about the date of composition for each of the Protestant "apocrypha," it is at least certain that they emerged during the period between Alexander the Great's conquests in the fourth century B.C.E. and the Bar Kokhba Revolt in 132-135 C.E. The writing of Tobit, Ben Sira, and Epistle of Jeremiah falls within the early part of this period, that is, from 300 B.C.E. until the Maccabean crisis in 175-164 B.C.E. Most of the books derive from the time between the Maccabean wars until the turn of the Common Era: 1 Esdras, Judith, Greek Esther, Prayer of Azariah, the Song of the Three Young Men, Susannah, Bel and the Dragon, 1 and 2 Maccabees, and possibly Prayer of Manasseh. The latest composition is *4 Ezra* (ca. 100 C.E.), which addresses circumstances arising from the destruction of the Second Temple in Jerusalem by the Romans.

The diverse linguistic origin, literary genre, and date of these works indicate why it was that they would not become a collection of books during the Second Temple period. Only with the development of the codex (which made larger collections of books possible) and only when decisions came to be made about canonicity were they formally brought together in different forms, first in Greek and then in Latin. Far from descriptive, then, the term "apocrypha" is anachronistic, and it remains a problem to find terminology that more accurately accords with the respective ways the books present themselves while at the same time recognizing their history of reception among Jews and Christians during the last two millennia.

The "Outside Books" in Jewish Tradition

A related problem to the early development of classifications for "Scripture," on the one hand, and books deemed heretical or rejected, on the other, is found in the rabbinic designation "outside books" *(sĕfārîm ha-ḥîṣōnîm)*, which first occurs in *m. Sanh.* 10:1, where a saying attributed to R. Akiba states that those who have no place in the World to Come include anyone "who reads the outside books." The Babylonian and Palestinian Talmud commentaries on this passage single out "the books of Ben Sira" as a poignant example. However, this condemnation is not unequivocal. For example, in the Babylonian Talmud (*b. Sanhedrin* 100b), after R. Akiba's condemnation is endorsed by a ruling of Rabbi Joseph, the latter himself is nonetheless made to permit the use of Ben Sira for instruction. This tension is underscored in the number of instances in which the Rabbinate continued to cite Ben Sira with the same respect shown to biblical works (*b. Berakot* 48a; *y. Berakot* 11b; *y. Nazir* 54b; *Bereshit Rabbah* 91:3; *Qohelet Rabbah* 7:11), presumably because its teaching could be seen as consistent with the Torah. In its condemnation of readers of Ben Sira, the Palestinian Talmud (*y. Sanhedrin* 10a) adds those who make use of the books of a so-called "Ben Laana." The text, however, states that a further category of literature, enigmatically called "the books of *hamiras*" (Homeric works?), is not problematic at all: "the one who reads them is like one who reads a letter" *(ha-qōrê' bā-hen kĕ-qōrê' bā-'igeret)*. Crucially, then, the text leaves the impression that the danger of Ben Sira consists in its potential for being confused with Torah, while no such difficulty exists for ancient literature held to be nonreligious. While it may be misleading to generalize from Ben Sira to other books, this broad classification suggests that for the rabbis the "outside books" would have at least consisted of the sort of Jewish writings that later Christian tradition would regard as "Old Testament Apocrypha" and "Old Testament Pseudepigrapha."

Apocryphal Collections in Medieval Jewish Manuscripts

The comparative devaluation of "outside books" in Jewish tradition did not mean an avoidance of them altogether. A number of Aramaic and Hebrew Jewish manuscripts from the Middle Ages contain short collections of works that to some extent resemble what would become the Protestant "apocrypha." Here, the texts for each of the works were either secondary versions (e.g., Tobit and Judith, translated from Latin and/or Greek; Epistle of Jeremiah), summaries (e.g., Baruch, Ben Sira, Esther, 1-4 Maccabees, Susanna, Prayer of Manasseh), or adaptations (Bel and the Dragon), related materials (to Esther: The Dream of Mordecai and the Books of Ahasuerus), and often additional obscure pieces (with titles such as the Book of Yashar, Proverbs of Solomon, the Book of Enoch [neither *1* nor *2 Enoch*], the Fables of Aesop, the Proverbs of Sandabar, The Deed of the Jerusalemite, The Speech of Aphar and Dinah, and so forth). The reason for such collections within manuscripts — that is, whether they were driven by an internal Jewish dynamic or in some sense were meant as counterparts to existing Christian compilations — has yet to be studied properly.

Pseudepigrapha

The Problematic Term "Pseudepigrapha"

The difficulties described above in relation to the use of "apocrypha" apply to "pseudepigrapha" as well. First, if "pseudepigraphon" refers to a work falsely ascribed to a figure who is not the real author, then it does not pertain to a discrete collection of works. Indeed, several books in the Hebrew Bible are arguably pseudepigrapha (e.g., Deuteronomy, Proverbs, Qoheleth, Daniel, and the Davidic Psalms), while the same may be said regarding "apocrypha" such as 1 Baruch, Epistle of Jeremiah, Prayer of Manasseh, Psalm 151 (and Syriac Psalms 154–155), Wisdom of Solomon, and *4 Ezra*. Second, as already noted, in Roman Catholic tradition it is pseudepigraphal works outside the "Deuterocanonicals" that are called "Apocrypha"; this accords with ancient usage of the term "apocrypha." Third, since the term does not describe a set of writings that can be distinguished from other existing collections (e.g., "biblical," "apocryphal"), it often refers today to an ever-growing and fluid corpus of documents preserved from antiquity. In this latter sense, the narrow definition of "pseudepigrapha" does not describe all documents which have occasionally been collected under this heading. A good case in point is James H. Charlesworth's edition of *The Old Testament Pseudepigrapha* (1983-1985), which, for example, includes a number of works or parts of works associated with their real authors' names (e.g., Aristeas the Exegete, Aristobulus, Artapanus, Cleodemus Malchus, Demetrius the Chronographer, Eupolemus, Ezekiel the Tragedian, and Theodotus).

Several considerations make a more precise understanding and definition of an ancient Jewish "pseudepigraphon" possible. (a) The designation is formally a subset of "anonymous" writings, that is, those compositions for which the historical author's identity remains unknown. This means that any information about the writers depends on what they reveal about themselves in the texts. (b) Following from this, a "pseudepigraphon" usually takes one of two basic forms: a writer either (i) communicates in the first person by directly taking on the name of an important or ancient paradigmatic figure (e.g., *1 Enoch, 2 Baruch, Testament of Job, Sibylline Oracles*); or, more loosely, (ii) composes a third-person account that attributes revelatory knowledge, instruction, or activity to such a figure (e.g., Jubilees [Moses], *Life of Adam and Eve, Proverbs of Ahiqar, Testament of Abraham*). (c) Thus, while the assumption of an ancient ideal figure's name is fictive in itself, it does not follow that ancient novella or legendary stories such as Tobit, Judith, *Joseph and Aseneth, Book of Giants,* or 11QMelchizedek are "pseudepigrapha" in the strict sense. (d) Sometimes ancient compositions combine these literary forms. Several examples illustrate this point. In the *Genesis Apocryphon* (1Q20) an anonymous author strings together a series of smaller first-person accounts attributed to different patriarchs such as Lamech, Noah, and Abraham to form a larger work that as a whole is not a pseudepigraphon. While the macro-genre of Tobit is that of a tale, part of it is presented as the words of the protagonist, Tobit; in this case, the first-person idiom, the extent of which differs among the versions of the book, forms a relatively small part of the work. Finally, in a number of works the predominant first-person discourse is introduced or framed by a brief third-person narrative that provides a setting (e.g., *Testament of the Twelve Patriarchs, Testament of Job, Testament of Moses, Ladder of Jacob*). It is not always clear in these cases whether the use of the third person is secondary or original to a given work.

Why "Pseudepigraphal" Writings?

To today's readers the notion of a falsely ascribed literary work can carry with it the connotation of "forgery." It is precisely this caricature that has made it difficult for religious communities to value "pseudepigrapha" for their theological ideas. To be sure, in antiquity a writer's use of another name was sometimes criticized, and the criterion of authenticity or nonauthenticity could be invoked as a reason, respectively, for a book's inclusion or noninclusion among sacred traditions. Josephus in the first century C.E., for example, treated the book of Daniel as written during the Babylonian exile by a prophet of that name; since what he prophesied about the Greeks' accession to power came true through the conquests of Alexander the Great, the "books" of Daniel (i.e., including the additions preserved in Greek) are to be found "among the sacred writings" (*Ant.* 10.210; cf. 10.190-281; 11.337-38; 12.322). Furthermore, insofar as 1 *Enoch,* for example, was treated as coming from the patriarch Enoch himself, it could be regarded as scripture (*Epistle of Barnabas* 4:3; 16:5-6; Tertullian, *De Cultu Feminarum* 3, *De Idololatria* 4; cf. Jude 14-15) or at least highly valued (Irenaeus, *Adversus Haereses* 4.16; Clement of Alexandria, *Eclogae Prophetarum* 2 and 53; Anatolius of Alexandria, *Paschal Canon* 5; Ethiopic Orthodox tradition), even though the main criterion for value was based more on the importance accorded to the contents of the book. On the other hand, as noted above, spuriousness was frequently held out by Jews and Christians as a reason to reject the use of certain writings (Tertullian, *De Cultu Feminarum* 3; cf. Origen, *Contra Celsum* 5.54; Augustine, *De Civitate Dei* 18.38).

For all the growing worry about pseudepigraphy expressed by Jewish and Christian writers during the first centuries of the Common Era, it remains true that the phenomenon itself was not only widespread but also widely received. This was so much the case that the notion of false ascription to authors could not be applied as a criterion for rejection in every case; the use of some books in faith communities had, for various reasons, gained an irreversible momentum. The main question to ask, however, is why pseudepigraphy was so popular, that is, why so many in antiquity were prepared to write under the name of an important personage. To this question several answers may be given.

First, libraries such as the great one in Alexandria were keen to collect copies of works by well-known writers. In response to such advertising, a supply of writings could be produced for purchase that met this demand.

Not only was the Greek translation of the Jewish Torah reportedly produced for such a reason during the third century B.C.E. (see the *Letter of Aristeas*), during the first several centuries many "heretical" works of suspicious value were brought to the Library of Alexandria, which perhaps on that account was subjected to destructive activities in 48 B.C.E. (Julius Caesar), 270-275 C.E. (Aurelian), and especially 391 C.E. (the decree by the emperor Theodosius) and 634 (by the order of the caliph Umar).

Second, writing under the name of someone important frequently served to gain a hearing for one's own views. Thus the analogies between the time of the real author and the ancient figure invoked could not always hide the very real and immediate concerns behind the composition. Examples of this abound, more obviously in pseudepigraphal documents that contain historical allusions to present or more recent events (so the *post-eventum* prophecies of *1 Enoch* 85–90 and 91:11-17; 93:1-10; Daniel 8-11; *2 Baruch*). For example, where the biblical book of Ezra is associated with the return from exile, the erection and rededication of a new Temple, and the reestablishment of the Torah among the people, *4 Ezra* is concerned more immediately with the aftermath of the destruction of the Second Temple by the Romans. Thus the affinities between biblical context and the time of writing were overwhelmed by the real author's pressing interests. Moreover, the process of transmission attempted to reshape or redirect received pseudepigraphal traditions to address new circumstances and theological issues; this can be observed in the later activities of Christian scribes who edited and even interpolated into the texts (e.g., *Testaments of the Twelve Patriarchs, Testament of Job, Testament of Abraham, 3 Baruch, 4 Baruch, 2 Enoch, Apocalypse of Zephaniah*).

Third, in some streams of tradition, such as philosophical schools or apocalyptic circles, the notion of writing in one's own name could simply be regarded as unethical. This was the case during generations subsequent to Pythagoras and Plato among students who produced a vast number of writings in the names of their teacher. Such a practice was regarded by the writers as a reasonable way for them to express their humility, indebtedness, and devotion in relation to the received tradition.

A fourth reason is related to the previous two: the name of a famous teacher or well-known figure of the past could be invoked in order to combat or refute other interpretations or views of the same tradition. This was especially true, again, in the literary output of philosophical schools and in the reception, transmission, and reappropriation of earlier pseudepigraphical tradition. An example of this is provided in the second-century-

B.C.E. *Epistle of Enoch* at *1 Enoch* 104:10-11, a passage preserved in Ethiopic and Greek texts:

Ethiopic	Greek
(10) And now I know this mystery, that many times the sinners will alter and pervert the word of truth; and they will speak evil words, and lie, and make big works and write my books in their own words.	(10) . . .] of truth they will alter; and the sinners co[py] and change many things, and lie and fashion great works and w[rit]e down books in their own names.
(11) And would that they would write down all the words accurately in their languages and neither pervert nor omit (anything) from my words, but accurately write down everything which I have testified before concerning you.	(11) An[d] would that [they wou]ld write all my words accurately in their names and [nei]ther omit nor change these words, but write all things accurately which I testify to them.

It has argued by some, especially on the basis of the Greek version, that the writer of this passage is engaged in a defense of his own work as a pseudepigraphon. If this is so, the possible charge of writing under someone else's name is met by reversing the accusation: those who write "in their own names" are the ones who perpetrate falsehood and corrupt the truth. It is not clear, however, that this reading reflects the sense of the text in its entirety. The emphasis in both versions on "my words" in verse 11 suggests that the writer's attack is predominantly concerned with those who, from his point of view, have subverted or misrepresented the Enoch tradition they have all received. The writer, in using Enoch's name, claims to be the authentic interpreter and transmitter of Enochic revelation and shows that he is aware of others who have deliberately taken it upon themselves to make improper use of it. While the polemic here may be directed against the construals of the figure of Enoch in works such as Ben Sira, *Jubilees,* or *Pseudo-Eupolemus,* the fictive character of the *Epistle of Enoch* momentarily gives way to an admission that the real author is not, in fact, Enoch himself. If this admission is sufficiently plain, then the text assumes a reception among its readers as a pseudepigraphon.

One should, of course, be cautious in regarding *1 Enoch* 104:10-11 as paradigmatic for how other pseudepigraphal authors understood what they were doing. In almost all the extant literature, the writers offer little or no direct hints about their *own* persona, and it is notoriously difficult to identify the context of origin and the groups for which they were writing. Nevertheless, from the perspective of the authors themselves, "pseudepigrapha" is a misleading label. They presented their works as divine revelation that is binding on its readers. "Truth" in content was more important than the literary genre or idiom chosen to convey it. By attributing the instructions and story lines to remote figures, the writers of pseudepigraphal works contextualized their messages within or in relation to master narratives that had been circulating widely and for a long time. Thus the effectiveness of their communication may have depended on what readers could be expected to be already familiar with from ancient tradition and, on the basis of such familiarity, be able to draw inferences from the analogies for themselves. On the other hand, the pseudepigraphal writings set their own terms of reference and already filtered through the ancient traditions in particular ways (as in the historical apocalypses or in reviews of the sacred past), so that direct acquaintance with such traditions would not have been necessary. To this extent, the implied readers are drawn into the sacred world being set before them: stark distinctions drawn between the faithful pious and the disobedient apostates in narratives and between divine or heavenly wisdom and errant knowledge in instructions invite readers, especially if they are ideally aligned with an author's intentions, to participate imaginatively in the religious *truths* being revealed to them. In those apocalyptic works that anticipate eschatological judgment, readers are presented with a decision: whether to align themselves with the way the righteous are described in the book and be rewarded or to reject the author's message, knowing that for this they will suffer the consequences of punishment. Thus, at the behest of the fictive protagonist, readers are transported into a "biblical" world that has extended into and beyond their time. Problems that beset the readers in the present — whether religious marginalization, social and political oppression, apostasy, or some other form of religious disorder — are resolved by an appeal to a paradigm in the remote past and imminent future. The pseudepigraphal idiom would have reminded readers that divine activity on behalf of the pious lies essentially outside the time in which they live. Now is the time for action, for a clear-cut decision to be faithful, whatever the circumstances.

Pseudepigrapha since the Enlightenment and the Dead Sea Scrolls

Since the beginning of the nineteenth century there has been a significant growth in textual witness to a number of pseudepigraphal writings. Many of these texts survive in the following languages: Latin, Greek, Old Slavonic, Armenian, Georgian, Rumanian, Coptic, Syriac, and Ethiopic; as such, they demonstrate how much the preservation of Jewish traditions composed during or derived from the Second Temple period depended on the activity of Christian writers, translators, editors, and copyists through many centuries since the first century C.E.

The discovery of the Dead Sea Scrolls in eleven caves from 1947 to 1956 made a significant impact on the study of ancient pseudepigraphy. This is so in two main respects. First, the Dead Sea materials have yielded non-Christian Jewish evidence for at least some of this literature. Among the previously known pseudepigrapha (if we take the technical meaning of the term as the point of departure), the following works have been confirmed as present at Qumran:

- *1 Enoch* (Aramaic)
    Book of Watchers (chaps. 1–36): 4Q201, 4Q202, 4Q204, 4Q205, 4Q206, XQpapEnoch
    Astronomical Book (chaps. 72–82): 4Q208, 4Q209, 4Q210, 4Q211
    Animal Apocalypse (chaps. 85–90): 4Q204, 4Q205, 4Q206, 4Q207
    Exhortation (91:1-10, 18-19): 4Q212
    Apocalypse of Weeks (93:1-10; 91:11-17): 4Q212
    Epistle of Enoch (92:1-5; 94:1–105:2): 4Q204, 4Q212
    Birth of Noah (chaps. 106–7): 4Q204

- Daniel (Aramaic): 1Q71, 1Q72, 4Q12, 4Q13, 4Q14, 4Q15, 4Q16, 6Q7

- *Jubilees* (Hebrew): 1Q17, 1Q18, 2Q19, 2Q20, 3Q5, 4Q176 frgs. 17-19, 4Q216, 4Q217, 4Q218, 4Q219, 4Q220, 4Q221, 4Q222, 4Q223-224, 11Q12

- Materials related to *Testaments of the Twelve Patriarchs*
    Testament of Judah [?]: 3Q7 Hebrew, 4Q484 Aramaic
    Testament of Naphtali: 4Q215 Aramaic
    Aramaic Levi Document (Aramaic): 1Q21, 4Q213, 4Q213a, 4Q213b, 4Q214, 4Q214a, 4Q214b

- Psalms 151, 154, 155: 11Q5
  Related, though not formally a pseudepigraphon, is the Aramaic *Book of Giants* (1Q23, 1Q24, 2Q26, 4Q203, 4Q206a, 4Q530, 4Q531, 4Q532, 4Q533, 6Q8).

Second, pseudepigraphal documents for which there has not been previous evidence have come to light through fragments from the Dead Sea:

- Traditions related to the biblical book of Daniel (Aramaic)
  Prayer of Nabonidus (4Q242)
  Four Kingdoms (4Q552, 4Q553)

- Testamentary material (Aramaic)
  Testament of Jacob (4Q537)
  Testament (or *Apocryphon*) *of Judah* (4Q538)
  Testament (or *Apocryphon*) *of Joseph* (4Q539)
  Testament (or *Apocryphon*) *of Levi* (4Q540, 4Q541)
  Testament of Qahat (4Q542)
  Visions of Amram (4Q543, 4Q544, 4Q545, 4Q546, 4Q547, 4Q548)
  Genesis Apocryphon (Aramaic) (1Q20)
  New Jerusalem (Aramaic) (1Q32, 2Q24, 4Q554, 4Q555, 5Q15, 11Q18)

Again, related materials to these include a number of documents which, in their preserved forms, show no evidence of being pseudepigrapha: *Pseudo-Daniel* (4Q243, 4Q244, 4Q245); *Aramaic Apocalypse* (4Q246); *Apocalypse?* (4Q489, 4Q490); *Noah* (4Q534, 4Q535, 4Q536; and 1Q19, 1Q19 bis); *Daniel Susanna?* (4Q551); and *Four Kingdoms* (4Q552, 4Q553).

While these materials, preserved in manuscripts dating from the third century B.C.E. until the first century C.E., both confirm and augment the existence of pseudepigraphal writing in Second Temple Judaism, two points should be noted. First, none of them are documents whose origins can be traced to the Qumran community, whose extant literature was invariably composed by (formally) anonymous writers. This means that, while the collection and, possibly, copying of these materials imply that the Qumran community did not reject them, the phenomenon of pseudepigraphy was fairly widespread among Hebrew and especially Aramaic-speaking Jews of the time. Second, these texts, especially those which can be said to pre-date the Maccabean revolt *(Book of Watchers, Astronomical Book)* or contain pre-Danielic tradition *(Aramaic Levi Docu-*

ment, Prayer of Nabonidus, Visions of Amram, Testament of Qahat), demonstrate that the practice of attributing wisdom and speech was well established during the third century B.C.E. This undergirds our confidence that a number of other works showing little or no overt sign of Christian editorial intrusion are originally Jewish and were composed during the Second Temple period (or at least before the Bar Kokhba Revolt): examples of this include *1 Enoch* 108 *(Eschatological Admonition), 4 Ezra, 2 Baruch, Apocalypse of Abraham, Testament of Abraham, Letter of Aristeas, Pseudo-Philo (= Liber Antiquitatum Biblicarum), Psalms of Solomon, Similitudes of Enoch (= 1 Enoch 37–71), Testament of Job, Testament of Moses, Joseph and Aseneth, Life of Adam and Eve, Pseudo-Phocylides,* 3 Maccabees, 4 Maccabees, and Prayer of Manasseh.

But for all their importance, the manuscripts from Qumran should not mislead one to assume that many or most of the "Old Testament" pseudepigrapha not attested at Qumran were also composed during the Second Temple period. To begin with, many of these compositions are simply Christian or contain very little trace of direct borrowing from non-Christian Jewish tradition (*Sibylline Oracles* books 6–8, *5 Ezra, 6 Ezra, Questions of Ezra, Greek Apocalypse of Ezra, Vision of Ezra, Apocalypse of Elijah, Apocalypse of Zephaniah, Apocalypse of Sedrach, Apocalypse of Daniel, Testament of Adam, Testament of Isaac, Testament of Jacob, Testament of Solomon, Ascension of Isaiah, Odes of Solomon*).

A number of others seem to be so predominantly Christian in outlook and tone that indicators of Jewish tradition seem best explained as a matter of reception or borrowing by Christian or Jewish-Christian writers (*Lives of the Prophets, Sibylline Oracles* books 1–2 and 14, *History of the Rechabites*).

More Jewish in outlook, several documents may derive from at least some Jewish written sources that have been edited, supplemented, or interpolated by Christian scribes (so, e.g., *Sibylline Oracles* books 3, 4 and 5; *3 Baruch; 4 Baruch;* the *Hellenistic Synagogal Prayers;* and *Testaments of the Twelve Patriarchs*). Here, some of the Christian interpolations are easy to identify (*4 Bar.* 8:12–9:32; *Sib. Or.* 1.324-400; *Sib. Or.* 3.776; *T. Levi* 4:4; 10:2-3; 14:2; 16:3, passim; *Hell. Syn. Prayers* 5:4-8 and 20-24; 7:4, etc.). Finally, some writings may have circulated in both Jewish and Christian circles, but show very little direct influence from either *(Ahiqar Proverbs, Sentences of the Syriac Menander)*. These classifications are not clear-cut; it sometimes remains difficult, if not impossible, to determine whether a given document or one of its passages without obviously Christian ideas therefore stems from a non-Christian Jewish tradition (e.g., many parts of *Testaments of the Twelve Patriarchs*).

Nevertheless, when non-Christian Jewish and Christian traditions have come together in a composition, scholarship in recent years has begun to shift from the assumption that a Jewish source has been reworked by Christians to a default view that attributes the essential form of the document to Christians who were inspired by Jewish traditions. Such a shift has been noticeable in recent treatments of *Testaments of the Twelve Patriarchs* (de Jonge, in numerous works from 1953 to 2003), *Ascension of Isaiah* (Norelli 1995), *Lives of the Prophets* (Satran 1995), *3 Baruch* (Harlow 1996), and *Joseph and Aseneth* (Kraemer 1998; Nir 2012). A methodological corollary to this shift is that, when the earliest evidence for such documents exists in Christian manuscripts, it is these Christian contexts that should provide the point of departure for study and analysis (Kraft 2001; Davila 2005). With regard to Early or Second Temple Judaism, then, it becomes crucial to identify and make use of criteria which might (or might not) assist in determining the extent to which pseudepigraphal writings originated among Jewish (or Jewish-Christian) groups. Scholars will continue to debate about how far each of these writings can be classified in precisely the ways outlined above. However, the different possibilities listed here illustrate (a) the complexities students of the materials face when attempting to determine their date and religious provenience, (b) the occasionally stark differences between Jewish and Christian tradition, and yet (c) how similar and, indeed, often indistinguishable, Jewish, Jewish-Christian, and non–Jewish-Christian traditions could be.

Conclusion

Today the terms "Apocrypha" and "Pseudepigrapha" refer to collections of writings of which many do not strictly reflect the literal meaning of these terms. The Apocrypha (or, for Roman Catholicism, Deuterocanonicals) is a fluid collection if one compares the lists of them among the different ecclesiastical traditions. However, within each ecclesiastical tradition, their identification has been remarkably stable. These writings may be confidently regarded as Jewish in origin; in addition, they all date to before the Bar Kokhba Revolt (132-135 C.E.) and, except for *4 Ezra*, were all originally composed before the destruction of the Second Temple (70 C.E.). At the same time, the free use of the term "apocryphon" for a number of documents discovered among the Dead Sea Scrolls reflects the ancient meaning of "hidden" traditions without, however, being "hidden" in the more technical sense found in Daniel, *4 Ezra,* and *2 Baruch.*

By contrast, collections of "pseudepigrapha" (or "apocrypha" in Roman Catholic tradition) have been anything but stable. This is due to a number of factors: (a) The term "pseudepigraphon" has often not been applied in its narrow meaning of a writing falsely ascribed. Instead, it has sometimes served as a broad category that refers to religious Jewish and Christian writings that are neither found in the "Bible" nor included in a church's list of "Apocrypha." (b) Since the beginning of the nineteenth century, when entrepreneurs and collectors brought ancient manuscripts to Europe from monasteries in Africa and the Middle East, and until the present, as manuscripts for new documents from Ethiopia, Armenia, and the Dead Sea have continued to come to light, collections of pseudepigrapha (however the term is defined) have been growing in number. (c) Modern collections of translated works — here we may take German and English publications since 1900 as an example — have each differed from one another in what to (and not to) include. Some of these differences can be attributed to nomenclature, that is, whether or not a given editor focused on "pseudepigrapha" per se (Kautzsch 1900, Charles 1913, Charlesworth 1983-1985, Sparks 1984: "apocryphal Old Testament"), more generally on works "outside the Bible" (Riessler 1927), or on Jewish writings from the Greco-Roman period (the series Jüdische Schriften aus hellenistisch-römischer Zeit [JSHRZ] 1973-present). These more widely disseminated collections, however, have fluctuated greatly on the number and selection of documents: Kautzsch (thirteen documents), Charles (seventeen), Riessler (sixty-one, including *Shemoneh Esreh, Megillat Ta'anit,* Heraclitus of Ephesus, Theodotus, *Caves of Treasures*), Sparks (twenty-five), Charlesworth (sixty-five, though ten nonpseudonymous works are included within a supplementary section entitled "Fragments of Lost Judeo-Hellenistic Works"), and JSHRZ (fifty, including "Apocrypha").

Beyond the writings included in these collections, a number of further documents could be included. The significance of the Dead Sea Scrolls has been noted for the addition of new materials, and there is little doubt that these materials were composed during the Second Temple period. A further project entitled *More Old Testament Pseudepigrapha* (MOTP), based at the University of St. Andrews under the direction of James Davila, is seeking to supplement the Charlesworth edition with an additional fifty pseudepigraphal writings, plus nearly thirty more that are found either in fragments or in quotations. The MOTP collection is casting its net more widely to include pseudepigrapha composed by Jews and Christians all the way up to 600 C.E. and the rise of Islam. With some notable exceptions (e.g., *Aramaic Levi Document, Book of Giants, Hebrew Naphtali, Balaam Text* [from Deir Alla], *Hebrew Apocalypse of Elijah, Geniza Wisdom Text, Sword of Moses, Massekhet Kelim, Midrash Vayissa'u, Eighth Book of Moses, Sepher ha-Razim, Sepher Zerubbabel*), many of the additional works in MOTP are Christian compositions and face the same issues regarding the relation between Jewish and Christian tradition outlined above. Accordingly, the net has been cast more widely here to include some pseudepigraphal documents in the Dead Sea Scrolls, but also works composed until 600 C.E. Thus the significance of each work for the Second Temple period varies widely and will require analysis on a case-by-case basis.

The problems that beset the terms "Apocrypha" and "Pseudepigrapha" have not prevented scholars from applying them to discrete collections of ancient works that stand alongside other recognized collections of works such as the Dead Sea Scrolls, rabbinic literature, the Hekhalot texts, the Nag Hammadi Library, and the works of Philo and Josephus. These different, though sometimes overlapping classifications of texts cannot hide the fact that in order to be interpreted, they need to be read together for a more comprehensive understanding of the diversities of Judaism that flourished during the centuries leading up to and after the turn of the Common Era.

BIBLIOGRAPHY

Baum, Armin Daniel. 2001. *Pseudepigraphie und literarische Fälschung im frühen Christentum.* Tübingen: Mohr Siebeck.

Charles, Robert H., ed. 1913. *The Apocrypha and Pseudepigrapha of the Old Testament.* 2 vols. Oxford: Clarendon.

Charlesworth, James H., ed. 1983-1985. *The Old Testament Pseudepigrapha.* 2 vols. New York: Doubleday.

Chazon, Esther G., and Michael E. Stone, eds. 1997. *Pseudepigraphic Perspectives: The Apocrypha and Pseudepigrapha in Light of the Dead Sea Scrolls.* Leiden: Brill.

Collins, John J. 1998. *The Apocalyptic Imagination: An Introduction to Jewish Apocalyptic Literature.* 2d ed. Grand Rapids: Eerdmans.

Davila, James R. 2005. *The Provenance of the Pseudepigrapha: Jewish, Christian, or Other?* Leiden: Brill.

de Jonge, Marinus. 2003. *Pseudepigrapha of the Old Testament as Part of Christian Literature: The Case of the Testaments of the Twelve Patriarchs and the Greek Life of Adam and Eve*. Leiden: Brill.

DeSilva, David. 2002. *Introducing the Apocrypha: Message, Context and Significance*. Grand Rapids: Baker.

Flint, Peter W. 1999. "'Apocrypha,' Other Previously-Known Writings, and 'Pseudepigrapha' in the Dead Sea Scrolls." In *The Dead Sea Scrolls after Fifty Years*. 2 vols. Ed. Peter W. Flint and James C. VanderKam. Leiden: Brill, 1:24-66.

Harlow, Daniel C. 1996. *The Greek Apocalypse of Baruch (3 Baruch) in Hellenistic Judaism and Early Christianity*. Leiden: Brill.

Harrington, Daniel J. 1999. *Invitation to the Apocrypha*. Grand Rapids: Eerdmans.

Henze, Matthias, 2011. *Jewish Apocalypticism in Late First Century Israel: Reading 'Second Baruch' in Context*. Tübingen: Mohr Siebeck.

Hollander, Harm W., and Marinus de Jonge. 1985. *The Testaments of the Twelve Patriarchs: A Commentary*. Leiden: Brill.

Kautzsch, Emil, ed. 1900. *Die Apokryphen und Pseudepigraphen des Alten Testaments*. 2 vols. Tübingen: Mohr.

Kraemer, Ross S. 1998. *When Aseneth Met Joseph: A Late Antique Tale of the Biblical Patriarch and His Egyptian Wife, Reconsidered*. Oxford: Oxford University Press.

Kraft, Robert A. 2001. "The Pseudepigrapha and Christianity Revisited: Setting the Stage and Framing Some Central Questions." *JSJ* 32: 371-95.

Nickelsburg, George W. E. 2001. *1 Enoch 1: A Commentary on the Book of 1 Enoch, Chapters 1–36, 81–108*. Minneapolis: Fortress.

———. 2005. *Jewish Literature between the Bible and the Mishnah*. 2d ed. Philadelphia: Fortress.

———, and James C. VanderKam. 2012. *1 Enoch 2: A Commentary on the Book of 1 Enoch, Chapters 37–82*. Minneapolis: Fortress.

Nir, Rivka. 2012. *Joseph and Aseneth: A Christian Book*. Sheffield: Phoenix.

Norelli, Enrico. 1995. *Ascensio Isaiae*, vol. 1, *Commentarius*. Turnhout: Brepols.

Riessler, Paul. 1927. *Altjüdisches Schrifttum ausserhalb der Bibel*. Heidelberg: Kerl.

Satran, David. 1995. *Biblical Prophets in Byzantine Palestine: Reassessing the "Lives of the Prophets."* Leiden: Brill.

Sparks, H. F. D., ed. 1984. *The Apocryphal Old Testament*. Oxford: Clarendon.

Stone, Michael E. 1990. *Fourth Ezra*. Minneapolis: Fortress.

———. 1996. "The Dead Sea Scrolls and the Pseudepigrapha." *DSD* 3: 270-96.

Stuckenbruck, Loren T. 2007. *1 Enoch 91–108*. Berlin: de Gruyter.

Wyrick, Jed. 2004. *The Ascension of Authorship: Attribution and Canon Formation in Jewish, Hellenistic, and Christian Traditions*. Cambridge: Harvard University Press.

The Dead Sea Scrolls

Eibert Tigchelaar

In a comprehensive sense, the Dead Sea Scrolls include all texts from Wadi Daliyeh, Ketef Jericho, Qumran, Wadi en-Nar, Wadi Ghweir, Wadi Murabbaʿat, Wadi Sdeir, Naḥal Arugot, Naḥal Ḥever/Wadi Ṣeiyâl, Naḥal Mishmar, Naḥal Ṣeʿelim, Masada, as well as Khirbet Mird. In common usage, and in this essay, the term "Dead Sea Scrolls" refers specifically to the texts found between 1947 and 1956 in the caves near Qumran, close to the northwestern shore of the Dead Sea. Some fragments that are reported to have been found in caves near Qumran may in fact stem from other sites that were discovered by the Bedouin in the same period, notably Wadi Murabbaʿat and Naḥal Ḥever/Wadi Ṣeiyâl. Likewise, the origin of some fragments in private collections is unknown.

The importance of the Dead Sea Scrolls for the history of early Judaism lies in the combination of the size, the antiquity, and the nature of the corpus. The scrolls are by far the largest collection of Jewish religious texts from the Second Temple period, preserving fragments of more than a hundred different religious compositions, most of which were hitherto unknown. For many different aspects of Judaism, the Dead Sea Scrolls provide the first literary evidence. Thus, for example, the corpus contains the oldest Hebrew and Greek biblical manuscripts, the first Aramaic translations of biblical books, the oldest *tefillin*, the earliest liturgies for fixed prayers, the oldest nonbiblical halakic works, as well as the oldest exorcistic prayers. In many cases we find hitherto-unknown precursors to or roots for phenomena found in rabbinic Judaism, such as the hymns embedded in the Hekhalot literature. At the same time, some scrolls attest to Second Temple practices and beliefs that did not become part of later normative Judaism, which is why they sometimes are called sectarian. This goes, for example, for so-called rule texts that discuss the membership of the movement of the "renewed covenant," exegetical works that apply scriptural prophecies to the contemporary history and future of the group, eschatological works dealing with the final war, and religious calendrical texts based on a 364-day calendar.

Because of the content of so-called sectarian texts, especially the *Rule of the Community,* scholars in the 1950s framed the Qumran-Essene hypothesis of the provenance of the Dead Sea Scrolls, which at the end of that decade had become the paradigm of scrolls scholarship. The scrolls were assumed to be the remnants of the library of an Essene, or Essene-like, sectarian community that dwelt at Qumran, composed and copied texts, and hid their manuscripts in various caves before the Romans conquered the site in 68 C.E. At present there are many different modifications of this paradigm. Most importantly, there is a broad recognition that not all the compositions and scrolls can be attributed to this one "sectarian" group, and that many texts may have been composed or written somewhere else, before they were brought to Qumran. Some archaeologists even deny that Qumran would have been a religious center and therefore assume that all the scrolls were brought from elsewhere. The following survey offers an overview of the corpus, a description of the texts and their contribution to our knowledge of Judaism in the Second Temple period, and critical reflections on the nature of the corpus.

The Contours of the Corpus

Although generally the Dead Sea Scrolls are discussed as one corpus, they comprise the inscribed material from eleven different caves in the vicinity of the ruins of Qumran. The finds in the caves share many commonalities but also differ in important respects. Largely or partially intact scrolls have been found only in Caves 1 and 11. The completely preserved Cave 3 *Copper Scroll* stands out because of its material, contents, and language. Cave 4, which yielded more than 15,000 fragments that can be assigned to at least 700 different manuscripts, surrendered far more manuscripts than all other caves together. In Cave 7 only fragments of Greek texts were found, and Cave 6 produced a relatively large number of papyrus texts. According to the current paleographical dating, the texts from Caves 1 and 4 are on average considerably older than those from Caves 2, 3, 5, 6, and 11. Caves 9 (one shred of papyrus with a few letters) and 10 (a shard of pottery with two letters) can be ignored in this overview.

The most characteristic feature of both the entire corpus and the collections of the individual caves is that virtually all the manuscripts contain texts of a religious nature or touching upon religious issues. Only a few, badly preserved fragments are the remnants of nonliterary texts such as letters, accounts, or deeds, and it cannot be excluded that some of those actually stem from Naḥal Ḥever.

The present inventory of Dead Sea Scrolls lists around 930 items. In most cases one item corresponds to one manuscript, but in view of the many unidentified fragments that have not been included in the lists, it is plausible that the materials known to us stem from more than a thousand different manuscripts. Only in a few cases do substantial parts of manuscripts remain, and often a manuscript consists of no more than a few identified fragments.

Most Dead Sea Scrolls were written on skins of domesticated goats and ibexes. Some exceptionally thick scrolls, like 11Q5, might be calfskin. Ten to fifteen percent of the manuscripts were written on papyrus. The Cave 3 *Copper Scroll* is the only text written on metal. Both in and near the caves (Caves 4, 6, 7, 8, and 10), and at the site of Qumran, jars and shards with inscriptions or incisions were found. Notable are the ostraca found at Qumran, as well as a small limestone plaque of five lines with what may be a literary text (KhQ 2207). Some fragments, both of skin and of papyrus, were found to be written on both sides.

The majority of the manuscripts are written in Hebrew. About 12 percent (or 17 percent of the nonbiblical, nondocumentary texts) are written in Aramaic. Almost 3 percent of the inventory items are written in Greek, but the percentage drops to less than 1 percent if we bracket out Cave 7. All but two Aramaic manuscripts and most Hebrew ones are written in the so-called square or Aramaic script. Two Aramaic manuscripts are written in a Nabatean script. Some Hebrew texts use the Paleo-Hebrew script, or several kinds of so-called cryptic scripts, the most common one being referred to as Cryptic A. The square script is attested in formal, semiformal, and semicursive hands, and a few of the documentary texts are written in a cursive hand. Some Hebrew texts display the orthography and morphology known from the Masoretic manuscripts of the Hebrew Bible; others have a distinct full orthography and special morphological features that are unattested or rare in Hebrew texts outside the corpus. Many manuscripts with those morphological features also have specific nontextual scribal features, so Emanuel Tov has proposed that we have within the corpus a large group of documents written according to a special "Qumran scribal practice."

The traditional paleographic dating of the manuscripts ranges from the mid-third century B.C.E. to the end of the first century C.E., but the vast majority of the manuscripts date to the first century B.C.E. Radiocarbon analysis of manuscripts by and large gives date ranges from the late third century B.C.E. to the early second century C.E., even though for specific samples paleographic and radiocarbon datings disagree. No manuscripts are internally dated, and the few texts that mention identifiable historical persons refer to figures that lived in the second century and especially in the first half of the first century B.C.E.

The near completion of the publication of all materials in the 1990s has enabled new approaches to the corpus, by allowing scholars to correlate different kinds of subsets within the corpus. For example, one may contrast collections from different caves, compare "biblical" texts written in the so-called Qumran scribal practice to other "biblical" texts, or use the date of the hands of manuscripts in order to trace chronological developments in the corpus.

Scholarly Categorizations Old and New

Classifications of the different kinds of Dead Sea Scrolls have shifted over time, as more scrolls became known, and as scholarly concepts, terminology, and interpretations changed. Initially, on the basis of the Cave 1 finds, the scrolls were roughly classified in three categories: (1) biblical or canonical; (2) apocryphal and/or pseudepigraphal; and (3) sectarian or Essene. This old categorization was partly based on genre and content of texts but also implied a historical view according to which (with the exception of Daniel) canonical books preceded apocryphal and pseudepigraphal ones, which in turn were older than the sectarian texts. At the same time, this three-part division was thought to reflect the literature of respectively all Jews, some Jews, and only the Dead Sea Scrolls sect. Gradually, the problematic categories of apocrypha and pseudepigrapha were subsumed in a broader general category of "parabiblical texts," and the initial tripartite scholarly categorization was in practice limited to two sets of oppositions, "biblical" versus "nonbiblical," and "sectarian" versus "nonsectarian," which influence scholarship up to the present.

The publication of all the Cave 4 materials and their subsequent analysis has required a thorough revision of those earlier classifications. The corpus does not conform to anachronistic assumptions connected to the term "biblical." This realization has provoked discussions of whether texts like the *Reworked Pentateuch* manuscripts are biblical, or whether *Jubilees* or the *Temple Scroll* had scriptural status for the group that collected the scrolls. Also, consideration of the corpus as a whole challenges the view that all the hitherto-unknown texts were written by only one group and suggests that they originated in different movements at different times. The result is that the sharp contrasts between the two sets of oppositions, "biblical" versus "nonbiblical" and "sectarian" versus "nonsectarian," has broken down; scholars now allow for different degrees of authoritativeness of scriptures and varying kinds of sectarianism. From a practical view, a classification with two sets of oppositions also has limited value, since most newly published manuscripts should have been assigned to the categories "nonbiblical" and "nonsectarian." The large increase in known materials does, however, enable one to classify the materials differently, according to literary form, content, or function of compositions. Such new classifications of the material can be found in the translations of García Martínez and Vermes, and in a more elaborate form in Lange's overview in DJD 39. In Lange's classification of the nonbiblical texts, which has been adopted by the *Dead Sea Scrolls Reader,* we find categories such as "parabiblical," "exegetical," "concerned with religious law," "calendrical," "poetical," "liturgical," "sapiential," "historical," "apocalyptic," "eschatological," and more.

The Texts and Early Judaism

The present survey does not aim at a strict categorization of the manuscripts but rather discusses the corpus and the most important texts thematically. It aspires to relate the materials to present scholarly discussion and to clarify what they contribute to the knowledge of early Judaism.

Authoritative Scriptures and the Formation of the Bible

In general the term "biblical" is used, anachronistically, but for practical reasons, for those scrolls which contained the text, or part of the text, of one or more compositions that would later be included in the Tanak. Altogether, the corpus contains more than two hundred Hebrew and Aramaic "biblical" manuscripts," five manuscripts with Greek translations of pentateuchal books, three with Aramaic translations *(targumim),* and thirty-three phylacteries and *mezuzot.* In addition, many of the "nonbiblical" manuscripts are in various ways intertextually related to the "biblical" books. While the "biblical" manuscripts give direct witness to the forms of the biblical books and their text in the period just before the final stage of the formation of the Hebrew Bible, the corpus as a whole gives indirect witness to those compositions and their text, but also sheds light on the authoritativeness of scriptures for the group(s) behind the corpus.

The "biblical" Dead Sea Scrolls reflect a wide diversity of textual variants and recensions. Whereas many manuscripts present a text that stands fairly close to the Masoretic Text (MT), there are also scrolls that preserve variants and even recensions that correspond to those of the Old Greek (e.g., 4QJer[b]), or to the Samaritan Pentateuch (4QpaleoExod[m], 4QNum[b], and 4QDeut[n]). But many other "biblical" manuscripts do not closely correspond to any of those three texts, since they either have multiple unique variant readings, or have readings that cannot be aligned with only one of the traditional texts. Therefore, with regard to textual readings, we do not have a limited number of text types but multiple texts. With regard to recensions, the manuscripts generally correspond with the types of recensions found in the MT or the LXX (where book by book the one or the other may be older), or with the harmonizing kind of recensions that are also found in the Samaritan Pentateuch (SP). Famous is the case of 4QJer[b], which displays the recensional differences in which the LXX differs from MT. But here again, some scrolls preserve recensions that are independent from other known texts (e.g., 4QJudg[a]). None of the variants or recensions has a clearly "sectarian" concern, though some of the 1QIsa[a] variants have been interpreted as expressing the self-understanding of the Dead Sea Scrolls community.

For the assessment of the LXX and the SP, the scrolls are invaluable because they demonstrate that divergent readings and recensions of the Old Greek (OG) often go back to a Hebrew *Vorlage* and are not tendentious innovations of the translator, and that the harmonizations in the SP were already present in the text the Samaritans chose. The variety of the "biblical" manuscripts from Qumran may be contrasted with the homogeneity of the post-70-C.E. "biblical" manuscripts found at Wadi Murabbaʿat, Wadi Sdeir, and Naḥal Ḥever/Wadi Ṣeiyâl, which preserve a text that is virtually identical to the MT. This contrast has been explained chronologically and sociologically: the Qumran "biblical" manuscripts, the majority of which stem from the first century B.C.E. and the early first century C.E., reflect the textual variety before the post-70-c.e. move toward textual standardization that influenced the other Judean Desert "biblical" manuscripts; or, mainstream (Pharisaic, proto-rabbinic) Judaism promoted a standardized text, whereas the group who collected or copied the Dead Sea Scrolls did not. The pre-73-c.e. "biblical" manuscripts found at Masada make the issue even more complex, since they are found at the same site as "nonbiblical" manuscripts comparable to those from Qumran but seem to display a text that is arguably closer to the MT than the "biblical" Dead Sea Scrolls are.

Equally important is the phenomenon of multiple, probably successive, recensions and rewritings of "biblical" books. For several biblical books, the LXX and the MT preserve two different recensions, and for the Pentateuch we have the systematically harmonizing recension of the SP. Yet another recension is found in the so-called *Reworked Pentateuch* manuscripts (4Q158; 4Q364-367), which contain editions of the Pentateuch characterized by harmonizations and relocations of materials, but also by additions of new text relating to, for example, the festival laws. Discussions of whether these manuscripts should be called biblical or authoritative scripture relate both to the analysis of the manuscripts and to suppositions regarding the concepts "biblical" and "authoritative." From a literary point of view, the recension in the *Reworked Pentateuch* goes one step beyond that of the SP by adding new materials, generally based on exegesis of the text. The techniques used in this recension are comparable to those used in some of the LXX recensions, for example, 3 Kingdoms and Esther. Whether these expansionist *Reworked Pentateuch* texts were biblical in the precanonical sense of authoritative depends on whether one assumes a strict boundary between texts or recensions of texts that were regarded as authoritative and those that were not.

From the perspective of the later canon, one may ask to what extent the books of the Tanak already were scriptural among the Dead Sea Scrolls. The partially reconstructed reference in 4QMMT to "the book of Moses, the books of the prophets, and David (?)" has been taken to refer to a threefold structure of scriptures, but this is only one of several possible readings, reconstructions, and interpretations of this passage. Copies of all books of the Hebrew Bible have been identified among the scrolls, with the exception of Esther (though the status of one fragment with a section of Chronicles and of another text is unclear). The quantity of preserved scrolls per book differs considerably, and one may contrast the large number of copies of the books of the Pentateuch, Isaiah, and Psalms (several of which are attested by twenty copies or more) with the small number of preserved copies (three or less) of Joshua, Judges, Kings, Proverbs, Qohelet, Ezra, and Chronicles. There are no *a priori* grounds for assuming that all the later biblical books of the Tanak were already scriptural or authoritative to the same degree. It seems that a core group of scriptures (Pentateuch, Isaiah, the Minor Prophets, and Psalms), were differently transmitted, interpreted, and granted a different degree of authority than other scriptures. For example, the textual transmission of Isaiah and the Minor Prophets is fairly stable: we have only one major recension. Also, there are pesharim interpreting those books, which indicates that the contents were seen as authoritative but in need of interpretation. In contrast, there are different recensions of Jeremiah and Ezekiel, and instead of pesharim we find parabiblical literature connected to those books. Some of the Ketuvim are extensively used in other Dead Sea Scrolls, such as the Psalms, Daniel, Proverbs, and Lamentations. Other Ketuvim, like Canticles, Ruth, Ecclesiastes, Esther, and Ezra, are not known to have been used or referred to in other texts.

Criteria that may cumulatively indicate the importance or authority that a group attached to a text include (a) the number of preserved copies of a composition, (b) the existence of commentaries on those works, (c) quotations or references to a text in other compositions, (d) the existence of translations of those texts, (e) implicit or explicit claims to authority in a work, and (f) attribution of a text to preexilic authors. Hence, it has been suggested that *Jubilees* and (some of) the books of *Enoch,* but possibly also texts like the *Aramaic Levi Document* and the *Apocryphon of Joshua,* may have been authoritative scriptures for groups behind the Dead Sea Scrolls. But here, too, the question is whether one should assume a sharp distinction between scriptural and nonscriptural.

Extending Scriptures by Interpretative Rewriting

Since the 1990s, the term "parabiblical" has gained popularity in Dead Sea Scrolls studies as an umbrella term for a large variety of texts that are closely related to texts or themes of the Hebrew Bible. This category includes both those texts that were formerly described as "rewritten bible" or "biblical interpretation," and those compositions that are attributed or connected to biblical figures and that often were characterized as pseudepigraphal and apocryphal. Even though there sometimes is an overlap, as in the case of rewritings attributed to Moses or Ezekiel, these are two distinct types, and the general but vague term "parabiblical" obfuscates the differences.

The first type consists of interpretative rewritings of earlier scripture, in the form of "rewritten scripture," or as a paraphrase or retelling of either entire books, or sections of books, or even as a pastiche of different passages. These rewritings sometimes have expansions that may go back to older sources or traditions, or derive from the interpretation of the author. The best-preserved examples of the first type are the book of *Jubilees* and the *Temple Scroll* (see fig. 46), both of which contain extensive interpretative rewritings of parts of the Torah, as well as parts that have no direct correspondence in the Torah and that may have been taken from other sources or traditions. Less well-preserved examples are the *Apocryphon of Joshua* and many other fragmentary manuscripts that deal with events from the Torah and Joshua. These include some parts of the *Genesis Apocryphon* (see fig. 42), some of the Moses Apocrypha, notably *Words of Moses* (1Q22) and *Apocryphal Pentateuch A* (4Q368) and *B* (4Q377). A few texts are related to the books of Samuel and Kings, such as *Vision of Samuel* (a misnomer for 4Q160) or *Paraphrase of Kings* (4Q382), and to the prophets, especially the *Pseudo-Ezekiel* manuscripts. We also find works of this type relating to the books later collected as Ketuvim, for example *Apocryphal Lamentation A* (4Q179), which rewrites parts of Lamentations, and *Wiles of the Wicked Woman* (4Q184) and *Beatitudes* (4Q525; 5Q16), which are copies of one or two works closely related to the text of Proverbs 1–9.

These compositions represent different degrees and kinds of rewriting. In the case of *Jubilees* and the *Temple Scroll,* the compositions both rewrite Torah and claim to be Torah themselves. They complement the pentateuchal Torah as its valid and authoritative interpretation. For other rewritten Mosaic texts, a similar relation to the Pentateuch may be assumed but cannot be established because the texts are too fragmentary. The *Apocryphon of Joshua* is a good example of different aspects of the process of rewriting: the author tackles exegetical problems in the scriptural book of Joshua, reworks Joshua according to his own agenda (the centrality of Jerusalem and the status of the land of Israel), and provides an interpretation of the prophetic curse in Josh. 6:26. In cases like this, it is not clear whether the *Apocryphon* intended to complement or supplement the book of Joshua. In any case, the preserved manuscripts of the *Apocryphon of Joshua* outnumber those of the scriptural Joshua. On the other hand, it is not clear to what extent the extensive use and reworking of

Proverbs 1–9 in 4QBeatitudes and 4QWiles of the Wicked Woman was meant as authoritative interpretation of scripture, or rather as imitation of a scriptural example.

In a few cases it is demonstrable that such rewritings of scriptures actually gained, at least in some circles, some kind of scriptural status. The quotation of Josh. 6:26 in *Testimonia* (4Q175; see fig. 49) follows the text of the *Apocryphon of Joshua*. A series of fragmentary manuscripts called *Pseudo-Jubilees* (4Q225-227, but also 4Q217 and perhaps 4Q228) are new rewritings based on the text of *Jubilees*.

This phenomenon of interpretative rewriting sheds an interesting light on the issue of scriptures in the second and first century B.C.E. The very act of interpretation and rewriting endorses the authoritative and foundational character of "biblical" scriptures, but at the same time extends this authority to the interpretative reworking of those scriptures.

Expanding Scripture by Ascribing
Traditions to Foundational Figures

Apart from new scriptures that are primarily based on interpretative rewriting of a scriptural text, there is a group of largely or entirely new compositions attributed or closely related to scriptural authors or figures. This second type is not based primarily on the text of Scripture but consists largely of a series of compositions, written in Aramaic, and ascribed to pre-Mosaic figures, from Enoch through Amram. Included in this category are several books of *Enoch,* the *Aramaic Levi Document,* the Lamech and Noah sections of the *Genesis Apocryphon,* a series of very fragmentary works that have been described as testaments of Jacob and several of his sons *(Testament of Qahat,* the *Visions of Amram,* and possibly the *New Jerusalem).* Also relevant here were compositions written in Hebrew that are attributed to Moses (especially the *Apocryphon of Moses* texts) and to Jeremiah *(Apocryphon of Jeremiah C),* and perhaps also those attributed to David (noncanonical psalms in 11Q5; the *Apocryphal Psalms* of 11Q11).

The Aramaic texts ascribed to Enoch, Noah, and the pre-Mosaic patriarchs should be considered a separate group of compositions. Here we find first-person narrative, generally with ancestral instruction, sometimes visionary reports, and, more rarely, exegetical expansions of scriptural narrative. The use of first-person narration is a feature common to other Aramaic literature (Ahiqar, Tobit) and may be regarded as a stylistic preference.

The contents of these Aramaic texts suggest that some might have a pre-Maccabean origin in priestly-Levitical circles who had knowledge of Mesopotamian lore and science. They were influenced by Persian ideas and emphasize revelation through dreams and visions, as well as the transmission of ancestral traditions above or alongside the interpretation of the Scriptures. Though some of these Aramaic texts include interpretative or paraphrastic sections, the main link is with the ancestral "scriptural" figure, not with the scriptural text.

The Hebrew examples of new writings attributed or connected to Moses, Jeremiah, and David belong to a somewhat different category than the Aramaic examples. The former may be seen as foundational figures according to the functions ascribed to them in the Scriptures. All the new texts attributed to Moses belong to a Mosaic discourse in which specific interpretations of the Law were regarded as divine revelation to Moses on Sinai. Likewise, the *Apocryphon of Jeremiah C* is based on the image of Jeremiah being the leader and teacher of the nation after the destruction of the Temple.

Most of these texts have in common that their ascription to ancestral patriarchs or foundational figures may be seen as an expansion of Scripture, although only in some cases is there evidence that they achieved scriptural status in some circles. This goes for the Enochic writings, the *Aramaic Levi Document,* and perhaps the *Apocryphon of Jeremiah C,* if 2 Macc. 2:1-4 is connected to that text.

More importantly, the Dead Sea Scrolls call for a more sophisticated approach toward the phenomenon of pseudepigraphy, which ranges from no more than a purely literary device in some texts (like the *Genesis Apocryphon*) to attribution of one's traditions to ancestral figures to an authority-conferring strategy of presenting one's new interpretation of authoritative Scripture.

Expounding Scripture in Commentaries and Pesharim

Whereas rewritten texts and paraphrases are implicitly interpretative, a special category of texts makes an explicit distinction between scripture and commentary. The clearest examples are the so-called continuous pesharim, such as the *Habakkuk Pesher* (see fig. 43) and *Nahum Pesher* and the pesharim on Isaiah, some Minor Prophets, and some of the Psalms. They feature a quotation of one or more verses from a "prophetic" Scripture, a commentary on the quoted verse(s), a quotation of the next verses, its interpretation, and so on. Characteristic is the explicit introduction of the commentary by means of the term *pišrô*, "its interpretation" (or *pešer ha-dābar*, "the interpretation of the passage"), which often involves the identification of the subject of the scriptural verse with subjects that were active just before or during the author's time, or expected to become active in the near future. Other commentaries, like *Florilegium* (4Q174) and *Catena A* (4Q177), which probably are two copies of one and the same composition *Eschatological Midrash*, as well as *Melchizedek* (11Q13), have been called either midrash (on the basis of the use of the term in 4Q174), or "thematic pesharim," since they do not interpret a running scriptural text but rather select different verses which, according to the interpretation, relate to the same theme. A special case is *Ages of Creation* (or *Pesher on the Periods;* 4Q180), which includes a series of notes commenting on the text of Genesis and explaining problematic issues in the text.

Some manuscripts seem to combine rewritten scripture with implicit exegesis and commentary with explicit exegesis. This holds, for example, for *Commentary on Genesis A* (4Q252), which starts out with a rewriting of the flood story in Genesis 7–8, consisting mainly of scriptural verses and chronological additions, continues with a discussion of problematic sections of Genesis, and ends with a commentary of Jacob's blessings, including the technical *pišrô* phrase. These different kinds of interpretative writing in 4Q252 may owe to a compilation of various sources. Or they may reflect the gradual transition from implicit interpretative rewriting (down to the first century B.C.E.) to explicit commentaries, which came into existence in the first half of the first century B.C.E. However, the explicit *pišrô* (and *pešer ha-dābar*) formula is used specifically with regard to "prophetic" texts, including Psalms and Jacob's prophecies in Genesis 49, which would explain the different exegetical techniques used in the same text. In 4Q180, and probably also in the fragmentary *Exposition on the Patriarchs* (4Q464), we find a different use of the phrase *pišrô ʿal*, "interpretation concerning," as a section heading for new topics. The official title of 4Q247, *Pesher on the Apocalypse of Weeks*, is misleading in at least two aspects. First, the sparse text of the extant fragment does not use the term *pesher*, nor are there any other indications that the text is exegetical. Second, though the scheme of weeks corresponds to that also found in the *Apocalypse of Weeks*, there is no indication that the fragment rewrites or interprets that specific text.

These different forms of extending, expanding, and expounding Scripture underline how by the early second century B.C.E. at the latest Judaism had become thoroughly scripturalized, even though the borders between scripture and interpretation may have been somewhat shifting, since some interpretation itself claims revelation and hence authoritativeness. Also fluid are the transitions from interpretative rewriting to explicit commentary, and from exegesis of texts to attribution of nonscriptural materials to foundational figures. The Dead Sea Scrolls therefore illustrate various kinds of exegetical techniques, as well as different strategies for conferring authority in early Judaism.

Special attention should be given to *Jubilees*, which combines rewritten Scripture, the adaptation of other traditions, and the attribution of the text to the founding figure of Moses. More importantly, *Jubilees* is related to many other texts in the corpus. It includes material found in the oldest Enochic books and in the *Aramaic Levi Document;* it shares halakic traditions with the *Temple Scroll;* it is in its turn imitated or rewritten in the *Pseudo-Jubilees* manuscripts; and diverse texts such as the *Words of Moses* and the *Apocryphon of Jeremiah C* are dependent on it.

Interpreting the Law in Legal Works

Some interpretative works deal partly or exclusively with the interpretation of the Law of Moses. But whereas the corpus includes much legal material, only a few texts are primarily focused on legal questions. Without a doubt, the two most important legal texts are the *Temple Scroll* and the so-called *Halakic Document,* now known as MMT for *Miqṣat Ma'aśê ha-Torah,* one of the phrases in the text (see fig. 48). Other legal texts include the legal section of the *Damascus Document,* the remnants of different *Tohorot* compositions, the Moses Apocrypha (including *Apocryphal Pentateuch A*), and compositions referred to as *Ordinances* (4Q159; 4Q513-514), *Halaka A* (4Q251) and *B* (4Q264a), and *Miscellaneous Rules* (4Q265).

The *Temple Scroll,* which is based on Deuteronomy but presented as God's word spoken in the first person at Sinai, contains the most extensive collection of legal material. It also discusses the construction of the sanctuary, its altar, and its courtyards, the festival calendar and festal sacrificial offerings; and purity laws. And it engages in a rewriting of Deuteronomy 12–23, into which are inserted the so-called Law of the King and other regulations regarding the Levites and crucifixion. The composition has been described as a utopian vision of the present age, and a polemic against Hasmonean policies and Pharisaic rulings.

MMT is as an epistolary treatise of which the central part (called B by the editors) consists of a survey of legal issues. They deal mainly with the purity of the sanctuary. The authors ("we") apparently disagree (sometimes with a direct appeal to Scripture) with either contemporary Temple practices or their opponents' views. In several cases, the points of discussion are known from rabbinic literature, where the "we" position of MMT is ascribed to the Zadokites/Sadducees and the opposite position to the Pharisees.

The publication of both texts and their subsequent study had a large impact on Scrolls studies. It became clear that the *Temple Scroll* did not fit in with the then known "sectarian" texts, and this confirmed the suspicion that the corpus contained works from different, albeit related, groups. MMT has been interpreted as a foundational document, summing up the calendrical and legal disputes with the Jerusalem priests and the Pharisees.

For the study of early Judaism, the legal texts confirm that the rabbinic descriptions of legal discussions between Sadducees and Pharisees were not anachronistic inventions but debates already current in the Hasmonean era. Also, the legal texts attest to practices that are much earlier than the rabbinic texts in which they are recorded. This goes, for example, for the *minyan* (minimum of ten men) described in *Rule of the Congregation* (1QSa), the *Rule of the Community* (1QS; see fig. 41), and the *Damascus Document* (CD). More generally, the mere existence of written law codes in Second Temple Judaism is at odds with the Pharisaic-rabbinic rule that extrabiblical legal traditions should remain oral.

The topics under discussion in the legal texts shed light on issues that had become important in the second and first century B.C.E., such as Sabbath and purity. This holds for purity concerns in general, and for the purity of the Temple and Jerusalem in particular, an issue that may reflect a reaction to the defilement of the Temple by Antiochus Epiphanes. Typical of the purity laws included in the corpus is that they are in general more stringent than the later rabbinic purity laws. Some texts extend the concept of purity from ritual to moral issues.

Harmonizing Times and Festivals: Calendrical Documents and Annals

The corpus contains a small amount of generally badly preserved calendrical documents, most of which are actually lists. These lists include enumerations of the number of days per month, registers of the holy festivals on their respective dates in a 364-day year, registers of the priestly watches or *mišmārōt* related to this calendar, lists relating phases in the monthly revolution of the moon to corresponding dates of the 364-day year, and the so-called *'Otot* list synchronizing the six-year *mišmārōt* cycles with the seven-year *shemitah* and the forty-nine-year jubilee cycle. In some cases calendrical lists are part of larger documents. For example, *'Otot* (4Q319) is actually the end of one of the Cave 4 copies of the *Rule of the Community* (4Q259), and a calendrical list is found at the beginning of one of the MMT manuscripts (4Q394). A special, related case is the two very fragmentary works (*Historical Texts D* and *E;* 4Q332 and 4Q333) that list historical events, including proper names, in relation to dates and priestly watches.

Virtually all the calendrical documents attest to the 364-day calendar defended in the Enochic *Book of the Luminaries* and in *Jubilees,* and implied in most other texts in the corpus — exceptions could be *Daily Prayers* (4Q503) and *Zodiology and Brontology* (4Q318). These documents are the result of exegetical activity and try to harmonize the different scriptural prescriptions for Sabbaths and dates of festivals, as well as priestly watches and larger cycles, into a coherent system. Many of the liturgical texts are based on this calendrical system, and the lists can therefore be seen as the legal basis for the priestly service and the liturgical and festal year. The difference between the 364-day calendar and the 354-day calendar known from other Jewish sources is crucial, since it implies a different festival calendar and would have provoked a major schism in early Judaism.

Performing Scripture: Liturgical and Poetical Manuscripts

Some poetical manuscripts in the corpus have explicit markers that indicate an intended liturgical or ritual use; other collections of poems lack such evidence. A large number of texts may be categorized as hymns and prayers. These include liturgies for evening and morning blessings for all days of the month, prayers for the days of the week, songs for the Sabbath sacrifice, and festival prayers. All of these texts are the oldest liturgies for fixed prayer times on record. Scholars are divided on two questions. First, whether these liturgies for fixed prayers were specifically sectarian or were rather representative of liturgies of Second Temple Judaism at large. Second, how these prayers relate to rabbinic prayer material. Because of the paleographic dating of *Words of the Luminaries*[a] (4Q504) around 150 B.C.E., and the lack of explicit sectarian terminology, it has been suggested that *Words of the Luminaries (Divre Ha-me'orot)* may plausibly be presectarian. The composition apparently utilized the same periodization of history found in the Enochic *Apocalypse of Weeks,* which may indicate a provenance in groups with affinities to the Enochic writings. Many thematic and vocabulary correspondences between the prayers in the Scrolls and rabbinic prayers have been adduced, but only very rarely are they unique. More generally, the vocabulary and character of both groups of prayers are dependent on Scripture, and specific shared features should probably be attributed to common streams of tradition rather than direct literary dependence. Even though there is no direct relation between the two corpora, the scrolls demonstrate that the fixation of prayer after Yavneh was not a new invention but the institutionalization of practices that already existed in Second Temple times.

Similar issues of comparison may be made for the *Songs for the Sabbath Sacrifice,* the *Blessings* (4Q286-290), and the hymnic material in *Mysteries*[c] (4Q301), which have been characterized as mystical due to the language of awe and mystery. Even though the medieval Hekhalot literature attests to a different kind of mystical practice, the style of the hymns in the Hekhalot seems to go back to such Second Temple precursors.

Whereas a specific ritual is assured for the *Blessings,* the *Purification Liturgies,* and the prayers and songs with an exorcistic character, it is disputed whether, for example, the *Hodayot,* the *Bless My Soul,* and the *Noncanonical Psalms* were composed for private prayer or reading or for communal recitation. The different collections of *Hodayot* from Caves 1 and 4 stand apart in the corpus on account of the highly unique and personal songs in the middle of the large Cave 1 *Thanksgiving Scroll.* These songs have been read as autobiographical expressions of a leading figure praising God for release from affliction, for the revelation of his wonders, and for having placed hymns in his mouth to instruct the lowly. More than other hymns, they contrast God's greatness to human smallness. The suggestion that the author may be the Teacher of Righteousness mentioned in the pesharim (hence the name "Teacher Hymns") is attractive but remains hypothetical. Some *Hodayot* collections also contain community hymns in which the "I" of the hymn may refer to individual members of the group.

Whereas older scholarship generally referred only to the anthological style of the hymns and prayers, it has become clear that they are often scripturalized in multiple respects. They use scriptural language but often interpret and allude to specific passages; they sometimes use scriptural patterns but also emulate or rework specific biblical sections, such as Psalm 18 in 1QH^a XI and in the *Prayer of the Man of God* in *Noncanonical Psalms B* (4Q381).

Understanding All There Is: Sapiential Texts

The term "wisdom literature" is used in a general way for those texts that have several, but not necessarily all, of the following characteristics: instructional or admonitory style; practical, proverbial, or didactic advice; intellectual reflection on the order of creation, human nature, and society; a concern with the meaning of human life and fate after death; and overtly sapiential terminology. The most substantial wisdom texts in the corpus are three very different works, 4QInstruction, the *Book of Mysteries,* and *Beatitudes.* 4QInstruction combines practical advice on many different matters of life with descriptions of eschatological judgment. The work contains discourses on the predestined order of creation and the nature of human beings. It is based in part on exegesis of Genesis and displays an interest in the angelic world. The multiple levels of discourse in the text and the different topics and addressees suggest that the composition may have been a handbook for a specific group of religious teachers, who in their turn had to instruct others.

The *Book of Mysteries* comprises many diverse materials, ranging from depiction of the eschatological judgment based on interpretations of the prophets, proverbial riddles, taunts of opponents, legal discussion of Temple issues, to a Hekhalot-like hymn in 4Q301. *Beatitudes* (and *Wiles of the Wicked Woman*) can be characterized as an eschatologizing rewriting of Proverbs 1–9 and is more homogeneous than the other sapiential works.

4QInstruction, and to some extent also *Mysteries,* attest to a transformation of older wisdom traditions. These works appropriate originally non-Jewish scientific concepts (such as the horoscope and Platonic ideas about the spirit) and expand the topic of wisdom to include not only earthly but transcendent realities. The acquisition of insight depends both on the pursuit of truth (including the exegesis of Scripture) and on divine enlightenment, which allows one to have insight into transcendent secrets. One may refer to this phenomenon as the apocalypticizing of wisdom. A less speculative concern with transcendent realities, but nonetheless a concern with divine judgment, is also found in wisdom texts such as

Sapiential Work (4Q185) and *Beatitudes*. The connection of practical and religious instruction with eschatology may have a parenetic function, but it seems to reflect the status of specific scribes or teachers as knowledgeable of everything.

Such scribal sapiential interest also explains the presence of various scientific texts in the corpus, such as 4QHoroscope (4Q186), 4QPhysiognomy (4Q561), 4QZodiology and Brontology (4Q318), and perhaps also the various astronomical texts, such as *Astronomical Enoch* and 4QLunisolar Calendar (4Q317).

The major contribution of the Dead Sea Scrolls sapiential texts is that they illustrate the merging of many different kinds of knowledge, including the appropriation of non-Jewish concepts, and the fusion of diverse literary genres. This is turn suggests the rise of a new kind of Jewish scholarship that tried to integrate all available disciplines and fields of knowledge.

Envisioning the End: Apocalypses and Other Eschatological Texts

The corpus contains a variety of texts that are in some way focused on the future. Those include many Aramaic apocalyptic and visionary texts, such as the texts assigned to *Enoch* and the *New Jerusalem* text, which may be a vision of Jacob, as well as texts related to the figure or the book of Daniel, such as *Apocryphal Daniel* (4Q246), the pseudo-Danielic compositions (4Q243-245), and perhaps the *Four Kingdoms* (4Q552, 4Q553, and 4Q553a). One may add the *Words of Michael* (4Q529, 4Q571, and 6Q23) and other small fragmentary visionary or prophetic Aramaic manuscripts. It is remarkable that most apocalyptic and visionary works are written in Aramaic, which may reflect a literary preference or a special provenance for those texts.

With the possible exception of *Vision and Interpretation* (4Q410) and *Narrative A* (4Q458), eschatological texts written in Hebrew rarely have a visionary form. Instead, there are poetic descriptions of the eschatological period, such as *Time of Righteousness* (4Q215a), *Renewed Earth* (4Q475), and *Messianic Apocalypse* (4Q521), a composition on the messianic period and resurrection, as well as rules for the congregation and blessings for the "last days" (1QSa, 1QSb). The corpus includes a series of related but different manuscripts on the eschatological war. They describe the final war between the children of light and the children of darkness, assisted by the angels and the troops of Belial, respectively, and prescribe the prayers to be said at different stages of the war. Other works, like the sapiential texts and the "Treatise of the Two Spirits" (1QS 3-4), contain eschatological sections.

These eschatological texts do not present a homogeneous worldview. For example, they do not seem to share the same messianic expectations. Three general aspects of the eschatological texts illustrate their contribution to the study of early Judaism. First, most Hebrew eschatological works are based on interpretation of Scripture, including perhaps the books of *Enoch*. For example, the rules for purity in the *War Scroll* are modeled on the prescriptions in Numbers, whereas the prayers in the scroll refer to other victories described in the Scriptures (e.g., David beating Goliath). Further, both *Time of Righteousness* and *Renewed Earth* are based on prophetic texts. Second, the fusion of descriptive and prescriptive elements in the war scrolls, 1QSa, and 1QSb — which include instructions for purity and other legal issues, as well as hymns, prayers, and blessings — suggests that these texts may have had a performative use. Third, these eschatological works attest to a series of different apocalyptic themes, such as the periodization of history, expectation of the end, communion with the heavenly world, and the eschatological war. These themes are also found in other works in and outside the corpus and may therefore be seen as reflecting a broader apocalyptic mentality.

Returning to the Law: Community Rules and Related Texts

The corpus contains several so-called community rules, the most important ones being the *Serekh ha-Yaḥad (Rule of the Community),* and especially its core as found in 1QS 5–9 and in 4Q256 and 4Q258; the so-called *Damascus Document;* and the *Serek ha-Edah (Rule of the Congregation).* Each of these documents gives rules pertaining to the entry into a specific group, the organization and officials of the group, responsibilities of the members, and organization of its meetings. The *Damascus Document* and *Rule of the Community* discuss such issues as transgressions and punishments, and they describe in some detail the aims of the groups. In general terms, these rules can be compared to other rules for ancient voluntary associations. These two large rules each contain sections not preserved in the other one. Thus, the *Damascus Document* has a large admonitory review of history and a substantial legal section, including Sabbath and purity laws. Some versions of the *Rule of the Community,* including 1QS, include a description of an annual covenant ceremony and the "Treatise on the Two

Figures 1A & 1B. Photograph and artistic rendering of decorated stone dome of the Huldah Gates, Jerusalem

Figure 2. One of the well-preserved polychrome mosaics in the lower bathhouse at Herodium, showing a rosette in the center, three balls in two corners, and pomegranates in the other corners *(www.HolyLand Photos.org)*

Figure 3. Mosaic
floors at Masada

Figure 4. Artistic renderings
stone tabletops from houses
in the Upper City, Jerusalem

Figure 5. Drawing of menorah and showbread table incised on a plaster fragment from the Upper City, Jerusalem

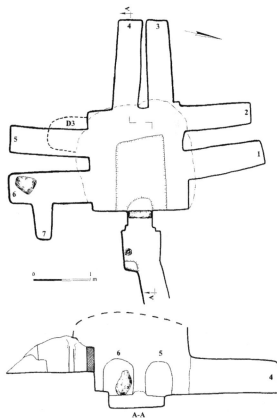

Figure 6. Plan of rock-hewn loculi tombs of the Second Temple Period

Figure 7. Plan of tombs at Qumran,
'Ein el-Ghuweir, and Jerusalem

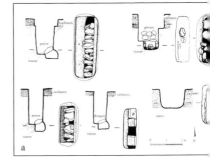

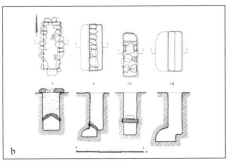

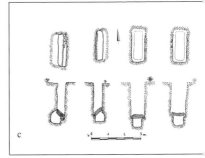

Figure 8. Four decorated ossuaries used for secondary burial of skeletal remains

9. Drawing of monumental tombs in the Kidron Valley, Jerusalem

10. Drawing of the "Goliath family" tomb at Jericho

11. Bronze prutah of Mattathias Antigonus (40-37 B.C.E.). Obverse: The Temple menorah
~~nded~~ unded by Greek legend, "The King Anti[gonus]." Reverse: The showbread table with Paleo-
~~w~~ legend, "Mattityah high priest." *(Israel Museum inventory nos. 3650, 14232)*

12. Shekel from year one of the First Jewish Revolt. The Hebrew shekel depicts a chalice on
~~verse~~ and a branch with three pomegranates encircled by a border of dots on the reverse.
~~d~~ in Jerusalem 66 C.E. *(Israel Museum, inventory no. 1475)*

Figure 13. The Siloam Hoard of Tyrian and Jewish shekels from the First Jewish Revolt (66–70 C.E.) originally held approximately 40 coins, of which only 12 remain. These coins provided one of the first clues for the correct dating of Jewish shekels from the First Revolt. *(Israel Museum)*

Figure 14. Silver denarius minted by Vespasian to celebrate suppression of the Judean revolt. Judea is personified as a woman seated in mourning beneath a Roman victory trophy, with IVDAE[A] written underneath. *(Richard Cleave)*

Figure 15. The Bar Kokhba Revolt Hoard (135 C.E.), a sampling of coins in circulation during the period. The hoard includes Roman and Bar Kokhba coins that were themselves struck over Roman originals. *(Israel Museum)*

Figure 16. Fragment of a papyrus contract
written in Greek from the Zenon Archive
(University of Michigan)

Figure 17. Marriage contract *(ketubba)*
from the Babatha Archive

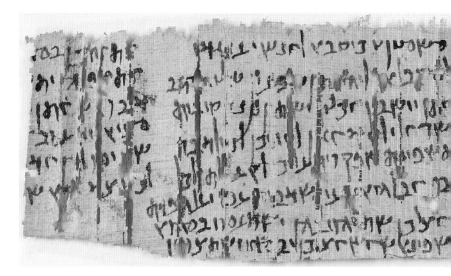

Figure 18. Hebrew letter of Ben Kosiba (Bar Kokhba) dispatched to 'Ein Gedi, reprim[anding] Masabala and Yehonatan for "living well, eating and drinking off the property of the Ho[use of] Israel, and [caring] nothing about your brethren" *(Photo Clara Amit, Courtesy Israel Ant[iquities] Authority)*

Figure 19. Two pages of a papyrus codex showing text from the book of Leviticus in [Greek.] Dating to ca. 200 C.E., this is one of the oldest Septuagint manuscripts extant for the book [of Le-] viticus *(The Schøyen Collection, MS 2649)*

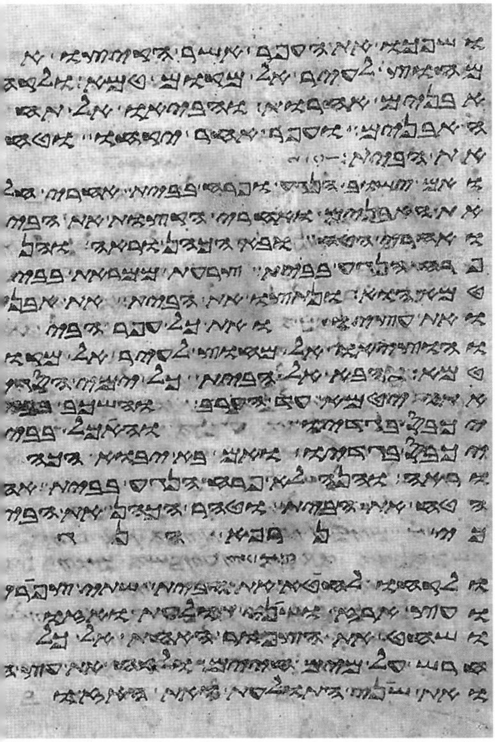

Figure 20. A page from Leviticus in a medieval copy of the Samaritan Pentateuch (Ascalon, Israel, 1189 C.E.) *(The Schøyen Collection, MS 201)*

Figure 21. Folio 422v (Ruth 3:13b–4:13a) of the Leningrad Codex *(Photograph by Bruce and Kenneth Zuckerman, West Semitic Research, in collaboration with the Ancient Biblical Manuscript Center. Courtesy Russian National Library [Saltykov-Shchedrin])*

Figure 22. Page of a fifteenth-century-C.E. Ethiopian Bible with the text of 1 Enoch in Ge'ez book script. The complete 1 Enoch is known only in the Ethiopic version. *(The Schøyen Collection, MS 1748)*

Figure 23. The Abba inscription on the wall of a tomb found north of the Old City of Jerusalem, is written in Aramaic using Paleo-Hebrew script. It describes the occupant of the tomb as "Abba, of the priest Eleaz(ar), son of Aaron the high (priest)." *(Courtesy Israel Antiquities Authority)*

Figure 24. The Theodotus inscription, marking the dedication of a synagogue in Jerusalem in the first century C.E. (CIJ 2.1400, Greek uncials on limestone, 75 cm. × 41 cm.) *(Courtesy Israel Antiquities Authority)*

Figure 25. A Greek inscription from the Jerusalem Temple forbidding entry by Gentiles into the courts of the Temple on pain of death *(Courtesy Israel Antiquities Authority)*

Figure 26. An inscription found in the theater at Caesarea Maritima: "Pontius Pilatus, Prefect of Judea, has presented the Tiberieum to the Caesareans" *(Phoenix Data Systems/Neal and Joel Bierling)*

Figure 27. Bronze mirrors with wooden mirror cases from the Cave of Letters in Naḥal Ḥever *(Israel Exploration Society)*

Figure 28. Wool tunics with colored stripes *(clavi)* from the Cave of Letters in Naḥal Ḥever *(Israel Exploration Society)*

e 29. Cosmetic items
dwellings of Jewish reb-
Masada, including a
en comb (lower right),
nze mirror case (upper
, and bronze eye-
w sticks (lower left)

Figure 30. A spindle whorl (upper left), wooden combs (center), and an iron cosmetic spoon (lower right) from the caves in Wadi Murabbaʿat

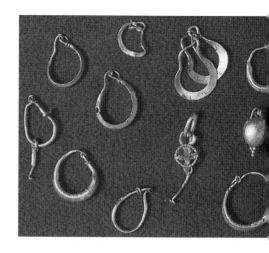

Figure 31. Gold earrings of the Roman period found in burial caves around Jerusalem *(Renate Rosenthal-Heginbottom)*

Figure 32. A carnelian intaglio with the zodiac sign of the scorpion from the Burnt House in Jerusalem *(Renate Rosenthal-Heginbottom)*

Figure 33. Carnelian and glass beads for a necklace, from a tomb at ʿEin Gedi *(Renate Rosenthal-Heginbottom)*

Figure 34. A set of Eastern Sigillata A dishes from the "Herodian Residence" in Jerusalem's Jewish Quarter *(Institute of Archaeology, Hebrew University, Jerusalem)*

e 35. Jerusalem painted or
do-Nabatean" bowls from the
entury-C.E. mansions in Jeru-
's Jewish Quarter *(Institute of
ology, Hebrew University,
lem)*

e 36. Overview of Khirbet Qumran and surrounding area *(Phoenix Data Systems/Neal and Joel
ig)*

Figure 37. Original entrance to Cave 4, first discovered by the Bedouin in 1954

Figure 38. Cylindrical pottery jars with lids ("scroll jars") found in caves near Qumran (height: 40-50 cm.) *(Courtesy Israel Antiquities Authority)*

39. View of the miqveh in L48-L49 at Qumran. Notice the low, plastered partitions on the [ ]nd the earthquake damage which has caused the left-hand side of the steps to drop. *[ ]agness)*

Figure 40. Fragment of an Aramaic papyrus manuscript of Tobit (4Q196) from Qumran (ca. 50 B.C.E.) *(The Schøyen Collection, MS 5234)*

Figure 41. 1QS Rule of the Community Scroll. This document contains rules and regulations for the community at Qumran.
(John C. Trever)

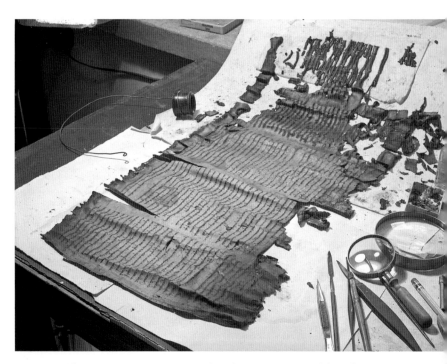

Figure 42. The Aramaic Genesis Apocryphon (1Q20 or 1QapGen) found in Cave 1 near Qum
(Israel Museum)

Figure 43. Column 8 of the Pesher on Habakkuk (1QpHab) found in Cave 1 near Qumran (*John C. Trever*)

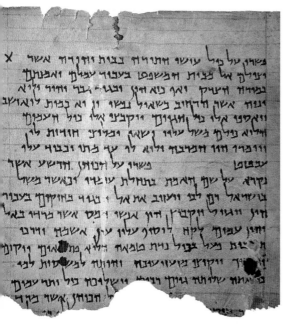

44. Column 6 of the Isaiah Scroll (1QIsaᵃ) in Cave 1 near an (*John C. Trever*)

Figure 45. Psalms Scroll from Qumran (11QPs^a) *(Courtesy Israel Antiquities Authority)*

Figure 46. Columns 43–44 of the Temple Scroll (11Q19 or 11QTemple^a) *(Photograph by Br... Kenneth Zuckerman, West Semitic Research. Courtesy Shrine of the Book)*

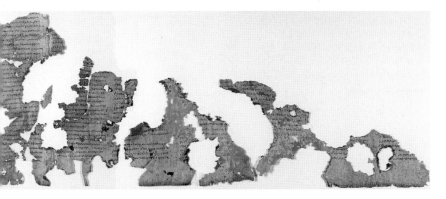

47. Fragments of the Greek Minor Prophets Scroll from Naḥal Ḥever (8ḤevXIIgr)
sy Israel Antiquities Authority)

Figure 48. 4Q394 MMTᵃ and 4Q395 MMTᵇ, fragments from the "Some of the Works of the Torah" document (*Courtesy Israel Antiquities Authority*)

Figure 49. 4Q175 Testimonia
(Photograph by Bruce and Kenneth
Zuckerman, West Semitic Research, in
collaboration with Princeton Theological
Seminary. Courtesy Department of
Antiquities, Jordan)

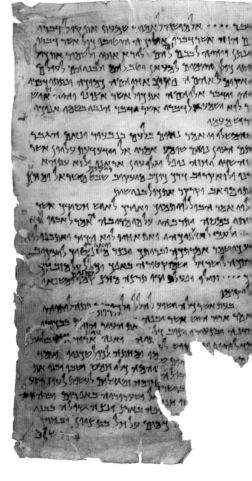

Figure 50. Phylactery cases from Qumran.
The case to the right (2.2 cm. × 1.2 cm.) is a
single-compartment case and was worn on
the arm. The two cases below (2-3 cm. × 1.2
cm.) contain four compartments and were
worn on the forehead. (Courtesy Israel
Antiquities Authority)

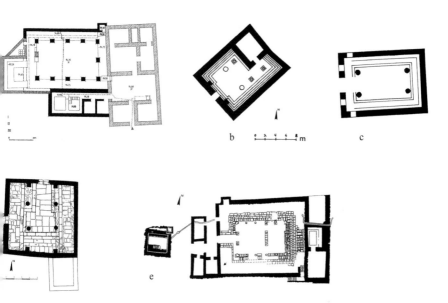

51. Synagogues of the Second Temple period

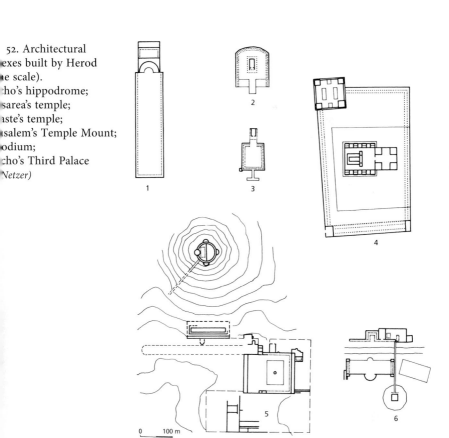

52. Architectural
exes built by Herod
e scale).
ho's hippodrome;
sarea's temple;
aste's temple;
salem's Temple Mount;
odium;
cho's Third Palace
Netzer)

Figure 53. The amphitheater-hippodrome built by Herod the Great at Caesarea Maritima *(www.HolyLandPhotos.com)*

Figure 54. View looking north at the northern *parados* — the vaulted entrance through portions of the audience would enter and exit the theater at Caesarea. On the right side of t age a portion of the *cavea* (seating area) is visible. *(www.HolyLandPhotos.com)*

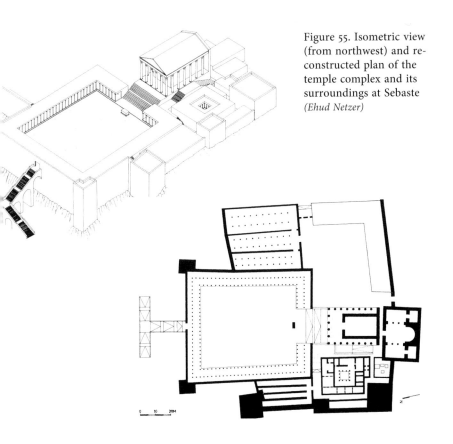

Figure 55. Isometric view (from northwest) and reconstructed plan of the temple complex and its surroundings at Sebaste (Ehud Netzer)

56. Herodium, mountain palace-fortress of Herod the Great (Hanan Isachar)

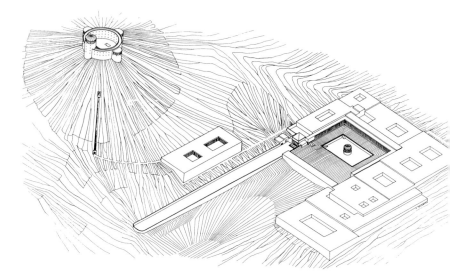

Figure 57. View of Greater Herodium from the northeast *(Ehud Netzer)*

Figure 58. Herod the Great's main palace in Jerusalem, with the three multistoried towers a[t] Antonia Fortress in the background *(www.HolyLandPhotos.com)*

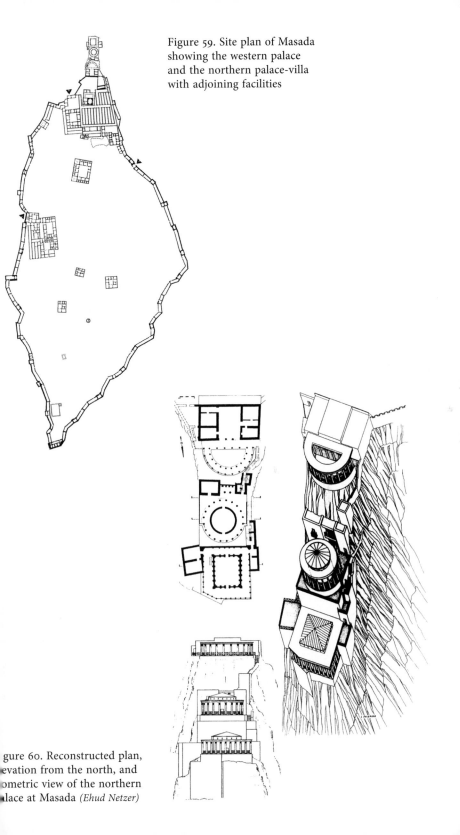

Figure 59. Site plan of Masada showing the western palace and the northern palace-villa with adjoining facilities

Figure 60. Reconstructed plan, elevation from the north, and isometric view of the northern palace at Masada *(Ehud Netzer)*

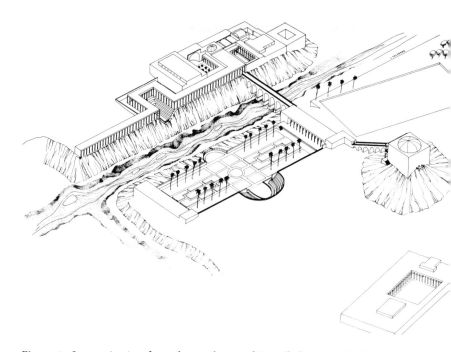

Figure 61. Isometric view from the southwest of Herod's first and third palaces at Jericho
(Ehud Netzer)

Figure 62. View of Jerusalem looking east-southeast, showing Herod's palace in the foreground
and the stadium and theater in the background *(www.HolyLandPhotos.org)*

63. View of Jerusalem looking north, showing the four towers of the Antonia Fortress on
ht (east) *(www.HolyLandPhotos.org)*

64. View of Jerusalem just north of the Herodian palace complex showing in the back-
d the Temple and, on the far left, two towers of the Antonia Fortress
HolyLandPhotos.org)

Figure 65. View looking west at the eastern facades of the Herodian Temple in Jerusalem. (balustrade surrounding the whole was a series of inscriptions forbidding Gentiles from er the more sacred areas of the Temple *(www.HolyLandPhotos.org)*

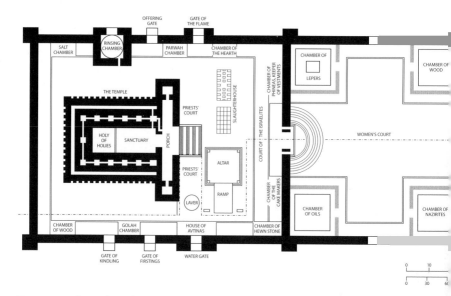

Figure 66. Floor plan of Herod's Temple *(Adapted from Encyclopedia Judaica)*

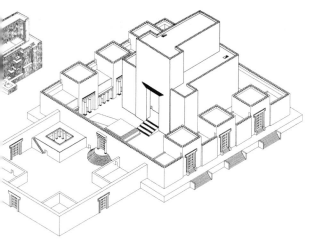

Figure 67. Isometric views of the temple (left: after Joseph Patrich; right: by Ehud Netzer) *(Ehud Netzer)*

68. Remains of the Burnt in Jerusalem, evidence of the tion of the city by the s in the year 70 C.E. *(Phoenix stems/Neal and Joel Bierling)*

Figure 69. Ballista balls used in the Roman siege of Masada *(Phoenix Data Systems/ Neal and Joel Bierling)*

Figure 70. Replicas of the Roman siege engines used at Masada in the mopping-up operat͏͏ the First Revolt *(Phoenix Data Systems/Neal and Joel Bierling)*

Figure 71. Arch of Titus, relief of the spoils of the Jerusalem (Second) Temple

Spirits," and end with a thanksgiving hymn, whereas the version preserved in 4Q259 ends with a calendrical text (*'Otot*).

The groups depicted in the main rules differ in various respects. The *Damascus Document* describes different groups but focuses on the congregation of those Israelite households or families who lived in cities and camps throughout the land, and who committed themselves to return to the Law of Moses as it should apply to all Israel, according to its correct interpretation. The *Rule of the Community* uses another word, *yaḥad*, to refer to groups at different locations. It never refers to women or families but only to the "men of the community." The work mentions an oath to return to the Law of Moses, stresses communal activities, emphasizes the handing over of one's property to the inspector, and describes a complex admission procedure. Both rules refer to a subgroup that aspires to a higher degree of holy perfection, but whereas this is mentioned only in passing in CD 7, the *Rule of the Community* discusses at length a real or ideal subgroup of twelve men and three priests who in some way had a higher degree of holiness. The example of the *Rule of the Congregation,* which refers to both "the congregation" and "the council of the *yaḥad*," cautions that one cannot make an easy distinction between the congregation and the *yaḥad*.

Several manuscripts in the corpus may be directly connected to the *Damascus Document* or the *Community Rule,* due to shared organizational expressions that are not found elsewhere. Thus, for example, the term "the Community" is very rare outside of the *Rule of the Community* and the *Rule of the Congregation,* and the few other manuscripts with this term would seem to refer to the same group. This goes for several of the pesharim, for legal texts like *Miscellaneous Rules* (4Q265) and *Harvesting* (4Q284a), and for the liturgical text *Blessings,* which includes blessings and curses that are very similar to those mentioned in 1QS 2. Another document, *Rebukes of the Overseer* (4Q477), records rebukes as described both in the *Damascus Document* and the *Rule of the Community,* and mentions the *yaḥad*. The Teacher of Righteousness appears in the *Damascus Document* and has a special role in several pesharim, specifically the *Habakkuk Pesher,* which also refers to the *yaḥad*. The fragmentary manuscripts *Communal Ceremony* (4Q275) and *Rule* (5Q13), which mention the "overseer" and refer to an annual ceremony, may be connected to either of the main rules.

Taken in themselves, these different rules give an unprecedented insight into aspects of the formation, organization, practices, and beliefs of early Jewish groups or movements on the basis of their different interpretation of the Law.

The Nature and Significance of the Corpus

Apart from specific organizational expressions, the rule scrolls attest to communal ritual, disagreements about calendrical matters, legal rulings with regard to everyday practices, a cosmological and ethical dualistic worldview, apocalyptic or eschatological expectations, and views on Scripture and authority. Many other texts in the corpus reflect the same or similar interests or views, sometimes expressed in identical formulations. For example, the introduction of 1QS is directly connected to 1QM since both oppose the "sons of light" to the "sons of darkness." Or, with hindsight, now that we know all the Cave 4 calendrical texts, it is easy to recognize how both the *Damascus Document* and the *Hymn of the Maskil* at the end of the *Rule of the Community* put forth a 364-day calendar, a point which is made even more explicit by the inclusion of the *'Otot* in one of the *Rule of the Community* manuscripts. A third example — in various compositions, including the two rules — is the attribution to the *maśkîl* of laws, hymns, and instructions, which probably indicates that this sage was to recite or teach them. In other cases, connections between texts consist of multiple shared locutions, such as those between the *Apocryphon of Jeremiah* and the *Damascus Document*.

Such connections illustrate that many works in the corpus are interlinked and should be related to a current in early Judaism that comprised the movements described in the *Damascus Document* and the *Rule of the Community*, and probably also to the circles responsible for *Jubilees* and the *Temple Scroll*. It is a challenge for scholarship to unravel the precise relationships among different texts and groups. However, the different versions of both the *Damascus Document* and the *Rule of the Community*, and the likelihood of different layers in those works, show that within this current the different movements and their compositions were in flux and that they changed and influenced one another. Likewise, manuscripts of other compositions may have been edited or revised in order to appropriate them, or to adjust them to the interests of specific copyists or movements, a phenomenon which can be seen, for example, in the Cave 4 versions of the *Aramaic Levi Document*.

There is no evidence that before their deposit in the caves all the manuscripts of the corpus were together as a single collection. Nor can one know, for that matter, whether all those manuscripts that were together at a certain time in the same place were actively read and studied or were merely deposited. Even the status of Cave 4 — as a library, repository, temporary place of concealment, or perhaps even a genizah — is unclear. And we do not know the precise historical events that led to their deposit in different caves near Qumran. But from the contents of the manuscripts, we may conclude that the corpus is not a random reflection of all kinds of available Jewish texts of the time but representative of a specific current in early Judaism.

Two vital perspectives are constitutive of the corpus. First, the corpus as a whole — from *Jubilees* and the *Temple Scroll* to the pesharim, legal texts, and Moses apocrypha — attests to a variety of strategies for interpreting Scripture, ranging from reworking and various degrees of rewriting, to expansion with new scriptures, exegesis, and commentary. Some texts in the corpus imply, others indicate explicitly, that the correct interpretation of Scripture is attained by exegesis, which may be confirmed by divine revelation of those things that hitherto had been hidden (i.e., not included in the Scriptures). The authority of interpreted Scripture may also go beyond the traditional "rewritten Scripture" texts and hold true for hymns and prayers like the *Hodayot*. For the study of the corpus, this perspective demands a more sophisticated approach in differentiating between the Scriptures and other writings, between revelation and interpretation.

Second, by and large the corpus represents a legal interpretive tradition that can be related to both *Jubilees* and the *Temple Scroll* (notwithstanding differences between those two works). The most decisive element is the 364-day calendar as the basis for the religious festival calendar, which is either stated explicitly or implied in a variety of texts of the corpus (e.g., *Jubilees, Temple Scroll, David's Compositions* in the Cave 11 *Psalms Scroll, Commentary on Genesis A, Songs of the Sabbath Sacrifice,* as well as a variety of calendrical texts). It is moot to what extent this 364-day festival calendar was actually designed on the basis of scriptural exegesis, or was practiced in some form in pre-Seleucid times. In both cases, the adherence to a 364-day calendar, as opposed to the one observed in the Temple, links the different circles and movements represented in the corpus.

From this perspective, and with the limited undisputed historical data we have, it makes most sense to study the corpus primarily as the product of a specific early Jewish current consisting of different interlinked groups and movements with a common interpretative approach to Scripture and a shared legal tradition.

BIBLIOGRAPHY

Alexander, Philip. 2006. *The Mystical Texts: Songs of the Sabbath Sacrifice and Related Manuscripts.* London: Clark.

Berthelot, Katell, and Daniel Stökl Ben Ezra. 2010. *Aramaica Qumranica: Proceedings of the Conference on the Aramaic Texts from Qumran in aix-en-Provence, 30 June–2 July 2008.* Leiden: Brill, 2010.

Collins, John J. 2002. *Apocalypticism in the Dead Sea Scrolls.* London: Routledge.

———. 2010a. *Beyond the Qumran Community: The Sectarian Movement of the Dead Sea Scrolls.* Grand Rapids: Eerdmans.

———. 2010b. *The Scepter and the Star: The Messiahs of the Dead Sea Scrolls in Context.* 2d ed. Grand Rapids: Eerdmans.

———. 2012. *The Dead Sea Scrolls: A Biography.* Princeton: Princeton University Press.

Dávid, Nóra, Armin Lange, Kristin De Troyer, and Shani Tzoref, eds. 2012. *The Hebrew Bible in Light of the Dead Sea Scrolls.* Göttingen: Vandenhoeck & Ruprecht.

Dimant, Devorah, ed. 2012. *The Dead Sea Scrolls in Scholarly Perspective: A History of Research.* Leiden: Brill.

Duhaime, Jean. 2004. *The War Texts: 1QM and Related Manuscripts.* London: Clark.

Falk, Daniel K. 2007. *The Parabiblical Texts: Strategies for Extending the Scriptures among the Dead Sea Scrolls.* London: Clark.

Fields, Weston W. 2009. *The Dead Sea Scrolls: A Full History.* Vol. 1. Leiden: Brill.

Flint, Peter W., and James C. VanderKam, eds. 1998-1999. *The Dead Sea Scrolls after Fifty Years: A Comprehensive Assessment.* 2 vols. Leiden: Brill.

García Martínez, Florentino. 1996. *The Dead Sea Scrolls Translated.* 2d ed. Grand Rapids: Eerdmans.

———. 2008. "¿Sectario, no-sectario, o qué? Problemas de una taxonomía correcta de los textos qumránicos." *RevQ* 23/91: 383-94.

Goff, Matthew J. 2007. *Discerning Wisdom: The Sapiential Literature of the Dead Sea Scrolls.* Leiden: Brill.

Grossman, Maxine, ed. 2010. *Rediscovering the Dead Sea Scrolls: An Assessment of Old and New Approaches and Methods.* Grand Rapids: Eerdmans.

Jokiranta, Jutta. 2005. "Identity on a Continuum: Constructing and Expressing Sectarian Social Identity in Qumran Serakhim and Pesharim." Dissertation, University of Helsinki.

Lange, Armin, with Ulrike Mittman-Richert. 2002. "Annotated List of the Texts from the Judaean Desert Classified by Content and Genre." In *The Texts from the Judaean Desert: Indices and an Introduction to the Discoveries in the Judaean Desert Series.* Ed. Emanuel Tov. Oxford: Clarendon, 115-64.

Lim, Timothy H. 2002. *Pesharim.* Sheffield: Sheffield Academic Press.

————, and John J. Collins, eds. 2010. *The Oxford Handbook of the Dead Sea Scrolls.* Oxford: Oxford University Press.

Parry, Donald, and Emanuel Tov, eds. 2004-2005. *The Dead Sea Scrolls Reader.* 6 vols. Leiden: Brill.

Reed, Stephen A. 2007. "Find-Sites of the Dead Sea Scrolls." *DSD* 14: 199-221.

Schiffman, Lawrence H. 2008. *The Courtyards of the House of the Lord: Studies on the Temple Scroll.* Leiden: Brill.

————, and James C. VanderKam, eds. 2000. *Encyclopedia of the Dead Sea Scrolls.* 2 vols. New York: Oxford University Press.

Schofield, Alison. 2009. *From Qumran to the Yaḥad: A New Paradigm of Textual Development for the Community Rule.* Leiden: Brill.

Shemesh, Aharon. 2009. *Halakhah in the Making: The Development of Jewish Law from Qumran to the Rabbis.* Berkeley: University of California Press.

Tov, Emanuel. 2004. *Scribal Practices and Approaches Reflected in the Texts Found in the Judean Desert.* Leiden: Brill.

Ulrich, Eugene. 1999. *The Dead Sea Scrolls and the Origins of the Bible.* Grand Rapids: Eerdmans.

VanderKam, James C. 2010. *The Dead Sea Scrolls Today.* 2d ed. Grand Rapids: Eerdmans.

————. 2012. *The Dead Sea Scrolls and the Bible.* Grand Rapids: Eerdmans.

Vermes, Geza. 1997. *The Complete Dead Sea Scrolls in English.* New York: Lane.

White Crawford, Sidnie. 2008. *Rewriting Scriptures in Second Temple Times.* Grand Rapids: Eerdmans.

Zahn, Molly M. 2011. *Rethinking Rewritten Scripture: Composition and Exegesis in the 4QReworked Pentateuch Manuscripts.* Leiden: Brill.

Early Jewish Literature Written in Greek

Katell Berthelot

A large number and great variety of early Jewish works were composed in Greek, but many of them survive only in excerpts quoted by church fathers. Our knowledge of Jewish thought and literature in the Greek-speaking Diaspora therefore depends to a large extent on the care with which Christian authors and scribes quoted and copied their Jewish sources. Yet the selective interests and apologetic agendas of the Christian transmitters means that they handed on only what was of use to them. These works not only enriched Judaism but also engaged Hellenism. Taken together, they demonstrate that Jews were able to embrace several aspects of Hellenistic culture while maintaining their Jewish identity in a creative, critical, and at times even subversive appropriation of Greek literary genres, mythological figures, and philosophical concepts. Many of these works take their inspiration from biblical traditions and attempt to solve exegetical problems or else refashion them. Others celebrate the superiority of Judaism over pagan religions in an attempt to strengthen the identity of their Jewish readerships.

The Nature of the Corpus

Several Greek texts will be set aside here, either because their original language was Hebrew or Aramaic (e.g., 1 Maccabees and Tobit), because their Jewish origin is uncertain (e.g., Thallus and Theophilus, who were probably pagan writers), because they have been significantly altered or perhaps even composed by Christians (e.g., *3 Baruch, 4 Baruch, Testament of Abraham*), or because their original language of composition is uncertain (e.g.,

2 *Enoch, Life of Adam and Eve*). The decision to put aside Greek translations of texts originally written in Hebrew or Aramaic means that we will
not deal with the Septuagint as such. We will, however, discuss writings in
the Septuagint that were composed in Greek and have occasion to emphasize that many Jewish authors writing in Greek used the Septuagint and
were influenced by its terminology.

Jewish writings composed in Greek are not the only documents to
qualify as Hellenistic Jewish literature or Judeo-Hellenistic literature. Every piece of Jewish literature produced during the Hellenistic and early
Roman periods may be labeled "Hellenistic" regardless of the language in
which it was written. For this reason, "Hellenistic" is too vague a term, except as a chronological label for the period extending from the conquests
of Alexander the Great in the fourth century B.C.E. to the end of the first
century B.C.E. It is also somewhat problematic: for those who think that
"authentic" Judaism necessarily expressed itself in Hebrew or Aramaic,
the term "Hellenistic" carries strong pejorative connotations. More to the
point, Hellenism was itself a mingling of different cultures, that of the
Greco-Macedonians and that of the Eastern peoples whom they conquered. To single out some Jewish texts written in Greek as "Hellenized"
implies that Hellenism and Judaism are two different and intrinsically an-
tagonist cultural phenomena, a view that is certainly advocated by the author of 2 Maccabees but that does not necessarily reflect the historical reality of that time. The relationship between Greek and Jewish culture was
far more complex.

Since some of the relevant texts adapt distinctively Greek genres, such
as tragedy (Ezekiel the Tragedian) and epic poetry (Theodotus), one might
well speak of Greek literature that is Jewish instead of Jewish literature
written in Greek. When the latter expression is used, the focus is laid right
from the start on the Jewish character of this literature, implying that the
linguistic dimension is secondary. But how are we to define Jewish literature in antiquity? What makes an ancient text Jewish? Scholars have traditionally appealed to two criteria: (1) content based on biblical tradition or
containing distinctively Jewish themes or terminology; (2) the Jewishness
of the author, which may be attested by reliable external sources or inferred from his name or from the topic (which takes us back to the first criterion). These criteria have their limits in some cases. The *Sentences* of
Pseudo-Phocylides offers a good example. For centuries this text was regarded as an original composition of Phocylides, a sixth-century-B.C.E.
Greek poet, and not as a Jewish text. It was only in the sixteenth century

that Joseph Scaliger pointed up its Jewish origin. The content is not so distinctively Jewish as to allow the reader to identify its author as a Jew. This interesting example should warn us that a Greek text attributed to a Greek philosopher or historian may be a Jewish text. Not all Jewish literature is "obviously Jewish."

Due to a lack of information, we must exclude from the corpus texts written by Jews who either had no commitment to their cultural heritage and religious tradition, or who chose to express themselves on topics that had little or nothing to do with the characteristic features of Judaism. Conversely, we will mention in passing authors who are not Jewish but who excerpted Jewish writings (e.g., Alexander Polyhistor) or who mentioned Jews and Judaism in a way that invited a response from early Jewish authors (Manetho, Apion).

One more reason to be cautious is that nearly all the Jewish texts written in Greek have been transmitted to us through Christian channels. Moreover, some of the church fathers — Clement of Alexandria and Eusebius, in particular — depended on Alexander Polyhistor, a Greek historian active during the first century B.C.E. The evidence we have is thus indirect, and it should not been taken for granted that we have the *ipsissima verba* of the Jewish authors whose works are now lost. What is more, the church fathers who quoted early Jewish writers such as Aristobulus, Eupolemus, and Artapanus did not attempt to preserve Jewish literature as such. They were looking for proofs of the antiquity of biblical revelation, in order to respond to pagan critics such as Celsus and Porphyry. What they ultimately wanted to show was that Christianity was not a new cult but a respectable religion with very ancient roots, even older than Greek civilization itself. Since Jewish authors had taken pains to demonstrate the antiquity of the Jewish people and the influence Moses exercised on Homer, Pythagoras, Plato, and others, their writings represented a providential pool of arguments for the church fathers. In Josephus, they also valued references to events contemporary with Jesus' life and the view that the Jewish defeat in the First Revolt was a punishment for the sins of the Jewish people, the Christian interpretation of what Josephus wrote being that the Jews had sinned in rejecting Jesus. The case of Philo is different, since many church fathers sincerely admired his work and took inspiration from his allegorical exegesis. Nevertheless, they used Jewish literature written in Greek with their own agenda in mind, an agenda that was clearly apologetic. They frequently manipulated the works they were quoting, either by omitting the context or by modifying the text. In short, the preservation and transmission of early Jewish literature written in Greek is itself problematic. This, in turn, helps explain why so many of the texts rewrite, explicate, or refer to the Bible: the corpus itself reflects to a great extent the church fathers' selective interests.

The Use of Biblical Traditions

Most early Jewish works composed in Greek that have come down to us deal with biblical topics. Obviously, in the case of works that survive only in fragments, we do not know exactly what topics were dealt with in the sections that have not been preserved. At any rate, the evidence we have looks roughly as follows: ten works deal partly or exclusively with the book of Genesis and eight with the book of Exodus; one is based on a story from the book of Judges; two refer in some way to the history of the kings of Judah (roughly 2 Samuel through 2 Kings); one is based on the book of Jonah; and two retell the story of Job. The works of Philo and Josephus, which are particularly long and well preserved, deal with a greater variety of biblical texts: the whole Pentateuch and even, in the case of Josephus, most of the books eventually included in the Masoretic canon, plus a few others.

Writings Based on Genesis

Among the Jewish writers who wrote about Genesis, Demetrius probably comes first. He evokes the episode of Isaac's sacrifice, the fate of Jacob, his two wives and his twelve sons, and the story of Joseph, focusing on chronological issues (frgs. 1 and 2). Then we have Artapanus, who recalls Abraham's descent to Egypt, mentions that he taught Pharaoh astrology, and retells the story of Joseph, attributing to him agricultural reform as well as the invention of measures (frgs. 1 and 2).

Other creative rewritings of the Genesis account include fragments of two authors known through Polyhistor: Cleodemus and Pseudo-Eupolemus. Cleodemus freely elaborates upon Gen. 25:1-4, which lists Abraham's offspring by his wife Keturah. He imagines that two sons of Abraham helped Heracles fight Antaeus, and that one of them, called Aphran, even gave him his daughter in marriage. Pseudo-Eupolemus, who probably was a Samaritan, and who seems to have used Berossus's *Bab-*

yloniaca, focuses on Abraham's discovery of astrology and astronomy, a science that he taught to the Phoenicians. He further refers to the war Abraham waged to free his nephew Lot, to the way he was welcomed in the sanctuary located on Mt. Gerizim (hence the identification of Pseudo-Eupolemus as a Samaritan), and to his encounter with Melchizedek. Like Artapanus, Pseudo-Eupolemus also mentions Abraham's stay in Egypt and says that he taught astrology and other sciences to the Egyptian priests. The first discovery of astrology is said to go back to Enoch, whereas the Babylonians attributed it to Belus and the Greeks to Atlas.

From a completely different perspective, the exegete and philosopher Aristobulus treats the significance of the Sabbath, which he connects to the creation account in Genesis 1 rather than to the liberation from Egypt, as in Deuteronomy 5. The epic poet Philo deals with the Binding of Isaac in Genesis 22 (frgs. 1 and 2), evidently construing it as a ritual that was pleasing to God. He also mentions the patriarchs Abraham, Isaac, Jacob, and Joseph (frg. 3). The epic poet Theodotus focuses especially on the story of Dinah and the vengeance against Shechem (Genesis 34), at least in the forty-seven lines that have come down to us from Eusebius, who took his excerpts from Alexander Polyhistor.

Philo of Alexandria deals at length with the book of Genesis in several of his works, especially in the allegorical commentary and in his *Questions and Answers on Genesis.* Josephus rewrites Genesis at the beginning of his *Jewish Antiquities.* Finally, the anonymous work entitled *Joseph and Aseneth* tells the story of the conversion of Aseneth, the daughter of an Egyptian priest, to Judaism, and of her marriage to the patriarch Joseph. Other texts allude here and there to characters or episodes from the book of Genesis — for instance, 4 Maccabees 13:12 and 16:20 refer to the *Aqedah* — but these matters do not constitute the main topic of the book.

Writings Based on Exodus

The book of Exodus is well represented too, sometimes in the same works. Demetrius addresses chronological as well as exegetical issues concerning the exodus (frgs. 3-5). Artapanus rewrites not only the story of Joseph but also that of Moses, whom he presents as the teacher of Orpheus and the inventor of several branches of learning, including philosophy. According to Artapanus, Moses was a great cultural benefactor who gave Egypt its political and religious institutions. Artapanus also retells the story of the exodus.

Eupolemus (frg. 1) writes that Moses was the first wise man as well as the first lawgiver and that he invented the alphabet and gave it to the Jews, who then passed it down to the Phoenicians, who in turn taught it to the Greeks. Aristobulus tries to explain some anthropomorphisms in the book of Exodus, such as the expression "the hand of God" (frg. 2), and addresses the issue of the date of the Passover (frg. 1).

A certain Ezekiel wrote a whole tragedy based on the story of the Exodus, in which he recalls the events from Moses's birth until the destruction of the Egyptian army. Fragment 16 mentions the arrival of the Hebrews at Elim (Exod. 15:27), and fragment 17 describes the extraordinary bird known as the phoenix. The Wisdom of Solomon also deals at length with the story of the exodus and the fate of the Egyptians, in order to demonstrate the perfection of God's justice.

Philo of Alexandria probably examined every verse of the book of Exodus in his *Questions and Answers on Exodus,* most of which is now lost. He also comments on the exodus in his *Life of Moses* and in several passages throughout his corpus. Josephus rewrites Exodus in the *Jewish Antiquities* and also deals with the historical accuracy of the biblical account in his apologetic book *Against Apion,* in which he tries to refute slanderous accounts of the origins of the Jewish people.

To this list one may add the *Letter of Aristeas* and 3 Maccabees, insofar as the biblical story of the exodus constitutes an implicit background for both. However, apart from very limited references, the exodus is not explicitly dealt with in these two works, which are concerned with more recent "historical" events.

Writings Based on Other Biblical Books

The other books of the Torah — Leviticus, Numbers, and Deuteronomy — were apparently given much less attention, but this is probably a misleading picture. The church fathers who quoted Jewish authors were not interested in their interpretation of specific commandments but were looking for testimonies about the patriarchs — hence their interest in passages from Genesis and the beginning of Exodus. However, the Wisdom of Solomon (chap. 12) alludes to specific passages from Deuteronomy (and perhaps from Joshua) that refer to the fate of the Canaanites. The works that deal most extensively with Leviticus, Numbers, and Deuteronomy are Philo's *On the Special Laws* and Josephus's *Jewish Antiquities* (3.208–4.331).

Occasionally, other biblical books inspired works written in Greek. Demetrius's work was actually entitled *Concerning the Kings in Judea,* and the sixth fragment is a chronological summary of Israel's history based on material from 2 Kings. One of Eupolemus's works is also known as *Concerning the Kings in Judea.* Fragments 2 to 4, which refer to another book by Eupolemus entitled *Concerning the Prophecy of Elijah,* rely on the Deuteronomistic History in general, especially 2 Samuel though 2 Kings, and perhaps Jeremiah as well. Eupolemus (frg. 5) also attempted chronological calculations, from Adam to the reign of Demetrius I Soter (162-150 B.C.E.). He seems to have been followed by Justus of Tiberias, who apparently wrote a *Chronicle of Jewish Kings* (from Moses to Agrippa II), perhaps a comprehensive world chronicle, which was used by later Christian chroniclers but has not survived. In his *Jewish Antiquities,* Josephus rewrites the history of the Jewish people from Adam to the time of Nero and therefore uses a great diversity of biblical books, including ones written in the Hellenistic period like Daniel and Esther. He also uses Jewish books that were not included in the rabbinic canon, such as the *Letter of Aristeas* and 1 Maccabees.

Among the Jewish authors quoted by the church fathers is a certain Aristeas, often called "the Exegete" to distinguish him from the narrator of the *Letter of Aristeas.* He wrote the book *On the Jews* and summarized the story of Job, probably at the end of his account of Genesis (since Job is presented as a son of Esau). The pseudepigraphic *Testament of Job* rewrites more extensively the story of this pious character, presenting him as a convert who purifies a nearby temple from its idolatrous cult and as a consequence is persecuted by Satan. Finally, two Jewish synagogal sermons originally written in Greek and wrongly attributed to Philo have been transmitted to us in an Armenian translation. The first one is based on the book of Jonah, the second on the story of Samson in the book of Judges.

Writings with Little or No Basis in Biblical Tradition

Before we turn to a different aspect of Jewish literature written in Greek, a few words should be said about the works that do not evoke biblical characters and topics in an explicit or significant way. To this category belong several pseudepigrapha: the Pseudo-Orphic verses, Pseudo-Hecataeus, the Jewish *Sibylline Oracles,* and Pseudo-Phocylides. To this group we may add the *Letter of Aristeas,* which is not a pseudepigraph *stricto sensu,* since no famous Greek writer named Aristeas is known to us, but which pretends to be written by a Greek instead of a Jew. That no reference to the Bible should be found in texts purportedly written by non-Jews comes as no surprise. However, there are biblical expressions or implicit references to biblical texts in works like the *Sibylline Oracles* and the *Sentences* of Pseudo-Phocylides. Sometimes explicit references can be found too, as in the *Letter of Aristeas,* in which the dietary laws of Leviticus 11 are openly discussed along with other biblical and Jewish notions. But even in the case of the *Letter of Aristeas,* the topic of the work does not come from a biblical book. Other works that do not have their point of departure in biblical tradition include those that deal with religious persecutions (2, 3, and 4 Maccabees), with Jewish history during the Hellenistic and Roman periods (Philo's *In Flaccum* and *Legatio ad Gaium,* Justus of Tiberias's history of the Jewish war, Josephus's *Jewish War* and the final part of his *Jewish Antiquities*), and with apologetics (Josephus's *Against Apion*).

The Literary Genres Represented

Jewish texts composed in Greek employ a great diversity of literary genres. The texts can be classified most broadly as poetry or prose. To the first category belong Philo the Epic Poet, Theodotus, Ezekiel the Tragedian, the *Sibylline Oracles,* Pseudo-Orpheus and other forged verses of Greek poets, Pseudo-Phocylides, and the Wisdom of Solomon. To the second belong Demetrius, Artapanus, Aristobulus, the *Letter of Aristeas,* Eupolemus, Pseudo-Eupolemus, Aristeas the Exegete, 2 Maccabees, Pseudo-Hecataeus, the Prologue to Ben Sira, Cleodemus Malchus, 3 Maccabees, Philo of Alexandria, Justus of Tiberias, Josephus, *Joseph and Aseneth,* 4 Maccabees, the *Testament of Job,* and the synagogal sermons *On Jonas* and *On Samson.* These texts can be further classified according to literary genre, even though one work may blend together several genres. The *Letter of Aristeas,* for instance, is a good example of the Hellenistic taste for *poikilia* — literary and stylistic diversity within a single work.

Prose Works Dealing with the Past

Several Jewish works composed in Greek are prose literature about the past, a rather loose category that includes genres such as chronography, historiography, and ethnography but also historical fiction (*Joseph and*

Aseneth). Several authors and texts belong to this group: Demetrius, Artapanus, the *Letter of Aristeas,* Aristeas the Exegete, Eupolemus, Pseudo-Eupolemus, Cleodemus Malchus, Pseudo-Hecataeus, 2 Maccabees, 3 Maccabees, Philo's *In Flaccum* and *Legatio ad Gaium,* Justus of Tiberius, Josephus's *Jewish War* and *Jewish Antiquities,* and *Joseph and Aseneth.* The term "history" has completely different meanings from one text to another. In several cases, history means biblical history, and the work may not look like history at all to the modern reader, who would classify it either as rewritten Bible (a rather anachronistic label) or as midrashic literature. However, these ancient writers certainly thought that they were writing history. Moreover, when dealing either with biblical history or with events more or less contemporaneous with the author, many texts contain sometimes glaring inaccuracies and frequently describe miracles and interventions by angels, so that the distinction between historiography and legend is blurred. Obviously, ancient texts should not be judged according to modern historiographic standards, especially given the variety of genres represented, from the nearly classical historiography exemplified by Josephus's *Jewish War,* to the very creative rewriting of Exodus by Artapanus, to the highly fictional story told in 3 Maccabees.

Sapiential and Parenetic Works

Sapiential and parenetic literature comprise a second group of texts, to which the following works belong: Prologue to Ben Sira, Pseudo-Phocylides, Wisdom of Solomon, *Testament of Job,* 4 Maccabees, and the synagogal sermons *On Jonas* and *On Samson.* Once again, nearly every text belongs to a specific subgenre, such as gnomic poetry (Pseudo-Phocylides), sermon, testament, and so on. The Prologue to the Wisdom of Ben Sira, written by Ben Sira's grandson, is not a sapiential work in itself but merely introduces the Greek translation of Ben Sira's ethical teaching, which closely resembles the biblical book of Proverbs. The Wisdom of Solomon is also strongly reminiscent of Proverbs (especially Proverbs 8) but is much more concerned with the fate of the righteous after death. 4 Maccabees can be considered both a diatribe and a panegyric, but it aims at religious edification. The work may have been delivered orally at some unknown commemorative festival.

Although most Jewish texts written in Greek deal with biblical traditions, there are very few exegetical works. Demetrius addresses the origin of the weapons held by the Israelites in the desert (frg. 5); because they departed from Egypt unarmed, the question of how they acquired weapons naturally presented itself. Similarly, in his *Jewish Antiquities* Josephus implicitly or explicitly deals with exegetical problems. But in neither case is the prime focus of the work on exegesis as such. Rather, the use of scriptural material for the purpose of historiography prompts the writer to analyze problematic aspects of the biblical text. In contrast, Aristobulus and Philo focus on the explanation of the biblical text as such and read the texts at different levels, both literally and symbolically or allegorically.

Philosophy

Philosophical treatises in the strict sense of the term are even rarer. Philo of Alexandria is the only early Jewish author known to have written whole treatises dedicated to philosophical questions (e.g., *De aeternitate mundi* and *Quod omnis probus liber sit*). The use of philosophical concepts or vocabulary in exegetical treatises such as Aristobulus's work, or in sapiential or parenetic texts such as the Wisdom of Solomon and 4 Maccabees, does not allow us to characterize these works as philosophical treatises *stricto sensu*.

Apology

There are at least two Jewish apologetic works written in Greek, Philo's *Hypothetica* (preserved only in part in Eusebius's *Praeparatio Evangelica*), and Josephus's *Against Apion*. However, there are many apologetic passages in the rest of Philo's and Josephus's works. Furthermore, Jewish works written in Greek often emphasize the superiority of Judaism over Greek culture and are therefore not devoid of apologetic overtones.

Autobiography

Josephus produced a work belonging to yet another literary genre, the *Life*, which is the fullest surviving example of Roman autobiography before Augustine's *Confessions*. It was appended to the *Jewish Antiquities* and was often read as an integral part of the latter but nevertheless remains an early example of personal memoir.

Epic Poetry and Drama

Epic poetry is represented by Philo the Epic Poet and Theodotus. Other poetic texts belong to different categories. The *Sibylline Oracles*, for instance, represent a specific type of oracular poetry. Finally, we have one Jewish tragedy on the exodus, written by an Egyptian Jew named Ezekiel who wrote in Alexandria in the middle of the second century B.C.E. He wrote his play in iambic trimeters, the standard meter used in Greek drama. He relied on the Septuagint but introduced several interesting haggadic embellishments. The most famous and debated scene has Moses report a dream that he had in which he was enthroned in heaven. His drama was certainly performed for a Jewish audience, perhaps in a synagogue.

The Influence and Reshaping of Greek Ideas

In most cases, the Jewish authors writing in Greek show a great familiarity with Greek literary themes and ideas, not only from the classical period but also from the Hellenistic age. This is especially true of the poetic texts. Theodotus uses Homeric expressions in a very skillful way, so that the fight of Simeon and Levi against Shechem and Hamor is reminiscent of Homeric battle scenes. In particular, the image of Shechem on his knees, clutching at the knees of Levi, recalls the image of Lycaon clutching the knees of Achilles, who slays him (*Iliad* 21.65). But Theodotus also uses non-Homeric terms that occur in Hellenistic epic poetry. Philo the Epic Poet's language is notably obscure, and his style has been characterized as pretentious, but it is actually quite typical of this form of Hellenistic epic. Pseudo-Phocylides was clever enough for his dactylic hexameters written in the old Ionic dialect to be considered authentic for many centuries.

Not only were Jewish authors writing in Greek able to imitate the styles and literary models of well-known Greek poets and tragedians, but they were also very familiar with Greek mythology, historiography, and philosophy. The Jewish "historians" were able to connect biblical figures to Greek, Babylonian, and Egyptian divine or heroic figures. For instance, Pseudo-Eupolemus identifies Bel with Cronos and presents him as the grandfather of Canaan, whom he considers the ancestor of the Phoenicians. He also equates Atlas with Enoch. In the *De Praemiis et Poenis* (23), Philo of Alexandria writes that Noah and Deucalion are the same person. At the beginning of his *Jewish Antiquities,* Josephus allusively establishes a relationship between the Nephilim (Gen. 6:4) and the giants, probably with reference to Hesiod's *Theogony* (*Ant.* 1.73). This is not unparalleled in Hebrew or Aramaic literature; both *1 Enoch* (10:2) and *Jubilees* (5:6) implicitly link the Watchers (the angels who mated with women) to the Titans bound in Tartarus. Josephus also endeavors to compare biblical chronologies with those of other cultures.

Although Justus of Tiberias's work has not been preserved, he seems to have made use of the Hellenistic universal chronicles even more intensively than Josephus did. Josephus himself was inspired by Greek precursors to a considerable extent, and he mastered the conventions of Greek historiography. He seems to have been particularly influenced by Thucydides and Dionysius of Halicarnassus. Before Josephus, Jewish authors who produced historiographical works or historical fiction, such as Eupolemus and the author of 3 Maccabees, also displayed great ability in imitating the language used in official Hellenistic and Roman documents.

Greek philosophy was also relatively well known by several Jewish authors, even if they generally did not write philosophical treatises. Aristobulus is introduced by Clement of Alexandria as a Peripatetic philosopher (*Stromateis* 1.15.72.4), whereas the fragments quoted show that he was well acquainted with Stoic allegorical readings of Homer and with Pythagorean theories of numbers. Philo's command of Greek philosophy and of the debates among the different philosophical schools of his time is remarkable and ranks far beyond that of any other Jewish author writing in Greek. Yet the way in which the author of 4 Maccabees freely presents Stoic notions such as the mastery of reason over the passions in Jewish garb also shows a familiarity with Hellenistic philosophical teachings.

In short, Jewish texts written in Greek are especially interesting for their complex intertextual relationship with biblical or Jewish literature on the one hand and with Greek literature on the other. Jewish authors had a rather good knowledge of Greek literature and philosophy, and even quoted Greek texts along with biblical ones to illustrate a specific point. Their efforts to adapt biblical narratives to Greek literary forms such as poetry and drama also led to significant literary achievements. Thus, Hellenistic culture was also the culture of these Jewish authors, especially in the case of Aristobulus, Theodotus, Pseudo-Phocylides, and Philo. It was *theirs*, even if not in the same way as biblical traditions were. Obviously, Jewish culture had its own integrity, whereas Greek culture was originally foreign to Judaism. But in Jewish authors writing in Greek, we may indeed speak of Greek-Jewish culture because both cultures were closely intertwined. The use of the Greek language was not a mere stopgap to make up for a deficient knowledge of Hebrew or Aramaic but an intrinsic part of the identity and worldview of early Jewish authors. And since words do not convey meanings in a neutral way, even the simplest statement of Jewish beliefs and customs in Greek took on a slightly different meaning than one formulated in Hebrew or Aramaic and gave birth to a different kind of Judaism. This is not to say that early Jewish writings composed in Greek did not share common themes or characteristics with their counterparts in Hebrew or Aramaic. A closer look at the issues tackled by the former will help us evaluate their connections with the latter.

Some Important Themes

Regardless of their literary genre, all early Jewish works composed in Greek convey a religious message at one level or another. Even Josephus's *Jewish War* contains considerable theological interpretation, and Philo's arguments against the rationality of animals in *De Animalibus,* to cite but one example, have an implicit biblical background: the first chapters of Genesis, which establish the superiority of human beings over animals. So there is no "profane" Jewish literature written in Greek, even if many texts perform functions besides religious edification and even aim at entertaining their audience. Humor, pleasure, aesthetics, polemics, and religious or moral instruction are not mutually exclusive goals.

Jews and Foreign Rulers

Beyond this general statement, several key issues can be emphasized. First, a strikingly recurrent theme of Jewish literature written in Greek consists in reflections about the relationship between the king or the emperor and his Jewish subjects. It represents a major topic in the *Letter of Aristeas,* 2 Maccabees, 3 Maccabees, Philo's *In Flaccum* and *Legatio ad Gaium,* Josephus's *Jewish War* and part of his *Jewish Antiquities*. It also appears, though to a lesser extent, in 4 Maccabees. All these works convey a certain vision of what a good king or emperor should be. The good monarch is the one who protects the Jews and grants them the right to live according to their ancestral laws and customs. In the *Letter of Aristeas,* the king even bows down in front of the Mosaic law and gives orders for the banquet to be prepared according to Jewish dietary laws. Moreover, he is willing to take advice on how to rule from the Jewish sages who come from Jerusalem. In works that describe a historical or fictional religious persecution, either perpetrated or only planned — Antiochus IV in 2 Maccabees and 4 Maccabees, Ptolemy IV in 3 Maccabees, Ptolemy VI in Josephus, *Against Apion* 2.51-55, Caligula, and Flaccus — a negative portrait of the ruler is drawn that helps to define what a good and just sovereign should be. In many instances, the monarch or his representatives repents of his wicked ways and recognizes the greatness of the God of Israel. This is the case with Heliodorus and Antiochus IV in 2 Maccabees and with Ptolemy IV in 3 Maccabees. The alternative scenario is the death of the impious ruler, as in the case of Flaccus and Caligula. However, a quite different picture emerges from Josephus's writings, due to his perspective on the First Revolt and his position as a protégé of the Flavians. In the *Jewish War,* he is at pains to describe Vespasian and Titus in a positive light, even if he is not as uncritical as some commentators have thought. In the *Antiquities,* he also insists on the "privileges" granted to the Jews by the Roman senate and the Roman emperors, who generally allowed the Jews to live according to their ancestral traditions. In this respect, Josephus's conception of the just ruler is similar to that of his predecessors from Alexandria.

Another leitmotiv in these texts is the Jews' faithfulness to the king. It is stressed again and again that the Jews are loyal subjects. According to these texts, the normal or ideal relationship between Jews and Hellenistic or Roman rulers is one of mutual trust and collaboration: the king protects the Jews and grants them the right to live according to their laws, at least in certain matters, and the Jews serve the king, pray for his welfare and that of his kingdom, dedicate *proseuchai* (houses of prayers) to him and his family, and even offer sacrifices at the Jerusalem Temple on his behalf. The same theme also appears in works composed in Hebrew and Aramaic, such as Daniel, Esther, and 1 Maccabees. Yet these works tend to depict non-Jewish sovereigns in a harsher light than do the Jewish texts written in Greek, and to present a less optimistic vision of the relationship between Jews and foreign rulers. There is no Hebrew or Aramaic counterpart of the *Letter of Aristeas.* This fact likely owes to the different ways in which Ptolemaic and Seleucid rule were experienced by Jews in Eretz Israel and in the Diaspora.

Jews and Non-Jews

A second issue is the relationship between Jews and non-Jews. Especially prominent is the topic of endogamy, the prohibition against marrying non-Jews. It is not always stated explicitly but can arise from small modifications to the biblical narrative. For instance, in Demetrius's account of the life of Moses (frg. 3), Zipporah, Moses's wife, whom the biblical text describes as a Midianite (Exod. 2:21), becomes a descendant of Abraham. Theodotus is more straightforward; when retelling the rape of Dinah, he omits Jacob's condemnation of his sons' violence. Moreover, the Shechemites are depicted as utterly wicked and are denied the possibility of joining the people of Israel through circumcision and of marrying the daughters of Israel. Philo is also quite explicit about the prohibition of marriage to foreigners (*Spec.* 3.29), but since he is merely paraphrasing Deut. 7:4, which refers to the Canaanites, it is not clear how he understood this interdiction in his own context. From the rest of his work, one may guess that he accepted intermarriage only with non-Jews who converted to Judaism. The synagogue sermon *On Samson* uses the example of Samson's unhappy relationship with Delilah (Judges 14–16) to insist on the danger represented by a union with a foreign woman (see especially §§22-23, 33). Similarly, in his *Jewish Antiquities* Josephus paraphrases the biblical account of the reign of Solomon and condemns his passion for foreign women (*Ant.* 8.190-96). In the *Testament of Job* (45:3), Job exhorts his children not to marry foreign women. Like Demetrius, the author of *Joseph and Aseneth* addresses a problem that stems from the biblical text: the reference to Joseph's marriage to the daughter of an Egyptian priest (Gen. 41:45). The author could have solved the problem by noting that Joseph lived before the Law was given at Mt. Sinai and therefore did not know the Mosaic legislation concerning forbidden unions, but he took a different approach. One passage in *Joseph and Aseneth* (8:6) bluntly emphasizes that Joseph hated foreign women. Aseneth therefore becomes a convert, an outcome that the very beginning of the work foreshadows by stating that she did not look like the daughters of the Egyptians but rather like the daughters of the Hebrews, and even like Sarah, Rebecca, and Rachel (1:7-8).

Jewish authors writing in Greek, then, seem unanimous in their condemnation of exogamy. However, there are a few exceptions. Artapanus and Ezekiel the Tragedian do not seem to have been bothered by the foreign wives of Joseph and Moses. Moreover, Artapanus apparently had a very open definition of the descendants of Israel. According to him, Joseph anticipated the conspiracy of his brothers and willingly traveled to Egypt with the help of the kings of the Arabs, who were "sons of Abraham and brothers of Isaac" and, as such, "descendants of Israel" (Eusebius, *Praep. Evang.* 9.23.1). Whereas the condemnation of forbidden unions can also be found in Jewish literature written in Hebrew (e.g., in *Jubilees*), Artapanus's and Ezekiel's lenient attitude is peculiar to Jewish literature written in Greek.

Circumcision is an issue closely connected with endogamy and with the preservation of Jewish identity, but it is not mentioned that often in Jewish texts written in Greek. Apart from Theodotus's epic poem, it is referred to in 2 Maccabees, in the context of the persecution ordered by Antiochus IV. The author tells us that circumcision was prohibited but that pious Jews resisted and even died rather than give up circumcising their children (2:10). 4 Maccabees also reports the fact, without building upon it except to introduce the story of the martyrs. Philo justifies the commandment of circumcision at some length at the beginning of the *Special Laws*, whereas Josephus refers to it only briefly in his retelling of the life of Abraham (*Ant.* 1.192) and mentions it again in connection with the conversion of non-Jews to Judaism (especially in *Ant.* 20.38-48, the story of the conversion of King Izates).

The dietary laws constitute yet another frequent theme pertaining to the general issue of the relationships between Jews and non-Jews. In the *Letter of Aristeas*, the high priest Eleazar explains the dietary laws in a symbolic way and emphasizes that they are supposed to lead to justice in social relationships (§§143-69), but he also states that they belong to the purity laws that are meant to separate the Jews from people who practice idolatry (§§139, 142). 3 Maccabees tends to equate faithfulness to the Torah with observance of the dietary rules. Moreover, its author acknowledges that these laws separate the Jews from their non-Jewish neighbors, and that this social *amixia* is perceived as a mark of hostility by those who are themselves hostile to the Jews. He does not give the commandments up for all that, but rather affirms that Jews have won for themselves a good reputation in social intercourse thanks to their righteousness (3:4-7). The issue of the dietary laws is found in the most dramatic way in 2 and 4 Maccabees, where it is linked to the story of the prohibition of Judaism by Antiochus IV. The old Eleazar, the seven brothers, and their mother are all put to death because they refuse to eat pork (2 Macc. 6:18–7:42; 4 Maccabees 5–18). Both Philo and Josephus frequently refer to the Jews' faithfulness to their ancestral laws, including the dietary laws. Philo explains them in a symbolic or allegorical way (*Spec.* 4.100-118) but also insists on the necessity of putting them into practice (*Migr.* 90–93). Finally, in *Joseph and Aseneth*, Joseph refuses to kiss Aseneth because she worships idols and eats impure food (8:5). Jewish texts written in Hebrew and Aramaic take up the issue of dietary laws too, but they tend to focus on halakic aspects rather than on the question of the laws' implications for the relationship with pagans. And in comparison with 2 Maccabees, 1 Maccabees is much less concerned with the dietary laws.

To conclude on the theme of the relationships between Jews and non-Jews, a few words should be said about the issue of conversion. Interestingly enough, converts and conversions appear in rather late texts. Philo praises proselytes who abandon idolatry or wrong conceptions about God and join Israel (see especially *Virt.* 179, 182, and 219). In the *Antiquities*, Josephus reports the story of the conversion of the king of Adiabene, and mentions other cases as well. In *Against Apion*, he follows Philo in stating that Judaism's openness to proselytes is a mark of *philanthrōpia* (2.261). But in the *Antiquities* and the *Life*, Josephus also confronts the issue of forced conversions to Judaism, in the context of the Hasmonean wars and the war against Rome (see *Ant.* 13.257-58; 318-19; *Life* 112–13). Other texts that refer to proselytes are *Joseph and Aseneth* and the *Testament of Job*, whose main characters are converts. They both date from the first century c.e. (if not later). This list probably reflects the fact that the very notion of conversion and the ritual surrounding it — which should be distinguished from mere recognition of the God of Israel as the one true God — emerged and developed only at the end of the Hellenistic period. Among Greek translations of Jewish texts originally written in Hebrew or Aramaic, Esther LXX (8:17) and Judith (5:5–6:20) allude to or explicitly deal with conversions, but these translations are late as well (and the original version of Judith itself only dates from the second century b.c.e.).

Judaism's Superiority over Paganism

A third theme frequently found in Jewish texts written in Greek, perhaps the most widespread of all, is the superiority of Judaism over paganism. This theme has important biblical roots but received a new impetus in the Hellenistic age. On the one hand, as in biblical texts, idols are condemned and mocked as handmade objects with no power to save, and those who worship them are depicted as foolish, wicked, or abominable. This is the case in several texts, including the *Letter of Aristeas* (134–38 in particular),

Pseudo-Hecataeus (who, through the story of Mosollamus, mocks pagan superstitious belief in omens), 3 Maccabees (4:16 in particular), Wisdom of Solomon, Philo, Josephus, *Testament of Job,* and *Joseph and Aseneth.* On the other hand, a monotheistic creed is attributed to well-known figures much admired by the Greeks, such as Orpheus, Homer, Hesiod, Pythagoras, Plato, and a few others, but they are said to have been inspired by Abraham, Joseph, or Moses. Thus, even if Greek culture is not utterly rejected as vile paganism, it is still considered inferior to Judaism since it derives its truth and its beauty from Judaism — hence the efforts of Josephus and others to demonstrate the great antiquity of the Jewish people and of the Mosaic revelation, which in their view predated the beginnings of Greek civilization. Hence, also, the use of pseudepigraphy in the pseudo-Orphic poem and the other verses attributed to famous Greek poets, and in the *Sibylline Oracles.*

All these works were conceived of as pagan testimonies to the truth and superior wisdom of Judaism. Even Artapanus, who presents Moses as the founder of Egyptian animal cults, was motivated by a sense of Judaism's superiority to Egyptian paganism. True, his perception of the latter is not as negative as in other Jewish texts (especially the *Letter of Aristeas* and Philo, who abhor Egyptian animal cults). But Moses's role as cultural benefactor in Egypt is still a mark of the superiority of Judaism over the culture of the natives. And the worship of animals is explained euhemeristically, implying that they are only animals that Moses judged to be useful. Moreover, Moses is identified with Mousaeus, the teacher of Orpheus. Thus, Artapanus celebrates the superiority of Judaism over both Egyptian and Greek culture, which is why his work can be considered an example of "competitive historiography."

The Mutual Faithfulness of God and Israel

A fourth theme prevalent in Jewish literature written in Greek is the mutual faithfulness of God and Israel. Several texts highlight God's justice and his providential care for Israel or reward of the righteous. For instance, in contrast to 1 Maccabees, 2 Maccabees introduces the episode of Heliodorus and of God's miraculous intervention to preserve the Temple in Jerusalem (chap. 3) and describes Antiochus IV's agony at length (chap. 9). Similarly, 3 Maccabees celebrates God's intervention at the Jerusalem Temple but also at the hippodrome in Alexandria (1:8–2:24 and 5:46–6:29, respec-

tively). Philo makes it very clear that Flaccus's disgrace was a divine punishment (*Flacc.* 180–91). Even Artapanus gives an example of divine retribution when he writes that, because of his treatment of the Jews, the
Egyptian ruler Chenephres was the first man to contract elephantiasis (frg.
3 in Eusebius, *Praep. Evang.* 9.27.20). The Wisdom of Solomon also recalls
God's intervention in favor of Israel and his chastisement of the Egyptians
and the Canaanites. Yet it argues first and foremost that the righteous will
be blessed with eternal life, whereas his adversaries will be punished and
disappear forever. Similarly, the *Testament of Job* describes the righteous
hero who suffers but is finally rewarded and achieves immortality, in contrast to the wicked Elihu, who is condemned to permanent destruction. In
all cases, what is at stake is divine justice and the ways it manifests itself, either in this world or in the afterlife, at a collective or individual level. In the
latter, eschatological concerns lead to the belief in bodily resurrection
(2 Maccabees, *Sibylline Oracles* 4) and the immortality of the soul (Wisdom of Solomon, Philo, *Testament of Job*). Messianic expectations do not
figure prominently in Jewish literature written in Greek, although some
hints may be found in Philo, Josephus, and *Sibylline Oracles* 5.

To God's faithfulness toward Israel corresponds Israel's faithfulness to
God and his Law. Jewish texts written in Greek tend to present the Jewish
people as pious. Apostates are few. In 2 Maccabees, impious Jews in Jerusalem try to introduce a Greek way of life and to alter the ancestral customs,
thus causing the wrath of God to fall on the Judeans (4:7-17). In 3 Maccabees, some Jews yield to Ptolemy's threats and promises, and apostatize
through their initiation into the Dionysian mysteries (2:31-33). However, in
both these books the vast majority of the Jews remain faithful to the covenant. At a more individual level, Aristeas and the *Testament of Job* retell
the story of Job, the righteous man who continued to trust in God despite
his great hardships. Particularly interesting are the stories of martyrdom
or readiness to undergo martyrdom in 2, 3 and 4 Maccabees, as well as in
several passages in Philo and Josephus (though martyrdom should be distinguished from noble death and suicide). Martyrdom is the supreme expression of the Jews' faithfulness to God's laws. Jewish readiness to die for
the Law is emphasized by several authors, including Philo and Josephus.
Conversely, apart from allusions in Daniel and 1 Maccabees (whose account is much shorter than that of 2 Maccabees and does not promote
martyrdom), this theme does not appear frequently in Jewish literature
written in Hebrew or Aramaic, even if apocalyptic literature often refers to
a period of trials before the final reward of the elect. However, the more

general issue of God's justice and Israel's faithfulness to the covenant is a recurring topic in Jewish literature written in Hebrew or Aramaic too.

This list of themes is not exhaustive; Jewish texts written in Greek engage other issues as well. But some themes are strikingly absent or marginal: messianism and cultic prescriptions, to name just a few. If one were to add to the corpus texts such as *3 Baruch, 4 Baruch (Paraleipomena Jeremiou), Testament of Abraham,* and *2 Enoch,* heavenly visions and angelic revelations would feature more prominently in the general picture. The Jewish or Christian provenance of these works, though, continues to be disputed. Also conspicuous is the lack of liturgical and halakic texts. Here again, though, the shape of the corpus likely reflects the selective interests of the church fathers.

Ideological Features

Jewish works composed in Greek do not display uniform ideological features. For instance, Theodotus's epic poem reflects a nationalistic and exclusive conception of Judaism. As mentioned above, he completely omits Jacob's condemnation of the aggression perpetrated by Simeon and Levi against the Shechemites (Gen. 34:30). By contrast, the author of 4 Maccabees refers to this condemnation and even quotes Gen. 49:7: "Cursed be their anger, for it is fierce, and their wrath, for it is cruel." According to him, the very fact that Jacob says about Simeon and Levi "May their anger be cursed" means that reason is able to restrain anger (4 Macc. 2:19-20). The violence with which the two brothers avenged their sister, which seemed so praiseworthy to Theodotus that he presented it as the fulfillment of an oracle from God, is depicted as a reprehensible passion by the author of 4 Maccabees. The same degree of disagreement can be noticed concerning other issues. For example, as we noted above, not all Jewish authors writing in Greek condemned marriages to foreign women. Moreover, had the writings of extreme allegorizers of Scripture (criticized by Philo in *De Migratione Abrahami* 89–90) been preserved, we would probably have an even more diverse picture.

The use of the Greek language and the mastery of Greek literary forms, then, does not in itself predetermine the ideological or philosophical orientation of the writer. In particular, writing in Greek is not synonymous with openness to Gentiles or universalism. Still, in Second Temple literature the most universalistic texts are indeed to be found among those written in Greek, especially those of Aristobulus and Philo. Universalism, though, is not based primarily on a willingness to welcome proselytes but rather on a broad understanding of God's law and of the cult at the Jerusalem Temple. Some Jewish authors writing in Greek boldly conceived of the Torah as a universal law that could appeal to every human being, mainly through reason. Philo goes so far as to present Israel as a priest offering sacrifices and prayers to God for the sake of all human beings (*Spec.* 2.163-67). It is especially in Jewish literature composed in Greek, then, that the relationship between Israel and the rest of humankind is thought out in its deepest and most positive way.

Scholars debate whether Jewish works composed in Greek should be labeled "apologetic" literature. On the one hand, this is not a missionary literature, even if the evidence shows that proselytes and God-fearers were welcome in the Jewish communities of the Diaspora. On the other hand, although the intended audience of the vast majority of these texts was Jewish, apologetic interests are not to be denied in some cases. To claim the superiority of Judaism over paganism and Greek philosophy, or to provide a rationale for dietary laws and circumcision, is to engage in apologetics. But the apologia was an affirmation of the superiority of Judaism directed in most cases to Jews themselves, to help them face the challenges of their Greco-Roman environment and to strengthen and comfort them in their religious and cultural identity.

Significance

Jewish literature written in Greek is significant for several reasons. First, it constitutes the main literary testimony to the ways people in the ancient Near East rose to the challenge of Hellenism. Although other cultures produced important works in Greek, these works have not survived, or only in fragments, as in the case of Manetho's *Aegyptiaca*, which is known mainly through Josephus's *Against Apion*. Jewish literature written in Hebrew or Aramaic during the Hellenistic and early Roman periods also offers important testimony to the encounter of Judaism with Greek civilization, at least in some cases. Moreover, the archaeological and documentary evidence (inscriptions, papyri, coins, and other artifacts) sheds crucial light on the processes of acculturation that took place during the Greco-Roman period. However, Jewish works composed in Greek remain our main and most explicit evidence for the Jewish engagement with Hellenism.

This literature documents a remarkable attempt to embrace Greek culture while maintaining a distinctive Jewish identity. On the one hand, it demonstrates the huge interest that Greek culture aroused among Jewish elites, and how much they could feel at home in the Greek-speaking world. On the other hand, it also shows that Jews remained very much aware of their distinctive cultural and religious identity. Admittedly, some Jews abandoned the ancestral customs of their people. We know, for instance, of Dositheos son of Drimylos and of Philo's nephew, Tiberius Julius Alexander. "Apostasy," if we may call it that, was probably more common among the elites than among the ordinary people. But in the case of Greco-Roman Egypt, which we know better than other places in the Diaspora, both the literary and the papyrological evidence show that, in general, Jews who expressed themselves in Greek did not indulge in religious paganism or give up the commandments of the Torah. Their culture and identity were bipolar and their relationship to Hellenism selective. They showed a great deal of creativity and boldness in appropriating Greek literary genres, Greek mythology, and Greek philosophical concepts, but used them for their own purposes. In other words, their relationship with Greek culture was not passive but active — and critical. Even when dealing with the biblical or Jewish traditions they inherited, however, they showed great exegetical freedom (a freedom not unparalleled in Hebrew and Aramaic compositions).

That Jews in the Hellenistic and early Roman eras borrowed concepts, literary motifs, and vocabulary from the surrounding culture was nothing new or exceptional. The biblical texts already attest many borrowings from Canaanite, Babylonian, and Persian cultures. Whatever its stage of development, Judaism was never impermeable or completely inward-looking. What was new was the attempt to translate the tradition into a language and cultural idiom that were not Semitic. Obviously, for texts to be translated one first needed to have them reach a certain state of completion. This was achieved in the course of the Hellenistic period, as the collection of manuscripts from Qumran shows. This was a major historical and cultural phenomenon that would leave important marks on the cultural history of the world.

This process of translation was not merely a linguistic one. Even the Septuagint — a collection of Hebrew and Aramaic texts translated into Greek — represented a *cultural* translation, an endeavor to transpose Jewish beliefs and traditions into a different key. Since Jewish beliefs and traditions were not set once and for all, this transposition also gave birth to new ways of expressing Jewish identity and faith. However, the term "syncretism," which is sometimes used in connection with Jewish texts written in Greek, is generally ill chosen. In most Jewish works composed in Greek, there is no syncretism at all, even if Greek terminology is used and Greek gods or heroes are referred to. For instance, that the narrator of the *Letter of Aristeas* compares the God of Israel with Zeus (16) is no proof of syncretism on the part of the real author of the *Letter*, since the narrator is a Greek. The comparison is part of playing the game of pseudonymous attribution. But even if "Aristeas" had been a Jew, the comparison with Zeus would still not count as religious syncretism but remain an example of cultural translation: in the mind of a Greek living in the second century B.C.E., the name "Zeus" did not necessarily conjure up all the mythological tales told by the poets. It could be used in a more philosophical way and refer to a more sophisticated conception of the divine. So an imperfect correlation could indeed be established between the God of Israel and what "Zeus" represented from a Greek philosophical perspective. Accordingly, "Aristeas" defines Zeus as the universal source of life and being, a definition not completely inappropriate to the God of Israel.

Above all, one should bear in mind that Jews writing in Greek frequently used Greek terminology in a subversive way. The use of a Greek term did not necessarily imply that the writer accepted the traditional Greek meaning of the word or all of its cultural implications. For example, the author of 3 Maccabees uses features of the Hellenistic kings to describe the God of Israel. One could argue that he was thoroughly Hellenized. His command of Greek and his knowledge of the language of the Ptolemaic court are certainly beyond doubt. However, the vocabulary he chose to use also conveys the idea that God alone is the true king of the world, above all human kingships. Similarly, the Wisdom of Solomon uses the term *mystēria* to designate both the holy revelations of Wisdom (2:22) and the abominable ceremonies of the Dionysian cult (14:23). Yet the use of the term *mystēria* in connection with Judaism is not a mark of religious syncretism but a way to oppose Judaism to pagan mysteries and to celebrate the superiority of the former. At a more distinctly philosophical level, Philo sometimes uses the Stoic term *oikeiōsis* ("appropriation"), which carried philosophical implications quite contrary to Jewish ethical principles. But he subverts its meaning by endowing it with the sense of *homoiōsis tō theō*, the Platonic "assimilation to God," which could easily be linked with the Jewish ideal of the imitation of God.

The encounter with Greek culture certainly represented a challenge to

Jews in the Hellenistic and early Roman periods. But it also prompted them to explore new ways of expressing their identity and to elaborate the very notion of *Ioudaismos*.

BIBLIOGRAPHY

Bar-Kochva, Bezalel. 1996. *Pseudo-Hecataeus on the Jews: Legitimizing the Jewish Diaspora*. Berkeley: University of California Press.

Barclay, John M. G. 1996. *Jews in the Mediterranean Diaspora*. Edinburgh: Clark.

Burchard, Christoph. 2003. *Joseph und Aseneth*. Leiden: Brill.

Collins, John J. 2000. *Between Athens and Jerusalem: Jewish Identity in the Hellenistic Diaspora*. 2d ed. Grand Rapids: Eerdmans.

―――. 2005. *Jewish Cult and Hellenistic Culture: Essays on the Jewish Encounter with Hellenism and Roman Rule*. Leiden: Brill.

Davila, James R. 2005. *The Provenance of the Pseudepigrapha: Jewish, Christian, or Other?* Leiden: Brill.

Denis, Albert-Marie. 1970. *Introduction aux pseudépigraphes grecs d'Ancien Testament*. Leiden: Brill.

―――. 2000. *Introduction à la littérature religieuse judéo-hellénistique*. 2 vols. Turnhout: Brepols.

Goodman, Martin. 1986. "Jewish Literature Composed in Greek." In E. Schürer, *The History of the Jewish People in the Age of Jesus Christ (175 B.C.–A.D. 135)*. Vol. 3, Part 1. Rev. and ed. Geza Vermes, Fergus Miller, and Martin Goodman. Edinburgh: Clark, 470-704.

Gruen, Erich S. 1998. *Heritage and Hellenism: The Reinvention of Jewish Tradition*. Berkeley: University of California Press.

Herr, Moshe D. 1990. "Les raisons de la conservation des restes de la littérature juive de l'Époque du Second Temple." In *La fable apocryphe I*. Ed. P. Geoltrain, E. Junod, and J.-C. Picard. Turnhout: Brepols, 219-30.

Holladay, Carl. 1983-1996. *Fragments from Hellenistic Jewish Authors*. 4 vols. Atlanta: Scholars Press.

Honigman, Sylvie. 2003. *The Septuagint and Homeric Scholarship in Alexandria: A Study in the Narrative of the Letter of Aristeas*. London: Routledge.

Inowlocki, Sabrina. 2006. *Eusebius and the Jewish Authors: His Citation Technique in an Apologetic Context*. Leiden: Brill.

Johnson, Sarah R. 2004. *Historical Fictions and Hellenistic Jewish Identity: Third Maccabees in Its Cultural Context*. Berkeley: University of California Press.

Lanfranchi, Pierluigi. 2006. *L'Exagoge d'Ezéchiel le tragique: Introduction, texte, traduction et commentaire*. Leiden: Brill.

Motzo, Raimondo Bacchisio. 1977. *Ricerche sulla letteratura e la storia giudaico-ellenistica*. Roma: Centro Editoriale Internazionale.

Rajak, Tessa. 2009. *Translation and Survival: The Greek Bible of the Ancient Jewish Diaspora*. Oxford: Oxford University Press.

————, Sarah Pearce, James Aitken, and Jennifer Dines, eds. 2007. *Jewish Perspectives on Hellenistic Rulers*. Berkeley: University of California Press.

Walter, Nikolaus. 1976. *Fragmente jüdisch-hellenistischer Historiker*. JSHRZ I, 2. Gütersloh: Gerd Mohn, 89-164.

————. 1983. *Fragmente jüdisch-hellenistischer Epik: Philon, Theodotos. Pseudepigraphische jüdisch-hellenistische Dichtung: Pseudo-Phokylides, Pseudo-Orpheus, Gefälschte Verse auf Namen griechischer Dichter*. JSHRZ IV, 3. Gütersloh: Gerd Mohn.

————. 1989. "Jewish-Greek Literature of the Greek Period." In *The Cambridge History of Judaism*, vol. 2, *The Hellenistic Age*. Ed. W. D. Davies and L. Finkelstein. Cambridge: Cambridge University Press, 385-408.

Philo

*Gregory E. Sterling, David T. Runia, Maren R. Niehoff,
and Annewies van den Hoek*

Philo of Alexandria (ca. 20 B.C.E.–ca. 50 C.E.) is one of the most important witnesses to Jewish exegetical traditions and practices of the Second Temple period. He was a prominent figure in the large Alexandrian Jewish community, coming from one of the wealthiest and most distinguished families. He is a good example of a writer from the East who used allegorical interpretation to find common ground between his ancestral tradition and Hellenistic philosophy. His impact on ancient Judaism appears to have ended with the destruction of the Alexandrian Jewish community in 115-117 C.E. At least direct awareness of his works is not discernible until Azariah dei Rossi (1513-1578) summarized some of his views in *Me'or 'Einayim*, and he was ambivalent about Philo's status. Philo's legacy did not, however, end with the destruction of his community; his achievement had such enormous appeal to early Christians that they preserved his writings and claimed him as one of their own, giving him a posthumous baptism (Prochurus, *Acts of John*) and even introducing him as a "bishop" in some Byzantine catenae (e.g., *Fragmenta Graeca, QG* 1.55).

Overview of His Life

We know very little about Philo's life. We have more contemporary evidence for his brother Gaius Julius Alexander, an exceptionally wealthy customs official in Alexandria, and his nephew Tiberius Julius Alexander, an ambitious social climber who gave up his ancestral traditions to make his way through the *cursus honorum*, than we do about Philo. Our evidence for Philo consists of the autobiographical asides that he makes in his writings and the tendentious *testimonia* of later Christians. The one exception is his role in the embassy to Gaius following the pogrom of 38 C.E.

Philo was born into a family with multiple citizenships: he was a citizen of the Jewish *politeuma* of Alexandria, the Greek city of Alexandria, and Rome. At least his brother and nephew must have held these citizenships, and it is likely that they were hereditary. His world was therefore complex. The complexities began with education. Philo received a thorough Jewish education, as his intimate familiarity with the LXX attests. It does not appear that he knew Hebrew or Aramaic; his Jewish education was apparently in Greek, as would have been true for most Diaspora Jews. It may have taken place in his home or perhaps in a house of prayer, although firm evidence for the latter is from a later period. He would also have received a standard Greek education. He would have attended a gymnasium for his primary training in grammar, mathematics, and music (*Congr.* 74–76). When he was thirteen, he would have officially enrolled in the gymnasium for the ephebate, a Greek cultural tradition carried over from the days when Greek city-states required it as preparation for military service. Its later Hellenistic form required training in literature and athletics, the latter as a remnant of its former function. It served as the right of entry to citizenship in Alexandria. Later in Philo's life, Claudius shut the door on Jewish claims to Alexandrian citizenship, a decision that closed the ephebate to them as well (*CPJ* 153 lines 83-95).

Philo's Jewish and Greek educations are reflected in his lifestyle. He was unambiguously committed to Jewish *halakot*. He criticized fellow Jews who thought that the underlying meaning of Jewish rituals negated the necessity of their observance. Philo argued that they were essential markers of community identity (*Migr.* 89–93). In particular, he emphasized the importance of circumcision (*Spec.* 1.1-12), Sabbath observance (*Somn.* 2.123), the celebration of Yom Kippur (*Spec.* 1.186), dietary regulations (*Spec.* 4.100), and endogenous marriage (*Spec.* 3.29) as essential markers of Jewish identity. On one occasion he made a pilgrimage to the Jerusalem Temple (*Prov.* 2.64). At the same time, he did not think that Jewish *halakot* prevented him from enjoying Hellenistic culture. He appears to have enjoyed a lifelong love of athletics, first as a participant while in the gymnasium and then as an observer (*Spec.* 2.230 and *Agr.* 113–15; *Prob.* 26, 110; *Prov.* 2.58). He commented on what he saw at the theater on at least two occasions (*Ebr.* 177; *Prob.* 141). While plays such as Ezekiel's *Exagōgē* may suggest that there was a Jewish theater in Alexandria, Philo explicitly commented on a Euripidean play, which indicates that he attended either a Greek theater or Jewish productions of Greek tragedies (*Prob.* 141). He also speaks of his attendance at banquets where he found it necessary to exercise moderation (*Leg.* 3.156). In sum, Philo did not feel restricted from participating in Hellenistic culture. The exception to this was participation in a pagan cult.

The pattern evident in his mores is also evident in his thinking. Philo went on to receive advanced training in rhetoric and philosophy. We are not certain how he acquired his advanced philosophical training. He may have read on his own as Augustine did centuries later or, like Cicero, hired a tutor and attended the lectures of well-known philosophers. We know of a number of philosophers who were active in Alexandria toward the end of the first century B.C.E., but we do not know with whom Philo studied. What is certain, however, is that he read and digested some of the most important works in the Platonic tradition. The two most important Platonic treatises for him were the *Timaeus* and the *Phaedrus.* He also appears to have known the *Laws,* the *Phaedo,* the *Republic,* the *Symposium,* and the *Theaetetus.* He undoubtedly knew the works of other philosophers such as Aenesidemus, but it is often difficult to know whether he read them first-hand or in fragmentary form as they were cited in a doxography.

Philo put his education to good use in his writings. An important question is the social location of his writing. As was true for his education, all of the evidence is indirect. It is hard to imagine that his works were private, intended solely for his own benefit as some have argued that Seneca's letters to Lucilius were and as Marcus Aurelius's *Meditations* were in fact. The variation in the nature of his treatises suggests that he was not their implied reader; the works assume multiple audiences. There are several possibilities for the social location. Some think that they reflect participation in a house of prayer, whether through worship or education or both. Philo described services in houses of prayer as if they were schools (e.g., *Mos.* 2.216; *Spec.* 2.62). Perhaps Philo taught in an Alexandrian house of prayer. Another possibility is that he owned a private school where he taught young Jews exegesis and philosophy.

There is one statement in his treatises that assumes a school setting, but it is difficult to know whether we should read this literally or as verisimilitude for the dialogue setting (*Anim.* 6). It is clear that Philo worked in an exegetical tradition and not as an isolated interpreter. He is keenly aware of other Jewish interpreters and includes their views in his commentaries, a fact that agrees with but does not require a school setting. The format of two sets of his commentaries, *The Questions and Answers* and the *Allegorical Commentary,* parallel the type of works that circulated in philo-

Treatise	Biblical Text	Textual Base
Questions and Answers		
QG 1	Gen. 2:4–6:13	Armenian QG 1
QG 2	Gen. 6:14–11:32	Armenian QG 2 + additions
QG 3	Gen. 12:1–17:27	Armenian QG 3 + additions
QG 4	Gen. 18:1–22:24	Armenian QG 4.1-70 + additions
QG 5	Gen. 23:1–25:18	Armenian QG 4.71-153 + additions
QG 6	Gen. 25:19–28:9	Armenian QG 4.154-95 + Latin 1-11 +
		Armenian QG 4.196-245
QE 1	Exod. 6:2–9:35	Lost (Eusebius, *Hist. Eccl.* 2.18.5)
QE 2	Exod. 10:1–13:16	Additions + Armenian QE 1 + additions
QE 3	Exod. 13:17–17:16	Lost (Eusebius, *Hist. Eccl.* 2.18.5)
QE 4	Exod. 20:25b–4:18	Armenian QE 2.1 + additions +
		Armenian QE 2.2-49
QE 5	Exod. 25:1–27:19	Armenian QE 2.50-102 + additions
QE 6	Exod. 27:20–30:10	Armenian QE 2.103-24 + additions
Allegorical Commentary		
	Gen. 1:1-31	Lost (*Alleg. Interp.* 1.1-2; significant lacuna)
Allegorical Interpretation 1	Gen. 2:1–3:1a	*Alleg. Interp.* 1–2
Allegorical Interpretation 2	Gen. 3:1b-8a	Lost (significant lacuna)
Allegorical Interpretation 3	Gen. 3:8b-19	*Alleg. Interp.* 3
Allegorical Interpretation 4	Gen. 3:20-23	Lost (*Sacrifices* 51; significant lacuna)
Cherubim	Gen. 3:24; 4:1	*Cherubim*
Sacrifices	Gen. 4:2-4	*Sacrifices*
	Gen. 4:5-7	Lost (significant lacuna)
Worse	Gen. 4:8-15	*Worse*
Posterity	Gen. 4:16-25	*Posterity*
	Gen. 5:32	Lost (*Sobriety* 52?)
Giants and *Unchangeable*	Gen. 6:1-12	*Giants* and *Unchangeable*
Covenants 1	Lost	(*Names* 53; Eusebius, *Hist. Eccl.* 2.18.3)
Covenants 2	Lost	(*Names* 53; Eusebius, *Hist. Eccl.* 2.18.3)
Agriculture	Gen. 9:20a	*Agriculture*
Planting	Gen. 9:20b	*Planting*
		End of treatise lost
Drunkenness 1	Gen. 9:21	*Drunkenness* (Note: This could be vol. 2,
		and vol. 1 could be lost.)
Drunkenness 2	Gen. 9:21b-23	Lost (Eusebius, *Hist. Eccl.* 2.18.2; Philo, *Sobriety* 1)
Sobriety	Gen. 9:24-27	*Sobriety*
		End of treatise lost (?)
Confusion	Gen. 11:1-9	*Confusion*
Migration	Gen. 12:1-4, 6	*Migration*
Rewards	Gen. 15:1	Lost (*Heir* 1)
Heir	Gen. 15:2-18	*Heir*
Preliminary Studies	Gen. 16:1-6a	*Preliminary Studies*
Flight	Gen. 16:6b-9, 11-12	*Flight*
Names	Gen. 17:1-5, 15-22	*Names*
God	Gen. 18:2	Armenian Fragment
Dreams 1	Gen. 20:3 (?)	Lost (Eusebius, *Hist. Eccl.* 2.18.4)
Dreams 2	Gen. 28:10-22; 31:10-13	*Dreams* 1

Treatise	Biblical Text	Textual Base
Dreams 3	Gen. 37:8-11; 40:9-11, 16-17; 41:17-24	*Dreams* 2
Dreams 4	Lost	(Eusebius, *Hist. Eccl.* 2.18.4)
Dreams 5	Lost	(Eusebius, *Hist. Eccl.* 2.18.4)
Exposition of the Law		
Creation	Gen. 1:1–2:5	*Creation*
Abraham	Genesis 4–25	*Abraham*
Isaac	Genesis 25–28, 35	Lost (*Joseph* 1)
Jacob	Genesis 25–50	Lost (*Joseph* 1)
Joseph	Genesis 37–50	*Joseph*
Decalogue	Deut. 5:1-20 (cf. Exod. 20:1-17)	*Decalogue*
Special Laws 1	Polytheism and idolatry	*Special Laws* 1
Special Laws 2	Oaths, Sabbath, parents	*Special Laws* 2
Special Laws 3	Adultery and murder	*Special Laws* 3
Special Laws 4	Stealing, false witness, and covetousness	*Special Laws* 4
Virtues:		
Justice		*Special Laws* 4.133-238
Courage		*Virtues* 1–50
Philanthropy		*Virtues* 51–227
Piety		Lost
Passions		Lost (*Alleg. Interp.* 3.139)
Rewards		*Rewards*
Introductory Work		
Moses 1		*Moses* 1
Moses 2		*Moses* 2
Philosophical Treatises		
Bad Person		Lost (*Good Person* 1)
Good Person		*Good Person*
Providence 1		Armenian *Providence* 1
Providence 2		Armenian *Providence* 2 + Greek fragments in Eusebius, *Praep. Evang.* 7.21; 8.14
Animals		Armenian *Animals*
Eternity 1		*Eternity*
Eternity 2		Lost (*Eternity* 150)
Numbers		Armenian Fragment
Apologetic Treatises		
Essenes		Lost (*Contemplative Life* 1)
Contemplative Life		*Contemplative Life*
Hypothetica		Fragments in Eusebius, *Praep. Evang.* 8.6.1-7.20 and 8.11.1-18
Virtues 1		Lost (Eusebius, *Hist. Eccl.* 2.5.1; 2.6.3)
Virtues 2		Lost (Eusebius, *Hist. Eccl.* 2.5.1; 2.6.3)
Virtues 3		*Flaccus*
Virtues 4		*Embassy*
Virtues 5		Lost (*Embassy* 373; Eusebius, *Hist. Eccl.* 2.5.1; 2.6.3)

Latin and English Abbreviations for Philo's Works

Abr. *Abraham*	*De Abrahamo* *On the Life of Abraham*	*Leg.* 1, 2, 3 *Alleg. Interp.* 1, 2, 3	*Legum allegoriae* I, II, III *Allegorical Interpretation* 1, 2, 3
Aet. *Eternity*	*De aeternitate mundi* *On the Eternity of the World*	*Legat.* *Embassy*	*Legatio ad Gaium* *On the Embassy to Gaius*
Agr. *Agriculture*	*De agricultura* *On Agriculture*	*Migr.* *Migration*	*De migratione Abrahami* *On the Migration of Abraham*
Anim. *Animals*	*De animalibus* *Whether Animals Have* *Reason* (= Alexander)	*Mos.* 1, 2 *Moses* 1, 2	*De vita Mosis* I, II *On the Life of Moses* 1, 2
Cher. *Cherubim*	*De cherubim* *On the Cherubim*	*Mut.* *Names*	*De mutatione nominum* *On the Change of Names*
Conf. *Confusion*	*De confusione linguarum* *On the Confusion of Tongues*	*Opif.* *Creation*	*De opificio mundi* *On the Creation of the World*
Contempl. *Contempl. Life*	*De vita contemplativa* *On the Contemplative Life*	*Plant.* *Planting*	*De plantatione* *On Planting*
Congr. *Prelim. Studies*	*De congressu eruditionis gratia* *On the Preliminary Studies*	*Post.* *Posterity*	*De posteritate Caini* *On the Posterity of Cain*
Decal. *Decalogue*	*De decalogo* *On the Decalogue*	*Praem.* *Rewards*	*De praemiis et poenis* *On Rewards and Punishments*
Deo *God*	*De Deo* *On God*	*Prob.* *Good Person*	*Quod omnis probus liber sit* *That Every Good Person Is Free*
Det. *Worse*	*Quod deterius potiori insidari* *soleat* *That the Worse Attacks the* *Better*	*Prov.* 1, 2 *Providence* 1, 2	*De providentia* I, II *On Providence* 1, 2
Deus *Unchangeable*	*Quod Deus sit immutabilis* *That God Is Unchangeable*	*QE* 1, 2 *QE* 1, 2	*Quaestiones et solutiones in* *Exodum* I, II *Questions and Answers on* *Exodus* 1, 2
Ebr. *Drunkenness*	*De ebrietate* *On Drunkenness*	*QG* 1, 2, 3, 4 *QG* 1, 2, 3, 4	*Quaestiones et solutiones in* *Genesin* I, II, III, IV *Questions and Answers on* *Genesis* 1, 2, 3, 4
Exsecr. *Curses*	*De exsecrationibus* *On Curses* (= *Rewards* 127–72)	*Sacr.* *Sacrifices*	*De sacrificiis Abelis et Caini* *On the Sacrifices of Cain and* *Abel*
Flacc. *Flaccus*	*In Flaccum* *Against Flaccus*	*Sobr.* *Sobriety*	*De sobrietate* *On Sobriety*
Fug. *Flight*	*De fuga et inventione* *On Flight and Finding*	*Somn.* 1, 2 *Dreams* 1, 2	*De somniis* I, II *On Dreams* 1, 2
Gig. *Giants*	*De gigantibus* *On Giants*	*Spec.* 1, 2, 3, 4	*De specialibus legibus* I, II, III, IV
Her. *Heir*	*Quis rerum divinarum heres sit* *Who Is the Heir?*	*Spec. Laws* 1, 2, 3, 4	*On the Special Laws* 1, 2, 3, 4
Hypoth. *Hypothetica*	*Hypothetica* *Hypothetica*	*Virt.* *Virtues*	*De virtutibus* *On the Virtues*
Ios. *Joseph*	*De Iosepho* *On the Life of Joseph*		

sophical schools. More importantly, the preservation of his treatises through Origen suggests that they were part of a Jewish library.

Sometime prior to the destruction of the Alexandrian Jewish community in 115-117 C.E., the works of Philo and other Jewish authors such as Aristobulus passed into Christian hands. Since Clement and Eusebius knew Aristobulus directly rather than through an intermediate source, it is likely that the works of Aristobulus and Philo were part of a common library. While it is possible that both were incorporated into the famous Alexandrian library and then copied by Christians, it is more reasonable to believe that a Jewish library that contained the works of Aristobulus and Philo passed into Christian hands. If Philo had a library for his school, he, like Aristotle (Strabo, *Geography* 13.1.54), would probably have made provisions for its transmission when he died. Either a later head of the school converted to Christianity and brought the library with him, or a well-to-do Christian attended the school and made copies of some of the most important works. Either way, it seems likely that the works of Aristobulus and Philo were transmitted together and belonged to a school library.

We are certain of one event in Philo's life. He served on the first Jewish embassy to Caligula following the pogrom in Alexandria that broke out during Agrippa I's visit in 38 C.E. The delegation left Alexandria in the fall of 39 C.E. and arrived in Rome in 40. According to Philo, there were five members of the delegation (*Legat.* 370; Josephus, *Ant.* 18.257-60, says that there were three). Josephus informs us that Philo was the head of the Jewish delegation (*Ant.* 18.259), a position probably due to his age and education (Philo, *Legat.* 182). The selection of Philo for this role suggests that he was a prominent and respected member of the Alexandrian Jewish community. E. R. Goodenough thought that Philo must have served on the Jewish senate in Alexandria prior to this. While this is possible, Philo's own description of his appointment suggests that he was taken from his intellectual work and thrust into the maelstrom of politics (*Spec.* 3.1-6). As is well known, the embassy enjoyed less success than they had hoped. Philo returned to Alexandria to his school. He probably died in the next decade.

Overview of His Writings

Philo was a voluminous author. Eusebius provided a list of his works that serves as a useful starting point but must be supplemented (*Hist. Eccl.* 2.18.1-9). Philo organized his commentaries into three major series: the

Questions and Answers on Genesis and Exodus, the *Allegorical Commentary,* and the *Exposition of the Law.* Modern scholarship generally recognizes two other groups of treatises: the philosophical and the apologetic works.

Philo's works have come down to us largely in Greek, although some are preserved in a rather literal sixth-century Armenian translation, and some material is extant only in Latin. The chart on pp. 256-57 assumes that the work is extant in Greek unless otherwise specified. It is important to note that the textual base of a number of treatises is problematic. There are times when treatises have been separated into two distinct works (e.g., *Alleg. Interp.* 2 = the current *Alleg. Interp.* 1 and 2; *Giants* = the current *Giants* and *Unchangeable*) and one case where short treatments have been clustered (*Virtues* = *Spec. Laws* 4.133-238; *Virtues;* and lost *Piety*). In other cases, we have only part of a treatise: sometimes the majority of the treatise (*Planting* and possibly *Sobriety*) and sometimes only fragments (*God, Hypothetica, Numbers*). There are a significant number of lost treatises. We know about them when either Philo or Eusebius mentioned them explicitly or when there is an obvious lacuna in a series of sequential treatises (labeled "significant lacuna"). There were undoubtedly other treatises that disappeared at an early date; for example, the *Questions and Answers on Genesis* may well have included a treatment of Genesis 1 and the *Questions and Answers on Exodus* probably dealt with Exodus 1–5, but we have not included any speculations about these.

We thus have thirty-six treatises fully or mainly extant in Greek, with fragments of another; plus an additional thirteen treatises fully or mainly extant in Armenian, with fragments of two others. This gives us a total of forty-nine fully or mainly preserved treatises and fragments of three others. We know or can reasonably speculate that Philo wrote another twenty-three treatises. We thus have approximately two-thirds of his work.

Questions and Answers on Genesis and Exodus

The *Questions and Answers on Genesis and Exodus* (Greek title, *Zētēmata kai lyseis eis tēn Genesin kai tēn Exodon;* Latin title, *Quaestiones et Solutiones in Genesin et Exodum*) is the least well-known of Philo's great scriptural commentaries. It is an exposition of the first two books of the Pentateuch but does not treat them in their entirety. It consists of lengthy series of questions that stay close to the biblical text, the answers to which form a kind of running commentary.

Text and Versions

The original work, written in Greek, consisted of six books for Genesis and five (or perhaps six) books for Exodus. The part on Exodus is recorded as such in the catalogue of Eusebius, but less than a century later only two of the five books had survived. The original Greek text of the work has been lost. For our knowledge of the surviving work, we are chiefly dependent on an Armenian translation made in sixth-century Byzantium.

Because the Armenian translators of the so-called Hellenizing school made a word-for-word translation, their version can give us a reasonably accurate impression of the original. In the edition of the Armenian text (with Latin translation) by Aucher (1826) and in modern translations, the *Questions on Genesis* has four books, but the fourth book contains books 4, 5, and 6 of the original division. There is also a rather idiosyncratic Latin translation of book 6 dating to the late fourth century, which contains twelve sections missing in the Armenian version. Numerous fragments of the original Greek have been preserved in patristic excerpt collections such as the *Catenae* and the *Florilegia*. These have been expertly collected and edited by Petit (1978), who also edited the Latin translation (1973). Two short extracts have been preserved in Greek manuscripts (*QG* 2.1-7; *QE* 2.62-68).

Contents

Genesis is dealt with as follows: book 1 treats Gen. 2:4–6:13 (100 questions); book 2, Gen. 6:14–10:9 (82); book 3, Gen. 15:7–17:27 (62); book 4 (Armenian 4.1-70), Gen. 18:1–22:18 (70); book 5 (Armenian 4.71-153), Gen. 23:1–25:18 (83); book 6 (Armenian 4.154-245 and Latin additions), Gen. 25:19–28:9 (92 + 12). The remains of the Exodus commentary are: book 1 on Exod. 12:2-23 (23 questions); book 2 on Exod. 20:25–28:34 (124 questions). Marcus (1953), followed by Royse (1976-1977), has noted the remarkable parallels between the scriptural coverage of Philo's books and the weekly readings *(parašiy-yôt)* of the Pentateuch in the annual cycle of the Babylonian synagogue. This suggests similar readings in the Alexandrian synagogues; that is, Philo's work may have covered six weekly readings for Genesis and five (or six) for Exodus. There is no evidence that the work extended to the remaining books of the Pentateuch.

Method of Interpretation

The method used by Philo in this work is straightforward and fairly uniform. A lengthy series of questions that closely follow the biblical text is followed by answers. Most questions begin with "why" *(dia ti)* or "what" *(ti estin)* and often incorporate direct quotes from the text. The length of the answers varies considerably, ranging from a few lines to more than five pages. Both literal and allegorical exegesis are practiced, with the exegete often explicitly moving from the literal *(to rhēton)* to the deeper sense *(to pros dianoian)*, for example in QG 3.50; QE 2.21. There is a greater focus on the exposition of numbers through arithmology than elsewhere in Philo.

Exegetical Origins, Affinities, and Context

The origin of the exegetical method employed in the *Questions and Answers* can partly be sought in Greek literature (*Peripatos,* Alexandrian Homeric exegesis), but there is no precedent for the practice of making a running commentary.

There are considerable parallels between the *Questions and Answers* and Philo's *Allegorical Commentary.* Scholars have pointed out that the questions posed in the former work often form the nucleus of the more sophisticated allegorical work. It has been argued that the work can be seen as a kind of prolegomenon to the other commentary (Sterling 1991), but this view may not do justice to the role of the literal exposition. It also has been argued that it precedes the other commentaries chronologically (Terian 1991), but this cannot be considered certain.

When describing the meetings of the community of Therapeutae, Philo tells us that their leader asks a question of Scripture or resolves a problem posed by another (*Contempl.* 75). The correspondence of the commentary's form with the *parašiyyôt* may also suggest a synagogal context. Nevertheless, given the scholastic form of the work, its social and intellectual context is more likely to have been a school of exegesis or a circle of exegetes. This does not preclude its use as a fund of material for preaching and exposition in the synagogue.

Influence

The legacy of the work is to be sought in early Christian rather than Jewish exegesis. Its contents were used by church fathers such as Origen, Didymus, Ambrose, and Augustine. Christians also took over the form of the question and answer, but they did not use it for running commentaries. Because of the poor transmission of the text, the *Questions and Answers* have been studied less intensively than other Philonic works. Much further research needs to be carried out on both form and content.

Allegorical Commentary

In modern scholarship the title *Allegorical Commentary* is applied to all the exegetical treatises of Philo that are included neither in his *Exposition of the Law* nor in his *Questions and Answers on Genesis and Exodus*. According to Eusebius, Philo himself gave to these treatises the title *Allegory of the Sacred Laws* (*Hist. Eccl.* 2.18.1). The treatises in the *Allegorical Commentary* numbered thirty-one; of these, nineteen survive in Greek but are usually referred to by their Latin titles (see the table on pp. 256-57). The *Allegorical Commentary* constitutes the most voluminous part of Philo's oeuvre. The treatises within the series cover important passages in Genesis 2–41 in a verse-by-verse commentary. In them Philo adapts the question-and-answer format. The questions, however, emerge from the exegesis of the passage, and the answers are lengthier and more complex than in his *Questions and Answers on Genesis and Exodus*. This series is of particular importance because it constitutes the first extant systematic inquiry into the book of Genesis, providing an in-depth analysis of each verse in light of its allegorical dimension as well as scholarly questions on the literal meaning. Philo addresses here a highly educated Jewish audience able to follow complicated discussions of minute details.

Exegetical Approach

The style of the *Allegorical Commentary* often strikes the modern reader as difficult and convoluted. It does not make for a fluent reading but demands the same kind of attention as rabbinic midrash, which similarly disregards the flow of the biblical stories and creatively engages each verse in its own right. Philo's style in the *Allegorical Commentary* is properly appreciated if we consider that he wished to put allegory on an academic footing, thus combining two genres which had hitherto not been connected. Academic investigations into foundational texts had a long tradition in Alexandria, having been practiced by both Homeric scholars and Jewish exegetes in the spirit of the *Aporemata Homerica* (works dealing with interpretive "difficulties" raised by Homer's epic poems, the *Iliad* and the *Odyssey*). In the second century B.C.E., the Jewish writer Demetrius provides crucial glimpses into this world of Jewish scholarship, which identified and solved problems of the biblical text, especially apparent contradictions between verses (Eusebius, *Praep. Evang.* 9.21.1-9; 9.29.1-3). This kind of literal and surprisingly critical scholarship on the biblical text became established in Alexandria at a very early stage, when Jewish exegesis in the land of Israel still proceeded in the style of "rewritten Bible" and the pesher commentaries from Qumran.

Philo was well aware of the scholarly enterprise of his colleagues, embracing some of it while vehemently opposing its more critical varieties. Overall he considered it very seriously, attempting to show that his own favored approach, namely spiritual allegory, was consistent with academic inquiry and even a natural continuation of it. This was a revolutionary step because allegorical interpretations had thus far been suggested rather freely, being justified at the most by etymological references. Philo's Jewish predecessors in the allegorical mode, such as Aristobulus and Aristeas, started with a question but offered their solution without providing an in-depth study of the literal meaning of the text. This is precisely what Philo aimed at in his *Allegorical Commentary,* thus setting new standards for allegorical interpretation.

The nature and origin of the allegorical method among Jews and Greeks are debated in modern scholarship. It is disputed whether allegory served merely as an apologetic means of defending a canonical text or whether it had a more creative function. Scholars have often identified allegory as a method invented by the Stoics, who sought ways of defending Homer's epics and thus suggested a more elevated, philosophical meaning to replace the literal, mythical level. This approach has been challenged with the observation that the Stoics did not introduce allegory, but were rather concerned with etymology, which investigated the root meanings of key words and eventually also led to allegory (Long 1992). Similarly, Philo has often been seen as adopting Stoic allegory in order to defend Scripture and render it more philosophical as well as Greek. This approach, too, has been challenged, with the counterclaim that Philo's method rather subjects Greek culture to the Jewish Scriptures (Dawson 1992). While Philo's allegory was conservative in the sense that it solved problems of the biblical text without considering radical literary solutions, such as emending the text, it is clear that he maintained the literal meaning of Scripture as far as the Law was concerned. It is well known that Philo opposed radical colleagues who substituted allegory for observance of laws like those pertaining to circumcision (*Migr.* 89–94). In his interpretations of the narrative parts of Scripture, the role of allegory varies: sometimes he offers an additional meaning, enriching Scripture by a further dimension (e.g., *Abr.* 68–80), while on other occasions he follows Aristobulus and uses allegory in order to uproot the mythological level of Scripture (e.g., *Leg.* 2.19).

Place in Philo's Corpus

The precise place of the *Allegorical Commentary* among Philo's works is still disputed today. Special attention has been given to the question of its relationship to Philo's *Questions and Answers,* which is most similar to it, because here, too, biblical verses are systematically quoted and then interpreted both literally and allegorically. It has been asserted that *Questions and Answers* is Philo's earliest work and that in it he was trying out ideas that he subsequently developed in the *Allegorical Commentary* (Terian 1991). Yet one could equally interpret the *Questions and Answers* as an abbreviation of thoughts presented in the *Allegorical Commentary.* The difference between the works is best understood as a difference of audience: while the *Allegorical Commentary* addresses specialized and highly educated readers, the *Questions and Answers* aims at more primary education, perhaps of young students in the Jewish community.

The Allegory of the Law *as a Representative Treatise*

The three books of the *Allegory of the Law (Legum allegoriae)* are the central piece of Philo's *Allegorical Commentary.* Philo presents here a close reading of clusters of running verses from the first two chapters of Genesis. Somewhat surprisingly he starts with Gen. 2:1, leaving out the creation of the world as described in Genesis 1. Either Philo's commentary on that chapter is lost (so Tobin 2000), or Philo decided not to comment on it allegorically because he considered it to be a separate unit (*Praem.* 1). Indeed, when treating it in his *Exposition of the Law,* he insisted that it may not be interpreted allegorically (*Opif.* 1–28). Philo's *Allegory of the Law* thus seems to have focused on the stories of the early heroes, which he regarded as belonging to the second part of the Torah dealing with "history" (*Praem.* 1).

Philo proceeds verse by verse in the *Allegory of the Law,* quoting a biblical passage, identifying a particular problem or question raised by it, and then discussing and ultimately resolving it on the allegorical level. A good example is *Leg.* 1.101-2, where Philo comments on Gen. 2:17, "But of the tree of knowledge of good and evil ye shall not eat." Using classical Greek terminology, Philo raises the difficulty why the command is here formulated in the plural, while in the previous verse God had addressed a single person, saying, "you may eat of every tree of the garden" (Gen. 2:16). Having defined the problem, Philo states his allegorical solution, again using standard academic terminology. He suggests that different forms of address have been chosen because the good is scarce but evil abounds.

Similar questions are raised in connection with the creation of man. Commenting on Gen. 2:7, Philo lines up several of them (*Leg.* 1.33):

> Someone may inquire why God generally considered worthy of the divine spirit the earthborn and body-loving mind . . . ; secondly, what is the precise meaning of the expression "breathed into"; thirdly, why was it breathed "into the face"; fourthly, why does he mention the word "breath" rather than "spirit" even though he knows the latter word, as when he said "and the spirit of God was lying upon the water"? (LXX Gen. 1:2)

Philo initially provides elaborate literal answers before embarking on the allegorical level. He thus insists, in response to the first query, that God is generous and happily provides good things to everyone; in response to the second, that the expression "breathed into" is the same as "blew into" or "put a soul into soulless things"; and, in response to the third, that there is a difference between "breath" and "spirit": the latter implies strength and vigor, while the former is like air. These explanations show how important the literal level was for Philo and how eager he was to integrate his allegorical approach with proper scholarship.

In terms of content, the *Allegory of the Law* covers some of the same ground that is treated in *De Opificio Mundi.* Most important of these is the issue of the double creation of man. Philo, for the first time in Jewish exegesis, addresses the question of why there are two creation stories that apparently convey contradictory accounts of man's creation. Philo solves this problem by arguing that the two stories refer to two types of man (*Leg.* 1.31; *Opif.* 34). Gen. 1:26 speaks of man's creation in the image of God, thus implying an ideal form of man who has nothing terrestrial about him, while Gen. 2:7 mentions man's creation out of the earth and thus speaks about a material creature. The ideal man was created first, serving as a model for his terrestrial equivalent. Philo thus adopts the Platonic notion of ideal forms, which are perfect and absolutely transcendental, serving as models for material creations. Although Plato himself did not yet speak about an ideal form of man, his students systematized his thought. Arius Didymus, an Alexandrian Platonist living a generation before Philo, is the first extant writer to mention an ideal form of man (Eusebius, *Praep. Evang.* 11.23).

When Philo dwells on the second account of creation, he gives special attention to the notion of divine breath entering the dust from the ground (Gen. 2:7). This gives him the opportunity to dwell on the relationship between mind and body. Philo assumes with Plato that the mind at first existed independently in a spiritual realm before it descended into the body, thus being imprisoned in the material world. Biblical writers still conceived of man in a holistic fashion and did not strongly distinguish his "spiritual" faculties from his material characteristics. A Jewish contemporary of Philo, however, as well as many rabbinic teachers, expressed similar notions of a body-mind dichotomy (Wis. 8:19; *Gen. Rab.* 34:10; *b. Sanhedrin* 71).

Other Treatises

Each of the treatises in Philo's *Allegorical Commentary* treats a particular passage in Genesis, focusing each time on a central subject or problem. Some even postulate an overall solution, such as the treatise *On the Unchangeableness of God,* which argues that the biblical indication of God's regret about the creation of man must not be read in an anthropomorphic vein, but taken allegorically as an affirmation of God's transcendence. Similarly, the treatises *On the Confusion of Tongues* and *On the Giants* treat biblical stories that appeared to many of Philo's Jewish contemporaries as mythological and parallel to stories in Greek literature. Applying both literal and allegorical methods, Philo aimed at showing that Scripture does not contain myth but only metaphysical truth.

Exposition of the Law

Philo's *Exposition of the Law* includes his treatise *On the Creation of the World (De opificio mundi)*, his lives of the Israelite patriarchs Abraham and Joseph *(De Abrahamo* and *De Iosepho)*, his treatise on the Ten Commandments *(De decalogo)*, and his four-volume commentary *On the Special Laws (De specialibus legibus)*. Two other treatises function as an epilogue to his treatment of the Mosaic Law: *On the Virtues (De virtutibus)* and *On Rewards and Punishments (De praemiis et poenis)*. These works are Philo's most accessible writings, in which he explains the principles of Jewish religion and history. While it has sometimes been assumed that the exoteric character of these writings presupposes a Gentile audience, it is now generally accepted that Philo primarily addressed fellow Jews in the community of Alexandria. Faced with multiple approaches and lively controversies, Philo aimed at expounding his own position. He hoped to gain a wider following and to expand his circle of students, who would ultimately also be able to read his more complicated works.

Stylistically, the *Exposition* clearly differs from Philo's other exegetical works. In his *Allegorical Commentary* and *Questions and Answers on Genesis and Exodus* he quotes Bible verses, offering respectively either an allegorical interpretation or a solution to a particular question. In the *Exposition*, by contrast, Philo freely paraphrases and rearranges biblical material, both in Genesis and in the legal passages of the Pentateuch. It is this style of "rewritten Bible" that makes these writings easily accessible to both ancient and modern readers.

In terms of contents, Philo pointed to a significant connection between the creation of the world, the lives of the patriarchs, and the specific laws. He wanted his treatises to be read in that order so that the discussion of the creation directly precedes the *Life of Abraham (Abr.* 2–3). This order is important and has been preserved in the Modern Hebrew edition of Philo's works, while the English edition interrupts the flow of the *Exposition*, introducing the *Allegorical Commentary* after the treatise on the creation.

The intended sequence of the *Exposition* rests on the notion that the Mosaic Law reflects the law of nature, which had already been enacted by the patriarchs even before the specific laws were given. Philo stresses that "Moses wished to show initially that the ordinances laid down are not at variance with Nature and, secondly, that it is not hard for those who wish to live in accordance with the established laws, seeing that . . . the forefathers readily and easily lived under them" *(Abr.* 5). The thread running through the whole *Exposition* is thus the coherence of norms attested in nature by the creation of the world, in history by the lives of the patriarchs, and in legislation by the specific laws of the Pentateuch.

The precise scope and place of the *Exposition* within Philo's overall work are still disputed today. It is difficult, for example, to know how Philo's two-volume *Life of Moses* relates to the *Exposition*. The second part in particular deviates significantly from the genres of the rewritten Bible and biography. This treatise, moreover, takes into account a wider, apparently also non-Jewish audience (*Mos.* 1.1-2). For these reasons it is usually not included in the *Exposition*, but E. R. Goodenough's plea to consider it as a "companion piece" has gained wide acceptance (Goodenough 1933; Morris 1987).

The place of the *Exposition* within Philo's overall work also remains a matter of debate. The question usually asked is whether it should be seen as the fruit of his ripe old age or as the precursor to his *Allegorical Commentary*. Formulated thus, the question probably misses the point, as it presupposes that Philo wrote each series *in toto* before approaching the other. The question also implies that the different series reflect an intellectual development on the part of Philo. According to some, he started as an allegorist and subsequently became a more literal expounder of the Torah, while others argue that he started with a more general type of exegesis, becoming more text-oriented and allegorical in his old age. It is, however, far more likely that Philo pursued different aims with different audiences, working alternatively on various kinds of treatises. He wanted each reader to be aware of the other works in the series without, however, intending a complete separation. Indeed, Philo freely introduced allegorical passages in his *Exposition* and *Questions and Answers on Genesis and Exodus*, while both questions-and-answers and literal paraphrases appear as well in his *Allegorical Commentary*.

On the Creation of the World (De opificio mundi)

The first part of Philo's *Exposition* is his treatise *On the Creation of the World*, which sets the tone for the whole series. Taking the story of creation as a fundamental theological issue (*Opif.* 170–72), Philo defines his own understanding over against other prevalent opinions. He fervently rejects a metaphorical reading of the creation, as offered by students of Plato and Aristotle as well as some fellow Jews, who all believed in the eternity of the world (*Opif.* 7–8, 26–28; *Aet.* 10–17). Insisting on the literal meaning of

Genesis as well as Plato's *Timaeus,* Philo stresses that Moses and the Greek philosopher perceived the true nature of the creator God, who is active and transcending the material world, but taking providential care of His creation (*Opif.* 8–22). Most scholars today recognize that, according to Philo, God's creation of the world was not *ex nihilo.* Living in an age when this notion did not yet exist, Philo rather assumed that God's creation consists in actively shaping the preexistent, passive material (*Opif.* 8–12).

Another issue of fundamental importance is discussed in the treatise on the creation: the nature and origin of mankind. Philo is the first known exegete to give serious attention to the crux of the two creation stories: one depicts man created together with woman in the image of God, while the other envisions man as having been created from the earth, but endowed with the divine spirit, while Eve was created secondarily, being molded from Adam's ribs. Philo suggests a reconciliation of these two stories, arguing that they refer to different types of man. While the first story describes, in his view, the ideal type of man, perfectly rational and sexless, the second speaks about the earthly type as a copy of the ideal man (*Opif.* 69–71, 134–35). While it is generally agreed that Philo employs the Platonic categories of ideal and copy, it is still disputed to what extent his exegesis betrays a particularly misogynist perspective. Does his discussion of the ideal type not imply male categories, constructing the archetype of man in masculine terms? Furthermore, does his praise of the earthly Adam, before "woman becomes for him the beginning of blameworthy life" (*Opif.* 51), not indicate a substantial rejection of women and femininity? Winston has countered these interpretations by proposing that we interpret such passages in their proper context. Philo, he stresses, also praises the "fellowship" between husband and wife (*Opif.* 152), while, more generally, his views on women are shared by many ancient writers (Winston 1998).

On Abraham (De Abrahamo) *and* On Joseph (De Iosepho)

The second part of Philo's *Exposition* is devoted to a biographical treatment of the major Israelite patriarchs. Philo's lives of the patriarchs are no longer fully extant. While the biographies of Abraham and Joseph are still available, those of Jacob and Isaac have unfortunately not survived. In telling the lives of the patriarchs, Philo was intrigued by the connection between a person's character and his actions. He was keen to show how traces of character visible in early infancy subsequently reach maturity and enable the hero to play his destined role in life. In Philo's view, all the forefathers, starting from Enosh, were men "yearning after virtue" (*Abr.* 48). Each did so in his own particular way, Enosh, for example, by setting his hope on the Creator. The exemplary triad, Abraham, Isaac and Jacob, however, were of an exceptionally high order, embodying virtue to such an extent that they practically transcended their human status and represented the pure virtues of teaching, nature, and practice (*Abr.* 54). Joseph, by contrast, is an appendix personifying the politician compromising virtue because of pressing circumstances.

The *Life of Abraham* is famous for its interpretation of Abraham's migration to the land of Canaan (*Abr.* 62–80). Philo offers two complementary perspectives, one literal and the other allegorical. Abraham's migration in the literal sense, Philo explains, was "more of the soul than of the body," because the patriarch showed an exceptional degree of detachment from earthly things, while proving to be wholly devoted to the divine command (*Abr.* 66). This attitude enabled him to take a solitary step, leaving behind all his material attachments. On the allegorical level, Abraham's migration signifies the path of a "virtue-loving soul in its search for the true God" (*Abr.* 69). The different stages of the journey thus represent different stages of spiritual development, Chaldea signifying reliance on visible phenomena and Haran trust in the senses, while the land of Canaan/Israel symbolizes the soul's ascent to God himself. In a passage that has sometimes been identified as descriptive of a mystical experience, Philo explains how God in his love for humankind does not turn away his face "when the soul approaches" (*Abr.* 79). The literal and the allegorical interpretation thus complement each other, one presenting a historical example of the correct spiritual attitude, the other envisioning any soul on its path to God.

On the Decalogue (De decalogo), On the Special Law (De specialibus legibus), On the Virtue (De virtutibus), On Rewards and Punishments (De praemiis et poenis)

The third part of Philo's *Exposition* is devoted to a treatment of the Mosaic legislation itself. His discussion is divided into five books, one treating the Decalogue *(De decalogo)*, the other four dealing with the specific laws *(specialibus legibus)*. Two additional treatises function as an epilogue:

treating the virtues *(De virtutibus)*, the other the rewards and punishments resulting from observance or nonobservance of the Law *(De praemiis et poenis)*. Philo argues that the Decalogue introduces the main categories underlying the specific laws, which are accordingly collected under the headings of the Ten Commandments. While in Philo's view all of Mosaic Law is a reflection of the law of nature and thus anchored in the creation of the world, it nevertheless distinguishes the Jews as a nation of spiritual pioneers. Following the Law, Jews implement the most stringent values and set a moral example for the world. The overall marker of Mosaic Law is its call to transcend the material world in the fields of cultic worship, sexuality, and food. Mosaic stringency isolates the Jews, clearly defining their identity vis-à-vis the Egyptians, Persians, Greeks, and Romans.

Philo's approach is decidedly different from that of the rabbis. Unlike them, he neither knows of the Mishnah nor considers the application of Mosaic Law to specific cases. He does not deal with halakic issues or reflect the hypothetical decisions of local Alexandrian law courts, as Goodenough suggested in a controversial argument. Philo's discussion of the Torah instead relies on a philosophical approach similar to that of Saadja Gaon in the Middle Ages. He attempts to categorize the laws and to explain their underlying meaning. He does not distinguish between rational and revealed commandments, as later Jewish philosophers do, but argues for the rationality of all the commandments. In his view, even the food laws were set up in order to teach spiritual values. Pork, for example, was forbidden precisely because it is the most delicious of meats. Abstinence from it is thus a perfect way of inculcating self-restraint.

Today it is widely recognized that both Philo's approach and the details of his discussion differ from the rabbinic discourse in the land of Israel. Ignorant of Hebrew and Aramaic, he was not inspired by contemporary teachers in Jerusalem. As a proud Diaspora Jew living in the cultural ᵉtropolis of Alexandria, Philo apparently saw no reason to seek instruc in Jerusalem.

ᵃl Works

ɪrks have been transmitted by early Christianity rather
ᵉsents a high point in the long-established Greek Jewish
ora. This tradition, which produced the Greek trans-

lation of the Hebrew Bible, connected Greek education and philosophy with Jewish culture, and adapted many elements of the surrounding culture, perhaps most importantly allegorical interpretation. This technique had been used by Stoics in their interpretation of mythology, but it has been questioned whether or not they influenced Philo directly. Earlier Jewish-Greek authors whose writings are almost entirely lost may also have had significance for the author. Other influences came from contemporary Platonism. Philo perceived the human soul as the central element in the ascent to divine contemplation. He considered the divine revelation manifest in the Scriptures equal to the highest form of philosophy. Another distinctive element of his thought was his perception of the divine Logos and its role in the creation of the world. The Logos, the active principle of God's thought, was at times perceived as the creator of the cosmos and at other times as the mediator between God and the world.

Scholars have debated at length which of the two, the philosophical or the exegetical aspects, were more dominant in Philo's writing. The question as formulated is overly simplified and therefore difficult to answer. Both aspects are important for Philo, but most of his treatises are allegorical commentaries on the Pentateuch, which may be considered the basis of his interests.

Most of Philo's treatises have been preserved, and the philosophical works represent only a small part. The works include *On the Eternity of the World, That Every Good Man Is Free, On Providence 1 and 2,* and *Whether Animals Have Reason.* The two former have been transmitted in the original Greek. The latter three are known through Armenian translations from the sixth century, although fragments of *On Providence* are extant in Greek.

Although Philo's writing shows a strong philosophical orientation in general, the five above-mentioned treatises have been singled out as "philosophical" because of the prevalence of philosophical argumentation and the lack of allegorical interpretation in them; in fact, they hardly contain any direct references to the Scriptures. For this and other reasons these works have often been treated as stepchildren in Philo's oeuvre. To explain the absence of scriptural references and some inconsistencies in Philo's philosophical views, scholars have argued that these treatises could have stemmed from his youth before he was fully immersed in his Jewish heritage. This argument, however, is problematic, contradicts details within Philo's works, and in the end has proven untenable.

In addition, some scholars have tried to dismiss these works as altogether inauthentic. In the last twenty-five years, however, closer attention has been given to the literary structure and the content of these treatises in an effort to explain their idiosyncrasies. New editions and translations have been published — some of the works, such as *About Animals,* had never been translated into a modern language. Scholars have also advanced specific reasons why these works appeared in their particular format and why they should be considered genuine.

The philosophical works are important in their own right, because they show that Philo was well acquainted with certain aspects of Hellenistic philosophy. They also provide valuable insight into the contemporary culture and the study of ancient philosophy in the first century. The five treatises deal with a variety of subjects that were common topics in ancient philosophy of the time.

On the Eternity of the World (De aeternitate mundi)

The main proposition in this work is the question of whether the world is destructible or not. The question is also raised whether the world came into existence or was uncreated. The work is typical of its time in linking the notions of coming into existence and ceasing to exist.

The treatise consists of an introduction, followed by a sequence of arguments which present various, often opposing, philosophical views. Philo offers arguments in favor of one or another position, although these may not necessarily reflect his personal views and may even be contrary to his own position. One section of the work is no longer extant, and there has been much speculation about what it would have contained. The most probable solution seems to be that the missing part reflected Philo's own position on the question of the indestructibility of the world.

After the introduction, in which he defines the meanings of the words for "world" and "destruction," Philo lists three main positions among philosophical schools: (1) The cosmos (or a plurality of worlds) is created and destructible, a view ascribed to Democritus, Epicurus, and most of the Stoics. Philo adds that the Stoics accept God as cause of the genesis of the world but not of its destruction; this is supposedly an editorial comment on Philo's part. (2) The cosmos is uncreated and indestructible — the Aristotelian position and that of certain Pythagoreans. Philo agrees with Aristotle on the perfection of the cosmos and its indestructibility, but disagrees that the world is uncreated. (3) The cosmos is created and indestructible — a view attributed to Plato and possibly Hesiod before him. This view also agrees with the biblical narrative in the book of Genesis. Philo maintains that long before Hesiod Moses was the source of inspiration for this doctrine and gives a (rare) biblical reference to the book of Genesis.

The doxographic sequence above shows that Philo envisioned an ascending order that finds its high point in Moses as the ultimate guarantee of the doctrine that the cosmos is created and indestructible. In his other major work, *On the Creation of the World* (7–12), Philo gives clarifications to the doxography outlined here. Together with most Platonists and against the Aristotelians, he accepts the view that the world is created. In theory it should come to an end, but it is preserved from destruction by the will and providence of the Creator. It remains unclear whether Philo thought that God created matter, out of which the world is fashioned, or that matter preceded the creation of the world. Moreover, Philo did not perceive creation as a creation in time, since time only originated with the world, but rather as depending for its existence on an external cause.

The exposition sets the stage for the remainder of the work, in which Philo continues at length arguing the three positions outlined above.

That Every Good Man Is Free
(Quod omnis probus liber sit)

That Every Good Man Is Free is about the freedom of the just according to Stoic principles. At the beginning of the treatise Philo informs his readers that it is the sequel of another work (now lost), entitled *That Every Bad Person Is a Slave*. Philo develops the Stoic paradox that only the wise person is free. The paradox states that things generally considered desirable belong only to the virtuous. The premise of this thought is that the only good is that which is morally good.

After a general introduction and praise of wisdom and the soul, Philo comes to his main point: that of true freedom. True freedom, like true sovereignty, means following God and freeing oneself from passions and desires. It can be postulated that in his previous work on slavery Philo would have argued the converse: that being a slave is being dependent on passions and desires. The idea is that wise persons alone master their emotions, desires, and fears. After some digressions on contempt of death, bravery, and obedience, Philo gives examples of free persons who, like Moses, are happy and friends of God. They are free because of their voluntary actions and because they cannot be compelled to do wrong. They also treat indifferent things with indifference; this refers to the Stoic concept of *adiaphora:* things that do not carry any positive or negative value in moral terms.

The remainder of the treatise deals with stories of people who are exemplary for the subject. Philo refers to traditional tales, such as of Calanos, Anaxarchos, Zeno, and Diogenes. He also includes a lengthy account of the Essenes; their ascetic way of life earns them a place in this treatise. He accentuates their innocence, rejection of slave labor, study of the law, devotion to God and neighbors, sharing of goods, and providing help for the sick and the poor. This account, which is quoted by the church historian Eusebius, is one of our few sources of knowledge about the Essenes.

On Providence 1 and 2 (De providentia)

These treatises on divine providence are stylized dialogues between Philo and his apostate nephew Alexander. The works are transmitted in an Armenian translation; a substantial part of the second book is extant in Greek. The first book offers an extensive account of the workings of God's providence. Alexander has doubts about the concept and brings in multiple objections, while Philo believes that it governs the world. Like other Platonists of his time, Philo tries to find a balance between an absolute free will and inflexible determinism. He maintains the autonomy of the will as a basis for ethical judgment, while at the same time preserving the doctrine of divine providence.

The second book continues the discussion. Starting with the problem of retribution, Alexander argues that wicked people often fare well and good people fare badly. Polycrates and Socrates are cases in point for Alexander. Philo responds that God does not necessarily punish evil immediately and that the wicked are never really happy. External goods have no value in the presence of God, and the true philosopher despises them. Sages defy poverty and ill-treatment — Socrates, Zeno, and Anaxarchos being the examples.

Other arguments deal with the theory of creation and the order of the world, all in the context of providence. The problem of evil in nature is part of the dialogue as well; natural nuisances, such as bad weather and savage animals, or disasters, such as earthquakes and floods, are discussed. Philo stresses the value of temperance, which is not dependent on natural causes but on moral behavior.

Whether Animals Have Reason (De animalibus)

Like the previous treatises, this work has been transmitted in Armenian. It again reflects a discourse between Alexander and Philo, but a third person is also involved, Lysimachus, a nephew of Alexander. In the first part of the work Alexander argues for the rationality of animals; the second part carries Philo's refutation. It again shows that Philo is heavily indebted to Stoic and Platonic points of view. He draws on Stoicism to prove the distance between humans and animals. An elaborate scheme of all existence lies in the background: divisions exist between corporeal and incorporeal, animate and inanimate, rational and irrational, mortals and divine beings, and ultimately between male and female. The discourse is, however, less about animals than about humans in their relationship with other beings. The divide between man and all other beings is the ability to reason. In his closing arguments Philo maintains that it would be unjust to grant equality to unequal entities. Philo considers it an insult to treat those endowed with reason in the same way as irrational creatures. In spite of Philo's preoccupation with human superiority, the treatise provides a wealth of information for zoological and botanical studies of early imperial times.

Apologetic Treatises

Philo appears to have written at least eight treatises that are generally considered to be apologetic. Unfortunately, only three of these and fragments of a fourth are preserved. As with the three commentary series *(Questions and Answers on Genesis and Exodus,* the *Allegorical Commentary,* and the *Exposition of the Law),* Philo did not conceive of these treatises as a single unit. While he grouped some of them into larger units, the category of apologetic treatises is a modern construct. Scholars apply it to these treatises because they situate Judaism in the Roman Empire. In some cases the treatises are direct responses to criticisms; in other cases, the works champion Jewish values in the context of the larger world. The implied audiences are non-Jewish, although this would not exclude Jewish readers from using them in their attempts to situate themselves in a Greco-Roman context.

Setting

While Philo might have written some of the treatises early in his life, the bulk of the treatises — and all those extant — were associated with the pogrom that broke out in Alexandria in 38 C.E. and its aftermath. The explosion occurred when Agrippa I visited Alexandria on his way to claim the kingdom that Gaius had given him. A group of Alexandrians mocked the king, and riots broke out. Two leading Alexandrians, Isodorus and Lampo, promised the governor Flaccus support with the new emperor if he, in turn, would support their efforts against the Jews. Flaccus, whose standing with the new emperor was shaky because of his ties to Tiberius, agreed, and the pogrom was on. He had, however, misread the political landscape. He was summoned to Rome, accused in part by none other than Isodorus and Lampo, and exiled. The new prefect, C. Vitrasius Pollio, moved the issue from the streets into the courtroom. Two embassies set out for Rome: an Alexandrian headed by Isodorus and Apion and a Jewish headed by Philo. After two hearings, it was apparent that the emperor favored the Alexandrians. Philo described the second reception of the Jewish delegation in these words: "When we entered, we immediately knew on the basis of his glance and body language that we had not come to a judge, but to an accuser, more hostile than those who opposed us" (*Embassy* 349). Following the assassination of Gaius on 24 January 41 C.E., hostilities broke out again. Claudius quickly suppressed them, heard both delegations, and issued a decree that attempted to reestablish the policies of Julius Caesar and Augustus (Josephus, *Ant.* 19.279). However, neither group of antagonists was ready to give up: both the Alexandrians and Jews sent second delegations (*CPJ* 153 lines 87-92). Claudius settled the matter with a famous letter that gave the Jewish community in Alexandria the right to practice their ancestral religion but closed the door for them to have more (*CPJ* 153).

Philo described his being thrust into these events in a famous passage: "There was once a time when by pursuing the study of philosophy and the contemplation of the cosmos and its contents, I enjoyed the beautiful, desirable, and truly blessed mind." These days were gone. "But the most troublesome of evils, good-hating envy, lay in wait for me. Suddenly it fell on me and did not stop pulling me down until it cast me down into a great sea of civil cares in which I am carried along — unable even to keep my head above water" (*Spec.* 3.1-6). While this might refer to a more general role that Philo played in the community, it probably alludes to his appointment as a member of the Jewish delegation that left Alexandria in the winter of

39 and arrived in Rome the next spring (Philo, *Legat.* 355; Josephus, *Ant.* 18.257-60). Philo suffered through the indignities of Gaius and the arrival of a second Jewish delegation. Philo probably returned to Alexandria following Claudius's letter. It was in the maelstrom of these "civil cares" that Philo wrote his apologetic treatises.

The Hypothetica

One of the most enigmatic works attributed to Philo is the *Hypothetica.* While Eusebius knew and accepted the work as Philonic, some modern scholars have registered doubts. The ambiguous position of the work is represented by its place in the standard critical edition: Cohn and Wendland omitted the fragments in their *editio major* but included it in their *editio minor.* Although the work is poorly preserved and has some unusual features, the majority of scholars consider it authentic.

Eusebius preserved two fragments. He attributed the first fragment to the first scroll of a work entitled the *Hypothetica* that "argued on behalf of the Jews against their accusers" (*Praep. Evang.* 8.5.11–8.7.20). Later the bishop quoted a fragment "from his apology on behalf of the Jews" (*Praep. Evang.* 8.10.19–8.11.18). The two excerpts are probably from the same work: Eusebius dropped the opaque title *Hypothetica* when he introduced the second fragment and repeated his description of the work as an apology. This is confirmed by his division of the Jewish people into two groups in his preface to the second fragment: the multitudes follow the literal meaning of the Law (first fragment), while the philosophical group of Essenes (second fragment) move to higher forms of contemplation (8.10.18-19). The relationship between the fragments is complicated by Eusebius's catalogue of Philo's works in the *Historia Ecclesiastica,* where the bishop does not mention the *Hypothetica* but includes a one-volume work *Concerning the Jews* (*Hist. Eccl.* 2.18.6). This title is a common heading for works that deal with the Jewish people and was probably a secondary title. While it is possible that *Concerning the Jews* refers to the *Hypothetica,* the fact that it is listed among the single-scroll works of Philo, while the *Praeparatio Evangelica* suggests that the *Hypothetica* contained at least two scrolls, makes the identification problematic.

The title *Hypothetica* does not help us understand the work. It has been taken variously to mean "Suppositions," based on the hypothetical approach of the opening of fragment 1; "Counsels or Admonitions," based on the use of *hypothēkē* elsewhere in Philo; "Imputations" in the sense of false opinions about Jews; or "Hypothetical Propositions," based on the use of the term in Stoic logic. While certainty is not possible, the last possibility would explain the setting of the work: it was probably intended to prepare Philo for his exchanges with his Alexandrian opponents who were influenced by Stoicism — in particular, Chaeremon (*CPJ* 153). Philo used Stoic logic to deflect the criticisms about Jewish origins.

The work deals with the exodus and settlement in the land (8.6.1-9), the law code (8.7.1-20), and the Essenes (8.11.1-18). The treatment of historical issues plays freely with biblical traditions in an effort to exonerate the Jews and Moses by arguing on the basis of logical probabilities rather than historical evidence. The fivefold epitome of the Law is similar to the summaries in Pseudo-Phocylides and Josephus's *Against Apion* 2.145-219, esp. 190-219. While there have been different explanations for the relationships among these treatments, it is likely that they drew from a common tradition, perhaps from common thematic treatments in Jewish ethical instruction. The treatment of the Essenes is similar to but not identical with Philo's treatment of them in other treatises.

On the Contemplative Life (De vita contemplativa)

Philo gave another brief account of the Essenes in *Quod Omnis Probus Liber Sit* 75–91. He also referred to a treatise devoted fully to them in the opening of his treatment of the Therapeutae (*Contempl.* 1). Since the statement presupposes an entire treatise, it cannot refer to the account in *Probus*. If the account of the Essenes in *Praep. Evang.* 8.11.1-18 is from the second book of the *Hypothetica*, it could refer to it. The alternative is that it refers to a lost treatise.

Philo treated the Essenes and Therapeutae similarly. Aristotle distinguished four eudaemonistic lives, of which the active and contemplative were the most important (*Ethica Nicomachea* 1.5.1-8). Stoics picked up Diogenes Laertius 7.92, while others added a third, the rational (Diogenes Laertius 7.130). Philo knew this discussion and, like the Stoics, thought that the active and contemplative lives could be united (*Mos.* 1.48). In his treatments of the Essenes and Therapeutae, he suggested that the Essenes were an example of the active life and the Therapeutae a model of the contemplative life.

Philo held both groups of Jewish philosophers out to the larger world as "athletes of virtue." The descriptions stand in the same tradition as the depictions of Egyptian priests in Chaeremon (in Porphyry, *De abstinentia* 4.6-8), the Indian sages in Arrian (*Indica* 11.1-8) and Philostratus (*Vita Apollonii* 3.10-51), the naked Egyptian sages in Philostratus (*Vita Apollonii* 6.6), the Neopythagoreans in Iamblichus (*Vita Pythagorae* 96–100), and the Essenes in Pliny (*Naturalis historia* 5.73) and Josephus (*J.W.* 2.120-61 and *Ant.* 18.18-22). While Philo may have known the Therapeutae personally, his account is shaped by the concern to present a Jewish counter to these other groups. He discussed the meaning of their name (2–12) and their lifestyle (13–39), and contrasted their symposium with those of the Greeks (40–90).

The most likely time for the composition of this work is in the aftermath of the pogrom. Philo may have written the treatise for the benefit of a Roman audience and could have thought of it as a counter to Chaeremon's presentation of the Egyptian priests.

On the Virtues (De virtutibus)

The setting for Philo's treatise *On Virtues* is suggested by the subtitle given in most of the manuscripts that refer to it as the fourth book of *Concerning the Virtues*. Some of the same manuscripts refer to the *Embassy to Gaius* as the first book of *Concerning the Virtues*. The relationship between the two is confused in the ancient sources. Eusebius mentioned that Philo had "related what happened to the Jews in the time of Gaius in five books" (*Hist. Eccl.* 2.5.1). He went on to mention the *Embassy* (2.5.6) and without indicating any shift in the work under consideration, the second book, *Concerning the Virtues* (2.6.3). When the bishop gave his catalogue of Philo's works, he said that "he came to Rome in the time of Gaius and in the time of Claudius is said to have read before the full Roman Senate the account that he wrote about Gaius's impiety that he — with tactful irony — entitled *Concerning the Virtues*" (2.18.8).

There are a number of ways to reconstruct the data from Eusebius and the manuscripts. If we follow the lead of the texts themselves, the following is reasonable. Philo opened his work *Against Flaccus* with "the next after Sejanus to continue his plot against the Jews was Flaccus Avillius" (*Flacc.* 1). This suggests that Philo wrote an earlier treatise about Sejanus. Eusebius tells us that this was the second book of *Concerning the Virtues* (*Chronicle*; cf. *Hist. Eccl.* 2.5.6-7). If the bishop is correct, our *Flaccus* would be the third treatise in the series. Philo ended the *Embassy* with a reference to the *Palinode* or *Reversal* (*Embassy* 373). If *Flaccus* and the *Embassy* belong to the same series, the first two volumes have been lost, the third is *Flaccus*, the fourth the *Embassy*, and the fifth has been lost. The association of *On the Contemplative Life* with this series correctly recognizes the social setting of the treatise, but appears to have associated it with *Concerning the Virtues* incorrectly.

Against Flaccus (In Flaccum) *and* Embassy to Gaius (Legatio ad Gaium)

The two treatises, *Against Flaccus* and the *Embassy to Gaius*, share a common perspective: they demonstrate how God has protected the Jewish people through crises and reversed the fortunes of those who have persecuted them. The structures of the two works make the point unambiguously: *Flaccus* 1–96 relates the pogrom in Alexandria and 97–191 narrates Flaccus's exile and eventual execution; the *Embassy* relates Gaius's insane opposition to the Jews while the missing *Palinode* related his assassination. Eusebius says that Philo read his account of Gaius to the Roman Senate (*Hist. Eccl.* 2.18.8). While this stretches credibility, the works were undoubtedly intended to demonstrate the folly of persecuting the Jews to any outsiders and the protection of God to insiders.

Achievement

Philo was not a systematic thinker, although there have been noble attempts to make him one. He was first and foremost an exegete or interpreter of Moses. He called himself "an interpreter" (*Anim.* 7, 74; cf. also *Opif.* 5). This does not mean that he did not have a comprehensive understanding of the cosmos, but that he did not work out a systematic presentation of it. He wrote commentaries and works that addressed specific issues. His lifelong project was to interpret the Jewish Scriptures allegorically through the lens of Hellenistic philosophy. In this regard his project was similar to Chaeremon's interpretation of Egyptian texts through Stoic philosophy or Plutarch's allegory of Egyptian myths through Middle Platonic thought (*Isis and Osiris*) or Numenius of Apamea's explanations of oriental traditions via Platonism (*On the Good*).

Philo did have a specific lens through which he read his ancestral Scriptures. It was captured in antiquity by the *bon mot:* "Either Plato philonizes or Philo platonizes" (Jerome, *On Famous Men* 11). Philo's task may have been to interpret Moses, but the Moses he read was a Platonized Moses. Unlike a number of Jews and later Christians who constructed a history of culture in which they subordinated Hellenistic thought to Jewish thought by making the "theft of philosophy" argument, Philo, who knew the argument and referred to it on occasion, appears to have believed that Moses and Plato had seen the same realities. Philo did not believe that he needed to read Plato into Moses, but out of Moses. For example, he argued that the "pattern of the tent" that Moses saw before he constructed the Tabernacle demonstrated the presence of Platonic ideas (Exod. 25:9, 40 in *Moses* 2.74, 76; Exod. 25:9 in *QE* 2.52; Exod. 25:40 in *QE* 2.82; and Exod. 26:30 in *QE* 2.90). It was from such a perspective that he interwove Plato's *Timaeus* into his treatises, especially *Creation* and the *Allegorical Interpretations* 1–3.

This does not mean that Philo was a Platonist; he was not if we understand him on his own terms. Nor does it mean that he restricted his philosophical lens to Platonism; he did not. Like most Hellenistic thinkers, he was eclectic. For thinkers like Antiochus of Ascalon, Eudorus, Arius Didymus, and many others, different systems of thought contributed to the understanding of reality. The best course of action was to draw the best from each tradition, even if a single tradition served as the overarching *Weltanschauung.* Philo falls easily into this perspective. He incorporated into his treatises not only Middle Platonic perspectives but also Stoic and Neopythagorean ones. Stoicism was the common coin of the Hellenistic and Roman worlds. Philo drew from a significant number of Stoic concepts, including cosmological, anthropological, and ethical views. His arguments for providence are largely Stoic. Similarly, he adopted Neopythagorean arithmology. His basic frame of thought was Platonic, but this was not an exclusive commitment for him.

Assessments of his contribution have been extreme. H. A. Wolfson thought that he created the system of thought that became the basis for medieval philosophy and theology until Spinoza deconstructed it. On the other end of the spectrum, Richard Goulet considered him to be a hack who spoiled a far more brilliant allegorical commentary on the entire Pentateuch. Most scholars fall between these two poles in their assessment, although there is no unanimity on specifics. One critical area where Philo did make a lasting contribution was in theology proper: he considered

God to be ontologically prior to everything else that was good. He identified the *ho ōn* of Exod. 3:14 with the *to on* of Platonism and emphasized divine transcendence (*Det.* 160; *Mut.* 11–15). Like other Middle Platonists, he posited an intermediary who was God's face to the cosmos and humanity's access to God, that is, the Logos. He thought that the Logos was God's image based on his interpretation of Gen. 1:27. In his thought there is God, the Image of God (the Logos), and human beings who were created in the image of God's Image (the Logos) (*Opif.* 24–25). Humanity can ascend to God through the Logos. The Scriptures are the key to understanding this reality. He understood that philosophy and the Scriptures taught the same thing about the Ultimate Cause (*Virt.* 65). Philosophy provided an intellectual framework, but it did not displace the legislation of Moses as the authoritative statement of the divine realities.

An assessment of Philo depends on how he is measured. If he is measured by the impact of his work on subsequent thinkers, then we may call this Jewish writer "the first Christian theologian." If, on the other hand, he is measured by what he accomplished, we may say that he is the most important representative and apex of the rich Jewish exegetical tradition that flourished in Alexandria from the end of the third century B.C.E. to the beginning of the second century C.E.

BIBLIOGRAPHY

General

Text
Cohn, Leopold, Paul Wendland, Siegfried Reiter, and Hans Leisegang, eds. 1896-1930. *Philonis Alexandrini opera quae supersunt.* 7 vols. Berlin: Reimer (2d ed. 1962).

Translations
Arnaldez, Roger, Clement Mondéseret, and Jean Pouilloux. 1961-1992. *Les Œuvres de Philon d'Alexandrie.* 34 vols. Paris: Cerf.
Cohn, Leopold, Isaak Heinemann, Maximilian Adler, and Willy Theiler. 1909-1938. *Philo von Alexandria: Die Werke in deutscher Übersetzung.* 7 vols. Breslau: Marcus (2d ed. Berlin: de Gruyter, 1962-1964).
Colson, Francis H., George H. Whitaker, and Ralph Markus. 1929-1962. *Philo.* 10 vols. and 2 supp. vols. LCL. Cambridge: Harvard University Press.

Bibliographies

Radice, Roberto, and David T. Runia. 1988. *Philo of Alexandria: An Annotated Bibliography 1937-1986*. Leiden: Brill.

Runia, David T. 2000. *Philo of Alexandria: An Annotated Bibliography 1987-1996*. Leiden: Brill (updated each year in *Studia Philonica Annual*).

―――. 2012. *Philo of Alexandria: An Annotated Bibliography 1997-2006*. Leiden: Brill.

Reference Works

Borgen, Peder, Karl Fuglseth, and Roald Skarsten. 2000. *The Philo Index: A Complete Greek Word Index to the Writings of Philo of Alexandria*. Grand Rapids: Eerdmans; Leiden: Brill.

Runia, David T., and Gregory E. Sterling, eds. 1989-. *The Studia Philonica Annual*. Atlanta: Society of Biblical Literature.

Sterling, Gregory E., ed. 2001-. The Philo of Alexandria Commentary Series. Leiden: Brill.

Studies

Borgen, Peder. 1997. *Philo of Alexandria: An Exegete for His Time*. Leiden: Brill.

Bréhier, Émile. 1950. *Les Idées philosophiques et religieuses de Philon d'Alexandrie*. Paris: Vrin.

Dillon, John M. 1996. *The Middle Platonists, 80 B.C. to A.D. 220*. Rev. ed. Ithaca: Cornell University Press.

Goodenough, Erwin R. 1935. *By Light, Light: The Mystic Gospel of Hellenistic Judaism*. New Haven: Yale University Press.

Goulet, Richard. 1987. *La philosophie de Moïse: Essai de reconstitution d'un commentaire philosophique préphilonien de pentateuque*. Paris: Vrin.

Hadas-Lebel, Mirielle. 2012. *Philo of Alexandria: A Thinker in the Jewish Diaspora*. Leiden: Brill.

Heinemann, Isaak. 1973. *Philons griechische und jüdische Bildung: Kulturvergleichende Untersuchungen zu Philons Darstellung der jüdischen Gesetze*. Hildesheim: Olms.

Kamesar, Adam, ed. 2009. *The Cambridge Companion to Philo*. Cambridge: Cambridge University Press.

Nikiprowetzky, Valentin. 1977. *Le commentaire de l'écriture chez Philon d'Alexandrie: Son caractère et sa portée; observations philologiques*. Leiden: Brill.

Runia, David T. 1986. *Philo of Alexandria and the Timaeus of Plato*. Leiden: Brill.

―――. 1993. *Philo in Early Christian Literature: A Survey*. Assen: Van Gorcum; Minneapolis: Fortress.

Tobin, Thomas H. 1983. *The Creation of Man: Philo and the History of Interpretation*. Washington, D.C.: Catholic Biblical Association of America.

Winston, David. 1985. *Logos and Mystical Theology in Philo of Alexandria*. Cincinnati: Hebrew Union College Press; Hoboken, N.J.: KTAV.

Wolfson, Harry Austryn. 1948. *Philo: Foundations of Religious Philosophy in Judaism, Christianity, and Islam.* 2 vols. Cambridge: Harvard University Press.

Zeller, Dieter. 2011. *Studien zu Philo und Paulus.* Göttingen: V&R unipress.

Questions and Answers on Genesis and Exodus

Armenian Text and Latin Translation

Aucher, Johannes Baptista. 1826. *Philonis Judaei Paralipomena Armena, Libri Videlicet Quatuor in Genesin, Libri Duo in Exodum.* Venice: Typis Coenobii PP. Aremnorum in Insula S. Lazari.

English Translation

Marcus, Ralph. 1953. *Philo of Alexandria.* Suppl. vols. 1 and 2. LCL. Cambridge, Mass.: Harvard University Press.

French Translation

Mercier, Charles, and Abraham Terian. 1979-1992, *Quaestiones in Genesin* and *Quaestiones in Exodum.* 2 vols. Les Œuvres de Philon d'Alexandrie. Paris: Cerf.

Greek Fragments

Petit, Françoise. 1978. *Quaestiones Fragmenta Graeca.* Les Œuvres de Philon d'Alexandrie. Paris: Cerf.

Paramelle, Joseph. 1984. *Philon d'Alexandrie: Questions sur la Genèse II 1–7: Texte grec, version arménienne, parallèles latins.* Geneva: Patrick Cramer.

Ancient Latin Translation

Petit, Françoise. 1973. *L'ancienne version latine des Questions sur la Genèse de Philon d'Alexandrie.* Berlin: Akademie Verlag.

Studies

Royse, James R. 1976-1977. "The Original Structure of Philo's *Quaestiones.*" *Studia Philonica* 4: 41-78.

Hay, David M., ed. 1991. *Both Literal and Allegorical: Studies in Philo of Alexandria's Questions and Answers on Genesis and Exodus.* Atlanta: Scholars Press.

Lombardi, Sara Mancini. 2010. *Studies on the Armenian Version of Philo's Works.* Leiden: Brill

Sterling, Gregory E. 1991. "Philo's *Quaestiones:* Prolegomena or Afterthought?" In *Both Literal and Allegorical: Studies in Philo of Alexandria's Questions and Answers on Genesis and Exodus.* Ed. David M. Hay. Atlanta: Scholars Press, 99-123.

Terian, Abraham. 1991. "The Priority of the *Quaestiones* among Philo's Exegetical Commentaries." In *Both Literal and Allegorical: Studies in Philo of Alexandria's Questions and Answers on Genesis and Exodus.* Ed. David M. Hay. Atlanta: Scholars Press, 29-46.

Allegorical Commentary

Borgen, Peder. 1997. *Philo of Alexandria: An Exegete of His Time*. Leiden: Brill.

Dawson, David. 1992. *Allegorical Readers and Cultural Revision in Ancient Alexandria*. Berkeley: University of California Press, 73-126.

Long, A. A. 1992. "Stoic Readings of Homer." In *Homer's Ancient Readers*. Ed. Robert Lamberton and John J. Keaney. Princeton: Princeton University Press, 41-66.

Morris, Jenny. 1987. "The Jewish Philosopher Philo." In Emil Schürer, *The History of the Jewish People in the Age of Jesus Christ*. Rev. and ed. Geza Vermes and Fergus Millar. Edinburgh: Clark, 3.2.840-68.

Niehoff, Maren. 2011. *Jewish Exegesis and Homeric Scholarship in Alexandria*. Cambridge: Cambridge University Press.

Runia, David T. 1990. "The Structure of Philo's Allegorical Treatises." In idem, *Exegesis and Philosophy: Studies on Philo of Alexandria*. Aldershot: Variorum, 202-56.

Terian, Abraham. 1991. "The Priority of the Quaestiones among Philo's Exegetical Commentaries." In *Both Literal and Allegorical: Studies in Philo of Alexandria's Questions and Answers on Genesis and Exodus*. Ed. David M. Hay. Atlanta: Scholars Press, 29-46.

Tobin, Thomas H. 2000. "The Beginning of Philo's Legum Allegoriae." *SPhA* 12: 29-43.

Winston, David, and John Dillon. 1983. *Two Treatises of Philo of Alexandria: A Commentary on De Gigantibus and Quod Deus Sit Immutabilis*. Chico, Calif.: Scholars Press.

Exposition of the Law

Borgen, Peder. 1997. *Philo of Alexandria: An Exegete for His Time*. Leiden: Brill, 65-77.

Goodenough, Erwin R. 1933. "Philo's Exposition of the Law and His De Vita Mosis." *HTR* 25: 109-251.

Loader, William R. G. 2011. *Philo, Josephus, and the Testaments on Sexuality: Attitudes towards Sexuality in the Writings of Philo, Josephus and in the Testaments of the Twelve Patriarchs*. Grand Rapids: Eerdmans.

Morris, Jenny. 1987. "The Jewish Philosopher Philo." In Emil Schürer, *The History of the Jewish People in the Age of Jesus Christ*. Rev. and ed. Geza Vermes et al. Edinburgh: Clark, 3.1: 840-68.

Niehoff, Maren R. 2001. *Philo on Jewish Identity and Culture*. Tübingen: Mohr Siebeck.

Runia, David T. 2001. *Philo of Alexandria: On the Creation of the Cosmos according to Moses: Introduction, Translation and Commentary*. Leiden: Brill.

Wilson, Walter. 2011. *Philo, On Virtues: Introduction, Translation, and Commentary*. Leiden: Brill.

Winston, David. 1998. "Philo and the Rabbis on Sex and Body." *Poetics Today* 19: 41-62.

Worthington, Jonathan D. 2011. *Creation in Paul and Philo: The Beginning and Before.* Tübingen: Mohr Siebeck.

Philosophical Works

Anderson, Charles A. 2011. *Philo of Alexandria's Views of the Physical World.* Tübingen: Mohr Siebeck.

Arnaldez, Roger, and Jean Pouilloux. 1969. *Philon d'Alexandrie, De aeternitate mundi.* Paris: Cerf.

Baldassarri, Mariano. 1993. "Le opere filosofiche di Filone Alessandrino." In *La filosofia antica.* Vol. 2. Como: Luca della Robbia, 173-202.

Dillon, John M. 1996. *The Middle Platonists, 80 B.C. to A.D. 220.* Rev. ed. Ithaca, N.Y.: Cornell University Press.

Frick, Peter. 1999. *Divine Providence in Philo of Alexandria.* Tübingen: Mohr Siebeck.

Hadas-Lebel, Mireille. 1973. *Philon d'Alexandrie, De providentia I et II.* Paris: Cerf.

Petit, Madeleine. 1974. *Philon d'Alexandrie, Quod omnis probus liber sit.* Paris: Cerf.

Reale, Giovanni. 1990. *A History of Ancient Philosophy.* Vol. 4. Albany: State University of New York Press.

Runia, David T. 1981. "Philo's De Aeternitate Mundi: The Problem of Its Interpretation." *Vigiliae Christianae* 35: 105-51.

———. 1996. "Philon von Alexandrien." In *Philosophie der Antike.* Vol. 2. Ed. Friedo Ricken. Stuttgart: Kohlhammer, 128-45.

Terian, Abraham. 1981. *Philonis Alexandrini, De Animalibus.* Chico, Calif.: Scholars Press.

Winston, David. 1996. "Hellenistic Jewish Philosophy." In *History of Jewish Philosophy.* Ed. Daniel H. Frank and Oliver Leaman. London: Routledge, 38-61.

Apologetic Treatises

Hypothetica

Barclay, John M. G. 2007. *Against Apion.* Leiden: Brill, 353-61.

Niebuhr, Karl-Wilhelm. 1987. *Gesetz und Paränese: Katechismusartige Weisungsreihen in der frühjüdischen Literatur.* Tübingen: Mohr Siebeck, 6-72.

Sterling, Gregory E. 1990. "Philo and the Logic of Apologetics: An Analysis of the *Hypothetica*." *SBLSP.* Atlanta: Scholars Press, 412-30.

———. 2003. "Universalizing the Particular: Natural Law in Second Temple Jewish Ethics." *SPhA* 15: 61-76.

On the Contemplative Life

Conybeare, Frederick C. 1895. *Philo about the Contemplative Life.* Oxford: Clarendon; rpt. New York: Garland, 1987.

Graffigna, Paola. 1992. *Filone d'Alexandria, De vita contemplative.* Genova: Melangelo.

Taylor, Joan E. 2003. *Jewish Women Philosophers of First Century Alexandria: Philo's Therapeutae Reconsidered.* Oxford: Oxford University Press.

Against Flaccus

Box, Herbert. 1939. *Philonis Alexandrini In Flaccum.* Oxford: Oxford University Press.

van der Horst, Pieter W. 2003. *Philo's Flaccus: The First Pogrom.* Leiden: Brill.

Embassy to Gaius

Smallwood, E. Mary. *Philonis Alexandrini Legatio ad Gaium.* Leiden: Brill, 1961.

Josephus

Steve Mason, James S. McLaren, and John M. G. Barclay

Josephus was a general during the First Jewish Revolt against Rome who later wrote historical, autobiographical, and apologetic works under the patronage of the Flavian emperors. His writings constitute the single most important source for Judaism in the early Roman period and, after the Bible, the most extensive ancient narrative of Jewish history.

Josephus was born Yoseph bar Mattityahu in Jerusalem in 37 C.E. Although his family did not belong to the small high-priestly circle, it must have enjoyed high standing in the city's hereditary aristocracy. Only so can we explain Josephus's Greek education, his dispatch to Rome on an embassy at the age of twenty-six (63-64 C.E.), his selection as regional commander of Galilee at the outbreak of war against Rome (late 66 C.E.), his land holdings in Jerusalem, and his network of high-level friendships in the city. After just four or five months of organizing Galilee's defenses against the 60,000-strong advancing Roman forces, by May of 67 C.E. he was driven back to the fortified hill at Jotapata (Yodefat). There he surrendered to Vespasian and his son Titus, after a siege of some weeks (July 1-2, 67). For most of the war he remained a captive, assisting the Romans with translation, interrogation, and negotiation, especially during the siege of Jerusalem under Titus's legions from May to September 70 C.E. After the city's fall, Josephus accompanied the victorious general, sailing back with him from Alexandria to Rome (71 C.E.) and observing the shared triumph of imperial father and son.

Before Vespasian's departure from Judea in 69 C.E., he reportedly freed Josephus from chains. At some point thereafter, Josephus received Roman citizenship and the traditional three-part name honoring his benefactors, "Titus Flavius Josephus." Although he uses only "Joseph(us)" in his writings, we know about the *nomen* "Flavius" from later writers, and it confirms the expected three-part citizen's name, derived from Titus Flavius Vespasianus (shared by Vespasian and Titus). Other benefactions from the imperial family, though not extravagant by contemporary standards, showed appropriate treatment of their dependent: at least initial accommodation in the family's private residence on Rome's Quirinal hill, some sort of maintenance money, and a parcel of land in Judea's coastal plains to replace the real estate in Jerusalem that had been spoiled by war and occupation.

As far as we know, Josephus lived the balance of his life in Rome. In the tradition of the retired statesman-soldier (though only 34), he began a literary career that would produce three substantial works in thirty books: the seven-volume *Jewish War* (mostly written by 79, completed by 81); the twenty-volume *Jewish Antiquities* with its appendix (*Life* of Josephus), completed in 93/94; and a sequel, the systematic treatment of Judean antiquity in two volumes known as *Against Apion*. Josephus may have died at any point from about 95/96 to the early second century C.E. A notice from the ninth-century Patriarch Photius puts the death of King Agrippa II, which Josephus mentions in his *Life*, at 100 C.E. Although the issue is still debated, most scholars think that this notice should not be given decisive weight, leaving Josephus free to have written his later works and to have died before 100 C.E. We have no way of determining his death date.

The *Vita*

The *Life of Josephus* provides a clear example of the difficulty of moving from story to history. In scholarship, this work has been thought to hold the key to Josephus's historical career for the following reason. At *Life* 40 and again in an excursus at 336–67, Josephus reports that his adversary Justus, a well-educated dignitary from Tiberias who later served on the staff of King Agrippa II, had written his own account of at least part of the war, in which Justus took issue with Josephus's *War*, especially as it concerned Josephus's behavior in Galilee. Scholars moved from that observation to the proposal that the entire *Life* must be a response to Justus, whose claims obviously stung Josephus. This appeared all the more likely because in *Life* Josephus often changes his story over against *War*. Now he claims, for example, that he was sent to Galilee with two others, to pacify the region, not as a sole general; his rival John of Gischala had much more understandable motives than *War* had allowed; and the delegation sent from Jerusalem to oust

Josephus was much more important and well connected in Jerusalem than *War* had volunteered. Scholars concluded that if the entire *Life* responds to Justus, we are in a good position to figure out the historical truth: we not only have Josephus's preferred account *(War)*, but we can reconstruct Justus's challenge by mirror-reading Josephus's responses. Thus, if Josephus claims to have rejected bribes and preserved every woman's honor (*Life* 80, 259), then Justus must have accused him on these accounts, and those charges provide a window into Josephus's historical career.

The fundamental problem with all this is that it ignores Josephus's own statements about his reasons for writing the *Life*. He introduces it at the end of the *Antiquities* as an autobiographical appendix, motivated by his desire to celebrate his credentials, including his ancestry, education, and events of his life; after that he will conclude his *Antiquities* (*Ant.* 20.262-67). Correspondingly, at the end of the *Life* (430) he declares that he will indeed now close the *Antiquities,* having surveyed the events of his life and offered material for assessing his character. The *Life* was clearly written as an autobiographical addendum to the magnum opus, to which it is joined in most surviving manuscripts, and it was understood by Eusebius to be part of the larger work (*Hist. Eccl.* 3.10.8-11). It did not need a separate motive.

The main reason for writing "lives" in antiquity was rhetorical, to demonstrate character with illustrative material. That is precisely what Josephus claims to be doing, and he follows the prescribed categories for such exercises, moving from illustrious ancestral pedigree (1–6) to prodigious education (7–12), to remarkable achievements in public life, featuring especially military exploits (13–412), to benefactions received from illustrious friends and bestowed on the less powerful. This is the material that constitutes his *Life;* he focuses on the five months between his appointment to Galilee and the beginning of the siege because that is the only period of his life from which he could illustrate his military-political achievements.

A standard technique in ancient rhetoric for exposing one's own good character was the polemical contrast with some convenient wretched person who behaved with despicable unworthiness. In the *Life* Josephus uses several such characters: Agrippa's commander Varus, his own priestly colleague, John of Gischala, the delegation sent from Jerusalem, and indeed Justus of Tiberias. But Justus is not targeted until near the end of the work, with a decisive turn to this new subject: "Having come this far in the narrative, I want to go through a few points against Justus, the very one who

Chronology of Josephus's Life	
37	Born Yoseph bar Mattityahu in Jerusalem
53	Samples the three major Jewish sects: Pharisees, Sadducees, and Essenes; begins three years of discipleship with the desert ascetic Bannus
56	Returns to Jerusalem; joins the Pharisees in his public life
63/64	Leads delegation to court of Emperor Nero in order to secure the release of imprisoned Jewish priests; gains support of Poppaea Sabina, Nero's mistress
66	Chosen by revolutionary council to command Jewish forces in Galilee at the start of the First Jewish Revolt; opposed in Galilee by John of Gischala
67	Surrenders to Vespasian's forces at Jotapata (Yodefat) after escape from Roman siege; predicts that Vespasian will become emperor
67-69	Held in Roman custody
70	Acts as mediator in Roman camp during siege of Jerusalem
71	Resides in Rome under imperial patronage, with Roman citizenship and name Titus Flavius Josephus
ca. 73	Publishes Aramaic edition of the *Jewish War*
75-79/81	Publishes Greek edition of the *Jewish War*
93/94	Completes the *Jewish Antiquities* and his *Life*
post 93/94	Publishes *Against Apion* (a defense of Judaism)
post 95/96	Dies

has written an *oeuvre* about these things" (336). It is difficult to see how Josephus's audiences could have understood him to be responding to Justus all along. He elsewhere demonstrates his ability to establish his targets at the outset of a work, when he devotes his work to combating them (*J.W.* 1.1-2; *Ag. Ap.* 1.1-5).

The *Life* thus appears to be Josephus's effort, in a rather hurried composition, to close his major work with an appendix "About the Author." His historical accounts have been an extension of his personal character and status, which he will now elaborate according to the accepted criteria.

If this approach to the *Life* is correct, the work does not (alas) offer us better historical traction than any other work. In fact, the text shows much the same relationship to the parallel stories in *War* 2–3 that *Antiquities* 13–20 shows in relation to *War* 1–2. In both cases Josephus exhibits an evident, sometimes breathtaking freedom in rewriting the story: rearranging the order of events, with sometimes different *dramatis personae* in different relationships to each other, and offering different moral evaluations. It is only more striking in *Life* because the subject is Josephus's own career. This freedom, although unsettling for historical work, accords with the prescriptions of rhetoric, particularly the mandate not to repeat the same things, and with his contemporary Plutarch's reuse of material in different ways (cf. also the Gospels, though by different authors). Josephus is unique only because we have such complete texts in which he retells the same events.

This new approach to *Life* tries to deal with his narrative as a whole, and this implies a concern also for the shape or structure. The structure of *Life* resembles that of his other works in that it reveals his taste for symmetrical or "periodic" (chiastic, concentric) design: matching opening and closing panels and then a movement toward and away from a central fulcrum, with paired "antiphonal" elements along the way. In the *Life* this is particularly obvious because only the opening and closing sections have to do with Josephus's family life; they also both include a voyage to Rome, benefactions from the wife of a ruling emperor, and providential rescue (1–16, 414–29). As we have noted, the references to Justus and his rival account come near the beginning and near the end of the work (40, 336). At the one-quarter and three-quarter marks are two revolts from Josephus's leadership in Tiberias, stories that share strikingly similar features (85–103, 276–308). The delegation from Jerusalem straddles the middle section (189–332), and at the center of everything sits *Life*'s only dream revelation (208–9), furnishing divine confirmation of Josephus's mission. It marks itself as a fulcrum by the repetition of key terms in reverse order before (206–7) and after (210–12) the episode.

Observing such a structure takes nothing away from others that may operate in the narrative at the same time. Dramatic structure, in this case building to a climax in Josephus's final confrontation with the delegation

(271–304), operates under its own logic. Concentric or ring composition is, however, a noteworthy aesthetic feature of Josephus's designs.

Jewish War

The first of the extant works written by Josephus, the *Jewish War* provides a vivid account of the conflict that resulted in the destruction of Jerusalem and its Temple in 70 c.e. The decision of Josephus to describe the work as the *Jewish War* (*J.W.* 1.1; *Ant.* 1.203; 18.11; 20.258; *Life* 412) has helped encourage the view that he was approaching the subject matter from a Roman perspective. Although the choice might indicate at least one possible target audience, a Roman readership, it most likely reflects the commonplace label being used at the time in Rome to describe the war, rather than the standpoint held by Josephus. It is clear that Josephus was not the first person, nor the last one, to write about the conflict (*J.W.* 1.1-2, 7-8; *Life* 336–38, 360). According to Josephus, there was an earlier version written in his native language, Aramaic, for those Jews who lived to the east of the Roman Empire (*J.W.* 1.3, 6). The precise nature of the relationship between the original version and the extant Greek work is not possible to establish. Given the extent to which the *Antiquities* 1–10 "translation" offers a rewriting of the biblical narrative, there is good reason to view the Greek version as far more than a literal translation of the earlier work. As acknowledged by Josephus, the process of constructing the text in Greek required assistance (*Ag. Ap.* 1.50), a claim that appears to be confirmed by the fact that *Judean War* displays a greater sophistication and eloquence in style than any of the latter works.

Date

There is no external evidence indicating when the text was written. A number of internal markers point to a date during the reign of Titus for books 1-6 and suggest that book 7 was added during the reign of Domitian. The latest datable event is the reference to the Temple of Peace constructed by Vespasian (*J.W.* 7.158-62), which was dedicated in 75 c.e. In the context of asserting the accuracy of his version of events, Josephus claims he presented copies of the text to Titus and Vespasian (*Ag. Ap.* 1.50-51). If this claim is accurate, it is best understood as Josephus sending selected extracts of what was still a work in progress. Elsewhere, Josephus states that he sent material to Titus and Agrippa II in order to receive their letter of recommendation (*Life* 363–67). Titus has a much larger profile than Vespasian; he is singled out in the preface (*J.W.* 1.10) and then dominates the account of the siege of Jerusalem. Even more significant for determining the dating is the negative reference to C. Caecina Alienus (*J.W.* 4.634-44). Such a depiction was plausible only after 79 C.E., when Caecina was executed for allegedly plotting against Titus. The attempt to promote the prowess of Domitian (*J.W.* 7.85-88), along with the disparate nature of the subject matter, suggests that book 7 was added at some stage during Domitian's reign.

Contents

The arrangement of the work into seven books was the choice of Josephus (*J.W.* 1.30; *Ant.* 18.11; *Life* 412). He intended the work to rival other accounts, deliberately modeling it along classical lines (*J.W.* 1.1-2, 7-8). A detailed preface stakes his claim to be writing an authoritative account of the war, as a participant and eye-witness concerned to provide readers with the truth of what happened (*J.W.* 1.13-16, 22, 30). The background to the war is outlined in books 1-2. Josephus makes the assault on the Temple by Antiochus IV the starting point (*J.W.* 1.31-35). He then outlines the rise of the Hasmoneans and their subsequent rule (*J.W.* 1.36-170). The vast bulk of book 1 describes the life and career of Herod (*J.W.* 1.171-673). The first part of book 2 provides a brief account of the activities of Herod's sons and the two periods of direct Roman rule interspersed with the reigns of Agrippa I and Agrippa II (*J.W.* 2.1-276). The remainder of book 2 provides a detailed account of when and how the war began and the first moves by the main protagonists (*J.W.* 2.277-654). In book 3 Josephus describes the campaign of Vespasian in Galilee, with the assault on Jotapata, where Josephus surrendered, forming the main focus of the narrative (*J.W.* 3.141-408). There are four different areas of interest in book 4: the completion of the campaign in Galilee (*J.W.* 4.1-120), of which the capture of Gamla formed the key component (*J.W.* 4.2-83); the state of affairs in Jerusalem, with a particular emphasis being placed on fighting among the Jews (*J.W.* 4.121-409); the isolation of Jerusalem in preparation for the final assault (*J.W.* 4.410-90); and the fighting among the Romans that resulted in Vespasian becoming emperor and Titus being dispatched to lead the attack on Jerusalem

(*J.W.* 4.491-663). The preparations for the siege and the detailed account of the actual assault on Jerusalem constitute books 5 and 6. The capture and destruction of the Temple dominate the narrative (*J.W.* 6.233-442). Book 7 is a rather eclectic collection of subject matter: the return of Titus to Rome and the subsequent triumph, which is described in detail (*J.W.* 7.1-157), interspersed with the description of several other revolts (*J.W.* 7.75-95); the aforementioned reference to the Temple of Peace; the capture of the remaining pockets of resistance (*J.W.* 7.163-408), of which the assault on Masada dominates (*J.W.* 7.252-406); and a brief account of the suppression of resistance in North Africa (*J.W.* 7.409-53). Josephus concludes his account with a short epilogue commending the work to his readers (*J.W.* 7.454-55).

Setting, Audience, and Purpose

The setting in which Josephus constructed the work is fundamental for any interpretation of what he wrote. Rome had been a city of much upheaval in its recent past. Romans had fought one another in the actual city in 69 C.E. in the battle for control after the death of Nero, with the symbolic temple of Jupiter destroyed in the process. The rebellion in Judea became an extremely important propaganda tool for the new Flavian ruler, Vespasian, to establish the credentials of his family to hold power, hence the triumph, the commemorative arch, coinage, and public buildings funded from the spoils. The decision of Titus and Domitian to continue to issue coinage celebrating the victory, and Domitian's construction of the now existing Arch of Titus, further reinforced the ongoing significance of the war. It is not surprising, therefore, that accounts of the conflict were in circulation and that Josephus, as a participant, decided to write his own version.

Josephus does not identify a target audience for his Greek version of the work. He asserts that the account was written in order to offer an accurate record of what took place (*J.W.* 1.6-8) and, in the context of explaining a long digression on the Roman army, that he wanted to discourage others from taking up arms against the Romans (*J.W.* 3.108-9). It is likely that Josephus saw his target audience as including Jews and interested Romans. Many Jews residing in Rome would have wanted to know more about what took place, especially given the public celebration and display of victory spoils from the war. At the same time, the numerous explanatory notes regarding Jewish customs and important historical figures, including Judas Maccabee, suggest an intended audience that was not familiar with the Jewish heritage. The submission of extracts to Agrippa II and to Vespasian and Titus suggests that Josephus wanted his work to be part of the public domain.

There has been a long-standing but misguided view that Josephus wrote his account as an instrument of Flavian propaganda. Crucial to this view are the exoneration of Titus for responsibility regarding the destruction of the Temple (*J.W.* 1.28; 6.236-66) and the numerous speeches of Titus pleading with the Jews to avoid allowing the Temple to become a battleground. It is important that these passages, along with the entire work, are read within the context of the contemporary literary and political environment. Criticism had to be veiled and expressed with due care since there was no freedom to voice opposition in an explicit manner. It is important to be open to reading Josephus's account of the war, and the role played by the Flavians, as one with nuance, in which irony was at play. Hence, although the inscription on the original Arch of Titus declared he was the first to capture Jerusalem (*CIL* 6.944), immediately after describing the destruction of the Temple in book 6, Josephus's reader was informed that the city had been captured on a number of previous occasions (*J.W.* 6.435-42). The work is a complex combination of a defense of the way Josephus and his associates behaved in the war and of the Jewish community at large as it sought to live under Roman rule in the postwar years.

Reception and Significance

Irrespective of who Josephus hoped would read and preserve his work, it was within a Christian setting that his account of the war received its most significant positive reception. Eusebius of Caesarea quoted large sections of the siege of Jerusalem as part of his claim that the destruction of city and its Temple were divine punishment (*Hist. Eccl.* 3.5.7; 3.7.1-9). Consequently, Josephus came to be regarded as an important source of the war. Assessment of what value should be placed on the text has been traditionally connected with discussion of the character of Josephus and the question of the way he used sources. The fact that Josephus, by his own admission, was a leader in the rebel forces (*J.W.* 2.569-71) who surrendered to the Romans (*J.W.* 3.383-408), and then offered advice and counsel to the rebels in Jerusalem that they should also surrender (*J.W.* 6.96-110), has often attracted strong criticism of his behavior. At the same time, Josephus has been criticized for relying heavily on the notes of Vespasian and Titus in constructing his account (*Life* 358; *Ag. Ap.* 1.56), and for uncritically drawing material directly from other sources (e.g., Nicolaus of Damascus).

There is no doubt that the text provides a rich resource of information on life in Judea in the first century C.E. and important aspects of Roman history, ranging from details of Roman military practice (*J.W.* 3.70-107) to the thorough description of the triumphal procession (*J.W.* 7.123-57). The various digressions, on topography and buildings, reflect an accurate knowledge of subject matter, and many of the archaeological excavations of locations described by Josephus have affirmed the general nature of his account. It is, however, important that material is not cited without due attention being paid to its context, within the text and within the political and literary context of Flavian Rome. Such elaborate elements as the speeches associated with major characters at key stages in the narrative indicate the extent to which the *Jewish War* is a crafted work (e.g., the speech of Agrippa II on the nature of Roman rule at the start of the war, *J.W.* 2.345-404). Most important, it must be remembered that the text was written after the event. The reconstruction of the situation in Judea before the war and of how the war unfolded was formed with the perspective of hindsight. It was written to explain how and why the disastrous events of 70 C.E. had taken place and what the future possibly entailed for the Jewish people. Josephus laid blame upon the Romans, depicting several governors as actively provoking the Jews to take up arms. He also interpreted what had happened as part of divine activity. God used the Romans as an instrument of punishment inflicted upon the Jews because of the actions of a rogue element within the community. Whatever claim to victory Rome asserted, Josephus assigned the control and direction of how events unfolded to the God of the Jews.

Jewish Antiquities

Josephus's *Jewish Antiquities* (or *Judean Antiquities*) is a twenty-volume primer of Jewish history and culture. Books 1–11 offer a paraphrase and reworking of the Bible, from creation to the return from the Babylonian Exile. Books 12–20 survey Jewish history in the Persian, Hellenistic, and early Roman periods down to the eve of the First Jewish Revolt against Rome.

Occasion and Date

Although the *Antiquities* turned out to be Josephus's *magnum opus*, he may not have initially intended it as a separate work. He claims that he had planned to include ancient history already in the *Judean War* (*Ant.* 1.6-7), which he wrote in the 70s C.E. and completed before Titus died in September 81 (*Life* 363). In the course of preparing such a comprehensive history, however, he realized that the older material was too copious and so crafted the *War* as a balanced monograph in its own right, with a matching beginning and end (*Ant.* 1.6-7). Presumably, this means that the first volume of prewar history, covering the Hasmoneans and Herod (*J.W.* 1), corresponded to the final volume on postwar events (*J.W.* 7). Reserving detailed treatment of the more distant past for a later study, alas, put him in the familiar writer's bind: the prospect of finishing the job was overwhelming. He credits a wealthier friend named Epaphroditus — a common name, not yet convincingly identified — with constant encouragement to complete the task (*Ant.* 1.8-9), something he achieved late in Domitian's reign (93/94 C.E.) at the age of 55 (*Ant.* 20.267).

Purpose

What exactly was Josephus's task in launching this separate major work? In speaking of his abandoned plan for a super-*War*, he relates that he had intended to discuss there *"who the Judeans were* from the beginning, what fortunes they had experienced, under what sort of lawgiver they were trained for piety and the exercise of the other virtues, and the number of the wars they had fought in the long ages past" before the recent conflict (*Ant.* 1.6; note the martial emphasis). This, then, is what he will narrate in the *Antiquities*. In casting about for a model of presenting Judean culture to foreigners, he seizes upon the high priest Eleazar, who had reportedly authorized the Greek translation of Scripture at the request of King Ptolemy II (cf. *Letter of Aristeas* 33). What Eleazar had given the king, in keeping with the Judean tradition of "not jealously hoarding beautiful things," was a Greek version of "our law and the framework of our constitution" (*Ant.* 1.10-11). Josephus brings all this together by declaring that his object now is to imitate Eleazar's magnanimity but also to go further: to render not only the laws but all the Judean sacred writings into Greek, thus presenting a history of "many strange undoings, fortunes of war, manly achievements of generals, and reversals of constitution" (*Ant.* 1.13; note again the military emphasis). He stresses the moral lesson to be learned from such an account: that those who follow these ancient prescriptions, which also embody the laws of nature, find success and happiness, whereas those who depart from them meet disaster (*Ant.* 1.14-50, 20).

This opening prospectus is striking for a number of reasons. First, it highlights the much overlooked connection between *Antiquities* and *War* in Josephus's conception. He begins *Antiquities* by recalling his reasons for writing *War* (*Ant.* 1.1-4) and assumes his audience's knowledge of the earlier work as he often refers to it for detailed information (*Ant.* 1.203; 13.173, 298; 18.11, 259). He thus offers *Antiquities* as a sort of prequel containing the earlier history. Most important is the connection of theme and tone between the two works. *War* had aimed at defending the Judean character from predictable calumnies following the catastrophe of 70 c.e. (*J.W.* 1.1-2, 6-8; *Ant.* 1.3-4). There Josephus foregrounded the Judean virtues — not given much exposure in other accounts — of manly courage, toughness, and contempt for death. Conspicuous in the above descriptions of *Antiquities* is the role of wars, generals, and manly deeds in the ancient Judean past. (The Greek and Latin words for "virtue" both meant, in the first instance, "manliness.") Just as *War* had sought to explore the Judeans' character from the recent conflict, so *Antiquities* will show "who they were *from the beginning.*"

This is where the language of "constitution" comes into play. Among Greek ethnographers, from at least a half-millennium before Josephus's time, it was a common assumption that the many peoples of the inhabited earth *(oikoumenē)* had different characters as a function of their diverse geographical and climactic situations, and that their various political constitutions, laws, and customs reflected those national characters. In some tension with this idea was the equally common view that constitutions were inherently unstable, constantly progressing and regressing in cycles, with monarchy degenerating to tyranny, democracy to mob rule, and aristocracy to oligarchy, so that each type yielded over time to another. Josephus sits on both sides of this fence, highlighting in the prologue *both* the superiority of the apparently unchanging Judean constitution *and* its many vicissitudes over time.

Intended Audience

A final noteworthy feature of *Antiquities'* prologue is its tone of outreach. In contrast to *War* and *Apion,* where he claims to feel compelled to counter the denouncers of his people, Josephus presents the *Antiquities* as a gift to a Greek-speaking audience that has demanded it (*Ant.* 1.5). This raises the question: Was he really writing for outsiders, or following the well-known apologist's tactic of "preaching to the converted" by appearing to address foreigners? If we lay aside his programmatic statements about writing for non-Jews (*Ant.* 1.5, 9; 20.262), which might have been easily added for rhetorical purposes, even in the most inconspicuous places the narrative sustains the impression that its expected audience was not Jewish. As in *War,* Josephus assumes that his audience knows Roman reference points but feels compelled to explain even the most basic elements of Judean culture, such as Sabbath, circumcision, and priesthood (*Ant.* 1.128-29; 3.317; 13.171; 297; 14.1-3, 186-87; 16.175; 17.254). He supports his account wherever possible with reference to non-Jewish evidence, makes frequent comparisons with Greek traditions, and feels it necessary to introduce the Judean laws or "constitution" with great care (*Ant.* 3.90-92, 222-86; 4.194-319). His consciousness of writing for outsiders is perhaps clearest when he concedes that he has had to rearrange the biblical text — in case any of his countrymen should happen to see this and complain (4.197).

But were there significant numbers of Gentiles in Rome so keen to learn of Judean culture that they would have remained alert through *Antiquities'* twenty volumes, let alone insisted that Josephus complete the work? As it happens, a surprisingly large proportion of the small amount of evidence we have concerning Judean culture in the capital at Josephus's time reflects a certain fascination in some quarters with Judean ways. Tacitus speaks with disgust about those who are converted to these foreign customs, abandoning their native land, families, and ancestral rites to support Jerusalem (*Historiae* 5.5). Suetonius (*Domitian* 12.2) mentions as a noteworthy feature of Domitian's reign his ruthless collection of the tax payable by Jews after 70, even from those who either covered up their Jewish origins or secretly lived Jewish lives without confessing it (suggesting sympathizers or quiet converts). Cassius Dio claims that Domitian executed his cousin, a serving consul, along with many others for the "atheism" implicit in their adoption of Judean ways (67.14.2); he later reports that the emperor Nerva stopped hearing accusations against people who had taken up a Judean life (68.1.2). Finally, Epictetus and Juvenal independently seize upon conversion to Judean customs to illustrate some other moral point (Arrian, *Epicteti Dissertationes* 2.9.20; Juvenal 5.14.96-106); so the phenomenon must have been obvious enough. This concentrated evidence for committed interest from foreigners, in authors who say little else about Judeans, is confirmed by incidental remarks in Josephus concerning various Greek cities of the East (*J.W.* 2.463, 560). It may help to explain his decision to feature stories of conversion to Judean law and piety near the beginning and end of *Antiquities*: Abraham's adoption of monotheism and efforts to convert Egyptians (*Ant.* 1.154-68) matches the Adiabenian royal family's risky embrace of a Judean identity in the first century (*Ant.* 20.17-96).

Josephus presents *Antiquities,* then, as a primer in Judean law, history, and culture, brought over into Greek from the sacred records, for interested outsiders in Rome represented by Epaphroditus. The nature of his biblical paraphrase (books 1–11) has attracted the lion's share of technical research on *Antiquities.* On the one hand, his obvious adjustments to the Bible by way of omission, rearrangement, and sometimes major addition — for example, his much elaborated story of Joseph and Potiphar's wife or Moses's Ethiopian campaign — are usually attributed to novelistic or Hellenizing tendencies (though the latter invites the question, to what extent he actually thought in common Mediterranean categories, rather than consciously bending his material). On the other hand, his extensive reworking of source material has greatly complicated the assessment of his underlying biblical text. Did he follow the Hebrew text throughout, as he implies? (His proper nouns often differ in form from those used by the LXX.) Was his Hebrew text significantly different from our Masoretic text, and would this help to explain some of his divergences? Did he change his procedure from making an original translation at the beginning to exploiting existing Greek models, as he wearied of the project? If he used existing Greek texts, which ones did he have at his disposal? Was he influenced by Aramaic, targum-like paraphrases? To what extent did he, consciously or unconsciously, incorporate existing oral traditions into his retelling of the biblical story, and how much of the narrative is original with him? These issues remain debated.

With much more space available for the early history than *War* had afforded him, Josephus also takes the opportunity to expand, in *Antiquities* 13–17, what he had compressed into *War* 1. Books 18–20 include often quite different versions of episodes from the first half of *War* 2, supplemented by substantial new Roman and Mesopotamian material.

Although scholars have understandably been tempted to view *Antiquities'* postbiblical material as an afterthought, since the prologue envisions only a rewriting of the sacred texts, that possibility seems excluded by *Apion* 1.54. There, writing after the completion of *Antiquities,* Josephus continues to describe the work as nothing more than his Greek version of the Judean sacred writings. Evidently, that is what mattered most to him: the later material must have continued or illustrated themes from the trunk of the work.

Scholarship

As recently as 1988 a comprehensive survey of Josephus scholarship reported the near absence of studies on either the aims or structure of *Antiquities* as a whole. Indeed, *Antiquities* has provided the clearest case of the general scholarly neglect of Josephus's compositional interests, in favor of a preoccupation with his sources. Most early critics did not even ask about his authorial aims but dissected *Antiquities* into large composite sources (e.g., books 1–13 *en bloc*), which anonymous authors had allegedly prepared for other uses — probably in Alexandria — and they did the heavy lifting of which our author was thought incapable. Josephus, these scholars imagined in keeping with the assumptions of the day, found such material ready-made and stitched it into the work we now possess.

With the studies of Richard Laqueur and Henry St.-John Thackeray in the early twentieth century, this radical source criticism was replaced with a biographical proposal: that having written *War* in the service of Flavian propaganda, Josephus later repented of this betrayal and turned to explicating his nation's laws and culture in a defensive-apologetic vein. For this he needed new patrons to replace the imperial family: hence the appearance of Epaphroditus (though there is no reason why the Greek patron should not have been among Josephus's audience for *War*). More or less loosely connected with this influential theory of a reconversion to nationalism was a subsidiary proposal — dominant through the 1970s to early 1990s and still occasionally found — that Josephus wrote *Antiquities* to ingratiate himself with the budding rabbinic movement at Yavneh and reconfigured his political allegiances to do so, in particular promoting the Pharisees as rabbinic progenitors.

Every piece of evidence for this construction has been seriously challenged in recent years. Careful reading of *War* does not commend it as Roman propaganda; Josephus claims to be writing against such partisan works. Josephus himself stresses the unity of purpose between his two major works, showing no hint of embarrassment over *War. Antiquities* introduces the Pharisees very late in the piece (13.171) and treats them with general disdain. Josephus's understanding of legal practice *(halakah)* shows no consistent correlation with rabbinic prescriptions. Finally, scholarship on the early rabbinic movement increasingly stresses its isolation and limited influence before the end of the second or even third century. The field thus remains open for closer inquiry into the overall purposes of such a large work as *Antiquities.*

One problem in generating comprehensive interpretations arises from scholarly specialization. As academic interest focused intently on what lies beneath Josephus's narratives rather than on the finished works, those who treated the biblical paraphrase of *Antiquities* 1–11 were required to have skills in comparative scriptural interpretation, to be specialists in Hebrew and Aramaic, rabbinic literature, Dead Sea Scrolls, and "rewritten Bible." Excellent and finely grained studies of the biblical paraphrase therefore flourished, but quite independently of any concern for the *Antiquities* as a whole. On the other end, a Roman historian could publish an excellent translation and commentary of *Antiquities* 19, covering the death of Gaius Caligula and the accession of Claudius, but paying no attention to the narrative of which the story is a part (Wiseman 1991). This piecemeal approach seemed justified when the leading Josephus scholar of the early twentieth century declared *Antiquities* a "patchwork," artificially drawn out to twenty volumes, with whatever sources Josephus could find, in order to match the earlier *Roman Antiquities* by Dionysius of Halicarnassus (Thackeray 1929: 56-69).

But what would a real audience in the first century have made of the entire work? Would they have found it so disjointed? Would they have needed the skills of a biblical scholar with access to the Hebrew Bible, LXX, Dead Sea Scrolls, and other resources to understand the first half? Would they have reached book 12 and declared that the rest was not for them? Evidently not. Josephus takes pains to develop the themes announced in the prologue throughout the whole narrative, and he leaves clear structural markers along the way to make the narrative coherent and manageable.

Structure

As to structure, we have noted Josephus's evident care in designing *War,* as well as the thematic correspondence between books 1 and 20 of *Antiquities:*

both are set in or near Mesopotamia and have to do with conversion. This correspondence is enhanced by Josephus's mention in the later story of Noah's ark, with the same language he had used to describe it in book 1 (20.24-26; 1.90-92). This suggests the same kind of symmetrical composition that his other works attest. *Antiquities'* unmistakable turning point, for example, comes precisely halfway through, at the end of book 10, with the fall of the First Temple and its implications for understanding divine providence *(pronoia)* — a marked theme of the work; book 20 ends on the eve of the Second Temple's destruction, referring the audience to *War* for the rest (20.258). Books 9–10 and 11–12 chart the path to the destruction of Solomon's Temple and its rebuilding afterward. Along the way, other matching panels command our attention: the elaboration of the peerless Judean constitution in books 3 and 4 corresponds to the Judean and Roman constitutional crises, caused by tyrannical monarchs and their succession woes, in books 17–19. The careers of King Saul (book 6) and King Herod (books 14–17) have striking similarities, as these outstanding representatives of manly virtue are undone by the fatal flaws of tyrants. The whole work thus reflects a coherent design. This design precludes the common but antecedently implausible assumption that Josephus made it up as he went along, filling the later volumes with a miscellaneous hodgepodge.

An Illustrative Theme: The Judean Constitution

The question of unity is decisively settled by the work's coherence of theme. Of the continuing themes from the prologue, one must suffice here as an illustration: that of the constitution, introduced above. In a later summary (*Apion* 2.287) Josephus reflects that he wrote the *Antiquities* in order to give a detailed account of the Judean laws and constitution. The prologue also establishes the theme as fundamental, and it remains prominent throughout. Thus at the end of book 20 he provides a summary of the constitutional changes, using the word *politeia* repeatedly (20.229, 251, 261): the nation began as an aristocracy, then was subject to monarchs (under judges and prophets), to kings, to priestly aristocrats again, to kings (later Hasmoneans and Herodians), and most recently to priestly aristocrats — including himself — after the removal of Archelaus in 6 c.e. Between the prologue and these concluding summaries, pointed asides keep the audience aware of the theme. It emerges that, although the form of government did change over time, its normative shape — so Moses and

Samuel already insisted (*Ant.* 4.223; 6.36, 84) — was that of an aristocracy anchored in the hereditary priesthood (cf. 5.135; 6.267-68; 11.111; 14.91). The high priest offers effective leadership, with many advantages of a monarch but only as *primus inter pares*. This system obviates the two main pitfalls of kingship: the inevitable tendency to tyranny (cf. Herodotus 3.80) and the problem of hereditary succession; even if a king should personally avoid tyranny, children are often not like their parents (*Ant.* 6.33-34). Collegial aristocracy, by allowing the prominence of one leader but from within a group of families, affords the advantages of unified direction without either tyranny or succession woes.

With such rare and partial exceptions as David and Solomon, Josephus portrays kingship as a disastrous aberration whenever tried, leading as Samuel had warned to outrages against the law, tyrannical behavior — marked especially by the murder and plunder of the nobility — and the downfall of the state. Here, incidentally, is the important backstory of *War:* in the earlier work it was precisely individuals whom Josephus styled "tyrants" who revolted against the collegial priestly aristocracy and thus fomented the civil strife that led to Jerusalem's recent fall (*J.W.* 1.9-10). In both works it is the Hasmonean Aristobulus who transforms the government into a monarchy, with disastrous consequences for native rule (*J.W.* 1.70; *Ant.* 13.401). In *Antiquities* Josephus apparently devotes so much space in the later work to the world-famous King Herod (books 14–17) because his reign furnishes a case study in kingship: it was a crucible of tyranny, undermined by his perpetual anxiety about succession as he clung to absolute power in the present. Herod had constantly to rewrite his will and groom new successors from the offspring of his various wives, not least because he would tyrannically execute those who seemed eager to replace him. His many violations of the law led to his predictably gruesome death (17.164-92).

Josephus goes on to apply these same themes and language clusters to Roman rulers in the early decades of his life (*Antiquities* 18–19). Tiberius, who tyrannically sent more nobles to death, at his personal whim, than anyone else (*Ant.* 18.226), faced a bizarre succession crisis that produced the miscreant Gaius Caligula, who himself thrived on harassing the Senate and those of noble birth (19.2). His grisly end after a short tyranny, recounted in minute detail, illustrates the same divine retribution that had overtaken Herod. Most remarkably, Josephus gives full play to the senatorial discussion that followed Gaius's death concerning the need to restore aristocratic-senatorial liberty, and he as narrator joins the senators in painting *all* the rulers from Julius Caesar onward as tyrants (19.169-74). This is striking, unparalleled in Roman literature of the time, and opposed to the strategies taken by Seneca or Dio Chrysostom in advocating virtuous kingship as a model for the Roman emperor. It is a fascinating question how Josephus's clear challenge to Roman (as well as Judean) monarchy actually fared among a Roman audience at the time of Domitian's tyranny, only a couple of years before his assassination in 96 C.E.

This we cannot know; nor can we get beyond speculation about the relationship between such political themes and the interest of Josephus's Roman audiences in Judean culture. At any rate, the constitutional theme provides one rich vein of narrative unity in *Antiquities*. There are several others, such as interest in temple and cult, the historiographical and rhetorical interest in rounded portraiture and moral assessment, and the philosophical character of both Judean culture as a whole and its leading representatives (Abraham, Moses, Solomon, Daniel, and the philosophical schools). In the absence of an ancient category matching our "religion," this philosophical color both grounds the political analysis and facilitates the adoption of Judean ways. As Josephus remarks to his eager audience at the beginning of the *Antiquities* (1.25): "For those who truly want to explore the reasons for each thing [in the laws], the investigation would be rich and highly philosophical."

Against Apion

The treatise known as *Against Apion* is the last of Josephus's extant works, written as a sequel to *Antiquities* and in place of his previously advertised treatise on *Customs and Reasons* (see *Ant.* 4.198; 20.268). The familiar title *Against Apion* represents only one quarter of its content; it is only in the first half of book 2 that Josephus responds to the Alexandrian scholar and politician, Apion. Josephus never gives a label to this work, and its range of topics led some early readers to call it *On the Antiquity of the Judeans* (Origen) or *Against the Greeks* (Porphyry), or to describe it in some composite expression of its themes (Jerome). It was written toward the end of Josephus's life, at the earliest in 95/96 C.E. (i.e., directly after the composition of *Antiquities* in 93 C.E.), but possibly later in the 90s or even the early 100s C.E.; since there are no unambiguous references in the text to contemporary circumstances, and because we do not know the date of Josephus's death, a more exact dating is impossible.

Contents

The work takes its starting point from a skeptical reception of *Antiquities*, as some reportedly doubted Josephus's claims for the extreme antiquity of the Judean nation (see *Ag. Ap.* 1.1-5). Josephus's first major task (1.6-218) is to prove this antiquity, primarily through the provision of "witnesses" to the existence (and achievements) of Judeans from non-Judean sources. An initial prolegomenon (1.6-56) discusses the methods and sources of historiography, in particular the deficiencies of the much heralded Greek historians, whose apparent ignorance of Judeans cast doubt on Judean claims to antiquity. Josephus turns the tables on such critics by undermining all trust in Greek historiography, and praising the accuracy of Judean records (notably their scriptures, 1.28-56). After a brief explanation of Greek ignorance of Judeans (1.60-68), he then marshals his main witnesses, Egyptian, Phoenician, Chaldean, and even Greek (1.69-218). The Egyptian evidence, drawn from Manetho (1.73-105), concerns the "Hyksos," whose violent rule of Egypt Josephus artificially takes to refer to Joseph and the Israelite sojourn in Egypt. Phoenician evidence (1.106-27), from Dios and Menander, concerns the legendary connection between Solomon and Hiram of Tyre. The chief Chaldean witness (1.128-60) is Berossus, whose account of Nebuchadnezzar made passing reference to "Syrian" captives transported to Babylon. Finally, seven authors are collected in a medley of Greek witnesses (1.161-214): Hermippus (on Pythagoras's interest in Judean customs), Theophrastus (on the Korban oath), Herodotus (on the "Syrian" use of circumcision), Cheorilus (on a race of warriors from the "Solyman hills"), Clearchus (on Aristotle's encounter with a philosophical Judean), Hecataeus (on Jerusalem and Judeans in the early Hellenistic era), and Agatharchides (on the capture of Jerusalem by Ptolemy I). In several cases, Josephus has to force the evidence to find some reference to Judeans, and the long quotations from "Hecataeus" probably derive not from the genuine Greek historian but from a Judean author writing under his name (Bar-Kochva 1996). Even the genuine material concerns Judeans of no great antiquity, and Josephus often changes the topic of discussion to Greek admiration of Judeans. Nonetheless, the accumulation of evidence encourages him to think he has proved to any reasonable person's satisfaction that Judean history stretches back, as he claims, to a period well before the Trojan War.

In the second part of the treatise (1.219–2.286), Josephus takes on a different task, the refutation of a large number of "slanders" that have been leveled at the Judean nation from a variety of sources. In the first place, he gathers and critiques three related "Egyptian" accounts of the expulsion from Egypt of a diseased/polluted people, variously connected with Judean origins. Josephus first cites and refutes Manetho's legend of a polluted mass of Egyptians, banished to Avaris, but aided by invading "Solymites" in their sacrilegious ravaging of Egypt (1.227-87); his extended critique (1.252-87) is a model of ancient literary criticism. He then compares and contrasts the parallel accounts in Chaeremon (1.288-303) and Lysimachus (1.304-20), pointing out inconsistencies or absurdities in (his abbreviated versions of) their stories.

Book 2 then raises the vitriolic tone of the treatise with an extended discussion of hostile comments made about Judeans by the Alexandrian scholar, Apion (2.1-144). Apion had made mischievous comments on Judean origins that Josephus briefly refutes (2.8-32), but he had also given an extended account of Judean history in Egypt from Alexander onward, painting the Judeans as a rebellious element in the population, hostile both to the Ptolemies and to the Romans. Josephus provides a lengthy riposte to this version of history (2.33-78), with particular focus on relations with Romans, since Apion, a prominent figure during and after the Alexandrian riots of 38 C.E., had clearly cast aspersions on the loyalty and legal/political claims of Alexandrian Jews. A third part of Josephus's response (2.79-114) answers Apion's slurs on Judean cult and culture — that Judeans worshipped in their temple the head of an ass; that they conducted an annual ritual slaughter of a Greek, with a cannibalistic feast and an oath of hostility against Greeks; that their miserable history showed their insignificance and religious impiety; and that their food laws and practice of circumcision proved their "barbarian" character. Josephus's rhetoric here rises to its greatest heights in counter-invective, climaxing in a passage gloating over Apion's miserable death (2.141-44). Throughout he makes great play on Apion's "Egyptian" ethnicity, exploiting Greek and Roman stereotypes about that supposedly unstable people with their absurd animal cults.

The refutation of slanders continues through the rest of book 2, but in a different mode (2.145-286, considered by some a separate and third part of the treatise). Starting from the attacks on Judean culture by Apollonius Molon, Josephus provides a positive description of Moses's legislation and the structure of his constitution (2.151-89), emphasizing the unity of word and action, and the superior understanding of the nature, rule, and providence of God ("theocracy") offered by Moses. He then gives a summary of select laws (2.190-218), focusing on the Temple, on sexual/family laws, and on friendliness to outsiders. Josephus next expands his emphasis on Judean endurance (2.219-35), by comparison with the famous resilience of the Spartans. In the final part of this section (2.236-86), he answers Apollonius's criticisms of Judean religious and social separatism; with an amusing assault on Greek mythology (heavily dependent on Greek philosophy), he defends Judean religious difference but finishes on a positive note by claiming that Moses has long been imitated by Greek philosophers, and that Judean customs continue to be copied by ordinary observers. A final peroration (2.287-96) sums up the work and claims that no greater constitution could be imagined or invented.

Genre

The genre of the treatise is primarily apologetic; even the first part, the proof of Judean antiquity, is presented within the larger frame of response to scurrilous libels and hostile doubts. The work constitutes, in fact, the only known example of ethnic "apology" from antiquity, and the first Judean text explicitly formulated in this originally legal genre (see Barclay 2007: xxx-xxxvi). In overall arrangement, and in many of its individual arguments, its rhetoric is highly skilled, enlivened by effective point-scoring, amusing character assassination, and clever manipulation of classical tropes. While there is evidence of some dependence on sources (e.g., in the overlap of materials in 2.145-286 with Pseudo-Phocylides and the Philonic tract *Hypothetica*), the bulk of the credit for this rhetorical performance must go to Josephus himself, by now sufficiently proficient in the Greco-Roman rhetorical tradition to use it for his own purposes.

Setting, Audience, and Purpose

The treatise was written in Rome in a context where highly diverse opinions about Judean culture were in circulation. Anti-Judean stereotypes flourished (witness those recycled and embellished by Tacitus a few years later), and in 95 C.E. Domitian staged political trials against individuals accused of "drifting into Judean ways" (Dio 67.14.1-2); but the hostility expressed in both cases was the flip side of the evident attraction of Judean culture to some Romans. The treatise declares itself to be addressed to sympathetic non-Judeans (1.1; 2.147, 296) and also implies, by its assumptions about readers' knowledge, values, and interest, an interested non-Judean audience, more likely to be identified with the label "Roman" than "Greek." The actual audience intended by Josephus is another matter, much harder to discern, but may have included both non-Judean sympathizers (hardly those genuinely hostile to Judeans) and educated (Romanized) Judeans in Rome. If it had this double intended audience, its purpose was also perhaps twofold: to instruct, encourage, and confirm Judeans that they stood on robust cultural ground, with a constitution better than any other, and to attract support and interest from actual or potential sympathizers among the non-Judean population (probably not to gain proselytes, though that purpose cannot be ruled out).

Impact and Significance

The treatise was of interest and value to early Christian apologists up to and including Eusebius, but became so marginal to the Josephan corpus that it barely survived; its thin textual tradition is incomplete in Greek, and a large lacuna (2.51-113) is filled only by the sixth-century Latin translation. In the modern era, however, the text has proven to be extremely significant, for a variety of reasons. Some of its citations (e.g., from Manetho and Berossus) are very precious evidence regarding ancient authors otherwise barely extant, of great interest to experts in Egyptian and Babylonian history. Moreover, Josephus's collection of material displaying hostility to Judeans has provided the richest and most diverse source for scholarly theories on ancient hostility to Judeans (sometimes inaccurately labeled "anti-Semitism"), even though Josephus often misrepresents its sources and motivations. More positively, this full-scale "apology" for Judean culture constitutes our most informative source on the concerns and techniques of Judean apologetics, and Josephus's skillful use of Greco-Roman cultural tropes is a fine example of Judean accommodation, susceptible in part to the sort of cultural analysis employed in postcolonial criticism. Particular attention has been focused on his presentation of the Judean constitution (2.145-286), whose semiphilosophical agenda bears many points of contact with Plato's Laws. Josephus appears to coin the potent term "theocracy" (2.165), and his particular collection of laws, with their continuing stress on the Temple and the priests (2.190-218), remains an intriguing product of the post-70 era. His selection of these laws, and his comment on their moral and cultural significance, remains one of the most impressive attempts to present Judean culture in terms understandable and attractive to those reared in the Greco-Roman tradition. Comparing Moses's constitution favorably with both the Athenian and the Spartan systems, Josephus indicates how Judean culture outclasses all its rivals, and why it attracts imitation by both philosophers and the ordinary "masses." Finally, the specifically Roman accents of this treatise, in its political stance and its adoption of Romanized values, suggests a partial trend toward the "Romanization" of Judean tradition, at least as envisaged by this articulate and culturally sensitive Roman citizen from Judea.

Josephus's Reception and Interpretation

In the ancient world members of the elite classes were educated to write in all genres, but always under the assumptions and principles of rhetoric (the art and science of convincing audiences). History was the statesman's genre par excellence: there he exercised his moral authority to expose the admirable and the execrable, to describe intractable problems and solutions, and to narrate catastrophes to be avoided in the future. Historians were valued not because of any independent verification of their accuracy, which was generally impossible, but because they were effective in conveying — by some combination of personal prestige, quality of writing, and moral appropriateness — a compelling account of human motives, foibles, and virtues.

In such a competitive context for the status of moral arbiter, it was natural that one author would typically win out and become "the authority" for his period. We know of several others who wrote histories overlapping with Josephus's, two by name (Nicolaus of Damascus and Justus of Tiberias) and unnamed Greeks and Romans who treated the Judean war before him (cf. *J.W.* 1.1-8). But whereas all of those are lost to us (except in those places where Nicolaus's 144-volume history overlapped with Josephus's history), Josephus's thirty volumes have reached us intact. At some point he became the exclusive authority for Judean history and geography from King Herod to the end of the Judean-Roman war in 73 C.E. Photius apparently still had access to Justus's writings, but he favored Josephus against Justus, even parroting Josephus's dismissal of his rival, and Justus's works did not survive much longer. The die had been cast long before.

How did this happen? The initial boost provided by the regime's endorsement of Josephus's *War* seems to have brought him to the attention of Christian authors in the second and third centuries C.E., who cite him with increasing emphasis through Origen in the third century. The influential fourth-century bishop and court panegyrist Eusebius is crucial for Josephus's legacy, because of his extensive use of Josephus and because of his own subsequent importance as the "father of church history." Eusebius's exploitation of "the most distinguished of historians among the Hebrews" (*Hist. Eccl.* 1.5.3) reflects the general Christian perception of the time: here is an outsider who cannot be accused of Christian tendentiousness, who yet describes in lurid detail the fall of Jerusalem (predicted by Jesus, according to the Gospels, as divine punishment on the Jews for failing to accept Jesus), and who excoriates the failings of his own people in the process. Josephus's heartbreaking story of the starving aristocratic woman who cooked and ate her own infant child during the siege of Jerusalem (*J.W.* 6.200-214) was particularly useful to Eusebius and later Christian teachers, who wished to claim that the Jews, obviously capable of such depravity, had been justly punished by God and excluded from their heritage in salvation history. Josephus's incidental mention of Jesus of Nazareth (*Ant.* 18.63-64: the *testimonium flavianum*), which treats him respectfully — though our existing version has undergone at least a little doctoring in the manuscript tradition — led to its being cited even more than the story of Maria's cannibalism.

The problem was that Josephus himself had entirely different points to make about the fall of Jerusalem, and about Jesus and the countless other individuals he mentions — as a Thucydidean-Polybian sort of statesman lamenting political folly. Whereas a scholar such as Eusebius could exploit Josephus's lack of association with Christian belief for rhetorical traction, by interweaving large quotations with Christian claims as if the two were providentially compatible, other writers of the period felt that his factual material should be liberated from his "Jewish unbelief." So, later in Eusebius's century, the unknown author we call Pseudo-Hegesippus reworked the Greek *War* into Latin, inserting pieces from *Antiquities* but removing what seemed too Jewish (replaced by abundant Christian glosses), to produce an account of Jerusalem's fall that would be safe for Christian readers. Centuries later the opposite tack was taken by the Cambridge mathematician William Whiston, who in his celebrated 1737 translation of Josephus, still in wide circulation today, understood him to be an Ebionite Christian.

From late antiquity and the Middle Ages we have little or no evidence of Jewish interest in the writings of this famous priest. This can be explained by his surrender to the Romans under conditions that smacked of betrayal and cowardice; his writing in Greek and in isolation from the growing rabbinic literature based in postwar Judea, Galilee, and Mesopotamia; and his enthusiastic use by Christian apologists, albeit without his approval, against the Jews. The wide-ranging tenth-century chronicle known as *Yosippon* does nothing to alter this picture, for the name is a corruption based on a mistake; even if it does use material from Josephus along with many other sources, its readers were interested in the legends and not in Josephus. His legacy has remained one of suspicion in the Jewish world until the present, although this has begun to change in the past three decades under the combined force of dazzling archaeological finds, for which Josephus's narratives provide explanations, and a new effort to read his narratives on their own terms, free of assumptions about his life and morals.

The modern critical study of Josephus, from the mid-nineteenth century, was curiously parallel to Pseudo-Hegesippus in its concern to rescue Josephus's "factual material" from its narrative framework, though for different reasons. This time he was simply not considered a writer worth exploring. What mattered — as in most ancient texts for these early critics — were the sources he used, which should take us as close as we can get to what actually happened. Isolating and excising Josephus's sources appeared to be a straightforward exercise. First, the critic should remove the obvious overlay of self-aggrandizement and moral evaluation, the very things that Josephus wrote to provide. In any case, Josephus's moral universe was thought to consist of little more than the rhetoric of an opportunist and coward: the mouthpiece of Roman masters in *War*, who later gave up writing propaganda to dwell on his native traditions, but still did little more than stitch together the work of others and call it his own. Since a Judean priest could not have had a very deep knowledge of Greek literature and rhetoric, according to older assumptions, he could not have personally investigated, understood, or written most of what goes under his name. By assiduous alertness to repetitions, changes of vocabulary for the same object, doublets, apparent changes of outlook, and *hapax legomena*, one could hope to identify the "seams" of his editing work and reconstruct his sources for reuse on a more scientific basis.

New Approaches

The past quarter-century has witnessed a sea change in the scholarly use of Josephus. The most important catalyst for this change was the completion of the *Complete Concordance* in 1983, followed quickly by the development of electronic databases that include Josephus along with countless other ancient texts. These fundamental new resources disabled at a stroke all the guesswork and speculation about Josephus's tendencies and interests as an author, and about his use of sources; one now has to prove one's claims. At the same time, scholars influenced by what has been called "the linguistic turn" in all areas of the humanities — the insight that language is always constructed, never neutral, and that it is a significant problem to get beyond language to objective truth — now have the tools to explore Josephus's language. For the first time they can undertake sustained analysis of his diction, phrasing, and even incidental traits (particles, Atticizing forms, neologisms), also in comparison with his literary context. This close analysis has opened the door to considering long-neglected compositional features known from contemporary writing: rhetorical devices, paradox, polyphony, and irony.

This kind of study, which has energized the burgeoning field of "Josephus studies," has already demonstrated a general unity of language and thought across the Josephan corpus, and the surprising sophistication of those parts that have received intensive study. A negative consequence is that the old criteria for source criticism have been disqualified as rules of thumb: Josephus himself, it turns out, tends to vary language for the same object; to use A-B-A patterns, repetitions, and doublets; to change narrative voice or outlook for effect; and to use new word forms that happen to come into vogue from Plutarch onward — and so cannot be attributed to older sources. Since these traits are evident also in Josephus's autobiography, they must be deliberate and not a clumsy effort to sew together poorly understood sources. There is no doubt that Josephus used sources for most of what he wrote about, since he could not have known the events personally. Extracting sources from his finished work, however, may be as difficult as reconstituting the eggs from a baked cake. What we have now is his artful creation. It always remains possible that any particular oddity might be explicable as the vestige of a source, but our first obligation is to understand it as part of the composition; only if it does not seem to fit should we turn to sources (along with clumsiness, literary assistants, manuscript transcription errors, or later doctoring) as a possible explanation. Study of Josephus's language also undercuts assumptions about any radical differences of purpose from his earliest work to his latest: they show a substantial continuity of concern to articulate, defend, and even promote Judean law, custom, and character as contributions to human existence.

This new approach has direct implications in two other areas: the use

of Josephus's works for historical study and our estimation of the historical man. As for history, it is no longer possible to imagine that some pieces
of his narratives are simply neutral or factual, begging to be stripped out
and presented in history books as facts. To remove elements from the story,
in which words and phrases are chosen in relation to others, merely de-
stroys their narrative meaning; it does not thereby produce facts. The logic
of recent analysis drives us toward viewing Josephus's (and other ancient
writers') historical narratives as artistic productions, not unlike historical
films that we may watch today. In both cases the art undoubtedly derives
from real events and lives, but we cannot simply move from the production to some underlying reality.

As for Josephus's life, it used to be that Josephus was understood first
of all by presumed facts of his life story, especially his "betrayal" at
Jotapata. He himself portrays his surrender at length and colorfully, with
his miraculous survival of the murder-suicide pact he first agreed to, on
the strength of his belief that he had a message from God. That story and
much of his reported behavior before Jotapata have suggested to modern
readers a distasteful duplicity and double-dealing with the people under
his care. Scholars used to feel justified, on the basis of these facts, in dis-
missing his writings as opportunistic.

The new approach emphasizes, by contrast, that we know nothing
about Josephus's life apart from what he chose to include in his narratives.
If we seek first to understand them, we quickly realize that the matrix of
double-dealing and misleading the public, which he openly declares as his
program (*Life* 17–22), was also part and parcel of elite political life in the
Roman Empire: these were not democratic societies with an educated
middle class and Enlightenment values. Josephus and his peers considered
it their *duty* to mislead "the masses" as the situation demanded, appearing
to support popular demands when necessary, seeking to terminate dangerous impulses when possible. Josephus must have portrayed his wily tricks
and deceptions in the expectation of respect, not condemnation, from his
audience. At any rate, since they are colorful literary creations, we cannot
extract them from the narrative, judge them negatively by our ethical principles, and make them the basis for our views of the historical Josephus.

If we postpone our speculations about what may lie *beneath* Josephus's literary legacy, and turn our attention to exploring the surviving
narratives in their literary and historical contexts, we begin to wonder at
the impact they must have made on whatever audiences he was able to assemble in Rome. He first, in *War*, explained the tragedy of the recent war as

a chain of small, typical situations and events that led to unintended consequences; in the process he tried consistently to redefine the standard
postwar image of the Judean national character. About fifteen years later,
in *Antiquities–Life,* he offered a detailed account of Judean history, culture,
and law from creation to his own time, masterfully distilling a single story
from the biblical narrative along the way. Again the focus is on the character of this people with such a rich and ancient heritage of noble laws. His
final work (*Apion*) is a forceful and sometimes rollicking attack, apparently designed for the same amenable audiences, on writers who have dis-
paraged the very aspects of the Judean character and constitution that his
Antiquities had celebrated.

Notwithstanding both traditional Christian and scholarly (ab)use, it is
becoming increasingly clear that we have in Josephus a major and energetic spokesman for Judean culture in the Roman period.

BIBLIOGRAPHY

General

Bilde, Per. 1988. *Flavius Josephus between Jerusalem and Rome: His Life, His Works
and Their Importance.* Sheffield: JSOT Press.

Cohen, Shaye J. D. 1979 *Josephus in Galilee and Rome: His Vita and Development as
a Historian.* Leiden: Brill.

Edmondson, Jonathan, Steve Mason, and James Rives, eds. 2005. *Flavius Josephus
and Flavian Rome.* Oxford: Oxford University Press

Feldman, Louis H., and Gohei Hata, eds. 1987. *Josephus, Judaism, and Christianity.*
Detroit: Wayne State University Press.

Feldman, Louis H., and Gohei Hata, eds. 1989. *Josephus, the Bible, and History.* Detroit: Wayne State University Press

Hadas-Lebel, Mireille. 1993. *Flavius Josephus: Eyewitness to Rome's First-Century
Conquest of Judea.* New York: Macmillan.

Klawans, Jonathan. 2012. *Josephus and the Theologies of Ancient Judaism.* Oxford:
Oxford University Press.

Laqueur, Richard. 1920. *Der Jüdische Historiker Flavius Josephus: Ein Biographischer
Versuch auf Neuer Quellenkritischer Grundlage.* Gießen: Münchow [English
trans. Caroline Disler at pace.cns.yorku.ca].

Mason, Steve, ed. 1998. *Understanding Josephus: Seven Perspectives.* Sheffield: Sheffield Academic Press.

———. 2001. *Flavius Josephus: Translation and Commentary,* vol. 9, *Life of Josephus.* Leiden: Brill.

————. 2003a. "Contradiction or Counterpoint? Josephus and Historical Method." *Review of Rabbinic Judaism* 6: 145-88.

————. 2003b. *Josephus and the New Testament.* 2d ed. Peabody, Mass.: Hendrickson.

McLaren, James S. 1998. *Turbulent Times? Josephus and Scholarship on Judaea in the First Century.* Sheffield: Sheffield Academic Press

Neyrey, Jerome H. 1994. "Josephus' *Vita* and the Encomium: A Native Model of Personality." *JSJ* 25: 177-206.

Olson, Ryan S. 2010. *Tragedy, Authority, and Trickery: The Poetics of Embedded Letters in Josephus.* Cambridge, Mass: Center for Hellenic Studies, Harvard University Press.

Parente, Fausto, and Joseph Sievers, eds. 1994. *Josephus and the History of the Greco-Roman Period: Essays in Memory of Morton Smith.* Leiden: Brill.

Pastor, Jack, Pnina Stern, and Menahem Mor, eds. 2010. *Flavius Josephus: Interpretation and History.* Leiden, Brill.

Pummer, Reinhard. 2009. *The Samaritans in Flavius Josephus.* Tübingen: Mohr Siebeck.

Rajak, Tessa. 2002. *Josephus: The Historian and His Society.* 2d ed. London: Duckworth.

Rodgers, Zuleika, ed. 2007. *Making History: Josephus and Historical Method.* Leiden: Brill

Sievers, Joseph, and Gaia Lembi, eds. 2005. *Josephus and Jewish History in Flavian Rome and Beyond.* Leiden: Brill.

Thackeray, Henry St. J. 1929. *Josephus: The Man and the Historian.* New York: Jewish Institute of Religion.

Jewish War

Brighton, Mark Andrew. 2009. *The Sicarii in Josephus's Judean War: Rhetorical Analysis and Historical Observations.* Atlanta: Society of Biblical Literature.

Cohen, Shaye J. D. 1982. "Masada: Literary Tradition, Archaeological Remains, and the Credibility of Josephus." *JJS* 33: 385-405.

Hata, Gohei. 1975-76. "Is the Greek Version of Josephus' *Jewish War* a Translation or a Rewriting of the First Version?" *JQR* N.s. 66: 89-108.

Linder, Helgo. 1972. *Die Geschichtsauffassung des Flavius Josephus im Bellum Iudaicum.* Leiden: Brill.

Mason, Steve. 2008. *Flavius Josephus: Translation and Commentary: Jewish War 1–4.* Leiden: Brill.

McLaren, James S. 2005. "A Reluctant Provincial: Josephus and the Roman Empire in *Jewish War.*" In *The Gospel of Matthew in Its Roman Imperial Context.* Ed. John Riches and David C. Sim. London: Clark, 34-48.

————. 2007. "Delving into the Dark Side: Josephus' Foresight as Hindsight." In

Making History: Josephus and Historical Method. Ed. Zuleika Rodgers. Leiden: Brill, 49-67.

Parente, Fausto. 2005. "The Impotence of Titus, or Flavius Josephus's *Bellum Judaicum* as an Example of 'Pathetic' Historiography." In *Josephus and History in Flavian Rome and Beyond.* Ed. Joseph Sievers and Gaia Lembi. Leiden: Brill, 45-69.

Price, Jonathan J. 1992. *Jerusalem under Siege: The Collapse of the Jewish State, 66-70 CE.* Leiden: Brill.

―――. 2005. "The Provincial Historian in Rome." In *Josephus and History in Flavian Rome and Beyond.* Ed. J. Sievers and G. Lembi. Leiden: Brill, 101-18.

Schwartz, Seth. 1986. "The Composition and Publication of Josephus' 'Bellum Judaicum' Book 7." *HTR* 79: 373-86.

Siggelkow-Berner, Birke. 2011. *Die jüdischen Feste im Bellum Judaicum des Flavius Josephus.* Tübingen: Mohr Siebeck.

Weber, Wilhelm. 1921. *Josephus und Vespasian: Untersuchungen zu dem jüdischen Krieg des Flavius Josephus.* Hildesheim: Olms.

Yavetz, Zvi. 1975. "Reflections on Titus and Josephus." *Greek, Roman and Byzantine Studies* 16: 411-32.

Jewish Antiquities

Attridge, Harold W. 1976. *The Interpretation of Biblical History in the Antiquitates Judaicae of Flavius Josephus.* Missoula, Mont.: Scholars Press.

Begg, Christopher T. 1993. *Josephus' Account of the Early Divided Monarchy (AJ 8,212-420): Rewriting the Bible.* Leuven: Leuven University Press.

―――. 2000. *Josephus' Story of the Later Monarchy.* Leuven: Leuven University Press.

―――. 2005. *Flavius Josephus: Translation and Commentary,* vol. 4, *Judean Antiquities 5–7.* Leiden: Brill.

Begg, Christopher T., and Paul Spilsbury. 2005. *Flavius Josephus: Translation and Commentary,* vol. 5, *Judean Antiquities 8–10.* Leiden: Brill.

Feldman, Louis H. 1988. "Use, Authority, and Exegesis of Mikra in the Writings of Josephus." In *Mikra: Text, Translation, Reading, and Interpretation of the Hebrew Bible in Ancient Judaism and Early Christianity.* Ed. Martin Jan Mulder and H. Sysling. Assen: van Gorcum, 455-518.

―――. 1998a. *Studies in Josephus' Rewritten Bible.* Leiden: Brill.

―――. 1998b. *Josephus's Interpretation of the Bible.* Berkeley: University of California Press.

―――. 2000. *Flavius Josephus: Translation and Commentary,* vol. 3, *Judean Antiquities 1–4.* Leiden: Brill.

Franxman, Thomas W. 1979. *Genesis and the Jewish Antiquities of Flavius Josephus.* Rome: Biblical Institute Press.

Mason, Steve. 1991. *Flavius Josephus on the Pharisees: A Composition-Critical Study.* Leiden: Brill.

Nakman, David. 2004. "The Halakhah in the Writings of Flavius Josephus." Ph.D. dissertation, Bar Ilan University [in Hebr.; Eng. summary at pace.cns.yorku.ca].

Nodet, Étienne. 1990. *Flavius Josèphe: Les Antiquités Juives.* Paris: Cerf.

Schwartz, Seth. 1990. *Josephus and Judaean Politics.* Leiden: Brill.

Semenchenko, L. 2002. "Hellenistic Motifs in the *Jewish Antiquities* of Flavius Josephus." Ph.D. dissertation, Russian Academy of Sciences, Moscow [in Russian; English summary at pace.cns.yorku.ca].

Smith, Morton. 1956. "Palestinian Judaism in the First Century." In *Israel: Its Role in Civilization.* Ed. Moshe Davis. New York: Harper & Brothers, 67-81.

Spilsbury, Paul. 1998. *The Image of the Jew in Flavius Josephus' Paraphrase of the Bible.* Tübingen: Mohr Siebeck.

Sterling, Gregory E. 1992. *Historiography and Self-Definition: Josephos, Luke-Acts, and Apologetic Historiography.* Leiden: Brill.

Wiseman, Timothy P. 1991. *Death of an Emperor: Flavius Josephus.* Exeter: University of Exeter Press.

Against Apion

Barclay, John M. G. 2007. *Flavius Josephus: Translation and Commentary,* vol. 10, *Against Apion.* Leiden: Brill.

Bar-Kochva, Bezalel. 1996. *Pseudo-Hecataeus "On the Jews": Legitimizing the Jewish Diaspora.* Berkeley: University of California Press.

Feldman, Louis H., and John R. Levison, eds. 1996. *Josephus' Contra Apionem: Studies in Its Character and Context.* Leiden: Brill.

Gerber, Christine. 1997. *Ein Bild des Judentums für Nichtjuden von Flavius Josephus: Untersuchungen zu seiner Schrift Contra Apionem.* Leiden: Brill.

Goodman, Martin. 1999. "Josephus' Treatise *Against Apion.*" In *Apologetics in the Roman Empire: Pagans, Jews and Christians.* Ed. Mark Edwards, Martin Goodman, and Simon Price. Oxford: Oxford University Press, 45-58.

Gruen, Erich S. 2005. "Greeks and Jews: Mutual Misperceptions in Josephus' *Contra Apionem.*" In *Ancient Judaism in Its Hellenistic Context.* Ed. Carol Bakhos. Leiden: Brill, 31-51.

Kasher, Arych. 1997. *Flavius Josephus: Against Apion.* Jerusalem: Zalman Shazar Center (in Hebrew).

Labow, Dagmar. 2005. *Flavius Josephus Contra Apionem Buch I.* Stuttgart: Kohlhammer.

Schäfer, Peter. 1997. *Judeophobia: Attitudes towards the Jews in the Ancient World.* Cambridge: Harvard University Press.

Troiani, Lucio. 1977. *Commento storico al 'Contra Apione' di Giuseppe.* Pisa: Giardini.

Archaeology, Papyri, and Inscriptions

Jürgen K. Zangenberg

Next to literary texts, the remains of material culture are an essential source for understanding Jews and Judaism in the Second Temple period. This article surveys archaeological, epigraphical, and papyrological material from Palestine and the Diaspora in chronological order. The criteria for defining an object as "Jewish" and for including it in this discussion are deliberately broad. Religion does not play the decisive role. While there can be no doubt that material culture can serve religious functions in a given society, many archaeologists rightly warn not to overemphasize the religious character of artifacts. Not all artifacts had a religious meaning, and religion was not the only meaningful component even of a religious artifact like an altar or a temple. Moreover, the question is often not whether an object can be identified as Jewish, but *what type* of Judaism it might reflect.

Ancient cultures, and among them early Judaism, were constantly in contact with each other. Responses to the "other" were never uniform but complex and diverse, dependent on prevailing regional and social conditions. Boundaries were often blurred. Some elements of material culture reflect no particular religious affiliation, others acquired different meanings according to the cultural context in which they were used, and still others are regional phenomena that would be absent if the same religious group had lived elsewhere. A large part of material culture sits right on the margins, where clear "decoding" is difficult. Consequently, this survey will discuss not only material that reflects early Judaism — that was made for and used by Jews to practice their religion — but also elements of material culture that were commissioned or built by Jews even if these structures had no particular religious functions. The survey will also touch on non-

Jewish material culture if it influenced developments and trends in the Jewish world or illustrates the conditions under which Jewish material culture developed.

Palestine in the Hellenistic Period (ca. 320-164 B.C.E.)

Although we have substantial material evidence for Jews and Judaism from the Persian period both from Palestine and the Diaspora (especially Egypt), the conquests of Alexander and their aftermath initially left no deep traces in the material record of early Judaism.

The situation in Palestine at the end of the Persian period is reflected through excavations and surveys in areas such as Galilee and Judea. Excavations in Jerusalem indicate the small size of the city, and seal impressions give evidence of administration. Among the remains in Samaria are fortifications, coins, and seal impressions. Excavations on Mt. Gerizim have revealed the beginnings of a large sanctuary on the acropolis. Papyri provide interesting details about social and legal conditions during the second half of the fourth century B.C.E. From Wadi ed-Daliyeh come fragments of about thirty-eight documents and ninety-seven legible seal impressions. From Jericho coins and stamped handles have been found, and from Idumea around 800 Aramaic ostraca (potsherds) have been uncovered.

Although Palestine was strategically important to Alexander the Great as a bridge between Egypt and Asia, he left few archaeological traces in the region. Andromachos, the first Macedonian governor, was killed by Samarians, but the revolt was quickly put down and a new governor installed. While few of the excavated structures in Samaria can be safely associated with the earliest Macedonian inhabitants (the three round towers on the acropolis being the most likely candidates), the skeletons and documents from Wadi ed-Daliyeh may represent remains of some of the insurgents.

For the first hundred years after the wars among Alexander's successors, the Diadochoi, Palestine belonged to the Ptolemaic kingdom. It is symptomatic of the situation in the first half of the third century B.C.E. that fortifications are among the best-known structures. The most impressive one is in Dor, but others are located in Ptolemais, Straton's Tower, Philoteria, Gaza, Shechem, and elsewhere. Ptolemaic rule was tolerant and did not interfere with local matters. The papyri archives of a Ptolemaic official named Zenon (260/59 B.C.E.) give insight into the mechanisms of economic exploitation in Palestine and the way local elites were used by the king to secure regular taxation.

From the second half of the third century B.C.E., both the growing contacts between the coastal cities and the larger Greek world and the rapid development of cities in Transjordan increasingly influenced the cultural context of the traditionally Jewish regions in central Palestine. From then on, the hill country of Judea, Samaria, and the Galilee was sandwiched between areas deeply influenced by Hellenism.

The Coastal Plain

Particularly important were developments in the coastal plain. The region functioned as a starting point for more permanent settlement of Phoenician colonists in the agricultural hinterland. In the south, Khirbet el-Qom and Aderet are good examples of rural sites having contacts with the coast. The hinterland provided agricultural goods (mostly wine and oil) that were consumed in or exported from the coastal cities. In turn, the inhabitants of settlements in the hinterland (above all, cities like Samaria) bought goods that had entered the country through the coastal plain harbors. Small amounts of Greek luxury ceramics had already served local elites since the fourth century B.C.E. Now, stamped amphorae indicate a growing demand for imported goods. Although perhaps only a few Jews lived in cities like Gaza, Ashkelon, Ashdod, Dor, and Ptolemais (Akko), the old cultural demarcation between coastal plain and hill country gradually decreased.

The Transjordan Plateau

The systematic reurbanization of the Transjordanian plateau created markets east of central Palestine that were to a large extent supplied by the cities on the coast. The exact circumstances of the transformation of older settlements into new, Hellenized urban centers during the first half of the third century B.C.E. are not entirely clear, but they quickly constituted an ever-growing cultural and economic factor. In cities like Gadara, Pella, Gerasa, Philadelphia, and Scythopolis (Beth Shean), which later combined with others to form the Decapolis, a lively blend of Greek and local pagan-Semitic culture developed.

Jerusalem

In contrast to these urban centers, only one place in Judea deserved the label *city:* Jerusalem. Its only source of income and status was the Temple. Early Hellenistic Jerusalem was fairly small (basically only the City of David was inhabited) and quite poor. Only the small priestly aristocracy enjoyed moderate wealth, mostly based on income from the Temple and revenues as landowners. Most people had access only to local goods. Handles of storage vessels stamped with YHD indicate taxation in kind, probably managed by authorized tax collectors or (in the case of stamps with YRSLM and a star) by members of the priesthood. These stamps first appear in the Persian period and were used well into the Ptolemaic age.

The situation in the hill country and especially in Jerusalem changed after 200 B.C.E. when Antiochus III defeated Ptolemy V Epiphanes in the battle of Paneion and the Seleucids took control of the region. The Seleucids supported the Temple out of their own politically inspired agenda, via members of the local elite who supervised the implementation of Seleucid policy.

The spectrum of finds from Jerusalem is notably different from that of the previous period. Now, large amounts of stamped amphora handles from Greek islands like Rhodes and Kos indicate frequent imports from the Aegean to meet the demands of elite who became increasingly attracted to Greek culture and had the means to acquire luxury goods. Few archaeological remains have survived from the pre-Hasmonean period. No remains of the Seleucid Akra have been identified securely, and only some stretches of the city walls in the City of David and around the citadel may date to the pre-Hasmonean period. Arrowheads and inscribed lead projectiles from the second century B.C.E. were found in Hellenistic layers at the citadel and probably belong to the siege by Antiochus VII in 133/32 B.C.E.

All other settlements in Judea were even smaller than Jerusalem. Bethel was a large village and Qalandiya no more than a large farmstead specializing in the production of wine. Fortresses continued to be built (e.g., at Maresha, Samaria, Beth-Zur, and Gebel Sartaba near Pella).

Samaria

In the region of Samaria, at least three sites can be called cities. The city of Samaria, the former seat of the Persian governor and later a Macedonian garrison, was certainly more important and cosmopolitan than Jerusalem. Several periods of excavation have uncovered substantial remains from the third century B.C.E., among them houses with painted stucco, Greek inscriptions, and imported Greek pottery. It seems that the population was largely pagan.

The second, certainly smaller city was the old site of biblical Shechem (Tell Balata), which was resettled at the end of the fourth century B.C.E. Contrary to many scholars who suppose that the new city was inhabited by Samaritans, the evidence points in the opposite direction. If Josephus is right (*Ant.* 11.344), we can assume that Shechem was a settlement of Sidonian colonists who wanted to control the strategically important valley between Mt. Gerizim and Mt. Ebal and the traffic crossing the fertile al-Askar plain. Material culture from Hellenistic Shechem was considerably poorer than from Samaria. All earlier structures on the tell were covered by a thick layer of fill; the Middle Bronze Age city wall was used as a foundation for new fortifications; and the interior was filled with regularly built private houses. 2 Maccabees 6:2 mentions a temple dedicated to Zeus Xenios on Mt. Gerizim, probably on Tell er-Ras, the eastern summit of Mt. Gerizim, which served as an acropolis for Shechem.

Around 200 B.C.E. at the latest, a third city existed on the summit of Mt. Gerizim, surrounding an older sanctuary. The sanctuary consisted of a large open courtyard measuring about 90 by 90 meters that was accessible over large stairways and surrounded by halls, rooms, and massive fortifications. Unlike the situation in Jerusalem, the sacred precinct does not seem to have housed a temple building but a large open altar. The remains of the altar were later obliterated by the construction of a Byzantine church. Outside the sacred precinct, archaeologists have excavated parts of a large city that, together with the sanctuary, was protected by a wide city wall. The houses were all very well built; many had large courtyards and rooms for processing agricultural produce (oil presses). Greek style bathtubs in some houses indicate a high standard of living. Many inscriptions in a recently published corpus of some 400 fragments (most of them dating to the third and second century B.C.E.) contain dedicatory formulae and mention names and titles of cultic personnel in Aramaic and Paleo-Hebrew. Although found in secondary use, it is possible that the inscriptions were once on display somewhere in the sacred precinct. On the basis of the epigraphic evidence, there can be no doubt that the city was the main settlement of the Samaritans, and that the sanctuary was their central place of worship, which included sacrifices and pilgrimages. Due to the lack of a natural spring on the summit, the city was not easy to defend despite strong fortifications (including chamber gates very much in the Iron Age tradition). Both city and sanctuary were destroyed by John Hyrcanus around 112/111 B.C.E. (Josephus, *Ant.* 13.254-57). Greek inscriptions from the second to fourth century C.E. witness to Samaritan pilgrimage to Mt. Gerizim long after the temple there had been destroyed.

The Galilee

Settlement activity in the Galilee seems to have been low and sparse before 100 B.C.E., but this impression will probably change as a result of more intensive surveys. Around the mid-third century B.C.E. veteran settlements were established at Philoteria, et-Tell (Bethsaida), and Gamla to guard the traffic arteries between the coast (especially Tyre) and the eastern plateau. A large public building at Hamath Tiberias dates from the later Seleucid period. Apart from that, there is growing material evidence of an indigenous, Semitic population in the hills of Upper and northern Lower Galilee. Some elements of its material culture seem influenced by the Phoenicians; others stand in the late Iron Age tradition. The sanctuaries at Dan and Paneion had regional importance in the second century B.C.E. A Phoenician presence itself is evident in the administrative center at Qedesh, the mountain sanctuary at Mitzpe Yamim, and the emporium at Tell Anafa. A fortification on the acropolis at Sepphoris, probably dating to sometime during the second half of the second century B.C.E., guarded the traffic route running inland from Ptolemais. The fort reflects the strategic value of the Galilee as a geographical link between harbors on the Mediterranean and the cities of western Syria.

Perea

Ever since the Persian period, Jews had lived in Perea east of the Jordan. Here the Ptolemies confirmed the descendants of the Persian governor "Tobiah the Ammonite" as landholders. Ptolemy III Euergetes appointed Joseph son of Tobiah as the highest civil functionary of the entire Ptolemaic province. He resided in ʿAraq el-Amir, a palace in a large estate seventeen kilometers west of Amman. The beginnings of the estate date back to the late Iron II period. The famous Tobiah inscriptions at the entrance to two caves date to the fifth century B.C.E., and a gateway was added in the late third century B.C.E. In the early second century B.C.E., the famous palace at Qasr el-Abd was built with monolithic columns, window fronts, and lion reliefs (Josephus, *Ant.* 12.230-33). The size of the estate and the lavish decoration of the palace, which shows a fine blend of Greek and oriental styles, offers a good indication of the Hellenizing tendencies of many members of the landowning Jewish upper class.

The Early Hellenistic Diaspora

Jewish communities in Egypt and Mesopotamia date back to the sixth century B.C.E. In the fourth century B.C.E. Jews are attested at Kition in Cyprus; epitaphs in Phoenician script mention names with a YHWH component. With the expansion of Hellenistic kingdoms and with Rome eventually controlling vast territories and connecting regions, Judaism reached Asia Minor, the Greek islands, mainland Italy, the area around the Black Sea, North Africa, Spain, and southern Gaul.

Although the origins of many of these Diaspora communities predate the Hasmonean period, most of our material dates to the late second century B.C.E. Inscriptions survive in sometimes great variety but are often distributed very irregularly. Jews generally enjoyed the protection of the rulers, but individual communities lived under very different cultural, legal, and social conditions. They took part in public life and used regionally available material culture.

Palestine in the Hasmonean Period (164-40 B.C.E.)

Antiochus IV Epiphanes' ill-fated attempt to forcibly stabilize Palestine around 167 B.C.E. with the help of the deeply Hellenized faction of the Jerusalem elite eventually resulted in the violent overthrow of Seleucid rule and the establishment of an independent Jewish state in Palestine under the Hasmoneans, a priestly family from rural Modein in Judea. The Hasmonean takeover of Palestine was a protracted process lasting well over two generations until John Hyrcanus's (134-104 B.C.E.) large-scale occupations in Samaria, Perea, the Galilee, and Idumea.

Hasmonean restoration did not mean the end of Hellenization. It was during the Hasmonean period that Judaism developed a distinct variant of eastern Hellenistic material culture. Hellenism became indigenous to Jewish Palestine, embedded in its culture and in the self-definition of its ruling dynasty. Symptomatic of that process is how Simon Maccabee (high priest and ethnarch 142-134 B.C.E.) integrated elements of Greek architecture into his renovated family tomb in Modein (1 Macc. 13:23-30; Josephus, *Ant.* 13.210-12).

Until well into the second century B.C.E., there are no criteria to distinguish a Jewish site from a non-Jewish one apart from general geographical considerations, inscriptions (still very rare), and textual information. Both Jewish and non-Jewish populations to a very large extent used the same pool of material culture, which often followed regional rather than religious patterns.

The Seleucid garrison in the Akra of Jerusalem was captured by Simon in 141 B.C.E. (1 Macc. 14:49-52). The subsequent territorial acquisitions by Simon, Hyrcanus, and Alexander Jannaeus followed a religiously inspired agenda. Pagans were expelled from cities such as Joppa and Gezer and repopulated by Jews; strongholds like Beth-Zur were destroyed and neutralized by settling Jews in the vicinity; and in the rural hinterland new, small settlements were established that guarded the hills and exploited regional agricultural resources.

John Hyrcanus I (134-104 B.C.E.) undertook an aggressive expansion that brought about much destruction especially in Samaria (Gerizim, Samaria, Shechem) and in the Galilee. Often the new settlements were oriented toward new markets and therefore lacked luxury pottery that had often abounded before (as in Gezer). The presence of *miqva'ot* (ritual baths) in houses signals new religious practices, as in Gezer and the Sepphoris acropolis. Next to expansion, Hyrcanus's activities were directed toward internal consolidation. Strongholds were erected at Masada, Machaerus, Hyrcania, and Alexandrion. Although these fortresses lack the highly complex palace structures characteristic of the subsequent Herodian period, they were not only intended for purely military purposes.

Palace Architecture

Palace architecture was not confined to fortresses, as the palace in Jericho demonstrates. Jannaeus integrated the residential complex there into a large estate and built a highly effective water supply system. The palace consisted of a fortified section situated on a moat overlooking Wadi Qelt, as well as several huge pools surrounded by gardens, pavilions, and storage facilities. Remains of stucco and wall paintings show that sumptuous decoration was already present in the initial phase of the palace. The ceramic profile, however, demonstrates that until the beginning of the Herodian period few foreign imports reached the palace; the residents used mainly local ware. Another, earlier example of Hasmonean palace architecture can be found in the second-century-B.C.E. phase of the Qasr el-Abd palace at ʿAraq el-Amir. Here, unlike west of the Jordan, free use was made of figurative art on a truly monumental scale.

Architecture in Rural Contexts

Architecture in rural areas was far less lavish than in the palaces of the ruling elite and more or less followed traditional lines. Typologically, houses in Hellenistic Palestine fell into two types: (1) polygonal courtyard complexes separated from each other by irregular streets; and (2) rectangular courtyard houses integrated into square neighborhoods in classical Greek, "Hippodamic" style. Towns and villages mostly followed traditional, irregular plans, as in Shechem, Shiqmona, and Bethel. At the end of the second century B.C.E., a new type of rural settlement made its appearance: the fortified farmstead consisting of rooms and installations arranged around a usually rectangular courtyard with a tower in one corner. The building type is similar to that of Hellenistic farmsteads in Asia Minor and the Black Sea area. It made its way into late Hellenistic and early Roman Palestine, in upper-class agricultural sites such as Ramat ha-Nadiv.

From around 100 B.C.E. onward settlement intensified in various regions. On the Dead Sea, ample evidence attests a systematic integration of the once rather thinly populated area. Settlements at Qumran, Khirbet Mazin, Qasr et-Turabe, Masada, and Machaerus signal growing interest in the region. After 100 B.C.E. settlement activity also dramatically increased in the Galilee and the Western Golan. Due to the destruction and abandonment of some sites (e.g., at Anafa and Qedesh) and the foundation of new settlements (e.g., at Gamla and Yodefat), settlement patterns and the flow of household goods changed. On Tel Anafa a small village with square houses of similar size was built a couple of years after the destruction of the large stuccoed building. The once fortified site on et-Tell was now built up with irregularly oriented, large farmhouses. New regional types of common ware developed (e.g., Kfar Hananiah ware), but the region was not entirely cut off from outside influence, as glass and some imported ware in the fishermen's village on et-Tell show.

Burial Practices

Burial practices offer a good example of how Jewish culture was suscepti-ble to symbiosis with surrounding cultures. Mourning and burial were family affairs in both the Jewish and non-Jewish worlds. Among the com-mon elements were preparing the body of the deceased for burial, wailing, playing music, marching in procession, and observing purity taboos. Early Hellenistic burial culture followed late Persian traditions for the most part. Sometimes single shaft tombs were used (e.g., in Dor and Atlit) along with chamber tombs (e.g., at Bat-Yam, Tell en-Nasbe, el-Azariye, and Lachish). Sometimes a cemetery was made up of one type alone. Architectural deco-ration is largely unknown, and grave goods are both poor and scarce.

The general situation changed in the first half of the second century. Traditional chamber tombs (e.g., at Maresha in about 200 B.C.E.) came under Hellenistic influence: funeral benches inside the burial chamber were replaced by longitudinal receptacles for the corpse hewn into the rock called *loculi* or *kokhim*, and the interior layout became more regularized (see fig. 6). Tombs were sometimes painted, and architectural decoration such as columns, capitals, and pilasters were used on façades. About two generations later the new style was adopted in Jerusalem's upper-class tombs, and from there it was taken over by more and more families. Espe-cially famous is Jason's Tomb, one of the oldest and most elaborate upper-class tombs in Jerusalem, built around 100 B.C.E.

Funeral culture demonstrates that traditional clan structures under-went a process of differentiation during the first century B.C.E. and C.E. in which individuals and smaller family units acquired a greater role. Instead of continuing the old Iron Age tradition of indiscriminate secondary burial in bone chambers, small limestone receptacles known as ossuaries became fashionable in the last decades of the first century B.C.E. and al-lowed for families to be buried in separate niches within the same tomb. About a third of these ossuaries bear names of the individuals buried in them, sometimes revealing information about the origin or the occupa-tion of the deceased. Archaeologists debate whether ossuaries reflect par-ticular beliefs about the afterlife such as resurrection of the body.

Pottery

Pottery is by far the most frequent type of material artifact and therefore extremely important for archaeological analysis. The question of how far pottery can directly define or identify the ethnicity of a given population is particularly controversial. Jews, like others, mostly used pottery that was produced locally, and in regions predominately populated by Jews, such as Palestine, Jews produced their own pottery, which was then regionally distributed. There is no such thing as explicitly and exclusively "Jewish pottery." Of course, pottery forms changed over time. Some early Hellenistic types developed from forms of the late Persian period; this was true of cooking pots and storage vessels. Others adapted and further developed Hellenistic forms, as is evident in the making of bowls and flasks. Apart from the coastal region, imported ware was very rare until the second half of the second century B.C.E. From then on, larger amounts of imported wares such as Eastern red-slipped pottery *(terra sigillata)* and mold-blown glass from Phoenicia became available and were readily absorbed by local customers.

Coins

The first clearly identifiable Jewish elements of material culture are coins. It is commonly accepted that John Hyrcanus I (134-104 B.C.E.) was the first ruler to issue coins. He did so under his Hebrew name, *Yehohanan.* Hasmonean minting started at around 120 B.C.E., when autonomous cities in the vicinity of Palestine also began issuing their own denominations. Hasmonean coins were issued in huge numbers only in bronze and are an important sign both of the independence of the Hasmonean state and of how firmly the realm was integrated into the material and political developments of the eastern Mediterranean (see fig. 11). Human and animal imagery was strictly avoided. Especially under Alexander Jannaeus (103-76 B.C.E.) and Mattathias Antigonus (40-37 B.C.E.), Hasmonean coins used generic Hellenistic symbols of prosperity and legitimate rule: cornucopias, pomegranates, stars, anchors, helmets, wreaths, and diadems. Many coins are decorated only on the margins and focus primarily on the title of the ruler ("priest"; "high priest"; "king") and of the ruled ("council of the Jews"). Legends are mostly written in Paleo-Hebrew, but Aramaic and later even Greek were used (e.g., one of Jannaeus's coins has the Greek legend

Alexandrou basileōs). Due to limited variation in iconography and nomenclature, many questions about precise chronology and iconographical development of specific types are still open.

Stepped, Plastered Pools

The earliest finds with a clear connection to Jewish religious practices are stepped, plastered pools. The earliest examples are attested in Sepphoris, where such pools were built into a former cistern sometime in the first half of the first century B.C.E., and in the palaces at Jericho. The houses of the new Jewish settlers in Gezer also had stepped pools, as did the palace-fortress of Masada, the wealthy mansions and small houses in Jerusalem, and the earliest phase of the settlement at Qumran. The evidence from Qedumim in Samaria shows that Samaritans also built stepped pools in the first century C.E. Although many of these installations served as ritual baths *(miqva'ot)*, it is far from certain that all stepped, plastered pools had ritual purposes or that their form was standardized.

The Late Hellenistic Diaspora

Archaeological evidence for Jewish life in the Diaspora during the second and first centuries B.C.E. is limited. While we know from numerous written sources that Judaism considerably expanded in the eastern Mediterranean basin during the Ptolemaic and Seleucid periods, no architectural structures and only a few inscriptions are known. Jewish "identity markers" such as *miqva'ot,* stone vessels, and ossuaries are virtually absent from the Diaspora.

Alexandria

Egypt must come first in our survey. One of the most influential events for Diaspora Judaism was the foundation of Alexandria at the mouth of the Nile in 321 B.C.E. Jews soon became a large and influential part of the city's inhabitants and enjoyed its economic opportunities, far-reaching contacts, and famous centers of Greek learning. Because few large-scale excavations have been carried out in the area of the ancient city, and because many older excavations in the surrounding necropolises remain poorly published, we know little about the actual living conditions of the city's Jewish community. The magnificent synagogue of Alexandria is known only from first-century-c.e. literary texts (Philo, *Legat.* 134; cf. the legendary version in *t. Sukkah* 4:6; *y. Sukkah* 5:1 [55ab]; *b. Sukkah* 51b). Its construction date is unknown, but its importance as a civic center for Alexandrian Jews is beyond doubt. It was destroyed during the uprisings under Trajan (116-117 c.e.).

Many Alexandrian Jews are attested in necropolises either through inscriptions (few of them *in situ*) or *in natura*. No separate cemeteries were used. Only the treatment of the corpse was somewhat different. Unlike the Egyptians, Jews did not practice embalming, and grave goods were rare. A number of decorated ossuaries indicate the sporadic practice of secondary burial.

Given the sprawling cultural interaction and the long tradition of Jewish life in Egypt, it is no surprise that the earliest evidence for a crucial Jewish institution comes from Egypt instead of Palestine: the dedication of a "prayer house" *(proseuchē)* by the *Ioudaioi* of Schedia, a suburb of Alexandria, from the time of Ptolemy III Euergetes (246-221 b.c.e.; *CIJ* 1:440). Because the building itself has not been found (indeed, no synagogue building has been excavated at all in Egypt), nothing is known about its shape and architectural context. Altogether, fifteen inscriptions and a number of papyri from the third century b.c.e. to the first century c.e. mention a synagogue (almost all use the term *proseuchē;* the term *synagōgē* is rare).

Leontopolis

Around 160 b.c.e. Ptolemy VI Philometor and Cleopatra III granted permission to the Jewish priest Onias IV to build a temple and a town at Leontopolis, a site in the Heliopolite nome thirty-two kilometers northeast of Cairo in the southeastern Nile delta (Josephus, *Ant.* 12.388; 13.63, 67, 285; *J.W.* 1.31-33; 7.427). The temple apparently flourished until the Roman prefect Lupus (71-73/74 c.e.) was instructed by Vespasian to destroy it (*J.W.* 7.421), an order that only Paulinus, Lupus's successor, followed (*J.W.* 7.433-35). Although it is disputed whether Onias's temple has indeed been identified at Tell el-Yehudiyyeh (it was excavated in 1887 and in 1906), a large number of tombs appear to have been used by Jews. As in Alexandria, the tombs usually follow contemporary forms. All of them are *hypogea* (underground chambers), most of them used for an entire family. The bodies were placed in *loculi* or *kokhim* (niches) hewn into the rock rectangular to the tomb's inner chamber. The head was often placed on an earthen "cushion," and the body received no embalming or decoration. More than eighty Greek tombstones (few found *in situ*) may be Jewish, but identification is notoriously difficult. The earliest inscription dates to 117 B.C.E., but most belong to the first century C.E. Both the size of the cemetery and the shape of the graves suggest that the population was well established and organized until its end in the uprisings of 116-117 C.E.

Other Sites in Egypt

Through inscriptions, ostraca, papyri, and burials, Jewish communities are also attested in many towns and villages in the Delta (Schedia, Athribis, Nitriai) and in Middle Egypt and the Fayyum (Arsinoe, Alexandrou Nesos, Oxyrhynchus, Hermoupolis Magna, Edfu, Sedment el-Gebel).

Greece

Archaeological evidence from Greece is scant before the second century C.E. Delos plays an especially prominent role. 1 Maccabees 15:23 attests a Jewish community there in 140 B.C.E. One building, built as a private home in the second century B.C.E., was rebuilt as a local assembly hall in two phases, first between the late second century B.C.E. and 88 B.C.E., and then in the first century B.C.E. The identification as a synagogue is based on the existence of a large assembly room and five dedicatory inscriptions mentioning *Theos Hypsistos* (the Most High God) and another inscription nearby mentioning a *proseuchē*. A cistern nearby could have been used as a *miqveh*, and a seat may have represented the "seat of Moses." Like synagogues in pre-70 Palestine, the assembly hall at Delos has a simple architecture and little decoration. The translation of *epi proseuchē* in the inscription as "house of prayer" is uncertain, since the phrase can mean "in (fulfillment of) a prayer/vow" (*IJO* 1:227). Several lamps with pagan motifs were also found in the house. The building itself followed the pattern set by other Delian associations, whose structures had a porticoed courtyard and a marble chair. The "mixed" profile of material culture leaves two alternatives: either a synagogue for a Jewish community deeply assimilated to local pagan culture (if so, then it would be the earliest one excavated in the Diaspora), or the assembly hall of a pagan guild. At present both options appear equally viable.

Two inscriptions from an unexcavated building near the possible synagogue demonstrate that Jewish communities were not the only ones to spread across the eastern Mediterranean; Samaritan communities did as well. Interestingly enough, the self-designation of the Samaritan community on Delos was "the Israelites in Delos who pay tribute to the holy sanctuary Argarizim," and they called their assembly hall a *proseuchē*. Two epitaphs inscribed before 88 B.C.E. were found on Rhenaia, the burial island of Delos. Each mentions the violent death of a woman and calls upon "*Theos Hypsistos*, Lord of the spirits and all flesh" to send "the angels of God" to avenge the crime. The terminology seems to indicate a Jewish milieu.

Evidence from other places in Greece is sparse. The second-century-B.C.E. date of an epitaph mentioning a certain Sim(e)on son of Ananias from Athens is debated (*IJO* 1:156-57). Especially interesting are two inscriptions incised on the polygonal wall of the temple of Apollo at Delphi dated to 163/62 and 158/57 B.C.E., respectively. The inscriptions document the manumission of a male slave named Ioudaios and a female slave named Antigone. In another inscription from Delphi from the second to first century B.C.E., Ioudaios son of Pindaros declares his slave Amyntas free (*IJO* 1:173-76). The oldest manumission inscription mentioning a *Ioudaios* ("Jew" or "Judean") comes from the Amphiareion at Oropus and is dated to 300-250 B.C.E. Here Moschus son of Moschion obeyed a dream sent by the gods Amphiaraos and Hygieia commanding him to erect an inscription documenting his manumission from an unknown master (*IJO* 1:177-80). On an inscription from Iasos, a certain Niketas son of Iason from Jerusalem is listed as one of two *metoikoi* (resident foreigners) who have together donated 100 drachmas for an unnamed pagan festival. If Niketas was indeed a Jew, the inscription, dated after 150 B.C.E., documents participation of Jews in public life. Another list of names from Iasos, dated to the early first century B.C.E., may also include Jews since the names Judas and Jason are mentioned (*IJO* 2:129-31). A list of benefactors from Smyrna dated 123/24 C.E. mentions that "a group of former Jews" pledged to give 10,000 drachmas. The phrase *hoi pote Ioudaioi* is unique and enigmatic: does it refer to inhabitants of Smyrna who used to live in Judea or who were apostate Jews? The term *Ioudaios* can indicate both regional origin and religious affiliation. Also unclear is whether the phrase is a self-definition or a label applied to them by the city officials who commissioned the inscription (*IJO* 2:177-79).

Asia Minor

For the growing Jewish communities in Asia Minor, literary texts are virtually our only sources before the second century c.e. Here the fragmentary nature of our archaeological material is especially deplorable.

Palestine in the Herodian Period (40 B.C.E.–39 C.E.)

The separation of the Hasmonean from the Herodian period is to a large extent artificial and follows historical rather than archaeological categories. In many respects, Herodian material culture not only builds upon earlier developments and inventions but also intensifies and differentiates them.

Herod's grandiose building projects put him in the first rank among his fellow eastern regents (see map 8). Usually, three phases of construction are distinguished. The first phase lasted from his accession to power in 40 B.C.E. to the Battle of Actium in 31 B.C.E. and comprised fortresses (the refurbishment of older ones at Alexandrion, Machaerus, and Masada and the construction of new ones at Antonia, Hyrcania, and Cyprus) and palaces (the western palace at Masada, the first palace at Jericho, and perhaps the palace at Callirhoe).

The second phase, which extended from the Battle of Actium until the visit of Augustus's friend Marcus Vipsanius Agrippa to Judea in 15 B.C.E., saw the most numerous and largest of Herod's building projects. Military architecture decreased; the focus now lay on development of the realm through cities, palaces, and buildings for entertainment and cult. After the construction of the theater and amphitheater in Jerusalem, Herod founded Sebaste, Herodium, and Caesarea Maritima; built the sanctuary in Paneas, his palace in Jerusalem, the second palace in Jericho, and the northern palace in Masada; and started expanding the Temple in Jerusalem.

The third phase of Herod's building program extended from the visit of Agrippa until Herod's death in 4 B.C.E. Few new accents appear in this phase. Many of the projects started in the second phase were continued. Complementary initiatives were the embellishment of David's tomb in Jerusalem, the foundation of military colonies in Trachonitis and Batanea, the construction of the third palace in Jericho, and the addition of the casemate wall at Masada. It is not clear if the sanctuaries in Mamre and Hebron and the foundation of the cities of Phasaelis, Antipatris, and Livias belong to the second or third phase. In addition to being enterprising in Palestine, Herod was an eager benefactor and donated money or commissioned buildings in many places around the Mediterranean.

Herod's sons readily followed their father, albeit on a lesser scale. In the southern Jordan Valley, Archelaus founded Archelais to better exploit the date palm groves; in Galilee, Antipas rebuilt Sepphoris and founded Tiberias in 18 C.E. as his two residential cities; and Philip refounded Bethsaida as Julias.

Herod's Building Style

Herod's building style mirrored the shrewdness of his political sensibilities and the multiethnic nature of his realm. He avoided almost entirely the use of figurative art in public and private contexts in regions where Jews were the predominant inhabitants. Here he brought the Hasmonean material culture to a new climax. This restriction went hand in hand with the intensified development of an alternative architectural and decorative idiom that had already begun in Hasmonean times. As before, the new style is inconceivable without contemporaneous architectural and decorative models borrowed from outside Palestine.

Herod's builders adapted building types and architectural models such as hippodromes, amphitheaters, Roman-style baths, domes, arches, vaults, triclinia (dining rooms with couches on three sides), gardens, peristyle courts (courts surrounded by a row of columns), and large piscinae (fish ponds) (see figs. 1, 52-54). Huge fortresses at Masada, Machaerus, and Herodium, palaces in Jericho and Jerusalem, and cities like Sebaste and Caesarea show new styles of wall construction, including *opus reticulatum:* the use of pyramidal blocks laid out diagonally with their bases facing outward (see figs. 55-61). The delicate geometrical patterns displayed on polychrome aniconic mosaics and on architectural elements of the Temple were based on Hellenistic and Roman decorative patterns of the first century B.C.E. but did not simply copy them (see figs. 2-3). The same trend seems to be evident in Herodian-period painting. There is evidence that Herod had some of his walls painted by artisans from Italy. Much of the new style also appears outside the court, as in the mosaics in the Upper City of Jerusalem and the wall paintings at Yodefat and Gamla.

The temples that Herod had built offer good examples of the complex blend of Hellenistic and indigenous traditions. The general layout of the Jerusalem Temple precinct resembles other contemporaneous sanctuaries in Heliopolis (Ba'albek), Damascus, and Palmyra (see figs. 65-67). The porticoes and stoa around the platform followed the best of Greek style and employed lavish classical decoration with meanders, rosettes, and floral designs. The sanctuary provided space for thousands of pilgrims, scores of cultic officials, and numerous installations. Although the Temple itself was built in centuries-old oriental fashion, the entire sanctuary reflected Herod's participation in the cultural koine of his time.

Herod's outlook is also visible in the promotion and architectural embellishment of traditional Semitic cult centers in Mamre, Hebron, and Paneion. In Mamre and Hebron the old cultic installations were surrounded with a monumental perimeter wall made in the same style as the Temple platform in Jerusalem. In Paneion the traditional cave sanctuary was embellished with a temple building placed directly in front of the grotto.

Settlement Activity

The Herodian age brought an intensification of settlement activity that was connected to and enabled a rise in population. Surveys in the Galilee have demonstrated that the decades after the turn of the era produced the greatest density in settlement before the Byzantine period. The same can be said of the area around the Dead Sea (see map 10). Here, old structures were expanded (Qumran) and new ones added ('Ein Feshkha). Entirely new settlements (e.g., Livias and Callirhoe) filled gaps in the regional infrastructure. Even the most luxurious palaces, such as those at Callirhoe and Jericho, were not isolated but integrated into large complexes.

Qumran

One of the most famous and controversial sites is Khirbet Qumran, located about fifteen kilometers south of Jericho on the western shore of the Dead Sea (see fig. 36 and map 12). Excavated by Roland de Vaux between

1949 and 1956, the site was soon identified as a settlement for a group of Essenes who had already been linked to scrolls found in a nearby cave in 1946/47. More caves and scrolls were discovered over the next decade (see fig. 37 and map 11). Due to the lack of a detailed report on the stratigraphy of the site and a complete presentation of finds, the history of the buildings and the stages of occupation are still not entirely clear. Many scholars accept the following chronology: after an initial phase of settlement in Iron Age II that lasted from about 630 to 580 B.C.E., a second phase of occupation began around 100 B.C.E. and lasted until about 9/8 B.C.E. or shortly thereafter (Period I). After a brief period of abandonment, the site was reoccupied from around 4 B.C.E. until it was destroyed by the Romans in 68 C.E. (Period II). A small Roman garrison was then stationed at Qumran until 73 or 74 C.E. (Period III).

More disputed is the function of the site in Periods I and II. While most scholars still more or less accept de Vaux's view that a sectarian community of Essenes inhabited Qumran during these phases, a significant minority regard Qumran as part of the economic infrastructure of the Dead Sea region. Advocates of the Essene hypothesis point to several features of the site that suggest its use as a religious community center: the high number and large size of the stepped pools, interpreted as *miqva'ot* (ritual baths; see fig. 39); the distinctive cylindrical jars (see fig. 38), thought to have been used to store scrolls and other valuables; the high number of ink wells, indicative of scribal activity; the animal bone deposits, suggestive of kosher communal meals; the communal dining rooms, with adjacent pantries containing more than a thousand dishes; the numerous workshops, including a kiln for the production of ritually pure pottery; and the large cemetery nearby that is hard to explain unless a community used it over time. Proponents of the Essene hypothesis also point to the nearby caves with scrolls, several of which describe the beliefs and practices of a sectarian group that resembles the Essenes as described by Pliny, Philo, and Josephus.

Several alternative identifications of the site have been proposed in recent years: a military fortress, a country villa, a commercial entrepôt, a fortified farm, or a center for ritual purification used by various Jewish groups. Most of these proposals doubt that there was a connection between the scrolls and the site. Some of them maintain that the pottery repertoire at Qumran is not distinctive and that neither the settlement's layout and location nor the nearby cemetery is unique or indicative of a religious community.

'Ein Feshka

In an oasis only two kilometers east of Qumran lies 'Ein Feshkha. The ceramic data indicate that the settlement was contemporaneous with Qumran Period II and was likewise destroyed in 68 c.e. 'Ein Feshkha is a good example of the continuity of traditional architecture in a rural context: a rectangular courtyard was surrounded on all sides by rooms; an industrial installation for processing dates or balsam lies immediately north of it, and stables to the south. Other sites such as Rujm el-Bahr, Qasr et-Turabe, and Khirbet Mazin show that the vicinity of Qumran was intensively used between 100 B.C.E. and 68 C.E.

Synagogues

In the Herodian period we find the oldest synagogues in Palestine. While the synagogue at Gamla may slightly predate the Herodian period, the ones at Qiryat Sefer and Horvat Etri and the added synagogues in Masada and Herodium are Herodian or later. The character of the "synagogue" in Jericho is uncertain. Since none of these buildings is explicitly identified as a synagogue through inscriptions, definition is a matter of conjecture based on form and functionality. All the structures have various shared architectural features: long halls divided by rows of columns into a central nave with surrounding aisles and stepped benches along all four walls. The earliest epigraphic evidence for synagogues in Judea is a building inscription in Greek found in a secondary context on Mount Ophel. No remains of the building itself have survived, but the inscription, which dates to the first decades of the first century c.e., names the dedicator of a synagogue, a man named Theodotus (see fig. 24):

> Theodotus, son of Vettanos, a priest and an *archisynagōgos,* son of an *archisynagōgos* grandson of an *archisynagōgos,* built the synagogue for the reading of Torah and for teaching the commandments; also the hostel, and the rooms, and the water installation for lodging needy strangers. Its foundation stone was laid by his ancestors, the elders, and Simonides.

Stone Vessels

Apart from *miqva'ot* and synagogues, two other types of objects connected to Jewish religiosity came into use during the later first century B.C.E.: stone vessels and ossuaries. Stone vessels are now known from more than sixty sites in ancient Palestine. They first appeared around 50 B.C.E. in Jerusalem and during the following decades flooded the market in an ever growing variety of forms, peaking just before the First Revolt and declining until the Bar Kokhba Revolt. After 150 C.E. they disappeared. Most widely used were small mugs with a handle (sometimes also with a lid) and round bowls mass produced by turning blocks of soft limestone on a lathe. Since the raw materials were especially easy to find near Jerusalem and in the vicinity of Nazareth, these two locations served as production centers. At the turn of the era, large crater-like vessels imitating luxurious Hellenistic marble ware were added to the repertoire of Jerusalem workshops, as were trays, tabletops (see fig. 4), decorative elements, small columns, and sundials. It is conceivable that the rapid distribution of simple stone vessels in first-century-B.C.E. and -C.E. Judea was inspired by stricter purity regulations, but it would go too far to link all products of the growing stone industry to religious attitudes or practices. Many products were simply fashionable, practical, and available in sufficient numbers to be successful on the market.

Ossuaries

Ossuaries are another product of the limestone industry. They came to be used only during the later decades of the first century B.C.E., starting in Jerusalem. They peaked just before the First Revolt and gradually disappeared in the second century C.E. Most of the ossuaries found in Jerusalem are not decorated, but most in Jericho are. The latter were ornamented with architectural, geometric, and plant motifs. The most frequent type of decoration involved incising or chip-carving a series of zigzag lines within two straight lines (see fig. 8). As noted above, some ossuaries have the names of the deceased inscribed on them and at times add details about the origin or the occupation of the deceased.

Menorahs

One of the most prominent symbols of Jewish culture and identity is the menorah, the seven-branched candelabrum. Originally part of the inventory of the Second Temple, the menorah came to be adopted in other contexts as well. The only archaeological witness to the Temple menorah itself is the famous relief on the Arch of Titus in Rome (81 C.E.; see fig. 71). There the candelabrum is depicted among other spoils of war, including the showbread table and trumpets, being presented in triumph by the victorious Roman army. The oldest depictions of the menorah, however, date to shortly before the Herodian period. In his struggle against Herod, Mattathias, the last Hasmonean king and high priest, minted coins depicting the menorah on the reverse and the showbread table on the obverse as the most prominent cultic objects in order to emphasize his priestly lineage and the legitimacy of his rule (see fig. 11). Later, menorahs were found incised on walls of rooms (the most famous from a wall in a house of the Upper City in Jerusalem dated to the first century C.E.; see fig. 5), on a sundial found in the vicinity of the Temple (its original context is unknown but it is dated to the first century B.C.E./C.E.), in tombs (the eastern wall of the porch of Jason's tomb from around 30 C.E.), on ossuaries (one example comes from the Goliath family tomb in Jericho), and on a cistern wall in a refuge cave in Naḥal Mikhmas. None of these contexts has a particularly cultic character. Evidently, the menorah was on its way to becoming a more generic symbol of the Jewish religion. The number of menorahs depicted before the second half of the second century C.E. is very low, and there are no depictions from the Diaspora before the third century C.E., except in the Arch of Titus.

Glassware

During the Herodian period, Palestine benefited from the stable political conditions in the early Empire and enjoyed unprecedented economic growth and prosperity. Consequently the variety of small objects, both locally produced and imported, grew considerably. Glass from the Lebanese coast and fine ware from Syria, Cyprus, and Italy were increasingly imported into Palestine, where they supplemented traditions of local pottery production. From the second century B.C.E. onwards, molded glass bowls, later complemented by beakers, were imported into Palestine. Blown glass quickly spread after its invention somewhere on the Phoenician coast in the very late first century B.C.E. or early first century C.E. Imported ware from Italy became available during the middle and latter part of the first century C.E. That glass is almost ubiquitous in first-century contexts indicates that it quickly lost its status as a luxury item and became a fairly common commodity. From the Herodian period onward, Palestine was firmly integrated into the empire-wide glass market, and its inhabitants showed no qualms in acquiring affordable vessels of the latest fashion, such as "Ennion" beakers in Jerusalem's Upper City and pieces of imported Italian glass found at Qumran. Some common household glass was even produced in local workshops in the Upper City of Jerusalem (including tools for blowing) before 70 C.E., but no large-scale glass factories are known from Palestine before the fourth century C.E.

Coins and Weights

Coins and weights provide important evidence about Herodian administration. Apart from one group (the Year 3 coins), Herod's coins are all undated. Minting took place first in Sebaste and then in Jerusalem. New imagery appeared, partly imitating Roman coins; among them was the *caduceus* (winged staff with two snakes wrapped around it), the ceremonial cap of an *augur* (Roman priest who specialized in divination), and the *aphlaston* (fan-like ornament at the stern of ancient galleys). But sometimes these images were balanced by a more traditional one on the reverse. One coin even shows an eagle. It is likely that Herod's Jerusalem mint copied Tyrian silver shekels after the completion of the Temple.

Of special importance is an Aramaic inscription on a stone weight, excavated in one of the houses in the Jewish quarter. It mentions "Bar Kathros," possibly the name of one of the four high-priestly families who according to the Mishnah (*m. Pesah.* 57:1) oppressed the people.

Inscriptions and Funerary Epitaphs

The number of inscriptions in both public and private contexts rose dramatically during the Herodian period. The rise no doubt owes to increased building activity especially under Herod himself, but it is particularly notable in the private sector connected with burial. One third of ossuaries are inscribed.

A number of inscriptions illustrate aspects of worship in the Jerusalem Temple and deserve particular attention. One of them was set up on the platform on the Temple Mount and threatens with death every foreigner who dares to enter the courtyard reserved for Israelites. Josephus reports that such warnings were set up in Greek and in Latin (*J.W.* 5.194; *Ant.* 15.417). A Greek specimen of the inscription was found in 1896 (see fig. 25), a second, fragmentary one in 1935.

Another fragmentary inscription was found in 1968 in the debris filling a pool south of the Temple Mount. It gives in Greek the name "[S]paris son of Akeson . . . in Rhodes," a man who donated an unknown number of drachmas for a floor dated to the twentieth year of Herod (18-17 B.C.E.). Despite its fragmentary state, the inscription indicates that private donations from the Diaspora played some part in erecting and decorating the Temple, and that donors did not have to be Jewish.

A third monumental inscription, found incomplete in the debris and written in square script is read by excavator Benjamin Mazar as "to the place of trumpeting to pr[oclaim the Sabbath]" (*lbyt htqy'h lhk*[). On another fragment only the Hebrew word "elders" (*zqnym*) is readable. Yet another, written in Paleo-Hebrew letters (only the word *bn* is discernible), was found in the fill below an Umayyad floor. It indicates that Paleo-Hebrew was still used for monumental inscriptions in Second Temple Jerusalem. It is impossible to say whether the use of Paleo-Hebrew reflects a special political or ideological intent. In any case, the material on which the inscription was made was marble imported from Greece or Italy.

Funerary epitaphs grant insight into the society of late Second Temple Jerusalem. Many of them are written in cursive Hebrew script, some in Aramaic, others in square script, still others in Paleo-Hebrew. Several ossuaries found in the burial complexes at Aceldama south of the Temple Mount demonstrate that Greek was also used. Monumental inscriptions on tomb façades are still rare, but inscriptions are numerous and instructive. Many of them mention the occupation or origin of the deceased, and several demonstrate that many Diaspora Jews wanted to be buried in Jerusalem. Some of the names on ossuaries have been identified with persons known from the New Testament: James the brother of Jesus (unprovenanced and highly disputed), Nicodemus, and Caiaphas (reading not entirely certain). Others name individuals who are otherwise unknown: "Simon the Temple builder," apparently one of the artisans who worked on the Temple; "Nicanor who made the Gates"; and Yehohanan from Giv'at ha-Mivtar, a man who was crucified. The longest inscription from a chamber tomb comes from the Giv'at ha-Mivtar neighborhood of Jerusalem. It was placed on the wall opposite the entrance of the tomb and written in Aramaic using Paleo-Hebrew script (see fig. 23). It is inscribed, very unusually, in the first person by the man who buried the deceased:

> I, Abba, son of the priest Eliez[ar] son of Aaron the Great; I, Abba, the oppressed, the pursued, who was born in Jerusalem and went into exile in Babylonia and (was) carried up (for interment), Mattathi[ah] son of Yud[ah], and I buried him in the cave that I purchased by the writ.

The Diaspora in the Early Roman Period

Compared to Palestine, the archaeological evidence for Jewish life in the Diaspora in the first century B.C.E. and C.E. is slim.

Inscriptions

In the first century B.C.E. the number of inscriptions from the Greek Diaspora in Achaia and Ionia grew. Between 37 and 27 B.C.E. the people of Athens honored King Herod (titled *philorhōmaios* [friend of the Romans] and *philokaisar* [friend of Caesar]) with at least two inscriptions for his benefaction *(euegersia)* and goodwill *(eunoia)*. A similar inscription was set up somewhere in the propylon (monumental gateway) of the temple of Apollo in Delphi by the "Athenian people and those living on the islands" in honor of the "Tetrarch Herod son of King Herod" (Herod Antipas). Obviously the Herodian family showed particular sympathy towards Apollo. A certain Justus son of Andromache from Tiberias is mentioned in an epitaph from Taenarum on the Peloponnesus dated to the first century C.E. or later.

Jews moved not only from the Diaspora to Palestine and especially Jerusalem but also in the opposite direction. A Greek epitaph from Smyrna dated to the early Imperial period mentions a certain Lucius Lollius Justus, "secretary of the people in Smyrna" *(grammateus tou en Zmyrnē laou)*. The word *laos* may refer to the Jewish people, but judging from the tripartite name Justus was a Roman citizen. During the first century C.E., Jews probably originating from Egypt began to leave traces in North Africa; evidence for this comes in two honorary inscriptions of Jews from Berenike in Cyrenaica. Although literary testimony leaves no doubt that Jews lived in Rome at least since the first century B.C.E., archaeological evidence there is rare. Most catacombs date to the second to fourth century C.E.

Synagogues

Archaeological evidence for Diaspora synagogues in the first century C.E. comes only from Ostia, beneath later building phases. There was a main hall with benches along the walls. Another first-century-C.E. synagogue is attested at Acmonia in Phrygia by its building inscription. Its socio-historical significance can be compared with the famous Theodotus inscription from Jerusalem. The inscription reads:

> the lifetime *archisynagōgos* P. Tyrronius Klados and the *archisynagōgos* Lucius son of Lucius, and the *archōn* Popilius Zotikos restored with their own means and those of the congregation the house that Julia Severa had built. They had the walls and ceilings painted, the safety of the windows restored and all the other decoration. They were honored by the congregation *(synagōgē)* through a gilded shield. (*IJO* 2:348-55)

Since the patron of the first synagogue, Julia Severa, belongs to the first century, the original synagogue must as well. The renovation may have been carried out in the second or third century C.E. Yet Julia Severa and her family are often mentioned in connection with the Imperial cult in Acmonia; she herself served as a priestess, so it is unlikely that she was Jewish. Judging from their names, the two *archisynagōgoi* and the *archōn* were Roman citizens. Honoring benefactors with a precious shield was not unusual in Greek cities but is unattested elsewhere in a synagogue context. The vast majority of Diaspora synagogues date to the later Roman period, a few to the late second or third century C.E. Again, Asia Minor is deeply underrepresented in the archaeological record.

Palestine before the First Revolt (ca. 6-66 C.E.)

Direct Roman rule in Palestine began after Archelaus was exiled from his ethnarchy Judea and replaced by a governor of equestrian rank in 6 C.E. From then on, Caesarea Maritima functioned as the capital of what was now a largely independent subunit of Syria under a subordinate official: a prefect of Judea *(praefectus Iudaeae)*. The other parts of Herod's former kingdom came under direct Roman administration only after their rulers Antipas and Philip had died, but they were not added to Judea. Only between 41 and 44 C.E. were all parts reunited under the Jewish king Agrippa I.

Few material remains can be securely attributed to the Romans, among them mostly inscriptions or building projects relating to infrastructure such as the aqueducts at Caesarea Maritima and Jerusalem. Caesarea is the only city where some building activity from the post-Herodian and pre-Revolt period can be observed. The governor probably resided in Herod's promontory palace, not far from the hippodrome. Administrative buildings were erected and the large storage vaults used for trade. Especially famous is an inscription discovered in 1961 that mentions Pontius Pilate (re)erecting a building dedicated to Tiberius (probably a lighthouse): *Tiberieum [Pon]tius Pilatus [Praef]ectus Iuda[eae]*. Large estates that formerly belonged to members of the Herodian family were now administered by *procuratores* of the emperor, who were mostly freedmen. A small garrison was stationed on Masada.

The First Revolt (66-73/4 C.E.)

The outbreak of the Jewish Revolt in 66 C.E. interrupted most integrative trends in Palestinian Jewish culture. Archaeological evidence for the activities and ideology of the insurgents is strong and varied. Coins serve as direct evidence of the ideology of the insurgents and their efforts to set up an effective administration (see figs. 12-13). The Jewish population was mobilized and cities, especially in the north, were fortified. Many of these fortifications are known from Josephus, only a few from the archaeological record. Apart from the wall surrounding Itabyrion (Mt. Tabor), it is especially the Zealot occupation at Herodium and Masada that has triggered the interest of scholars. Both strongholds and their supplies were seized from the Romans in the year 66. At Herodium and Masada, triclinia were converted into assembly rooms (synagogues) by changing the layout of the room (Masada) and adding benches around the walls (Herodium and Masada). The casemate walls at Masada were subdivided into workshops, and living quarters for families and headquarters were set up in the western palace. According to the excavators, the construction of numerous stepped pools *(miqva'ot)* and the use of special types of pottery ("dung ware" made from a mixture of animal dung and clay) testify to the purity concerns of the inhabitants. Toward the end of the revolt, many people fled to caves in the Judean desert or took refuge in underground hideouts. The coins from Sepphoris with their blunt designation as NEPWNIA CPFW . . . EIPHNOPOLI ("Neronias-Sepphoris, city of peace") are a rare indication of refusal to join the revolt.

Archaeology also allows detailed insight into the tactics and skills of the Roman occupational force, further illustrated by detailed descriptions in Josephus. Among the best-preserved archaeological remains of Roman battlefields are the breach in the wall of Gamla and the destruction of its main tower, and the siege works at Narbata, Yodefat, Machaerus, and Masada. Weapons such as arrowheads, swords, *ballistae* (heavy missile weapons), and parts of military equipment such as catapults have been found at Gamla and Masada (see figs. 69-70).

Qumran provides a good example of the destruction of a smaller settlement. Remains of the Jewish defenders are rare but telling. In the Burnt House in Jerusalem (see fig. 68), a spearhead and a severed arm of a woman were found, as were two skulls in the Kenyon excavations in the City of David. The famous skeletons discovered by Yadin on Masada, however, belonged to the occupants of the post-revolt garrison.

Excavations in the Old City of Jerusalem show signs of profound destruction. The sanctuary was damaged during the siege and the Roman assault. The Temple had gone up in flames. Large blocks tumbled from the platform and covered the paved streets west and south of the sanctuary. All shops were destroyed, many showing signs of burning. In the city, entire residential quarters were destroyed. The Burnt House in the Lower City and the area around the Palatial Mansion in the Upper City are telling witnesses of the devastation. From then on, the *Legio X Fretensis* (Roman Tenth Legion) guarded the interests of Rome in the region. The Romans celebrated their victory by issuing the famous IVDAEA CAPTA (Judea Captured) coins (see fig. 14), dedicating monuments like the Arch of Titus (see fig. 71) and the Coliseum, and setting up inscriptions, some of which are known from Rome and Jerusalem.

Palestine between the Two Revolts (73/74-132 c.e.)

Archaeological evidence for Roman influence after 73/74 is continually growing. While only little research has been carried out in Joppa (Jaffa) and Nikopolis, second-century-c.e. Neapolis is much better known. A theater, a hippodrome, and a temple dedicated to Zeus on Tell er-Ras and parts of the necropolis have been excavated. Caesarea Maritima continued to flourish as governor's seat and mercantile center, with the Latin presence becoming even more prominent. Soldiers built a new aqueduct and repaired the old one. Tombstones and military diplomas attest many of the auxiliary units stationed in the region along with the *Legio X Fretensis,* and they provide prosopographic and administrative information. The first governor of Judea after the conquest of Jerusalem, Sextus Lucilius Bassus, governor from 71-73 and conqueror of Herodium, is mentioned in a fragmentary building inscription found in the vicinity of Abu Ghosh at the Roman road from Joppa to Jerusalem. Lucilius Bassus also seems to be named on a milestone reused as support for a pillar in an Umayyad palace.

In Jerusalem, many remains of the Herodian city were gradually removed. Remains of the Temple were completely obliterated from the platform, and large parts of the *temenos* (Temple precinct) walls were torn down. Herod's palace on the western side of the city in today's Armenian quarter was completely razed to make room for the camp of the *Legio X Fretensis.* Parts of the Ophel/City of David were used as a dump and a quarry. In other areas, especially in the northwest and northeast, the Romans slowly began to rebuild the city. Pottery workshops at the outskirts of Roman Jerusalem mass-produced building material for the army, including tiles with the stamp of the Legion. A bakery built into former shops at the southwestern corner of the Temple Mount catered to the army. Roman soldiers introduced cremation to the region. Although Jerusalem's population gradually became pagan, the city retained its old name, Hierosolyma, until 130/131 c.e. Foreign cults must have found their way into the city after 70 c.e., providing the basis for the second-century paganization under Hadrian.

Archaeological traces of a Jewish presence in the decades between the two revolts are scant. Often tendencies and impulses from the late Herodian period continued, such as the first display of the menorah on lamps dating to the early second century c.e., and of grapes, fruit, and other symbols. Similar designs were used on ossuaries.

The Diaspora between the Revolts

The First Revolt had little direct support from the Diaspora, and the devastating uprisings in Egypt, Cyprus, Cyrenaica, and Mesopotamia during the reign of Trajan in 115/116-117 C.E. evidently had little effect on Palestine. Archaeological evidence for these uprisings remains extremely scarce, but papyri do shed some light. One dated to 19 June 116 indicates that the *stratēgos* Apollonios, who took part in the conflict, had requested the purchase of new arms (P.Gissenses 47), and another shows that at the beginning of September Apollonios's wife Aline was deeply concerned for his safety (*CPJ* 2:436). Epigraphic evidence indicates that Jews attacked temples and other centers of Greek civic life. In the city of Cyrene, in the sanctuary of Apollo, the baths and other neighboring buildings were burned to the ground. The temple of Hecate was also destroyed, as were the Caesareum and the temple of Zeus. Papyri from Egypt show that the uprising spread over vast sections of the country and that Jews won some early victories. Eventually, though, the uprisings brought total disaster on the Jews. In Egypt, Jewish property was confiscated by the Roman government (*CPJ* 2:445, 448; P.Berolensis inv. 7440; P.Berolensis inv. 8143), and evidence for Jewish life in Egypt, Libya, and Cyprus virtually disappears after 117 C.E.

A number of inscriptions shed light on some aspects of Jewish life in the late first and early second century C.E. Manumission inscriptions from the first to second century C.E. in Pantikapaion, Phanagoria, and Gorgippia on the Black Sea mention a "community of the Jews" (sometimes the phrase *theon sebōn* — "who worship God" — is added) that served as the slaves' guardian upon their manumission (*IJO* 1:268-86, 295-301, 303-19). In that respect, the "prayer house" *(proseuchē)* functioned like pagan temples.

The Bar Kokhba Revolt (132-135 C.E.)

Unlike the First Revolt, which was documented in great detail by Josephus, the history of the Second Revolt is not well known. When Hadrian set off for his famous oriental journey and traveled to Egypt through Judea in 130 (Cassius Dio, *Epitome* 69.11.1), many local councils took the chance to demonstrate their loyalty by renaming their city and commissioning public buildings in honor of the emperor. Coins proclaimed the ADVENTVS AVGusti IVDAEAE ("Arrival of Augustus in Judea") and inscriptions were erected. Hierosolyma was renamed Aelia Capitolina in honor of Aelius Hadrianus and the Capitoline Trias. With it came a prestigious building program: an equestrian column was erected on the Temple platform, other sanctuaries were founded or refurbished, and public buildings erected or commissioned. Coins announced the new city: COLonia AELia CAPITolina CONDita ("Founding of the Colony of Aelia Capitolina"). Before many of these building projects could be implemented or even completed, the Second Revolt broke out in 132.

As in the First Revolt, coins provide the most prominent evidence of the ideology of the Jewish insurgents. All coins refrained from displaying offensive images but deliberately used traditional imagery with clear religious connotations: the façade of the Temple, grapes, the four species (lulav, ethrog, willow, myrtle), Temple vessels, palm tree, and musical instruments (lyre, harp, trumpets). The only symbol that has classical predecessors is the wreath. The titulature of the coins expressed hope for the liberation of Jerusalem and the restoration of the Temple and its cult. The leader of the revolt, Shimon bar Kosiba (nicknamed Bar Kokhba, "Son of a Star," after Num. 24:17), is designated "prince (naśi') of Israel." As in the previous revolt, years were counted from the beginning of the insurgency (year one to four of the "redemption"). The coins were struck in bronze and silver and were inscribed in square or Paleo-Hebrew script. Often Roman coins were simply overstruck (see fig. 15). In caves by the Dead Sea, refugees hid precious goods (documents, keys, textiles, basketry, coins) that they had either brought from their own homes or, as in the case of incense shovels, plundered. Some of the bronze jugs even had pagan images defaced.

Initially, Roman resistance was uncoordinated, and the revolt spread through various parts of central Palestine. Three very different kinds of archaeological sources can be used to reconstruct the geographical range of the rebellion: the distribution of rebel coins, the distribution of characteristic hiding places, and place names mentioned in documents written by insurgents. The focus of the revolt clearly was Judea, including the Judean Desert, and the Jewish-populated hill country to the west, east, and south and 'Ein Gedi. New papyrological evidence suggests that Jerusalem was under the control of the insurgents at least for a short period, but this is not yet corroborated by coin finds. Jewish communities in western Transjordan were also affected. Material evidence from Galilee is not yet sufficient to determine whether the region actively took part in the revolt. The final battle at Bethar, west of Jerusalem, is documented by archaeological remains (siege works, military equipment).

The results of the Second Revolt probably were even more devastating for the Jews than those of the First. Judea was renamed Syria Palestina to erase the rebellious Jews' name from memory. The plans to rebuild Hierosolyma as Aelia Capitolina were carried out. A large arch was built north of the city (Damascus Gate), and in the second half of the second century C.E. another arch was built to demarcate the civil and military parts of the city (Ecce Homo Arch). The chance find of a cuirassed bronze torso of Hadrian in 1975 near Tel Shalem, twelve kilometers south of Scythopolis, and the results of subsequent excavations (more bronze fragments, a bronze head of a boy, and a fragmentary inscription) throw fascinating light on one particular victory celebration. Both the statue and the inscription belonged to a triumphal arch that was erected by the senate and people of Rome after the fighting had ended in early 136, to commemorate Hadrian's personal efforts in suppressing the revolt and to celebrate the reorganization of Judea as Syria Palestina.

The surviving Jewish population shifted south to Darom and north to the Galilee, where Jewish cultural life was gradually reconstituted along new lines that included prayer in synagogues and study of religious law. Material traces of the revival do not begin to appear until one or two generations after the crushing of the Second Revolt, so they fall beyond our chronological scope.

It is significant that Hellenization did not end during the period of Jewish reconstruction but was resumed and even intensified by the new elite comprised of rabbis and other scholars. Crucial institutions were directly continued (above all the synagogue), while other elements of material culture, such as stone vessels and ossuaries, gradually disappeared. Elements of Hellenistic art and architecture played a much greater role than before the revolt. Late Roman and Byzantine synagogues are a good example; they were lavishly decorated with mosaics representing complex theological concepts and central scenes of salvation history, but the frequent use of animals and human figures goes well beyond the limits of what most Jews would have considered tolerable before the year 70.

Textual Discoveries from Palestine

Apart from Egypt, where large numbers of texts on perishable material such as papyrus, leather, and wax tablets made of wood have been found, the Judean Desert, especially its caves on the western side of the Dead Sea, has proved the major source for such texts since the late 1940s. Popularly known as the Dead Sea Scrolls, they are more properly referred to as documents from the Judean Desert. The texts were found at different places, come from different periods, and fall into various categories.

Qumran

Undoubtedly the most famous and most widely discussed texts among the Dead Sea Scrolls are those found between 1946-1947 and 1956 in eleven caves near Qumran. As noted above, most scholars regard the texts as remains of a library associated with a group of Essenes. Discovered were around 100,000 fragments of approximately 800 to 900 manuscripts representing some 350 literary compositions, penned between the third century B.C.E. and around 50 C.E. The distribution of manuscripts between the caves is very uneven. No less than 70 percent of the manuscripts were found in Cave 4, while the most complete ones come from Caves 1 and 11. Caves 2, 3, 5, 6, 8, 9, and 10 produced very few texts. In Cave 7 only Greek papyrus fragments were found.

The Qumran texts differ from all other manuscript finds from the Judean Desert by their number and their religious character. About a quarter of the corpus, around 220 manuscripts, are multiple copies of biblical works, though Nehemiah and Esther are apparently lacking. The biblical manuscripts not only throw important light on the development of the biblical text and the history of the Jewish canon, but they also allow new insights into techniques of copying and transmitting biblical manuscripts. Another quarter of the corpus, close to 200 manuscripts, represents a wide variety of religious texts, a few previously known but most heretofore unknown. Slightly more than a third of the corpus, around 250 manuscripts, are recognized by most scholars as documents that reflect the ideology and practices of a particular sect, usually identified as Essene. This category includes such works at the *Rule of the Community* (1QS), the *Rule of the Congregation* (1QSa), the *Rule of Blessings* (1QSb), the *Thanksgiving Hymns* (1QH), the *War Scroll* (1QM), and the pesharim (e.g., 1QpHab).

The great majority of books from the Qumran corpus were written in Hebrew, only a few in Greek, among them copies of LXX manuscripts in Cave 4 and a small number from Cave 7. Aramaic is represented by a significant minority of texts, among them reworkings and expansions of biblical traditions (e.g., *Genesis Apocryphon; Aramaic Levi Document*) and apocalyptic works, mostly from the Enoch cycle. Most of the texts use the square Aramaic script regardless of whether their language is Hebrew or Aramaic. Paleo-Hebrew appears in a small number of copies of pentateuchal books (e.g., 4Q11; 4Q22), Job (4Q101), and theological texts (4Q123). In some manuscripts Paleo-Hebrew is used only for the Tetragrammaton. Besides square script, Paleo-Hebrew, and Greek, a small number of texts were written in three types of a "cryptic" Hebrew script attested nowhere else.

Seventeen documentary texts from Cave 4 written in Hebrew, Aramaic, Greek, and Nabatean probably did not originally come from Qumran. The Aramaic economic list 4Q355, Hebrew documentary texts 6Q26-6Q29, and Hebrew ostraca KhQ 1-3, however, are connected to the site.

Several graffiti and ostraca (fifty-one in Hebrew and Aramaic, eleven in Greek, and three in Latin) were found at Qumran and at ʿEin Feshkha, in addition to seven graffiti of uncertain content and ten recently discovered ones. The vessels used for the graffiti are of various origins and document the connection between settlement and the Dead Sea region, not only the caves.

Wadi Murabbaʿat

Many other texts of a different character were found south of Qumran in caves perched in the eastern cliffs of the Judean Desert. Apart from traces of habitation from the Chalcolithic, Bronze, and Iron Ages and the Arab period, the four caves in Wadi Murabbaʿat (Naḥal Dargah) examined in 1952 yielded important finds from the late Second Temple period to the time of the Bar Kokhba Revolt (pottery, coins, textiles, Roman military equipment, and documents). The oldest document from Murabbaʿat dates to the Second Temple period and is a record of a court decision (Mur 72; paleographically dated to between 125 and 100 B.C.E.). A few private legal documents suggest that refugees from the Jerusalem area fled to the region at the end of the First Revolt; these include an acknowledgment of debt (Mur 18); a writ of divorce dated to "year 6" (Mur 19); deeds of sale of land (Mur 21, 23, 25); and a marriage contract (Mur 20)

The majority of texts, however, date to the Bar Kokhba period when refugees brought private documents on papyrus (letters as well as legal documents) and religious texts on scrolls with them. The private documents cover a wide range: marriage contracts, a certificate of remarriage, farming contracts, and fiscal and administrative documents. Two letters are directly written by Bar Kokhba to Yeshua Ben Galgula (Mur 43-44). Mur 29 and 30 are especially important because they indicate that Jerusalem recognized the authority of a Jewish state as late as September-October 135.

Nahal David

Apart from a number of graves dated to the Hasmonean and Herodian periods in caves in and around Nahal David (Wadi Sudeir), one cave was used as a place of refuge during the Chalcolithic and Iron Age and especially the Bar Kokhba period. During their treasure hunt through caves in the 'Ein Gedi area in 1952 and 1953, the Bedouin took the remains of at least three manuscripts from the Cave of the Pool (named after a large pool at the entrance similar to the ones in Cave 1 in Wadi Murabba'at and Cave 40 in Nahal Harduf): fragments of a Genesis scroll on leather and remains of two fiscal documents on papyrus, one in Greek and the other in Aramaic dated to 134 C.E. In 1961/62 Yohanan Aharoni and Nahman Avigad found pottery, glass vessels, combs, food remains, and a bow and arrowheads in the same cave.

Nahal Hever

When Nahal Hever (Wadi Habra) was surveyed by Yohanan Aharoni in 1953, ten caves were discovered, and three of them were examined in 1953 and 1955. In 1960 and 1961 intensive excavations were conducted by Yigael Yadin. It turned out that these caves were primarily used as shelter by refugees during the Bar Kokhba period. Two Roman camps, one on each side of the wadi, show that the Romans besieged the caves. Unfortunately, the manuscript caves had been searched by Bedouin before Aharoni and Yadin arrived. Three of the caves in Nahal Hever proved especially important.

In a large cave with two openings, located under the northern bank of the wadi (5/6Hev, called the Cave of Letters), Yadin discovered a burial chamber in 1960 that contained skeletons of nineteen individuals, coins, pottery, a fragment of a Hebrew Psalms scroll (5/6Hev 1b), a couple of bronze objects, and a leather flask with fifteen letters written by Shimon Bar Kosiba and his comrades. A year later, Yadin found more pottery, glass vessels, metal objects, fragments of a scroll of the book of Numbers (5/6Hev 1a), and again a large number of papyrus documents. In all, the papyri from 5/6Hev (now named P.Yadin) represent four separate archives.

The first of these archives, the Bar Kokhba Archive discovered in 1960, is especially famous (P.Yadin 49–63). Most of these letters were addressed to Yehonatan ben-Be'ayan and Masabala, two of Kosiba's commanders from 'Ein Gedi who took refuge in the cave (P.Yadin 49–56, 58–60). Only four of the documents were written in Hebrew (P.Yadin 49, 51, 60, 61; see fig. 18), two in Greek (P.Yadin 52, 59), the rest in Aramaic. These letters give interesting insight into the legal authority of Bar Kokhba and the social and economic implications of his command.

The second archive is hardly less famous. It consists of thirty-six legal documents written in Aramaic (P.Yadin 7-8, 10), Greek (P.Yadin 5, 11–35), and Nabatean (P.Yadin 1–4, 6, 9; also P.Yadin 36, originally published as XHev/Se nab 1) that date from between 11 August 94 and 19 August 132 C.E. They belonged to a Jewish woman named Babatha, who had fled from her hometown Maḥoz Eglatain on the eastern shores of the Dead Sea to the region of 'Ein Gedi (see fig. 17).

Five other documents, belonging to Eleazar ben-Samuel, a farmer from 'Ein Gedi, were also found; these include private legal deeds, mostly leases and receipts from the time of Bar Kokhba (P.Yadin 42–43 in Aramaic, P.Yadin 44–46 in Hebrew, and P.Yadin 47a/b in Aramaic), possibly belonging to the same archive. These texts offer important insights into the land administration in 'Ein Gedi by Bar Kokhba.

Other documentary texts written in Hebrew, Aramaic, and Greek come from a fourth archive, one belonging to the family of Salome Komaise, daughter of Levi: P.Hever 12 (Aramaic) is a receipt for dates; P.Hever 60-64 (Greek) are deeds; P.Hever 65 (Greek) is a marriage contract. The Nabatean document catalogued as XHev/Se nab. 1, first published by Jean Starcky in 1954 and now called P.Yadin 36, may also come from this archive, as may the rest of the Nabatean documents from XHev/Se. Salome came from the same town as Babatha. Her archive contained deeds of sale and of gifts, petitions, land registrations, receipts, mortgages, promissory notes, and marriage contracts covering a period from 30 January 125 until 7 August 131 C.E.

Six papyrus documents written in Nabatean (XHev/Se nab. 1-6), most of which were found by Bedouin, and one document in Greek probably belonging to the archive of Salome Komaise (P.Yadin 37) were also found in the Cave of Letters, as were two fragments that were wrongly assigned to the Qumran corpus but match texts from Naḥal Hever (4Q347 and 4Q359). All these texts — the documents from the Bar Kokhba circle, the archives of private persons, and documents concerning property — closely resemble text finds from Wadi Murabbaʻat and Wadi Seiyal.

A second cave on the southern bank, designated 8Hev and also known as the Cave of Horror, was excavated by Aharoni in 1961. It contained more than forty skeletons together with three ostraca with names of the deceased and Hebrew scroll fragments (8Hev 2). The nine fragments from a Greek scroll of the Minor Prophets found in 8Hev (8HevXIIgr; see fig. 47) matched fragments already handed over by the Bedouin to the Rockefeller Museum in 1952 and 1953. Two fragmentary personal documents in Greek and Aramaic complement the textual finds from this cave.

Also found by Bedouin was another group of documents that probably originated from a cave further up the wadi. The documents evidently belonged to refugees from neighboring villages in the Judean Desert. This cave was excavated in 1991 by Hanan Eshel and David Amit (P.Hever 9 and 69).

Naḥal Mishmar

After three very badly fragmented documents and two ostraca, all probably from the Bar Kokhba period, entered the antiquities market with documents said to have come from Naḥal Se'elim (Wadi Seiyal) in 1952 and 1953, the Israel Exploration Society launched the Judean Desert Expedition in 1960 and 1961. Expedition B, directed by Yohanan Aharoni and Nahman Avigad, concentrated on several caves in Naḥal Se'elim and Naḥal Harduf (Wadi Abu Maradif), about four kilometers north of Masada. Four caves on the northern bank, one in Naḥal Harduf (Cave of the Reservoir) and three in Naḥal Se'elim (Cave of the Arrows, Cave of the Skulls, Cave of the Scrolls), yielded remains from the Bar Kokhba period. In addition, four Roman forts that guarded the area were identified.

Although most of the caves had been pillaged by Bedouin, they fortunately missed a small cave on the northern bank of the wadi (Cave 34). Here, eight written documents were found (34Se 1-8), together with a couple of personal objects, among them a coin from the Severan period. Among the texts are two phylacteries on parchment with passages from Exodus (34Se1 frgs. A and B), one fragmentary legal papyrus in Aramaic, and remains of two others in Greek. Fragments of a census list (34Se 4) and an account in Greek (34Se 5) complement the collection from Seiyal and were published in DJD 38.

A number of other caves yielded additional documents from the time around the First and the Second Revolt. Many of these documents are still unpublished; others have been collected and made accessible in DJD 38 (among them nineteen papyri from Jericho). The excavation of the large cave complex (Cave VIII/9) and the Cave of Avior (Cave VIII/10) during an expedition in 1993 yielded nine additional documents in Aramaic, six in Greek, and four in Hebrew. Five as yet unpublished Greek and Semitic documents on parchment and papyrus are listed in the PAM archives (Palestinian Archaeological Museum, now the Rockefeller Museum) as coming from Wadi en-Nar (Kidron Valley).

Masada

The last site in the Dead Sea area that has yielded written documents is Masada, excavated by Yigael Yadin between 1963 and 1965. The character and composition of the Masada finds reflect the turbulent history of this stronghold from its construction in the second century B.C.E. to the deposition of Archelaus in 6 C.E. Masada was the location of a Roman garrison until the outbreak of the First Revolt (4 B.C.E./6 C.E. to 66). It offered the last refuge for Zealots during the First Revolt (66-73/74 C.E.) and again housed a Roman garrison guarding the eastern flank of *Provincia Iudaea* from 73/74 to around 112/113 C.E. Centuries later, it was used as the site for a small Byzantine monastery.

All the Latin *tituli picti* (labels on amphorae written in ink, nos. 795-850) and Latin amphora stamps (nos. 946-51) belong to the Herodian period. The dated ones come from the period between 27 and 14 B.C.E. Stamps and labels represent large shipments of imported wine and luxury goods, mostly from Italy, such as apples and garum (a Roman fish sauce), for the court of Herod, who appears with his official title REX IVDAICVS (King of Judea).

It is unlikely that any of the Latin, Greek, and Semitic documents can be associated with the first Roman garrison, given the widespread nature of the destruction and cleaning up in 73/74 and the lack of supporting dates on any of the documents. It can be assumed, however, that during the first half of the first century a peaceful coexistence between Roman soldiers (all of them auxiliaries) and local Jews developed; some Greek ostraca written by Jews and mentioning deliveries (nos. 772-77) and Greek *tituli picti* (nos. 854-914) may indicate as much, if the latter are not to be dated to the Herodian phase of the site. The only Latin document to be dated to before or during the siege is P. Masada 722, a legionary pay record brought by its owner to the site.

Several biblical scrolls, including fragments of Genesis, Leviticus, Deuteronomy, Ezekiel, and Psalms, were discovered at Masada, as were fragments of other religious texts that include Ben Sira, the *Genesis Apocryphon*, the *Joshua Apocryphon, Jubilees,* and *Songs of the Sabbath Sacrifice.* These texts were probably brought to Masada by refugees before the Roman siege had the fortress effectively closed off. Seven fragments were found in casemate room 1039, which apparently was used as a garbage dump by the Romans. All fourteen literary texts are written in Hebrew (one in Paleo-Hebrew on papyrus) with one possible exception in an Aramaic text that remains unclassified.

A second class of finds from Masada is comprised of ostraca that are usually associated with the Sicarii. Among them are shards inscribed with letters, personal names including the famous "lots," and lists of priestly shares. The ostraca are written in Hebrew or Aramaic cursive script; twenty are in Paleo-Hebrew script. Some of them can be connected to the internal administration of the fortress by the Sicarii, such as the distribution of provisions; others mention names of owners of store jars (O. Masada 462) or give instructions for supplying bread (O. Masada 557-84). Still others may have been used as food coupons, as tags for a "population registry," or as lots for watch duties. A somewhat more intimate view of those who occupied Masada is given by three personal letters on ostraca, one of them written with charcoal. All other texts are written in ink.

After the siege, a small Roman garrison remained on Masada. No Greek documents date to the period after 73/74. The Latin papyri and ostraca written by members of the Tenth Legion do not provide an official archive but a random collection that affords insight into the life and duties of Roman soldiers. Among these items are a line from Virgil, a legionary pay stub, and a list of hospital supplies.

Jewish Papyri from Egypt

Among the tens of thousands of papyri found in Egypt are many that were written by Jews or refer to Jews. These papyri come from all regions of Egypt and document all phases, areas, and aspects of Jewish presence along the Nile. Among the most important corpora are the Elephantine Papyri, written by members of a Jewish military colony that lived on the island of Elephantine between 495 and 399 B.C.E. and even ran their own temple. Also important are the papyri in the Zenon Archive. Zenon was a Ptolemaic official who toured Palestine in 260/59 B.C.E. The documents in his archive, which include accounts, lists, receipts, and memoranda, provide valuable information on the social and economic situation. There are also many papyri from Alexandria reflecting various private and public affairs such as private letters, requests directed to city officials, pagan warnings against Jewish moneylenders, a letter of Claudius to the city of Alexandria demanding peace and unity between pagans and Jews, and documents connected to the revolt of 116-117.

One unique document from Egypt is the Nash Papyrus, which contains the Hebrew text of the Decalogue with wording drawn from both the Exodus and Deuteronomy versions. It was acquired by an antiquities dealer but may have come from the Fayum. Its first editors dated it to the first or second century c.e., but recent studies date it to the second century b.c.e. A fragmentary Hebrew prayer after meals found at Dura-Europos in Mesopotamia (P.Dura 10) joins the Nash Papyrus in providing rare evidence for the use of Hebrew as a liturgical language in the Diaspora.

We also have papyri from the Jewish *politeuma* (a council of an acknowledged ethnic community) of Herakleopolis dating to 143-132 b.c.e. That Jews in Herakleopolis apparently enjoyed as high a degree of autonomy as their fellows in Alexandria and Leontopolis is attested in literature and papyri. They yearly elected their officials *(archontes)* under a *politarchēs* and were allowed to run their own internal affairs. Many aspects of the privilege of living according to their ancestral customs are addressed in the papyri; these include civil law, synagogue courts, oaths, Sabbath, and pilgrimage.

Papyri also attest various practical and legal aspects of Jews living together with Greeks, Egyptians, and members of other ethnic groups. Many legal practices documented in Jewish papyri from Egypt are reminiscent of issues and formulas in papyri from the Judean Desert.

Ostraca

As a special case of written documents, a few notes on ostraca are appropriate. Ostraca are texts incised on pottery shards or written on them with ink. In Hellenistic and Roman Palestine, the same languages appear on ostraca as on papyrus and in inscriptions. The variety of texts on ostraca is notably broad, although they are usually short and confined to mundane matters. Especially frequent are writing exercises or abecedaries, written in Hebrew and Aramaic in square script; several of these are known from Qumran, Wadi Murabba'at, Masada, and other sites. A few are written bilingually in Greek and Latin. In many cases ostraca provided a good and cheap alternative to papyrus. Texts on ostraca were not necessarily less carefully written in terms of grammar or orthography, and they are a good indication that writing was widespread and even employed for the most profane purposes.

Often single personal names or lists of names in Hebrew or Aramaic appear on ostraca (Mur 74-77), sometimes also in Greek (Mur 165-76) or Latin (Mur 168). The earliest examples come from second-century-B.C.E. Gezer. The most famous corpus of this kind is the more than 700 shards from Masada bearing names, single letters, or combinations of letters on them.

A clearly economic purpose is evident in a list scratched onto the lid of an ossuary found in 1910 in a tomb at Bethpage. The lists gives twenty-three names along with sums of money. It is evidently a roster of workers in an ossuary workshop and indicates their daily wages. It was found only 1.5 kilometers from the large limestone quarries of Hizma.

Other ostraca parallel papyrus documents. One of the most famous and controversial examples is KhQ 1, the largest of three ostraca found in 1996 atop Roland de Vaux's excavation dump at Qumran. This Hebrew ostracon is probably the draft of a deed documenting the sale of an orchard by a certain Honi to Eleazar son of Nahmani. The deed was written in Jericho and is dated to "year two," which for paleographical reasons must refer to the First Revolt (67 C.E.). Unfortunately, the text is fragmentary. It gained some attention when the first editors read a partial word in line 8 as *yaḥad* and interpreted the ostracon as another link between the Qumran settlement and the texts from the caves. This reconstruction has rightly been rejected by several specialists. An Edomite ostracon from Maresha dated to summer 176 B.C.E. is also documentary in nature and represents so far the only marriage contract on an ostracon from ancient Palestine. One of the very few examples of a "narrative" text on an ostracon from the Hellenistic and Roman periods is Mur 72, which describes the activities of a certain Yohahan. Unfortunately, the fragmentary nature of the text provides little information on the context and purpose of the narrative passage.

BIBLIOGRAPHY

General

Berlin, Andrea M. 2005. "Jewish Life before the Revolt: The Archaeological Evidence." *JSJ* 36: 417-70.

————, and J. Andrew Overman, eds. 2002. *The First Jewish Revolt: Archaeology, History, and Ideology.* London: Routledge.

Binder, Donald D. 1999. *Into the Temple Courts: The Place of the Synagogues in the Second Temple Period.* Atlanta: Scholars Press.

Chancey, Mark Alan, and Adam Lowry Porter. 2001. "The Archaeology of Roman Palestine." *Near Eastern Archaeology* 64, 4: 164-203.

Galor, Katharina, and Gideon Avni, eds. 2011. *Unearthing Jerusalem: 150 Years of Archaeological Research in the Holy City.* Winona Lake, Ind.: Eisenbrauns.

Hachlili, Rachel. 1988. *Ancient Jewish Art and Archaeology in the Land of Israel.* Leiden: Brill.

————. 1998. *Ancient Jewish Art and Archaeology in the Diaspora.* Leiden: Brill.

————. 2005. *Jewish Funerary Customs, Practices and Rites in the Second Temple Period.* Leiden: Brill.

Hezser, Catherine, ed. 2010. *The Oxford Handbook of Jewish Daily Life in Roman Palestine.* Oxford: Oxford University Press.

Leibner, Uzi. 2009. *Settlement and History in Hellenistic, Roman and Byzantine Galilee: An Archaeological Survey of the Eastern Galilee.* Tübingen: Mohr Siebeck.

Levine, Lee I. 2000. *The Ancient Synagogue: The First Thousand Years.* New Haven: Yale University Press.

————. 2002. *Jerusalem: Portrait of the City in the Second Temple Period (538-70 C.E.).* Philadelphia: Jewish Publication Society.

Magen, Yizhak, Haim Misgav, and Levana Tsfania. 2004-2008. *Mount Gerizim Excavations I: The Aramaic, Hebrew and Samaritan Inscriptions,* vol. 2, *A Temple City.* Jerusalem: Israel Antiquities Authority.

Magness, Jodi. 2011. *Stone and Dung, Oil and Spit: Jewish Daily Life in the Time of Jesus.* Grand Rapids: Eerdmans.

————. 2012. *The Archaeology of the Holy Land: From the Destruction of Solomon's Temple to the Muslim Conquest.* Cambridge: Cambridge University Press.

Mazar, Eilat. 2011. *The Temple Mount Excavations in Jerusalem 1968-1978 Directed by Benjamin Mazar, Final Reports Volume IV: The Tenth Legion in Aelia Capitolina.* Qedem 52. Jerusalem: Institute of Archaeology, the Hebrew University of Jerusalem.

Meyers, Eric M., and Mark A. Chancey. 2012. *Alexander to Constantine: The Archaeology of the Land of the Bible.* Vol. 3. New Haven: Yale University Press.

Netzer, Ehud, with R. Laureys-Chachey. 2006. *The Architecture of Herod, the Great Builder,* Tübingen: Mohr Siebeck.

Ovadiah, Asher, and Yehudit Turnheim. 2011. *Roman Temples, Shrines and Temene in Israel.* Rome: Bretschneider.

Overman, J. Andrew, and Daniel N. Schowalter, eds. 2011. *The Roman Temple Complex at Horvat Omrit: An Interim Report.* Oxford: Oxford University Press.

Patrich, Joseph. 2011. *Studies in the Archaeology and History of Caesarea Maritima: Caput Judaeae, Metropolis Palaestinae.* Leiden: Brill.

Pucci Ben-Zeev, Miriam. 2005. *Diaspora Judaism in Turmoil, 116/117 CE: Ancient Sources and Modern Insights.* Leuven: Peeters.

Richardson, Peter. 2004. *Building Jewish in the Roman East.* Waco, Tex.: Baylor University Press.

Schäfer, Peter, ed. 2003. *The Bar Kokhba War Reconsidered: New Perspectives on the Second Jewish Revolt against Rome.* Tübingen: Mohr Siebeck.

Egypt

Porten, Bezalel, and Ada Yardeni, eds. 1986-1999. *Textbook of Aramaic Documents from Ancient Egypt,* 4 vols. Jerusalem: Hebrew University (vol. 1 = *Letters;* vol. 2 = *Contracts;* vol. 3 = *Literature and Lists;* vol. 4 = *Ostraca and Assorted Inscriptions*).

Masada

Aviram, Joseph, Gideon Foerster, and Ehud Netzer, eds. 1989-2007. *Masada: The Yigael Yadin Excavations 1963-1965. Final Reports.* 8 volumes. Jerusalem: Israel Exploration Society and Hebrew University of Jerusalem.

Qumran

Frey, Jörg, Carsten Claußen, and Nadine Kessler, eds. 2011. *Qumran und die Archäologie: Texte und Kontexte.* Tübingen: Mohr Siebeck.

Galor, Katharina, Jean-Baptiste Humbert, and Jürgen Zangenberg, eds. 2006. *Qumran: The Site of the Dead Sea Scrolls: Archaeological Interpretations and Debates.* Leiden: Brill.

Hirschfeld, Yitzar. 2004. *Qumran in Context: Reassessing the Archaeological Evidence.* Peabody, Mass.: Hendrickson.

Humbert, Jean-Baptiste, and A. Chambon, eds. 1994. *Fouílles de Khirbet Qumrân et de Aïn Feshkha I: Album de photographies, repertoire du fonds photographique, synthese des notes de Chantier du P. Roland de Vaux OP.* Fribourg: Editions Universitaires.

————. 2003. *Excavations of Khirbet Qumran and Ain Feshka: Synthesis of Roland de Vaux's Notes.* Trans. S. J. Pfann. Fribourg: Academic Press (Eng. trans., with corrections, of the French ed.).

————, and Jan Gunneweg, eds. 2003. *Khirbet Qumran et 'Ain Feshkha II: Studies of Anthropology, Physics and Chemistry.* Fribourg: Academic Press.

Magness, Jodi. 2002. *The Archaeology of Qumran and the Dead Sea Scrolls*. Grand Rapids: Eerdmans.

Vaux, Roland de. 1973. *Archaeology and the Dead Sea Scrolls*. Rev. ed. London: Oxford University Press.

Coins

Ariel, Donald Zvi, and Jean-Philippe Fontanelle. 2012. *The Coins of Herod: A Modern Analysis and Die* [sic] *Classification*. Leiden: Brill.

Meshorer, Ya'akov. 1989. *The Coinage of Aelia Capitolina*. Jerusalem: Israel Museum.

———. 2001. *A Treasury of Jewish Coins from the Persian Period to Bar Kokhba*. New York: Amphora Books.

———, and Shraga Qedar. 1999. *Samarian Coinage*. Jerusalem: Israel Numismatic Society.

Inscriptions

Ameling, Walter. 2004. *Inscriptiones Judaicae Orientis*. Vol. 2. *Kleinasien*. Tübingen: Mohr Siebeck.

———, et al., eds. 2011. *Corpus Inscriptionum Iudaeae et Palaestinae, Volume 2: Caesarea and the Middle Coast: 1121-2160*. Berlin: de Gruyter.

Boffo, Laura. 1994. *Iscrizioni Greche e Latine per lo Studio della Bibbia*. Brescia: Paideia Editrice.

Cotton, Hannah M., et al., eds. 2010. *Corpus Inscriptionum Iudaeae et Palaestinae, Volume 1: Jerusalem, Part 1: 1-704*. Berlin: de Gruyter.

———. 2012. *Corpus Inscriptionum Iudaeae et Palaestinae, Volume 1: Jerusalem, Part 2, 705-1120*. Berlin: de Gruyter.

Frey, Jean-Baptiste. 1936-1952. *Corpus Inscriptionum Judaicarum: Recueil des inscriptions juives qui vont du IIIe siècle avant Jésus-Christ au VIIe siècle de notre ére*. 2 vols. Rome: Pontificio istituto di archeologia Cristiana.

Horst, Pieter W. van der. 1991. *Ancient Jewish Epitaphs: An Introductory Survey of a Millennium of Jewish Funerary Epigraphy (300 BCE–700 CE)*. Kampen: Kok Pharos.

Lüderitz, Gert, with Joyce M. Reynolds. 1983. *Corpus jüdischer Zeugnisse aus der Cyrenaika*. Wiesbaden: Reichert.

Noy, David. 1993-1995. *Jewish Inscriptions of Western Europe*. 2 vols. Cambridge: Cambridge University Press.

———, and William Horbury. 1992. *Jewish Inscriptions of Greco-Roman Egypt*. Cambridge: Cambridge University Press.

———, Alexander Panayotov, and Hanswulf Bloedhorn. 2004. *Inscriptiones Judaicae Orientis*. Vol. 1. *Eastern Europe*. Tübingen: Mohr Siebeck.

———, and Hanswulf Bloedhorn. 2004. *Inscriptiones Judaicae Orientis*. Vol. 3. *Syria and Cyprus*. Tübingen: Mohr Siebeck.

Textual Discoveries from Palestine

The manuscripts from Qumran Caves 1-11, Wadi Murabbaʿat, Jericho, and Wadi Seiyal, as well as many texts from Naḥal Ḥever, are presented in the series Discoveries in the Judean Desert (DJD), published by Oxford University Press. Another large part of the Naḥal Ḥever corpus is available in the series Judean Desert Studies (JDS).

Papyri from Palestine

Cotton, Hannah M., and Ada Yardeni, eds. 1997. *Aramaic, Hebrew and Greek Documentary Texts from Naḥal Ḥever and Other Sites, with an Appendix Containing Alleged Qumran Texts.* DJD 27. Oxford: Clarendon.

Lewis, Naphtali, Yigael Yadin, and Jonas C. Greenfield, eds. 1989. *The Documents from the Bar Kokhba Period in the Cave of Letters: Greek Papyri, Aramaic and Nabatean Signatures and Subscriptions.* Jerusalem: Israel Exploration Society.

Yadin, Yigael. 1963. *The Finds from the Bar Kokhba Period in the Cave of Letters.* Jerusalem: Israel Exploration Society.

———, Jonas C. Greenfield, Ada Yardeni, and Baruch Levine, eds. 2002. *The Documents from the Bar Kokhba Period in the Cave of Letters: Hebrew, Aramaic and Nabatean-Aramaic Papyri.* Jerusalem: Israel Exploration Society.

Yardeni, Ada. 2000. *Textbook of Aramaic, Hebrew and Nabataean Documentary Texts from the Judaean Desert and Related Material.* Jerusalem: Hebrew University.

Papyri from the Diaspora

Cowey, James M., and Klaus Maresch, eds. 2001. *Urkunden des Politeuma der Juden von Herakleopolis (144/3-133/2 v. Chr.) (P.Polit.Iud.): Papyri aus den Sammlungen von Heidelberg, Köln, München und Wien (Gebundene Ausgabe).* Wiesbaden: Westdeutscher Verlag.

Porten, Bezalel, et al., eds. 1996. *The Elephantine Papyri in English.* Leiden: Brill.

Tcherikover, Victor, and Alexander Fuks, eds. 1957-1963. *Corpus Papyrorum Judaicarum.* 3 vols. Cambridge: Harvard University Press. (A fourth volume is in preparation by I. Fikhman.)

Jews among Greeks and Romans

Miriam Pucci Ben Zeev

The relations of Jews with Greeks and Romans during the Second Temple period were complex. On the one hand, a variety of source materials including inscriptions, papyri, and formal documents quoted by Josephus show that Jews were thoroughly integrated into the economic, social, and political life of Hellenistic cities, that they embraced several aspects of Greco-Roman culture, that they enjoyed certain rights and privileges pertaining to the practice of their ancestral customs and laws, and that they even attracted the admiration of non-Jewish sympathizers, adherents, and converts. On the other hand, these same sources indicate that Jews frequently encountered competition, resentment, and even overt hostility from their non-Jewish neighbors and at times ran afoul of their Greek and Roman overlords. They also suggest that Jewish rights were neither permanent nor inherently stable. Greek and Roman rulers could rescind those rights or simply choose not to enforce them. When the government did intervene in support of the Jews, oftentimes little was done to solve the underlying problems. On a few occasions, direct intervention actually exacerbated the problems, not least when rulers sided with the Greeks against the Jews.

At the root of these sometimes tense relations was Jewish exclusiveness or separatism: Jews not only formed their own communities and practiced a measure of political autonomy, but they refused to participate in the cults of the patron deities of Greek cities. Precisely because religion was an integral part of civic identity in the Greco-Roman world, Jewish nonparticipation was felt keenly. Jewish monotheism and aniconism led to pagan accusations of atheism and misanthropy. As a result, Jewish life in the Greco-Roman world was somewhat precarious even as it flourished.

The Jews under Hellenistic Rule

The Legal Status of Jews under the Ptolemies and Seleucids

Already in the Persian period (539-332 B.C.E.), the Torah was officially recognized as the law to which the Jews of Judea had to conform their lives and by which their judicial cases were to be adjudicated (Ezra 7:25-26). The same probably applied to Jews living in other provinces of the Persian Empire, namely, in Egypt and in Babylon. It was not that the Persians had a special regard for the needs of the Jews; they simply found it useful to codify the laws of subject peoples in order to consolidate their control. Thus, for example, Darius ordered that "the law of Egypt that had formerly been valid" be written down. The codified law, written in Aramaic and in Demotic, was thereby introduced as the provincial law of Egypt. The same policy was implemented after the conquests of Alexander the Great. Josephus has Alexander grant the Jews of Judea the right "to observe their country's laws" (*Ant.* 11.338), which was probably extended, *de iure* or *de facto,* also to Jews living in the Diaspora.

In third-century-B.C.E. Egypt, the Greek translation of the Torah was officially recognized by its integration into the judicial system created by King Ptolemy II. It became a statute *(nomos)* to which Ptolemaic judges had to accord their official sanction, in conformity with a royal decree directing them to render judgments when a matter was not dealt with in the royal legislation. In other words, the Greek Torah, as part of the legal system of Ptolemaic Egypt, became one of the political laws, a kind of "civic law for the Jews of Egypt." In return, the Jews stressed their loyalty to the government by dedicating their houses of worship *(proseuchai)* to the king, his wife, and their children *(JIGRE* 9, 13). In all the countries under Ptolemaic rule — Judea, Libya, Cyprus, and Egypt — the Jews were free to live according to their ancestral laws.

Evidently no major changes took place when Judea came under Seleucid rule at the beginning of the second century B.C.E. A document quoted by Josephus states that King Antiochus III allowed the Jews "to have a form of government in accordance with the laws of their country" *(Ant.* 12.142); and in Asia Minor, too, the Jews seem to have had the right "to use their own laws" *(Ant.* 12.150). Yet there was probably no binding royal legislation, and so Jewish rights could be revoked at any time for any reason. In the first half of the second century B.C.E., when internal Jewish struggles for power in Judea were interpreted by King Antiochus IV Epiphanes as a rebellion against Seleucid rule, this provoked not only a military reaction but also an enforced Hellenization. Jews were compelled "to depart from the laws of their fathers and to cease living by the laws of God. Further, the sanctuary in Jerusalem was to be polluted and called after Zeus Olympius" (2 Macc. 6:1-2). This forced Hellenization lasted only a few years, but it made clear that Jewish freedom always depended on the personal goodwill of the ruler who happened to be in power.

Cultural Antagonism between Jews and Greeks in Egypt

Since the beginning of their settlement in Egypt early in the third century B.C.E., the Jews were active in most branches of economic activity. Extant papyri show them as farmers, artisans (*CPJ* 1:33-47), tax farmers and tax collectors, bankers, granary officials (*CPJ* 1:48-124, 127, 132, 137), and soldiers, even officers, in the Ptolemaic army (*CPJ* 1:18-32; Josephus, *J.W.* 1.175, 190-92; *Ant.* 14.99, 131-32; *Ag. Ap.* 1.200-204; 2.64). The Jews were a strong presence in the economic life of the country, a fact that created competition and perhaps friction between them and their Greco-Egyptian neighbors. This was all the more the case because the Jews insisted on forming their own separate communities and refused to participate in the religious activities of the Greek cities. The issue was particularly problematic because these activities often had civil and economic underpinnings; identification with the gods of one's city was a fundamental aspect of civic identity, as in the cases of the cult of the deified Alexander and Ptolemies and of the patron deities of the Greek city.

Cultural antagonism may have developed in the third century B.C.E. also on account of the translations of the Pentateuch into Greek that were circulating in Egypt — the best known was the Septuagint — which made generally known the account of the Exodus, with its strong anti-Egyptian bias. No source tells us how extensively it may have been read and known, but there are a number of parallels between the biblical account of the Exodus and its counter-version in the work of Manetho, a priest of the Greco-Egyptian god Serapis who was influential in the court of Ptolemy Philadelphus. One of the two passages of Manetho quoted by Josephus associates the Jews with the tyrannical Hyksos regime, a foreign dynasty that had ruled Egypt harshly. After five hundred years of domination, they left Egypt "with their possessions . . . and journeyed over the desert into

Syria. . . . There . . . they built in the land now called Judea a city . . . and gave it the name of Jerusalem" (*Ag. Ap.* 1.73-91).

The other account of Manetho quoted by Josephus draws on popular legends and recounts the segregation of a crowd of lepers, led by a priest named Osarseph, identified with Moses, who advocated social isolation and taught them not to worship the Egyptian gods but rather to sacrifice the Egyptian sacred animals. In the end, the Egyptian king defeats the lepers and expels them from Egypt, pursuing them to the frontiers of Syria (*Ag. Ap.* 1.228-52). Similar stories with different details were recounted between the second century B.C.E. and the first century C.E. by other Greco-Egyptian authors such as Lysimachus, Chaeremon, Ptolemy of Mendes, and Apion. Written in Greek, these accounts deeply influenced public opinion even outside Egypt, as the later Roman *Histories* of Tacitus witness (5.3.1–5.4.2).

These are not the only manifestations of antagonism preserved by our sources. 3 Maccabees reflects memories of a conflict between the Jews and the Egyptian ruler — a persecution sparked by Jewish religious practices that was thwarted thanks to divine intervention. The conflict probably belongs to a later historical period, but it remains significant that the author of the book places it in the Hellenistic age, at the time of Ptolemy IV Philopator in the third century B.C.E. (Josephus dates the event to the reign of Ptolemy Physcon [Euergetes II] in the second century B.C.E.)

Toward the end of the Ptolemaic period, the rule of the kings weakened under the strain of dynastic strife, and the security that the Jews had enjoyed in the early period could no longer be taken for granted. In the first half of the first century B.C.E., a papyrus dealing with commercial issues warns that in Memphis "they loathe the Jews" (*CPJ* 1:141).

Jewish Engagement with Hellenism

At the end of the fourth century B.C.E., the conquests of Alexander the Great brought a real revolution not only on the political level but also in the cultural sphere. All over the Near East, people came in close contact with the thought, cultural values, and institutions of the Greeks; among them, a special role was played by the gymnasium, where people trained in physical exercises and devoted themselves to letters, music, rhetoric, and philosophy. Through the medium of a common language — the Hellenistic form of Greek, the so-called *koine*, which soon became the lingua franca of the East — Greek culture spread widely and reached all the countries under Hellenistic governments, influencing every aspect of life. The world became a small world — the "inhabited world" *(oikoumenē)* — where each people followed their own traditional customs and beliefs, participating at the same time in the new common supernational culture, which was open to everybody since it was based not on birth but on education.

The Jews, too, participated in this formidable movement of peoples and ideas. In Egypt, they learned to speak and write in Greek, appealed to Greek tribunals when the need arose, and gave Greek names to their children. The onomasticon attested by the papyri shows that Jewish names amount to no more than 25 percent; most names are Greek. Literary works composed by Jews in Egypt also attest a high degree of integration between Greek culture and traditional Judaism, and similar developments may well have characterized other Diaspora communities. Scholars emphasize the appropriation of Hellenistic themes, genres, forms, and styles for Jewish purposes. The Jews appropriated Hellenism to the goals of rewriting biblical narratives, recasting the traditions of their fathers and shaping their distinctive identity within the larger world of Hellenic culture. In a world where Hellenic culture held an ascendant position, they strove to present Judaic traditions and express their own self-definition through the media of the Greeks. Literary models and rhetorical devices were often Greek, while the content related specifically to Jewish interests.

An author such as the epic poet Theodotus (second to first century B.C.E.) writes on biblical themes, while his language betrays Homeric influences. The tragedy composed by Ezekiel (second century B.C.E.) is based on the biblical story of the Exodus but reflects Euripides' influence. Aristobulus, the second-century-B.C.E. philosophic writer and supposed teacher of Ptolemy VI, maintains that Greek philosophy is to be found in the Pentateuch, which he interprets allegorically. The same line of thought is followed by the author of the *Letter of Aristeas,* who strives to demonstrate that Hellenistic and Jewish traditions are only two different expressions of the same metaphysical reality. He, too, gives an allegorical interpretation to the text of the Pentateuch that explains the Jewish law according the principles of Greek thought and presents Judaism and Hellenism as two different forms emanating from the same divine entity, venerated under different names.

Historical works composed by Jews also reflect the influence of Greek literary models while centering on Jewish cultural and theological values.

In 2 Maccabees, which deals with the history of the Jewish people in Judea at the time of Antiochus IV Epiphanes (175-164 B.C.E.), history is presented according to a Jewish interpretative scheme in which the causes of events are sought in the spiritual rather than the political realm. Accordingly, the religious persecution is regarded as punishment for the sins committed by the Jews, sins which are identified with the extreme Hellenization of those Jews who had been ready to give up the exclusivity of Judaism in order to become an integral part of the Hellenistic world. From a theological point of view, this book is a distinctly Jewish work, while formally and literarily it is completely Greek.

Yet there are early Jewish works that reflect cultural antagonism of one sort or another. One of them is the Wisdom of Solomon, in which considerable learning, sophisticated vocabulary, developed rhetorical features, and Hellenistic philosophical influences are employed not to integrate Judaism with its environment but to construct a sophisticated attack upon it, focusing on worship of animals and idolatry, which are presented as the height of folly and the root of immorality. Another case is that of 3 Maccabees, where the narrative centers on the hostility between Jews and Gentiles, and *Joseph and Aseneth,* a work fiercely antagonistic to all non-Jewish religion. Similar features are displayed by the third book of the *Sibylline Oracles,* which may reflect a revival of Jewish nationalistic sentiment in the wake of the Maccabean revolt. Directed against the unjust regimes of Greece, Macedonia, and Rome, it predicts woes and cosmic disasters, followed by visions of worldwide repentance and the worship of all nations at the Temple of God.

In the practical domain, too, Hellenism influenced Jewish life in different ways. Recent scholarship distinguishes between assimilation (social integration) and acculturation (linguistic, educational, and ideological integration). At one end of the spectrum, we find a complete submersion of Jewish cultural uniqueness, well illustrated by the cases of Dositheos son of Drymilos in the third century B.C.E. and of Tiberius Julius Alexander in the first century C.E. Both of these men abandoned Jewish ancestral traditions and made brilliant carriers in the Ptolemaic and Roman administrations. At the other end of the spectrum are the Therapeutae, who closely resembled the Essenes while including women; they were an ascetic Jewish community living in the vicinity of Alexandria who devoted themselves to study and contemplation. Philo calls them "the citizens of heaven and of the universe." In the middle between these extremes, there were "mainstream" Jews whose cultural identity was well defined and who adhered to Jewish practices. Hybrid cases are also attested, as that of a certain Moschios, son of Moschios, who is mentioned in an inscription erected at Oropus, Greece, in the temple of Amphiaraos (*CIJ* 1:82); he calls himself a Jew but mentions the instructions he received in a dream from the gods Amphiaraos and Hygieia. For Jews to live in a deeply Hellenized milieu and maintain their Jewish identity over generations was certainly a challenge.

The Jews under Roman Rule

Religious Freedom

No significant change took place when the Romans conquered the East. The Roman government had a conservative character that tended to preserve the existing frameworks. In Judea, a decree issued by Julius Caesar allowed the Jews to live according to their ancestral laws and customs (*JRRW* 1), possibly confirming a decree issued by Pompey after the conquest of Jerusalem in 63 B.C.E. that has not been preserved.

Religious freedom was also granted to Diaspora Jews. From Josephus's narrative and from a number of documents quoted by him, we learn that in different centers of the Mediterranean the Jews were allowed to follow Jewish law, assemble, perform their rites on Sabbaths and festivals, send their contributions to the Temple in Jerusalem, have autonomous internal administration and jurisdiction, build sacred and profane buildings, and have kosher food in the local markets.

The right to follow Jewish customs and laws, however, was by no means stable or permanent. In 38 C.E., Emperor Caligula's desire to impose his own worship on all his subjects encouraged the Gentile population of Yavneh (Jamnia) in Judea to set up an altar to him. This altar was promptly destroyed by the Jews, an act to which Caligula responded by ordering a golden statue of himself to be set up in the Jerusalem Temple. His purpose was probably to stress his power over the Judean population, but for the Jews it was a serious infringement of religious freedom; a statue in the Temple would have polluted it and automatically suspended its cult. Thanks to the successful delaying tactics of the local Roman governor and to the assassination of the emperor early in 41 C.E., the statue was not set up, but the incident shows that Jewish religious rights were intrinsically precarious.

The Jews in Rome

Even though a foreign labor force had increasingly become a necessity in the Roman economy, the Romans did not particularly enjoy the presence of foreigners in their city. They feared that foreign manners, customs, and cults — which often differed significantly from their own — might influence their society negatively and contaminate Roman values and ancestral traditions, the so-called *mores maiorum*. Between the second century B.C.E. and the first century C.E., foreigners were periodically expelled from Rome. In the second century B.C.E., the Jews were kicked out along with the astrologers, who were accused of disturbing fickle and silly minds with a fallacious interpretation of the stars, while the Jews were accused of "infecting" the Roman customs with their cult (Valerius Maximus, *Facta et Dicta Memorabilia* 1.3.3). In the early years of Tiberius's reign, a strong reaction occurred against foreign cults, and the Jews were expelled along with the adherents of the Egyptian cult of Isis (Josephus, *Ant.* 18.81-84; Cassius Dio, *Roman History* 57.18.5a).

The attitudes toward Jews preserved in Latin literature are not particularly friendly. In the middle of the first century B.C.E., some years after the conquest of Jerusalem by Pompey, Cicero, the well-known Roman politician, lawyer, and statesman, held that, since they resisted Pompey's troops, the Jews were to be regarded as enemies. He stressed the great cultural discrepancy between the Roman and the Jewish people: even "when Jerusalem was still standing and the Jews were at peace with us, the practice of their sacred rites was at variance with the glory of our empire, the dignity of our name, and the customs of our ancestors" (*Pro Flacco* 28, 69). Poets such as Tibullus, Horace, and Ovid were less interested in political issues; what provoked their satire and ridicule were Jewish customs such as observance of the Sabbath, circumcision, and abstinence from pork. Pompeius Trogus, the first historian to deal at some length with the past history of the Jewish people, displays a rather objective tone but quotes anti-Jewish Egyptian sources that were percolating into Roman consciousness, thereby making them more widely known in the capital.

The attitude of the Roman upper classes became more rigid and hostile in the course of the first century C.E., perhaps as a result of the spread of Jewish customs in Roman society and of the intensified rebel movements in Judea. Seneca resented the popularity of Jewish customs in Rome, singling out for adverse comment especially the observance of the Sabbath and the custom of lighting Sabbath lamps, a visible and apparently attractive feature of Jewish observance. Caustic comments on the Jews appear in the work of Juvenal, in a combination of cultural and class snobbery. In the second century c.e., Tacitus, a Roman senator and historian, wrote extensively about the Jews, calling their rites "base and abominable" and declaring that they "owe their persistence to their depravity. . . . the Jews are extremely loyal toward one another . . . but toward every other people they feel only hate and enmity." In particular, Tacitus lamented their influence on Roman society, since they teach converts "to despise the gods, to disown their country, and to regard their parents, children, and brothers as of little account." His account of Jewish customs ends with the observation: "the ways of the Jews are preposterous and mean" (*Histories* 5.5.1-5).

On the other hand, extant sources show that the Jews of Rome also attracted sympathy, winning admirers and imitators among ordinary citizens and even, in certain cases, among the higher echelons of society. We hear of notable figures who supported the Jews, among whom was Nero's wife, Poppaea Sabina, who exerted her patronage on behalf of Judean priests who had been sent to Rome on trial.

Concerning the social integration of the Jews in Roman society, we know very little. They left no written records at all, a fact for which different explanations have been put forward in contemporary research, all of them speculative. Philo and Josephus tell us that the bulk of the Jewish population of the capital descended from Jewish prisoners brought to Rome and sold as slaves after the conquest of Pompey in 63 b.c.e. Other slaves arrived after the numerous failed revolts that followed, and a conspicuous number reached Rome after the defeat of the Judean rebellion in 70 c.e. In time, many Jews gained their freedom. Josephus was certainly not the only Jew granted Roman citizenship (*Vita* 423). Many Jews were entitled to the corn dole (Philo, *Legat.* 158) and may have gained citizenship on manumission. Yet, on the whole, it appears that Jews did not achieve leading positions in Roman society. Philo states that in the reign of Augustus Jews were settled mainly on the right bank of the Tiber, in an area of generally poor residences, far from the heart of Rome, a location that suggests a generally humble mode of life. That Jews were not an economically and socially significant presence in the city may explain why we do not hear of episodes of tension or conflict between them and their neighbors. The case of the relations between the Jews and their neighbors in the eastern parts of the Mediterranean, however, is different.

Jews and Greeks in the Eastern Mediterranean Diaspora

A Problem of Sources

We have far better information concerning the relations between Jews and Greeks in the eastern Mediterranean Diaspora. The problem is that our sources — a few papyri and inscriptions, quoted fragments of several Greek and Roman documents, and literary records — always concentrate on a given place at a given time and fail to provide a comprehensive historical context. Moreover, we often get the impression that our literary sources — mainly the narratives of Philo and Josephus — omit as much as they include, so that we have to read between the lines. Great caution is required when drawing general conclusions from our scraps of evidence. Nevertheless, all of our sources clearly point both to the integration of Jews in society and to controversies between Jews and Greeks.

Social and Economic Integration

Josephus tells us that in Cyrene there were three thousand well-to-do Jews (*J.W.* 7.445). The numbers are certainly exaggerated, but the existence of a high Jewish society is confirmed by the epigraphic material, which attests the presence of Jews among the ephebes of Cyrene, in the highest rank of the administration (*CJZC* 6 [late first century B.C.E.] and 7 [3/4 C.E.]). A Jew named Eleazar son of Jason is found in the list of the "guardians of the law" *(nomophylakes)* (*CJZC* 8 [60/61 C.E.]), a position that entailed considerable responsibility and required education, experience, and the confidence of the civic leaders. At Teucheira, among the names scratched on the walls of the gymnasium are some that are probably Jewish (*CJZC* 41), and an inscription attests the rise of individual Jews into positions of civic responsibility (*CJZC* 36). Josephus mentions that wealthy Jews in Asia Minor were required to perform liturgical duties (*Ant.* 16.28), a role that suggests a high degree of civic responsibility. At Iasos there was at least one and probably several Jewish ephebes, and an inscription from Hypaepa indicates the existence of an association of Jewish youths, apparently ephebes, who had graduated from the gymnasium while retaining their Jewish identity (*CIJ* 755).

In Alexandria, Egyptian Jews actively participated in the economic life of the city. Philo mentions Jewish shipowners, merchants, and moneylenders (*Flacc.* 57). Alexander the Alabarch, Philo's brother, belonged in the highest stratum of Jewish society and held an important administrative role probably connected with customs collection on the Nile. He was rich enough to donate nine massive gates of silver and gold to the Jerusalem Temple (Josephus, *J.W.* 5.205). Philo himself no doubt received a thorough training in a gymnasium, and his familiarity with theatrical and sporting events suggests that he enjoyed the regular entertainments of Alexandrian citizens.

Cases of local inhabitants being attracted to Judaism are also well attested. According to Josephus, each city in Syria had its "Judaizers" (*J.W.* 2.463); at Damascus, many women had "submitted to the Jewish religion" (*J.W.* 2.559-61); at Antioch, the Jews were constantly attracting to their religious practices "a considerable body of Greeks, whom they had in some measure made a part of themselves" (*J.W.* 7.45). Attraction to Judaism may have taken various forms, from a general interest and sympathy to real adherence to Jewish practices. The statement of the New Testament that the Pharisees "compass sea and land to make one proselyte" (Matt. 23:15) may be exaggerated, but the testimony of later Jewish sources — which take pride in the claim that some of the greatest Jewish figures descended from proselytes — suggests a policy of acceptance.

Friendly relations, however, are not attested always and everywhere. Josephus also reports that serious controversies and disputes arose between the Jews and their Greek neighbors in various places around the Mediterranean. A reconstruction of these episodes and their causes is extremely difficult, since we get only the Jewish point of view. Even when Josephus quotes non-Jewish documents, for example, his choice is always subjective and leads him to cite only those texts attesting favorable decisions concerning the Jews.

Controversies between Jews and Greeks

Mesopotamia

Jews arrived at Seleucia in the first part of the first century c.e., having escaped from Babylon, where they had been always "quarreling with the Babylonians because of the contrariety of their laws" (*Ant.* 18.371). In Seleucia they got caught up in conflicts between Syrians and Greeks. An armed attack against the Jews ensued in which an enormous number of

Jews were killed (*Ant.* 18.372-76). Those who managed to escape fled to Ctesiphon, a Greek city near Seleucia, but there too the local Greek population did not receive them favorably, so they had to leave and take refuge at Nearda and Nisibis (*Ant.* 18.377-79).

Syria

According to Josephus the Jews in Syria enjoyed "the protection of the Seleucid kings" (*J.W.* 7.43) and were granted citizen rights "on equality with the Greeks" (*J.W.* 7.44), a claim that is difficult to accept at face value. In any case, the resentment of the Greek population reached its peak in 66 C.E. when the Jewish rebellion started in Judea and "hatred of the Jews was everywhere at its height" (*J.W.* 7.47). Josephus writes that at Antioch a Jew named Antiochus approached the Greek magistrates and accused his fellow Jews of conspiring to burn the whole city to the ground. Then a real fire broke out that destroyed the market square, the magistrates' quarters, the record office, and the basilicas. The Greeks "rushed for the Jewish masses, believing the salvation of their native place to be dependent on their prompt chastisement." Antiochus sought to furnish proof of his conversion and of his detestation of Jewish customs by sacrificing after the manner of the Greeks. He recommended that other Jews be compelled to do the same. As a result observance of the Sabbath was prohibited not only in Antioch but also in other cities (*J.W.* 7.46-62). Possibly in this context, efforts were made to abolish the privileges of the Jews to get their own non-Gentile oil (Josephus, *Ant.* 1.120).

Another episode reported by Josephus took place in Damascus. Learning of the disaster that had befallen the Romans at the beginning of the Jewish revolt in Judea, the Greeks "were fired with a determination to kill the Jews who resided among them. As they had for a long time past kept them shut up in the gymnasium . . . they fell upon the Jews, cooped up as they were and unarmed, and within one hour slaughtered them all with impunity, to the number of ten thousand five hundred" (*J.W.* 2.559-61). Then, at the end of the war, the Greeks of Antioch asked Titus to expel the Jews, or at least to have their rights abolished (*J.W.* 7.100-111).

Asia Minor

In Asia Minor Jewish settlements were apparently a conspicuous element of the local population. The Jews had formed vital and influential communities dating back to the third century B.C.E., but on several occasions the Greeks prevented the Jews from observing their traditional customs. We learn about these incidents from a number of documents quoted in part by Josephus. The authenticity of these texts has often been challenged in modern scholarship, and Josephus has even been accused of forging the documents in order to prove that the Jews had always been held in high esteem by Rome. This view, however, is not tenable. Parallels in structure, phraseology, and content can be readily found in authentic contemporary Greek and Roman documents preserved on stone, bronze, and papyrus. Moreover, if the documents were forgeries they would not contain so many errors; an informed forger would have taken pains to replicate standard formulas and conventional structures correctly. Paradoxically, the textual corruptions and factual errors constitute the strongest argument for authenticity and indicate that the original texts had probably been copied several times before they reached Josephus.

From these documents, which date to the second half of the first century B.C.E., we learn that at Delos the Jews were denied religious freedom by a decree issued by the Greek city (*JRRW* 7). In Laodicea, the Greek magistrates wrote to the Roman proconsul agreeing to let the Jews observe their Sabbaths and rites in accordance with their native laws, but that the people of Tralles were dissatisfied and would not easily comply with the Roman requests (*JRRW* 17). At Miletus, the Roman governor resented that, "contrary to our expressed wish, you are attacking the Jews and forbid them to observe the Sabbaths, perform their native rites, and manage their produce in accordance with the laws" (*JRRW* 18). At Halicarnassus, Roman pressure forced the Greek city to issue a decree allowing the Jews to follow their customs (*JRRW* 19). That the Jewish observance of the Sabbath was liable to a fine we learn from another decree, issued this time at Ephesus, where, again under Roman pressure, the Greeks agreed that "no one shall be prevented from keeping the Sabbath days nor be fined for so doing" (*JRRW* 21). Kosher food also represented a problem; special permission was necessary at Sardis for "having suitable food for them [the Jews] brought in" (*JRRW* 20).

Not surprisingly, the Roman letters and decrees were not very effective. A few generations later, during the reign of Augustus, some of the same issues were still pending. Quoting the work of Nicholas of Damascus, Herod's secretary, who personally witnessed the episode, Josephus presents us with two reports of a visit to Ionia in 14 B.C.E. by the Roman statesman Agrippa and King Herod. In the first report (*Ant.* 12.125-27) the Ionians are said to have requested from Agrippa that the citizenship (*politeia*) granted by Antiochus Theos should be restricted to them alone and should not include the Jews, who declined to worship the gods of the Ionians. This statement is illuminating: the Jews are not entitled to the same rights of the Greeks since they refuse to acknowledge the city's gods. Economic and religious issues were intermingled because religion was central in the maintenance of civic patriotism. A local cult with a world-famous temple, for example, was vital to a city's identity and crucial to its economy.

The second report (*Ant.* 16.27-28) centers on Jewish claims. The Jews do not mention civic rights and the city's gods, but rather their mistreatment by the Greek cities, which forbade them to observe their religious laws, compelled them to attend judicial hearings on their holy days, stripped them of the monies destined for the Temple in Jerusalem, pressed them into military service, and forced them to spend their income on unwanted civic duties "although they had been exempted from these duties because the Romans had always permitted them to live in accordance with their own laws." These "unwanted civic duties" may have been liturgies, that is, public services assumed by, or rather imposed upon, the wealthier citizens as a compulsory duty toward the community. In the difficult economic situation following the Roman civil struggles of the last years of the Republic, which had drawn heavily on Asian resources, liturgies had become a problematic feature in the life of Greek cities in the East. The Jews of Ionia based their refusal to participate in these duties on their religious freedom, which was legally recognized by the Roman government. But why did they justify their refusal on religious grounds and expect Agrippa to agree with them? Their appeal makes sense only if the liturgies in question were somehow incompatible with Jewish religious scruples. The obligations may have included something like underwriting the cost of pagan festivals or the expenses of the local gymnasium.

The same issues may have been at stake in an episode reported by Josephus, in which the Jews complained that the Greeks "were persecuting them to the extent of taking their sacred monies away from them and doing them injury in their private concerns" (*Ant.* 16.160-61). In hard times, the Greeks may have resented that the Jews made no contribution to renovate the dilapidated temples in their own cities but sent their monies to a temple way off in Jerusalem. They therefore took steps to rectify this lack, which was felt as injustice, and seized the monies that the Jews had collected to be sent to the Jerusalem Temple. The situation must have been grave, since Augustus had to provide a special penalty for those caught stealing Jewish sacred monies or sacred books (*JRRW* 22).

Libya

In Libya as well we hear of friction between Jews and Greeks over taxation. Josephus quotes a letter in which Agrippa, Augustus's best general and son-in-law, writes to the magistrates of Cyrene: the Jews complain that "they are being threatened by certain informers and prevented (from sending their monies) on the pretext of their owing taxes, which are in fact not owed" (*Ant.* 16.170). Scholars suggest that this statement may refer to the *metoikion,* which all noncitizens had to pay. If so, the claim would have been that some or all of the Jews of Cyrene had the same (or equivalent) rights as those of the members of the Greek city, the *polis,* and therefore did not have to pay the taxes owed by noncitizens. But other suggestions may be offered too. For example, the taxes here may have been related to pagan worship, as was the case in Ionia in the same period. In any case, attempted tax evasion was apparently a common feature of the time. During Augustus's reign, the Greek cities also appealed to the emperor against Roman citizens who claimed exemption from taxation and liturgy duties (*SEG* 9, 8, section III). Moreover, since the Greek cities were engaged in a war against native tribesmen, economic pressure may have exacerbated financial disputes.

Egypt

Theoretically, there was no dramatic change when Egypt fell under Octavian's control in 31 B.C.E. after the Battle of Actium. Octavian, now Augustus, implemented the traditional policy of the Ptolemies toward the Jews and confirmed their traditional rights. The testimonies of Josephus (*J.W.* 2.488; *Ant.* 14.282) and Philo (*Legat.* 159, 291; *Flacc.* 50) are confirmed by a Greek papyrus that mentions the religious freedom enjoyed by Alexandrian Jews "in the time of the god Augustus" (*CPJ* 2:153).

Yet significant changes, both good and bad, occurred in other areas. The abolition of Ptolemaic monopolies opened new possibilities in the local economy, so that a few generations afterward we find wealthy Jews living in Alexandria as shipowners, merchants, and moneylenders (Philo, *Flacc.* 57). This status may well have increased the competition that already existed between the Jews and the upper strata of the Greek population.

Not all Jews, however, benefited from the change in rule. Jews serving in the Ptolemaic army, for example, lost their source of income when it was disbanded. Jews working in the administration simply disappear from the papyri of the Roman period, a fact that scholars relate to the preference now accorded to Greeks.

Frustration on both sides may have exacerbated underlying competition. The Greeks resented the loss of their political freedom when Augustus abolished their civic council, the *boulē*. They regarded this act as an injustice, especially in view of the confirmation of Jewish religious rights. Other changes of policy were resented by the Jews, among them the special status granted to the Greek cities *(poleis),* which allowed them a kind of fictitious freedom. Alexandria, for example, was called *Alexandria ad Aegyptum* — "by Egypt," not "in Egypt" — as if to underline its (obviously fictitious) independent status. More significantly, the Greek cities received economic privileges such as exemption from the poll tax *(laographia),* which all Egyptians had to pay on the principle that a conquered people should render tribute. Descendants of mixed marriages had to pay the tax at reduced rates. To obtain an exemption, it was necessary to demonstrate one's right to citizenship in one of the country's Greek cities.

No legal source tells us whether the Jews were considered Greeks or Egyptians, but from the very beginning of the Roman period Jews began lodging complaints. In a petition written to the prefect of Egypt under Augustus (*CPJ* 2:151), a Jew named Helenos son of Tryphon complains of an injury done to him by a financial office of the government. Helenos contested the decision, which evidently concerned payment of the poll tax, and asserted his right to be exempt since his father was an Alexandrian citizen and he himself had always lived in the city of Alexandria and received "the appropriate education" as far as his father's means allowed. Helenos styled himself "an Alexandrian," but the scribe who wrote the letter for him struck out this word and in its place wrote "a Jew from Alexandria." This is an extremely significant change, since "Alexandrian" meant a citizen of the Greek city, while "a Jew from Alexandria" meant a person who lived in the city as a simple resident. The scribe's rewording may well indicate that a legal dispute lay behind the issue.

A generation later, Philo observes that the Jews were "anxious to obtain equal rights with the burgesses and are near to being citizens because they differ little from the original inhabitants" (*Mos.* 1.34-35) — a claim strongly rejected by the Greeks. From a Greek papyrus we learn that Isidorus, one of the fiercest Alexandrian leaders in the time of Caligula, accused the Alexandrian Jews of being of the same character as Egyptians because both nations had to pay the poll tax (*CPJ* 2:156c). Scholars have debated whether these rights had to do only with membership in the Greek *polis* or included additional rights for the Jewish community. The scarcity of the sources, their fragmentary state, and their obvious bias make it extremely difficult to reach a definitive conclusion. Yet one thing clearly emerges from all the sources: Jewish claims were strongly contested by their Greek neighbors.

The reasons for these objections may have to do with Jewish religious separatism. Josephus puts an important question in the mouth of Apion, a grammarian and Homeric scholar of Egyptian origin who played a prominent part in the cultural and political life of the first century c.e.: "Why, then, if they are citizens do they not worship the same gods as the Alexandrians?" (*Ag. Ap.* 2.65). This may be a rhetorical question intended to conceal more practical concerns. Recent scholarship emphasizes that it may represent a maneuver to limit other Jewish rights. By focusing on religious issues, the Greeks would have pushed the Jews on the most sensitive matters. If the Jews insisted on maintaining their practices, as of course they would, the municipal governments could regard this as their opting out of civic responsibilities and debar Jews from the services and benefits of the community.

In any case, Jewish refusal to participate in the cult to the gods of the city may have been difficult for Greeks to understand in a syncretistic world where cults and mythologies freely intermingled. Moreover, this refusal was made in the name of the Jewish god, who could not be seen or represented in the form of a statue or image. This aniconism made the Jewish god a nonentity in Greek eyes — hence the accusation of atheism found in Apollonius's work (*De Iudaeis* in Josephus, *Ag. Ap.* 2.148). A cult in a temple that had no image in its inner sanctum was also difficult for Greeks to understand. Apion claimed that the Jews worshiped the head of an ass in their temple. In this accusation he was relying on a supposed relation of the Jews with Seth, the god of evil, chaos, and confusion who was often identified with the donkey, an animal abhorred by the Egyptians (*Ag. Ap.* 2.79-80).

Another feature of Judaism criticized in Egypt from the time of Hecataeus in the third century B.C.E. was its social separateness: "The sacrifices he [Moses] established differ from those of the other nations, as does their way of living, for as a result of their own expulsion from Egypt he introduced an unsocial and intolerant mode of life" (*Aegyptiaca*, apud Diodorus Siculus, *Bibliotheca Historica* 60.3.4). In time, Jewish separateness was interpreted as misanthropy — hence the accusation of hatred of humanity and of ritual murders. Its first formulation is found in the work of Apion, who claims that the Jews used to "kidnap a Greek foreigner, fatten him up for a year, and then convey him to a wood, where they slew him, sacrificed his body with their customary ritual, partook of his flesh and, while immolating the Greek, swore an oath of hostility to the Greeks" (*Ag. Ap.* 2.91-95).

Intellectual antagonism materialized at the time of Emperor Caligula. In the year 38 C.E., the arrival of King Agrippa in Alexandria was the occasion of a popular riot, described at length in Philo's *Against Flaccus*. Stirred up by a group of extremists, the Alexandrians installed images of the emperor in the synagogues, so that the Jewish cult automatically ceased. Jews were proclaimed "foreigners and aliens" (*Flacc.* 54) and shut up in one quarter of the city. When forced by the scarcity of food to leave the quarter and to appear in the marketplace, they were pursued and slaughtered; their houses were plundered and their goods stolen or destroyed. Members of the Jewish senate were flogged with whips in the theater. Jewish traditional autonomy was officially abolished. Seeking reconciliation, the Jewish aristocracy sent a delegation to the emperor in Rome, but it failed in its purposes. As soon as Caligula was killed in 41 C.E., Jews in Alexandria rose in arms and retaliated against the Greeks. Josephus tells us that "upon the death of Gaius, the Jews, who had been humiliated under his rule and grievously abused by the Alexandrians, took heart again and at once armed themselves." Claudius commanded the prefect of Egypt to put down the uprising (*Ant.* 19.278-79). Peace was restored but the dispute was not solved; there were continuous clashes between Jews and Greeks in which each crackdown by the authorities further exacerbated the quarrel between the two sides (*J.W.* 2.489).

Two generations later, amidst the prevailing anti-Jewish attitudes at the time when the First Jewish Revolt broke out in Judea in 66 C.E., another episode of violence took place in the theater of Alexandria (*J.W.*

2.487-98). And some years later, in the aftermath of the First Revolt, the citizens of Alexandria appealed to Titus to strip the Jews of their rights (*Ant.* 12.121-24)

Two additional episodes of conflict in Alexandria took place at the beginning of Trajan's reign, about which we learn from Greek papyri. One of them (*CPJ* 2:157) belongs to the so-called *Acts of the Alexandrians,* which deal with historical facts by inserting them in a fictional framework and manipulating them with strong political bias. Precise historical details are impossible to reconstruct, but a conflict between Jews and Greeks had taken place, probably at some point between 110 and 113 C.E. Another episode of strife between the Greeks and the Jews occurring a couple of years later is reported by an official Roman document written in October 115 (*CPJ* 2:435). The Jews complain about "fire and weapons" prepared against them, and a Roman authority, possibly the Roman prefect, displays a critical attitude towards the Greeks. Obscure references are made to disorders and to a demonstration held in the theater of the city, and the arrival of a judge sent by the emperor to investigate is noted. Other fragmentary papyri appear to allude to the eventual condemnation of those responsible for the disorders: sixty Alexandrians were exiled and their slaves beheaded (*CPJ* 2:158a, 158b).

Some months later, in the spring of 116 C.E., there was an uprising of Jews not only in Egypt but also in Libya, Cyprus, Mesopotamia, and Judea. The catalyst for the uprisings has unfortunately left no trace in extant sources. In Libya, Egypt, and Cyprus, the Jews attacked their Greek and Roman neighbors, destroying temples, statues of gods, and centers of Greek civic life (*CJZC* 17-23). The attacks were led by Andreas (according to Dio), or by Lukuas (according to Eusebius), to whom Eusebius ascribes the title "king," a fact that has led some scholars to assume that the uprising had a messianic background. The evidence, however, is scanty. In Cyprus, the Jews were led by a certain Artemion (Dio 68.32.2), and here too we get an impression of great destruction. In Egypt, where the local Jews acted in cooperation with those of Libya (*Hist. Eccl.* 4.2.3), the uprising covered large sections of the country, and for a while Jews had the upper hand (*CPJ* 2:438). The Greeks fought back, led by their *stratēgoi* — the most well known is Apollonios — and helped by the Egyptian peasants and the Romans. The Jewish uprisings were crushed only when Trajan decided on a massive intervention. Order was restored by the autumn of 117 (*CPJ* 2:443), and at Oxyrhynchus the victory over the Jews was commemorated by a festival that was still observed some eighty years later (*CPJ* 2:450).

Assessment

These long-running disputes could arise only if the Jewish communities were a significant presence in the cities concerned. In Asia, for example, a small and insignificant community would have been ignored by the city magistrates or coerced into submission. But in the extant documents and in Josephus's narrative, one senses the presence of Jews sufficiently prominent in city life for their refusal to attend court or do business on the Sabbath to be deemed highly awkward if not even offensive. Some modern interpreters consider Jewish integration as the dominant reality and treat controversies as minor episodes, while others suggest the opposite. In fact, however, no real contradiction exists when social, cultural, and political integration, on the one hand, and antagonism and conflicts, on the other, are regarded as two sides of the same coin.

Jews, Greeks, and Roman Policy

In the regions under their rule, the Romans always tried to pursue a policy that would give them full control but allow the inhabitants to remain reasonably satisfied. That is why the existing organizational framework was usually preserved and the local laws typically endorsed. The status quo of the Jews was likewise preserved and their traditional rights endorsed. All the decrees and edicts quoted by Josephus that were issued between the middle of the first century B.C.E. and the middle of the first century C.E. by Roman commanders, the Roman senate (the so-called *senatus consulta*), Roman governors, and Roman emperors point in the same direction. They all proclaim that the Jews are free to follow their traditional laws and customs: to assemble, to feast and hold common meals, to perform their cult, to have a measure of internal administration and jurisdiction, to build sacred and profane buildings, and to have kosher food in the markets of their cities. It was not a pro-Jewish policy per se; inscriptions and papyri attest that permission to follow local laws was usually granted to conquered peoples by the Romans.

From these same documents quoted by Josephus, however, we also understand that Roman grants had a somewhat theoretical character. Asians, Libyans, Alexandrians, and perhaps other Greeks had their own good reasons for ignoring the Roman ordinances and for preventing the Jews from following their traditional customs and laws. The Jews requested Roman support and, as far as we can judge from the evidence quoted by Josephus, they often got it, but the new letters and the new decrees issued by the Roman government did not get better results, and few practical consequences followed.

This somewhat apathetic attitude on the part of the Romans should occasion no surprise since it was a common feature of Roman politics. The Romans seem to have had a very limited interest in what happened in the provinces and perhaps did not even expect their decisions to be implemented. It was therefore only theoretically that the Romans sided with the Jews and only, it must be emphasized, when religious issues were at stake.

In other areas, the situation was ambiguous. The issue of taxation provides a case in point. Several times the Jews appealed to the Roman authorities, claiming that they did not have to pay the taxes imposed upon them by the Greek cities. In spite of the Jewish sources' desire to present the Romans as generous partners, it appears that the Romans simply refrained from dealing with the matter. A dispute concerning taxes owed to a Greek city took place in Asia in the time of Augustus. Josephus tells us that the emperor granted the Jews "the same equality of taxation as before" (*Ant.* 16.161), but this is not confirmed by the edict quoted immediately below (*JRRW* 22), which deals only with Jewish traditional rights and does not mention taxation at all. Josephus's remarks, therefore, are misleading. In Libya, too, a letter written by Agrippa to the magistrates and the people of Cyrene (*JRRW* 25) mentions the Jewish claim to the effect that they do not owe the taxes imposed upon them by the Greek city. Agrippa's own statement, however, concerns only the Jewish sacred monies, not taxes.

Philo and Josephus would often like us to believe that the Romans sided with the Jews, but this was not always the case. When the Alexandrians introduced images of the emperor Caligula into Jewish synagogues in the city — effectively terminating the Jewish religious cult, in open violation of their traditional rights — the Roman prefect Flaccus could have ordered the statues removed, but he did not, possibly out of fear that his act might be interpreted in Rome as hostility toward the emperor. Whatever the reasons, Flaccus sided with the Greeks, had the leaders of the Jews taken and publicly scourged in the theater, and issued an edict proclaiming that Alexandrian Jews were "foreigners and aliens" in the city (Philo, *Flacc.* 54). Modern scholars have labored to explain and even justify Flaccus's behavior in an attempt to counterbalance the perspective of Philo and Josephus. But the fact remains that Flaccus was either unwilling or unable to stop the anti-Jewish pogrom, and that is why he was later condemned for his behavior, exiled, and then put to death (*Flacc.* 109–15, 121–26, 147–51, 169–70, 181, 185–91).

When the next emperor took power, the need to settle the Alexandrian question on a more stable base was urgent, and this time we are fortunate enough to have a reliable document. Preserved in a Greek papyrus (*CPJ* 2:153), it is a letter written by Emperor Claudius to the Alexandrians showing that the situation was far less complimentary to the Jews than Josephus would like us to believe. Again, an apathetic attitude emerges: Claudius states right away that he does not wish "to make an exact inquiry" into what transpired and limits himself to ordering the two parties "to keep peace": "I adjure the Alexandrians to behave gently and kindly towards the Jews who have inhabited the same city for many years . . . [and] . . . to allow them to keep their own ways." The Jews, on the other hand, are ordered not to aim at more than they have previously had "since they enjoy what is their own, and in a city which is not their own they possess an abundance of all good things" (*CPJ* 2:53). This statement is amazing. The claim of Alexandrian Greeks that the Jews were strangers in Alexandria, which had been accepted by the prefect Flaccus some years before, is now endorsed for the first time by a Roman emperor.

Obviously, Claudius's policy did nothing to solve the underlying conflict. Two generations later, when a violent clash took place in Alexandria in the theater of the city, the Roman prefect, Tiberius Julius Alexander, a nephew of Philo and a renegade Jew who had made a brilliant carrier in Roman administration, seems to have crushed the disturbance with ruthless cruelty (*J.W.* 2.487-97).

When public order was menaced, the Roman response was typically immediate and harsh. This happened also when the Jews took up arms during the reign of Trajan in 116 to 117. The Roman prefect, Rutilius Lupus, seems to have participated in the engagements, and Trajan took serious measures to suppress Jewish disorder by sending his best generals: Gaius Valerius to Cyprus, with a detachment of soldiers on a military expedition (*ILS* 3:9491), and Marcius Turbo to Egypt, with land and sea forces including cavalry. Turbo "waged war vigorously . . . in many battles for a considerable time and killed many thousands of Jews, not only those of Cyrene but also those of Egypt" (Eusebius, *Hist. Eccl.* 4.2.3-4). In Libya, during the war against the Jews, a Roman *praefectus castrorum* mentioned by Artemidoros Daldianus (*Oneirocriticon* 4.24) was killed. In Egypt, a victorious battle against the Jews took place in the vicinity of Memphis (*CPJ* 2:439), and the Roman historian Appian states that in his day Trajan "exterminated" the Jewish race in Egypt (*Bella Civilia* 2.90). As always, maintenance of peace and order was the main goal Roman policy.

BIBLIOGRAPHY

Barclay, John M. G. 1998. *Jews in the Mediterranean Diaspora: from Alexander to Trajan (323 BCE–117 CE)*. Edinburgh: Clark.

Bartlett, John R., ed. 2002. *Jews in the Hellenistic and Roman Cities*. London: Routledge.

Berthelot, Katell. 2003. *Philanthropia Judaica: Le debat autour de la "misanthropie" des lois juives dans L'antiquite*. Leiden: Brill.

Cappelletti, Silvia. 2006. *The Jewish Community of Rome: From the Second Century BCE to the Third Century BCE*. Leiden: Brill.

Collins, John J. 2005. *Jewish Cult and Hellenistic Culture: Essays on the Jewish Encounter with Hellenism and Roman Rule*. Leiden: Brill.

Feldman, Louis H. 1993. *Jew and Gentile in the Ancient World*. Princeton: Princeton University Press.

Gambetti, Sandra. 2009. *The Alexandrian Riots of 38 C.E. and the Persecution of the Jews: A Historical Reconstruction*. Leiden: Brill.

Goodman, Martin. 1994. *Mission and Conversion: Proselytizing in the Religious History of the Roman Empire*. Oxford: Clarendon.

Gruen, Erich S. 2002. *Diaspora: Jews amidst Greeks and Romans*. Cambridge: Harvard University Press.

Horbury, William, and David Noy, eds. 1992. *Jewish Inscriptions of Graeco-Roman Egypt*. Cambridge: Harvard University Press.

Lüderlitz, Gert, ed. 1983. *Corpus jüdischer Zeugnisse aus der Cyrenaika*. Wiesbaden: Reichert.

Modrzejewski, Joseph M. 1995. *The Jews of Egypt: From Rameses II to Emperor Hadrian*. Philadelphia: Jewish Publication Society.

Pucci Ben Zeev, Miriam. 1998. *Jewish Rights in the Roman World: The Greek and Roman Documents Quoted by Josephus Flavius*. Tübingen: Mohr Siebeck.

Rajak, Tessa. 2001. *The Jewish Dialogue with Greece and Rome: Studies in Cultural and Social Interaction*. Leiden: Brill.

Schäfer, Peter. 1997. *Judeophobia: Attitudes toward the Jews in the Ancient World*. Cambridge: Harvard University Press.

Smallwood, E. M. 1981. *The Jews under Roman Rule from Pompey to Diocletian*. Leiden: Brill.

Stern, Menahem. 1972-1984. *Greek and Latin Authors on Jews and Judaism*. 3 vols. Jerusalem: Israel Academy of Sciences and Humanities.

Tcherikover, Victor. 1979. *Hellenistic Civilization and the Jews*. New York: Atheneum.

Tcherikover, Victor, and Alexander Fuks, eds. 1957-1964. *Corpus Papyrorum Judaicarum.* 3 vols. Cambridge: Harvard University Press.

Trebilco, Paul. 1991. *Jewish Communities in Asia Minor.* Cambridge: Cambridge University Press.

Williams, Margaret H. 1998. *The Jews among Greeks and Romans: A Diasporan Sourcebook.* Baltimore: Johns Hopkins University Press.

Early Judaism and Early Christianity

Daniel C. Harlow

Today it is a commonplace to acknowledge that Jesus and his first followers were Jews thoroughly embedded in the Judaism of their day. But this has not always been the case. Well into the twentieth century, New Testament scholarship tended if not to separate Jesus from his Jewish milieu then at least to view him as transcending its "legalism" and "ritualism." Only in the post–Holocaust era have Christian scholars overcome the negative caricature of ancient Judaism and reckoned with the essential Jewishness of Jesus. The group he inspired began as a movement within Second Temple Judaism, so for much of the first century C.E., the term "Christianity" is inappropriate if taken to suggest a non-Jewish religion. The term itself (Gr. *Christianismos*) was invented in-house in the early second century (Ignatius, *Rom.* 3:3; *Magn.* 10:3; *Phld.* 6:1; *Mart. Pol.* 10:1), while the epithet "Christian" *(Christianos)* was coined by outsiders several decades before (Acts 11:26, 28; 1 Pet. 4:16). Initially, though, even "Christian" did not designate adherents of a non-Jewish faith but followers or partisans of *Christos* the Jew.

Our main sources for the early Jesus movement are the New Testament writings, which were composed over the course of about seventy years, from roughly 50 to 120 C.E. These documents provide valuable historical evidence not only for Jesus and his first followers but also for the wider Jewish world they inhabited. Apart from the ancient Jewish historian Flavius Josephus, the apostle Paul — the earliest and major writer of the New Testament — is the only (former) Pharisee to have left behind a literary legacy. The Synoptic Gospels of Matthew, Mark, and Luke are a mine of information about first-century Palestinian Judaism: they mention such figures as Herod the Great and his son Antipas, the tetrarch of

Galilee; they witness to the beliefs and practices of various Jewish groups; and they supply evidence for Jewish institutions like Temple and synagogue, Jewish rituals like hand washing and kosher table fellowship, Jewish festivals such as Passover, and Jewish theological ideas like angelology, eschatology, and messianism. The Gospels also offer examples of Jewish modes of scriptural interpretation and of early Jewish exegetical traditions. The Gospel of Luke and its sequel, the book of Acts, are especially rich in details of Jewish tradition. The third gospel gives the earliest narrative portrait of pilgrimage to Jerusalem and of synagogue worship in the land of Israel. For its part, Acts mentions Gamaliel, Theudas and "the Egyptian," Judas the Galilean, and Agrippa I, figures known from Josephus and rabbinic sources, and describes a communal organization for the Jerusalem congregation of Jesus' followers which has some points of similarity with that of the Qumran sect. It also distinguishes the Pharisees and Sadducees in their beliefs concerning angels and resurrection, and affords insight into synagogues in the Jewish Diaspora, including the presence there of God-fearing Gentiles. Of course, this material has to be evaluated critically, but it remains nonetheless important.

Any attempt to discuss the relation between early Christianity and early Judaism must confront two main difficulties. The first is the sheer variety that characterized both of them, a variety so pronounced that some scholars prefer to speak of "Judaisms" and "Christianities." Nothing like an official or normative Judaism existed in the earliest centuries of the Common Era; it was probably not until the fourth century or later that the rabbinic movement could lay serious claim to be the dominant form of Judaism. The same is true, *mutatis mutandis,* of early Christianity. Although the New Testament writings do not fully reflect the range of diversity that characterized Christianity in the first century, they still reveal considerable variety and tension.

The second difficulty lies in the recognition that in some settings the boundaries between "Judaism" and "Christianity" were fluid even after the latter had become overwhelmingly non-Jewish in its ethnic composition. Among Jews and Christians, there was considerable overlap in areas of theological identity owing in part to their common scriptural heritage, and to the Christian preservation and transmission of most of the extant literature of Second Temple Judaism. There is also some evidence that Jews and Christians interacted with one another in social and even liturgical contexts into late antiquity and beyond.

Despite these difficulties, it is still proper to speak of early Judaism and early Christianity without resorting to the plural. For all the manifest variety in Second Temple Judaism, a set of core beliefs and practices characterized the piety of most observant Jews. This "common Judaism" centered on the exclusive and imageless worship of the one God, the notion of covenant election, reverence for the Torah, and devotion to the Jerusalem Temple; it included practices such as circumcision for males, Sabbath and festival observance, and kosher diet. To be sure, groups like the Essenes at Qumran defined election in narrow sectarian terms, and in the Hellenistic Diaspora Jews had to negotiate their Jewish identity rather differently than did their compatriots in the homeland. It is also true that in some early apocalypses neither covenant nor Torah is constitutive of Jewish identity. But even these caveats do little to erase the impression of a common Judaism, which receives confirmation in archaeology and in the observations of Greek and Latin authors who wrote about Jews and Judaism. Likewise, all varieties of early Christianity shared in revering Jesus, even if their doing so took on different forms, from simply remembering him as a miracle worker or venerating him as a great teacher to worshiping him as the incarnate Son of God. Further, although "Judaism" and "Christianity" were never airtight categories, the initially Jewish Jesus movement did eventually become a non-Jewish religion, not least in the sense that most of its adherents were Gentiles who did not observe Torah.

In order to highlight some of the major areas of continuity and discontinuity between Second Temple Judaism and early Christianity, it will be useful to examine Jesus in his Jewish context, the Jewish character of the early Jesus movement, and the relation of Paul to Judaism. From there the discussion will proceed to the range of perspectives on Jews and Judaism reflected elsewhere in the New Testament, and conclude with some reflections on the "parting of the ways" between Judaism and Christianity.

Jesus within Judaism

Even after a critical sifting of the Synoptic Gospels of Matthew, Mark, and Luke, our principal sources, Jesus fits securely within Second Temple Judaism. He was an apocalyptic prophet who proclaimed and symbolically enacted the imminent arrival of God's kingdom on earth. In his prophetic role, he bears some resemblance to Jesus ben Hananiah, Theudas, and other popular prophets in first-century Palestine mentioned by Josephus. In his reputation for performing healings and exorcisms, he shows certain affinities with charismatic holy men like Hanina ben Dosa and Honi the Circle Drawer recalled in rabbinic tradition. Scholars debate whether and in what sense Jesus called himself the "Son of Man" and whether he accepted the titles "Messiah" or "Son of God" (the latter in its royal, messianic sense). But he almost certainly regarded himself as God's final envoy to the people of Israel, urging his countrymen to heed his message and calling on some of them to follow him. That both Jesus' former mentor John the Baptist and the movement Jesus left behind were steeped in apocalyptic eschatology argues strongly in favor of seeing him as an apocalyptic figure. The point bears emphasizing since some scholars construe Jesus as a nonapocalyptic sage and social reformer, an understanding of him that is suspect on several counts (see below).

Jesus symbolized the eschatological restoration of Israel by calling twelve disciples to represent the twelve tribes of Israel (Mark 1:16-20 pars.), and he dramatized the eschatological reversal of fortunes by sharing table fellowship with the outcast, including prostitutes, tax gatherers, and other "sinners" — those who lived in flagrant violation of the Torah. He believed that he and his disciples would have places of leadership in the coming kingdom (Mark 10:29-31, 35-40; Matt. 19:28-29) and that those who accepted his message would be included in it. He also predicted the destruction of the Temple (Mark 13:1-2 pars.).

Careful analysis of the Synoptic tradition shows that Jesus was an observant Jew who did not directly oppose any significant aspect of the Torah. He was circumcised, he observed the Sabbath, he attended the synagogue, he taught from the Torah, he went on pilgrimage to Jerusalem and celebrated the Jewish festivals, and he accepted the atoning efficacy of sacrifice at the Temple (Mark 1:44 pars.; Matt. 5:23). When asked about the greatest commandment, he affirmed the Shema and the obligation to love one's neighbor, innovatingly combining the two (Mark 12:28-34 pars.). He never denounced Moses or the Law and never denied the covenant election of the Jewish people. The Synoptics portray him in conflict with scribes and Pharisees over such halakic matters as healing on the Sabbath, fasting, tithing, food purity and meal practices, oath taking, and divorce. On at least one occasion he debated with some Sadducees about the resurrection of the dead (Mark 12:18-27 pars.). But these issues were commonly disputed among Palestinian Jews, and since no group represented the "official" position on any matter — there was none — Jesus cannot be said to have opposed the Judaism of his day.

Unfortunately, the original contexts of these disputes were soon forgotten as oral traditions about Jesus began to circulate, so it is impossible to gain a full sense of his attitude toward aspects of Torah piety. Nevertheless, even granting the historicity of the halakic disputes in the Synoptics (which stand in some doubt), the positions attributed to Jesus fall within the bounds of acceptable Jewish behavior. Healing on the Sabbath, for instance, was not considered a violation of Sabbath law in pre-70 Judaism (at least no pre-70 Jewish text indicates that it was), and Jesus' stance on marriage and divorce (Mark 10:2-12 pars.) was not less but more stringent than what the Torah requires. Although his disciples were allegedly criticized by some Pharisees for plucking grain on the Sabbath and not washing their hands before meals (Mark 2:23-28 pars.; Mark 7:1-23/Matt. 15:1-20), these perceived infractions would have been relatively minor. On the face of it, Jesus' statement "Let the dead bury their own dead" (Matt. 8:22/Luke 9:50) conflicts with Torah piety, but the eschatological urgency of his mission must be taken as a mitigating factor. The single major infringement of Jewish halakah attributed to Jesus comes with the statement in Mark that "he declared all foods clean" (Mark 7:19b). But this is the evangelist's editorial comment and reflects an attitude that probably goes beyond Jesus' own position. It is quietly dropped in Matthew's redaction of the passage (Matt. 15:17-18).

Whence then the opposition? What Jesus' Pharisaic and Sadducean interlocutors found most objectionable was probably not so much his particular stance on matters of Torah praxis but the way he articulated his stance. He propounded his views by uttering authoritative pronouncements in the first person, and not by entering into debate in the style of a contemporary scribe or rabbi. Instead of citing the opinions of revered teachers, he went straight to the Scriptures. This practice appears most dramatically in the series of antitheses that now make up the Sermon on the Mount, which are introduced with the formula "You have heard it said to the men of old . . . but I say to you . . ." (Matt. 5:21-48). Some of the antitheses are polemical and go beyond the literal meaning of the Torah, but they effectively intensify Torah commandments by trying to get at their root intention. The formula "You have heard it said . . . but I say to you" does not imply a demotion — far less a rejection — of the Torah but only a challenging of traditions of scriptural interpretation. An analogous formula, "You know . . . but we say," features in the halakic document from Qumran (4QMMT). On occasion, Jesus also pronounced sins forgiven when he healed people (Mark 2:1-12 pars.), but the passive verb form he used, "Your sins are forgiven," bears the implication "by God." In making such statements he certainly invited censure, but he was not necessarily claiming divine status for himself, only an authority that relativized the prerogative of the priests. That in itself would have made him plenty controversial.

No doubt Jesus *was* controversial in his day, but it seems unlikely that it was anything that he said or did during his Galilean ministry that got him killed. This suspicion is confirmed by the observation that in the gospel passion narratives it is not the Pharisees who have him arrested and handed over to Pilate but the Jerusalem Temple leadership. Some of his parables, notably the Vineyard and Tenants (Mark 12:1-12 pars.), imply criticism of the Jerusalem priesthood, but the critique is scarcely harsher than what we find in the sectarian writings from Qumran. Jesus' proclamation of the coming kingdom of God might have been regarded by Pilate as politically subversive had it come to his attention, since it implicitly challenged the kingdom of Rome. More likely, however, it was the messianic enthusiasm of large crowds that greeted Jesus on his entry into Jerusalem and his demonstration in the Temple that brought him to the lethal attention of the chief priests and the Romans. Both of these incidents are reported in the Synoptics and independently in John with an overlay of interpretation (Mark 11:1-10 pars. and John 12:12-19; Mark 11:15-17 pars. and John 2:13-25), but there is no good reason to doubt their essential historicity. What prompted Jesus' disrupting the commerce in the Temple is unclear. Perhaps his ire was aroused by Herod's remodeling program, which had transformed the Temple's outer court from a sacred space into a commercial venue. Equally offensive to him, perhaps, was the type of coinage required to pay the half-shekel Temple tax: Tyrian silver issues that bore the image of the Canaanite god Melqart. Whatever provoked his gesture, he may have intended it to symbolize the Temple's impending doom and perhaps also its eschatological replacement. This understanding of the event finds support in the tradition of his predicting the Temple's destruction, a prediction that need not be taken as an *ex-eventu* prophecy (Mark 13:1-2 pars.).

The Markan trial narrative and its parallel in Matthew depict false witnesses offering conflicting testimony before the Judean council that Jesus threatened to destroy the Temple himself (Mark 14:57-58/Matt. 26:60-61; cf. Jesus' symbolic threat in John 2:19). The charge is not sustained but replaced with the accusation of blasphemy (Mark 14:64). What actually transpired at Jesus' interrogation by the high priest is beyond recovery. In the Markan account he is accused by Caiaphas of blasphemy after confessing to be the messiah and declaring, "You will see the Son of Man seated at the right hand of Power and coming with the clouds of heaven" (Mark 14:62). Among Jews, claiming to be the messiah was not a blasphemous assertion, but the Son of Man saying as Mark words it implies that Jesus arrogated divine power and status to himself. Had Jesus made such a claim, it would indeed have been regarded as blasphemy. But again, what he actually said cannot be known.

The clearest indication of why Jesus was crucified comes from his Roman executioners, in the *titulus* that Pilate had affixed to Jesus' cross: "King of the Jews" (Mark 15:26 pars.). With mocking irony, the inscription suggests that he was executed on grounds of political sedition. This does not mean that Pilate regarded Jesus or his followers as a potent political threat to the Roman Empire as such, only that Jesus' provocative demonstration in the Temple had to be dealt with so as to quell potential unrest in Jerusalem during the politically charged atmosphere of Passover, a Jewish festival celebrating liberation from foreign domination. In turning him over to Pilate, the chief priests no doubt sought to avoid the vigorous police action from the Romans that any further disturbances in the city would have risked (cf. John 11:48, "If we let him go on like this, everyone will believe in him and the Romans will come and destroy both our holy place and our nation" — a statement attributed to the chief priests apropos of the raising of Lazarus that would make excellent historical sense in relation to the Temple incident). Indeed, the chief priests may have been working with Pilate to preserve public order and may have arrested Jesus with Pilate's approval.

The Early Jesus Movement(s)

Within a few weeks of Jesus' death around the year 30, several of his followers began boldly proclaiming that he had appeared to them risen from the dead. Over the next months and years, their reflection on Jesus' life, their study of the Jewish scriptures, and their experience of his spiritual presence in their midst led them to elaborate on their core proclamation: God had sent Jesus to redeem all humankind; his death was necessary to inaugurate God's sovereign rule in the earth; and faith in the saving death and resurrection of the one now exalted to God's right hand would prepare all who turned to him for the coming judgment and grant them eternal life in the coming kingdom.

Initially the members of "the Way" or "the Assembly" *(ekklēsia),* as the group called itself, would have appeared to outsiders as yet one more messianic movement within Palestinian Judaism. In their social organization and religious practice, they resembled other Jewish groups: they met in one another's homes for table fellowship, prayer, and study, in the manner of the later Pharisaic *havurot;* some continued to worship in the Temple and to participate in the life of their local synagogue communities.

The early years of the Jesus movement in Palestine remain sketchy because of the sparse quantity and apologetic nature of the source material. The book of Acts is the principal source for the first three decades, but its narrow focus and idealizing tendencies present some obstacles. Acts portrays the movement having its center in Jerusalem under the aegis of the Twelve and expanding under their auspices, with Peter and James, the brother of Jesus, as the chief leaders. In itself the account is credible, but it probably does not tell the whole story, and for many historians it fits too neatly with Luke's understanding of salvation history. It is also countered by the putative existence of other groups in other locales. Independent traditions in the Gospels of Mark and Matthew and in the epilogue of John point to appearances of the risen Jesus in Galilee. Moreover, a small handful of passages in the Synoptic Gospels (e.g., Matt. 10:5-15) seem to reflect the interests and lifestyle of traveling bands of miracle-working teachers and prophets in Galilee, Syria, and the Decapolis, figures attested more clearly at the end of the first century in the *Didache.* These wandering charismatics would have been active alongside more settled clusters of followers in towns and villages, relying upon them to support their itinerant, mendicant existence.

Some scholars have posited the existence of a Galilean community on the basis of the Q document, a Greek source for Jesus' sayings adapted by the Gospels of Matthew and Luke. Recent reconstructions suggest that the group revered Jesus as a countercultural wisdom sage and attached no redemptive significance to his death and resurrection. These reconstructions, though, are as problematic in their own way as the idealized picture in Acts. Some literary stratifications of the Q source rely on dubious assumptions regarding the generic incompatibility of the wisdom sayings (supposedly early) and apocalyptic sayings (allegedly later) attributed to Jesus. Just as questionable is the notion that Q exhausts everything that its author(s) and community believed about Jesus. Most speculative of all is the correlation of Q's alleged literary layers with stages in the history of the "Q community."

The Jesus movement likely did take root in different places rather quickly, assuming different forms in a variety of social settings. But the fact remains that no significant community is attested for Galilee in the early decades. After Jesus' death and resurrection, the principal Galilean disciples either remained in or relocated to Jerusalem, which became the effective center of the movement. The city's status as such receives independent confirmation from the letters of Paul, whose relations with the Jerusalem congregation were often tense but who shows no awareness of any other major community in Palestine. There were many locales but only one true center.

For several decades, the ethos of the Jerusalem community remained Jewish. According to Acts, its members sacrificed in the Temple and experimented with a communal sharing of goods now seen to resemble the organizational life of the Qumran sectarians (Acts 2:44-45; 4:32-35; cf. 1QS 6:19-20, 22). They also attracted priests and Pharisees to their ranks, and three decades later were still "all zealous for the law" (Acts 21:20). Until the First Jewish Revolt disbanded the community, it practiced traditional forms of Jewish piety such as fasting, almsgiving, Torah study, and observance of holy days.

One thing that did distinguish the early Jesus movement from other forms of Second Temple Judaism was its strong missionary impulse. Initially, it evangelized other Jews and not Gentiles, but as it extended its outreach into urban areas of Palestine and neighboring regions, contact with Gentiles became inevitable and even desirable. According to Acts, the impetus for expansion beyond Jerusalem came as an unforeseen but providential consequence of the stoning of Stephen, a leader of the movement's Hellenist wing comprised of Greek-speaking Jews from the Diaspora who were critical of the Temple (Acts 6:8–8:1a). After his martyrdom, Stephen's fellow Hellenists were driven from the city, taking their message about Jesus with them into wider Judea and Samaria, to Phoenicia, and as far as Cyprus and Syrian Antioch (Acts 8:1b–11:27). Several early evangelists and apostles in the movement were Diaspora Jews. Acts names Philip, Barnabas (from Cyprus), Paul (Tarsus), Prisca and her husband Aquila (Pontus), and Apollos (Alexandria). All but Philip are mentioned in Paul's letters as well. In addition, Acts refers to several unnamed men from Cyprus and Cyrene as the first to proclaim the new message to Gentiles in Antioch.

An important focus of missionary effort centered on Jewish synagogues in cities of the Mediterranean Diaspora, whose Gentile attendees and benefactors were open to embracing the new, multiethnic variety of Judaism on offer. Diaspora synagogues supplied the Jesus movement not only with potential Gentile converts but with religious resources and models of communal organization. Although hard evidence is lacking, Christian hymns and prayers probably borrowed freely from the liturgies of synagogues, and Christian house churches imitated the social intimacy, international networking, and practice of hospitality that characterized synagogue communities. Perhaps most importantly, the Diaspora synagogues bequeathed to early Christianity a massive literary and theological legacy in the form of the Greek Scriptures, alongside numerous other works written in an astonishing range of genres that today make up the Old Testament Pseudepigrapha — histories and novellas, apocalypses and testaments, philosophy and wisdom, drama and poetry.

As increasing numbers of non-Jews joined the movement, their table fellowship with Jewish believers raised a critical issue: whether Gentile converts should be required to accept kosher food restrictions. The matter was pressing because early Christian worship took place in the context of a communal meal. To most Jewish believers and to many Gentile converts as well, both this requirement and that of circumcision would have made obvious sense; after all, they were mandated by Jewish Scripture, had the weight of tradition, and were sanctioned by the example of Jesus and his disciples. Others disagreed, however. The best known and most controversial dissenter was Saul (Paul), a Diaspora Jew who joined the Hellenist wing of the movement after his persecuting it was brought to an abrupt end by a vision of the risen Jesus. Both Acts and Paul's letter to the Galatians indicate that the issue came to a head in Antioch and was settled at a meeting of the Jerusalem apostles (ca. 49 c.e.) in a way that did not require circumcision of Gentile converts (Acts 15:1-35; Gal. 2:1-10). Beyond these bare facts, the two sources disagree over several details. Most notably Acts reports that, although Gentiles did not have to be circumcised, they were expected to "abstain from idol meat, from sexual immorality (possibly including close kinship marriages), from what has been strangled, and from blood" (Acts 15:20, 29). According to Galatians, however, no such ritual restrictions were imposed. In any case, the accommodation opened the way for increasing numbers of Gentiles to enter the movement without adopting the traditional sign of covenant membership. It was a fateful development and had a major impact on the Christian movement's eventually becoming a religion separate from Judaism.

Paul

Next to Jesus, Paul was the most significant figure in the movement during the first century. In some respects, he was even more controversial than Jesus. We know a lot more about him thanks to the second half of Acts and to some letters of his that survive. (His authoring seven of them is undoubted, but the other six were probably written in his name by his associates in the decades after his death.) The two sources are not completely at odds, but they do present rather different portraits of Paul's relation to Judaism. Acts depicts him as an observant Jew even after he joined the Jesus movement. He continues to follow Jewish laws and observe Jewish customs. He has Timothy circumcised, frequents Diaspora synagogues, gets his hair cut to fulfill a vow, travels to Jerusalem to give alms to his nation and offer sacrifices, undergoes ritual purification in the Temple, pays the expenses of a Nazirite ceremony for four men, and announces before the Sanhedrin that he is a Pharisee. For Luke, then, Paul was basically a Jew who added faith in Messiah Jesus to his Judaism.

Paul's letters (which Acts nowhere mentions) confirm several elements of this profile. In them he claims to be a Hebrew born of Hebrews who was circumcised on the eighth day (Phil. 3:5). He proudly calls himself an Israelite and a descendant of Abraham (Rom. 11:1). He concedes that circumcision is of value if one practices the Torah (Rom. 2:25). He speaks of the Jewish people as his "kinsmen according to the flesh" and avers that "to them belong the adoption, the glory, the covenants, the giving of the Law, the worship, and the promises"; they are beloved for the sake of the patriarchs, and to them belongs the messiah (Rom. 9:3-5; 11:28). And he staunchly insists that even though Christ came to save Gentiles, God has not abandoned the Jewish people; in fact, their election is "irrevocable" and all "Israel will be saved" (Rom. 11:26, 29). He pronounces the Torah "holy, just, and good" (Rom. 7:12) and protests that faith does not abrogate the Law but establishes it (Rom. 3:31). "It is not the hearers of the Law who are righteous before God but the doers of the Law who will be counted righteous," he writes to Christians in Rome (2:13). Indeed, the "just requirements of the Law" (the moral demands of the Torah) are to be fulfilled in the lives of believers as they cooperate with the Spirit of God at work within them (Rom. 8:4).

These strong affirmations of Jewish identity, however, reveal only part of the picture. Most of Paul's positive statements about the Torah appear in a single letter, Romans, his last; and they look like strategic backpedaling, written out of deference to Jewish believers in Rome and with an eye toward his upcoming visit to Jerusalem. His letter to the Galatians is far more negative. There Paul speaks of his "former life in Judaism" in a way that distances him from it (Gal. 1:13). In lines written to believers in Thessalonica so harsh that many regard them as an interpolation, he says of the Jews in Judea that they "killed both the Lord Jesus and the prophets and drove us out; they displease God and oppose all people, hindering us from speaking to the Gentiles so that they may be saved, so as to fill up constantly the measure of their sins. But God's wrath has come upon them at last!" (1 Thess. 4:15-16). As for circumcision, it ultimately counts for nothing (Gal. 5:5; 6:15; 1 Cor. 7:19). More, if his Gentile converts have their foreskins cut off under compulsion, they will cut themselves off from Christ (Gal. 5:4). The Jew is one whose Jewishness is "inward" *(en tō kryptō)*, and real circumcision is a matter of the heart, spiritual not literal (Rom. 2:29; Phil. 3:3). The Torah presided over a ministry of condemnation (2 Cor. 3:9) as an unwitting ally of Sin (understood as a cosmic power) that brought only death (Rom. 7:9-11). Because it cannot "make alive" (Gal. 3:21), its fading glory has been set aside in Christ (2 Cor. 3:10-11), who is the "end" but also "goal" *(telos)* of the Law (Rom. 10:4). "No one is counted righteous by works of the Law [i.e., by observing the Torah's ritual commandments] but by the faithfulness of Jesus Christ" (Gal. 2:16), and all who rely on works of the Law, especially circumcision, are under a curse (Gal. 3:10).

For Paul, Jesus himself is more than just the messiah of Israel; he is the universal Savior and Lord. He never calls Jesus "God," and no Pauline prayer is addressed *to* Jesus but to God *through* Jesus. Even so, his Christology goes beyond the veneration of any other mediator figure in early Judaism. In a proto-binitarian rewriting of the Shema, he includes Jesus in the life of the one God and identifies him as the divine agent in creation: "for us there is one God, the Father, from whom are all things and for whom we exist, and one Lord, Jesus Christ, through whom are all things and through whom we exist" (1 Cor. 8:6). Christ's preexistence, divinity, and incarnation are also alluded to in the statement that, though he was in the form of God, he emptied himself by being born in human likeness (Phil. 2:6-11). Like Paul's midrash on the Shema, this poem (probably of pre-Pauline origin) effectively identifies Christ with heavenly Wisdom. Here messianism encroaches on monotheism.

It is important to note that Paul addressed none of these letters to Jews or Jewish believers in Jesus but to his Gentile converts (though the non-Pauline congregations in Rome probably numbered some Jews), so in none of them does he engage Judaism directly. Even the Judaizing advocates of Gentile circumcision whom he attacks in Galatians and Philippians — he calls them "the dogs, the evil workers, the mutilation" (*katatomē*, a wordplay on *peritomē*, "circumcision"; Phil. 3:2) — may have been Gentile, not Jewish, believers. Nevertheless, Paul's statements regarding covenant election and salvation being possible only in Christ clearly apply to both Jews and Gentiles. Over the past several decades, a small but vocal minority of scholars has claimed that Paul envisioned two paths to salvation: Torah for Jews and Jesus for Gentiles. For the sake of religious pluralism, one would like for this to be so, but the argument rests on wishful thinking rather than sound exegesis. In 2 Cor. 3:13-18 Paul interprets the veil that Moses wore at Sinai (Exod. 34:29-35) as an indicator that the glory of the old covenant was being abolished. The minds of the Israelites were "hardened," he says. "Indeed, to this very day, when they hear the reading of the old covenant, that same veil is still there, since only in Christ is it set aside" (3:14). In Romans 9–11 Paul faces the problem that most Jews have rejected Jesus, and he attributes their rejection to the same divine hardening. In a key passage, he says

> Brothers, my heart's desire and prayer to God on their behalf is for their salvation. For I can testify about them that they have a zeal for God but not in accord with knowledge. For by ignoring God's righteousness and seeking to establish their own, they did not submit to God's righteousness. For Christ is the end of the Law so that there may be righteousness for everyone who has faith. (Rom. 10:1-4)

At the end of Romans 11 Paul envisions the eschatological salvation of "all Israel" coming about by a mass *apokalypsis* of the Redeemer coming from Zion, evidently a reference to the second coming of Christ (11:25; cf. LXX Isa. 59:20-21). This is how Paul himself came to Jesus — by way of divine revelation, not missionary proclamation (cf. Gal. 1:16). Paul's hope, then, was that nonbelieving Jews would come to acknowledge Jesus as their messiah.

Paul does not seem to have objected to Torah observance as such, and evidently had no problem with Jewish believers in Jesus abiding by Jewish laws and customs. It is even conceivable, though very unlikely, that he would not have objected to Gentile converts doing so as long as they did not regard such observance as necessary for inclusion in the covenant or salvation. As a practical missionary expedient, he himself could live as a Jew under the Torah in order to win Jews (1 Cor. 9:19-21). In spite of all this, he considered himself free from the Law and wanted his Gentile congregations to do the same.

Except for their worshiping the God of Israel and adopting the Bible's sexual ethics, the communities that Paul founded and nurtured in Asia Minor and Greece were not Jewish in their ethos. True, the theological motivation for his mission to them was thoroughly Jewish, being predicated upon the biblical vision of the Nations worshiping the God of Israel in the last days. But the Hebrew prophets who envisioned the inclusion of Gentiles in the eschatological restoration of Israel had been rather vague, mentioning no entry requirements beyond worshiping God (e.g., Isa. 60:8-12; Mic. 4:1-2). Paul concluded that there were not to be any — except faith in Christ. Significantly, there is no hint in his letters that his Gentile congregations had social contacts with Diaspora synagogue communities, even though in his three-decade mission he himself visited synagogues often enough to receive the "forty lashes less one" on five occasions (2 Cor. 11:24). So in their *ethnos* and *ethos,* the Pauline churches were not Jewish.

If with E. P. Sanders we agree that Judaism's "pattern of religion" in the first century can be characterized as "covenantal nomism," what can be said of Paul's pattern of religion? The essential components of covenantal nomism look like this:

God's gracious election of Israel at Sinai
↓
Israel's grateful response of obedience to the Torah
↓
final judgment with rewards and punishments

The basic structure of Paul's religion looks very similar:

God's gracious act in Christ
↓
grateful response of "the obedience of faith" in Christ
↓
final judgment with rewards and punishments

It is not that Paul's theology reflects a fundamentally different pattern of religion than Judaism, as Sanders maintains. The pattern is the same, but its crucial element — Christ instead of Torah — differs. Christ is the only true offspring of Abraham and sole heir to God's promises, and only those who are "in him" — who are united to him by being baptized into his death and having his life formed in them by the Spirit — become fellow heirs to those promises. This notion, that the Abrahamic covenant and union with the messiah trump the Sinai covenant and living by Torah, has no precedent in early Judaism. And there is nothing in early Jewish thought to account for why the coming of the messiah should dethrone the Torah. (Paul, of course, would protest that he and his Gentile converts were indeed living by Torah, in accord with its true intention. He says as much in Rom. 3:31, "Do we then nullify the Law through faith? Absolutely not! Rather, we uphold the Law.")

Since Paul was a Jew who regarded faith in Christ as the fulfillment of Judaism, it is wrong to call him "anti-Jewish." It is also unfair to call him an "apostate" since he considered his Gentile mission to be a prophetic vocation within his native religion, not the consequence of a conversion to a new one. But in redefining the notion of covenant election so radically, he struck at the heart of the Jewish identity of most Jews. Disagreement over who is elect was certainly part of intra-Jewish debate in the Second Temple period. This is clear enough from the sectarian Dead Sea Scrolls. Paul, however, went a step beyond the covenanters at Qumran: for them not all Jews are elect, but all the elect are still Jews. Not so for Paul: only those in Christ are in the covenant and among the elect. In his vision of a new humanity destined for a new creation, ethnicity — so essential to Jewish identity — disappears. If his theology implies no wholesale rejection or supersession of Israel, it does imply a new definition of "Israel" and a displacement of historic Israel's covenantal self-understanding as a community formed by physical descent and ritual observance.

Other New Testament Perspectives on Jews and Judaism

Paul's theology is the most complex — and on the subject of the Law, the most convoluted — in the New Testament. The rest of the corpus presents a range of attitudes toward Jews and Judaism. At one end of the spectrum are writings that engage in a constructive and relatively positive appropriation of Jewish scripture and tradition without vilifying or even referring directly to Jews or non-Christian Judaism. At the other end are those that were written to communities of believers who were in competition with Jewish communities and that therefore reflect varying degrees of polemic, separation, and supersession.

The General Epistles and Revelation

Representative of the more irenic end of the spectrum are the "general" or "catholic" epistles of James, Peter, Jude, and Hebrews. Although Acts and Galatians remember James as an advocate of ritual Torah observance, the pseudonymous epistle that bears his name deals only with the ethical teachings of the Torah. It is a fine specimen of Hellenistic Jewish wisdom literature, addressed to "the twelve tribes of the Diaspora" (Jas. 1:1), a designation that ostensibly suggests Jewish believers. The body of the letter consists of a series of short aphorisms and admonitions followed by a sequence of mini essays that pick up and elaborate on the key themes of the sayings. The work contains no Christology to speak of — and in fact mentions Jesus only twice — but it does contain echoes of Jesus' teachings. It understands the "royal law" or "law of liberty" (1:24; 2:8, 12) not as a body of instruction distinct from the Torah but as the Torah's command to love the neighbor, now ratified, at least by implication, in the teaching and example of Jesus. All of this is stated with absolutely no polemics against Jews or non-Christian Judaism.

The epistles attributed to Peter and Jude also arrogate Jewish tradition to themselves without indulging in anti-Jewish invective. The latter is attributed to "Jude a servant of Jesus Christ and brother of James" (Jude 1) and addressed to believers whose location is not specified, though if the attribution is genuine a Palestinian provenance would be likely. As with James, the authorial attribution to a brother of Jesus is regarded by many scholars as pseudonymous. The body of this short document condemns false teachers, evoking various figures and groups in the Jewish Scriptures as examples of wickedness that merited divine punishment. Among its accusations is that the ungodly teachers "slander the glorious ones" (v. 8), a charge that occasions mention of an extrabiblical tradition about the angel Michael disputing with Satan over the body of Moses (v. 9). It also quotes *1 Enoch* as Scripture (vv. 14-15; *1 Enoch* 1:9).

Most of Jude was taken up into 2 Peter, a letter almost universally regarded as a pseudonymous writing of the early second century. Like Jude, 2 Peter shows no concern with Jews or Judaism as it co-opts Jewish tradition. So also with 1 Peter, a circular letter from Rome (called "Babylon," 5:13) sent to Gentile believers in Asia Minor who are addressed as "exiles in the Diaspora" (1:1). Composed by a Roman Christian in the late first century, it is a letter of moral exhortation designed to bolster its audience in the face of slander and ostracism from their pagan neighbors. One of its major means of identity formation is to confer on its Gentile readers the prestige of Israel's sacred rites and institutions. The readers are "living stones" being built into a "spiritual house" in which they serve as members of a "holy priesthood" and offer "spiritual sacrifices" (2:5). They are a "chosen race," a "holy nation," and "God's own people" (2:9; cf. LXX Exod. 19:6; Isa. 43:20; Hos. 2:25). Again, not a single reference to non-Christian Jews surfaces.

Falling roughly at the same point on the continuum of positive appropriation to negative engagement is the Epistle to the Hebrews. The traditional title is a complete misnomer. With epistolary features coming only in the closing lines, it is more a sermon than a letter. It was directed not to Hebrews but Christians, perhaps from a Jewish background but possibly from a Gentile one. Rome may be the intended destination. The addressees have experienced persecution, though of what sort and by whom are not specified. They have grown weary in their commitment to Christ and are in danger of falling away. There is no clear support in the text for the traditional view, frequent among commentators, that the author wrote to dissuade a Jewish-Christian audience from reverting to Judaism. The homily's poetic prologue contains some of the highest christological affirmations in the New Testament: Christ as divine Son is mediator, heir, and Lord of the entire cosmos. He is "the exact imprint of God's very being" — an honorific that early Jewish tradition conferred on the figure of divine Wisdom personified (Heb. 1:3; Wis. 7:26). Hebrews asserts Christ's superiority to angels, to Moses, and, most extensively, to the levitical priesthood, employing a variety of sophisticated rhetorical devices and frequent exposition of passages in the Psalms and other Jewish Scriptures (e.g., Gen. 14:17-20; Jer. 31:31-34; Pss. 2:7; 8:4-6; 95:7-11; 110:4). Its signal contribution to New Testament Christology is its designation of Jesus as an eternal, heavenly priest in the line of Melchizedek whose atoning death has established a new covenant ratified in the heavenly sanctuary (chaps. 7–10). Strikingly, though, the author of Hebrews never so much as glances at a living Judaism or at the Jerusalem Temple and priesthood of the first century. The points of comparison, contrast, admonition, and warning are made rather with respect to the newly formed levitical priesthood in the days of Moses and Aaron, the desert tabernacle, and the Israelites of the exodus generation. The author is familiar with interpretive traditions concerning Melchizedek, Moses, and angels known from a variety of Second Temple texts, and his Platonism has affinities with the thought of Philo of Alexandria. He engages in typological, midrash-like, and promise-and-fulfillment exegesis of the Scriptures. His acquaintance with Jewish tradition seems to be pure book learning.

All these so-called general epistles virtually ignore Jews and Judaism of the first century, either because their social settings were distant from Jewish communities or because their authors' varied agendas simply required no direct engagement. The same is true of the Deutero-Pauline and Johannine epistles. Ephesians, for instance, has a moving statement about how in Christ Gentiles have been brought near to the "commonwealth of Israel" and the "covenants of promise," and how the "dividing wall" of hostility between Jews and Gentiles has been torn down. Yet the union of Jew and Gentile in one new humanity is bought at the price of Christ's nullifying the "law [made up] of commandments in decrees" (Eph. 2:11-22; cf. Col. 2:16-19 for a disparaging reference to Jewish dietary practices). It is a unity that effectively erases Jewish distinctiveness. Nevertheless, Ephesians and the other epistles appropriate early Jewish tradition mostly by treating it as a resource for constructing and strengthening Christian identity. Their authors ransack the Septuagint for self-defining language in order to forge a link with Israel's sacred past and to write Christian believers into her story. To judge only by what they wrote, the Christians reflected in these documents look less like competitors of Jews than aspiring imitators and heirs.

With a few notable exceptions, the situation is largely the same in the book of Revelation, an apocalypse with an epistolary framework written by a Jewish prophet of Christ named John, and dispatched to seven communities in as many cities in Asia Minor. It was probably written (in an often awkward Semiticizing Greek) during the reign of the emperor Domitian (81-96 C.E.). It calls for radical cultural disengagement, urging Asian Christians not to assimilate to the idolatrous political, economic, and religious system of the Roman Empire, and preparing them for the prospect of persecution. The work has a high Christology: although it does not explicitly assert Christ's preexistence or divinity, Jesus nevertheless shares completely in the sovereignty of God. Unlike angels (Rev. 19:10; 22:8-9), Jesus *legitimately* receives worship in a heavenly throne room scene precisely parallel to one focused on God (4:1–5:14; cf. 7:10; 11:15; 12:10-12; 19:6-8). He also shares with God the title "the alpha and omega" (1:8 and 22:13; cf. 1:17 and 21:6) and is petitioned in prayer (22:20). Virtually every line of the work is steeped in the language of Jewish scripture, though never by way of direct quotation; and at more than one point, the full complement of God's faithful people is defined in terms of the twelve tribes of Israel (7:4-8; 21:12). The apocalyptic visions in chapters 4–22 — the bulk of the book — do not mention Jews or attack non-Christian Judaism, but early on, in the proclamation to the congregation in Smyrna, John has the exalted Christ say, "I know the slander *(blasphēmia)* on the part of those who say they are Jews *(Ioudaioi)* and are not, but are a synagogue *(synagōgē)* of Satan" (2:9). The message to believers in Philadelphia includes a similar statement (3:8). The word *Ioudaioi* here is a positive epithet with a negative thrust. The Jewish author thinks highly of it, so highly as to imply that he and his fellow believers have exclusive claim to it. The Jews down the street have forfeited their right to the title, having rejected the proclamation about Jesus while enjoying the legal privileges and exemptions that the Romans granted the Jewish people. It may be that these Jews were denying the title to partisans of Christ, and perhaps taking measures to exclude Christian believers from access to the privileges it afforded by denouncing them before Roman authorities. But this is not clear. In any event, this sort of name-calling was typical in intra-Jewish conflicts, as in the Qumran sect's labeling its opponents the "congregation of Belial."

The Gospels and Acts

At various points along the negative part of the spectrum of attitudes toward Jews and Judaism are the Gospels and Acts. The Gospel of Mark and Luke-Acts are the least vituperative, while Matthew and John are at once the most "Jewish" and "anti-Jewish." The anonymous Gospel of Mark was written either just before or (less likely) just after the destruction of Jerusalem and the Temple in 70 C.E. It is traditionally assigned a provenance in the city of Rome but more likely stems from somewhere in the Roman East, perhaps in close proximity to the Jewish homeland. The closest Mark comes to reflecting a supersessionist stance toward Judaism is in the Parable of the Vineyard and the Tenants (12:1-12). There he invites his readers to regard the chief priests, scribes, and elders of the people as the landlords of God's vineyard (Israel) who seized and killed Jesus, God's "beloved son." "What will the owner of the vineyard do?" the Markan Jesus asks. "He will come and destroy the tenants and give the vineyard to others." It is not clear who Mark means by "the others" who inherit the vineyard — that is, the patrimony of Israel in the coming kingdom of God. On Jesus' original telling of the parable, the "others" were probably to be understood as himself and the Twelve, who would be the nation's new leaders. Mark, however, may have in mind the leaders of his own and other largely Gentile communities who accept Jesus as the messiah. This acceptance may not imply the rejection of Israel as a whole, but it would exclude most of ethnic Israel.

Luke-Acts was composed around 80-90 C.E. using Mark, Q, and other sources. Its place of composition is unknown; Antioch is often suggested on the basis of tradition, but almost any major city around the Mediterranean is possible. The two-volume work stresses the salvation-historical continuity between Israel and the Christian movement more explicitly and extensively than any other New Testament writing. Luke alone among the evangelists has a positive attitude toward the Temple: his gospel both begins and ends there (Luke 1:5-23; 24:52-53); Jesus does not abandon it after cleansing it but teaches in it (19:47; 20:1; 22:53); in Acts the apostles continue to worship and teach within its precincts (Acts 3:1-8; 5:21, 25). His attitude toward Jerusalem is more ambivalent. On the one hand, it symbolizes positively God's relationship with the people of Israel. On the other, it is the place of Israel's rejection of its Prophet-Messiah. Like Joseph and Moses, Jesus is at first rejected by his brethren but eventually vindicated by God (in the resurrection and outpouring of the Spirit on his followers) in a way that empowers him to save the very ones who rejected him. In Acts, the apostles are the new leaders of Israel, but God has not written off the Jewish people. The history and story of Israel are continued and fulfilled in the work of Jesus and the community he formed, which is not a renegade sect but the authentic form of the restored people of God. In Luke's view, membership in the people of God is no longer limited to those who are Jews by birth but open to "anyone in every nation who fears him and does what is right" by "believing in Jesus and receiving forgiveness of sins through his name" (Acts 10:34, 43). To be a part of the "people" *(laos)* of God, Gentiles do not have to convert to the "nation" *(ethnos)* of the Jews by following their "custom" *(ethos)* of circumcision. Yet the inclusion of Gentiles in the restored people of God does not mean the replacement of Israel but its expansion. And the exemption of Gentiles from circumcision does not trumpet the dismissal of the Torah but the fulfillment of its true, prophetic intention "made known from long ago."

The most negative portrait of Jews in Luke-Acts comes in the account of Paul's missionary journeys in Asia Minor and around the Aegean rim. Jews in synagogues of the Diaspora treat him to the ancient equivalent of tar and feathering, sometimes stalking him from city to city. When he gets to Jerusalem, a number of Jews from Asia accuse him of defiling the Temple and almost beat him to death before he is taken into Roman custody

(Acts 21:27-31). Soon after, more than forty Jews swear an oath to assassinate him (23:12-15). At the end of Acts, the leaders of the Jewish community in Rome greet him coolly but ask to hear more about "this sect *(hairesis)* . . . everywhere spoken against" (28:22). The response of Jews to Paul's message about Jesus is mixed; some accept it, but most reject it. Throughout Luke-Acts, Israel remains divided. Is the work "anti-Jewish"? The label is no less dubious than when applied to Paul. Yet, although there is no overt supersession of Israel by Gentiles, no "true" or "new" Israel to replace the old one, there is a supersession of Israel's ethnically exclusive covenantal election.

The Gospel of Matthew was written around the same time as Luke-Acts and draws on Mark and Q as the two-volume work does. It was composed in and for a community of believers in Jesus that considered itself Jewish in every respect — ethnic, cultural, religious. Located perhaps in Antioch or a city such as Caesarea, Sepphoris, or Scythopolis, it was in fierce competition with Pharisaic Judaism in a nearby synagogue community. The Jewishness of the Matthean community is reflected in several subtle but noticeable ways, such as the omission of Mark's explanation of Jewish customs and of the Markan narrator's comment that Jesus "declared all foods clean." More overt examples of Matthew's limning of Jesus' Jewishness include a genealogy that traces his ancestry to Abraham (Matt. 1:1-17) and an extensive typological correspondence between Jesus and Moses drawn in the infancy narrative, the Sermon on the Mount, and other passages. Like Moses in the books of Exodus and Deuteronomy, Jesus is a liberator who has come to set his people free from their bondage and to give them the Torah anew. The Matthean Jesus does not nullify the Torah; he is its true and final interpreter. In a saying unique to Matthew, Jesus says,

> "Do not think that I have come to abolish the Law or the Prophets; I have come not to abolish but to fulfill. For truly I tell you, until heaven and earth pass away, not one letter, not one stroke of a letter, will pass from the Law until all is accomplished. Therefore, whoever breaks one of the least of these commandments, and teaches others to do the same, will be called least in the kingdom of heaven. For I tell you, unless your [Torah-based] righteousness exceeds that of the scribes and Pharisees, you will never enter the kingdom of heaven." (Matt. 5:17-20)

On the negative side, Matthew underscores the distinction or even separation of his community from Pharisaic Judaism by referring to "*their* synagogues" and having Jesus speak of "*your* Law" when debating with Pharisees. He also darkens the Markan portrait of the Pharisees in his Galilean section and the profile of the Jerusalem authorities in his passion narrative. Most notoriously, he has "the people as a whole" tell Pilate, "His blood be on us and our children!" (27:25).

Even so, Matthew's community represents a type of Judaism. It was comprised largely of Jews who continued to observe Sabbath (12:1-8; 24:20), to practice tithing (23:23), and to engage in almsgiving, prayer, and fasting (6:1-19) — and who were not ready to dispense completely with ritual purity concerns such as kashrut even though they set a priority on matters of moral purity (15:17-18; contrast Mark 7:19b). It is not Judaism that Jesus' followers are to reject but the hypocrisy, burdensome halakah, casuistry, ostentatious piety, and status-seeking of the Pharisees (Matthew 23). But they must also recognize that ethnic Israel no longer holds exclusive elect status since God's plan of salvation now includes the Nations as well. The Matthean community's debate with Pharisaic Judaism can be seen in large part as an intra-Jewish argument, but the community reflected in this gospel pushed the boundaries of the common Judaism of the day to the breaking point.

The Gospel of John vies with Matthew for the distinction of being the most "Jewish" and "anti-Jewish" of the Gospels. Like the Matthean community, the Johannine community pitted itself against Pharisaic Judaism. By the time the Fourth Gospel was written (ca. 90-100 C.E., somewhere in the Diaspora, possibly Ephesus), it had broken off all contact with the synagogue and was so deeply alienated from its formative roots in Judaism that it called Jesus' opponents (and its own) "the Jews." The term does not refer to all Jews in all times and places but primarily to the Jewish leadership, who in this Gospel are identified, anachronistically, with the Pharisees. (In a few passages, *hoi Ioudaioi* is a neutral designation for the inhabitants of Judea, and in 4:22 it is used positively in Jesus' remark to a Samaritan woman that "salvation is from the Jews.") In the narrative, the Jews function as a dramatic foil to Jesus and in symbolic terms are equivalent to "the world" in its ignorance, unbelief, and rejection of him.

The Fourth Gospel was written independently of the Synoptics, though its author knows some Synoptic traditions and was probably aware of one or more of the other gospels. Although it has some affinities with them, especially in its passion narrative, and though it shares half a dozen episodes from Jesus' public ministry with them, it is largely unique in content, style, and theology. Its Jewishness is evident in its regard for major marks of Jewish identity such as Torah, Temple, Sabbath, and Festivals. But in John Jesus fulfills and replaces these key institutions. And it alone among the gospels has an explicit Christology of pre-existence, divinity, and incarnation — not only in its prologue ("In the beginning was the Word, and the Word was with God, and the Word was God. . . . And the Word became flesh and dwelt among us," 1:1, 14) but on Jesus' own lips: "No one has ascended to heaven except the one who descended from heaven. . . . Before Abraham was I am. . . . The Father and I are one. . . . Whoever has seen me has seen the Father" (3:13; 8:58; 10:30; 14:9). Jesus is the one and only path to God and to eternal life: "I am the way, the truth, and the life; no one comes to the Father except through me" (14:6).

Instead of teaching in parables and aphorisms, the Johannine Jesus delivers long monologues. Their subject is not the kingdom of God but Jesus' identity as the only Son of the Father come down from heaven to reveal and to save. In dialogues with his opponents, which frequently turn into monologues, the subject of controversy centers not on aspects of Jewish halakah but on Jesus' identity and self-claims. Gone in John are debates over fasting, tithing, food purity, oath taking, and divorce. Instead, Jesus' healing on the Sabbath quickly provokes the charge that he makes himself out to be "equal to God" (John 5:18; cf. 10:33). When the Jews assert their Abrahamic paternity and deny Jesus' divine paternity, he replies, "You are of your father, the Devil" (8:44). Though he submits to the Father's will and declares "the Father is greater than I" (14:28), he does not hesitate to claim unity with God (e.g., 10:30, 38; 14:10-11; 17:21). From the narrator's point of view, though, this is not blasphemy, since Jesus is no mere man but the Logos incarnate. Doubting Thomas does well to bow before Jesus and call him "My Lord and my God!" (20:28).

The most revealing passage in the Fourth Gospel for the Johannine community's separation from the synagogue comes in the story of the man blind from birth in John 9. The passage starts off as a Synoptic-like healing story, but after he heals the man Jesus is absent for most of the chapter, so that the focus falls on the man. He is hauled before "the Jews" twice and interrogated. The more they pressure him to denounce Jesus as a sinner, the higher and bolder his claims about Jesus become. In the scope of some twenty verses, he goes from referring to him as "the man called Jesus" to saying "he is a prophet" to declaring "he is from God." His Pharisaic interrogators expel him from the community, "for the Jews had already agreed that anyone who confessed Jesus to be the messiah would be put out of the synagogue (*aposynagōgos*, 9:22; cf. 14:42; 16:2). When Jesus later finds him and elicits faith in himself as the Son of Man, the fellow replies, "'Lord, I believe.' And he worshiped him" (9:38). This remarkable passage seems to telescope a years-long process of conflict in a synagogue community. In a narrative palimpsest, the conflict has been inscribed onto the story of Jesus. Debates over whether Jesus was the messiah had escalated into heated arguments over claims about his divine status, claims forged in the fires of the conflict itself. The Fourth Gospel is not anti-Jewish — far less anti-Semitic — in any ethnic sense, but in it Judaism without Jesus is no longer a viable path to God.

The Parting of the Ways

Without question the Christian movement began as a messianic renewal movement within Judaism and for several generations retained much of its Jewish character. Yet the seeds for a gradual distancing and eventual separation from Judaism were planted early on with the movement's high Christology, which led to veneration of Jesus in a way that infringed on Jewish monotheism, and in its outreach to Gentiles, which led to a demotion of the Torah and a dismantling of covenant election by descent or conversion. Both of these developments were underway within a few years of Jesus' death and resurrection, though certainly not in every quarter.

In the last two decades, the leading metaphor for Christianity's separation from Judaism has been the "parting of the ways." The metaphor is salutary insofar as it grants Judaism its own integrity, but it is also problematic because it conjures up images of two neat and tidy religious groups who began as happy siblings but ended completely estranged. When, why, and how the separation took place remains contested. Some see it occurring, at least *in nuce,* as early as Jesus' own career; others date it to the time of the First Jewish Revolt in 66-73 or to the Bar Kokhba Revolt of 132-135 C.E. More recently some have pushed it as late as the fifth and even sixth century. Decisive historical moments have been sought in the Apostolic Council around the year 49, the alleged flight of the Jerusalem congregation to Pella in Transjordan in the mid 60s, the destruction of Jerusalem and the Temple in 70, the convening of a rabbinic summit at Yavneh around 90 and the supposed promulgation there of the *Birkat Ha-minim* (a formal curse designed allegedly to expel believers in Jesus from Jewish synagogues), or the failure of the Bar Kokhba Revolt in 135. Others have focused less on historical factors than theological ones, such as the Gentile-inclusive tendencies of Jesus' ministry, the Law-free gospel of Paul and other Hellenist believers, and the high Christology evident in several New Testament writings.

Both the historical and theological factors invoked as determinative for the separation entail difficulties. In the theological domain, the downplaying of the ritual aspects of the Torah has some precedent in Diaspora Judaism, and high Christology has parallels in early Jewish logos and wisdom theology and in ideas about divine mediation centered on principal angels like Yahoel and Metatron and on human figures like Enoch and other exalted patriarchs. Some of the historical arguments are equally shaky. The earliest mention of the Pella tradition comes from the fourth-century church father Eusebius and stands in some doubt. Similarly, the traditions concerning Yavneh and the *Birkat Ha-minim* date to the Talmudic period. The rabbis at Yavneh did not have the Christian movement on their agenda, and the *Birkat Ha-minim* was not current in the first century in a form that would have targeted believers in Jesus; indeed, it may not have been added to the *Amida* or *Eighteen Benedictions* until the third century. There are also indications of ambiguity, contact, and overlap between "Judaism" and "Christianity" in the second through fifth centuries, factors that to many interpreters are most evident in the phenomena of "Judaizing" and "Jewish-Christianity."

The verb "Judaize" — "to live like a Jew" — is used in several Christian sources for Gentile believers in Jesus who adopted Jewish practices like circumcision, Sabbath observance, and kosher diet (e.g., Gal. 2:14; Ignatius, *Magn.* 10:2-3). Yet in the patristic literature, the label just as often has nothing to do with following Jewish customs. In some of the church fathers it is a polemical label for Christians whose Christology is too "low" or who interpret the Old Testament literally instead of figuratively. Like the phenomenon "anti-Judaism," "Judaizing" need not imply direct contact with or influence from Jews or Judaism. More often it reflects intra-Christian theological disputes and seems not to have been encouraged by non-Christian Jews.

The category "Jewish-Christianity" is no less slippery, complicating rather than clarifying the parting of the ways. The ambiguous label is a modern creation that can refer either to ethnic Jews who believed in Jesus or to people of any ethnicity — Jew and non-Jew alike — whose devotion to Christ included aspects of Torah observance. Jewish-Christianity in both these senses is attested in the New Testament and other early Christian sources. Further muddying the waters, some scholars use the label

"Jewish-Christian" loosely to describe Christian writings that draw extensively on Jewish scripture and tradition, regardless of whether their settings reflect Jewish ethnicity or practice. Others restrict the designation to groups such as the Ebionites and Nazoreans, marginal groups regarded as heretical sects by church fathers like Eusebius and Epiphanius whose members occupied a shrinking no-man's-land between emergent orthodox Christianity and ascendant rabbinic Judaism.

There can be no denying that the borderlines between Judaism and Christianity were not clear-cut everywhere in the early centuries of the Common Era, or that the separation between them was uneven and complex. It was at least *possible* to live both as a Jew — a member of a Jewish synagogue — and as a believer in Christ until Theodosius I made Christianity the only religious option in the Roman Empire (380 C.E.). Nevertheless, Christianity did separate from its Jewish matrix in substantive ways already in the first century. Because early Christianity was characterized by considerable diversity, speaking constructively about the parting of the ways requires precision about whether one has ethnic-demographic, sociological-cultural, or theological-religious factors in view, and which regions, settings, and times one is investigating. Some generalizations in each of these three areas, however, are inevitable and even necessary.

(1) In sheer demographics, the Jesus movement was overwhelmingly non-Jewish in its constituency by the end of the first century, and in that sense was a largely Gentile religion. Since ethnic descent was a fundamental identity marker in early Judaism (except for proselytes), this datum is significant.

(2) In terms of social identity, Pauline and other congregations of the middle and later decades of the first century were separate from Jewish synagogue communities. Although Jewish and Christian individuals continued to interact with one another for centuries, by the second half of the first century Jews and Christians as social groups were going their separate ways, organizing themselves around distinctive beliefs and practices. Then, too, by the latter decades of the first century, the Romans seem to have begun distinguishing Christians (Lat. *Christiani*) from Jews, as the Neronian persecution in Rome in 64 C.E. and the imposition of the *fiscus Iudaicus* ("Jewish tax") after the First Revolt suggest. This is undoubtedly the case by the time of the Pliny-Trajan correspondence ca. 110 C.E. (*Epistles* 10.96, 97). Further, the evidence for contact between Jews and Christians in the patristic period is almost exclusively literary, and most of it comes from the Christian side. To be sure, church fathers like Justin, Origen, and

Jerome had scholarly exchanges with learned Jews, and several patristic sources gladly incorporate Jewish exegetical and haggadic traditions. But on the whole the rabbis simply ignored Christianity. It is also true that Judaism continued to be a vital religion that continued to attract Christian believers into late antiquity. This is most evident in fourth-century Antioch, where John Chrysostom preached a series of homilies against the Judaizing proclivities of Christians in the city who were consulting with rabbis, attending synagogue services, and participating in Jewish festivals. This sort of evidence, however, is not abundant in late antiquity and has no counterpart on the rabbinic side.

(3) Finally, although early Christianity is unthinkable apart from its reliance on Jewish scripture, theology, and ethics, there remain two crucial areas in which the Jesus movement diverged from the rest of Judaism at a very early date: covenant election and monotheism. The moment Gentiles began to be welcomed into the Jesus movement without being required to adopt the chief ritual marks of Jewish identity — especially circumcision — the Jewish notion of covenant election was radically spiritualized, and the defining role that Torah observance had for most Jews was effectively demoted. Further, the moment that Jesus began to be identified so closely with the one God as to be petitioned in prayer and worshiped, Christian messianism collided with Jewish monotheism. It is not that high Christology did not build upon early Jewish logos and wisdom theology (it did), or that the worship of Jesus was not prepared for by the veneration of mediator figures like exalted patriarchs or principal angels (it was). But the worship of the crucified and risen Jesus — a man of living memory and not a figure of hoary antiquity — as the incarnation of a preexistent divine being represents a quantum leap beyond any form of Second Temple Judaism. Neither of these theological developments nor their sociological corollaries are late phenomena but early realities that can be dated with some precision to the 30s and 40s C.E. in texts like the pre-Pauline Christ hymn in Philippians. If a definitive separation between Rebecca's children was long in the making, the seeds for it were sown very early on.

BIBLIOGRAPHY

Barclay, John, and John Sweet, eds. 1996. *Early Christian Thought in Its Jewish Context*. Cambridge: Cambridge University Press.
Bauckham, Richard. 2008. *Jesus and the God of Israel*. Grand Rapids: Eerdmans.

Becker, Adam H., and Annette Yoshiko Reeds, eds. 2003. *The Ways that Never Parted: Jews and Christians in Late Antiquity and the Early Middle Ages.* Tübingen: Mohr Siebeck.

Bieringer, Reimund, and Didier Pollefeyt, eds. 2012. *Paul and Judaism: Crosscurrents in Pauline Exegesis and the Study of Jewish-Christian Relations.* London: Clark.

Boyarin, Daniel. 1994. *A Radical Jew: Paul and the Politics of Identity.* Berkeley: University of California Press.

———. 2004. *Border Lines: The Partition of Judeo-Christianity.* Philadelphia: University of Pennsylvania Press.

———. 2012. *The Jewish Gospels: The Story of the Jewish Christ.* New York: New Press.

Brooke, George J. 2005. *The Dead Sea Scrolls and the New Testament.* Minneapolis: Fortress.

Cohen, Shaye J. D. 1999. *The Beginnings of Jewishness: Boundaries, Varieties, Uncertainties.* Berkeley: University of California Press.

Dunn, James D. G. 2003-2008. *Christianity in the Making.* 2 vols. Grand Rapids: Eerdmans. (A third volume is forthcoming.)

———. 2006. *The Parting of the Ways between Christianity and Judaism and Their Significance for the Character of Christianity.* 2d ed. London: SCM.

Eisenbaum, Pamela. 2009. *Paul Was Not a Christian: The Original Message of a Misunderstood Apostle.* New York: HarperOne.

Fredriksen, Paula. 1999. *Jesus of Nazareth, King of the Jews: A Jewish Life and the Emergence of Christianity.* New York: Knopf.

Hengel, Martin, with Anna Marie Schwemer. 2007. *Geschichte des Frühen Christentums I: Jesus und das Judentum.* Tübingen: Mohr Siebeck.

Hurtado, Larry. 1998. *One God, One Lord: Early Christian Devotion and Ancient Jewish Monotheism.* 2d ed. Edinburgh: Clark.

Jackson-McCabe, Matt, ed. 2007. *Jewish Christianity Reconsidered: Rethinking Ancient Groups and Texts.* Minneapolis: Fortress.

Jossa, Giorgio. 2006. *Jews or Christians? The Followers of Jesus in Search of Their Own Identity.* Tübingen: Mohr Siebeck.

Levine, Amy-Jill, and Marc Zvi Brettler, eds. 2011. *The Jewish Annotated New Testament.* Oxford and New York: Oxford University Press.

Lieu, Judith M. 2005. *Neither Jew nor Greek? Constructing Early Christianity.* Edinburgh: Clark.

Marcus, Joel. 2006. "Jewish Christianity." In *The Cambridge History of Christianity,* vol. 1, *Origins to Constantine,* ed. Margaret M. Mitchell and Frances M. Young, 87-102. Cambridge: Cambridge University Press.

McCready, Wayne O., and Adele Reinhartz, eds. 2008. *Common Judaism: Explorations in Second-Temple Judaism.* Minneapolis: Fortress.

Meier, John P. 1991-2009. *A Marginal Jew: Rethinking the Historical Jesus.* 4 vols. New Haven: Yale University Press.

Murray, Michelle. 2004. *Playing a Jewish Game: Gentile Christian Judaizing in the First and Second Centuries C.E.* Waterloo, Ont.: Wilfrid Laurier University Press.

Nickelsburg, George W. E. 2003. *Ancient Judaism and Christian Origins: Diversity, Continuity, and Transformation.* Minneapolis: Fortress.

Sanders, E. P. 1977. *Paul and Palestinian Judaism.* London: SCM.

―――. 1985. *Jesus and Judaism.* London: SCM.

―――. 1990. *Jewish Law from Jesus to the Mishnah.* London: SCM.

―――. 1992. *Judaism: Practice and Belief 66 BCE–66 CE.* London: SCM.

Sandmel, Samuel. 1978. *Anti-Semitism in the New Testament?* Philadelphia: Fortress.

Schiffman, Lawrence H. 1985. *Who Was a Jew? Rabbinic and Halakhic Perspectives on the Jewish-Christian Schism.* Hoboken, N.J.: Ktav.

Segal, Alan F. 1990. *Paul the Convert: The Apostolate and Apostasy of Saul the Pharisee.* New Haven: Yale University Press.

Setzer, Claudia. 1994. *Jewish Responses to Early Christians: History and Polemics, 30-150 C.E.* Minneapolis: Fortress.

Simon, Marcel. 1986. *Verus Israel: A Study of the Relations between Christians and Jews in the Roman Empire AD 135-425.* London: Littman Library of Jewish Civilization.

Taylor, Miriam S. 1994. *Anti-Judaism and Early Christian Identity.* Leiden: Brill.

Tomson, Peter J. 2001. *'If This Be from Heaven': Jesus and the New Testament Authors in Their Relationship to Judaism.* Sheffield: Sheffield Academic Press.

Udoh, Fabian E. et al., eds. 2008. *Redefining First-Century Jewish and Christian Identities: Essays in Honor of Ed Parish Sanders.* Notre Dame: University of Notre Dame Press.

Vermes, Geza. 1993. *The Religion of Jesus the Jew.* Minneapolis: Fortress.

Wilson, Stephen G. 1995. *Related Strangers: Jews and Christians 70-170 C.E.* Minneapolis: Fortress.

Yarbro Collins, Adela, and John J. Collins. 2008. *King and Messiah as Son of God: Divine, Human, and Angelic Messianic Figures in Biblical and Related Literature.* Grand Rapids: Eerdmans.

Early Judaism and Rabbinic Judaism

Lawrence H. Schiffman

One of the central issues of the history of Judaism is the periodization of its early history. Behind this issue lurks a much more central question: To what extent may we trace continuity between the various bodies of Jewish literature and the religious ideas that they embody? When we study the development of Judaism from the late books of the Hebrew Bible, through the texts of the Second Temple period, into rabbinic literature, to what extent do we observe continuity and to what extent do we see change? This question is made more complex by the variegated nature of Second Temple Judaism, to the extent that some would prefer to use the designation "Judaisms." At issue, then, is not only the fact of historical change but also competing forms of Judaism at various times — a phenomenon best documented and understood for the Hasmonean period but no doubt also present at other times. Within this complex framework, one may ask how Judaism in the Second Temple period as represented in the Apocrypha, Pseudepigrapha, Philo, Josephus, and Dead Sea Scrolls relates to the Judaism of the Mishnah, Talmud, and Midrash, that is, to the rabbinic or talmudic tradition. What has been continued, and what has been changed; what is old and what is new?

To a great extent this question is complicated by a related issue. In the transition from the period of the Hebrew Scriptures to Second Temple times, the earlier period bequeathed a massive literary legacy to the subsequent history of Judaism: the Hebrew Bible. This religious, literary, and historical legacy remains a permanent, indeed formative, ingredient in all subsequent Jewish development. Yet although Second Temple Judaism passed the Bible on to rabbinic Judaism, it did not pass on its own literary productions. There is only one text from the Second Temple period that fell into the hands of the talmudic rabbis in its entirety: Ben Sira. Beyond that, they did not have, or perhaps did not want to read, the Dead Sea Scrolls or the writings that now comprise the Apocrypha and Pseudepigrapha, nor the works of Philo and Josephus. This hiatus in culture, indeed an abyss from a literary point of view, remains largely unexplained. This gap is not unique; after all, some twenty-two books are mentioned in the Hebrew Bible that did not survive into later periods. Still, that virtually nothing passed from Second Temple times to the talmudic era stands in stark contrast to the large body of Israelite literature that was transmitted to Second Temple Judaism.

If there was no direct literary influence, we will have to content ourselves with seeking common ideas and approaches that were passed down as part of a general religious ambience. Because the halakic and theological forebears of the rabbis were the Pharisees, we have to expect that rabbinic literature and rabbinic Judaism are dependent primarily on the Pharisaic teachings. But here we have no existing Second Temple texts written by Pharisees. This situation most probably owes to the penchant for oral tradition among the Pharisees, as known from Josephus, even if the ideological notion of oral revelation and transmission was actually articulated only in the tannaitic period. At the same time, some Pharisaic texts may have lost popularity as oral tradition came to dominate Pharisaic Judaism. Obviously, such texts would not have been preserved in the Qumran sectarian collection, since the sect was so anti-Pharisaic. In any case, the Pharisees bequeathed no literary materials to the talmudic enterprise but only extensive oral traditions. It is possible that as Pharisaic Judaism emerged as the only real survivor of the Second Temple period, the other books were ignored or suppressed, under the category of "outside (apocryphal) books."

Indirect Influences and Continuities

There are very few explicit references to apocryphal works in rabbinic literature. In fact, rabbinic texts mention only two such works, one being Ben Sira, which the rabbis apparently knew and quoted. Another is Sefer ben La'ana (*y. Sanhedrin* 10a), of whose contents nothing is known. The rabbis explicitly prohibit the reading of such books, but there is some uncertainty regarding the meaning of this prohibition. On the one hand, it might be a blanket prohibition forbidding the reading of these texts under any circumstances. The assumption would be that it is forbidden to write, and therefore to read, any books other than those of Scripture. On the other hand, the prohibition may have extended only to the public reading of these books as part of the lectionary. In this case, it would be permitted to read such books privately. Such an approach would explain the use of Ben Sira by the rabbis.

An interesting example of the indirect influence of Second Temple books on the rabbis comes in their fundamental agreement with a theme central to the book of *Jubilees,* that the patriarchs observed all of the laws later to be given at Sinai. Apparently, this notion was part of the common heritage of Second Temple Judaism and was taken up by some rabbis.

Numerous sectarian groups are in fact mentioned in rabbinic literature. These groups, however, while apparently practicing modes of piety similar to those known from the Dead Sea Scrolls, seem in no way to be identifiable with the specific literary works of the Second Temple period. Rather, it appears that the later rabbis were aware of the general nature of Judaism in the period before 70 C.E. Indeed, they blamed the phenomenon of sectarianism for the disunity that led to the destruction of Jerusalem and the Temple. However, none of the reports that they preserve can be directly associated with the textual materials from Second Temple times. We can only assume, again, that they did not or would not read these texts.

The sect of the Essenes is not mentioned by name in rabbinic literature. Attempts to identify the Essenes with the Boethusians *(baytôsîn* or *baytûsîn)* have failed to garner significant support because of the philological difficulties involved. While it is possible that some practices of the Essene sect might be described somewhere in rabbinic literature, it is more likely that the Essenes described by Philo and Josephus shared the Sadducean-type halakic tradition polemicized against in rabbinic texts.

One area in which rabbinic literature provides fruitful parallels to sectarian organization is the system of entry into the sect and the close link between purity law and sectarian membership. A similar system was in effect for the *havurah,* a small group that practiced strict purity laws, extending Temple regulations into private life even for non-priests. Scholarly literature has tended to associate this group with the Pharisees, most probably correctly, but the textual evidence seems to separate these terms. In any case, the detailed regulations pertaining to entering the *havurah* (*m. Dem.* 2:3-4; *t. Dem.* 2:2–3:4) are more closely parallel to the initiation rites of the Qumran sect (1QS 6:13-23) than they are to the descriptions of the Essenes in Josephus, with which they also share fundamental principles.

Some practices typical of the Qumran sect are indeed mentioned in rabbinic polemics against heterodoxy, termed *derek aḥeret*. But these practices are too few to indicate any kind of real knowledge of the Qumran sect or its practices or of other sectarian groups.

One interesting area is that of calendar disputes. Alongside the calendar of lunar months and solar years used by the Pharisaic-rabbinic tradition, other groups, including the Dead Sea sectarians and the authors of *1 Enoch* and *Jubilees,* called for use of a calendar of solar months and solar years. Although numerous problems still beset study of the calendrical situation in Second Temple Judaism, some part of it was clearly known to the rabbis. Rabbinic sources report that certain sectarians, Sadducees, and Boethusians practiced such a calendar, insisting that Shavuot fall on a Sunday and, hence, that the start of the counting of the omer commence on a Saturday night. If indeed these rabbinic notices refer to the calendar controversy known from the Scrolls and pseudepigraphal literature, then it seems that the rabbis' knowledge was quite fragmentary or that they chose to pass on only a small part of the picture. From rabbinic sources alone one would never have gathered that this sectarian calendar was based on solar months and that it represented an entirely alternative system. All we would have known is that they disagreed on the date of Shavuot.

Rabbinic Engagement with Second Temple Issues

From what we have said so far, one would assume that there simply is very little relationship between the literature of Second Temple Judaism and the rabbinic corpus. Yet when we examine the Judaism of the Dead Sea Scrolls sect and of the literature they preserved, we find both similarity to and interaction with views preserved in rabbinic texts. Further, fundamental ideas preserved in the Apocrypha and Pseudepigrapha found their way into the rabbinic tradition. And still to be fully explained, rabbinic literature preserves a variety of reflections on historical data preserved by Josephus, either in his words or those of his sources. In what follows, we will concentrate on examples illustrated by materials preserved in the Qumran corpus, including some that stem from books otherwise preserved in the Apocrypha and Pseudepigrapha.

Jewish Law

Qumran sectarian law was characterized by a clear distinction between the "revealed law" — that is, the written Torah — and the "hidden law" derived by sectarian exegesis and known only to the sectarians. This concept is clearly different from the rabbinic concept of a dual Torah, which includes a written law and an oral law. Further, the sectarian view makes no attempt to trace its second Torah to divine revelation at Sinai, seeing it rather as something that emerged with divine inspiration from the life of the sect and its leadership. At the same time, the sectarian system and the Pharisaic-rabbinic dual Torah both provide for a supplement to the fundamental written Torah, solving in slightly different ways the difficult problem of applying the written Torah to the life of the community. Further, both groups share the notion that the second Torah was divinely inspired. True, the *Temple Scroll* seems to be based on a very different approach; it assumes that only one Torah was revealed at Sinai, and it enshrines the author's interpretations in his law. Such a one-Torah system is at serious variance with that of the rabbis, but the revealed/hidden approach more broadly typical of the Qumran texts seems to share some of their fundamental concepts.

As is well known, tannaitic literature contains two kinds of halakic texts: collections of apodictic laws arranged by subject matter (mishnah) and those organized according to Scripture (midrash). The Qumran legal materials display both of these options in a "proto-rabbinic" mode. Laws such as those pertaining to the Sabbath, to courts and testimony, and to forbidden sexual unions often appear as a series of apodictic laws organized by subject and titled accordingly. These collections parallel in form the mishnaic tractates and even have similar titles. Further, texts like the *Temple Scroll* and certain fragments of legal texts indicate that some authors chose to express their legal views in the context of Scripture. There is one essential difference, though. Whereas in rabbinic literature midrashic exegesis maintains a strict distinction between the words of the Bible and the words of the rabbinic explanations, the *Temple Scroll* freely rewrites the biblical text in accord with sectarian assumptions. Such an approach would have been anathema to the rabbis. A further difference involves the very apodictic statements preserved in Qumran texts. Whereas in rabbinic literature such statements are composed in mishnaic Hebrew, and therefore are linguistically distanced from the biblical texts upon which they might depend, many Qumran apodictic laws make use of the language of the Bible and even allow us to determine their biblical midrashic basis from their phraseology.

When we come to the actual subject matter of the laws, the situation is also complex. Some laws and their derivation from Scripture seem to be virtually the same, as, for example, the statement that the Sabbath begins on Friday at sunset. Although some of the laws are very similar, such as the requirements to wear clean clothes on the Sabbath, others differ more extensively, such as the establishment of two separate Sabbath limits or the setting up of courts of ten for judging issues of Jewish civil law. These differences almost always derive from differing interpretations of Scripture. This is certainly the case with the *Temple Scroll,* whose laws and interpretations are often at variance with those of the rabbis.

Nevertheless, these differences often constitute a conceptual link between the Second Temple texts and the rabbinic corpus. In many cases, it is only the alternative interpretations in the Dead Sea Scrolls that allow us to understand the intellectual world within which the talmudic views were being put forth. Much research remains to be done in this area, and one example must suffice here: It is clear that rabbinic laws pertaining to ritual purity and prayer are closely linked to Temple purity laws preserved in the *Temple Scroll* and other Qumran documents. There is simply no other way to understand these laws, even as presented in the Babylonian Talmud.

It is generally accepted that ancient Judaism knew two separate approaches to Jewish law, that of the Zadokite priestly tradition and that of the Pharisees and rabbis. The former approach typifies the codes of the Qumran sect and such works as *Jubilees* and the *Aramaic Levi Document.* These trends were opposed by the Pharisaic-rabbinic approach preserved for us in talmudic literature. Due to the strictures of the Pharisees against writing down their traditions or other vicissitudes of preservation, the Pharisaic-rabbinic tradition is represented only in the later corpus of the talmudic rabbis. Nonetheless, it is possible to reconstruct the early layers of that material and in so doing often to reconstruct the Pharisaic views that were opposed, explicitly or implicitly, by the authors of the Dead Sea Scrolls. The Scrolls have enabled us to uncover an earlier layer of history in which the approach later ensconced in rabbinic works competed with the priestly approach for dominance in the halakic market. The importance of this perspective in understanding rabbinic literature cannot be overestimated.

This is especially the case when rabbinic literature itself preserves evidence for the content of the Zadokite tradition. After the removal of those references to Sadducees *(Ṣĕdûqîm)* that owe to scribal alterations, there remains a series of passages that seem to describe this alternative halakic tradition and that stand in general agreement with the information available from the Scrolls and other Second Temple texts. In this manner, some sense of the general authenticity of rabbinic materials that report on the Second Temple period has been gained, and scholars have begun to discard more skeptical approaches of the last generation. This situation is exemplified, perhaps exceptionally, by the collection of Pharisaic-Sadducean disputes in Mishnah *Yadayim* and the parallel collection in the halakic document found at Qumran, *Miqṣat Maʿaśê ha-Torah* (MMT). What is astounding here is the presence of a group of traditions in both places, of course stated from the opposing perspectives. In general terms, the rabbinic literature and Second Temple texts often represent opposite sides of the same coin, that is, two separate approaches to the same set of problems. Without the Second Temple materials, we would never have known this.

Phylacteries, Mezuzot, and "Bibles"

Scribal practice constitutes a distinct area of halakah. Here it seems clear that much of the scribal art transcended sectarian religious affiliation. This would explain why scribal law in rabbinic texts and indeed in later Jewish tradition is so close to that found in the Dead Sea Scrolls and other biblical texts from the Judean desert. Rabbinic Judaism received a scribal tradition from the earlier Jewish community and, for the most part, simply passed it down, following virtually the same mechanics for the preparation and production of hides, writing, and the storage of scrolls. Further, in the case of mezuzot and phylacteries, there is an intersection of the common scribal arts with the varying interpretations of the contents. Apparently, the sectarians were willing to include passages from the previous and following literary context, beyond those required by the Pharisaic-rabbinic tradition, which limited itself and did not allow any additional material. But the commonality in the preparation and construction of phylacteries and in the practice of mezuzot shows clearly that these were elements inherited from the common Judaism of Second Temple times. This is the case even though rabbinic traditions connect these religious objects closely to oral law, an approach eschewed by the Qumran sectarians and other priestly groups.

However, the Second Temple biblical materials contrast greatly with rabbinic statements on the subject and with what seems to be the evidence of Pharisaic influence at Masada and in the Bar Kokhba caves. Rabbinic texts assume a much greater standardization of the biblical text than what is in evidence in the Qumran texts and in the secondary use of biblical material in the Scrolls. Further, the Septuagint and the use of biblical materials in the Apocrypha and Pseudepigrapha often support the looser construction of biblical texts known to us from Qumran, where a variety of texts and text types coexisted. While this stands in contrast with rabbinic texts, despite some textual variants in biblical materials preserved there, we cannot be totally certain that Pharisaic Jews in Second Temple times would have had "Bibles" as standard as those assumed by the Mishnah and Talmud. Josephus writes as though this was the case at the end of the first century c.e., but we cannot be certain about the Pharisees of the earlier period.

Biblical Exegesis

Despite the absence of direct literary influence, and all the fundamental historical changes, a central aspect of continuity between Second Temple Judaism and rabbinic Judaism may be seen in the area of biblical exegesis. But even here, the issues are complex.

The translation of the Scriptures represents one area of continuity. The two translations at issue are the Greek (Septuagint) and the Aramaic (Targumim). Regarding the Greek, one might gather from the tannaitic parallel to the account of the seventy-two elders in the *Letter of Aristeas* (*b. Megilla* 9b; *y. Meg.* 1:9) that the rabbis saw the translation as a tragic step in the Hellenization of the Jews and yet approved of the actual translation, at least of the modifications supposedly made by the elders for polemical reasons. However, scholarly investigation of these variants shows that the account reflects no actual familiarity with the Septuagint, which, like the rest of Greek Jewish literature, was apparently lost to the rabbinic Jewish community. This is the case even though additional Jewish translations (Theodotion, Aquila, and Symmachus) were created or adapted after the Septuagint to bring the Greek closer to the Masoretic Text, which became the standard for Jews. The Greek Bible simply became identified with Christianity, despite the use of the Septuagint by Josephus and/or his assistants. Even so, rabbinic texts attribute special status to the Greek language and its use in Bible translation — clearly an echo of its former status.

With Aramaic translation the situation is more complex. Although the fragmentary Qumran Leviticus targum has exegetical parallels with the later Leviticus targums and rabbinic exegesis, the actual text from Qumran was not taken up by the rabbis. Nor was the Job targum found at Qumran. Like the targum to Job preserved by the rabbinic community, this is a very literal translation. Rabbinic tradition (*t. Šabb.* 13:2) mentions that both Rabba Gamliel I and II buried Job targums in the belief that translation was part of the oral law and so should not be written down. No mention of sectarian provenance appears, and in any case there is nothing at all sectarian about the (pre-) Qumran Job targum. Yet there is no literary relationship between the two Job targums. The Second Temple version apparently fell into disuse and was replaced later by a much younger one, probably dating to the Byzantine period. The rabbinic tradition, then, continued the pattern of translation but initially rejected putting it in writing. All pre-70-C.E. targums were lost, and later texts, composed or at least recorded after the rabbis, loosened up their prohibition of writing down the oral law and replaced the old, lost ones.

Another type of biblical interpretation that deserves mention has come to be called "rewritten Bible." Some of the exegetical presumptions of these texts are similar to those of rabbinic aggadah. Here we need to distinguish form from content. Whereas the Second Temple texts among the Pseudepigrapha and numerous Dead Sea Scrolls allow the authors to invade the actual biblical texts, as is done in the *Genesis Apocryphon, Jubilees,* and for halakah in the *Temple Scroll,* it seems that the barrier between written and oral tradition for the rabbis meant that such books were totally forbidden.

The rabbis maintained this distinction strictly, even with the gradual abeyance of the prohibition of writing down the oral law, with the result that not a single literary connection can be established between these early Jewish texts and rabbinic literature. However, parallels are also evident in the specific units of interpretation and sometimes in the actual content. In general terms, specific passages in the Second Temple texts use exegetical techniques similar to those of the rabbis. The interpretations of the rabbis are often quite different, though. At times there are common interpretations, and these were no doubt part of the traditions inherited by the rabbis from Second Temple times, but more often rabbinic tradition directly contradicts the interpretations found in earlier books.

One type of exegesis found in the Dead Sea Scrolls with no real resonance in rabbinic literature is the pesher. This form of contemporizing exegesis assumes a two-step process of prophecy and fulfillment, on the conviction that the Hebrew prophets did not really speak to their own times but to Second Temple circumstances. Parallels between pesher and rabbinic exegesis usually concern only the basic interpretation of the text, and not the pesher form itself. The theological presumptions of pesher exegesis were not in agreement with rabbinic notions of prophecy, and the rabbis tended in general to minimize apocalyptic trends.

Sectarian versus Rabbinic Theology

Both Second Temple texts and rabbinic literature were heir to the complex and often contradictory theological views of the various biblical books. Both corpora also share basic Jewish theological ideas such as belief in God the creator, the revelation of the Torah, and hope in a coming redemption. An important question is whether ideas in Second Temple texts that differ substantially from the biblical tradition were taken up in rabbinic Judaism. The extreme dualism and determinism taught in the sectarian Dead Sea Scrolls offers an interesting case in point. This set of beliefs assumes that God has preplanned the entire course of the cosmos and certainly of humans, who are divided into two lots, as are the heavenly beings, who struggle eternally against one another. Individual actions, for good or evil, seem in this system to be beyond one's own power, and yet individuals are punished for transgressing God's law, even including prescriptions that are not known beyond the sect. There is no basis for such ideas in the Hebrew Scriptures, and it is widely assumed that these concepts are somehow influenced by Persian dualism. In the rabbinic corpus, predestination is not accepted, although human free will can be countermanded by God. There is no cosmic dualism but rather an inner spiritual dualism of the good and evil inclination *(yeṣer)* in each person. Later, this concept merged with Hellenistic notions so that the two inclinations came to be identified closely with the spiritual and physical aspects of humanity. But free will is the basis of God's judgment of people, and all are responsible for their actions.

Another notion found in the Scrolls and other Second Temple texts but at variance with rabbinic theology is that prophetic or revelatory phenomena did not end with the story line of Scripture ca. 400 B.C.E. but rather continued into Greco-Roman times. This point of view underlies a lot of Second Temple literature but is virtually absent in rabbinic texts. The rabbis state explicitly that prophecy ended with the last of the Hebrew Bible prophets — Haggai, Zechariah, and Malachi. In fact, the end of

Malachi is probably an addition emphasizing the completion of the prophetic canon. The only remnant of prophecy, the *bat qol,* some kind of echo of a divine voice, is explicitly declared to be null and void. Clearly the system of Oral Torah obviated the need for direct divine inspiration. Perhaps most importantly, the rise of Christianity seems to have confirmed the rabbis in their belief that the end of the biblical period meant the end of prophecy and the end of writing scriptural books.

A few words need to be said about eschatology and messianism. Both of these themes are very important in rabbinic literature, with extensive materials devoted to them. This is not to speak of the apocalyptic-type messianic materials that appear in posttalmudic writings and that resemble such texts as the Qumran *War Scroll.* Here we must distinguish as two separate issues the nature of the messianic figure or figures and the nature of the messianic expectations. We need to ask first how many and what kinds of messiahs are expected and then what kind of events are expected to lead up to the messianic era and what its nature will be.

Second Temple texts contain three different types of messianism. Some texts make no explicit mention of any messiah. We cannot be certain that in these instances no such leader is expected; it is simply that no messianic figure appears in the texts. A second variety, perhaps the most common, awaits a Davidic messiah. The third approach, known to us from certain Qumran sectarian texts and from the *Testaments of the Twelve Patriarchs,* is the notion of two messiahs, one of Aaron and one of Israel. Many scholars simply assume that the messiah of Israel is Davidic, but this may not be the case. In any event, rabbinic Judaism assumes that there must be a messianic figure, even though some rabbis argued that the messiah had already come. The dominant expectation centers on one messiah, a scion of David. No serious rabbinic parallel at all can be adduced for the notion of a priestly messiah. Talmudic tradition does, however, speak of a second messiah, a messiah son of Joseph. This Josephite messiah (referred to in some later apocalyptic texts as a son of Ephraim) may be mentioned in a recently published stone inscription dated to the late first century c.e. known as the *Vision of Gabriel,* which refers to Ephraim in a messianic context (A. Yardeni and B. Elizur in *Cathedra* 123 [2007]: 155-66). However, such a figure is otherwise not found in any Second Temple text. The upshot of this is that the dominant notion in Second Temple times, carried over into rabbinic tradition, was the expectation of a Davidic messiah who would bring about the redemption and rule over Israel as the messianic king. While this approach has extensive rabbinic parallels, other competing approaches seem to have become extinct and not to have crossed the literary abyss that separates Second Temple from rabbinic tradition.

A significant difference of opinion among Second Temple texts regarding the onset of the messianic era itself is carried over into rabbinic texts. Two trends have always been observable in Jewish messianism: the first trend, the restorative trend, assumed that the messianic era would constitute a return to the great glories of the ancient Jewish past. A second trend, the catastrophic or utopian, assumed that the messianic era would usher in an era of total perfection, one that never had existed before, in which all evil and suffering would be eradicated. While the restorative approach assumed that the messianic era could be created by the gradual improvement of the world, the catastrophic one assumed that a great war, often termed the Day of the Lord, would lead to the total destruction of the wicked and the onset of the eschaton. Both of these views existed in Second Temple times, but the Dead Sea Scrolls particularly emphasize the apocalyptic belief that a great war between the sons of light and the sons of darkness, in which all but the sectarians would be destroyed, would bring on the messianic era. These two trends are reflected in rabbinic texts and constitute an aspect of the common Judaism of the Greco-Roman period that passed, with no literary framework, into the thought of the rabbis. In the aftermath of the Great Revolt (66-73 C.E.) and the Bar Kokhba Revolt (132-135 C.E.), the rabbis tended toward more quietist types of messianism. The militant apocalyptic notions, however, resurfaced in amoraic times and were further ignited when the Byzantine period gave way to the Muslim conquest.

There was also a debate during Second Temple times about the nature of the messianic age. On the one hand, Jews who awaited a Davidic messiah expected him to restore Jewish national independence and to rebuild the Temple. On the other hand, those who expected two messiahs and who believed that the messiah of Aaron would have precedence over the messiah of Israel anticipated the restoration of the Temple to the standards of holiness and sanctity that it deserved. In the aftermath of two Jewish revolts, the rabbis longed for a restoration of the Davidic glories of old, of a political entity secure and independent. Apparently, in their view this would ensure the proper rebuilding of the Temple. Yet they did not see the Temple as the central act in the messianic drama but as only a part of the process. For this reason, the Aaronide messiah has no parallel in rabbinic literature. This is the case even though Eleazar the Priest appeared with Bar Kokhba on coins, conjuring up the messianic pair of the *naśi* ("prince") and *kōhēn* ("priest").

Prayer and Poetry

Prayer was a significant part of the individual piety of a fair number of Israelites in First Temple times. Individual prayer was accompanied apparently by poems written for the collective people of Israel. Such prayers seem definitely to have attained a place in the psalmody of the Temple by the Second Temple period. In various Second Temple texts there are individual and collective prayers, and toward the end of the Second Temple period, prayer was becoming institutionalized increasingly, at least as appears from the tannaitic evidence. From the set liturgical texts preserved at Qumran, it seems that daily statutory ritual had become part of the life of the sectarians, who had separated from the Temple, which they regarded as impure and improperly conducted. These texts appear not to be of sectarian origin and may typify wider trends in the Jewish community. Further, the Dead Sea Scrolls give evidence of the twice-daily recital of the Shema and the use of mezuzot and phylacteries, some of which were prepared in a manner similar to that required by Pharisaic-rabbinic tradition.

Some tannaitic practices may have derived from those in evidence in Qumran liturgical texts. Both corpora require that a benediction of lights be part of the service each morning and afternoon-evening. This seems to be the only required benediction in the daily prayer texts preserved at Qumran. However, it seems to be equivalent to one of the two blessings before Shema required by the rabbis.

Qumran liturgical texts include also supplication texts similar to later rabbinic propitiatory prayers, and festival prayers seem to share similar motifs. However, not a single prayer preserved in the Scrolls is part of the rabbinic liturgy, and no text of rabbinic prayer was found in the sectarian collection. Again, the parallels in practice seem to derive from the common Judaism of Second Temple times, not from any literary or other direct connection.

Second Temple literature also seems to have played a major role in the development of the Jewish religious poetry known as piyyut. Before the discovery of the Dead Sea Scrolls, the evidence for Hebrew poetry in the postbiblical period was ignored. The poems in 1 Maccabees, for example, and even in the New Testament, not to mention early Jewish liturgy preserved in rabbinic texts or capable of being reconstructed from the later prayer texts, went largely overlooked. It was assumed that biblical psalmody was a dead-end tradition to be continued only later by a new form of Hebrew liturgical poetry that developed virtually *ex nihilo*. When the first scrolls were discovered, the *Hodayot* were taken to be an inferior version of Psalms poetry. No one seemed to realize that we were dealing with the next stage in the history of Hebrew poetry. Indeed, elements of Qumran religious poetry point in various directions toward the style, though not the content, of the later piyyut. This is clear now especially in the reuse of biblical material to form postbiblical poems and in the tendency to create grammatical forms not previously known. Yet, as a corpus related closely to rabbinic literature, the piyyut takes the rabbinic liturgical calendar and its content as a starting point and is suffused with rabbinic midrashic material and legal rulings, even if some of them are at variance with those taken as normative in the rabbinic legal texts.

Conclusion

How can we explain the contradictory observations that we are making here? On the one hand, we have emphasized the lack of a literary pipeline from early Judaism into rabbinic Judaism, beyond that of the Hebrew Scriptures themselves. On the other hand, we have pointed to rich parallels and apparent intellectual interaction between those who left us Second Temple texts and those who were apparently the spiritual ancestors of the Tannaim, namely, the Pharisees. It would seem that the existence of a "common Judaism" provides the answer.

As we have noted, Pharisaic-rabbinic Judaism was at odds with sectarian and apocalyptic trends, both in Second Temple times and after the destruction. The relationship between early Judaism and rabbinic Judaism, then, is characterized not by dependence but dialogue, disputation, and sometimes polemic. We lack adequate documentation of the Pharisaic side of the debate beyond reconstructing it on the basis of rabbinic literature. However, the license to perform such a reconstruction is inherent in the anti-Pharisaic polemics of the Second Temple texts, especially the Dead Sea Scrolls. The texts hint at a rigorous debate replete with polemics back and forth. This polemic must have been quieted greatly in the aftermath of the destruction of the Temple, when the Pharisaic-rabbinic approach gradually emerged as the consensus. From this point on, in an atmosphere of rabbinic debate, various aspects of the common Judaism of Second Temple times were preserved in the rabbinic movement and its literature. All kinds of ideas crossed the literary abyss without the rabbis having read Second Temple texts. It is these ideas that constitute the heritage of Second

Temple literature and the Dead Sea Scrolls for the rabbis, but they were vastly outnumbered and overpowered by the Pharisaic heritage, which was transmitted as an unwritten tradition and served as the real basis of rabbinic Judaism.

BIBLIOGRAPHY

Cohen, Shaye J. D. 2006. *From the Maccabees to the Mishnah*. 2d ed. Philadelphia Westminster John Knox.

Collins, John J. 2010. *The Scepter and the Star: The Messiahs of the Dead Sea Scrolls in Context*. 2nd ed. Grand Rapids: Eerdmans.

Edrei, Aryeh, and Doron Mendels. 2007-2008. "A Split Jewish Diaspora: Its Dramatic Consequences." *Journal for the Study of the Pseudepigrapha*, vol. 16, no. 2: 91-137; vol. 17, no. 3: 163-87.

Jaffee, Martin S. 2001. *Torah in the Mouth: Writing and Oral Tradition in Palestinian Judaism 200 BCE–400 CE*. Oxford: Oxford University Press.

Neusner, Jacob. 1994. *Introduction to Rabbinic Literature*. New York: Doubleday.

Nickelsburg, George W. E., and Robert A. Kraft, eds. 1986. *Early Judaism and Its Modern Interpreters*. Atlanta: Scholars Press.

Reif, Stefan C. 1993. *Judaism and Hebrew Prayer: New Perspectives on Jewish Liturgical History*. Cambridge: Cambridge University Press.

Sarason, Richard S. 2001. "The 'Intersections' of Qumran and Rabbinic Judaism: The Case of Prayer Texts and Liturgies." *DSD* 8: 169-81.

Schiffman, Lawrence H. 1989. *From Text to Tradition: A History of Judaism in Second Temple and Rabbinic Times*. Hoboken, N.J.: Ktav.

———. 1994. *Reclaiming the Dead Sea Scrolls*. Philadelphia: Jewish Publication Society.

———. 1998. *Texts and Traditions: A Source Reader for the Study of Second Temple and Rabbinic Judaism*. Hoboken, N.J.: Ktav.

Shanks, Hershel S., ed. 1992. *Christianity and Rabbinic Judaism: A Parallel History of Their Origins and Early Development*. Washington, D.C.: Biblical Archaeology Society.

Shemesh, Aharon. 2009. *Halakhah in the Making: The Development of Jewish Law from Qumran to the Rabbis*. Berkeley: University of California Press.

Urbach, Ephraim E. 1987. *The Sages: Their Concepts and Beliefs*. Cambridge: Harvard University Press.

VanderKam, James C., and Peter W. Flint, eds. 1998-1999. *The Dead Sea Scrolls after Fifty Years: A Comprehensive Assessment*. 2 vols. Leiden: Brill.

Index of Authors

435

Index of Subjects

Index of Scripture and Other Ancient Literature